HANDBOOK OF CREATIVE CITIES

T0327724

Handbook of Creative Cities

Edited by

David Emanuel Andersson

Associate Professor, Institute of Public Affairs Management, National Sun Yat-sen University, Kaohsiung, Taiwan

Åke E. Andersson

Professor, Department of Economics, Jönköping International Business School, Jönköping, Sweden

Charlotta Mellander

Associate Professor, Department of Economics, Jönköping International Business School, Sweden and Martin Prosperity Institute, Rotman School of Management, University of Toronto, Canada

Edward Elgar
Cheltenham, UK • Northampton, MA, USA

Published by
Edward Elgar Publishing Limited
The Lypiatts
15 Lansdown Road
Cheltenham
Glos GL50 2JA
UK

Edward Elgar Publishing, Inc.
William Pratt House
9 Dewey Court
Northampton
Massachusetts 01060
USA

A catalogue record for this book
is available from the British Library

Library of Congress Control Number: 2011925746

ISBN 978 0 85793 768 1
Printed and bound by CPI Group (UK) Ltd, Croydon, CR0 4YY

Contents

Contributors

Patrick Adler, Research Associate, The Martin Prosperity Institute, Rotman School of Management, University of Toronto, Toronto, Canada.

Åke E. Andersson, Professor, Department of Economics, Jönköping International Business School, Jönköping, Sweden.

David Emanuel Andersson, Associate Professor, Institute of Public Affairs Management, National Sun Yat-sen University, Kaohsiung, Taiwan.

David F. Batten, Senior Research Fellow, Commonwealth Scientific and Industrial Research Organization, Aspendale, Victoria, Australia.

Terry Nichols Clark, Professor, Department of Sociology, University of Chicago, Chicago, Illinois, USA.

Roberta Comunian, Lecturer, School of Arts, University of Kent, Canterbury, UK.

Elizabeth Currid-Halkett, Assistant Professor, School of Policy, Planning and Development, University of Southern California, Los Angeles, California, USA.

Pierre Desrochers, Associate Professor, Department of Geography, University of Toronto, Mississauga, Ontario, Canada.

Gus diZerega, PhD, independent political theorist, Sebastopol, California, USA.

Alessandra Faggian, Reader in Economic Geography (Associate Professor), School of Geography, University of Southampton, Southampton, UK; Visiting Associate Professor, AED Economics, Ohio State University, Columbus, Ohio, USA.

Søren Find, Head of Department, DTU Analysis and Research Promotion Centre, D'ARC, Technical University of Denmark, Copenhagen, Denmark.

Richard Florida, Professor of Business and Creativity, The Martin Prosperity Institute, Rotman School of Management, University of Toronto, Toronto, Ontario, Canada.

Fred E. Foldvary, Lecturer, Department of Economics, Santa Clara University, Santa Clara, California, USA.

Todd M. Gabe, Professor, School of Economics, University of Maine, Orono, Maine, USA.

Peter Gordon, Professor, School of Planning, Policy and Development, University of Southern California, Los Angeles, California, USA.

Cristopher Graziul, PhD Candidate, Department of Sociology, University of Chicago, Chicago, Illinois, USA.

David F. Hardwick, Professor Emeritus of Pathology and Pediatrics, University of British Columbia, Vancouver, British Columbia, Canada.

Randall G. Holcombe, DeVoe Moore Professor of Economics, Department of Economics, Florida State University, Tallahassee, Florida, USA.

Sanford Ikeda, Associate Professor of Economics, Purchase College, State University of New York, Purchase, New York, USA.

Börje Johansson, Professor, Department of Economics, Jönköping International Business School, Jönköping, and the Royal Institute of Technology, Stockholm, Sweden.

Arielle John, Mercatus Center Graduate Fellow and PhD Candidate, Department of Economics, George Mason University, Fairfax, Virginia, USA.

Charlie Karlsson, Professor, Department of Economics, Jönköping International Business School, Jönköping, Sweden.

Karen M. King, Postdoctoral Fellow, The Martin Prosperity Institute, Rotman School of Business, University of Toronto, Toronto, Ontario, Canada.

Carol Marie Kiriakos, PhD, Research Fellow, Department of Marketing and Management, Aalto University School of Economics, Helsinki, Finland.

Johan Klaesson, Associate Professor, Department of Economics, Jönköping International Business School, Jönköping, Sweden.

Charles Landry, Comedia, author and advisor to cities on how to creatively make the best of their assets, London, UK.

Samuli Leppälä, Research Associate, Department of Economics, University of Turku, Turku, Finland.

Christian Wichmann Matthiessen, Professor, Department of Geography, University of Copenhagen, Copenhagen, Denmark.

Charlotta Mellander, Associate Professor, Department of Economics, Jönköping International Business School, Jönköping, Sweden and Visting Research Fellow, Martin Prosperity Institute, University of Toronto, Toronto, Ontario, Canada.

Stefano Moroni, Associate Professor, Department of Architecture and Planning, Milan Polytechnic, Milan, Italy.

Philip S. Morrison, Professor, School of Geography, Environment and Earth Sciences, Victoria University of Wellington, Wellington, New Zealand.

Peter Jason Rentfrow, University Lecturer, Department of Social and Developmental Psychology, University of Cambridge, Cambridge, UK.

Annette Winkel Schwarz, Director of Development, Technical University of Denmark, Copenhagen, Denmark.

Daniel Silver, Assistant Professor, Department of Sociology, University of Toronto, Scarborough, Ontario, Canada.

Dean Keith Simonton, Distinguished Professor, Department of Psychology, University of California, Davis, California, USA.

Kevin M. Stolarick, Research Director, The Martin Prosperity Institute, Rotman School of Management, University of Toronto, Toronto, Ontario, Canada.

Virgil Henry Storr, Senior Research Fellow, Mercatus Center; Research Associate Professor, Department of Economics, George Mason University, Fairfax, Virginia, USA.

Tara Vinodrai, Assistant Professor, Department of Geography and Environmental Management & School of Environment, Enterprise and Development, University of Waterloo, Waterloo, Ontario, Canada.

PART 1

FOUNDATIONS

1 Analysing creative cities
David Emanuel Andersson and Charlotta Mellander

With the publication of *The Rise of the Creative Class* (Florida, 2002), the 'creative city' became the new hot topic among urban policymakers, planners and economists, especially in North America and Western Europe. But Richard Florida was not the first scholar to study the relationship between creativity and economic development. Already in 1985, the regional economist Åke E. Andersson published a book (in Swedish) that claimed that creativity represents the future of the metropolis, and that creative 'knowledge handlers' will become increasingly important in the emerging post-industrial economy (Andersson, 1985a). In 1989, Andersson co-authored another book that explained how the establishment of critical infrastructural links may cause phase transitions that result in far-reaching economic restructuring (Andersson and Strömquist, 1989). But since these books were published in Swedish, and the corresponding contributions in English were both much shorter and much less accessible to non-economists (Andersson, 1985b, 1985c; Andersson et al., 1990), the sphere of influence of Andersson's theory of the 'creative knowledge society' was limited to academic regional economists. The exception is Scandinavia, especially Sweden and Denmark, where Andersson's ideas have reached a wider audience.

This is not to say that Andersson's and Florida's theories are identical. They are not. While Andersson has always emphasized the importance of inter-regional network connectivity and the role of investments in transport infrastructures, for Florida these factors became a concern much later in conjunction with his work on mega-regions and post-crash structures (Florida, 2010). Conversely, Florida's interest in the various attributes that members of the creative class are more likely to share with one another than with others (see, for example, Florida, 2002, 2008; Florida et al., 2008) has no direct counterpart in Andersson's *oeuvre*. The focus on creativity in a new type of society where cities play a leading role is however something that Andersson and Florida shares. This implies that both Andersson's 'knowledge handlers' and Florida's 'talent' include artists, designers and entertainers as part of the human capital stock. Traditional economists tend to leave out such occupations when they use formal educational attainment as equivalent to human capital accumulation. The differences that remain between these two scholars could be summed up by contrasting their theoretical emphases: *infrastructure* (Andersson) versus *diversity and tolerance* (Florida).

Another original thinker in creativity research is the psychologist Dean Simonton. Since the 1970s he has analysed both the inherent personality traits of unusually creative individuals and what type of social interactions encourage creativity (see, for example, Simonton, 1984a, 1984b). More recently, Simonton has considered the relationship between creative milieus and political institutions (Simonton, 2004). Simonton's contributions represent a micro-level perspective on creativity that in many ways complement Andersson's and Florida's more aggregated analyses, and which Andersson has attempted to integrate in his more recent contributions (see, for example, Andersson and Andersson, 2006 and Chapter 2 in this volume).

It is our conviction that Åke E. Andersson, Richard Florida and Dean Simonton are the three leading theorists that have investigated the social aspects of creativity. It is therefore fortunate that this handbook is the first book that includes separate chapters by each of the 'Big Three'.

FOUNDATIONS

Since the most comprehensive treatises on creative people, cities or societies are associated with the regional economist Åke E. Andersson, the urban planner Richard Florida and the psychologist Dean Simonton, it is appropriate that these three creative thinkers provide the foundations for the more partial and applied contributions that follow in later parts of the book. In addition to Andersson, Florida and Simonton, Charlie Karlsson is also included as a contributor to the foundational part of the book, since he is one of a very small number of scholars who can provide an exhaustive account of the nascent literature on creative cities and its relation to adjacent fields such as cluster theory and the economics of innovation.

Åke E. Andersson (Chapter 2) sets the stage by connecting the micro, meso and macro aspects of creative cities. Drawing on some of the psychological findings of Simonton and others, he points to the human need for external stimulation as the underlying cause of knowledge-related agglomeration economies.

Andersson also shows that while creativity has become more widespread with the advent of post-industrial society, there is nonetheless a great deal of continuity between the most creative cities of the past and the globalized creative cities of the present. He uses examples ranging from ancient Athens to fin de siècle Vienna in order to show that there are a few time-invariant preconditions that must be present if human creativity is to flourish. For example, creative cities are and have always been associated with substantial and diverse inflows of migrants and traded goods as well as with the free exchange of artistic and scientific ideas.

Looking back at the phenomenal impact of Florida (2002), Richard Florida and co-authors (Chapter 3) take stock of past achievements and look ahead to what Florida's creative class theory can accomplish in the future. Does Florida's theory amount to a new paradigm in the social sciences? Florida, Charlotta Mellander and Patrick Adler think it does, as the chapter title makes clear. The new paradigm represents the confluence of a variety of pre-existing theoretical components, ranging from Marxian notions of class over Schumpeterian 'creative destruction' to the relentlessly evolving urban neighbourhoods of Jane Jacobs. The authors argue that the creative class paradigm – which includes associated ideas such as the three Ts of talent, technology and tolerance – has been better at explaining and predicting urban development trajectories than any single competing theory.

Creative cities and the creative class rely on creative individuals, implying that the starting point of any multi-layered analysis must include an understanding of what makes some individuals more creative than others. Dean Simonton (Chapter 4) explains how psychological research can shed light on creative processes in urban environments.

In particular, empirical psychological research shows that human creativity is related to a number of personality traits, including not only openness to experience and intelligence but also psychopathology.

Simonton speculates that creative cities act both as attractors and stimulators: they attract creative migrants and stimulate those already there. One of the stimulants of creativity is a diverse population, which is not only associated with big cities, but also with institutional features such as political fragmentation and decentralization.[1]

Charlie Karlsson's contribution (Chapter 5) provides the main literature review in this handbook, connecting the contributions of Andersson, Florida and Simonton to the wider literature on clusters, innovation and urban development. As the editor of numerous books (including handbooks) on clusters and innovation and as President of the European Regional Science Association at the time of writing, Karlsson is arguably uniquely qualified to offer the mainstream view in regional science (regional economics and economic geography) on the state of the art in creative city theorizing. Like many of the other contributors to this volume, he emphasizes the importance of economic diversity, such as when different clusters in a creative city spawn 'offspring' clusters that combine ideas from different sources.

PEOPLE

Florida's notion of a creative class builds on the assumption that a certain group of individuals are united by a number of attributes such as remuneration for creating new knowledge, tolerant values and perhaps even shared psychological traits. While there is a positive correlation between the share of a region's workers that belong to the creative class and the region's average educational attainment, this correlation is far from perfect. The creative class is therefore distinct from the highly educated segment of the population.

Peter Jason Rentfrow (Chapter 6) analyses the spatial distribution of responses to the well-known Five Factor Model of personality traits. Certain cities and regions may disproportionately cultivate certain personality traits, while at the same time attracting an inflow of people who have similar psychological predispositions as their established residents. Rentfrow's chapter represents an empirical study that makes explicit the spatial sorting processes that Simonton discusses at a conceptual level (see Chapter 4).

The main finding is that cities combine psychological traits, economic specialization and political values in a way that is both non-random and where psychological and non-psychological city attributes complement one another. For example, San Francisco, Los Angeles, Austin and New York are the cities whose residents attain the four highest average scores on the 'openness to experience' factor in the Big Five personality test. They are also among the most creative of American cities (Florida's top four creative cities are San Francisco, San Diego, Austin and Boston). A statistical analysis shows that the openness of a city's residents is most strongly correlated with its 'gay index', followed by its proportion of international migrants and the Milken Institute Tech-Pole Index.

While Rentfrow shows that openness to experience is related to many more factors than educational attainment levels, Todd Gabe (Chapter 7) shows that wage differences are not reducible to some education-based measure of human capital accumulation. He does this by showing that there is a 'creativity wage premium' that is not explained by differences in educational attainment, using detailed wage data from American metropolitan regions. In addition, the econometric analysis shows that the creativity wage premium is greater in more economically diverse regions, which implies that there are increasing returns to scale as a region diversifies economically. In contrast, the creativity wage premium is smaller in the most creative industries, implying diminishing returns to creativity within the same industry.

Design work characterizes some of the most creative occupations, such as fashion designer, graphic designer and architect. Tara Vinodrai (Chapter 8) shows that Canadian employment in design occupations grew much more rapidly than overall employment between 1991 and 2006. Toronto was, however, the only city in which designers accounted for more than 1 per cent of the total workforce at the end of the analysed period, indicating that Toronto is Canada's design capital in both absolute and relative terms. But many other cities are catching up by posting faster growth of design employment than Toronto, for example, Calgary and Vancouver.

Karen King (Chapter 9) writes about another aspect of Canada's post-industrial economy. Her focus is on inter-regional migration and the question of whether Florida's creative, service and working classes exhibit different migration propensities as regards the characteristics of their respective destination regions. Perhaps surprisingly, King finds that this is not clearly evident. While creative class people are more prone to migrate to regions that are high in tolerance and technology than to other regions, this demonstrated preference is not limited to creative class migrants; service and working-class people also exhibit greater-than-average migration propensities to such regions. Another unexpected result is that while creative class workers are attracted to tolerant and technological destinations, they are repelled (*ceteris paribus*) by regions that are rich in talent. While this result may appear counterintuitive, one should perhaps interpret it as the effect of diminishing returns as talent becomes progressively less scarce.

A subset of the creative class that is supposed to demonstrate unusually pronounced creative class attributes are the 'bohemians', which is the occupational grouping that Florida (2002) uses for his so-called 'boho index'. Roberta Comunian and Alessandra Faggian (Chapter 10) note that many of these bohemians have attended arts-related courses in higher education.

In the United Kingdom, arts-related education is over-represented in certain localities, which implies that bohemian students are likely to cluster there. The question then arises whether they stay in the same location after graduating from college. Comunian and Faggian show that although there are positive correlations between the number of bohemian students, graduates and workers in a location, there are nevertheless some British locations that are favoured to a greater extent than is accounted for by the spatial distribution of bohemian students. No such place is more favoured than London, which dominates bohemian employment to an even greater extent than it dominates bohemian education. In particular, the western part of inner London seems to have taken on a role as the 'artistic Mecca' of the British economy.

NETWORKS

The network perspective is closely connected to Åke E. Andersson's focus on how critical infrastructural links enable cities to create more new knowledge than would otherwise be possible (cf. Andersson, 1985a; Andersson and Strömquist, 1989). According to this 'infrastructure-centred' view, creative cities not only need sufficient population diversity, tolerant values and investments in scientific research, they also need sufficient infrastructural connectivity to other creative cities around the world.

In what is perhaps the key empirical contribution of this book, Christian Wichmann Matthiessen, Annette Winkel Schwarz and Søren Find describe and analyse the spatial distribution and connectivity of scientific research, using linkages between academic institutions and functional urban regions to assess the relative weight of the world's metropolitan regions. Their findings support Florida's (2008) assertion that the world is 'spiky' rather than flat, and that the scientific world is even spikier than other economic spatial configurations. The existence of agglomeration economies guarantee spikiness, but spatial patterns in science, engineering and medicine imply even stronger agglomeration economies in the production of science than elsewhere, as well as an even spikier map of the world.

Matthiessen, Schwarz and Find show that there is a great deal of path dependence in the spatial structure of science, with northwestern Europe and North America hosting most of the leading creative city regions. But there is also a dissemination tendency that is demonstrated by the fact that the scientific output of Asian and southern European cities is growing more rapidly than the output of the dominant cities along the main European and North American corridors.

Scientific connectivity is measured as journal paper co-authorships involving different cities while scientific volume is measured as the total number of journal papers originating in a city. Combining the connectivity and volume measures results in a spatial structure with several levels and regional 'bands'. The image that emerges from this spatial analysis is one in which London is the world's most important science city. This is a striking conclusion for two reasons. First, London is also the city where land prices reach a global maximum, which points to the connection between science and other types of production. Second, the centrality of London in the world of science exemplifies the importance of lock-in effects and path dependence: London was the city where the scientific method was invented in the seventeenth century in conjunction with the establishment of the Royal Society of London for Improving Natural Knowledge (see Chapter 2).

Daniel Silver, Terry Nichols Clark and Christopher Graziul (Chapter 12) expand our view by looking at the role of creativity in urban development, but in a very different way from the conventional economic focus on either industries or occupations. Their focus is instead on how the mixture of scenes (consumption clusters) of various types interact with different local performance measures such as population growth or income growth. The authors identify and survey different types of such creative scenes, including a city's 'glamorous', 'bohemian' and 'traditional' scenes.

Silver, Clark and Graziul find that there is no simple recipe between one type of scene and one type of urban development. Many different types of scenes may generate growth, and what type of scene generates the greatest growth-enhancing properties depends on a number of local and regional attributes. For example, bohemian scenes 'are strongest in areas that are breaking with tradition and taking off in artistic and economic activity'.

In Chapter 13, Elizabeth Currid-Halkett and Kevin Stolarick show that artistic specialization tends to be specific rather than general within the spatial context of American metropolitan areas. Only in New York and Los Angeles does it make sense to speak of a general specialization in a variety of artistic skills and artistic industries.

Currid-Halkett and Stolarick also show that many visual artists, musicians and writers do not work in artistic industries. Conversely, many of the workers in the artistic industries are non-artists. Different places specialize in different arts, and some places may combine over-represented artistic skills with under-represented artistic industries and vice versa.

David Batten (Chapter 14) identifies the Dutch Randstad region as an original network city which also serves as an example of the economic potential associated with a new trend: the development of networks of overlapping cities with complementary economic functions. Newer examples of this type of emergent network region include Scandinavia's Øresund and Japan's Kansai regions.

The economic justification of a network region is its ability to combine diverse specializations and diverse residential environments within an integrated market for jobs and housing. It therefore becomes possible to serve a greater variety of skills and residential preferences than is possible in a traditional monocentric region. Batten contends that networks of mutually accessible city centres, residential neighbourhoods and green areas may become increasingly common (and competitive) as part of the evolution of the new post-industrial society.

It is not only locally that people network; in today's globalized world networks may span the globe, as is evidenced by interactions between information technology professionals as far apart as Silicon Valley and Finland. But while it is true that telephone and computer networks facilitate long-distance interaction, Carol Kiriakos argues (Chapter 15) that such technologically assisted interaction is insufficient for certain types of interpersonal exchange.

Not only does transmission of tacit knowledge often require face-to-face interaction; being in a locality may also build trust and provide an environment in which serendipitous discoveries happen. In interviews with Finnish residents of Silicon Valley, she shows how advantageous an on-the-scene presence is for those who desire to take full advantage of the local knowledge that is hosted by a specific region. As one Silicon Valley Finn puts it: 'from a distance, you can access what you know you are looking for, but when living in the locality, you can access what you did not know you needed'.

PLANNING

Friedrich Hayek (1945) shows how central planning leads to knowledge losses, because planners cannot access or process knowledge of the 'particular circumstances of time and place' (Hayek, 1945, p. 521). Economic progress depends on the existence of a multitude of decentralized economic experiments that are both guided by and influence market prices.

David Emanuel Andersson (Chapter 16) argues that a more complex economy implies more diverse preferences, which in turn implies that the Hayekian knowledge problems that afflict all planning are even more serious in a post-industrial than in an industrial society. While the set of shared objectives is small in an industrial society, we can expect it to be smaller still in a society where people are not only more diverse in their geographic origins, but also more diverse in the skills that they make use of as producers and consumers.

D.E. Andersson therefore suggests that the success of government initiatives in creative cities depends on their being modest and severely constrained. While it may sometimes be worthwhile to tax residents in order to fund major infrastructure projects, any attempt to fine-tune land-use patterns or to plan elaborate social policies can only diminish the set of local creative experiments that jointly decide the creative accomplishments of a city.

In a similar vein, Stefano Moroni (Chapter 17) argues that creative cities do not need 'creative land-use plans'; stable, rigid and uncreative land-use regulations are necessary for allowing the full potential of creative market interactions to materialize. Moroni's point of view is that these land-use regulations should be universal and based on a simple, non-discriminatory and easily understood system of rules that is the same everywhere (cf. Hayek, 1979). More active and locally differentiated public planning is only desirable when it concerns public property. There should therefore be a stricter differentiation between private property (with minimal planning constraints) and public property than is usually the case. This would facilitate the emergence of creative new uses of land.

While using a similar theoretical approach as D.E. Andersson and Moroni in that it employs the Hayekian notion of a 'spontaneous order', the conclusions of Gus diZerega and David Hardwick (Chapter 18) are much less similar. Rather than treating the market as an unusually efficacious spontaneous order (the views of D.E. Andersson and Moroni), they claim that a balance has to be achieved between three complementary and sometimes contradictory such orders: the market, democracy and civil society. According to this view, markets privilege a narrow rationality centred on the accumulation of money, while democracies privilege the accumulation of votes. There is therefore a need for balancing the systemic forces so that no single spontaneous order reigns supreme.

Gus diZerega and Hardwick use Vancouver as an example of what they consider to be an unusually successful example of balancing markets, politics and civil society. It is this balance that has enabled the city to prosper as one of North America's most successful creative cities. Markets have been creative, but so have democratic decision-making and non-governmental grassroots organizations.

MARKETS

Both Åke E. Andersson and Richard Florida explain creative cities as spatial manifestations of market processes. In Åke E. Andersson's theory, new networks and new institutions have caused a phase transition from an industrial society based on manufacturing and large-scale infrastructures to a new type of society in which the creation of knowledge is central. And the creation of knowledge tends to benefit from being located in cities with good and 'fine-grained' connectivity to the rest of the world. Florida's creative class theory is similarly economic: increasing market demand for creative endeavours has resulted in many more people earning a living from the creation of new ideas and new designs than in the past.

Randall Holcombe (Chapter 19) argues that since the creative class is defined as consisting of people who receive market remuneration for their services, notions of entrepreneurship become central to our understanding of the creative class. He uses Israel Kirzner's (1973) theory of entrepreneurship to show that creative work really is entrepreneurial work: it amounts to directly or indirectly profit-seeking creative changes from the habitual way of doing things within an evolutionary market process.

The implication, according to Holcombe, is not only that policies that favour entrepreneurship are exactly those that favour the creative class. It is also that sufficiently favourable policies may expand the creative class to encompass almost all workers. Holcombe contends that a society with well-protected property rights, low barriers to market entry for newcomers and low taxes would be especially important for cultivating an environment in which people are likely to engage in work that is both creative and remunerative.

Arielle John and Virgil Henry Storr (Chapter 20) claim that markets are not only important as a process which encourages and rewards socially beneficial creativity and entrepreneurship. Markets also encourage values that are conducive to creative cities. Among other such values, they claim that markets encourage the very tolerance that Florida asserts is associated with the creativity of urban environments. They note that Voltaire was an early exponent of this view, writing that in 'the Exchange in London . . . the Jew, the Mohametan, and the Christian deal with one another as if they were the same religion' (Voltaire [1733] 2003, p. 26).

The modern economic explanation for the connection between markets and tolerance is that markets raise the cost of discrimination and therefore discourage it (Friedman, 1962). John and Storr use the Reading Terminal Market in Philadelphia as one specific example of how real-world markets encourage interactions that serve to defuse ethnic and other cultural tensions.

Inventors are a category of people who are natural members of the creative class and who should benefit from locating in creative cities. Pierre Desrochers and Samuli Leppälä (Chapter 21) describe their interviews with numerous inventors in Québec and Ontario, which were conducted with the aim of finding what connections and local conditions are especially conducive to coming up with new ideas.

Echoing Jacobs (1969), Desrochers and Leppälä conclude that inventors benefit not only from an urban environment, but from a diverse urban environment. The interviewed inventors gave detailed descriptions of how they benefited from being able to encounter dissimilar ideas within a limited spatial context.

In Chapter 22, Peter Gordon and Sanford Ikeda look at another of Jacobs's prescriptions, which is that density is essential for creativity and innovation. With this as their starting point, they investigate whether members of the creative class are disproportionately attracted by dense areas.

When looking at the migration pattern of people with advanced degrees in the United States, they find that there is no clear preference either way: both high-density

Manhattan and low-density Silicon Valley are among the main destinations for such migrants. On the other hand, dense areas get more in-migrants, other things being equal. But districts with high population densities areas attract people in general rather than members of the creative class in particular. Generally speaking, high-income and high-density neighbourhoods in small conurbations are most favoured, especially if located on the west coast or in New England.

Gordon and Ikeda speculate that while density may continue to be important due to superior interaction opportunities, the relevant density may take other forms than Jacobs's favoured inner-city neighbourhoods with short blocks and mixed uses. They argue that in a society where most people travel by car, what is important is not so much being in a traditional downtown, but rather in any kind of space that provides informal meeting places with good accessibility vis-à-vis residents.

Stockholm is one of the most creative cities in the world. It is not only one of the top 30 global research centres (see Chapter 11) with one of the highest number of published papers per person, it also has an unusually tolerant population according to the results of the 2005 wave of the World Values Survey. It is therefore appropriate that Börje Johansson and Johan Klaesson (Chapter 23) dig deeper in order to survey and analyse the economic structures and interactions that characterize the metropolitan area.

They show that knowledge-intensive services are over-represented in the Stockholm region as compared with Sweden as a whole. It is possible to identify five important clusters with high location quotients in the Stockholm region, of which four are unusually knowledge-intensive in terms of their cognitive requirements.

An especially important finding is that Stockholm is Sweden's key import region. This corroborates Jacobs's (1984) contention that successful metropolitan regions are import centres. Inflows of new ideas and products facilitate the creation of a diverse local economic environment, which in its turn encourages local creativity and innovativeness. But Johansson's and Klaesson's analysis shows that the benefits of imports are not limited to the cultivation of creativity within the region itself. While their analysis shows that imports flow disproportionately to Stockholm and that imported novelties are a source of innovation in its dominant clusters, it is perhaps even more significant that the innovative changes to the economic structure that take place in the Stockholm region foreshadow similar structural changes in the rest of the Swedish urban hierarchy. Imports make Stockholm more creative, and this creativity demonstrates feasible directions of change for firms in smaller Swedish regions.

Philip Morrison (Chapter 24) analyses the spatial structure of Wellington, a small creative region and an antipodean capital city. Unlike Johansson and Klaesson, Morrison concentrates on a feature that may be interpreted as a less desirable consequence of knowledge-driven economic restructuring. He argues that the inflow of high-income creative class people to the city centre of Wellington has resulted in increasing levels of socio-economic residential segregation. This spatial segregation has had the effect of forcing many less-educated workers to accept long commutes in order to provide essential services for the high-end creative workers that populate the downtown area and adjacent neighbourhoods.

While acknowledging that Wellington's economic restructuring has benefited the region in terms of aggregate wealth, Morrison argues that there may be certain segments of the population that are becoming increasingly marginalized. This is especially evident in the housing market, as market forces may price many long-established residents out of previously attainable locations.

VISIONS

The contributors to this volume agree that the creative city is here to stay. The new post-industrial society has arisen due to greater network connectivity and increasing economic complexity, and the strong agglomeration economies that are associated with most knowledge-intensive services guarantee that some cities must become creative centres.

But what a desirable scenario of future urban development should look like is not self-evident. In the final part of the book, Fred Foldvary and Charles Landry offer competing visions that could hardly be more different. While different, they offer relevant contrasts, since the (mostly unstated) policy implications of the book's contributors seem to range from Foldvary's decentralized minimal-state conception to Landry's highly interventionist creative city. While most contributions could perhaps be construed as implicitly prescribing a vague middle ground, it is appropriate that the explicitly normative contributions represent contrasts that can serve as useful foils to each other.

Foldvary (Chapter 25) offers an unabashedly libertarian vision. He argues that market processes are virtually always best at encouraging desirable forms of creativity in an urban setting. Drawing partly on the ideas of Henry George, he envisions a future creative society that consists of a multitude of voluntary communities, where collective goods are funded through contribution assessments that are derived from land rents. The voluntary communities that Foldvary proposes have a great deal in common with contemporary condominium associations, although on a larger spatial scale. The community of Arden, Delaware, is one of several examples of contractual governance that Foldvary thinks stimulates creativity to a greater extent than is possible with conventional urban institutions.

In contrast, Landry (Chapter 26) offers up a variegated menu of possible policy interventions that he thinks will encourage cities to become more creative. These policies range from targeted housing policies over encouragement of various aspects of creativity in the education system to architectural landmarks that symbolize the specific character of a creative city. While accepting that markets have an indispensable role in urban development and rejecting the idea that all cities should adopt identical policies, his chapter reads very much like a manifesto for an updated (or 'post-modernized') social democracy.

We believe that it is a desirable attribute of this book that it accommodates a wide variety of policy views; it complements the diversity of analytical approaches that the contributors represent. The goal of this book is not to provide a unified and mutually consistent theory, nor is it to pursue shared ideological commitments. What we wish to provide is a diverse framework that may stimulate future creative attempts to understand creative cities. Creativity benefits from the presence of diverse ideas, whether they manifest themselves as diverse individuals in a city or as diverse chapters in a book.

NOTE

1. This aspect is elaborated by Åke E. Andersson in Chapter 2 (the role of political fragmentation and disunity) and by David Emanuel Andersson in Chapter 16 (the creative potential of political decentralization).

REFERENCES

Andersson, Å.E. (1985a), *Kreativitet, Storstadens framtid*, Stockholm: Prisma.
Andersson, Å.E. (1985b), 'Creativity and regional development', *Papers of Regional Science*, **56**(5), 5–20.
Andersson, Å.E. (1985c), 'Creativity and economic dynamic modelling', in D.F. Batten, J. Casti and B. Johansson (eds), *Economic Evolution and Structural Adjustment*, Berlin: Springer, pp. 27–45.
Andersson, Å.E. and D.E. Andersson (2006), *The Economics of Experiences, the Arts and Entertainment*, Cheltenham, UK and Northampton, MA, USA: Edward Elgar Publishing.
Andersson, Å.E. and U. Stömquist (1989), *K-samhällets framtid*, Stockholm: Prisma.
Andersson, Å.E., C. Anderstig and B. Hårsman (1990), 'Knowledge and communication infrastructures and regional economic change', *Regional Science and Urban Economics*, **20**, 359–76.
Florida, R. (2002), *The Rise of the Creative Class and How It's Transforming Work, Leisure, Community, and Everyday Life*, New York, NY: Basic Books.
Florida, R. (2008), *Who's Your City? How the Creative Economy is Making Where to Live the Most Important Decision of Your Life*, New York, NY: Basic Books.
Florida, R. (2010), *The Great Reset, How New Ways of Living and Working Drive Post-crash Prosperity*, New York, NY: Harper Collins.
Florida, R. C.M. and K.M. Stolarick (2008), 'Inside the black box of regional development: human capital, the creative class and tolerance', *Journal of Economic Geography*, **8**(5), 615–49.
Friedman, M. (1962), *Capitalism and Freedom*, Chicago, IL: University of Chicago Press.
Hayek, F. A. (1945), 'The use of knowledge in society', *American Economic Review*, **35**(4), 519–30.
Hayek, F.A. (1979), *Law, Legislation, and Liberty*, Chicago, IL: University of Chicago Press.
Jacobs, J. (1969), *The Economy of Cities*, New York, NY: Random House.
Jacobs, J. (1984), *Cities and the Wealth of Nations*, New York, NY: Random House.
Kirzner, I.M. (1973), *Competition and Entrepreneurship*, Chicago, IL: University of Chicago Press.
Simonton, D.K. (1984a), *Genius, Creativity, and Leadership: Historiometric Inquiries*, Cambridge, MA: Harvard University Press.
Simonton, D.K. (1984b), 'Artistic creativity and interpersonal relations across and within generations', *Journal of Personality and Social Psychology*, **46**, 1273–86.
Simonton, D.K. (2004), 'Creative clusters, political fragmentation, and cultural heterogeneity: an investigative journey though civilizations East and West', in P. Bernholz and R.Vaubel (eds), *Political Competition, Innovation and Growth in the History of Asian Civilizations*, Cheltenham, UK and Northampton, MA, USA: Edward Elgar Publishing, pp. 39–56.
Voltaire [1733] (2003), *Philosophical Letters: Letters Concerning the English Nation*, Mineola, NY: Dover.

2 Creative people need creative cities
Åke E. Andersson

The proper study of creativity requires an interdisciplinary approach. At the micro level most of the research has been done by psychologists, neurologists and other cognitive scientists. Herbert Simon (1955) was the first economist to stress the need for cognitive psychology as a part of microeconomic analysis in the age of information technology. The main reason is the fact that ideas emerge and are developed in the brain of some individual. In the following sections considerable space is devoted to an analysis of the incentives, capacities and other individual conditions that are relevant at the micro-analytic level of creative individuals.

However, the ideas that arise in the brain of an individual may develop further in the interaction with other individuals. The potential for further development implies an important role for organizations that favour creative interaction. Such organizations can be informal gatherings like the Bloomsbury Group in London or highly formalized organizations such as university departments, research institutes or art schools.

Much of the research on creativity has stressed the importance of accessibility to informal and formal organizations for creative individuals. In addition, there is ample evidence that a great diversity of ideas supports the creative processes of scientists and artists. Large metropolitan urban regions are therefore the most important and accessible 'macro-organizations', since they tend to host a great number of formal and informal creative (lower-level) organizations.[1]

CREATIVITY AS AN ECONOMIC CONCEPT

Creativity is a common phenomenon. Small children are creative when they discover new ways of expressing themselves through sentences, pictures or games. This kind of small-scale creativity is of course relevant to schooling and child rearing. However, in this chapter the focus is on creativity as a public phenomenon; on creativity as it occurs in science, the arts and in industrial research.

Creativity in its role as a public phenomenon is a process that generates useful new ideas in a general sense. This process is inherently dynamic and thus important for the development of culture, technology and institutions (Andersson and Sahlin, 1997; Sahlin, 2001). Formally, I define creativity as follows:

Creativity is a process that gives rise to a flow of ideas from an individual or a group of individuals. For the process to be regarded as creative, relevant experts will – sooner or later – have to judge the flow of ideas as new and at least potentially useful for consumers, producers or other creators.

Table 2.1 Impacts and characteristics of creative capital

	Capital	
	Tangible	Intangible
Impact		
Private (Individual)	Innovation of prototypes	Innovation of ideas Diffusion of ideas (for example, in universities)
Public (Collective)	Diffusion of copies Diffusion in markets of artefacts Derived ideas on communication networks	Creation of ideas (for example, new compositions, models or blueprints)

The creation of new ideas is – in economic terms – related to the subsequent innovation of these ideas in the form of useful and testable prototypes in relevant arenas such as laboratories, lecture halls or local markets. The size, wealth and diversity of large cities such as New York or London explain the predominant role of such cities as arenas for the market innovation of new products (Andersson, 1985; Glaeser and Mare, 2001). The intimate connections between creation, innovation and direct diffusion of ideas are a primary explanation of why large cities are the historical and contemporary hubs of creativity. Table 2.1 shows the relations between creation, innovation and diffusion of new ideas.

The diffusion process may start as direct diffusion of new ideas within research universities, or as production and marketing of an innovated new product. In the latter case, it tends to be based on a prototype which is frequently protected by patents so as to secure private returns. After the patents or copyrights expire successful innovations tend to give rise to widespread production of generic copies and the new idea will then become available as a public good.

The patent protection time is relatively short, while the copyright protection time is irrationally long.

CREATION OR DISCOVERY?

A hotly disputed issue, especially among mathematicians and physicists, is the nature of new theories. Do they exist independently before humans discover them? Would the natural number system or the Pythagorean Theorem be true even if no mathematician had ever formulated the relevant concepts? Alternatively, is the natural number system or Euclidian geometry creations of individual human minds in some social and natural context?

These questions have been debated among philosophers since ancient times. Leslie White (1947) scrutinizes the arguments for and against discovery and creation within mathematics. The reason for concentrating on mathematics is the purely syntactic nature of mathematics, which makes it somewhat similar to music. White's first group of examples includes mathematicians such as G.H. Hardy and Isaac Newton, philosophers such as Rene Descartes and Immanuel Kant and even a musical composer such as Johann

Sebastian Bach, all of whom shared a belief in eternal truths rather than purely human creation. They believed that they had been lucky in their process of discovery and that no human, social or cultural factor had facilitated their creative acts. The implication is that agglomerations of scholars in cities or regions could not have been the ultimate causal factors behind their achievements. The city would then just be a convenient place for marketing such discoveries.

The opposite belief – in human mathematical creativity as an outcome of a social and cultural process – was shared by an equally influential group of thinkers that included the physicists Albert Einstein and Erwin Schrödinger as well as the mathematicians Jacques Hadamard and Henri Poincaré.

The confusion among the believers in eternal truths – to be discovered by a lucky few – is caused by their disregard of the importance of inherited accumulated knowledge and interactions with other knowledgeable people. And it is in the context of the evolutionary nature of history and its impact on the accessibility of knowledge that one must search for explanations as to why some cities and regions have become especially good at cultivating human creativity.

INFRASTRUCTURAL AND VARIATIONAL CREATIVITY

Inventions and discoveries are different manifestations of created ideas. An invention or a discovery mostly starts with the conception of a rather superficial structure, which is later followed by a sudden realization that below this surface structure there is a more important deep structure. A new deep structure may encompass the formation of a new principle of composition or a new theory which may be used as a starting point for new creations.

Margaret Boden (1990) draws on this observation in her dichotomization of creativity. The first class of creativity implies invention of a completely new principle of construction, composition or set of concepts, which thereby provides a new generative structuring of some problem area. This type of creativity is fundamental or infrastructural. The second class of creativity is built on variations of themes, which uses some pre-existing creative infrastructure as its foundation. Joseph Schumpeter (1954) and Thomas Kuhn (1962) had earlier made the same distinction as Boden. Schumpeter claimed that there tended to be alternating periods of creative and relatively static periods that he called a 'classical situation', with the latter periods encompassing marginal improvements to the previously created theories. A classical situation was characterized by 'a large expanse of common ground . . . and a feeling of repose, both of which create an expression of finality – the finality of a Greek temple that spreads its perfect lines against a cloudless sky' (Schumpeter, 1954, p. 754).

Schumpeter (1934), John von Neumann ([1937] 1975), von Neumann and Oscar Morgenstern (1944) and John Maynard Keynes (1936) are four obvious examples of creativity in the infrastructural sense, while Paul Samuelson ([1947] 1983), Gerard Debreu (1959) and Robert Solow (1956) are obvious examples of classical or variational creators.

A few further examples from the arts and from mathematics suffice to clarify the difference. Arnold Schoenberg created the most important principles for composing dodecaphonic music and should consequently be seen as the creator of the infrastructure of dodecaphony. In contrast, Alban Berg and Anton von Webern exemplify variational creativity in their application and further development of Schoenbergian principles. Applied to the visual arts, this same dichotomy would imply that Paul Cezanne was the creator of the infrastructure of modernist painting, while Georges Braque and Pablo Picasso would be its most important variational creators (Andersson and Andersson, 2006). A third example from the world of science is a treatise entitled '*Inequalities*' by G.H. Hardy, John Edensor Littlewood and George Pólya ([1934] 1967). By reformulating many mathematical equations as inequalities they created a basis for many of the contributions in mathematical programming that were developed and innovated from the 1940s onward. In this context, George Dantzig (1984) and Harold Kuhn (1956) – with their respective formulations of linear and non-linear programming – would be examples of variational creators.

This dichotomization of creativity does, however, not imply that one type of creativity is more important in the short run. The only qualitative difference is that infrastructural creativity harbours a greater potential for expanding the domain of feasible variational creativity.

CREATIVITY VERSUS PRODUCTIVITY: ADAM SMITH ON AN ECONOMIC DILEMMA

In *Wealth of Nations*, Adam Smith ([1776] 2006) discusses the trade-off between the requirements of a productive society (in the short run) and the need to preserve inventiveness for the long-term progress of productivity. In his famous passage on pin production, Smith shows how a far-reaching division of labour may lead to a 400-fold increase in productivity as compared with production without specialization:

> To take an example, therefore, from a very trifling manufacture; but one in which the division of labour has been very often taken notice of, the trade of the pin-maker; a workman not educated to this business (which the division of labour has rendered a distinct trade), – nor acquainted with the use of the machinery employed in it (to the invention of which the same division of labour has probably given occasion), could scarce, perhaps, with his utmost industry, make one pin in a day, and certainly could not make twenty. But in the way in which this business is now carried on, not only the whole work is a peculiar trade, but it is divided into a number of branches, of which the greater part are likewise peculiar trades. One man draws out the wire, another straights it, a third cuts it, a fourth points it, a fifth grinds it at the top for receiving the head; to make the head requires two or three distinct operations; to put it on, is a peculiar business, to whiten the pins is another; it is even a trade by itself to put them into the paper; and the important business of making a pin is, in this manner, divided into about eighteen distinct operations, which, in some manufactories, are all performed by distinct hands, though in others the same man will sometimes perform two or three of them. – I have seen a small manufactory of this kind where ten men only were employed, and where some of them consequently performed two or three distinct operations. But though they were very poor, and therefore but indifferently accommodated with the necessary machinery, they could, when they exerted themselves, make among them about twelve pounds of pins in a day. There are in a pound upwards of four thousand pins of a middling size. Those ten persons, therefore, could make among them upwards of forty-eight thousand pins in a day. Each person, therefore, making a tenth part of forty-eight thousand pins, might be considered as making four thousand

eight hundred pins in a day. But if they had all wrought separately and independently, and without any of them having been educated to this peculiar business, they certainly could not each of them have made twenty, perhaps not one pin in a day; that is, certainly, not the two hundred and fortieth, perhaps not the four thousand eight hundredth part of what they are at present capable of performing, in consequence of a proper division and combination of their different operations. (Smith, 2006, Vol. 1, pp. 4–6)

In Volume V, Smith reconsiders the long-term consequences of such a far-reaching division of labour:

In the progress of the division of labour, the employment of the far greater part of those who live by labour, that is, of the great body of the people, comes to be confined to a few very simple operations; frequently to one or two. But the understandings of the greater part of man are necessarily formed by their ordinary employments. The man whose whole life is spent in performing a few simple operations, of which the effects are, perhaps, always the same, or very nearly the same, has no occasion to exert his understanding, or to exercise his invention in finding out expedience for removing difficulties which never occur. He naturally loses, therefore, the habit of such exertion and generally becomes as stupid and ignorant as it is possible for a human creature to become. The torpor of his mind renders him, not only incapable of relishing or bearing a part in any rational conversation, but of conceiving any generous, noble or tender sentiment, and consequently of forming any just judgment concerning many even of the ordinary duties of private life. Of the great and extensive interest of his country he is all together incapable of judging; and unless very particular pains have been taken to render him otherwise he is equally incapable of defending his country in war. The uniformity of his stationary life naturally corrupts the courage of his mind, and makes him regard with abhorrence the irregular, unset, adventurous life of a soldier. It corrupts even the activity of his body, and renders him incapable of exerting with vigour and perseverance, in any other employment than that to which he has been bred. His dexterity at his own particular trade seems, in this manner, to be acquired at the expense of his intellectual, social and martial virtues. But in every improved and civilized society this is the state into which the labouring poor, that is the great body of a people, must necessarily fall, unless government takes some pains to prevent it.

It is otherwise in the barbarous societies, as they are commonly called, of hunters, of shepherds and even of husband-men in that rude state of husbandry which precedes the improvement of manufacturers, and the extension of foreign commerce. In such societies varied occupations of every man oblige every man to exert his capacity, and to invent expedience for removing difficulties which are continuingly occurring. Invention is kept alive, and the mind is not suffered to fall into that drowsy stupidity, which, in a civilized society, seems to numb the understanding of almost all the inferior ranks of people. (Smith, 2006, Vol. V, p. 782)

Division of labour is closely related with short-run productivity, while creativity is oriented towards increasing productivity in a much longer (and more uncertain) time perspective.

THE INCENTIVES TO CREATE AND THE SECULAR RISE IN THE DEMAND FOR CREATIVITY

The incentive to create new ideas can be exogenous or endogenous to the scientist or artist.

Exogenous incentives to create can come from the market or some policy-maker, by expressing a willingness to pay for the expected creative output. These incentives are becoming increasingly important as demand-side determinants of industrial research and development. But exogenous incentives can also be somewhat harder to observe. The creator may, for instance, be stimulated by expectations of future fame or by citations and other signs of appreciation from peers.

Endogenous incentives include the creative individual's curiosity and other such intrinsic psychological urges. Endogenous incentives have always been and remain important for mathematicians, philosophers and most other scientists with highly uncertain long-term consequences of their creative output. Much artistic work is of the same kind, whereas creative entertainment tends to be exogenously demand-driven to a greater extent.

The industrial society that was emerging in Britain at the time of Adam Smith was orientated towards quantitative productivity growth. This required a far-reaching division of labour all the way down to the individual worker within a hierarchically organized firm. The stability of this organizational principle implied – in a certain sense – a sort of arrested technological development. Industrial research and development became a kind of tinkering that aimed at improving the techniques for producing a given set of goods. Genuine creativity was looked upon as a socially marginal activity for a small group of artists, scientists and inventors.

Knowledge accumulation was rarely analysed by economists before the 1980s. Creativity – if it was mentioned at all – was only analysed indirectly, for example as an implicit and obscure part of 'human capital', 'technology' or 'innovation'. The recent interest in the role of creativity in economic growth is closely related to the consequences of the secular expansion of education in the industrial economies, the rapid growth of producer services and other knowledge-based industries and the increasing focus of manufacturing firms on industrial research and development (R&D).

In the early stages of industrialization, scientific and technological research has always been of minor importance. Even today, newly industrialized countries such as Greece, Turkey or Mexico allocate no more than half a per cent of their total resources (as measured by GDP) to investments in R&D. The GDP share allocated to R&D was probably even lower when countries such as the United States, Britain or Germany started industrializing in the nineteenth century.

By 2005 the picture had changed somewhat, as Table 2.2 illustrates. In the Organization of Economic Cooperation and Development (OECD) region, 2.25 per cent of total combined GDP was allocated to R&D expenditures. In Sweden, Finland and Japan the share allocated to R&D investments exceeded 3 per cent. There is, however, substantial variability among developed economies. Some wealthy countries – for example, Spain, Italy and Portugal – only allocated about 1 per cent of their respective GDPs to R&D.

The relative role of industrial R&D is remarkable. Fundamental scientific creativity – as measured by higher education research and development (HERD) – is less than one-fifth of total R&D expenditures (Gross Domestic Expenditures on Research and Development, GERD) in the OECD region. This is in stark contrast to the early twentieth century, when the small universities of Europe and the United States held most of the scant resources for research, while industrial entrepreneurs scavenged for those parts of scientific research output that could form a new base for industrial manufacturing. Technological development could then be seen as exogenous to economic processes

Table 2.2   Research and development (R&D) in OECD economies, 2005; percentages

	R&D/ GDP	R&D employment/ total employment	HERD[a]/GDP
Sweden	3.89	1.25	0.8
Finland	3.48	1.65	0.7
Japan	3.33	1.10	0.4
South Korea	2.99	0.79	0.3
Switzerland	2.93	0.61	0.7
United States	2.62	0.97	0.4
Germany	2.46	0.70	0.4
Denmark	2.45	1.02	0.6
Austria	2.42	0.68	0.6
OECD	**2.25**	**0.73**	**0.4**
France	2.13	0.80	0.4
Canada	1.98	0.77	0.7
Belgium	1.82	0.76	0.4
United Kingdom	1.78	0.55	0.5
Australia	1.76	0.84	0.5
Luxembourg	1.56	0.68	0.0
Norway	1.52	0.92	0.5
Czech Republic	1.42	0.48	0.2
Ireland	1.26	0.59	0.6
Spain	1.12	0.57	0.3
Italy	1.10	0.30	0.4
Hungary	0.94	0.41	0.3
Portugal	0.80	0.41	0.3
Greece	0.49	0.37	0.2

Note: [a]HERD is R&D in higher education institutions.

Source: OECD Science and Technology Indicators (2007).

(cf. Schumpeter, 1934). The situation is different in modern economies. Research and education is to an increasing extent developed interdependently with material invest-ments and the harnessing of economies of scale and scope. Scientific, technological and economic expansions are becoming important components of an endogenous growth process (Andersson and Beckmann, 2009). It is fairly clear that scientists have strong economic incentives to favour industrial research rather than those creative activities that form an integral part of research in the purer sciences. The increasing demand for applied research is therefore likely to have caused a brain drain from infrastructural creativity.

A genuine integration of creative research and technological development did not come to fruition until the end of the industrial era in North America and Western Europe. Manufacturing in the classical industrial mode was in decline both in North America and Western Europe as early as the 1950s. By the 1970s, manufacturing had seen its share of employment stagnate and – in some cases – even decline. The implication was that the most economically advanced societies could no longer expect

Table 2.3   Characteristics of efficient, creative and ordinary scientists

Individual characteristics	Very creative	Productive (efficient)	Very intelligent	Rich in ideas	Original	Personally absorbed in research
Group characteristics						
Productive (efficient)	0	Positive correlation	Positive correlation	0	0	0
Creative	Positive correlation	0	Positive correlation	Positive correlation	Positive correlation	Positive correlation
Ordinary	Negative correlation	0	0	Negative correlation	Negative correlation	0

Source: Smith (1993).

increasing employment from producing standardized producer or consumer goods. At that time, many economists expected conventional household services to be the new guarantors of full employment. Some economists even expected economic stagnation or decline, with increasing unemployment and lower living standards as unavoidable consequences.

Few economists expected creativity in science, technology, art and entertainment to become the most important factor for the future growth of real incomes and employment in an emerging post-industrial society. In reality, the occupational restructuring of some regions, notably the San Francisco Bay Area with Silicon Valley, Route 128 near Boston, Massachusetts as well as Cambridge, England, were early examples of a new type of interdependence between creative scientists, designers and innovative producers of new complex goods. The new occupational networks alluded to a new and increasingly important role for creativity in the economic system, which would eventually cause a realignment of the spatial distributions of employment, income and wealth (Andersson and Mantsinen, 1980; Andersson and Beckmann, 2009).

INDIVIDUAL INTELLIGENCE: A NECESSARY BUT NOT SUFFICIENT CONDITION FOR CREATIVITY

The psychologist Gudmund Smith and his colleagues have studied individual psychological traits among scientists. In one study (Smith and Carlsson 1990; Smith, 1993), all the sampled scientists were categorized according to their productivity (static efficiency) as well as their creativity as judged by a peer group. The results of the study are given in Table 2.3. The statistical method used by Smith is inverted factor analysis.

This study shows that a member of the creative group is not necessarily productive, while a member of the productive group cannot be expected to be more creative than average. But both groups comprise very intelligent individuals.

What is then meant by intelligence? One definition agreed upon by a sample of 52 psychologists and other cognitive scientists is the following:

> Intelligence is a very general mental capability that, among other things, involves the ability to reason, plan, solve problems, think abstractly, comprehend complex ideas, learn quickly and learn from experience. It is not merely book learning, a narrow academic skill, or test-taking smarts. Rather, it reflects a broader and deeper capability for comprehending our surroundings – 'catching on,' 'making sense' of things, or 'figuring out' what to do. (Gottfredson, 1997, p. 13)

Cognitive scientists and psychologists (Gardner, 1993) have expanded the notion of intelligence to reflect the following distinct cognitive abilities:

1. Visual-spatial
2. Verbal-linguistic
3. Logical-mathematical
4. Bodily-kinaesthetic
5. Musical
6. Interpersonal
7. Intrapersonal
8. Naturalistic
9. Existential

In contrast to the group of psychologists to which Gottfredsson (1997) refers, the cognitive scientist Howard Gardner uses a very broad definition:

> To my mind, a human intellectual competence must entail a set of skills of problem solving – enabling the individual to resolve genuine problems or difficulties that he or she encounters and, when appropriate, to create an effective product – and must also entail the potential for finding or creating problems – and thereby laying the groundwork for the acquisition of new knowledge. (Gardner and Moran, 2006, pp. 227–32)

Gardner's broad definition does not work in the context of creativity as analysed by Gudmund Smith, because Smith has defined and measured intelligence as a concept that is independent of creativity. It seems as if Smith is more in line with the ideas of most other psychologists.

The cognitive ability to solve problems of the nine types listed above has a long history in philosophy and, specifically, within epistemology. In much of philosophical analysis the focus has been on the individual's capacity to engage in logical deductive analysis in fields such as geometry, mathematics, linguistics or music. Recently, however, a number of philosophers have questioned the methods of classical logical analysis, with the most cogent arguments against narrow definitions being formulated by the philosopher Jaako Hintikka (1999) of Boston University. His view of intelligence uses analogies that bring to mind the fictional strategies of Sherlock Holmes: they go beyond the limits of classical logical deduction.

The four fundamental steps of successful and thus intelligent reasoning are, according to Hintikka (1999):

1. logical deduction from a set of axioms;
2. expansion of the process of reasoning by interrogation;
3. introduction of fruitful analogies;

4. introduction of new and often surprising elements (for example, facts, objects, hypotheses).

These steps constitute a decision loop whereby steps one through four are repeated until the problem is finally solved during the final application of step one. The approach implies that there is a fundamental difference between human and artificial intelligence (AI). AI is usually constrained to narrowly confined problem-solving of the type represented by step one.

An example from Sherlock Holmes is the story of the lost racehorse, which illustrates the critical importance of steps two and four. The story starts with the fact that a valuable horse has disappeared from a stable the preceding night. A number of employees and strangers might be suspected of having stolen the animal. The crucial question turns out to hinge on the reaction of the dog. The fact that the dog did not bark prompted the logical conclusion that the owner (of the dog and the horse) must have been the thief: the thief 'stole' the horse from himself.

An example from mathematics illustrates the interrogation approach. Let us assume that we have observed the following sequence:

1 = 1 squared
1+3 = 2 squared
1+3+5 = 3 squared
1+3+5+7 = 4 squared
1+3+5+7+9 = 5 squared

We can now start a Hintikka-type interrogation by asking the following question: could there be a theorem that is such that it states that the sum of n consecutive odd numbers is equal to n squared? If this can be assumed, is there then a way to prove beyond reasonable doubt that the theorem is true? What would be the best method for proving the theorem?

One way would be to use induction and to introduce the formula for the entity $n+1$ and then to proceed to step one. When this is done we can safely reduce all calculations of such sums to a single calculation of the square of n (= the number of numbers).

It is claimed that the great mathematician Carl Friedrich Gauss used similar reasoning when Gauss's primary school teacher asked him to calculate the sum of all integers from 1 to 100. To the astonishment of his teacher he did this in a couple of minutes. Gauss had thereby demonstrated (mathematical) intelligence. And he had also demonstrated creativity, because he must have invented the necessary theorem.

The broader conception of intelligence as demonstrated by mathematicians as well as detectives thus requires a combination of logical deduction; the ability to formulate new questions; and the use of analogies. The joint presence of these three elements in problem-solving implies a capacity to introduce new and sometimes surprising entities into the analysis.

THE MICRO-FOUNDATIONS OF CREATIVITY: ARE INDIVIDUAL CAPABILITIES ACQUIRED OR INHERITED?

We need to understand the creative processes at the micro level if we aspire to understand creativity at the social level, even if our focus is as narrowly delimited as the role of cities in the spatial organization of creativity. The creativity of an individual is a process which must rely on certain capabilities. As a process it is dynamic, because creativity causes the emergence of something that is genuinely new. Discoveries and inventions are the two most important outcomes of a creative process. It is nevertheless impossible to account for all cognitive capabilities and social contexts that jointly comprise the necessary and sufficient conditions for individual creativity. In this section the analysis is limited to a few important necessary capabilities that empirical studies have shown to be typical of creative personalities. There are also some pertinent complementary questions such as the question of whether all people are born creative. Another such question concerns the role of the social environment in supporting or reinforcing various creative capabilities.

There are a number of indicators that imply that creativity is not a genetic deviation from the norm but rather a generic human capability. One indicator is the development of the ability to speak. Even a small child can create completely new sentences in their communication with other children and adults. Sometimes they even seem surprised at their own linguistic discoveries and inventions. Linguistic creativity seems to develop by social interaction throughout a normal human lifespan.

The concentration of mathematical, musical and visual creativity in a minority of the population may very well be a consequence of too little daily training during the early childhood years for the bulk of the population. Most creative musicians and other artists have had the benefit of an education in the arts from their earliest years. Surprisingly many artists have grown up in an environment that is rich in artistic activities. Simonton (1984) used extensive empirical information to show that early exposure to scientifically or artistically creative personalities influences the creative capabilities of young people.

The education system does not generally compensate for the lack of artistic and other creative inspiration in the homes of children. Most school instruction in both the old and new industrialized countries focuses on the diffusion of established knowledge that is useful in manufacturing firms or bureaucracies. This implies that schools give priority to discipline, adaptation and group co-operation. Rote learning has been favoured at the expense of creativity training in almost all primary and secondary schools.

Gudmund Smith (Smith and Carlsson, 1990; Smith, 1993) has in his studies of the psychology of creativity found that the development of creativity during childhood and adolescence follows a typical cyclical pattern. During some phases of the cycle, learning and knowledge absorption is easy, while in other periods creativity develops rapidly. The creative phases typically occur between the ages of five and seven, ten and twelve as well as seventeen and nineteen. In most educational systems the two latter creativity periods are used for memorization exercises and exams. Such activities are inimical to the development of creativity. Smith has even claimed that creativity development benefits from an absence of fixed curricula.

COGNITION OF HIDDEN PATTERNS

Discoveries rely on the capacity to find patterns in a seemingly chaotic world. Peter Gärdenfors (2006, 2007, 2010) shows that the human brain is more or less permanently trying to discover meaningful patterns, even if no such pattern is at hand. A prominent example is the Rorschach test, where tested persons interpret meaningless pictures as conveying meaningful patterns or messages. One of the important creative capacities is the ability to discover and give meaning to visual patterns.

The detection of a hidden pattern and its transformation into something meaningful is often something that occurs suddenly in the brain – indicating dynamic non-linearity at work. Stewart and Peregoy (1983) use experiments to show how the brain discovers hidden structures. Their main finding is that the brain may be represented as a non-linear dynamic system with zones of structural instability, bifurcations and hysteresis as typical ingredients. Figure 2.1 shows how the perception of a man may suddenly change into a clear perception of a woman after three to six steps from left to right, while the perception of a woman is suddenly transformed into a man, when starting from the right and moving three to five steps to the left.

This implies that the brain tends to 'anchor' the original perception and needs a considerable inflow of new information before it can give up the initial interpretation in favour of a new one. The human mind tends to reinforce what it already knows, which creates stability. Creativity, however, benefits from a certain degree of instability in the

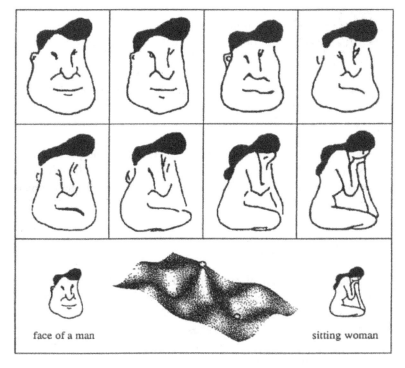

face of a man   sitting woman

Figure 2.1   The bi-stability of perception

human mind. Some instability is present in all who can experience cognitive instability when looking at patterns of the kind shown in the picture in Figure 2.1.

APPRECIATION AND USE OF PARADOXES

In the monumental treatise *Principia Mathematica*, Alfred North Whitehead and Bertrand Russell (1925/1927) – the two leading rationalists of philosophy and mathematics – tried to develop a new foundation of mathematics that would permanently set mathematics free from paradoxes. The key paradox arises from the question of whether the set of all sets is also a conventional set. This paradox harks back to paradoxes formulated by the philosophers of ancient Greece. One example is Epimenides of Knossos on Crete, who claimed that 'all Cretans are liars'. Can this be a true sentence? Another example is as follows: 'The next sentence is false. The preceding sentence is true.'

Most such examples are amusing. But some paradoxes are provocative from the vantage point of social scientists or politicians. A famous instance is the paradox of thrift, which was first stated by Bernard Mandeville ([1732] 1988) and elaborated by John Maynard Keynes (1936). According to this paradox it is prudent for a single household to increase its propensity to save if a recession is expected in the near future. If such a decision is taken by all members of a society, it may however cause a recession or even a depression. The rational political response might then be to encourage people to reduce their savings. The economist Thomas Schelling presents a number of similar economic paradoxes in *Micromotives and Macrobehavior* (1978). Such paradoxes are often helpful as a starting point for the creative thinker. An expansion of the analysis to a larger set of variables that present new interdependencies with the original variables may subsequently lead to a resolution of the initial paradox.

Frank Ramsey ([1931] 1977), Alan Turing (1937) and Kurt Gödel (1931) all show that there are a number of irreducible paradoxes in mathematics (Sahlin, 1990). In the arts, Oscar Reutersvärd and M.C. Escher demonstrated analogous irreducible paradoxes in the visual arts. The illustration by Reutersvärd in Figure 2.2 depicts a number of such visual paradoxes.

These irreducible paradoxes are aggregations of two possible parts that after their fusion into one seamless entity become impossible. The need for reducible as well as irreducible paradoxes as a starting point for creative processes in both art and science has been pointed out by Douglas Hofstadter (1979) among others.

EXPLOITING ANALOGIES

Based on the thinking of the Greek philosopher Pappos, the mathematician George Pólya claims that the most important capability in creative problem formulation and solving is shown in the use of analogies: 'Analogy pervades all our thinking, our everyday speech and our trivial conclusions as well as our ways of expression and the highest scientific achievements' (Pólya, 1945, p. 37). This is obvious in mathematics but seems to be even more important in artistic, scientific and technological creativity. The role of analogies in the creative process is obvious from Johannes Kepler's work on

Figure 2.2   Paradoxical projections to the plane

astronomical phenomena (Gentner et.al., 1997). Arthur Koestler – in his *Act of Creation* (1969) – also stressed the use of analogies when Gutenberg invented the printing process.

ON THE ART OF USING STRUCTURAL INSTABILITY CREATIVELY

The structural instability of technological or social systems is often seen as a major problem. However, it is frequently the only reasonable starting condition when searching for a creative solution to an apparently impossible design problem.

At the end of the nineteenth century, a number of engineers with an interest in aviation tried to create a manoeuvrable, motorized aeroplane. In spite of considerable expertise in aerodynamics and other disciplines, all early attempts at creating a manoeuvrable motor-powered airborne vehicle failed. The ambition had been to combine dynamic controllability with aerodynamic equilibrium and stability. The Wright brothers, by contrast, constructed an aeroplane that was structurally unstable. To the surprise of many, their construction proved manoeuvrable without superhuman strength, even if it required pilots to have rapid reflexes and reaction speeds.

Structural instability is also a precondition for much creativity in the arts, including architecture. Stable equilibrium states are in general only achieved in conjunction with the completion of the creative process. The initial phase of the process amounts to a search with several different stable equilibrium states as potential outcomes. The Necker cube (Figure 2.3) shows that what can be perceived as a stable hexagon (if inner lines are disregarded) can be transformed into an unstable cube by inclusion of the inner lines. The observer perceives each of the two focal points of the unstable cube to suddenly shift

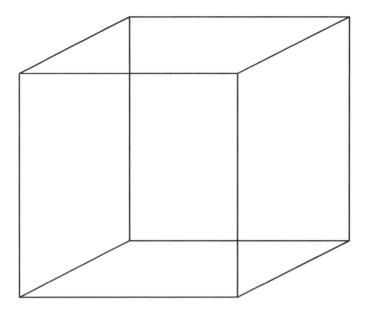

Figure 2.3   Perception instability of the Necker cube

between two perceived locations: the nearest point becomes the most distant point and vice versa.

The remarkable thing about this cube is that it is perceived as increasingly unstable the longer one observes it. Such a degree of instability creates a creative potential. By various minor changes it becomes possible to make the figure unambiguous, but which stable figure that will result is not predetermined; it is a decision problem for the designer.

We can also illustrate creative structural instability with a development tree. Apparently immaterial choices at an early stage can have dramatic effects on later outcomes. The dependence of creative processes on this type of instabilities – bifurcations – is used in origami, the Japanese art of folding sheets of paper.

Figure 2.4 shows a number of possible objects that result from folding a quadratic sheet of paper with a few predetermined folds, which all objects in the picture have in common. Every resulting object has a structurally stable composition of forms and folds. Origami-folding is a structurally unstable development process: the transformation paths from an unfolded paper with predetermined potential patterns to the nine objects run via a few strategic bifurcation points. After three folds out of nine or eleven, respectively, one has to decide whether to make a duck or a horse. The vase and the tulip are the most complicated objects in terms of the number of folds. The process also demonstrates that the originally quadratic sheet of paper attains an increasing number of characteristics. The sequencing of the folds is decisive for the final result, even if the intermediate steps do not reveal anything that anticipates the resulting object. It is that stage of the folding process where it is impossible to guess if the sheet will become, say, a seagull or a dog, which is the structurally unstable stage. This stage is fundamentally uncertain and is therefore also the critical point in the creative process. Tönu Puu (2006, pp. 160–8) analyses an analogous process as it relates to the development of technology. It should

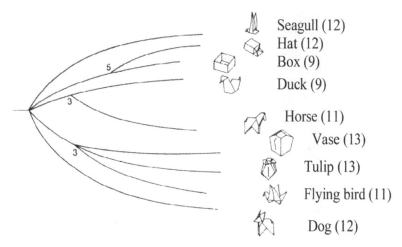

Seagull (12)
Hat (12)
Box (9)
Duck (9)

Horse (11)
Vase (13)
Tulip (13)
Flying bird (11)
Dog (12)

Figure 2.4   Origami folding as a bifurcating process

at this point be obvious that three-dimensional pattern formation, which is common in architecture, urbanization and in the creation of organizations of an even higher dimensionality, offers similar creative opportunities for exploiting structural instability.

Unlike creativity, a well-structured production process requires predictability and structural stability in order to be efficient. Creation has almost nothing in common with efficient production. The creator has to accept fundamental uncertainty and its unavoidable companion: structural instability. This implies that creative individuals must accept a career with uncertain production processes. They must therefore also accept uncertain income flows and in the end uncertain wealth.

A potentially creative society is – metaphorically speaking – like a stream of flowing ideas, where structural stability is the dominant feature of the dynamic process. During structurally stable periods, the creative acts that do occur amount to variations on a few established paradigmatic themes. There are, however, also short and infrequent periods of structural instability that generate potential bifurcations. Such bifurcations imply that many different creative trajectories are possible outside of the dominant paradigm. It is these short periods that give rise to revolutionary (infrastructural) creativity.

DYNAMICS AND STRUCTURAL INSTABILITY: FORMAL ANALYTICAL POSSIBILITIES

Most classical analytical techniques use the assumption that the system of interest exhibits stable equilibrium properties. In contrast, I have in this chapter argued in favour of using structural instability as a starting point in the analysis of individual and organizational creativity. The question then becomes this: is it possible to use formal theories and models that incorporate a generic situation of non-linearity that leads to structural instability?

Creative processes are highly dependent on non-linear synergies between people and their different ideas. The dynamics of synergies are possible to handle formally with the methods developed in synergetics. The field of synergetics owes much of its methodological development to the contributions of the German physicist Hermann Haken (1978). In a number of path-breaking studies, Haken has highlighted certain elements that are involved in synergetic processes. If we disregard certain less important components of this paradigm, we arrive at the following two conditions that must be fulfilled in synergetic analysis:

1. *The variables that are involved are dynamically and non-linearly interactive.*
2. *Timescales are separable, according to the relative velocity of change in the dynamic sub-processes.*

The first requirement, non-linear interactivity, excludes many of the standard and basically linear economic and psychological models from synergetics. Synergetics starts at the level of second-order interactions, which means that the interactions cannot be transformed into linear relations. Included among synergetic phenomena are catalysts, enzymes and similar interactive and collective phenomena. One example from psychology is given above (Stewart and Peregoy, 1983).

Fundamental to synergetic theory is the possibility of adiabatic approximation. This concept refers to the possibility of solving for an approximate equilibrium, using the actual difference in the timescales of different processes as a vehicle for approximating constancy of sub-processes. This implies that synergetics is a theory and modelling procedure for real rather than idealized systems.

Synergetics is a theory containing possibilities of bifurcations (that is, phase transitions). Although an evolutionary equilibrium may be a typical outcome, every synergetic system contains the potential for revolutionary changes to the structure. Stochastic phenomena can be essential to such phase transitions in synergetic models. Although of minor consequence during the stages of the evolutionary equilibrium of a specific system, there are situations – such as in the vicinity of a bifurcation – where and when even small stochastic swings can trigger a transfer from one evolutionary trajectory onto another, by way of a revolutionary disruption of the overall structure. In this sense, synergetics comes rather close to the thinking of Ilya Prigogine (Prigogine and Nicolis, 1989).

We can use synergetic reasoning in the context of modelling the development of creative ideas. Let us assume that such ideas are accumulated in nodes of an intellectual network. Let us further assume that some of these ideas are of a paradigmatic (infrastructural) nature, which means that they are changing extremely slowly and only through continuous confirmations or falsifications by fast, variation-oriented processes.

We can then consider the Modernist paradigm in the arts, as formulated by Cezanne, Picasso and Braque; the theory of quantum physics, as formulated by Planck, Bohr and Heisenberg; or Keynesian macroeconomics as examples of such slowly changing, paradigmatic, processes. Each process exists within networks of composition principles, that is to say, within networks of theoretical constructs. Assuming that the components of such a paradigm are interconnected with each other into a consistent and stable network of ideas, the consequence is then that the network (paradigm) can co-exist with a very fast process which generates derived models and compositions that are supported by the network. The network provides a source of composition principles for practical crea-

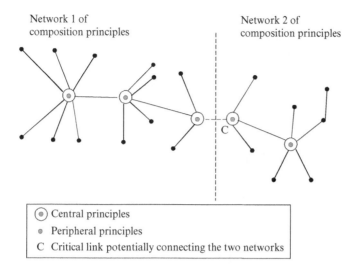

Network 1 of
composition principles

Network 2 of
composition principles

⊙ Central principles
● Peripheral principles
C Critical link potentially connecting the two networks

Figure 2.5   Interdependency of principles of composition

tive work. We can illustrate the synergetic principle as applied to a creative process with Figure 2.5.

Newly generated ideas can be either critical or non-critical. A critical idea must belong to the slowly changing part of a theoretical or aesthetic paradigm. A critical idea links or interconnects large subsets of the different networks of ideas, generating an expanded infrastructure for further development. Such a synergetic, critical idea (for example, a new theory, model or hypothesis) has two characteristics:

1.   It provides a short cut between otherwise unconnected networks of ideas.
2.   It can trigger a large increase in the development potential of the field as a whole, in spite of being small in itself.

Both these phenomena introduce fundamental non-linearity into theories of creative development. The introduction of a small but sufficiently critical idea implies that a small change in one of the slowly changing variables causes a much greater shift in the structure of ideas as a whole. Thus we arrive at a generic situation, where an infinitesimal change in one variable causes substantial changes in (a possibly large number of) other variables.

There are many examples of how critical (although innocuously small) contributions can trigger the development of totally new approaches to theoretical or aesthetic work. One theoretical example is the aforementioned *Inequalities* (Hardy et al. [1934] 1967). In that book, the three mathematicians reformulated many relations as inequalities rather than as equalities, which was the standard procedure before the publication of their book. This new approach was an example of a critical idea, which made it possible to use set theory in practical problem formulation and problem-solving. Most of modern mathematical programming needed this critical link between applied mathematical modelling and its theoretical foundation.

In the same way, Leon Battista Alberti's fourteenth-century book on painting was a similar trigger in that it linked the mathematics of the time (Euclidian geometry) with aesthetic composition principles (Alberti [1435–1436] (1966), [1485] (1988)). The critical idea was the vague but basically correct idea of a reasonable projection from three to two dimensions as perceived by the recipient of visual stimuli. By using that simple idea, Euclidian geometry was brought into contact with the visual arts. This illustrates how an apparently small idea can have enormous consequences when the creative system is in a structurally unstable state.

CREATIVE PSYCHOLOGICAL PERSONALITY TRAITS

The transformation from an industrial society into a society based on the exploitation of knowledge and creativity in numerous domains will need better development and use of human creativity. Finding and supporting individuals who are suitable for creative work has become increasingly important. Gudmund Smith (Smith, 1993; Smith and Carlsson, 1990) has conducted a number of empirical analyses of creative personality traits. There are seven important conclusions that can be drawn from Smith's studies.

First, a typical characteristic of the creative personality is the capacity to formulate a problem and energetically work towards its solution. Sometimes the problem is not regarded as especially interesting by anyone else, and may even be considered somewhat strange or bizarre by others.

Second, a part of the creative personality is that the creative process gives rise to an increasingly subjective and emotional relationship between the creative individual and his or her independently formulated problem. The solution to the problem is however often perceived by others as being rather unimportant.

Third, the creative personality tends to exhibit an orientation towards aesthetic solutions to the formulated problem.

Fourth, a general characteristic of creative individuals is the 'oceanic capacity'. This is a capacity to perceive almost infinite possibilities after a new creative solution has been achieved. The oceanic capacity implies an instant – yet sustainable – reward of greater impact than what is possible through external rewards such as money or fame.

Fifth, creative individuals tend to be victims of angst, which according to Smith is the natural companion of creative activities.

Sixth, the creative personality includes an unusually strong interest in one's childhood. Creative people often think about their childhood and childhood experiences are important parts of their dreams. Dreaming is also in itself a more frequent and intense experience than among less creative people. One of the surprising properties of these dreams is that creative individuals are apt to describe their dreams as involving strong colours.

Seventh, it does not seem to be the case that goal-oriented or wealthy homes are the best environments for creativity development among children. Creative individuals surprisingly often come from poor or dysfunctional homes.

For these and possibly other reasons, there is a tendency among creative people to combine immature and even childish behavioural traits with a capacity to concentrate and be quite serious in the process of formulating and solving problems. It would of course be possible for employers or schools to be reasonably successful in identifying suitable creative individuals if creativity tests would be based on these findings. But history shows that creativity has not been one of the more highly appreciated traits in the labour market. Creative people have instead tended to develop their qualities in isolation or in combination with other creative individuals. Finding these rare combinations has for the most part compelled creative individuals to move to urban centres with their attendant greater – albeit still low – probability of finding suitable creative partners for joint creative projects.

CREATIVITY ON THE BORDER TO CHAOS

A Karolinska Institute study (de Manzano et al., 2010) investigated the role of factors that are correlated both with brain disorders and creativity as indicated by 'divergent thinking'. The experimentally based study supports the hypothesis that dopaminergic neurotransmission plays a role in creative thought and behaviour. It provides statistical estimates of the relationship between creative ability and dopamine D2 receptor expression in healthy individuals:

> [The] focus [is] on regions where aberrations in dopaminergic function have previously been associated with psychotic symptoms and a genetic liability to schizophrenia. Scores on divergent thinking tests (Inventiveness battery, Berliner Intelligenz Struktur Test) were correlated with regional D2 receptor densities, as measured by Positron Emission Tomography, and the radioligands [^{11}C]raclopride and [^{11}C]FLB 457. The results show a negative correlation (–0.64) between divergent thinking scores and D2 density in the thalamus, also when controlling for age and general cognitive ability. Hence, the results demonstrate that the D2 receptor system, and specifically thalamic function, is important for creative performance, and may be one crucial link between creativity and psychopathology. We suggest that decreased D2 receptor densities in the thalamus lower thalamic gating thresholds, thus increasing thalamocortical information flow. In healthy individuals, who do not suffer from the detrimental effects of psychiatric disease, this may increase performance on divergent thinking tests. In combination with the cognitive functions of higher order cortical networks, this could constitute a basis for the generative and selective processes that underlie real life creativity. (de Manzano et al., 2010, p.1)

The statistical estimates imply that one-third of the variability in creativity can be attributed to the 'D2 factor'. There thus seems to be a continuous positive association between creativity and bi-polar (that is, manic-depressive) and schizophrenic disorders.

ARTIFICIAL CREATIVITY?

> One hallmark of the progress of mature science is that it eventually begins to appreciate its own boundaries. In the present century we have seen many examples of this. In an attempt to extend a theory in new ways what has often been discovered is some form of 'impossibility theorem' – a proof using the assumptions of the theory that certain things cannot be done or certain questions cannot be answered. The most famous examples are Heisenberg's Uncertainty Principle in physics, Einstein's speed-of-light limiting of signalling velocities, Gödel's incompleteness theorem in mathematical logic, Arrow's theorem in economics, Turing uncomputability, the intractability of NP-complete problems like the 'Travelling Salesman Problem', and Chaitin's Theorem about the unprovability of algorithmic randomness. . . . it is known that nature has found a way to fold complex proteins quickly. If it carries out this searching process by the

process that we would use to program it computationally, then it would seem to be uncomputable in the same way that the 'Travelling Salesman Problem' is uncomputable. However, nature has found a way to carry out the computation in as fraction of a second. As yet we don't know how it's done. Again we are led to appreciate the gap between the limitations on nature and the limitations upon the particular mathematical, computational or statistical descriptors that we have chosen to describe its actions. (Barrow, 1992, pp. 7–9)

I have argued in the strongest possible terms for the importance of cities as incubators of human creativity. My conviction has not been weakened by the increasing interest among some cognitive scientists in computer-based AI. A number of empirical studies indicate that intelligence is a necessary condition for creativity. AI would then – even if increasingly important – become a necessary condition for 'artificial creativity'.

But a deeper question still remains: is artificial creativity possible? Artificial creativity would then render the creative function of cities obsolescent. A computer that performs all the processes that are needed for a good life could be located anywhere, including the creative processes involved in creating new creative computers.

Theoretical debates about AI have been intense and have primarily involved philosophers, computer scientists and mathematicians. The proponents of artificial creativity are remarkably few. Alan Turing seems to have believed in computers that are able to think and create (see Turing, 1950). Douglas Hofstadter (1979) is explicit in his belief in creative algorithms and John Casti (1997) even attempts to demonstrate the creativity of computers by using examples from music and abstract art. Nevertheless, what is most striking about these examples is that there is a conspicuous lack of semantic or pragmatic creativity in their proposed computer algorithms.

The critics of artificial creativity are numerous and have primarily relied on the impossibility features of the recursive algorithm in Universal Turing Machines (UTMs), which are commonly used for representing the workings of the human brain. The mathematical physicist Roger Penrose (see Penrose, 1989) and the philosophers John Lucas (1971, 1972) and John Searle (for example, 1980, 1990) have formulated influential criticisms of AI and – at least implicitly – of artificial creativity.

Roger Penrose (1989) claims that we should view the brain as a macro-system that is ruled by principles from quantum theory. He argues against the strong AI theory that the rational processes of the mind are completely algorithmic and may thus be duplicated by a sufficiently complex computer. Penrose's theory is however controversial within the scientific community, since it has not been subjected to rigorous empirical testing; it remains an interesting hypothesis.

John Lucas (1971, 1972) takes the liar paradox as a starting point for connecting Gödel's theorems to the hypothesis that AI is impossible. 'This sentence is false' constitutes the liar paradox. An analysis of the liar paradox shows that it cannot be true, because then it is false. Nor can it be false, since then it must be true. He then formulates a question to a computer that is assumed to be 'artificially intelligent':

> You ask the computer, 'Dear computer, what is your procedure for telling that problem number n cannot be solved by procedure number n?' And if he answers '7,777,777' – supposing he gives this as his answer for his procedure for telling that problem number n cannot be solved by procedure number n, then naturally the next thing to do is to ask him 'Can problem number 7,777,777 be solved by procedure number 7,777,777?' and if he is a very arrogant computer he may say 'yes'. If he says 'yes', then you point out that that procedure is one which tells him that

that problem cannot be solved by that procedure. So perhaps he is a more modest computer and will say 'no', and then either you could start niggling and induce him again into an inconsistency or you might be generous and allow his humility at the price of getting him to admit his humanity, and show that here is a problem that he can solve, but not by that procedure. (Lucas, 1972, lecture 5, p. 3)

In this example, Lucas uses Gödel's theorem, which states: 'For every consistent formalization of arithmetic F, there exist arithmetic truths that are not provable within that system. Therefore F is incomplete.' Moreover, Turing (1937) shows that Gödel's theorem is equivalent to the theoretical impossibility of guaranteeing the eventual cessation of a computer program: 'Given a program P and an input data set I, there is no way in general to determine whether P will ever finish processing the input I.'

Lucas (1971, 1972) claims that this is a problem for computers but not for intelligent humans. Humans are able to perceive that certain statements that are not provable in a computer algorithm can be deemed to be true by some gifted humans, to the extent that they use non-algorithmic reasoning. Lucas writes:

> I have been arguing that the algorithms don't answer all the questions. We can't reduce all the operations of the human mind to working according to some set of definite decision-procedures; but we should not conclude from that that in those cases where there actually is a decision-procedure, one is, nevertheless, still at liberty to decide something else. My argument against Longuet-Higgins doesn't mean that either the computer or I am at liberty to say that two and two equal five. Rather what is wrong with the doctrine of complete reducibility to decision-procedures is the completeness. We can formalise different parts of logic, and we can formalise some different sorts of legal procedure and insofar as we do it and do it well we are able to set up procedures which will enable us to see what ought to be done or what ought to be believed, but it will never be a complete job. The lesson that we should draw from the incompleteness theorems is not that formalism is always wrong but that, however far we go in laying down formal procedures for deciding different questions, there will always be other questions which will not be decided by this method. We may then be able to produce another method which will do that other problem but then there will be other problems still, which will elude both the first and the revised decision-procedure. What is wrong with the algorithmic approach is partly that it tries to prevent us asking certain questions, partly that it encourages us to ask certain other questions. (Lucas, 1971, 1972, p. 5)

THE PROBLEM OF DISCRETE CHOICES

Economic and political decisions often involve integer variables. A typical case is the problem of assigning a number of employees to different jobs. This problem is quite easily solved by computers as long as the choice criterion is linear. The problem in which the efficiency of the different employees depends on the assignment of other employees is different. The efficiency criterion would then become non-linear and the search for an optimal solution would imply a complete enumeration of all possible assignment combinations: assigning n persons to n different jobs implies an assessment of $n!$ combinations. By way of example, 20 interdependent employees who are to be assigned to 20 jobs involves a comparison of 2432902008176640000 (that is more than 2.4 quadrillions) employee-job combinations. A similarly intractable problem is the Travelling Salesman Problem, which requires a salesman to find the shortest route for a salesman who must visit n cities. These problems are not only impossible to optimize for the unaided human mind; they also become impossible to solve for computers as soon as a critical – and usually quite modest – number of agents or locations affects the decision criterion (Gray and Rowe, 2000).

A Diophantine equation is an equation of the form

$$p(x_1, x_2, \ldots, x_n) = 0, \tag{2.1}$$

where p is an integer-valued polynomial with integers as coefficients. It took many years for mathematicians to conclude that Hilbert's Tenth Problem is insoluble. Matyasevich (1971, 1973) showed that no such algorithm can be proved to exist in the general case. This insolubility has serious practical implications, since it points to the impossibility of solving various common applied economic planning problems, all of which require integer solutions to non-linear equations (Koopmans and Beckmann, 1957). Yet creative decision-makers tend to develop heuristic methods to cope with such apparently intractable decision problems.

THE PROBLEM OF EVOLUTIONARY SEMANTICS AND PRAGMATICS

Arguments against AI that rely on theorems by Gödel and Turing are all within the domain of syntactic and logical reasoning. The American philosopher John Searle (1980, 1990) has formulated critical arguments that belong to a different domain. Searle's critique of AI does not refer to Gödel or Turing, nor does it examine the logical or syntactic completeness of algorithms. The focus is instead on the limitations that are imposed by analyses that focus exclusively on the properties of algorithms.

Searle's vantage point is different. He emphasizes the lack of understanding that is implicit in any algorithm, since algorithms constitute a rather mechanistic stepwise conversion of a set of inputs into a set of outputs. Searle illustrates his view of the problem by making use of his famous Chinese box example of a simple but typical algorithm:

> Imagine a native English speaker who knows no Chinese locked in a room full of boxes of Chinese symbols (a data base) together with a book of instructions for manipulating the symbols (the program). Imagine that people outside the room send in other Chinese symbols which, unknown to the person in the room, are questions in Chinese (the input). And imagine that by following the instructions in the program the man in the room is able to pass out Chinese symbols which are correct answers to the questions (the output). The program enables the person in the room to pass the Turing Test for understanding Chinese but he does not understand a word of Chinese. . . . The point of the argument is this: if the man in the room does not understand Chinese on the basis of implementing the appropriate program for understanding Chinese then neither does any other digital computer solely on that basis because no computer, qua computer, has anything the man does not have. (Searle, 1980, p. 418)

Searle concludes that a computer is constrained to handle syntactic problems only; it can never have access to semantics. Any semantic content would have to be attached by humans before and after the algorithmic procedures.

Proponents of AI have disputed such criticisms. Gödel himself had a humble view of the future of artificial intelligence as a vehicle of theorem-proving: '. . . it remains possible that there may exist (and even be empirically discoverable) a theorem-proving machine which in fact is equivalent to mathematical intuition (to the human mind), but cannot be proved to be so, nor even proved to yield only correct theorems of finitary number theory (Gödel, as quoted by Casti and De Pauli, 2000, p. 144).

Gödel thus thought that the long-term evolutionary emergence of such an AI device might be possible. However, it would still be constrained to mathematical proofs, logic and similar purely syntactic problems. Needless to say, AI has at the time of writing not given rise to any artificial creativity in pure, applied or motivated mathematics. It is unlikely that there will ever be such a thing as semantic or pragmatic creativity.

The cognitive psychologist Gerd Gigerenzer has recently discussed the prospects for artificial creativity (see Gigerenzer, 2000, 2007). One of his questions concerns the potential for computer-generated music. Could the music of Bach, Beethoven or Mozart be generated by some computer program that is based on a search for optimal solutions? Gigerenzer doubts this on bio-evolutionary grounds. Most important decisions of an integer character, which are extremely frequent in all creative decision processes, are determined by our evolved brains:

> It supplies us with capacities that have developed over millennia but are largely ignored by standard texts on decision making. It also supplies us with human culture, which evolves much faster than genes. These evolved capacities are important for many important decisions and can prevent us from making crude errors in important affairs. . . . we need to understand that there is an evolved human brain that allows us to solve problems in our own way – different from that of reptiles or computer chips . . . Because many of our evolved capacities are not well understood, we can't endow machines with the same abilities. . . . Composition, like cognition, is based on capacities that vary from man to mouse to microchip. (Gigerenzer, 2007, pp. 55 and 66)

COMPUTERIZED AND HUMAN MEMORY SYSTEMS

For many decades it was assumed in psychology and cognitive science research that the memory of the brain is like the memory of a computer. Thus it was believed that the information was coded into the memory and stored there in order to be picked up at some later instance. Modern memory research has radically changed the modelling of the human memory system. No longer is it believed that memory is static. Instead, the new models are dynamic and the focus is on the memorizing process (Nilsson, 1988; Bäckman and Nyberg, 2009). This dynamic memory is a process of interdependencies between different cognitive capacities of perception, formation of concepts, problem-solving, questioning and decision-making as determined by the temporal, spatial and social context. Memory theorists therefore understand memorizing as a process that engages almost all parts of the brain, rather than as an entity that is located in some distinct part of the brain.

My conclusion is that 'artificial creativity' is currently unthinkable on at least five grounds:

1. Creativity depends on the capacity to disentangle paradoxes of different kinds. This requires a switch to heuristic or intuitive decision methods if standard recursive procedures do not work.

2. Computers and their programs are semantically blind.
3. The creativity of humans is based on interactions with other humans, yielding social problem formulation and social experiences – computers are pragmatically blind.
4. The human memory is an evolved system of interactions between most of the cognitive capacities and not similar to the memory of a computer.
5. Human creativity is a consequence of slow processes of biological and social evolution – a sufficiently long period of time might lead to an analogous evolution of computers and programs, but the end result might be a completely different set of cognitive capabilities.

Computers are nonetheless important for human creativity. In creative processes, substitution of human skills by computers is not the best strategy. On the other hand, computers often function as complements to the human mind within creative processes, thereby exploiting the respective comparative advantages of humans and computers. Computers have great (and increasing) advantages in static information storage, algorithmic speed and in the precision of various types of calculation. Most creative individuals and teams are aware of the gains from increasing their use of computers, whether in science, art or entertainment. Some pure mathematicians have become open to the use of computers as is evidenced by the new field of 'experimental mathematics' (Chaitin, 1997; Wolfram, 2002), even though many mathematicians of a more classical bent remain sceptical to these developments.

Computer art provides another example of the interaction between human creative teams and computers. Peitgen and Richter (1986) view the role of computer art in the following way:

> But every tool (computer) requires a creative mind that puts it to good use. It would be unfair to discredit our pictures as being purely the result of machine work. They are not.. . . . Choices must be made. . . . In the assignment of colors, for instance, there is a very subjective choice of balance between integration and differentiation: some information is discarded by the use of the same color for different points; other features are being enhanced by carefully adjusting their display to our aesthetic intuition. (Peitgen and Richter, 1986, pp. 20–1)

To me, there is an obvious need for interaction between people with different characteristics and knowledge and between people and computers in the creative process. Cities are useful in this context as agglomerations of diversity that facilitate human as well as human-machine creative interaction.

CITIES AS HUBS OF CREATIVE REVOLUTIONS

Creative artists, scientists or designers may be organized into formal groups such as academies, universities or firms. The idea behind the original organizational plan is in most cases the generation of revenues that support the creative individuals and possibly also yield reasonably certain profits for the entrepreneurial planner. Such planned organization of creativity tends to be based on incremental creativity, with the aim of quickly transforming the new ideas into economically advantageous innovations. This is because such tightly organized creativity tends to be incapable of the type of major breakthrough that is associated with new paradigms and foundational theories. Another type of 'organization' is needed for this.

The creative city as an informal and spontaneously evolving spatial organization has been the arena for all large-scale creative revolutions. In the course of the past 2500 years, a small number of relatively large cities have functioned as hotbeds of revolutionary creativity. These cities attracted a disproportionate share of migrants with creative inclinations, and they also facilitated the growth of creativity among those already present. Such cities were both used as arenas for presenting findings from elsewhere – as in the case of Isaac Newton in London – and as fertile locations for developing new ideas in collaboration with other creative people (Andersson et al., 1984).

The following four sections illustrate the importance of creative cities by discussing four examples from four different eras: Athens at 400 BC, Renaissance Florence, Enlightenment London and *Fin de Siècle* Vienna.

CLASSICAL ATHENS

The fist intellectual revolution with a lasting impact occurred around 400 BC. The centre of this revolution was the city state of Athens – the most important city in ancient Greece. The war against Persia had ended in 449 BC. The Greek victory had given Athens power over an area that extended from present-day Macedonia to eastern Turkey.

For its free citizens, Athens had introduced an early form of democracy. The Athenians had amassed substantial wealth under the leadership of Pericles. Much of this wealth was used for the construction of the path-breaking architectural monuments of the Acropolis: the Parthenon, the Erechtheum and the Temple of Athena Nike.

The architectural inventions constituted the starting point for a cumulative creative process among Athenian sculptors and painters; creative artists such as the painter Polygnotus decorated the edifices of the Acropolis. New architectural ideas were not only innovated as religious buildings and monuments. Innovative architects also designed numerous secular buildings such as theatres and stadiums. The design of the *agora* was especially important, since it was the centre of both intellectual and commercial interactions. Athenians and others met in the *agora* not only to buy and sell merchandise, but also to discuss philosophical, scientific and political issues.

From early on, Athens had both imported and originated ideas and theories. The foundations of mathematics and astronomy derived from the older civilizations of Asia Minor. From other parts of the region came new musical impulses, which were given a mathematical and philosophical interpretation by Pythagoras. Probably Socrates but certainly Plato integrated musical and mathematical structures with their normative analyses of statecraft. Philosophy merged with the arts and science to become an integrated intellectual world view. Creativity blossomed not only in music, but also in literature and theatre. Sophocles, Euripides and Aristophanes made lasting contributions to the development of theatre as an art form. Many of the ancient Greek dramas as well as philosophical treatises dealt with similar themes: the psychological, social and moral dimensions of social conflicts.

What were the mechanisms behind the creative expansion of Athens in the fifth century BC? It is likely that the expansion of trade and other forms of interaction with other parts of the Mediterranean and with the Orient were decisive. At the peak of Athenian creativity, circa 400 BC, Greece's trading area reached a maximum of five million square kilometres. Trading relationships spawned new cultural impulses that in turn gave rise to a diversity of ideas, which supplied wide-ranging creative 'raw material' for the residents of Athens. Both democracy and the informal institutions of the *agora* supported the circulation and adoption of recently articulated ideas. The perceived structural instability of the political system with its attendant power shifts gave Plato and other Athenian philosophers empirical observations that piqued their interest in the potentials and limitations of the political system.

In nuce:

1. Accumulation of wealth followed the expansion of Athenian power.
2. Migration from other parts of the empire enlarged the population of Athens.
3. Political change culminating in the world's first democracy enhanced freedom of expression.
4. Athens became a centre for long-distance trade and communication.
5. The creation of the public square – the *agora* – and the establishment of Plato's Academy facilitated the exchange of philosophical and artistic ideas among the residents of Athens, whether citizen or *metic*.
6. The structural instability of the political and other institutions seems to have been an important contributing factor to the remarkable agglomeration of creative individuals in Athens.

RENAISSANCE FLORENCE

Florence is perhaps the best historical example of a creative city. It was for two distinct periods between 1250 and 1500 Europe's most important creative centre.

From the middle of the thirteenth century the Italian city states began their transformations into centres of knowledge and culture. In Sicily, new republican city councils – *signorias* – had been created in an earlier era; it was this institutional structure that was adopted by the cities and towns of northern Italy. The new governance structure facilitated the formation of informal co-operation networks, which enabled cities such as Genoa, Milan, Naples, Venice and Florence to become important trading nodes, each of which was surrounded by hinterlands specializing in early textile manufacturing.

In the city of Florence, trading capitalists, scientists and artists could benefit from the growth in trade, wealth and population. The development base of the city was its accessibility to markets. Located at the intersection of the river Arno and the major road towards Lombardy and Northern Europe, Florence could exploit trading advantages associated with the rapid growth of the Hanseatic trading system. The economy of Florence was thus based on three pillars: long-distance trade, the manufacture of textiles and banking.

The Florentine bourgeoisie took advantage of the conflicts between the feudal lords in the region and the Roman Catholic Church. Eventually the leadership of the city managed to secure special privileges, including substantial economic freedom for the region's manufacturers and traders. The Guelphs attained effective control over the city and established a political system without any important role for the Church or the nobility. One effect was that the economic base in terms of assets associated with trade and production could grow without being burdened with the severe institutional constraints that were common in most other Southern European towns.

Florence's accessibility to Bologna, Paris, Bruges and other mediaeval knowledge centres provided the city with another advantage as a centre of creativity in science and the arts. With most of the traditional feudal and clerical constraints gone, cultural creativity flourished on the basis of substantial accumulations of wealth. The unstable political power structure meant that there were few if any political limits to artistic experimentation. From about 1270 until 1340 Florence experienced its first creative era. Cimabue, Giotto and Dante Alighieri are three names that are intimately associated with this era.

In connection with the baptistery Florence had a large workshop that, in fact, became an academy of Florentine painting. The most important of the students from this academy was Cimabue, who developed the Florentine school of painting. Cimabue's most important apprentice was Giotto, who was to become the greatest painter of his time. Through Giotto's work, the reputation of Florentine painting spread to other parts of Europe. The philosopher and author of *La Divina Commedia*, Dante Alighieri, was the third central figure of this period. He was born in Florence as a member of one of its most respected families.

Florence's politics and cultural life were inextricably linked during these decades. Both Dante and Giotto became involved in the political administration of Florence. In Dante's case his political activities caused him to attain the position of a *prior* – an engagement that later led to his expulsion from the city. During his exile Dante wrote *La Divina Commedia*, in which he referred to ancient Greek ideals such as the importance of philosophy in society.

The growing role of Florence as a centre of creativity was reinforced by two of Dante's followers – Francesco Petrarca and Giovanni Boccaccio – who ironically also were expelled from the city. With their expulsions the first period of creativity in Florence had come to an end.

The second revolutionary creative period in Florence is associated with the Medici family of bankers. In 1434, Cosimo di Medici attained political power in Florence. For more than three decades he ruled a city whose cultural and political development made it emerge as the pre-eminent creative centre of Europe. Cosimo di Medici used his considerable wealth to assemble an impressive group of philosophers, mathematicians, artists and authors. He initiated *L'accademia neoplatonica*, which was an academy where scholars discussed the basic principles of art, philosophy and science.

Cosimo di Medici was also a great supporter of architecture. The most influential Florentine architect was Filippo Brunelleschi, who was commissioned to design the *Duomo* (the cathedral of Florence) with its remarkable dome. Brunelleschi became the first architect to employ mathematical theory to establish new rules of proportionality and symmetry.

Brunelleschi's most important follower was Leon Battista Alberti, who besides his work as designer of buildings became the most important aesthetic theorist of the Renaissance. *De Re Aedificatoria* (Alberti, [1485] 1988) was his theoretical masterpiece. Like Vitruvius's *Ten Books on Architecture*, *De Re Aedificatoria* consists of ten books.

Alberti's books are a set of analyses of how buildings should be built rather than a description of architectural masterpieces of the past. *De Re Aedificatoria* remained the most important treatise on architecture for more than two centuries.

Painting developed in parallel with the advances in architecture. Basing much of his theories on the creative work of Masaccio, which explored perspectives, shadows and light, Alberti also developed a theory of painting in his book *De Pictura*. Alberti's creativity was as multifaceted and revolutionary as Leonardo da Vinci's.

Florentine revolutionary creativity comprised more individuals than Brunelleschi and Alberti, however. It suffices to mention Luca della Robbia, whom Alberti praised as a genius on a par with the sculptors Donatello and Lorenzo Ghiberti.

Cosimo di Medici's wealthy grandson Lorenzo – *Il Magnifico* – became the principal patron of creativity in the arts and sciences in the last decades of the fifteenth century. Not only did he support many creative individuals, he was also instrumental in promoting the revival of Greek philosophy and humanism as pursued by the philosophers Marsilio Ficino and Giovanni Pico della Mirandola. In Pico della Mirandola's ([1486] 2010) famous oration *On the Dignity of Man* we find a strong plea for the open society:

> I shall not, in the first place, have much to say against those who disapprove this type of public disputation. It is a crime – if it be a crime – which I share with all you, most excellent doctors, who have engaged in such exercises on many occasions to the enhancement of your reputations, as well as with Plato and Aristotle and all the most esteemed philosophers of every age. These philosophers of the past all thought that nothing could profit them more in their search for wisdom than frequent participation in public disputation. Just as the powers of the body are made stronger through gymnastic, the powers of the mind grow in strength and vigour in this arena of learning. (Pico della Mirandola [1486] 2010)

Towards the end of the fifteenth century Florence nevertheless declined as a dominant creative city. Although the great masters of the High Renaissance – Michelangelo, Leonardo and Raphael – were educated in Florence, they were eventually more or less forced to leave Florence for cities that later became more tolerant than Florence of creative work. After the death of Lorenzo di Medici the balance of power shifted as the Dominican priest Girolamo Savonarola gained the upper hand. Savonarola launched a violent but successful campaign against what he considered the immorality of Renaissance books and art.

Some of the characteristics of Florence as a creative city can now be summarized:

1. Accumulation of wealth through trade and banking preceded and later fuelled Florentine creativity.
2. The attraction of migrants from other city states transformed Florence into a relatively large city.
3. The integration of the Mediterranean trading system with the Hanseatic League caused a phase transition from a regional to a continental trading network.
4. The increasing interactivity among Italian city states and wealthy Hanseatic towns (particularly Bruges) implied ever greater flows of ideas along the trading links.
5. *L'accademia neoplatonica* became an important *agora* for the free exchange of scientific and artistic ideas.

6. The structural instability of various political and economic power centres that was associated with the emergence of new institutions caused a necessary openness vis-à-vis revolutionary creative endeavours in Florence and a few other European cities.

ENLIGHTENMENT LONDON

The types of ship that were common during the First Logistical Revolution – the times of the Renaissance in Italy – were appropriate for relatively short voyages. The *cog* and its Mediterranean counterparts were designed for coastal shipping. Intercontinental voyages were therefore impossible. But a new type of ocean-going sailing ship, the *caravel*, was developed during the second half of the fifteenth century. This was an Iberian ship with two to four masts; Christopher Columbus sailed a *caravel* on his transatlantic voyage. The ship opened up the high seas, and shifted the centre of gravity of the European trading system towards the Atlantic coast. Lisbon became the centre of European trade flows for a short period, but its centrality was soon obscured by the rise of the competing northern Atlantic cities of Antwerp, Amsterdam and London (Andersson and Strömquist, 1988).

The Dutch had developed a ship that was highly suitable for trade, the *flute*. The *flute* was voluminous and yet slender, and could be sailed by a relatively small crew. With this innovation, the Dutch had created one of the conditions for Amsterdam's emergence as a new centre of world trade.

All trade needs credit. Already in the twelfth century, it became common to use bills of exchange rather than direct monetary transfers in Italy, which led to the creation of the first banks. Florence became a leading centre of early banking. But these early private banks, which were created by the Medicis, Fuggers and other merchants, were often regarded as unreliable because of their role in bankrolling the Church and the nobility. There were attempts to create banks with public guarantees in northern Italy, but these attempts turned out to be insignificant in quantitative terms.

The steadily increasing distances over which goods were exchanged led to an increasing need for credit. Trade with Asia, the Americas and other distant regions required access to long-term credit. It became necessary to find a reliable method for funding trading projects that were both risky and protracted; the demand for secure and predictable instruments of credit mounted. New transport technology, which made transoceanic trade possible, set the stage for the Second Logistical (or Commercial) Revolution. The resulting expansion of trade caused a severe shortage of credit.

These shortages were redressed by the introduction of publicly guaranteed banks, first in Amsterdam and later in London with the creation of the Bank of England in 1694. A number of commercial innovations preceded the increasing role of the British economy in the eighteenth century. Sir Thomas Gresham founded the Royal Exchange between 1566 and 1568. The first modern joint stock companies were established in the early seventeenth century, which had the objective of ensuring a reliable source of funds for colonial projects in North America and the Far East.

The centre of gravity in the European and world economy moved from the Mediterranean-Hanseatic network to the North Atlantic coast during the sixteenth century. Amsterdam and London expanded, while Hanseatic and Mediterranean cities stagnated or declined. The newfound wealth of North Atlantic cities, particularly Amsterdam and London, also provided the financial foundation for their emergence as the most important centres of science and culture. It was in these cities, with London as the outstanding centre, that philosophers and mathematicians laid the foundations of modern science.

Two factors contributed to London's increasingly predominant role. First, the massive construction of 1160 miles of inland waterways increased the accessibility of London as the most important trading gateway for almost all British production nodes. Second, the British pound of the London-based banking system had become the most important currency in world trade through a process of expansion that involved a transformation from the silver to the gold standard and thereafter from the gold standard to a standard based on guaranteed credit. These transformations took place without inflationary or other disruptions of the credibility of the pound. One of the early defenders of policies aiming at stabilizing the pound was the philosopher John Locke. It was seen as the primary precondition for British domination of world trade.

Although total British trade volumes are uncertain, estimates of British exports to the American colonies imply a ten-fold increase in North Atlantic trade in the eighteenth century. In his *Essays on Mankind and Political Arithmetic*, William Petty ([1689] 2004) estimated total British exports to be on the order of ten million pounds. By 1720 the value of British exports has been estimated to have amounted to 13 million pounds, while in 1760 exports may have reached 31 million pounds (Maddison, 1982). These figures correspond to an annual export growth of 2.2 per cent. The growth of trade in goods (paralleling the very rapid growth in the slave trade) was safeguarded by a massive increase in the number of war ships. By 1760, Britain had achieved its goal of controlling the seas.

Fernand Braudel ([1979] 1986) estimates that the port of London handled approximately four-fifths of the rapidly growing English exports and imports. The rapid increase in shipping led to congestion in the port of London. By the 1720s, according to Daniel Defoe (1748, p. 147), there were 'about two thousand ships of all sorts, not reckoning barges, lighters or pleasure boats or yachts' using the quays.

Amsterdam had grown from a population of about 30 000 in 1580 to 200 000 in 1650. The latter population figure remained relatively stable until 1800. In the seventeenth century, the geographical centre of economic development shifted from Amsterdam to London. This is evidenced by London's population growth as compared with Amsterdam's stagnation after 1650. As London became the principal North Sea port, migrants arrived from other parts of England and from overseas. The population rose from an estimated 225 000 in 1605 to as many as 700 000 by 1700; London became not only the undisputed economic capital of the world but also the global focal point of scientific creativity.

The history of science since 1660 is intimately related to the history of the Royal Society of London. The Royal Society was where Isaac Newton presented his paradigmatic scientific and mathematical theories, which paved the way for the remarkable growth of scientific and technological knowledge that occurred during the following two centuries (Gleick, 2003). The origin of the Royal Society is sometimes traced to the meetings of natural philosophers in the 1640s. The official founding occurred on 28 November 1660, when 12 of the participants met at Gresham College after a lecture by

Table 2.4   Important seventeenth-century members of the Royal Society of London for Improving Natural Knowledge

Member	Discipline(s)	Origin
Isaac Barrow	Linguistics; theology; mathematics	England
Robert Boyle	Chemistry	England
William Brouncker	Mathematics	England
Robert Hooke	Mathematics; physics	England
Christian Huygens	Physics	Netherlands
Gottfried Wilhelm Leibniz	Mathematics	Germany
Nicolaus Mercator	Mathematics	Germany
Abraham de Moivre	Mathematics	France
Isaac Newton	Mathematics; physics	England
Henry Oldenburg	Natural philosophy	England
John Wallis	Mathematics; cryptography	England
John Wilkins	Natural philosophy	England
Christopher Wren	Astronomy; mathematics; architecture	England

Christopher Wren. At that meeting, they formally declared the founding of a 'Colledge for the Promoting of Physico-Mathematicall Experimentall Learning'. This group included Wren, Robert Boyle, John Wilkins, Robert Moray and William Brouncker. The Society was to meet weekly to observe experiments and discuss what we would now call scientific topics. Robert Hooke was the first Curator of Experiments while Moray secured the approval of the King of England. The King's approval explains its official name: The Royal Society of London for Improving Natural Knowledge.

Already in 1662 the Society was permitted by Royal Charter to publish its first two books; John Evelyn's *Sylva* and Hooke's *Micrographia*. More important was the publication of the first issue of *Philosophical Transactions*, which was edited by the secretary of the Society, Henry Oldenburg. The Royal Society assumed formal responsibility over the publication a few years later and *Philosophical Transactions* is now the oldest scientific journal in the world. Another important milestone in the early development of the Royal Society was Isaac Newton's lasting influence on its activities. Table 2.4 lists the most important members in the seventeenth century.

The list of the seventeenth-century members gives a clear indication of the wide mathematical, physical and philosophical interests of the founders of modern science, all of whom had chosen London as an appropriate meeting place for intellectual discussions. Philosophically, the members of the Royal Society were converging on a new hypothetico-deductive paradigm that can be summed up as follows (Wedberg, 2003):

1. A deductive system can be formulated (primarily in mathematical terms).
2. The truth values of the system are considered as probable rather than certain.
3. This system is regarded as probably true as long as the implied (that is, logically deduced) consequences are consistent with empirical observations.

These ideas were central to John Locke's earlier analysis of knowledge and the creative process in *An Essay Concerning Human Understanding* (Locke, [1690] (1975); Wedberg,

2003). According to Locke, we have two types of experience. The first type is 'sensation' and the other type is 'reflection'. The sensation is the impact on our consciousness of artefacts and other observable phenomena, while reflection is the impact of ideas on our consciousness. Locke seems to have been of the opinion that reflection is the finite capacity of our imagination to combine sensations and ideas into some new and complex idea.

The creativity of the members of the Royal Society was complemented by the parallel emergence of other intellectual meeting places such as London's coffee houses. The coffee houses provided a gathering place where, for a penny admission charge, any man who was reasonably dressed could smoke, enjoy his coffee, read the newsletters and converse with other men. As journalism was in its infancy, the coffee house provided a centre for the dissemination of news: 'runners' reported major events of the day. New gazettes were also distributed in the coffee houses, which thereby endowed them with a reading-room character. The cost of newspapers and pamphlets was included in the admission charge. Naturally, this dissemination of news led to the dissemination of ideas, and the coffee house served as a forum for their discussion. The social historian George Macaulay Trevelyan observed that 'the "universal liberty of speech of the English nation" . . . was the quintessence of Coffee House life' (Trevelyan, 1942, p. 324).

In addition, bulletins announcing sales, sailings and auctions covered the walls of the establishments, providing valuable information to the businessman who conducted much of his business from a table at his favourite coffee house. As important a financial organization as Lloyds was named after a coffee house, Lloyd's Coffee House in Lombard Street, which was frequented by merchants and ship-owners.

'Creative destruction' leading to increasing and new demand is a key concept in Schumpeter's theory of economic and cultural development (Schumpeter, 1934). And London had its share of creative destruction in the seventeenth century with plagues, political upheaval and, particularly, the Great Fire of London, which is perhaps the best illustration of the creative forces that are unleashed by destruction.

The Great Fire developed rapidly. After two rainy summers in 1664 and 1665, London had a long period of drought from November 1665 until the summer of 1666. The fire started in a bakery in Pudding Lane and spread rapidly, owing to the prevailing gale-force winds. The fire swept through the central parts of London from 2 September to 5 September 1666. It destroyed 13 200 houses, 87 parish churches, the old St Paul's Cathedral and most official buildings in the City of London.

After the usual hunt for scapegoats, some of the most creative thinkers of the period demonstrated the new possibilities of a reconstructed London. The five most influential planners and architects were Christopher Wren, John Evelyn, Robert Hooke, Valentine Knight and Richard Newcourt, all of whom proposed rebuilding plans. However, for various institutional reasons none of the grand schemes for a baroque city were realized. Instead, much of the old street pattern was recreated in the new city, albeit with improvements in hygiene and fire safety: wider streets as well as open and accessible wharves along the Thames. The new construction materials were brick and stone rather than wood. New public buildings were created in the old locations. The most famous of these public buildings are St Paul's Cathedral and 50 smaller churches, all of which were designed by the mathematician and astronomer Christopher Wren, who became the most influential architect of the time, even though he was largely self-taught.

What were then the main factors causing London to become the most important creative city in seventeenth-century Europe? As many as nine distinct factors are likely to have played a partial causal role:

1. The slow but inexorable shift of trade and finance from Amsterdam to London, which caused London to become a global economic centre with an unsurpassed agglomeration of wealth.
2. Rapid population growth, with migration as the driving force.
3. Expansion of demand and the creative reconstruction of London's infrastructure that followed the Great Fire.
4. Unstable political and religious institutions.
5. The formation of the Royal Society of London, which admitted both British and foreign members.
6. Increasing intellectual openness, as demonstrated in the writings of John Locke, Daniel Defoe and Jonathan Swift.
7. The formation of the first international network of scientists.
8. The emergence of coffee houses and other *agoras* for discussing and disseminating new economic, political and intellectual ideas.
9. The first newspapers and scholarly journals.

FIN DE SIÈCLE VIENNA

A number of books describe Vienna in the late nineteenth and early twentieth centuries. The most important ones are arguably Carl Schorske's *Fin de Siècle Vienna* (1981) and Allan Janik's and Stephen Toulmin's *Wittgenstein's Vienna* (1973). These two studies both focus on the period between 1880 and 1914, up to and including discussions relating to the later economic crises and political upheavals. This means that the analyses concentrate on the stagnation and collapse of the Habsburg monarchy, and the liberal and nationalist movements that arose in the aftermath of the collapse. The later political tensions are perhaps best illustrated by the fact that the creators of Zionism and National Socialism, Theodor Herzl and Adolf Hitler, were living in Vienna at the same time. Both of them were moulded in their political life by Vienna's anti-Semitic mayor Karl Lueger.

A recurrent theme in *Wittgenstein's Vienna* is the question: how was it possible that the seemingly unrelated fields of philosophy, economics, medicine, psychology, mathematics, literature, music, painting, architecture, theatre and journalism could be in such a rapid creative flux at the same time and in the same city? *Fin de Siècle*, on the other hand, delves more deeply into the cross-fertilization of ideas from music, literature, painting, design and architecture, with a special emphasis on the impact of the Freudian psychological revolution on these different art forms.

One of the causes that can be detected in all these examples is the disequilibrium or structural instability that characterized the social, institutional and political structures of Vienna. The Vienna of the last decades of the Habsburg monarchy could be compared to a pressure cooker on a hot stove. A quite authoritarian political regime in combination with the rigid values of the Viennese bourgeoisie increasingly constrained the cultural, social and economic experiments that were demanded by the intellectual – liberal or socialist – elites.

Table 2.5   Vienna's infrastructural creators, 1880s to 1920s

Discipline	Individuals
Architecture	Otto Wagner; Adolf Loos; Josef Hoffmann
Economics	Carl Menger; Joseph Schumpeter
Fine arts	Gustav Klimt; Oskar Kokoschka; Egon Schiele
Mathematics and physics	Ernst Mach; Ludwig Boltzmann
Music	Gustav Mahler; Arnold Schönberg; Alexander Zemlinsky
Philosophy	Ludwig Wittgenstein; members of the *Wiener Kreis*
Political journalism	Karl Kraus; Theodor Herzl
Psychology	Sigmund Freud

The conflicts between different creative groups and between the intellectuals and the obsolete institutional structure became increasingly antagonistic from the 1880s onward. One well-known example is the conflict concerning legitimate scientific problems and methods between Sigmund Freud and the medical establishment. Another example is the recurring battles between the journalist Karl Kraus and Vienna's conservative politicians.

The growing structural instability that set the stage for such a wide range of scientific, social and cultural experiments was for the most part due to the inability of the declining monarchy to control the dynamic process of change. The old-fashioned rules and regulations were entirely inappropriate for dealing with a diverse and cosmopolitan urban population.

Vienna had experienced unprecedented economic growth during the second half of the nineteenth century. It was in this period that Vienna had become a city with modern boulevards and monumental architecture. Otto Wagner was the leading architect who transformed the city with his vision of a modern metropolis. The mediaeval walls were replaced with the circular *Ringstraße*, which was lined with palaces, churches, museums and theatres. And all these new buildings created additional demand for sculptures and paintings. Intellectuals from all parts of the Austro-Hungarian Empire were attracted by the economically dynamic city with its expanding population. In the first decade of the twentieth century, the population of Vienna increased by almost 20 000 per year.

Knowledge and skills are necessary conditions for creativity, both in science and in the arts. Vienna had an impressive number of highly skilled scientists and artists at the onset of its creative 'take-off' in the late nineteenth century, as is indicated by Table 2.5.

The creative expansion of Vienna was built on an impressive infrastructure of knowledge. In the arts and sciences creative processes extended and transformed established knowledge. The history of music is a well-known example of the role of established knowledge for revolutionary new ideas. Arnold Schoenberg is known to have claimed that composers of new music – whether late romantic, dodecaphonic or atonal – needed a thorough knowledge of the classical or early romantic composition principles of musical composers such as Wolfgang Amadeus Mozart and Ludwig van Beethoven.

The international and inter-regional exchange of goods and ideas had a long history in Vienna. The city was the capital of a large empire with few constraints on the mobility

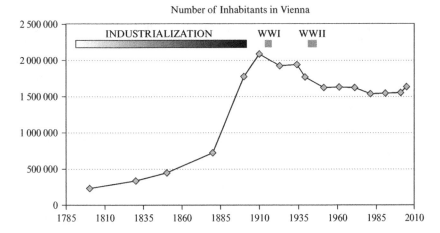

Figure 2.6 Vienna's population growth, 1800–2005

of people. Long-distance roads intersected in Vienna. The Danube connected the city with Germany and the Black Sea. From northern Italy, Slovenia and Croatia there was a steady flow of goods into Vienna along inland roads. Vienna had a unique role as the cultural, institutional and economic centre that connected all the diverse parts of the Double Monarchy of Austria-Hungary.

The extreme density of the city had unexpectedly beneficial effects. Although Vienna's level of specialized knowledge was impressive, creative processes always require cross-fertilization. The ease of transport between different parts of the city facilitated contacts between specialists, while the high population density made unplanned meetings between academics, writers and artists likely; housing standards had been declining over the decades as a consequence of the massive migration into Vienna. From 1850 to 1900 the population increased by 2.3 per cent annually and reached almost two million in 1900 (Figure 2.6).

The people of Vienna had no choice but to spend most of their leisure time outside of their crammed apartments in more or less public spaces. Similar to London in the seventeenth and eighteenth centuries – and for the same reasons – this crowdedness stimulated the creation of a remarkable number of coffee houses.

People came to Viennese coffee houses not primarily to have a cup of coffee but to meet friends, to close business deals or to discuss scientific, cultural and political issues. Coffee houses thus took on the function of a network of *agoras* in which to meet journalists, authors or scientists. They provided a space where spontaneous communication was possible to an extent that went far beyond the normal boundaries that were determined by one's ethnicity, religion or academic discipline. The coffee houses were thus the best exponents of the virtues of 'the open society', to use a phrase that was coined by the Viennese philosopher Karl Popper (1945).

By the end of the first decade of the twentieth century, the first meetings of the informal Vienna Circle were taking place, which were promoted by the physicist Philipp Frank, the mathematician Hans Hahn and the economist and philosopher Otto Neurath. Their meetings were held in Viennese coffee houses on a regular basis from 1907 onward. After the Great War this group was formally established as *der Wiener Kreis* (the Vienna Circle of philosophy). The history of the *Kreis* illustrates how the enemies of the open society caused the downfall of Vienna as a creative city a decade later. Many of the founding members of the group left Vienna in conjunction with the fascist takeover of the Austrian government. It is but one illustration of the dynamic instability that always affects truly creative cities.

The major factors behind Vienna's creativity can now be summarized:

1. Vienna was the major node of transport and trade in the Habsburg Empire and Central Europe.
2. The city experienced a massive growth of its population that was driven by migration from the different parts of the empire.
3. Many of the most creative individuals had migrated from other regions.
4. New political movements reinforced the disequilibrium and structural instability of the political system.
5. The city had a population consisting of many ethnic groups; a disproportionate share of the creative scientists and artists were Jews.
6. The growing population and the resulting housing shortage sparked an increase in the demand and supply of public meeting places, especially coffee houses in the city centre.
7. The coffee house culture and Vienna's ethnic and intellectual diversity facilitated discussions across traditional disciplinary and cultural boundaries.
8. The city was remodelled with a ring road around the city centre and numerous construction projects increased the demand for new architecture and decorative art.
9. The creative period ended with the establishment of a fascist government in the late 1920s.

CREATIVE CITIES: WHEN THE TIME AND PLACE IS RIPE

Many different factors seem to be co-operating in the formation of a city as a creative milieu. The time has to be ripe. The scientific and/or the artistic world must be in a state of creative flux. An example is the birth of calculus in the seventeenth century. Based on older mathematical findings, these new ideas were emerging in Germany, England and Japan at the same time – but with very different motivations. For Leibniz in Germany the reasons seem for the most part to have been intra-mathematical, while the Japanese mathematician Seki Kowa aimed at a new form of mathematical entertainment. In contrast, Isaac Newton viewed calculus as a necessary means for understanding spatial and dynamic physical phenomena.

Already in the 1920s, Ogborn (1923) noted the temporal confluence of new scientific ideas. Some notable examples are:

1. The law of inverse squares: Isaac Newton (1666) and Edmond Halley (1684).
2. Logarithms: John Napier (1614), Henry Briggs (1624) and Jost Bürgi (1620).
3. Least squares estimates: Carl Friedrich Gauss (1809) and Adrien-Marie Legendre (1806).

4. Non-Euclidian geometry: Carl Friedrich Gauss (1829), János Bolyai (1826–33) and Nikolai Lobachevski (1836–40).
5. The duality principle of geometry: Jean-Victor Poncelet (1838) and Joseph Diaz Gergonne (1838).
6. Discovery of oxygen: Carl Wilhelm Scheele (1774) and Joseph Priestley (1774).
7. The periodic system: Julius Lothar Meyer (1869) and Dmitri Mendeleev (1869).

The creativity of individuals forming the creative core of a city can be seen as a synergetic process in which their interactions are reinforcing overall creativity. The force of these interactions is determined by the quality and size of the environment. In the historical examples given above, the creative milieus have been described as large in scale and wide in cultural scope. The milieus have been rich in the sense of knowledge that is both deep and diverse; the combined depth and diversity have provided unusual interaction opportunities among the creators of new philosophical, scientific or aesthetic ideas.

The size of the organization (such as a university or an academy) that employs each creator does not seem to be of great importance. While the relative scale and growth of the city as a whole seems to be of great import, it does not seem to matter whether the scale and growth of the constituent organizations are equally impressive. The creative city is thus a large whole with a multitude of interactive and diverse individuals and organizations.

My conclusion is that there are at least seven conditions that must all be present for a city to be truly creative:

1. A critical mass of accumulated wealth and positive economic growth.
2. A large and increasing population with a substantial inflow of migrants.
3. A pool of knowledgeable people.
4. Large and diversified trade and communication flows with other regions.
5. An 'open society' – tolerant and with accessible arenas for exchanging new ideas.
6. Imbalances between perceived public and private needs and their actual provision. That is to say that there should be excess demand for numerous goods and services in both qualitative and quantitative terms.
7. Structural instability and uncertainty in the development of institutions and of philosophical, scientific and artistic paradigms.

Richard Florida (2002, 2008) provides extensive empirical studies and evidence of the importance of conditions three and five from contemporary cities. The importance of these factors cannot be falsified according to these studies.

CONCLUSIONS

Creativity is an inherently dynamic concept, which is applicable to individuals, organized social groups and informal agglomerations such as cities and regions. Creativity is necessary for – and always precedes – innovation and diffusion. Creativity is exhibited by individual artists and scientists whose genetic and acquired personality traits are necessary determinants. This implies that one's family upbringing and one's education are important influences on personal creativity development. It is also obvious that standardized education programmes that have been designed to meet the needs of manufacturing firms or bureaucracies can extinguish the creative powers of young people. Large cities with a multitude of educational options provide better opportunities for creativity than elsewhere.

Many individual capabilities are necessary for creativity – among these are the capabilities to intelligently exploit analogies, paradoxes, ambivalence, disequilibrium, fundamental uncertainty and instability. Structural instability and its companion, fundamental uncertainty, are especially important factors in the analysis of creativity. A paradigm and its associated theorems, models and unquestioned truths reside in some stable equilibrium basin. Any fundamental creative act will lead towards a new paradigm, which always resides in a different stable equilibrium basin. Fundamental creativity thus requires a move across a structurally unstable zone or ridge.

Moves across instability zones lead to cultural, political or intellectual conflicts. This can be exemplified by Florence at the end of the fifteenth century, Enlightenment London or Vienna at the beginning of the twentieth. Conflicts between schools of thought have been even more antagonistic. Examples include the disputes between Newtonians and their opponents regarding the nature of light (particles versus waves), and the fundamental disagreement that separated Albert Einstein from Niels Bohr on the role of uncertainty in physics.

Cities have always been important for creative processes. This is because their size and density allow for synergies and have the intrinsic potential of effecting structural instability. My conclusion is that both the time and the place must be ripe for revolutionary creativity to occur in a city. Revolutionary creativity requires a window of structural instability. Thus no city can be permanently creative.

NOTE

1. In 1983 I received sufficient financial means from the County of Stockholm to study the role of big cities as macro-organizations that favour creative processes in science, industry and the arts. Mr Bo Wijkmark, Chief Executive Officer of the Regional Planning Office of the Stockholm County Council was instrumental in this process, leading to the publication in 1985 of my book *Kreativitet – Storstadens Framtid* (Creativity – the Future of the Metropolis), where many of my ideas regarding creative cities were developed for the first time.

REFERENCES

Alberti, L.B. [1435–1436] (1966), *On Painting*, translated by J.R. Spencer, New Haven CT, Yale University Press.
Alberti, L.B. [1485] (1988), *De Re Aedificatoria. On the Art of Building in Ten Books*, translated by J. Rykwert, N. Leach and R. Tavernor, Cambridge, MA: MIT Press.
Andersson, Å.E. (1985), *Kreativitet – Storstadens Framtid*, Stockholm: Prisma.
Andersson Å.E. and D.E. Andersson (2006), *The Economics of Experiences, the Arts and Entertainment*, Cheltenham, UK and Northampton, MA, USA Edward Elgar Publishing.
Andersson, Å.E. and M.J. Beckmann (2009), *Economics of Knowledge. Theory, Models and Measurements*, Cheltenham, UK and Northampton, MA, USA: Edward Elgar Publishing.

Andersson, Å.E. and J. Mantsinen (1980), 'Mobility of resources, accessibility of knowledge and economic growth', *Behavioral Science*, **25**, 353–66.

Andersson , Å.E. and N.-E. Sahlin (eds) (1997), *The Complexity of Creativity*, Dordrecht: Kluwer.

Andersson, Å.E. and U. Strömquist (1988), *K-samhällets framtid*, Stockholm: Prisma.

Andersson, Å.E., F. Snickars, G. Törnqvist and S. Öberg (1984), *Regional mångfald till rikets gagn: En idébok från ERU*, Stockholm: Liber.

Barrow, J.D. (1992), *Pi in the Sky: Counting, Thinking and Being*, Oxford and New York, NY: Oxford University Press.

Boden, M. (1990), *The Creative Mind. Myths and Mechanisms*, London: Weidenfeld & Nicholson.

Braudel, F [1979] (1986), *Civilisation matérielle, économie et capitalisme, XVe–XVIIIe siècle*, Paris: Armand Colin.

Casti, J.L. (1997), *Would-be Worlds*, New York, NY: John Wiley and Sons.

Casti, J.L. and W. De Pauli (2000), *Gödel: A Life of Logic*, Cambridge, MA: Perseus.

Chaitin, G.J. (1997), *The Limits of Mathematics: A Course on Information Theory and the Limits of Formal Reasoning*, Berlin: Springer.

Dantzig G.B. (1984), 'Reminiscences about the origins of linear programming', in A. Schlissel (ed.), *Essays in the History of Mathematics, American Mathematical Society, San Francisco, Calif., January 1981*, Providence, RI: American Mathematical Society, pp. 1–11.

Debreu, G. (1959), *Theory of Value: An Axiomatic Analysis of Economic Equilibrium*, New Haven, CT and London: Yale University Press.

Defoe, D. (1748), *A Tour Through the Whole Island of Great Britain: Divided into Circuits or Journeys*, London: S. Birt & T. Osborne.

Florida, R. (2002), 'Bohemia and economic geography', *Journal of Economic Geography*, **2**(1), 55–71.

Florida, R. (2008), *Who's Your City?*, New York, NY: Basic Books.

Gärdenfors, P. (2006), *How Homo Became Sapiens – On the Evolution of Thinking*, Oxford and New York, NY: Oxford University Press.

Gärdenfors, P. (2007), 'Understanding cultural patterns', in M.M. Suarez-Orozco (ed.), *Learning in the Global Era: International Perspectives on Globalization and Education*, Berkeley, CA: University of California Press, pp. 67–84.

Gärdenfors, P. (2010), 'The role of understanding in human nature', in D. Evers, A. Jackelen and T.A. Smeds (eds), *How Do We Know? Understanding in Science and Technology*, London: TRClarke, pp. 3–22.

Gardner, H. (1993), *Multiple Intelligences: The Theory In Practice*, New York, NY: Basic Books.

Gardner, H. and S. Moran (2006), 'The science of multiple intelligences theory: a response to Lynn Waterhouse', *Educational Psychologist*, **41**(4), 227–32.

Gentner, D., S. Brem, R. Ferguson et al. (1997), 'Analogical reasoning and conceptual change: a case study of Johannes Kepler', *Journal of the Learning Sciences*, **6**, 3–39.

Gigerenzer, G. (2000), *Adaptive Thinking: Rationality in the Real World*, New York, NY: Oxford University Press.

Gigerenzer, G. (2007), *Gut Feelings: The Intelligence of the Unconscious*, New York, NY: Viking.

Glaeser, Edward L. and David C. Mare (2001), 'Cities and Skills', *Journal of Labor Economics*, **19**(2), 316–42.

Gleick, J. (2003), *Isaac Newton* (translated into Swedish), Lund: Historiska Media.

Gödel, K. (1931),'Über formal unentscheidbare Sätze der Principia Mathematica und verwandter Systeme I', *Monatshefte für Mathematik*.

Gottfredsson, L.J. (1997), 'Mainstream science on intelligence (editorial)', *Intelligence*, **24**, 13–23.

Gray J.J. and D. Rowe (2000), *The Hilbert Challenge*, Oxford: Oxford University Press.

Haken, H. (1978), *Synergetics – An Introduction*, Heidelberg: Springer Verlag.

Hardy, G.H., J.E. Littlewood and G. Pólya [1934] (1967), *Inequalities*, Cambridge: Cambridge University Press.

Hintikka, J. (1999), *Inquiry as Inquiry: A Logic of Scientific Discovery*, Dordrecht and Boston, MA: Kluwer.

Hofstadter, D.R. (1979), *Gödel, Escher, Bach*, New York, NY: Vintage Books.

Janik, A. and S. Toulmin (1973), *Wittgenstein's Vienna*, New York, NY: Simon and Schuster.

Keynes, J.M. (1936), *The General Theory of Employment, Interest and Money*, Cambridge: Cambridge University Press.

Koestler, A. (1969), *The Act of Creation*, New York, NY: Macmillan.

Koopmans, T.C. and M.J. Beckmann (1957), 'Assignment problems and the location of economic activities', *Econometrica*, **25**(1), 53–76.

Kuhn, H.W. (1956), *Linear Inequalities and Related Systems (AM-38)*, Princeton, NJ: Princeton University Press.

Kuhn, T.S. (1962), *The Structure of Scientific Revolutions* (2nd edition), Chicago, IL: University of Chicago Press.

Locke J. [1690] (1975), *An Essay Concerning Human Understanding*, Oxford: Oxford University Press.

Lucas, J. (1971, 1972), 'The autonomy of mind', in *The Nature of Mind* (1971–1973), The Gifford Lectures, Edinburgh: University of Edinburgh Press.

Maddison, A. (1982), *Phases of Capitalist Development*, Oxford: Oxford University Press.

Mandeville, B. [1732] (1988), *The Fable of the Bees or Private Vices, Publick Benefits*, Vol. 1 of two volumes, with a critical, historical and explanatory commentary by F.B. Kaye, Indianapolis, IN: Liberty Fund.

de Manzano, Ö., D. Cervenka, A. Karabanov, L. Farde and F. Ullén (2010), 'Thinking outside a less intact box: thalamic dopamine D2 receptor densities are negatively related to psychometric creativity in healthy individuals', *PLoS ONE*, 5(5), e10670, doi:10.1371/journal.pone.0010670

Matyasevich, Y. (1971, 1973), 'On recursive unsolvability of Hilbert's tenth problem', in *Proceedings of Fourth International Congress on Logic, Methodology and Philosophy of Science, Bucharest, 1971*, Amsterdam: North-Holland, pp. 89–110.

Nilsson, L-G. (1988), 'Psykologi och Kommunikation', in Å.E. Andersson, *Universitet – Regioners Framtid*, Värnamo: Fälths.

OECD (2007), *OECD Science and Technology Indicators*, Paris: Organization for Economic Cooperation and Development

Penrose, R. (1989), *The Emperor's New Mind*, Oxford: Oxford University Press.

Petty, W. [1689] (2004), *Essays on Mankind and Political Arithmetic*, available at http://www.gutenberg.org/ebooks/5619.

Pico della Mirandola, G. [1486] (2010), *Oration on the Dignity of Man (De hominis dignitate)*, Adelaide: eBooks@Adelaide.

Pólya, G. (1945), *How to Solve It: A New Aspect of Mathematical Method*. Princeton, NJ: Princeton University Press.

Popper, K. (1945), *The Open Society and Its Enemies*, London: Routledge and Kegan Paul.

Prigogine, I. and G. Nicolis (1989), *Exploring Complexity*, New York, NY: W.H. Freeman.

Puu, T. (2006), *Arts, Sciences, and Economics: A Historical Safari*, Berlin: Springer.

Ramsey F.P. [1931] (1977), *Foundations – Essays in Philosophy, Logic, Mathematics and Economics*, New York, NY: Humanities Press.

Sahlin, N.-E. (1990), *The Philosophy of F.P. Ramsey*, Cambridge: Cambridge University Press.

Sahlin, N.-E. (2001), *Kreativitetens filosofi*, Nora: Nya Doxa.

Samuelson, P.A. [1947] (1983), *Foundations of Economic Analysis* (enlarged edn), Cambridge, MA: Harvard University Press.

Schelling, T. (1978), *Micromotives and Macrobehavior*, New York, NY: Norton.

Schorske, C. (1981), *Fin de Siècle Vienna*, New York, NY: Vintage Books.

Schumpeter, J.A. (1934), *The Theory of Economic Development*, Cambridge, MA: Harvard University Press.

Schumpeter, J.A. (1954), *History of Economic Analysis*, New York, NY: Oxford University Press.

Searle, J. (1980), 'Minds, brains and programs', *Behavioral and Brain Sciences*, **3**, 417–57.

Searle, J. (1990), 'Is the brain's mind a computer program?', *Scientific American*, January, 26–31.

Simon, H.A. (1955), 'A behavioral model of rational choice', *Quarterly Journal of Economics*, **69**, 99–188.

Simonton, D.K. (1984), *Genius, Creativity, and Leadership – Historiometric Inquiries*, Cambridge, MA: Harvard University Press.

Smith, A. [1776] (2006), *An Inquiry into the Nature and Causes of the Wealth of Nations*, London: W. Strahan and T. Cadell.

Smith, G.J.W. (1993), 'The creative person', in Å.E. Andersson, D.F. Batten, K. Kobayashi and K. Yoshikawa (eds.), *The Cosmo-creative Society*, Berlin: Springer Verlag.

Smith, G.J.W. and I.M. Carlsson (1990), *The Creative Process: A Functional Model Based on Empirical Studies from Early Childhood Up to Middle Age*, Madison, WI: International Universities Press.

Solow, R.M. (1956), 'A contribution to the theory of economic growth', *Quarterly Journal of Economics*, **70**(1), 65–94.

Stewart, I.N. and P.L. Peregoy (1983), 'Catastrophe theory modeling in psychology', *Psychological Bulletin*, **94**(2) 336–62.

Trevelyan, G.M. (1942), *English Social History: A Survey of Six Centuries – Chaucer to Queen Victoria*, London: Longmans, Green & Co.

Turing, A.M. (1937), 'On computable numbers, with an application to the Entscheidungsproblem', *Proceedings of the London Mathematical Society*, **2**(42), 230–64.

Turing, A.M. (1950), 'Computing machinery and intelligence', *Mind*, **LIX**(236), 433–60.

Vitruvius (1914), *The Ten Books on Architecture*, translated by Morris Hicky Morgan, London: Humphrey Milford, Oxford University Press.

von Neumann, J. [1937] (1975), 'Über ein ökonomisches Gleichungssystem und eine Verallgemeinerung des Brouwerschen Fixpunktsatzes', in M.J. Beckmann and R. Sato (eds), *Mathematische Wirtschaftstheorie*, Köln: Kiepenheuer & Witsch.

von Neumann, J. and O. Morgenstern (1944), *Theory of Games and Economic Behavior,* Princeton, NJ: Princeton University Press.

Wedberg, A. (2003), *Filosofins historia: Nyare tiden till romantiken,* Stockholm: Thales.

White, L.A. (1947), 'The locus of mathematical reality: an anthropological footnote', *Philosophy of Science,* **14**, 289–303.

Whitehead, A.N. and B. Russell (1925/1927), *Principia Mathematica* (3 volumes; 2nd edition), Cambridge: Cambridge University Press.

Wolfram, S. (2002), *A New Kind of Science,* Champaign, IL: Wolfram Media.

3 The creative class paradigm
Richard Florida, Charlotta Mellander and Patrick Adler

The Rise of the Creative Class (Florida, 2002a, hereafter *Rise*) has enjoyed unusual impact both on the practice of economic development and on academic debate. It has been less than a decade since the book was published and it already stands as one of the most referenced texts in economic development and urban sociology. A Google Scholar search in early 2010 showed that 2584 subsequent works had cited it to that point, edging out Jane Jacobs's (1969) seminal, *The Economy of Cities* (2403 citations) and Louis Wirth's (1938) 'Urbanism as a way of life' (2433 citations).

What accounts for the book's academic traction and the ensuing debate it generated? First and foremost, *Rise* was the first work that really synthesized the emerging construct of 'creativity', coursing through psychology, economic history and regional science in the kind of straightforward language that practitioners as well as academics could understand. It draws off earlier work by Jane Jacobs (1961) and especially by Åke Andersson (1985) on the role of creativity and of the intersection of people's creative capacities and place to situate creativity in the context of regional development. *Rise* also successfully integrated two divergent streams of thinking in urban economics: one which held industry and university location paramount to growth, and a second, more recent stream which focused on the autonomous decisions of human capital or skilled labour. By adopting place as the organizing unit of economic growth, replacing the corporation which played that role in the industrial age, its 3 Ts model of economic development attempted to unify the chicken-and-egg question of whether jobs or people lead economic development.

THE CREATIVE CLASS APPROACH IN BRIEF

So what exactly is the creative class approach? Florida, drawing off earlier seminal contributions by Karl Marx (1906), Joseph Schumpeter (1942) and more recently Peter Drucker (1993), Daniel Bell (1961, 1973) and others, points to the rise of a new social class rooted in knowledge work or mental labour. The class is made up of workers spanning industries such as science and technology, arts, culture and entertainment and the knowledge-based professions. It has grown from roughly 5 to 10 per cent of the workforce at the turn of the twentieth century to roughly a third or more of the workforce in the advanced economies by the early twenty-first century. It draws attention to the role of occupation as opposed to industry as a key lens in understanding economic change and regional development.

Rise presents a model for urban growth called 'The 3 Ts of Economic Development'. It suggests that in the post-industrial era, successful regional economies need to cultivate an ecosystem incorporating high levels of talent, high-technology industry concentration, low barriers to entry for talent and high degrees of social heterogeneity (or tolerance).

While its effect was transformative, Florida's book essentially draws together several branches of economic development theory with long histories. Marx (1906) and Schumpeter (1942) focused on the intersection of innovation and socio-economic structures in powering economic growth. Robert Solow (1956), Robert Lucas (1988) and Paul Romer (1986, 1987, 1990) explored the relationship between technological innovation and economic growth, emphasizing in particular the role of high-tech workers. Studies of Silicon Valley and Route 128 (such as Saxenian, 1996) highlighted the dynamics through which technology played a role in the emergence of those two highly productive regions. *Rise* also builds on contributions by the likes of Robert Barro (1991), Edward Glaeser (1994, 1998) and Glaeser et al. (2001) that emphasize the role of skilled labour in development – more specifically, the role of skilled workers in explaining urban and national growth. In highlighting the importance of diversity, the 3 Ts theory extends the work of national-level theories (Inglehart, 1977; Dei Ottati, 1994; Welzel et al., 2003) that posit a relationship between social openness and growth.

This chapter seeks to situate the contribution of *Rise* and the creative class approach in the context of the broader literatures on technological change, economic development, socio-economic class and regional development. It begins with a review of the regional growth literatures that *Rise* drew upon and sought to contribute to and a discussion of how the book sought to contribute to this broad and important field of research. The last section highlights the debate and dialogue about the book and advances in understanding regional development that comes from this ongoing dialogue.

WHERE *RISE* COMES FROM

Rise took the primacy of the firm as a core unit of analysis in economics, economic geography and regional science as one of its core challenges. For much of its history, the study of regional economic growth focused on the firm as the primary scale of analysis. As the basic unit of industrial districts, the central unit in industrial organization, and the source of technology, the firm was said to be central to increasing productivity and growth. Locations encouraged economic growth by attracting investment from elsewhere and by commercializing local knowledge.

The geographic clustering of firms that do not formally cooperate (and may even compete) with one another was said to be an important contributor to regional growth. Clusters realize at least four economies by co-locating. Alfred Marshall (1890) was the first to describe them, and his work has found contemporary resonance in the likes of Michael Porter (1994) and Gabi Dei Ottati (1994). The first economy is access to a larger and specialized pool of subcontractors. The second is more efficient communication, thanks to closer proximity and more opportunities for ideas to be transmitted and absorbed. The third is access to a shared labour market with a specialized set of skills. The fourth is less concrete, relating to the un-transacted and immeasurable 'atmosphere' of trust (Dei Ottati, 1994) that results when humans are in the same place for a long time.

According to numerous studies in the 1980s and 1990s, these spillovers, in particular the final one, found their embodiment in the regions of Emilia Romagna, Italy and Baden-Württemberg, Germany (Piore and Sabel, 1984; Bellandi, 1989; Goodman, 1989; Sforzi, 1989; Cooke and Morgan, 1990). Silicon Valley and Los Angeles were cited as the

North American archetypes of industrial clusters. Each of these districts was dominated by a large number of small producers with fairly even power relations. But the forces of agglomeration did not apply solely to small firms. Dominated by large firms and the state, more hierarchical clusters were observed in other places (Markusen, 1996), and they reinforced the importance of industrial clustering.

There is also a strong tradition of work known as the (New) Urban Economics (NUE) that explains agglomeration economies and locational choices as a function of transportation costs (Alonso, 1960, 1964; Fujita, 1985, 1988; Krugman, 1991). Based on the tradition of J.H. von Thünen ([1826] 1966), Walter Christaller (1933) and August Lösch (1940), the NUE provides a micro-fundamental basis for urban spatial structure studies (Alonso, 1960, 1964; Muth, 1961, 1969; Mills, 1967). Based on von Thünen-like models, the regional structure is envisioned as a flat plain with a single, well-defined central business district and equal transport costs in all directions. The structure of the city is determined by incomes, tastes, housing, commuting conditions and the relative use and pricing of urban/non-urban land. From this, an optimal level of population or housing density can be derived as a function of the distance from the central business district. The approach implies that all regions have an optimal size, and that they are monocentric, with just one city core.

Research into industrial districts cannot be divorced from the larger issue of 'post-Fordist' economic organization that dominated economic geography in the last part of the twentieth century. The process of deindustrialization in the last quarter of the twentieth century and the migration of capital away from the large factories of the Midwestern 'rust belt' prompted scholars to seek out a new economic and regulatory system of accumulation to serve as an heir to Fordism.

Industrial clusters were said to possess features of a new type of capitalism: flexible specialization (Piore and Sabel, 1984; Storper, 1994). Greater agglomeration among similar industries was one feature. The products produced by these districts were less standardized, and the machinery used to produce them was less specialized. Technological plasticity enabled workers to have expertise in a wider range of products (Storper, 1994), and led to more continuous firm learning. The role of learning under flexible specialization was emphasized in Florida and Kenney's early research on the organization of Japanese firms (1993). They found that the flexible and extremely successful 'Toyota System' involved shop floor workers in the innovation process and was rooted in continuous learning.

Innovation itself becomes a topic of inquiry for those interested in the post-Fordist accumulation. The work of Solow (1956) carved out a new role for technology in economic growth theory. Technological change was said to be an important component of productivity growth in the post-war period, and an area in which increasing economic returns could be realized. Regional economists were interested in how this process was initiated at the local level. It would be perilous to summarize the entire 'regional innovation literature' in such a short space, but the strand with the clearest links to the creative thesis is concerned with the role of the university in the development of technology. The view that universities might be engines of innovation was widely subscribed to. According to the 'linear model of innovation', innovations flow from university science to commercial technology (Smith, 1990) through regional channels. Adam Jaffe (1989) concludes that university research made corporate research more efficient. Anselin et al., (1997) found that university research tends to attract corporate research labs.

While this strand of research was concerned with how universities produce knowledge, it was every bit as firm-focused as the industrial districts literature. The impact of the university was measured at the firm level, through variables like new firm formation and patent licensing. It was concerned with the co-location of institutions, industries and firms, and largely elided regional factors such as occupational mix, amenities or built form which might explain why some strong universities spawn significant regional growth (Stanford, MIT, Harvard) and others (Carnegie Mellon, Rochester Institute of Technology) do not. While many studies examined the firm characteristics that contributed to commercialization (see Cohen and Levanthal, 1990; Anselin et al., 1997) there was not a similar focus on the broader factors that contribute to a place.

HUMAN CAPITAL THEORIES

Rise also was influenced by and sought to broaden the emphasis on talent or human capital. To do so, it sought to shift attention from education as a key determinant of human capital to *occupation*. Spurred by Marx's (1906) insistence that it is the work people do that really matters, *Rise* sought to shift attention to the way the shifting role of the worker in production – that is, in actual work – shapes society and regional development. *Rise* argues that occupation provides a better and more nuanced measure of skill than education on two dimensions. One, it enables those who engage in knowledge-based or creative work but do not have college degrees, such as many leading entrepreneurs, to be counted. And two, it provides a way to look at the actual composition of regional economies strategically. Education-based measures are quite broad, but occupations can be analysed in a way that is similar to industries. Regional economies can be broken down and analysed in terms of their leading component occupations.

In the extant literature, labour had always been viewed as an important input in the process of firm location but was not, until the turn of the century, posited as an independent factor that might contribute to urban growth.

The theories we have reviewed up to this point considered human capital to be an important feature of firm location. Skilled workers were, alternatively, the source of agglomeration economies, an input increasing in value under post-industrialism and a connection between universities and firms. The arrival of human capital theory disentangled the education decisions of skilled people from those of firms.

This new perspective on human capital originated primarily in economics. Gary Becker (1964) and Jacob Mincer (1974) establish that regional wage levels vary with the level of human capital. Romer (1986, 1987, 1990) suggests that the rate of invention is a local feature, determined both by the presence of a knowledgeable workforce and the pre-existing stock of knowledge. This countered Solow's contention that technology was exogenous to the production system. Lucas (1988) shows that knowledge not only improves an individual's productivity, it also improves the productivity of the people around her. This insight that clustered knowledge workers create positive externalities for the local economy added formal support to Jacobs's long-held argument that cities are able to 'make old work out of new' (Jacobs, 1969).

Research in regional economics began to link educational attainment (one measure of knowledge and skill) to regional economic performance. Building on the work of Barro (1991), who linked national economic performance with attainment, Glaeser and colleagues (1995, 2001; Berry and Glaeser, 2005) chronicled a positive relationship between high educational attainment and the growth of local incomes and populations. Glaeser's work on the growth of sunbelt cities and high-amenity urban centres helped to demonstrate that the locational preferences of human capital were distinct from those of firms. Vijay Mathur's (1999) important paper in *Economic Development Quarterly* brought the new focus on human capital into the regional development literature.

Explanations for why human capital concentrated in certain places centred on the presence of local amenities. Jennifer Roback's early work on amenities (1982) explains wage differentials in American cities via a battery of amenities such as weather, housing quality and crime, a series of variables that more recent research has examined more closely. Other studies have highlighted the correlation between the presence of cultural amenities (cafes, artistic institutions) and growth (Glaeser et al., 2001; Lloyd and Clark, 2001; Lloyd, 2002). Amenity-based theories of economic growth find that the consumption preferences of skilled individuals play an increasing role in regional growth.

THE CREATIVE CLASS APPROACH

So it was with all this in mind that the creative class approach appeared. And in this sense – drawing from these broad literatures and Florida's previous work – the approach represents an important fusion of the 'firm (or technology)-centred' and 'people (or human capital)-centred' growth literatures, with place, as noted before, as the central organizing principle bringing them together. Like the work on human capital, it emphasizes the role of knowledge location for regional economic growth while suspending the assumption that workers 'go where the jobs are'. Like some of the most useful firm-centred growth literature, its focus is on the fundamental mechanisms of economic growth, eliding factors such as individual taste and generational tendencies that amenity-based theories of economic growth (for instance, Glaeser et al., 2001; Clark et al., 2002) tend to hold as paramount. While some (see Storper and Scott, 2009) have criticized the human capital work for its over-simplicity, the 3 Ts theory incorporates some of the human capital school's perspective that education will impact growth to a greater extent in the post-industrial era.

THE '3 TS' OF ECONOMIC DEVELOPMENT

The creative class model of economic development views place as the most significant economic unit where human capital and firms resolve their location preferences. Growth does not simply occur in the places that lower firm costs or improve output in an aim to be as 'business-friendly' as possible. Instead, it occurs in places that allow individuals to 'maximize their utility and not just their income' (Clark et al., 2002, p. 496). The 3 Ts theory assumes that firms which rely on skilled labour will have to trade inefficiencies in other areas for access to human capital. For instance, they might locate in places that have higher taxes if those places also provide access to a skilled labour force. As economic units that rely on income, skilled labour must likewise consider the availability of jobs when they make their location decisions. Each of talent, technology and tolerance are necessary but not sufficient conditions of place. Economic growth occurs in regions with substantial levels of all three.

The first set of variables is related to technological activity. Drawing upon contributions from Marx (1906) to Schumpeter (1942), Solow (1956) to Romer (1986, 1987, 1990), the theory views economic growth as a function of technology and innovation. The Technology Index is composed of two technology- and industry-related location quotients. The first captures the percentage of regional output contributed by high tech as a percentage of a nation's high-tech output. The second measures the share of regional output contributed by high tech.

Talent is the second T. While place is the most significant economic unit in the 3 Ts model, talented workers are its most significant actors. The first group of variables that explain growth fall under the umbrella of 'talent'. Talent is a direct measure of the share of high-skill workers in a region at a given time. Skill is measured in two ways in 3 Ts models: on an educational basis and on an occupational one. The latter constitutes the creative class. Occupational skill is measured as the percentage of people engaged in 'non-routine occupations that require creative problem solving and/or the generation of new forms'. Occupations in this creative class include occupations related to: computer and programming, architecture, engineering, social science, education and library, arts and entertainment, sports, media, managers, finance, law, health related and high-end sales (Florida, 2002a). In keeping with previous work on human capital, educational skill is measured by the attainment of a bachelor's degree or higher. Like other models of human capital growth (Becker, 1964; Mincer, 1974; Glaeser, 1994, 1998), the 3 Ts model assumes that high-skill workers are more productive and command higher wages and incomes than workers at large, and thus help to improve income and wage accumulation across the region in which they live.

Tolerance is the third T. Florida has elsewhere said that he believes this focus on socio-cultural or non-market factors may be the greatest contribution of the approach. Economists have long neglected these factors. As noted above, they view both talent and technology as stocks that are accumulated in places. But it is clear from the empirical literature that both are highly mobile factors. They are more aptly characterized as flows, not stocks. But what accounts for these flows? While *Rise* makes a series of arguments about physical place-based characteristics and what is termed quality of place, emphasis is placed on a key factor in realizing these flows – openness to human capital or openness to people. This openness requires tolerance, which is measured not through opinion surveys or attitudes but observed locational preferences. The three tolerance variables are based on key indicators of these observed locational preferences which reflect low barriers to entry for people. Each measures a population that has traditionally faced considerable discrimination and segregation and has been treated as outsiders. The Mosaic Index measures the percentage of a region's residents born in another country. The Bohemian Index measures the share of artists – a population that trades in challenging convention perhaps more than any other. The Gay Index measures the fraction of the population made up of same-sex partners who reside in the same household.

This emphasis on talent accessibility is based in the assumption that human capital is a dynamic 'flow' and not a stock (Florida, 2005). Unlike many physical resources, skilled labour is mobile. Where it locates is dependent on a multiplicity of factors, most of which have not yet been accounted for. But places with high barriers of entry to outsider groups are less likely to be welcoming and supportive of outsiders in general – including skilled outsiders.

THE CENTRALITY OF PLACE

Rise situates place at the very centre of regional development, and it is through the lens of place that the approach seems to unify 'firm-focused' and 'people-focused' theories of urban growth.

Like the rest of the human capital literature, it severs the assumed relationship between the geography of industry and the geography of talent. Human capital has ceased to be merely an input into the production process, a resource to be tapped by a firm, or shared by similar firms in the same industrial cluster. Instead of locating where other costs are lower or where agglomeration economies exist, skill-intensive firms must also locate where they can access skilled labour. Instead of treating skilled labour as a permanent stock of a place, firms must treat it as a flow, the amplitude of which varies with qualities of place.

The firm has only had to consider the location preferences of skilled labour with the advent of the post-industrial economy. Under early industrialization, the fixed nature of transport networks (canals, seas, rivers) and power generation (canals, rivers) kept production and producers close to these sources. With the advent of electricity, transport, power and communication became less fixed to a specific place, but the sunk costs of advanced industrialization were still high. Once large factories were established in a place, they were hard to move and much less mobile compared with labour. Large factory towns such as Hershey, Pennsylvania, were the embodiment of this firm-led system. Here, the consumption preferences of workers were not only subservient to the microeconomic demands of the firm, but the firm also controlled worker housing and consumption. The development of industrial suburbs at the periphery of cities during the late nineteenth century (Walker and Lewis, 2001) is another example of the industrial firm's primacy over the industrial worker.

Today, the skilled post-industrial worker enjoys more autonomy over where they live because post-industrial production is relatively footloose. Firms can relocate offices, studios and laboratories with greater ease than assembly plants. Communications technology allows them to maintain multiple sites of production with much greater ease than before, and to separate command and control functions that might once have been centralized at one office. Most importantly, since skilled labour is a greater source of competitive advantage and firm differentiation in this era, firms must bid for skilled labour in order to gain competitive advantage. They do this in part by locating in places that appeal to the lifestyle of high-human-capital individuals and reflect their values. Research that sees industrial location as the leading determinant of economic growth (for example, Storper and Scott, 2009) tends to overlook the ways in which the fundamental forces of economic growth are themselves subject to change.

The theories of technological generation identified in the first section see place as a container for economic innovation and nothing more. The 3 Ts perspective sees innovation as dependent on a series of forces that operate at the regional level. The talent level of the local region – not just the local university or firm – is seen as an important determinant of new firm formation and knowledge formation. The openness of a region to this talent becomes an equally important characteristic, alongside the technological production and innovation of the region's industries.

This place-based perspective on innovation is useful in explaining why similar universities seem to have different effects on regional technological growth. Pittsburgh and Boston, for instance, both have strong university bases, but they have different rates of commercialization and different average regional incomes. Higher talent, technology and tolerance scores for Boston suggest that the regional environment plays an important role in absorbing and commercializing new knowledge creation.

It would be a mistake to see amenity-based human capital theories as being completely blind to firm geography. The location decisions of human capital are determined by both income and amenities in early human capital models (Glaeser et al., 2001; Clark et al., 2002). In the 3 Ts approach, the ability to earn an income, or a higher income, is one of many local features that determine a place's talent-friendliness. Firm geography plays a more significant role in the 3 Ts model than in other human capital models. Both of its technology variables are based on industrial data, suggesting that places without concentrations of high-tech activity will not achieve significant levels of growth, regardless of their other measures.

The 3 Ts model is also distinguished by its focus on tolerance, a more fundamental and deeply rooted characteristic of place. It seeks to go beyond and go deeper than the previous focus on lifestyle, tastes and amenities. In fact, the very measures developed were developed in response to the limited and at times non-systematic nature of data associated with amenity and lifestyle variables. Data on observed locational preferences of artistic and cultural creatives, foreign-born people and gay and lesbian people is far more systematic and unbiased. The experiential amenities identified by Terry Nichols Clark and his collaborators are united by a specific aesthetic sensibility (Clark et al., 2002; Florida, 2002a), which is not uniformly shared across all skilled workers (Markusen and Schrock, 2006), and which might change with time. Likewise, the climactic, educational and safety amenities identified by Glaeser (1994, 1998) are specific to skilled labour with a particular set of lifestyle demands, and largely neglect cohorts such as the young and childless. *Rise* sought to go beyond the limits of these variables and measures.

Thus, the third T – tolerance – is not simply an amenity compatible with lifestyles and tastes, but a mechanism that can attract mobile labour. Inglehart's work at the national level (Welzel et al., 2003) has found a relationship between openness to outsiders and economic performance. The 3 Ts approach has extended this established research into an even more fundamental unit of economic activity. Even the life-stage amenities identified by Florida in his later work are much more variable.

The 3 Ts model values racial diversity at a regional scale through its mosaic index. This approach fails to capture that some regions that are relatively diverse at a regional level are composed of socially homogeneous neighbourhoods that rarely interact. Certainly, regions with high shares of segregated visible minorities and immigrants but also a high degree of segregation do not accrue the same benefits from heterogeneity that regions with integrated communities do, or signal low barriers to human capital in the same way. When *Rise* was first published there was no measure of racial integration at the sub-metropolitan scale, and numerous authors have pointed out this limitation (Thomas and Darnton, 2006: Hansen and Niedomysl, 2009; Storper and Scott, 2009). This was later updated when the paperback edition of *Rise* was published, with a new Integration Index added to the tolerance measures (Florida, 2004), as well as by Høgni Hansen and Thomas Niedomysl (2009), who formulated their own integration measure in their study of Sweden's creative class. The new measure gauges the degree of racial mix at the neighbourhood scale of US metropolitan areas. The extent to which integration is positively integrated to economic outcomes is not fully known, but according to recent research there is at least some evidence that pockets of ethnic homogeneity persist in even the most prosperous regions (Thomas and Darnton, 2006).

The 3 Ts approach departs most from human capital theory in challenging how human capital is defined. Since Becker (1964), Mincer (1974) and Romer (1986), educational attainment has been the proxy for human capital. However, the 3 Ts approach holds that knowledge is not the only cognitive resource that improves productivity. Creativity, intelligence and intuition have also been found to be separate and important sources of productivity growth (Smith et al., 1984), and are encountered separately from formal education.

Florida's 'creative class' defines human capital in occupational terms (as well as educational ones) because occupation captures skills that are directly put to use by the economy. His theory holds that while a region's share of educated people may indicate the supply of people who have acquired a threshold of skill, its share of creative workers indicates a region's demand for this skill. Resources that are not engaged in economic activity will not by themselves be a part of the growth process. For instance, Saudi Arabia's large oil reserves are only relevant to its economic trajectory because the oil there is extracted from the ground. If the country's reserves could not – for whatever reason – be mined from the ground, then its strength as an oil economy would be significantly impaired. A large supply of skilled workers can, likewise, only be expected to account for growth if the resource is absorbed and utilized by the local economy.

Another strength of the occupational measure is that it captures segments of the labour force that did not acquire their skills in school. In some lines of work skills are acquired informally on the job and not recognized by a formal, measurable credential. The revolutionary and disruptive nature of entrepreneurial work often makes it incompatible with the proven lessons and established thinking that characterize university curriculums. Recent research for Sweden estimates that while 90 per cent of degree holders have a creative job, only 25 per cent of the creative class has a degree (Mellander, 2009).

THE GREAT CREATIVE CLASS DEBATE

It is an understatement to say that *Rise* instigated a robust debate. Science – as Thomas Kuhn (1962) long ago noted – advances through challenge and debate. And the debate over *Rise* has helped propel the field forward in important ways. The debate has evolved across several dominant streams which we address below.

The first relates to how to define human capital. The 3 Ts theory challenged the educational definition for human capital, based on the notion that the absorptive capacity for talent (captured by occupation) is more useful from the standpoint of economic growth. The education and training definition of human capital had been pre-eminent for economists going back to Becker (1964) and Mincer (1974), and heirs to this tradition such as Glaeser (1994, 1998) resisted alternative frameworks, claiming that they added no additional explanatory power. More recent critical work holds that human capital is still paramount. Glaeser (2005) finds that the educational measure correlates with regional population growth better than share of a region in the super-creative core or the share of bohemian occupations. In other calculations, Stephen Rausch and Cynthia Negrey (2006) find that the traditional measure of human capital correlates better with their measure of gross municipal product when regional and state capital affects are controlled for. In their analysis of German regions, Ron Boschma and Michael Fritsch (2009) find that the effect of educational attainment on patenting is more significant than the creative class, although both are significant. Yet other studies have pointed in other directions. Charlotta Mellander and Florida's study of Sweden (2009) finds that creative class measures do a better job of accounting for wage levels. Gerard Marlet and Clemens Van Woerkens (2004) conclude that for the Netherlands, their refined formulation of the creative class outperforms educational attainment in accounting for job growth.

Which is better at accounting for regional growth, human capital or the creative class? The most recent empirical evidence on the subject suggests that the answer depends on how you define regional growth. Florida et al. (2008) compare human capital and the creative class on how they accounted for metropolitan wage and income. They find that human capital is more strongly associated with wages, while creative class is correlated better with income. This result suggests that education and creativity act in different ways to affect economic outcomes, even as the two measures correlate with one another. Wage level is said to reflect a region's overall productivity, while the income level is said to reflect its overall wealth (Florida et al., 2008). Since both are important policy goals, both clearly have a long-term place in the analysis of regional economic growth

Second, recent research has aimed to disaggregate the occupational groups contained within the creative class, associations between the creative class and economic growth notwithstanding. Some have criticized the creative class concept for being too broad to develop policy around. Ann Markusen (2006) argues that the creative class groups together people with drastically different lifestyles, mobility tendencies, political views and amenity preferences, and that the 'creative class' writ large cannot be courted with the same set of policies. Artists, for instance (Markusen and Schrock, 2006), appear to be relatively more mobile, socially liberal and sensitive to price levels when compared to other members of the creative class. The call to disaggregate the creative class is rooted, partially, in the desire to establish understandings that will allow jurisdictions to more directly enact policies to attract and retain members of the creative class.

Recent research has sought to distinguish creative class occupations from each other by using the precise skills that each occupation demands (McGranahan and Wojan, 2007: Abel and Gabe, 2008; Asheim and Hansen, 2009). Asheim and Hansen (2009) claim that the location preferences of creative types are affected by the predominant knowledge bases required by local industry. They find that workers who require a synthetic knowledge base tend to favour a better climate for business and industry, while workers with analytical and symbolic knowledge bases tend to worry more about a place's 'people climate'.

David McGranahan and Timothy Wojan (2007) use ONET, a database that assigns various skill ratings to each occupation in order to remove occupations related to education and health, which Florida did not have access to when doing the research for *Rise*. This is an important, empirically grounded advance. It should be noted, however, that the new ONET-based definition is closely correlated with the original one and subsequent research by Florida's stream and others indicates that the updated definition does not alter the key findings of the original research. Gabe and colleagues (2007) find that – while wage returns to the creative class are only significant in metropolitan counties – the returns to mathematical and technical skills are significant in both metropolitan and non-metropolitan areas.

Florida et al. (2008) find that excluding education and health occupations does help to achieve stronger growth relationships. They also find significant differences in how various creative occupations impact regional development. For instance, they find that educators and healthcare professionals are evenly distributed across the population nationwide, and thus do not tend to affect regional productivity or wealth. Likewise, artistic occupations, which tend traditionally to be thought of as non-traded industries, are found to 'exert considerable direct influence on regional development' (Florida et al., 2008). Occupations relate to computer science, management and engineering (Florida et al., 2008) and producer services and information (Abel and Gabe, 2008) have also been found to influence economic growth.

The third debate is concerned with the conditions that affect the distribution of human capital and, ultimately, economic growth. Whether human capital is defined according to an attainment or an occupational measure, it is assumed to flow to places that are most suited to it. Prior to *Rise*, there was little theoretical consensus on which conditions favour human capital agglomeration. Although numerous studies had hinted that human capital co-located with consumer amenities, industrial clusters and universities, it was unclear how the full complement of these factors worked to channel human capital.

The introduction of 'tolerance', as a new condition, has added to the list of variables that can be analysed and empirically tested. And this has been an area of contentious debate. Numerous studies have looked at the influence of tolerance on the distribution of human capital, exploring whether the tolerance measures, as indicators of barriers to human capital, are related to urban growth. The significance of the tolerance variable on growth appears to vary depending on the specific independent and dependent variables that are employed. Rausch and Negrey (2006) find that tolerance, and the Melting Pot Index specifically, is more strongly related to gross municipal product than is the creative class. Clark (2003) finds that the significance of tolerance only holds for large metropolitan regions. Glaeser (2005) finds that the Gay Index is negatively related to US metropolitan growth and that the Bohemian Index is not significantly related. Employing a path analysis technique, Florida et al. (2008) are able to suggest a broader relationship between tolerance, the concentration of human capital and regional outcomes (income and wages). They conclude that tolerance is significantly and directly related to both measures of the creative class, and both regional outcomes.

They find evidence that tolerance acts though human capital to promote regional growth, but that it also acts on its own. How might tolerance work independently of human capital to affect growth? The authors offer two additional mechanisms – each supported by additional research.

First, a tolerant region is said to be necessarily more ripe for interaction and positive spillovers. Bohemian workers are said to be highly mobile across industries and employers – allowing for them to transmit knowledge and best practices (Vinodrai and Gertler, 2006; Markusen and Schrock, 2006; Currid, 2007). In addition, a region that is more open to outsiders may house employees that are more open to new co-workers. In keeping with this theme, they suggest that tolerant regions value openness and self-expression, the same values that have been linked to economic growth in studies at the national level (Welzel et al., 2003; Berggren and Elinder, forthcoming).

These recent contributions to 3 Ts research have also found that consumer amenities and the presence of a university are related to the location of both types of human capital (Florida et al., 2008). This squares with another, even more recent finding. Alessandra Faggian and Philip McCann (2006) find that the presence of a university does not explain growth, once the presence of human capital has been controlled for. This suggests that the university's primary economic role is in attracting human capital to a region, and not necessarily in spinning off or generating technological activity directly.

The revelation that all these conditions can simultaneously affect both human capital and economic growth is perhaps the most important indication thus far that the region is the primary organizing unit of post-industrial economic growth.

The 3 Ts framework has been most influential as an alternative method of accounting for regional economic growth. In introducing a new variable for socio-economic differences, however, the theory has opened up research that seeks to grapple with increased social polarization in advanced capitalist societies. A fourth genre of debate is concerned with how differences at the occupational level correspond with distinct income, health and wellbeing outcomes.

Florida discussed early findings on the relationship between occupational class and income in *Rise,* finding that creative occupations earned dramatically higher annual incomes than non-creative ones. Mary Donegan and Nichola Lowe (2008) studied the relationship between a region's creative class share and its wage polarization. Although they conclude that 'traditional' institutional factors such as unionization and the minimum wage are important mechanisms for easing inequality, the presence of the creative class outperforms all other variables in their correlation analysis.

The wide gulf in income between the creativity-oriented and routine-oriented classes hints that the content of jobs might be a leading mechanism of social polarization. Subsequent research has confirmed this hypothesis by analysing wage and income returns to skills (Feser, 2003; Martin and Florida, 2009; Scott, 2009). A recent skills-based analysis of North American occupations finds that earnings increase dramatically as the level of analytical and social skills required by an occupation increase. Earnings were found to increase by between US$24 000 and US$32 000 as the level of analytical and social intelligence skills required by a job increased from the 25th to the 75th percentile. But earnings decreased as the physical skills required at a job went up. Members of different occupations are not only rewarded differently, but the value of their skills also varies. The growing disparity in regional incomes is another dimension of social polarization, and recent work (Feser, 2003; Scott, 2009) has linked regional income to the concentration of cognitive skills in metropolitan areas.

Commentary on the creative class thesis has also linked the consumption practices of high-income workers to high levels of income inequality where creative workers are found. By some accounts, creative workers are highly dependent on an underclass of service workers, earning low wages to do tasks that creative workers do not have time to perform on their own (Peck, 2005; Scott, 2006; McCann, 2007). The livelihoods of these service workers, it is said, are further complicated by gentrification and displacement processes which, by necessity, accompany the influx of wealth and capital to a city (Peck, 2005: Scott, 2006; Atkinson and Easthope, 2009). In subsequent work, Florida and colleagues have also noted the occupational and income polarization that seems to accompany the creative economy (Florida, 2005; Martin and Florida, 2009). Viewing wage polarization through an occupational lens, as these authors have done, might be a useful step towards addressing the problem, since the challenge of changing occupational content is much more direct than the problem of 'paying workers more'. Recently Florida (2010; see also Martin and Florida, 2009) has speculated that a small cohort of leading-edge service companies may be developing ways to increase the productive output of traditionally low-paid service jobs by integrating the creative capabilities of front-line workers into their business models. If service workers contribute more value to their firms, then it should be possible to compensate them better as well. Future research will no doubt examine if such efforts can moderate the social 'bifurcations' of the post-industrial economy (Scott, 2006).

In the end the ongoing debate has been extremely fruitful and valuable. Florida always says he learns the most from his critics: they spur him – and all of us – to think hard about our assumptions, our constructs and our work. In the end, our understanding of the social, economic and geographic world occurs through debate. We – all of us – stand on the shoulder of giants. Our task is to move that understanding forward slowly and gradually most of the time and much less frequently in great lurches. Our economy and society have changed enormously over the past several decades, and just this sort of debate is what advances our understanding. In this the greatest contribution of *Rise* is the debate it has given rise to.

REFERENCES

Abel, J. and T. Gabe (2008), 'Human capital and economic activity in urban America', *Federal Reserve Bank of New York*, **332**.

Alonso, W. (1960), 'A theory of the urban land market', *Papers and Proceedings of the Regional Science Association*, **6**, 149–58.

Alonso, W. (1964), *Location and Land Use*, Cambridge, MA: Harvard University Press.

Andersson, Å.E. (1985), 'Creativity and regional development', *Papers of Regional Science*, **56**(5), 5–20.

Anselin, L., A. Varga and Z. Acs (1997), 'Local geographic spillovers between university research and high technology innovations', *Journal of Urban Economics*, **42**(3), 422–48.

Asheim, B. and H.K. Hansen (2009), 'Knowledge bases, talents, and contexts: on the usefulness of the creative class approach in Sweden', *Economic Geography*, **85**(4), 425–42.

Atkinson, R. and H. Easthope (2009), 'The consequences of the creative class: the pursuit of creativity strategies in Australia's cities', *International Journal of Urban and Regional Research*, **33**(1), 64–79.

Barro, R.J. (1991), 'Economic growth in a cross section of countries', *Quarterly Journal of Economics*, **106**(2), 407–43.

Becker, G. (1964), *Human Capital: A Theoretical and Empirical Analysis, with Special Reference to Education*, Chicago, IL: University of Chicago Press.

Bell, D. (1961), *The End of Ideology: On the Exhaustion of the Political Ideas in the Fifties*, New York, NY: Collier Books.

Bell, D. (1973), *The Coming of Post-industrial Society: A Venture in Social Forecasting*, New York, NY: Basic Books.

Bellandi, M. (1989), 'The industrial district in Marshall', in E. Goodman, J. Bamford and P. Saynor (eds), *Small Firms and Industrial Districts in Italy*, London and New York, NY: Routledge, pp. 136–52.

Berggren, N. and M. Elinder (forthcoming), 'Is tolerance good or bad for growth (or both)?', *Public Choice*.

Berry, C.R. and Glaeser, E.L. (2005), 'The divergence of human capital levels across cities', *Papers in Regional Science*, **84**(3), 407–44.

Boschma, R. and M. Fritsch (2009), 'Creative class and regional growth: empirical evidence from seven European countries', *Economic Geography*, **85**(4), 391–423.

Christaller, W. (1993), *Die zentralen Orte in Süddeutchland*, Jena: Gustav Fisher.

Clark, T.N. (2003). '3. Urban amenities: lakes, opera, and juice bars: do they drive development?', in *The City as an Entertainment Machine (Research in Urban Policy, Volume 9)*, Emerald Group Publishing, pp. 103–40.

Clark, T.N., R. Lloyd, K. Wong and P. Jain (2002), 'Amenities drive urban growth', *Journal of Urban Affairs*, **24**(5): 493–515.

Cohen, W. and D. Levinthal (1990), 'Absorptive capacity: a new perspective on learning and innovation', *Administrative Science Quarterly*, **35**(1), 128–52.

Cooke, P. and K. Morgan (1990), *Learning Through Networking: Regional Innovation and the Lessons of Baden Wurttemberg*, Cardiff: University of Cardiff.

Currid, E. (2007), *The Warhol Economy: How Fashion, Art, and Music Drive New York City*, Princeton, NJ: Princeton University Press.

Dei Ottati, G. (1994), 'Trust, interlinking transactions and credit in the industrial district', *Cambridge Journal of Economics,* **18**(6), 427–48.

Donegan, M. and N. Lowe (2008), 'Inequality in the creative city: is there still a place for "old-fashioned" institutions?', *Economic Development Quarterly,* **22**(1), 46–62.

Drucker, P.F. (1993), *Post-capitalist Society*, New York, NY: HarperCollins.

Faggian, A. and P. McCann (2006), 'Human capital flows and regional knowledge assets: a simultaneous equation approach', *Oxford Economic Papers*, **58**(3), 475–500.

Feser, E.J. (2003), 'What regions do rather than make: a proposed set of knowledge-based occupation clusters', *Urban Studies,* **40**(10), 1937–58.

Florida, R. (2002a), *The Rise of the Creative Class*, New York, NY: Basic Books.

Florida, R. (2002b), 'The economic geography of talent', *Annals of the Association of American Geographers*, **92**(4), 743–55.

Florida, R. (2004), *The Rise of the Creative Class. And How It's Transforming Work, Leisure, Community & Everyday Life*, New York, NY: Basic Books.

Florida, R. (2005), *The Flight of the Creative Class*, New York, NY: Harper Business.

Florida, R. (2010), *The Great Reset: How New Ways of Living and Working Drive Post-crash Prosperity,* Ontario: Random House Canada.

Florida, R. and M. Kenney (1993), *Beyond Mass Production: The Japanese System and its Transfer to the United States*, New York, NY: Oxford University Press.

Florida, R., C. Mellander and K. Stolarick (2008), 'Inside the black box of regional development: human capital, the creative class and tolerance', *Journal of Economic Geography*, **8**(5), 615–49.

Fujita, M. (1985), *Urban Economic Theory: Land Use and City Size*, Cambridge, MA: Cambridge University Press.

Fujita, M. (1988), *Urban Economic Theory*, Cambridge, MA: Cambridge University Press.

Gabe, T.M., K. Colby and K.P. Bell (2007), 'The effects of workforce creativity on earnings in US counties', *Agricultural and Resource Economics Review*, **36**(1), 71–83.

Glaeser, E.L. (1994), 'Cities, information, and economic growth', *Cityscape*, **1**(1), 9–47.

Glaeser, E.L. (1998), 'Are cities dying?', *Journal of Economic Perspectives*, **12**, 139–60.

Glaeser, E.L. (2005), 'Review of Richard Florida's "The Rise of the Creative Class"', *Regional Science and Urban Economics*, **35**(5), 593–96.

Glaeser, E.L., L. Scheinkman and A. Shleifer (1995), 'Economic growth in a cross-section of cities', *Journal of Monetary Economics*, **36**(1), 117–43.

Glaeser, E.L., J. Kolko and A. Saiz (2001), 'Consumer city', *Journal of Economic Geography*, **1**(1), 27–50.

Goodman, E. (1989), 'Introduction: the political economy of the small firm in Italy', in E. Goodman, J. Bamford and P. Saynor (eds), *Small Firms and Industrial Districts in Italy*, London and New York, NY: Routledge, pp. 1–3.

Hansen, H.K. and T. Niedomysl (2009), 'Migration of the creative class: evidence from Sweden', *Journal of Economic Geography*, **9**(2), 191–206.

Inglehart, R. (1997), *The Silent Revolution: Changing Values and Political Styles Among Western Publics*, Princeton, NJ: Princeton University Press.

Jacobs, J. (1961), *The Death and Life of Great American Cities*, New York, NY: Random House.

Jacobs, J. (1969), *The Economy of Cities*, New York, NY: Random House.
Jaffe, A.B. (1989), 'Real effects of academic research', *American Economic Review*, **79**(5), 957–70.
Krugman, P. (1991), *Geography and Trade*, Cambridge, MA: MIT Press.
Kuhn, T. (1962), *The Structure of Scientific Revolutions*, Chicago, IL: University of Chicago Press.
Lloyd, R. (2002), 'Neo-bohemia: art and neighborhood redevelopment in Chicago', *Journal of Urban Affairs*, **24**(5), 517–32.
Lloyd, R. and T.N. Clark (2001), 'The city as an entertainment machine', *Critical Perspectives on Urban Redevelopment*, **6**, 357–78.
Lösch, A. (1940), *Räumliche Ordnung der Wirtschaft*, Jena: Gustav Fischer (English translation (1954), *The Economics of Location*, New Haven, CT: Yale University Press).
Lucas, R.E. Jr (1988), 'On the mechanics of economic development', *Journal of Monetary Economics*, **22**(1), 3–42.
Markusen, A. (1996), 'Sticky places in slippery space: a typology of industrial districts', *Economic Geography*, **72**(3), 293–313.
Markusen, A. (2006), 'Urban development and the politics of a creative class: evidence from a study of artists', *Environment and Planning A*, **38**(10), 1921–40.
Markusen, A. and G. Schrock (2006), 'The artistic dividend: urban artistic specialisation and economic development implications', *Urban Studies*, **43**(10), 1661–86.
Marlet, G. and C. Van Woerkens (2004), 'Skills and creativity in a cross-section of Dutch cities', discussion paper No. 04-29, Tjalling C. Koopmans Research Institute, Utrecht.
Marshall, A. (1890), *Principles of Economics*, London: Macmillan.
Martin, R.L. and R. Florida (2009), *Ontario in the Creative Age*, Toronto: Martin Prosperity Institute.
Marx, K. (1906), *Capital*, New York, NY: Modern Library.
Mathur, V.K. (1999), 'Human capital-based strategy for regional economic development', *Economic Development Quarterly*, **13**(3), 203–16.
McCann, E.J. (2007), 'Inequality and politics in the creative city region: questions of livability and state strategy', *International Journal of Urban and Regional Research*, **31**(1), 188–96.
McGranahan, D. and T. Wojan (2007), 'Recasting the creative class to examine growth processes in rural and urban counties', *Regional studies*, **41**(2), 197–216.
Mellander, C. (2009), 'Creative and knowledge industries: an occupational distribution approach', *Economic Development Quarterly*, **23**(4), 294–05.
Mellander, C. and R. Florida (2009), 'Creativity, talent, and regional wages in Sweden', *Annals of Regional Science*, 1–24.
Mills, E. (1967), 'An aggregative model of resource allocation in a metropolitan area', *American Economic Review*, **57**, 197–210.
Mincer, J. (1974), *Schooling, Experience, and Earnings, Human Behavior & Social Institutions No. 2*, New York, NY: National Bureau of Economic Research.
Muth, R. (1961), 'The spatial structure of the housing market', *Papers and Proceedings of the Regional Science Association*, **7**, 207–20.
Muth, R. (1969), *Cities and Housing*, Chicago, IL: University of Chicago Press.
Peck, J. (2005), 'Struggling with the creative class', *International Journal of Urban and Regional Research*, **29**(4), 740–70.
Piore, M.J. and C.F. Sabel (1984), *The Second Industrial Divide: Possibilities for Prosperity*, New York, NY: Basic Books.
Porter, M.E. (1994), 'The role of location in competition', *International Journal of the Economics of Business*, **1**(1), 35–40.
Rausch, S. and C. Negrey (2006), 'Does the creative engine run? A consideration of the effect of creative class on economic strength and growth', *Journal of Urban Affairs*, **28**(5), 473–89.
Roback, J. (1982), 'Wages, rents, and the quality of life', *Journal of Political Economy*, **90**(6), 1257–78.
Romer, P.M. (1986), 'Increasing returns and long-run growth', *Journal of Political Economy*, **94**(5), 1002–37.
Romer, P.M. (1987), 'Growth based on increasing returns due to specialization', *American Economic Review*, **77**(2), 56–62.
Romer, P.M. (1990), 'Endogenous technological change', *Journal of Political Economy*, **98**(5), S71–S102.
Saxenian, A.-L. (1996), *Regional Advantage: Culture and Competition in Silicon Valley and Route 128*, Cambridge, MA: Harvard University Press.
Schumpeter, J.A. (1942), *Capitalism, Socialism and Democracy*, New York, NY: Harper and Brothers.
Scott, A.J. (2006), 'Creative cities: conceptual issues and policy questions', *Journal of Urban Affairs*, **28**(1), 1–17.
Scott, A.J. (2009), 'Human capital resources and requirements across the metropolitan hierarchy of the USA', *Journal of Economic Geography*, **9**(2), 207–26.

Sforzi, F. (1989), 'The geography of industrial districts in Italy', in E. Goodman, J. Bamford and P. Saynor (eds), *Small Firms and Industrial Districts in Italy*, London and New York, NY: Routledge, pp. 153–73.

Smith, B. (1990), *American Science Policy Since World War II*, Washington, DC: Brookings Institution Press.

Smith, G., I. Carlsson and A. Danielsson (1984), *Experimental Examinations of Creativity*, Lund: Lund University.

Solow, R.M. (1956), 'A contribution to the theory of economic growth', *Quarterly Journal of Economics,* **70**(1), 65–94.

Storper, M. (1994), 'The transition to flexible specialisation in the US film industry: external economies, the division of labour and the crossing of industrial divides', in A. Amin (ed.), *Post-Fordism: A Reader*, Hoboken, NJ: Wiley-Blackwell, pp. 195–226.

Storper, M. and A.J. Scott (2009), 'Rethinking human capital, creativity and urban growth', *Journal of Economic Geography*, **9**(2), 147–67.

Thomas, J.M. and J. Darnton (2006), 'Social diversity and economic development in the metropolis', *Journal of Planning Literature*, **21**(2), 153–69.

Vinodrai, T. and M.S. Gertler (2006), 'Creativity, culture and innovation in the knowledge-based economy', paper prepared for the Ontario Ministry of Research and Innovation, 1 October.

von Thünen, J.H. (1966), *Isolated State; an English Edition of Der isolierte Staat* [1826], translated by C. Wartenberg and edited by P. Hall, Oxford and New York, NY: Pergamon Press.

Walker, R. and R. Lewis (2001), 'Beyond the crabgrass frontier: industry and the spread of North American cities, 1850–1950', *Journal of Historical Geography*, **27**(1), 3–19.

Welzel, C., R. Inglehart and H.D. Kligemann (2003), 'The theory of human development: a cross cultural analysis', *European Journal of Political Research*, **42**(3), 341–79.

Wirth, L. (1938), 'Urbanism as a way of life', *American Journal of Sociology*, **44**(1), 1–24.

4 Big-C creativity in the big city
Dean Keith Simonton

I was born and raised in metropolitan Los Angeles, not far from famed Hollywood. I even got my BA from a local liberal arts institution there, namely Occidental College. Although I left for the US East Coast to earn my MA and PhD degrees, and eventually transplanted myself to a college town in northern California, I still have some roots in the 'Southland'. Besides having family members who continue to live there, I occasionally listen to LA's classical music station KUSC, which streams its programmes over the internet. On one such occasion, I recently heard the radio announcer refer to my former home city as 'The Creative Capital of the World'. This appellation was a most refreshing change from the usual nicknames, whether LA's 'Lalaland' or Hollywood's 'Tinseltown'. But, also, surprising.

After googling the expression, I discovered that this little bit of self-promotion had some factual basis. Purportedly, one out of six denizens of the metropolitan area is employed in some creative field. Of course, the fields are not necessarily the same as those that brought splendour to Periclean Athens, Renaissance Florence or even Paris between the two big wars. LA is more the land of entertainment, fine and performing arts, communication arts, digital media, toys, design, fashion and even art galleries. Still, as an expatriate Angelino, I could not help but feel a little pride. My basking in reflected glory was intensified by the fact that ever since my undergraduate years at Oxy, I have been preoccupied with the scientific study of creativity. Now, hundreds of publications later, my preoccupation has helped me more fully comprehend this most complex but fascinating phenomenon.

My goal in this chapter is to provide a brief overview of what we know about creativity, with an emphasis on how that knowledge might shed light on how cities can become loci of creative ideas. Because I am a psychologist rather than a sociologist or economist, my perspective will have an obvious disciplinary twist. Yet because I received my doctorate in social psychology, my point of view will extend beyond the individual creator. Plus, because I am an academic by profession, I have to begin by defining my terms.

DEFINITIONS: WHAT IS CREATIVITY?

Creativity is often conceived as an idea that satisfies two essential requirements (Simonton, 2000). First, the idea must be novel or original. Without novelty or originality, the idea can only be considered routine, even mundane. Hence, someone trying to 'reinvent the wheel' cannot be engaged in creativity. Second, the idea must be useful, functional or adaptive. It must work. This requirement is what separates creative ideas from the crazy ideas of the psychotic. If some inventors announce that they have devised a kitchen stove out of soap bubbles, we will likely question their sanity as well as their creativity. Note that both novelty and utility are matters of degree rather than kind. One person may come up with a 'better mousetrap' whereas another might create a safe and effective means of keeping all pests from ever entering the house in the first place.

Not all creativity researchers believe that the above two criteria are rigorous enough. Instead, we should add a third stipulation, the same one imposed by the US Patent Office on applications: to receive a patent, the inventor must prove not only that the idea is new and useful, but also that it is non-obvious (http://www.uspto.gov/inventors/patents.jsp). If the idea is an obvious extension or elaboration of an already patented idea, then the patent is rejected. An inventor cannot just take a mousetrap made with a pine base and substitute an oak base – even if the latter has never been tried before and works better. Naturally, this third criterion is not as easily applied as the first two.

An interesting example is what became known as the Pelton water wheel, a highly efficient water turbine used to generate hydroelectricity (Constant, 1978). Although another inventor had come up with the same idea, his conception was closer to an already existing invention, whereas Pelton's idea was a non-obvious extension of a more remote invention. So Pelton received both the patent and the eponymic credit! Expressed differently, Pelton's creative idea was more surprising.

In light of the foregoing, perhaps creativity should be defined as the conjunction of novelty, utility and surprise. Ever since I began conducting research on cinematic creativity about a decade ago, I have come to prefer this three-part definition. One of the problems of many Hollywood movies is that they can be novel and useful – earn a decent box office – but be almost completely devoid of surprise. I am thinking of remakes and sequels. Although the data quite plainly show that remakes and sequels are more profitable than the average film, the data also prove that such movies are less likely to receive critical acclaim or movie awards (Simonton, 2011). Whatever novelty and utility remakes or sequels may have is often undermined by the complete obviousness of it all. Moviegoers have seen the protagonists before, and even the plot may be no more than a recycling of tired ideas. No wonder, then, that these movies often try to obscure the diminished creativity by adding more bells and whistles! Sequels, especially, will rely on increasingly more expensive special effects (Simonton, 2011).

To appreciate better the nature of creativity, we need to delve into some refinements. These concern perspectives, magnitudes and domains. These refinements will enable us to narrow discussion to those research findings most pertinent to understanding creativity in cities.

What Perspective?

Creativity is a multifaceted phenomenon. As a result, researchers have tended to study creativity from rather distinct perspectives. Of special importance are 'the three Ps' of creativity research.

First, creativity entails a process. Or, probably it is more accurate to say that creative thought involves a set of processes, both conscious and unconscious, deliberate and involuntary, domain-specific and domain-general (Simonton and Damian, forthcoming). Creative thought is what produces the creative idea. This perspective is favoured by cognitive psychologists who study creativity.

Second, creativity concerns a person. The creative individual generates creative ideas, presumably using the creative process. In this sense, creativity might be considered an ability rather than a process. This perspective is the favourite of personality and differential psychologists who are interested in how people vary.

Third, creativity yields a product. This product may be a patent, poem, painting, composition, film, game, design, recipe, slogan, calendar and so on. Most often, these products will be packed with multiple ideas that vary immensely in creativity. The typical feature-length film provides a conspicuous example: characters, plots and subplots, casting, cinematography, music, art production and costume design, editing, sound mixing, visual effects and so forth – some creative, some not. Interestingly, psychologists are quite divided on how to study the creative product. Some focus on artistic products and look at aesthetic factors, while others concentrate on scientific products and examine methodological and theoretical factors. In any case, the creative product is the outcome of a creative person or persons applying the creative process or processes.

Although all three of these perspectives are equally important to our understanding of creativity, the person perspective may be especially valuable when we speak of creativity in cities. That's because a hallmark of creativity is very often the concentration of creators in specific population centres. I've already mentioned the cases of Athens, Florence, Paris and (perhaps) Los Angeles!

What Magnitude?

No matter which perspective we adopt, it must be apparent that creativity varies in magnitude. Thus, some processes are more likely to produce a creative idea than others. For instance, algorithms demonstrate a lower level of novelty, utility and surprise than do heuristics. Similarly, unconscious processes tend to be more creative than conscious processes. Regarding the person perspective, it is obvious that some people are far more creative than others. At one end are the practitioners of everyday creativity, such as creativity seen at home or the workplace. At the other end are the exemplars of creative genius. Of course, this difference in creativity from the person perspective has repercussions for the product perspective. Where the creative genius will produce a masterpiece that will ensure the person lasting fame – such as Beethoven's Fifth Symphony, Michelangelo's Sistine Chapel ceiling frescoes, Cervantes's *Don Quixote*, Descartes's *Discours de la méthode* or Newton's *Principia* – the more everyday creator will generate a product that promises a more limited impact. The latter might be an effective solution to an irksome problem at work or home – like a new system for distributing assignments or a new approach to manage the household budget.

Creativity researchers will often distinguish between little-c and Big-C creativity (Simonton, 2000). The distinction between lower- and upper-case reflects the distinction between ideas that are low in novelty, utility and surprise and those that are high on all three criteria. This contrast is most frequently applied to the person perspective, the creative geniuses being carefully separated from the everyday creators. Even so, it must be recognized that little-c creators and the Big-C geniuses do not form homogeneous populations. The former can vary in creativity, and so can the latter.

On the one hand, individual differences in little-c creativity are often assessed using some so-called 'creativity test', especially measures of 'divergent thinking' (Simonton, 2003b). The latter is the ability to generate multiple alternative responses to a given stimulus. A well-known instance is the unusual uses tests that ask people to come up with numerous ways of using a commonplace object, such as a paperclip or brick (Guilford, 1967).

On the other hand, individual variation in Big-C creativity is most frequently gauged in terms of actual creative achievement or products (for example, Simonton, 1997a). For example, an inventor's creativity would be assessed by the number of patents, a filmmaker's creativity by the number of films and a scientist's creativity by the number of journal articles. The bottom end of the distribution would be represented by an inventor who had only one patent, a filmmaker one film and a scientist one article. The top end of the distribution is more ambiguous, besides varying from one area to the next. A lyric poet can write many more poems than a novelist can write novels. Nevertheless, the shape of the frequency distribution is remarkably similar regardless of the area of creative achievement (Simonton, 1997a). In general, a small proportion of the creators are responsible for most of the contributions. Whereas most creators contribute only one product each, a small percentage, usually the top 10 per cent in lifetime output, are credited with about half of everything in the field. This highly skewed distribution stands in marked contrast to scores on creativity tests, which tend to be described by a normal or 'bell-shaped' curve.

What distinguishes the little-c from the Big-C creators? A great deal, it turns out. For instance, higher levels of creativity are positively associated with such personality traits as openness to experience, social independence and even some modest tendencies toward psychopathology (Simonton, 2009a). There is a grain of truth to the 'mad genius' even if it is not justified to say that genius must be mad. Nonetheless, another contrast has to do with domain-specific expertise. Unlike practitioners of everyday creativity, high-impact creative individuals have acquired considerable expertise in their chosen domain of achievement (Simonton, 2009a). This necessity is often expressed in the research literature as the ten-year rule (Ericsson, 1996). It usually requires a full decade of devoted study and practice to master the knowledge and skills requisite for world-class contributions. Even the highly precocious Mozart could not escape this period of apprenticeship, his earliest works being imitative rather than innovative (Hayes, 1989; but see Simonton, 1991).

Once we acknowledge that Big-C creativity depends on domain-specific expertise, then we also have to concede that such creativity has become a social rather than individual phenomenon (Csikszentmihályi, 1990, 1999). In addition to the specific domain, the creator operates with respect to a specific field – the collection of colleagues, associates, collaborators and competitors who have acquired expertise in the same domain. Members of the creator's field are often responsible for making decisions about what gets published or presented, as illustrated by the peer-review of grant proposals and submitted manuscripts in the sciences. In fact, we can often speak of a creativity cycle: (a) the individual draws a sample of domain-specific ideas that are then transformed into creative ideas; (b) the field then evaluates the individual's ideational offerings; and (c) the domain expands with those ideas that survived the selection process (Csikszentmihályi, 1990, 1999). In this view, it is not appropriate to say that the individual is creative until after a given contribution completes the cycle. For some unfortunate souls, the so-called 'neglected geniuses', the final disciplinary judgement may constitute a posthumous appraisal. Gregor Mendel and Emily Dickinson come immediately to mind.

What Domain?

I just observed that Big-C creativity is associated with a domain and the corresponding field. The choice of domain is not a trivial decision. The creativity of a scientist is not equivalent to the creativity of the artist (Simonton, 2009b). Indeed, creativity can vary across various scientific disciplines or various artistic disciplines. In the former case, we can distinguish the natural sciences from the social sciences, for example, and in the latter case, the formal arts from the expressive arts. Although domains differ in many ways, probably the most critical contrast concerns the amount of constraint that is placed on the creative process (Simonton, 2004b). Creativity in highly paradigmatic domains like physics is governed by stronger logical and factual constraints than is creativity in a highly expressive art, such as lyric poetry. Poets are allowed 'poetic licence', physicists never are. Because domains differ so much in how much creators must operate under disciplinary constraints, creators active in different domains will exhibit different dispositional traits and developmental experiences (Simonton, 2009b). For example, in comparison with physicists, poets tend to display higher rates of psychopathology and to grow up in unstable, unconventional and culturally heterogeneous environments.

Some of these disciplinary contrasts suggest that different environments may favour one or another domain of creative achievement. And, of course, urban life provides a very distinct environment from rural life.

SPECULATIONS: WHY CREATIVITY IN CITIES?

The distinction between little-c and Big-C creativity presumes the emergence of population centres during the course of cultural evolution. This assumption is illustrated by the research that cultural anthropologists have conducted on evolutionary scales (Carneiro, 1970; cf. Peregrine, et al., 2004). Human communities normally reach a size of 100 or more persons before craft specializations can emerge. Not until towns appear with populations of 2000 or more will religious or political leaders employ artisans to glorify their regimes, and not until cities reach a size of around 10000 citizens do full-time painters, sculptors, architects and engineers become conspicuous. At this point, we can probably talk about bona fide instances of Big-C creators. But an even larger population size may be required before we can expect creative geniuses of the highest order. Thus, Athens had acquired a population of more than 90000 freeborn persons by the time it hosted a golden age of creativity (Galton, 1869).

This relation between population growth and creative genius may be partly explained in terms of the distribution of human abilities. For illustrative purposes, it is useful to think of this relation using general intelligence, or 'IQ'. If a 140 IQ demarcates the minimal qualification for a genius-level intellect, then the population would have to consist of at least 100 persons to claim just one intellectual genius. Likewise, a population of around 10000 would yield someone with an IQ of 150 and around 30000 to get an individual with an IQ of 160. An IQ of 170 or more would not be anticipated unless the population reached a million. To put these figures in context, the average estimated IQs of geniuses in modern Western civilization range between about 150 and 160 (Simonton, 1976a; Simonton and Song, 2009).

Admittedly, there is much more to creative genius than just a high IQ (Simonton, 2009a). A Big-C creator must also have the right personality profile for his or her chosen domain (Simonton, 2008b). In addition, high achievement in any domain requires a very high level of energy, drive and determination (Cox, 1926; Duckworth et al., 2007). Even so, the inclusion of these other individual factors serves only to render genius much more rare than if it were dependent on IQ alone (Simonton, 1999). Big-C creators must then prove exceptional on multiple cognitive and dispositional traits. As a consequence, obtaining creative geniuses of a very high order would require an even larger population than suggested in the previous paragraph.

Still, it must be acknowledged that the positive connection between population growth and Big-C creativity does not necessitate that the population growth be concentrated in urban areas. In theory, one can imagine a primarily agricultural economy with a more evenly spread population. The potential number of creative geniuses would be the same as another region with the same population size but with a higher urban concentration. Therefore, it is imperative to inquire into why Big-C creativity has a direct association with the big city. The potential reasons can be roughly divided into two categories: (a) cities as creativity attractors and (b) cities as creativity stimulators.

Cities as Creativity Attractors

The first possibility is the least interesting: cities may attract creative individuals without necessarily making those individuals more creative. I say that this is uninteresting because I am a psychologist. An economist or sociologist may feel differently. Cities often provide job opportunities unavailable elsewhere. The inflow increases the population, and that growth alone enhances the odds that a creative genius might appear. Even so, on a per capita basis cities would not necessarily feature a greater supply of creative individuals. The number of Big-C creators might be merely proportional to the size of the population.

However, it is conceivable that certain urban areas may attract Big-C creators at a faster rate than they attract non-creators. This differential selection would happen if the city is especially conspicuous in the creative industries. In such cases, the per capita representation of Big-C creators will exceed what holds in the nation as a whole. The film industry in Los Angeles provides an obvious example. Directors, screenwriters, cinematographers and other film talent are certainly more strongly represented in LA relative to Chicago, an otherwise comparable metropolitan area.

Nonetheless, as a psychologist I find another possibility far more intriguing. Cities may attract the immigration of persons, whether foreign or domestic, who possess the personal characteristics strongly associated with creativity. Let me focus on just two, namely openness and psychoticism.

Openness
Openness to experiences is one of the Big-Five personality factors, and thus describes a major dimension by which people differ from one another (Goldberg, 1993). Persons who score high on this factor are characterized by such descriptors as intelligent, original, imaginative, insightful, curious, wide interests, sophisticated, clever, sharp-witted, inventive, artistic, ingenious, creative, wise and anti-authoritarian (John, 1990).

It is readily surmised that persons who possess these personal attributes might find life particularly attractive in the Big City, with its unusually diverse and conveniently concentrated exhibition of museums, galleries, restaurants, libraries, educational institutions, entertainment venues, sports events and historical monuments. Hence, a disproportionate percentage of urban immigrants may score unusually high on openness to experience.

It is critical to observe that this selective immigration does not require that these new urbanites themselves be Big-C creators. On the contrary, the high-openness immigrants could be filling entry-level jobs in service and manufacturing industries. Yet their offspring would inherit the same personal proclivities, and thus use them when taking advantage of opportunities unavailable to their parents. This inheritance is plausible given that openness to experience features a very high heritability, one of the highest of the Big Five (Loehlin et al., 1998). In this light, it is telling that a disproportionate number of eminent persons, including Big-C creators, are first- or second-generation immigrants (for example, Bowerman, 1947; Helson and Crutchfield, 1970; Goertzel et al., 1978). To be sure, not all of these luminaries will end up in urban centres. Some fraction will be attracted to towns that house major universities. Yet a university town has many of the same attractions as a major metropolitan area even if on a smaller scale – art galleries, museums, concert performances, drama productions and lecture series.

Psychoticism
Judging from the descriptors associated with openness, this characteristic must be deemed a beneficial attribute, even a virtue. In this respect, cities seem to be making a positive contribution to a nation's gene pool by attracing highly open immigrants. Even so, this selective immigration may have a dark side as well. Let us go back to the earlier comment that Big-C creativity (unlike little-c creativity) appears to have some relation with traits associated with psychopathology (Eysenck, 1995; Simonton, 2005). To illustrate, high-level creativity positively correlates with psychoticism, a dimension of the Eysenck Personality Questionnaire (Eysenck, 1995). Although people who score higher than the norm on psychoticism are not outright psychotic, they do tend to be more aggressive, cold, unempathetic, anti-social, impulsive, impersonal, egocentric and tough-minded. One can conjecture that some of these traits might increase the probability that a person might leave their native community to seek a new life in a major metropolitan area. These persons are not going to have close and stable personal ties with family and friends in their hometown. Nothing prevents them from pulling up their roots and transplanting themselves elsewhere.

Furthermore, psychoticism bears an intimate connection with the hypomanic personality (Eysenck, 1995). Without being manic to a pathological degree, but only 'sub-manic', hypomanic persons are extremely energetic, enthusiastic, imaginative and optimistic risk-takers who like to pursue ambitious plans and projects. Hypomanics are just the kind of persons who dream of making it big by venturing into the big city to try out their fortunes. And, in fact, such individuals may be over-represented among Big-C creators (Gartner, 2005).

Significantly, both psychoticism and hypomania are genetically inheritable (for example, Keller et al., 2005). If that inheritance is too intense, the result may be outright psychopathology (Simonton, 2005). It is thus no accident that Big-C creators often come from family lines that exhibit higher than average rates of mental illness (Karlson, 1970; Andreasen, 1987; Jamison, 1993). Moreover, those nations with higher immigration rates tend to display higher rates of mania, an affective disorder where the manic symptoms become too extreme to be adaptive (Gartner, 2005).

Yet the increment to mental institutions and the street homeless may be a small price to pay for the corresponding augmentation in Big-C creativity. This enhancement would take place not just immediately, with the direct addition of creative genius, but also with a generational lag, by the presumed alterations in the gene pool.

Cities as Creativity Stimulators

I have presented some reasons for believing that cities might serve as attractors of creativity, and especially Big-C creativity. Not only may highly creative persons be more strongly inclined to move to metropolitan areas, producing an instantaneous enhancement, but also cities may attract immigrants who have inheritable personality characteristics that can enhance high-impact creativity after a delay of a generation or two. Nonetheless, selective immigration appears to constitute such a passive process. Might life in the Big City make a more active contribution to Big-C creativity? Based on the empirical research, we can offer two speculations. First, cities stimulate creative development. Second, cities stimulate creative performance.

Creative development

Research has indicated that the larger socio-cultural context can have a profound impact on childhood and adolescent growth, including the development of creative potential (Simonton, 2003a). For this reason, Big-C creators are most likely to grow up in particular socio-cultural milieus. Creative genius is not randomly distributed across time or space but rather is concentrated into periods of florescence interspersed with periods of stagnation and even decadence or decay (Sorokin and Merton, 1935; Kroeber, 1944; Simonton, 1975, 1988). Yet these ups and downs in Big-C creativity, while not cyclic, are not random either. Instead, the fluctuations are contingent on various political, cultural, economic and disciplinary circumstances (Simonton, 2003a). Of these many influences, the following three have some relevance for comprehending how cities might stimulate creative development:

1. One of the main reasons why creative genius tends to cluster into golden ages separated by dark ages is that creators cannot emerge *de novo*. Instead, creators must be exposed during early adolescence and early adulthood to role models and mentors in their field of creativity. Indeed, within any given field, the number of Big-C creators in a generation is a positive function of the number in the prior generation (Simonton, 1975, 1988, 1997b; cf. Simonton, 1976c, 1977). Although it is not necessary for a creative talent to have direct exposure to role models – who can be admired and emulated from a distance – that distance learning is not possible with mentors. Consequently, creative geniuses will typically spend some time working under a distinguished teacher or master (Simonton, 1984, 1992a, 1992b). This period is especially crucial for picking up the tacit knowledge and skills associated with a

particular domain. Now to the extent that such mentors are more likely to be found in urban areas, this apprenticeship phase will necessarily occur in city environments. In fact, research on talent development indicates how often exceptional gifts will have to move to metropolitan areas once they reach a certain stage in their intellectual or artistic growth (Bloom, 1985; Gardner, 1993). Of course, this city-centred centrifugal force will not hold in domains where the masters are more likely to be found in rural retreats. Yet in those domains in which this process applies, the Big City can be said to stimulate Big-C creativity.

2. The clustering of creative genius cannot be completely explicated according to the cross-generational impact of role models and mentors (Simonton, 2003a). Other factors must come into play, and among the most important is political fragmentation (Simonton, 2004a). By this I mean the circumstance when a given civilization area is fragmented into a large number of sovereign states. With few exceptions, political fragmentation is positively associated with an upsurge in Big-C creativity (for example, 1975, 1976c). Indeed, revolts and rebellions against large imperial states are often connected to creative resurgence as well (for example, Simonton, 1975, 1976d). Notably, political fragmentation may operate as developmental influence. This suggests that growing up in a relatively small sovereign state surrounded by similarly sized sovereign states is conducive to creative development. Finally, it should be obvious that often these independent political units take the form of the city-state. The city-states of classical Greece and Renaissance Italy provide familiar examples.

3. Various investigators have offered reasons for the positive relation between political fragmentation and the emergence of Big-C creators (Vaubel, 2008). For example, the developmental connection might be attributed to greater personal freedom within each state or to enhanced competition among the states (see, for example, Candolle, 1873). However, I would like to discuss a third possibility: increased cultural heterogeneity (Simonton, 2004a). Large, inclusive empires often tend to encourage a homogenization of a given civilization area with respect to language, religion, art, literature and a host of other cultural traits (for example, Simonton, 1976b). Yet creative development may be enhanced by early exposure to ideational diversity and conflict, enabling the individual to engage in cultural 'hybridization' or 'cross-fertilization' as an adult creator (Sorokin [1947] 1969; Simonton, 1997b). To the degree that a free exchange takes place between distinct cultures or subcultures, this exposure will likely take place. It is more likely that urban centres will be the locus of these exchanges than rural areas. After all, cities are more likely to be the centres of economic growth as well as educational or cultural institutions that help mix up the broth.

Apropos of the last paragraph, it is of interest that recent research suggests that creative development is reinforced by extensive multicultural experiences (Simonton, 1997b; Leung et al., 2008). To the extent that cities facilitate such multicultural experiences, they are necessarily accelerating the emergence of future Big-C creators.

Creative performance

To understand how cities might contribute to the adulthood creative performance, we must first recognize that such creativity occurs at individual and group levels.

1. It is customary to think of creativity as being a completely individual phenomenon. This tendency is particularly strong in the case of Big-C creativity – as evinced in the recurring image of the 'lone genius'. Yet, as pointed out earlier, this perspective is misleading: even Big-C creators operate with ideas belonging to a particular domain and have their ideas judged and extended by members of the same field (Simonton, 2004b). In short, creators belong to a discipline. Even so, it remains true that many times creators function in a highly individualistic manner and thereby assume primary if not exclusive responsibility for the products of their intellects. Nevertheless, even in this lone-creator scenario we would anticipate that the Big City might facilitate Big-C creativity. One clear-cut example concerns the so-called incubation period of the creative process (Wallas, 1926). Frequently creators have to confront a problem that does not lend itself to a ready solution. After trying out various straightforward solutions to no avail, the person then lapses into a period in which the problem is temporarily put aside. During this phase, the creator will work on other problems and, of course, engage in the tasks of everyday life – commuting to work, shopping for groceries, picking up the kids at day care and so on. These diverse activities will expose the creator to sundry stimuli that will prime various associations in a haphazard fashion. Given sufficient time, one of these stimulated pathways may lead to a solution to the problem – a solution that would not have been conceived otherwise. Archimedes had his famed Eureka moment when he stepped into a public path; Gutenberg conceived the 'press' part of the printing press by inadvertently observing wine presses. It goes without saying that an urban environment will afford a more diverse variety of potential priming stimuli than will a rural environment. The former, relative to the latter, is more likely to offer a world replete with different languages, cultures, religions and lifestyles.

   It may also be appropriate in this context to mention the positive relation between bilingualism and creativity (Simonton, 2008a). It is not unlikely that a linguistically heterogeneous metropolis – with its ethnic neighbourhoods, shops and restaurants – facilitates the maintenance of such bilingualism in first- and second-generation immigrants.

2. The concept of the solitary creator notwithstanding, much of the creativity in modern societies emerges in groups (Paulus and Nijstad, 2003; Sawyer, 2007). Examples include research laboratories, cinematic collaborations and architectural teams. Naturally, the members of these problem-solving or brainstorming groups are most often recruited from the immediate environment, whether suburb, town or city – persons who are at least within commuting distance. This likelihood would often hold even when outsiders, such as consultants, may be brought in to enhance group functioning. Thus, we would expect these groups to be more diverse to the degree that the available workforce is diverse. This expectation is important because diversity of membership enhances group creativity (Nemeth and Nemeth-Brown, 2003; Page, 2007). This heterogeneity stimulates group members to conceive original ideas that would not be thought of in a homogeneous setting. In addition, the diversity of perspectives enables the group to evaluate better whether a new idea will in fact work.

TWO COMPLICATIONS: SOMETHING OLD AND SOMETHING NEW

I have just offered several speculations about why Big-C creativity may be more probable in major metropolitan areas. The reasons include both major cities as attractors of creators and major cities as stimulators of creativity – the latter with respect to both development and performance. Nevertheless, this discussion failed to consider two critical complications.

The first complication goes back to my earlier assertion that creativity varies according to the domain (Simonton, 2009a). Certainly scientific creativity operates differently than artistic creativity. As a result, some of the preceding connections between Big-C creativity and city life may also differ for the sciences and the arts. For example, young talents in the arts are more likely to come from homes that have parents who come from different backgrounds, whereas talents in the sciences tend to have parents who are far more similar in ethnic and geographic origins (Schaefer and Anastasi, 1968). Given that urban settings are probably more prone to support the former rather than the latter, we would expect that creative artists would be more disposed to grow up in metropolitan areas. If valid, this argument may hold for as long as there has been Big-C creativity and Big Cities.

The second complication concerns a far more recent development: the truly awesome technical advances in human communication. In ancient times, it would take years, even decades, for creators to exchange new ideas. This interchange could only be accelerated if creativity was concentrated in a small number of proximate urban centres. Indeed, until the nineteenth century, an idea could travel by land no faster than a horse, travel by sea no faster than a sailing vessel – and travel by air was impossible until the twentieth century. The velocity of communication certainly increased with the advent of the railroad, steamboat, telegraph, telephone and airplane. The emergence of the internet in the latter part of the twentieth century has increased both the speed and volume of potential exchanges. By various means, it is now possible for creative individuals to share ideas virtually instantaneously, and with virtually no restrictions on what can be shared. Scientists can exchange huge data sets, while artists can upload their portfolios. Creators can collaborate on joint projects even if separated by thousands of miles. Moreover, now that even a small portable computer will feature microphone, speakers and video cam, the possible exchanges are increasingly proximate to face-to-face communication. Given these expanding possibilities, one wonders when the Big City will face stiff competition from electronic media as the key facilitator of Big-C creativity – if that centralization has not already taken place. Rather than Los Angeles being the 'Creative Capital of the World', creativity may burst out from the synergistic interactions of creators scattered all over the world.

REFERENCES

Andreasen, N.C. (1987), 'Creativity and mental illness: prevalence rates in writers and their first-degree relatives', *American Journal of Psychiatry*, **144**, 1288–92.
Bloom, B.S. (ed.) (1985), *Developing Talent in Young People*, New York, NY: Ballantine Books.

Bowerman, W.G. (1947), *Studies in Genius*, New York, NY: Philosophical Library.

Candolle, A. de (1873), *Histoire des sciences et des savants depuis deux siècles*, Geneva: Georg.

Carneiro, R.L. (1970), 'Scale analysis, evolutionary sequences, and the rating of cultures', in R. Naroll and R. Cohn (eds), *A Handbook of Method in Cultural Anthropology*, New York, NY: Natural History Press, pp. 834–71.

Constant, E.W. II (1978), 'On the diversity of co-evolution of technological multiples: steam turbines and Pelton water wheels', *Social Studies of Science*, **8**, 183–210.

Cox, C. (1926), *The Early Mental Traits of Three Hundred Geniuses*, Stanford, CA: Stanford University Press.

Csikszentmihályi, M. (1990), 'The domain of creativity', in M.A. Runco and R.S. Albert (eds), *Theories of Creativity*, Newbury Park, CA: Sage, pp. 190–212.

Csikszentmihályi, M. (1999), 'Implications of a systems perspective for the study of creativity', in R.J. Sternberg (ed.), *Handbook of Creativity*, Cambridge: Cambridge University Press, pp. 313–38.

Duckworth, A.L., C. Peterson, M.D. Matthews and D.R. Kelly (2007), 'GRIT: perseverance and passion for long-term goals', *Journal of Personality and Social Psychology*, **92**, 1087–101.

Ericsson, K.A. (1996), 'The acquisition of expert performance: an introduction to some of the issues', in K.A. Ericsson (ed.), *The Road to Expert Performance: Empirical Evidence from the Arts and Sciences, Sports, and Games*, Mahwah, NJ: Erlbaum, pp. 1–50.

Eysenck, H.J. (1995), *Genius: The Natural History of Creativity*, Cambridge: Cambridge University Press.

Galton, F. (1869), *Hereditary Genius: An Inquiry into Its Laws and Consequences*, London: Macmillan.

Gardner, H. (1993), *Creating Minds: An Anatomy of Creativity Seen Through the Lives of Freud, Einstein, Picasso, Stravinsky, Eliot, Graham, and Gandhi*, New York, NY: Basic Books.

Gartner, J.D. (2005), *The Hypomanic Edge: The Link Between (a Little) Craziness and (a Lot of) Success in America*, New York, NY: Simon & Schuster.

Goertzel, M.G., V. Goertzel and T.G. Goertzel (1978), *300 Eminent Personalities: A Psychosocial Analysis of the Famous*, San Francisco, CA: Jossey-Bass.

Goldberg, L.R. (1993), 'The structure of phenotypic personality traits', *American Psychologist*, **48**, 26–34.

Guilford, J.P. (1967), *The Nature of Human Intelligence*, New York, NY: McGraw-Hill.

Hayes, J.R. (1989), *The Complete Problem Solver* (2nd edn), Hillsdale, NJ: Erlbaum.

Helson, R. and R.S. Crutchfield (1970), 'Mathematicians: the creative researcher and the average Ph.D.', *Journal of Consulting and Clinical Psychology*, **34**, 250–7.

Jamison, K.R. (1993), *Touched with Fire: Manic-depressive Illness and the Artistic Temperament*, New York, NY: Free Press.

John, O.P. (1990), 'The "Big Five" factor taxonomy: dimensions of personality in the natural language and in questionnaires', in L.A. Pervin (ed.), *Handbook of Personality Theory and Research*, New York, NY: Guilford Press, pp. 66–100.

Karlson, J.I. (1970), 'Genetic association of giftedness and creativity with schizophrenia', *Hereditas*, **66**, 177–82.

Keller, M.C., W.L. Coventry, A.C. Heath and N. Martin (2005), 'Widespread evidence for non-additive genetic variation in Cloninger's and Eysenck's personality dimensions using a twin plus sibling design', *Behavior Genetics*, **35**, 707–21.

Kroeber, A.L. (1944), *Configurations of Culture Growth*, Berkeley, CA: University of California Press.

Leung, A.K., W.W. Maddux, A.D. Galinsky and C. Chiu (2008), 'Multicultural experience enhances creativity: the when and how', *American Psychologist*, **63**, 169–81.

Loehlin, J.C., R.R. McCrae, P.T. Costa Jr and O.P. John (1998), 'Heritabilities of common and measure-specific components of the Big Five personality factors', *Journal of Research in Personality*, **32**, 431–53.

Nemeth, C.J. and B. Nemeth-Brown (2003), 'Better than individuals? The potential benefits of dissent and diversity', in P.B. Paulus and B.A. Nijstad (eds), *Group Creativity: Innovation Through Collaboration*, New York, NY: Oxford University Press, pp. 63–84.

Page, S.E. (2007), *Difference: How the Power of Diversity Creates Better Groups, Firms, Schools, and Societies*, Princeton, NJ: Princeton University Press.

Paulus, P.B. and B.A. Nijstad (eds) (2003), *Group Creativity: Innovation Through Collaboration*, New York, NY: Oxford University Press.

Peregrine, P.N., C.R. Ember and M. Ember (2004), 'Universal patterns in cultural evolution: an empirical analysis using Guttman scaling', *American Anthropologist*, **106**, 145–49.

Sawyer, R.K. (2007), *Group Genius: The Creative Power of Collaboration*, New York, NY: Basic Books.

Schaefer, C.E. and A. Anastasi (1968), 'A biographical inventory for identifying creativity in adolescent boys', *Journal of Applied Psychology*, **58**, 42–8.

Simonton, D.K. (1975), 'Sociocultural context of individual creativity: a transhistorical time-series analysis', *Journal of Personality and Social Psychology*, **32**, 1119–33.

Simonton, D.K. (1976a), 'Biographical determinants of achieved eminence: a multivariate approach to the Cox data', *Journal of Personality and Social Psychology*, **33**, 218–26.

Simonton, D.K. (1976b), 'Ideological diversity and creativity: a re-evaluation of a hypothesis', *Social Behavior and Personality*, **4**, 203–7.

Simonton, D.K. (1976c). 'Philosophical eminence, beliefs, and zeitgeist: an individual-generational analysis', *Journal of Personality and Social Psychology*, **34**, 630–40.

Simonton, D.K. (1976d), 'The sociopolitical context of philosophical beliefs: a transhistorical causal analysis', *Social Forces*, **54**, 513–23.

Simonton, D.K. (1977), 'Eminence, creativity, and geographic marginality: a recursive structural equation model', *Journal of Personality and Social Psychology*, **35**, 805–16.

Simonton, D.K. (1984), 'Artistic creativity and interpersonal relationships across and within generations', *Journal of Personality and Social Psychology*, **46**, 1273–86.

Simonton, D.K. (1988), 'Galtonian genius, Kroeberian configurations, and emulation: a generational time-series analysis of Chinese civilization', *Journal of Personality and Social Psychology*, **55**, 230–8.

Simonton, D.K. (1991), 'Emergence and realization of genius: the lives and works of 120 classical composers', *Journal of Personality and Social Psychology*, **61**, 829–40.

Simonton, D.K. (1992a), 'Leaders of American psychology, 1879–1967: career development, creative output, and professional achievement', *Journal of Personality and Social Psychology*, **62**, 5–17.

Simonton, D.K. (1992b), 'The social context of career success and course for 2,026 scientists and inventors', *Personality and Social Psychology Bulletin*, **18**, 452–63.

Simonton, D.K. (1997a), 'Creative productivity: a predictive and explanatory model of career trajectories and landmarks', *Psychological Review*, **104**, 66–89.

Simonton, D.K. (1997b), 'Foreign influence and national achievement: the impact of open milieus on Japanese civilization', *Journal of Personality and Social Psychology*, **72**, 86–94.

Simonton, D.K. (1999), 'Talent and its development: an emergenic and epigenetic model', *Psychological Review*, **106**, 435–57.

Simonton, D.K. (2000), 'Creativity: cognitive, developmental, personal, and social aspects', *American Psychologist*, **55**, 151–8.

Simonton, D.K. (2003a), 'Creative cultures, nations, and civilizations: strategies and results', in P.B. Paulus and B.A. Nijstad (eds), *Group Creativity: Innovation Through Collaboration*, New York, NY: Oxford University Press, pp. 304–28.

Simonton, D.K. (2003b), 'Creativity assessment', in R. Fernández-Ballesteros (ed.), *Encyclopedia of Psychological Assessment*, vol. 1, London: Sage Publications, pp. 276–80.

Simonton, D.K. (2004a), 'Creative clusters, political fragmentation, and cultural heterogeneity: an investigative journey though civilizations East and West', in P. Bernholz and R. Vaubel (eds), *Political Competition, Innovation and Growth in the History of Asian Civilizations*, Cheltenham, UK and Northampton, MA, USA: Edward Elgar Publishing, pp. 39–56.

Simonton, D.K. (2004b), *Creativity in Science: Chance, Logic, Genius, and Zeitgeist*, Cambridge: Cambridge University Press.

Simonton, D.K. (2005), 'Are genius and madness related? Contemporary answers to an ancient question', *Psychiatric Times*, 1 June, **22**(7), 21–3.

Simonton, D.K. (2008a), 'Bilingualism and creativity', in J. Altarriba and R.R. Heredia (eds), *An Introduction to Bilingualism: Principles and Processes*, Mahwah, NJ: Erlbaum, pp. 147–66.

Simonton, D.K. (2008b), 'Scientific talent, training, and performance: intellect, personality, and genetic endowment', *Review of General Psychology*, **12**, 28–46.

Simonton, D.K. (2009a), *Genius 101*, New York, NY: Springer.

Simonton, D.K. (2009b), 'Varieties of (scientific) creativity: a hierarchical model of disposition, development, and achievement', *Perspectives on Psychological Science*, **4**, 441–52.

Simonton, D.K. (2011), *Great Flicks: Scientific Studies of Cinematic Creativity and Aesthetics*, New York, NY: Oxford University Press.

Simonton, D.K. and R.I. Damian (forthcoming), 'Creativity', in D. Reisberg (ed.), *Oxford Handbook of Cognitive Psychology*, New York, NY: Oxford University Press.

Simonton, D.K. and A.V. Song (2009), 'Eminence, IQ, physical and mental health, and achievement domain: Cox's 282 geniuses revisited', *Psychological Science*, **20**, 429–34.

Sorokin, P.A. [1947] (1969), *Society, Culture, and Personality*, New York, NY: Cooper Square.

Sorokin, P.A. and R.K. Merton (1935), 'The course of Arabian intellectual development, 700–1300 A.D.', *Isis*, **22**, 516–24.

Vaubel, R. (2008), 'A history of thought on institutional competition', in A. Bergh and R. Höijer (eds), *Institutional Competition*, Cheltenham, UK and Northampton, MA, USA: Edward Elgar Publishing, pp. 29–66.

Wallas, G. (1926), *The Art of Thought*, New York, NY: Harcourt, Brace.

5 Clusters, networks and creativity
Charlie Karlsson

In the last decade we have seen a rapidly increasing interest in creativity among research-ers. A search using Google Scholar for the concept creativity for 1990 generates about 20 000 hits, while a similar search for 2008 generates more than three times as many hits. For the disciplines of business administration, finance and economics the number of hits increases about four times during the same period. There are strong reasons to assume that the publications on the emergence, importance and behaviour of the crea-tive class by Richard Florida have substantially contributed to this increased interest.[1] However, it is important to remember that creativity has always been an important human activity in all fields of human activity, stretching from the generation of new knowledge, new inventions, innovations and new enterprises to the generation of new artistic expressions.

Today, creativity is more than ever before looked upon as a crucial resource not only for the cultural sector, but also for contemporary economic development and indeed, for personal growth (O'Connor, 2007). Hence creativity does not only reside in the arts, the cultural industries and/or the media industries, but it has become a central and increasingly important input into all sectors where design and content form the basis for competitive advantage (Flew, 2002). Creativity is critical for research. The production of new knowledge implies that creative processes must take place somewhere in the research process. In particular, creativity is related to innovation, which increasingly is seen as the key to economic competitiveness. Researchers try to isolate the qualities that give rise to new thinking and new visions upon which innovation can build (Negus and Pickering, 2004). What creativity is supposed to contribute to innovation is an artistic quality, something deemed to be intuitive rather than calculative (Banaji et al., 2007). Thus crea-tivity has emerged in recent decades as a prime contemporary value and not least as a resource that has to be mobilized by the business community (Leadbeater, 1999; Rifkin, 2000; Howkins, 2001; Tepper, 2002). However, creativity has also come into focus in recent decades as a new role has been identified for the arts and the cultural industries as generators of economic value and as important to quality of life, the 'image' of cities and regions, tourism and ancillary service industries (Myerscough, 1988; Gibson, 1999, Throsby, 2000; Andersson and Andersson, 2006).

Koestler (1964) and Simon (1985) stress that exceptional creativity calls for an ability to bring together habitually incompatible ideas and combine them in a way that gives deep new insights. Törnqvist (1983), on the other hand, considers the influence of place or context (milieu) on the individual act of creating something new. Törnqvist's perspec-tive is important since creativity as well as innovation is a localized process (Karlsson and Johansson, 2006). Bringing these two perspectives together implies that the milieu shall play an important role in creativity by supplying both a large number of incompatible ideas and good conditions for bringing them together. The supply of incompatible ideas is among other things a function of the local accessibility (clustering) of incompatible ideas, and the inter-regional accessibility to incompatible ideas in other regions, which both are a function of the network characteristics of the local milieu.

There is a long research tradition in regional economics and economic geography dealing with clustering, going back to the nineteenth century and associated with names such as von Thünen, Marshall, Weber, Ohlin, Hoover, Christaller, Palander, Lösch, Isard and Beckmann (Karlsson, 2008a). Despite substantial research on clusters, there is still much confusion concerning the proper conceptualization of a cluster, except that it is generally conceived as a non-random spatial concentration of (economic) activities (Ellison and Glaeser, 1997). Typically, most research on clusters has focused on industrial clusters and less interest has been paid to other types of clusters. However, whatever the type of cluster, we may in line with Krugman (1991a) assume that the phenomena of clustering are evidence of the pervasive influence of one or several types of increasing returns. Typical of clusters is the existence of one or several forms of direct and/or indirect interaction between the agents in the cluster location. Increasing returns are obtained when such interaction generates positive externalities for the agents in the cluster. Also agents engaged in creative activities show clear tendencies to cluster. Thus, it is relevant to ask what types of positive externalities they get from clustering.

Concerning the network characteristics of a locality, we make a simple distinction between local and non-local networks. Here we focus on networks between agents. We define a network as consisting of economic agents connected by links, which together constitute the structure defining a specific network (Karlsson et al., 2005). When all the agents in a network are located in the same locality, we talk about a local network whereas when at least one agent is located elsewhere, we talk about a non-local network. Networks and network relations have five important characteristics (cf. Cappelin, 2003): (i) networks can be open or closed; (ii) the relationship (link) between two agents is characterized by a precise direction, which identifies either a mutual relationship or a relationship of control or dependence of an agent with respect to another agent; (iii) each agent has a specific function, which depends not only on its relationship with other agents, but also on its position in the overall network; (iv) each network is normally linked to other networks, so that many networks are interconnected with each other; and (v) the relations existing at a given moment in a specific network are normally affected by the relations that existed in the same network in previous periods, due among other things to the existence of cumulative learning (Nelson and Winter, 1982) and of general path dependence. To the extent that creativity depends upon the interaction opportunities of agents, the network characteristics of localities and regions might have a decisive impact on creative performance as well as the direction of the creative efforts. There are also strong indications, not least in science, that interaction opportunities are important for creativity. For example, Laudel (2001, p. 763) remarks that '[o]ne of the most important changes scientific research has undergone in the 20th century is the change from being something undertaken by single individuals into being a chiefly collective enterprise'. The reason behind this is, on the one hand, the increasing complexity of many research problems and, on the other hand, the intense and rapid dynamics of many research fields which require scientists to specialize, to take advantage of the division of labour and to collaborate.

The purpose of this chapter is to analyse the role of networks and place and the characteristics of creative regional economic milieus.

CREATIVITY IS A FUZZY CONCEPT

Creativity is a fuzzy concept, which is difficult to define, measure and confine. It has been conceptualized as: (i) the personality traits of individuals that facilitate the generation of new ideas; (ii) the process of generating new ideas; (iii) outcomes of creative processes; and (iv) milieus conducive to new ideas and behaviour (Rhodes, 1961; Im, 1999). Andersson (1985a), for example, defines creativity as the ability to combine knowledge (familiarity and insights) and competence (the ability to use knowledge for one or several purposes, to create something new, which implies that change is at the centre of creativity).[2] However, it is beyond the scope of this chapter to try to come up with some unifying and unambiguous definition of the concept. Instead, we use the rather clear definition suggested by Boden (2004, p. 1). She defines creativity as 'the ability to come up with ideas that are new, surprising, and valuable',[3] stressing a general ability that is not limited to the creation of cultural artefacts and expressions. Thus, creativity can be interpreted as the ability of individuals or groups of individuals to generate ideas, which are perceived by relevant specialists to be new and at least potentially useful for other creators, consumers and/or producers. The creative process is both a mental and a social process involving discovery of new ideas or concepts, or new associations between existing ideas or concepts, implying novelty by combination (Schumpeter, 1934). Thus, the creative ability of individuals and groups depends upon their absorptive capabilities – on their ability to find, evaluate and use information, ideas and concepts (Cohen and Levinthal, 1990).

Any discussion of creativity presupposes some degree of understanding of the creative processes at the micro level, within individuals or small teams of individuals working together. Unfortunately, the knowledge about creative processes at the micro level is rather limited. The human brain has, however, certain interesting abilities (Andersson, 1985a). They include the ability to:

- Use heuristic reasoning such as to associate ideas, to formulate problems, to be perceptive, to discover and so on.
- Remember important facts and theories.
- Detect deep structures in a system of overlaid and interdependent structures.
- Detect and use ambiguity and manifoldness such as the ability to deal with seriously non-linear psychological processes.
- Appreciate paradoxes and surprises.
- Use and react upon experienced disequilibria.
- Use fundamental uncertainties and structural instabilities.

According to some specialists, creativity consists of three components – domain-relevant skills, creative processes and intrinsic task motivation – components which all can be developed through informal and formal learning (Robinson, 2000; Simonton, 2000; Sternberg, 2007). There seems also to be some sort of consensus around the opinion that creativity is both a way of thinking 'associated with intuition, inspiration, imagination, ingenuity and insight' and 'novel and appropriate response to an open-ended task' (Byron, 2007).

It is possible to make a distinction between different types of creativity (cf., Florida,

2002): (i) scientific creativity; (ii) technological or innovative creativity; (iii) economic or entrepreneurial creativity;[4] and (iv) artistic or cultural creativity. These different types of creativity are probably to a certain extent mutually dependent in the sense that they may stimulate and reinforce each other when located in the same urban region. However, it is well known that artists such as painters may develop a high level of creativity when forming artistic communities also in peripheral rural regions.

To illustrate the creative process, Wallas (1926) introduces a phase model with six steps: (i) preparation, that is acquisition of the skills, knowledge and information that allow a person to create; (ii) incubation; (iii) intimation; (iv) illumination or insight – the 'Eureka moment' of Archimedes; (v) verification; and (vi) communication. However, despite the substantial research using laboratory studies as well as detailed examinations of historical accounts of major discoveries of men like Newton, Darwin and Einstein, the underlying mechanisms of illumination remains elusive (Schilling, 2005). Koestler (1964, p. 95) identifies the capacity to 'perceive . . . a situation or an event in two habitually incompatible associative contexts' as the decisive phase of creativity. Thus, the capacities to select, reshuffle, combine or synthesize already existing facts, ideas, faculties and skills in original ways may be understood as evidence of creativity at work.[5] Perkins (1981) insists that skills like pattern recognition, creation of analogies and mental models, the ability to cross domains, exploration of alternatives, knowledge of schema for problem-solving, fluency of thought and so on are all indicators of creativity as a set of learning dispositions or cognitive habits.

The use of the term creative process implies that we can talk about a start and an end, where of course the duration may vary very substantially. However, we may also characterize a process with a start and an end as a project – in this case a creative project. Thus we should never look upon creative processes as a continuous process akin to commodity production. This observation has important implications for the organization and location of creative activities.

Much of the earlier research on creativity has focused on creative individuals in the arts as well as in the industrial domain. This research has built upon the fundamental idea that creativity is connected with imaginative and uniquely gifted individuals. Research on creativity has therefore mainly analysed individual cognitive characteristics and traits that are assumed to generate creative outcomes (Sternberg, 1985; Tardif and Sternberg, 1988; Glynn, 1996). In fact, the majority of studies on creativity have drawn tight boundaries around the individual as the locus of analysis (Montuori and Purser, 1996).

It is certainly well known in the industrial domain that many creative individuals, such as Thomas Edison, Gottlieb Daimler, John Dunlop, Alexander Graham Bell, George Eastman and Guglielmo Marconi, all obtained their first patents working in their own basements or in a building in their backyards. However, even these highly creative individuals soon became members of larger creative teams. Today, creative activities in the industrial domain increasingly are organized with teams in research labs within large firms, specialized research and development firms and universities. Individual inventors, however, still get a substantial share of the patents awarded. Nevertheless, developments during the last century indicate that it is the community and not the individual that matters most for creativity (Csikszentmihályi, 1999).

The general trend in creativity research seems to be to release creativity from 'artiness', individual genius and idiosyncrasy, and to focus on creativity as something that is economically valuable, team-based, observable and learnable (McWilliam, 2007). This implies a broadening of the concept of creativity to include ways of thinking and doing that are observable and replicable processes and practices within daily economic and social life. The influence of various contextual factors, including the social environment on individual creativity, has been documented by, for example, Amabile (1988) and Amabile et al. (1996). Woodman et al. (1993) stress that the group constitutes the social context within which creative behaviour occurs, and Hargadon and Bechky (2006) present evidence that many creative solutions are the product of collective creative processes (social creativity) (Cattani and Ferriani, 2008).

It is common to relate creativity to innovation but it is important to stress that it is essential to make a clear distinction between the two concepts. 'All innovation begins with creative ideas. . . . We define innovation as the successful implementation of creative ideas within an organization. In this view, creativity by individuals and teams is a starting point for innovation; the first is a necessary but not sufficient condition for the second' (Amabile et al., 1996, pp. 1154–5).[6] Creativity is thus typically used to refer to the act of producing new ideas, approaches or actions, while innovation is the process of both generating and applying such creative ideas in some specific context.

PLACE, CREATIVITY AND CREATIVE PROCESSES

It seems to be a generally accepted fact that some places or milieus are more creative than others (Storper, 1997; Florida, 2002), even if their creative specialization differs. Why then are some milieus more creative than others? Are the underlying factors the same in all fields of creativity or different? How do creative milieus emerge, develop, mature and possibly decline? Are the life cycles the same for all fields of creativity or do they differ? Are there mutual positive interactions between different fields of creativity stimulating different fields of creativity to agglomerate in the same milieus?

It is beyond the scope of this chapter to answer these questions. The ambition here is to highlight the role of clusters and networks for creativity and in particular for the spatial concentration of creativity. But to do this we have to go a bit deeper into the nature and characteristics of the creative processes. Despite substantial research on creativity and creative processes, it seems fair to state that creative processes are uncertain and unpredictable and characteristics of these processes are partly unknown. As a result, there is substantial disagreement among scientists regarding the factors that stimulate or restrain creative processes.

Starting with the role of the milieu it is clear that there is no general agreement concerning its importance. Rank ([1932] 1989), for example, claims that exceptional creativity requires that the creative mind is able to develop complete autonomy, which would imply that creative individuals and creative teams may need a degree of isolation. Koestler (1964) and Simon (1985), on the other hand, stress that exceptional creativity calls for an ability to bring together habitually incompatible ideas and combine them in a way that gives deep new insights. This implies that creative individuals and creative teams will be more creative the more exposed they are to a variety of ideas and further that this cannot be achieved in isolation. Simon (1985) stresses that the process of learning from diverse knowledge databases is a highly important source of invention and innovation and, thus, for creativity.[7]

In recent decades, we have witnessed a veritable explosion of new information, new ideas and new knowledge at the same time as the complexity of these items has increased (Quantas, 2002). Under these circumstances, it is becoming increasingly difficult for creative individuals to command all the resources that are needed for being creative. This makes it necessary to integrate creative activities in creative networks (Powell and Grodal, 2005) with frequent formal and informal interaction to stimulate creativity, to overcome unforeseen obstacles, to reduce uncertainty and to build confidence (Christensen et al., 2004). The effectiveness of creative networks depends on their ability to search for and exchange information, ideas and resources, in other words, on the navigability of the network (Watts, 1999). In this connection it is important to observe that the larger the network of people from which creative individuals and creative teams can learn, the greater will be the prospects for creativity and invention. However, it is only with nearby people that we can have frequent face-to-face interaction and learn effectively, since many ideas are not spelled out and much knowledge is tacit.

The emergence and consolidation of creative networks depend on a number of factors, among which a catalysing agent is one of the most important (Ekboir, 2002). Such an agent induces other economic agents to engage in the network and to invest time and resources in it. However, once a creative network has been established, the importance of the catalyst may decrease and the importance of linking agents may increase, because the incentives for other economic agents to contribute increase when they can take advantage of network interactions and when the rules for interaction and governance become known by all participants.

What are the factors that stimulate creativity? Already Adam Smith (1776) dealt with this issue. According to Smith, the division of labour stimulates creativity and

> the invention of all those machines by which labour is so much facilitated and abridged seems to have been originally owing to the division of labour. Men are much more likely to discover easier and readier methods of attaining an object when the whole attention of their minds is directed towards that single object than when it is dissipated among a great variety of things. . . . A great part of the machines made use of in those manufactures in which labour is most subdivided, were originally the inventions of common workmen, who, being each of them employed in some very simple operation, naturally turned their thoughts towards finding out easier and readier methods of performing it. (Smith, 1776 [1937], p. 9)

Smith's analysis implies that creativity will be stimulated in milieus with a large market potential, since a large market potential stimulates the division of labour and specialization. However, even Smith (1776 [1937], p. 734) admits that there is a limit to the creativity-stimulating potential of specialization: '[t]he man whose whole life is spent in performing a few simple operations, of which the effects are perhaps always the same. Or very nearly the same, has no occasion to exert his understanding or to exercise his invention.' If the division of labour does not itself promote creativity, the intelligence that is necessary for creativity and invention must come from other sources.

Smith (1776 [1937], p. 10) however also offers another aspect of creativity by noting that 'those who are called philosophers or men of speculation, whose trade is not to do anything, but to observe everything; and who, upon that account are often able of combining together the powers of the most distant and dissimilar objects'. When Smith writes that someone's trade is 'not to do anything', the implication is that the person is a theorist, and when he records that such a person observes everything, the meaning is that he or she must talk to many; Smith introduces a network perspective. The observation that the same person is good at 'combining together' additionally implies a superior ability to combine disparate and dissimilar knowledge. Almost 150 years later, Alfred Marshall (1920, p. 225) elaborated on Smith's insights by describing the process by which knowledge variety stimulated the emergence of new ideas: '[I]f one man starts a new idea, it is taken up by others and combined with suggestions of their own; and thus becomes the source of further new ideas'. Joseph Schumpeter described this as 'novelty by combination'.

Combination and reorganization of existing ideas and knowledge is a fundamental part of the creative process, so-called 'bisociation' (Koestler, 1964). The scope for bisociation is greatest where there can be creative interaction in heterogeneous groups, in particular at the 'creative margin'. However, frictions may emerge, since different disciplines lack a common language and/or common concepts.

New knowledge combinations are, according to Desrochers (2000, 2001) accomplished by (i) multidisciplinary teams working within a firm; (ii) employees adding to, or switching, their product line; (iii) individuals moving from one type of production to another; (iv) individuals observing a product/process in another setting and incorporating it into their main activity; or (v) individuals possessing different skills and working for different firms, collaborating with each other.

Another important question relates to why people are creative. This question is also discussed in Andersson (1985a), and he makes a distinction between individual or intrinsic and social or extrinsic motivations.[8] It seems as if internal reinforcement mechanisms have greater importance for explaining the total creativity level of individuals than simple reward or coercion arguments. This possibly implies that it is difficult to stimulate the creative output of individuals, and thus that the creative output of regions is dependent upon the total number of creative persons. It is also important to observe that exaggerated demands for discipline and organization might strangle the creative potential. Concerning the social motivation for creativity it seems as if workers' right to initiate plans as well as low levels of work supervision and employment and income security are important for generating creative working conditions.

There must obviously be rewards to creativity, since the creative process is a costly, uncertain process that includes the risk of failure, stress and other negative effects. Creative ideas challenge established norms and might bring disorder, which implies a risk for creative people. This implies that they tend to be met by resistance and scepticism, which is typical not least within science (Kuhn, 1962) but also within the arts, music and poetry (Boden, 2004), where the orthodoxy works as a constraint on novelty and new means of individual expression. On the other hand, to change the established norms might be the intrinsic motivation for creative people. It is also probable that persons with intrinsic motivation are less worried about breaking 'the rules of the game'.

Creative capabilities are important because the creative processes of economic agents are characterized by a frequent interaction in formal and informal creative networks. Creative capabilities cannot normally be bought or easily copied; they have to be learnt through sustained investments, experimentation and employment of – or interaction with – the right specialists. They may also be supported by the commitment of management in organizations and of participants in relevant creative networks (Christensen et al., 2004). Creative capabilities are embedded in individuals, in teams and in the strategies, routines and cultures of organizations (Argote and Darr, 2000). What is critical here is not that all employees in an organization are creative but that the creative individuals can exercise their creativity and influence the behaviour of other employees. However, the management of creative processes must be regarded as a managerial challenge, since creativity always involves some degree of novelty and contingency (Mumford, 2000) that can neither be fully planned nor fully controlled.

Economic agents depend on their creative capabilities to be proactive as well as reactive in relation to changes in their technological, economic and cultural milieu. Creative capabilities are built by learning – by the absorption and creation of knowledge. Because the stock of information, ideas and knowledge is growing, complex, diverse and partly short-lived, learning requires strong absorptive capabilities when searching for useful information, ideas and knowledge and also transformative capabilities as these inputs enter a creative process that produces new ideas and knowledge. These absorptive capabilities depend upon endogenous as well as exogenous factors. The endogenous factors include the strategies, routines and cultures of individuals, groups and organizations, the supply of creative personnel, the investments in creative processes and the internal and external network structures of the economic agents. The exogenous factors include the general economic and cultural milieu and the institutional context where the economic agents are located as well as the general economic conditions.[9]

From an organizational point of view, creativity also involves collective sense-making and framing of issues that builds on existing social practices of problem-solving, agenda-setting and 'creative interaction' (Ford, 1996; Drazin et al., 1999). Creative processes in organizations are therefore partly governed by group norms, organizational structure and leadership (Woodman et al., 1993; Mumford, 2000). Openness and dynamic contacts between individuals, teams and departments facilitate the acceptance of new perspectives and seem to be particularly relevant traits in organizational cultures able to stimulate creativity (Mumford et al., 2002; Martins and Terblanche, 2003).

LOCAL NETWORKS AND CREATIVITY

As was stressed in the preceding section, the local milieu – including its culture and knowledge base – appears to act as a critical success factor for creative processes. Apparently, the local milieu also offers various types of local networks that stimulate creative processes. The probability that creative processes will be successful can be increased through participation or involvement in local as well as broader inter-regional and international networks. In general, urban milieus offer many opportunities for strategic network involvement, whether material or virtual. Large and dense urban milieus appear to offer fruitful conditions for network behaviour, because of benefits from density, suitable communication modes and associative cultures (including a scientific milieu). Such a milieu – with an abundance of formal and informal contacts – may offer a protective shell for creative activities.

Networks may, in general, relate to physical configurations (such as air, road, railway and telecommunication networks) or to virtual networks (such as industrial clubs and knowledge and information networks) (Karlsson and Manduchi, 2001). Such networks may have a local character, but may also extend towards global levels. Networks may be intentionally organized for a particular purpose but they can also be self-organized and self-governing. Networks are said to facilitate the relations of economic agents in a way that falls somewhere between the flexibility of the market and the rigidity of the hierarchy. Through networks, individual economic agents are engaged in reciprocal, preferential and mutually supportive actions.

All networks tend to create diversity in terms of information and knowledge and to stimulate the creative spirit. In general, local networks between economic agents may be seen as supporting mechanisms for creative processes; as such, networks are a blend of openness and protection. Information and knowledge provided via various networks is a *sine qua non* for successful creative processes. A variety of network configurations, such as supplier and customer networks, local networks of neighbouring firms, professional networks and knowledge networks may all contribute to more effective creative processes.

Network analysis views economic agents as interdependent and linked parts of a connected whole, rather than as independent units of observation (Uzzi et al., 2007). It is obvious that creativity can be better understood and analysed by applying the principles of network theory and network analysis, since many of the ideas and much of the information and knowledge that are critical for creative processes are accessed via various professional, commercial and private networks. In his study of creativity in science, art and philosophy, Collins (1998) shows that the creative breakthroughs of individuals such as Pythagoras, Freud, Picasso, and Watson and Crick were a consequence of a particular type of personal network that stimulated exceptional personal creativity.[10] In recent decades, scholars in organization science have also started to analyse the network aspects of individual creativity (Simonton, 1984; Brass, 1995; Perry-Smith and Shalley, 2003; Burt, 2004; Perry-Smith, 2006). Networks offer three unique advantages (Uzzi and Dunlap, 2005): private information, access to diverse skill sets and power.

It is possible to understand the importance of networks for creativity by applying network theory. Networks provide horizontal links that cross institutional boundaries to put people and organizations in direct contact with one another. First, networks using modern information and communication technologies facilitate rapid information transfer over any distance but they also help create information. As people connected to the network receive information they synthesize it and new information emerges since information partly builds upon information. These networks also help in sharing and creating ideas. Both information and ideas are important inputs in creative processes.

Second, personal networks play a critical role in the transfer of tacit knowledge, which often is a critical input in creative processes. The transfer of tacit knowledge often requires frequent face-to-face interaction over longer periods, which implies that local personal networks have strong advantages when it comes to the transfer of tacit knowledge.

Third, creative processes are characterized by the manipulation of information, ideas and knowledge but the characteristics of information, ideas and knowledge are very different from ordinary goods. One basic common characteristic of information, ideas and knowledge is that its production cost is independent of its scale of use, which implies increasing returns. This factor has traditionally conferred benefits to the early movers in the creative process.

One type of network that is of special interest for creativity research is small-world networks, which is a type of networks in which (i) the links among economic agents are highly clustered, in the sense that there is a high probability that the connections of one economic agent are also connected to another; (ii) the average number of intermediaries needed to connect any two economic agents is low; and (iii) the average path length is relatively short. Thus, small-world networks offer a unique combination of high clustering and short path lengths, which offer an especially potent organizing mechanism for increasing performance, not least in terms of creativity. Milgram (1967) shows that small-world networks have short path lengths despite a high level of clustering; even in a very large small-world network actors are separated by an average of only six degrees of separation (six intermediaries). Thus, it is natural to assume that small-world networks create unique performance benefits in activities such as creative processes. The reason is that many separate clusters enable the incubation of a diversity of specialized ideas, while short paths allow ideas and resources to mix into novel combinations (Uzzi and Spiro, 2005; Fleming and Marx, 2006).

CLUSTERS AND CREATIVITY

There are numerous historical examples of how creative people and creative activities tend to cluster. The examples stretch from painters of the late nineteenth century clustering in Skagen in Denmark to creative software developers in Silicon Valley. Even if there are examples of creative people clustering in small places such as Skagen, the majority of the historical examples occurred in cities.

The tendency of creative activities to cluster or co-locate have been noted in the scientific literature (cf. Mommaas, 2004).[11] What advantages does clustering bring to creative activities? The obvious answer would be competitive advantage if we apply a traditional value chain discourse (Porter, 1998). But when discussing creative activities it is probably better to talk about creative advantages. We can thus formulate the question as follows: what creative advantages does clustering bring to creative activities? Do these advantages differ for different types of creative activities? Do these advantages change over time, given improvements in transport and communication infrastructures? With reference to analyses of value chains in commodity production one can ask whether creative clusters are 'stand-alone' or if they are nodes in creative value chains, where creative impulses are transferred between different creative clusters. One interesting issue here is of course whether the importance of creative impulses varies between different creative activities. The relationships between creative clusters will be discussed in the next section where we discuss the role of inter-regional networks for creative activities.

In the introduction, we emphasized that creative processes involve both mental and social processes that – if they are successful – lead to the discovery of new ideas or concepts, or new associations between existing ideas or concepts. We can assume that the discovery of new ideas or concepts is very rare and that creative processes that are successful normally come up with a new association between existing ideas or concepts. The probability that such new associations shall emerge is – all other things being equal – a function of the accessibility of existing ideas in a location, as well as the variety and diversity of these ideas (Lazzeretti, et al., 2008). The accessibility of existing ideas increases with the size and density of locations, which implies that creative individuals as well as organized creative activities are attracted to larger and denser regions with higher idea accessibility but also with greater variety and diversity of ideas. This implies that the productivity of creative activities will tend to increase with size and density of a region.

If we further assume that we can evaluate the creative output and make a distinction between small and large creative steps (between incremental and radical creativity), we may assume that the size and density of regions influence the probability for large creative steps. The reason is that radical creativity demands the combination of diverse ideas and that large and dense regions offer a much more diverse set of ideas than small regions. Partly these ideas can be perceived 'as being in the air' (Marshall, 1920, p. 271), and the larger and denser the region is, the larger will be the number of ideas that are 'in the air'. However, many ideas are not fully articulated and therefore reside in the heads of people until they are released. We may also assume that face-to-face interaction between people increases the probability that such 'trapped' ideas will be released and that such release will be stimulated by the greater face-to-face interaction opportunities in large and dense as opposed to small and sparse regions.

Given these basic considerations, we may now discuss more broadly the factors that tend to stimulate the clustering of creative people and creative activities in general and in large and dense regions in particular. Researchers have identified different properties of those locations that attract clusters of (modern?) artists, such as artistic freedom (Vaubel, 2005), ideological diversity (Simonton, 1976) and political fragmentation (Naroll et al., 1971). Ley (2003) discusses the tendency of artists to cluster in large cities and explains the clustering by the need to come close to the art-related community, close to their market,[12] and – perhaps most important (!) – 'close to each other'. Large cities offer artists a suitable milieu in which to generate networks, relationships, facilities and creative spillover effects within and across creative communities (Becker, 1982; Bain, 2003; While, 2003), but also opportunities to learn in arts colleges and through instruction from peers. Artists in a cluster may develop a common language, joint interpretative contexts and a shared knowledge base (Lawson and Lorenz, 1999). Bonds of trust and common goals are complemented by shared local knowledge, which is rooted in local social structures, institutions and cultures.

Co-location facilitates the establishment of common interpretative schemes (Grabher, 2002a), especially through 'hanging out' in local 'communities of practice' (Wenger, 1998). This implies that one distinguishing feature of clusters of artists is that they provide unique opportunities for the transmission of sticky, non-articulated, tacit forms of knowledge between the artists located there. When this locally embedded knowledge is combined with codified knowledge from other regions new artistic expressions can be created. In terms of radical creativity, one can observe that different avant-garde movements have been closely associated with large and dense cities and this remains true in the developed West (Ley, 2003; Grosenick and Stange, 2005).

When discussing the role of Paris and New York as centres of artistic creativity and innovation, Norton (2004, p. 172) summarizes most of the above arguments when he argues that 'these avant-garde art clusters provided localized knowledge networks in which artists, dealers, gallery owners, and critics could keep abreast of the latest artistic advance'. He mentions five factors that created positive feedback cycles in these centres: (i) the efficiency of communication; (ii) the ready availability of new knowledge; (iii) the cumulative building of a specialized knowledge base; (iv) the education of an art-buying public; and (v) the development of a public infrastructure of museums, schools, galleries, auction houses and the like.

Thus artists tend to cluster together to share ideas, offer mutual support and provide a sympathetic audience for one another (Kim, 2007). Furthermore, the rapid changes in artistic styles in contemporary art require of those artists who want to be in touch with current trends and the latest developments to be near important art galleries (Kostelanetz, 2003; Grosenick and Stange, 2005). The results reported by Hellmanzik (2009) indicate that works that have been produced in artistic clusters are more valuable than paintings produced elsewhere; there exists a cluster premium that is due to the favourable production and demand conditions in artistic clusters. It is this quest for superior rents that lures artists to clusters, even though they may also search for potentially useful external knowledge pools and impressions by means of study tours (cf. Maillat, 1998; Scott, 1998a).

Obviously, learning opportunities is one critical factor in explaining the formation of creative clusters. A main argument in the contemporary literature on learning and creativity is that these are the result of interactive processes in which different artists come to collaborate directly and indirectly to create new artistic expressions. Thus, it is important to understand the learning processes that take place within a cluster of artists as well as the types of interaction that are involved.

Learning within artistic clusters can take place in many different ways (cf. Simon, 1991) but is often closely related to ongoing activities that extend the internal pool of knowledge and competence (cf. Fuchs, 2001; Tracey et al., 2002). An artistic cluster offers a common interpretative context based on artistic visions, values and memories, which exist in the form of artefacts, routines and experiences. This helps to ensure that what each artist learns is in some way connected to what other artists know or learn. However, as knowledge is in itself an important source for future learning and knowledge creation, small initial individual differences tend to increase over time even when individual experiences are shared. As a cluster grows and matures, its knowledge stock will grow but in an uneven fashion and gradually becomes more coherent. The larger the cluster becomes, the fewer the experiences that are shared among all artists. This implies that what was presumably from the beginning a homogeneous body of knowledge and competence becomes fragmented into a complex pattern of only partly overlapping fields of knowledge, competence and expertise, with limited connections and objectives no longer in full accordance with each other. Such developments create incubators for new types of artistic expressions based upon some sort of dedicated vision and targeted effort. Thus, we here have a mechanism by which an artistic cluster may renew its artistic expressions.

Overall, the shared knowledge and idea base enables artists in clusters to continuously combine and recombine similar and non-similar knowledge and ideas to create new ideas and new artistic expressions. This stimulates artistic specialization within the cluster and results in the development of localized capabilities (cf. Maskell and Malmberg, 1999a, 1999b) that are available to the artists in the cluster. Living within an artistic cluster has further advantages that are not available to artists located elsewhere. Making an analogy with the famous notion by Marshall (1927) of 'industrial atmosphere' as being something 'in the air', we could talk about a 'creative artistic atmosphere' that is limited to the artists living within and possibly visiting a particular artistic cluster. In a similar vein, Storper and Venables (2002), for example, recently have identified what they see as a particularly important subset of cluster advantages, which they label 'buzz'.[13] 'Buzz' represents the idea that clusters can be vibrant in the sense that there are lots of piquant and interesting processes going on simultaneously. These processes generate lots of information, ideas and inspiration, which can then stimulate the creativity among perceptive artists in different clusters. 'Buzz' refers to the information and communication ecology generated by face-to-face interaction by the co-presence and co-location in the cluster of artists and of other people interacting with the artistic community such as customers, critics, dealers, tourists, policy makers and so on. The 'buzz' consist of specific ideas, information and knowledge, which are continuously updated and revised. It also consists of intended and unanticipated learning processes in organized as well as accidental meetings, the application of paradigm-specific interpretative schemes,[14] a mutual understanding of new knowledge and techniques, as well as shared cultural traditions and habits within the specific paradigm. All this stimulates the establishment of paradigm-specific conventions and other institutional arrangements. Artists continuously contribute to and benefit from the spread of ideas, information, techniques, gossip and news by just being there (Gertler, 1995).

Participation in the 'buzz' requires personal investments in links with other persons in the cluster, leading to network formation and the creation of communities of practice. All persons who are located in the cluster do not automatically receive ideas, information and knowledge. Instead, it is necessary for the artists to participate in various professional, economic and social spheres. In this context, artists are, on the one hand, deliberately scanning their regional milieu in search for ideas, information and knowledge at the same time as they are surrounded by a concoction of rumours, impressions, recommendations, trade folklore and strategic information (cf. Grabher, 2002b). It is almost unavoidable to receive some information, rumours and news about other artists in the cluster and their creations, behaviour and success. This occurs in negotiations with gallery owners, in phone calls with colleagues, when having lunch or dinner together with colleagues, at art exhibitions and so forth. Thus part of the 'buzz' is spontaneous and fluid. Co-presence within the same professional and social context generates manifold opportunities for face-to-face meetings and communications. These meetings can be planned or occur spontaneously in a non-designed, non-targeted and more or less accidental way. However, the probability that such a meeting will occur depends on the size and density of the artistic cluster.

The links in the different artistic networks link cluster actors in multiple ways (Uzzi, 1997). The longer the history of the cluster, the more likely it is for the networks and connections between different networks to develop. Over time, these structures of professional and social relations stimulate fine-grained information transfer, joint problem-solving, creative sessions and the development of trust and reciprocity (Granovetter, 1985; Uzzi, 1997). Different modes of communication operate in the professional and social context of a cluster (for example, chatting, gossiping, brainstorming and in-depth discussions). Co-location and visibility generate potentials for efficient interpersonal translation and interpretation of news, information and knowledge between the actors in the cluster (Latour, 1986; Allen, 1997). Specific learning processes, path dependence and selection environments (Murdoch, 1995) establish paradigm coherence within clusters. Being located in the same place also enables artists to understand the local 'buzz' in a meaningful and useful way. This is because co-location within a cluster stimulates the development of a particular informal institutional structure, such as similar language and interpretative schemes that are shared by those who participate (Lawson and Lorenz, 1999).

Under these circumstances, a high level of 'ordinary' creativity may develop under the prevailing artistic paradigm. But what factors trigger 'exceptional' creativity? Under what circumstances are artistic clusters able to generate new artistic paradigms?

To understand the factors driving the clustering of artists we can use the famous scheme developed by Marshall (1920): (i) a common labour pool; (ii) a supply of intermediate inputs; and (iii) information and knowledge spillovers. These supply-side factors generate local proximity effects (Glaeser et al., 1992) – accessibility – which allow economic agents to benefit from otherwise unattainable tacit knowledge and externalities of the trade that is located in a particular region, which can be internalized through learning. It is obvious that information and knowledge spillovers are the critical factor on the supply side for artists. Artists share ideas, information and knowledge and generate a collective knowledge that is embedded in the locality. In particular, they are well informed about the characteristics of the creations of other artists in the cluster due to more or less continuous monitoring and comparing. Individual artists can thereby effectively compare their performance with that of other artists in the cluster. Overall, this creates rivalry and serves as an incentive for differentiation and variation of the artistic expressions.

The tacit character of much of the new knowledge implies that the potential for knowledge spillovers varies considerably over space. Tacit knowledge demands frequent face-to-face interaction for knowledge transfer and knowledge sharing to take place (Karlsson et al., 2004). Since face-to-face interaction over long distances is both time and resource consuming, it is natural for economic agents who are dependent on knowledge spillovers to cluster in a limited number of locations. Consequently, one important reason why creative activities cluster in large urban regions is that these regions offer physical proximity, which facilitates the integration of multidisciplinary knowledge that is tacit and therefore 'person-embodied' rather than 'information-embodied', as well as allowing the rapid decision-making that is needed in order to cope with uncertainty (Patel and Pavitt, 1991). Due to urbanization economies, these regions also offer diversity, that is, economies of scope in information, skills, knowledge, competence, producer services and other inputs, which are crucial in creative, innovative and entrepreneurial processes (Karlsson et al., 2009).

Individual artists are not dependent upon a common labour pool and the supply of intermediate inputs is certainly not critical but may make life easier for artists. However, what might be more critical is the supply of outlets for their creations in the form of, for example, art galleries. The demand side matters too. The supply-side and the demand-side aspects were synthesized by Krugman (1991b) in his New Economic Geography Model, where he illustrated that economic agents will be located where demand is large and that demand will be large where many economic agents are located.

Proceeding from the factors that stimulate the clustering of creative individuals to the factors that stimulate the clustering of organized creative activities, such as the production of theatre performances, concerts and movies, it is obvious that Marshall's factors play a critical role. The presence of these specialized creative inputs in a geographically constrained area creates both static and dynamic localized advantages for creative activities. Of particular importance are the localized dynamics of collective learning and creativity (Keeble and Wilkinson, 1999). Both cultural production and R&D are organized in the form of projects. Projects are unique but organized endeavours that are undertaken by heterogeneous teams of specialized economic agents who collaborate to fulfil complex and interdependent tasks for specific purposes (Lundin and Söderholm, 1998). In these projects, various creative economic agents are linked together with other economic agents, each of whom performs a series of specialized tasks in a complex web, leading to the collective creation of a creative output.

'Cultural commodity production' often involves high levels of human input that are organized as temporary networks of small firms and professional individuals (freelancers) that work on a project basis (Scott, 2000). Teams, partnerships and alliances tend to dissolve and reorganize in an irregular manner over time (Bilton, 2007). These networks provide dense flows of information, knowledge, goods and services and create economies of scale and, in particular, economies of scope in skills-sourcing and know-how. They involve a complex division of labour and specialization that are supported by developments in information and communication technologies, which tend to tie professional people and small firms to places with a particular specialization known as clusters (cf. Pratt, 2004). Such clusters can normally only develop and survive for extended periods in large urban regions. This implies that cultural commodity production is strongly related to the city (Scott, 2004). Only large urban regions can provide those facilities, institutions, and embedded knowledge and practices – the urban ecosystem – which are crucial for sustainable creative milieus. Cities are thus 'collectives of human activity and interest that continually create streams of public goods – . . . – that sustains the workings of the creative field' (Scott, 2001, p. 13).[15] The underlying reason is of course that 'creative production' often has a collective nature, is dependent upon the development and maintenance of creative teams with diverse skills, and often needs to be coordinated within a relatively short and often finite time frame (Caves, 2000).

Few researchers have made an attempt to analyse how 'creative work' in projects comes about in the different contexts where they are embedded (Manning and Sydow, 2007). One interesting observation that can be made here is that the more project cycles that are short term and unforeseeable in terms of mission, the more important it becomes that project partners are co-located (Sassen, 1995; Scott, 1997, 1988b; Hutton, 2000). This implies that project networks increasingly gravitate towards local concentrations of creative talent, specialists, professionals and producer service firms as relations become driven by availability, speed of delivery (Grabher, 2002a) and an ambition to reduce geographical transaction costs.

At this point it is important to note that it is not only creative activities within 'cultural commodity production' that have a tendency to cluster and that such clustering is not a new phenomenon. It has, for example, been observed that American inventors and in particular great inventors in the first half of the nineteenth century had a strong tendency to cluster disproportionately in regions (such as New England and the Middle Atlantic) and in particular counties where low-cost transport (such as navigable inland waterways) as well as patent agents and lawyers were more accessible (Sokoloff, 1988; Kahn and Sokoloff, 1993, 2004; Lamoreaux and Sokloff, 1996, 1999a, 1999b).[16]

NON-LOCAL INTERACTION AND CREATIVITY

Above we have discussed the importance of clustering and local interaction for learning and creativity. However, some researchers question the superiority of local over non-local interaction (Malecki and Oinas, 1999; Oinas, 1999; Bathelt, 2001; Gertler, 2001; Vatne, 2001). There is according to these authors too little research on actual processes of learning and creativity that support claims about the importance of localized learning and creativity that is based mainly on local interaction. As processes of learning and creativity are not well documented empirically, the mere clustering of creative persons such as artists is assumed to prove the existence of localized processes of learning and creativity. Since these clusters do not exist in isolation but are connected to other regions, of which some contain similar clusters, it could be the case that learning and creativity are the result of a combination of local and non-local interactions.

The channels used for non-local interaction have been referred to as 'pipelines' in the literature (Owen-Smith and Powell, 2002). The basic idea is that decisive, non-incremental knowledge flows are often generated through 'network pipelines'. Creative people are embedded in social and professional networks, which are not geographically bounded and ideas, information and knowledge can be acquired through partnerships and cooperation of inter-regional and international reach. The resulting interaction is greatly impacted by the degree of trust that exists between the persons involved. When pipelines are established to new partners, new trust has to be built in a conscious and systematic way – a process that takes time and involves costs (Harrison, 1992). The non-local networks are essential since ideas, information and knowledge tend to be fragmented and specialized. It is then only through interaction in non-local networks that it is possible to sort out, interpret and evaluate these fragments and additions to the current stock of ideas, information and knowledge (cf. Törnqvist, 1983).

It seems natural to assume that ideas, information and knowledge spread through local 'buzz' interact synergetically with ideas, information and knowledge spread through 'pipelines' to stimulate learning and creativity in a cluster. The more the persons who are active in a cluster engage in the build-up of inter-regional and international 'pipelines', the more ideas, information and knowledge about, for example, new artistic trends are pumped into the local networks and the more dynamic the 'buzz' from which these persons benefit. Burt (1992) emphasizes the importance of those actors in a cluster who are able to make connections to otherwise remote networks, thereby bridging 'structural holes'. Because of their potential to stimulate and intensify local interaction, the 'pipelines' support a cluster's cohesion and strengthen its internal relations and interaction processes between cluster participants (Murdoch, 1995). Openness of cluster relations and active search for external ideas, information and knowledge may be critical to understand the rise of successful clusters (Maillat, 1998; Scott, 1998a; Bresnahan et al., 2001).

The importance of non-local networks can be understood from another perspective. The need for non-local networks emerges partly from the fact that local networks can be too closed, too exclusive and too rigid (Uzzi, 1996, 1997). External network relations are important to avoid lock-ins in clusters (Kern, 1996). There is a significant difference between 'introvert' and 'extrovert' clusters (cf. Malecki, 2000), but even if a cluster over time achieves a successful balance between an inward and an outward orientation, it is nevertheless only able to handle a limited number of external linkages (cf. Grabher, 2001, 2002a). The reason for this is that the establishment and maintenance of external linkages require substantial time and are costly.

Communication processes in non-local networks are contingent by nature and are characterized by high uncertainty. Non-local networks encompass, for example, artists from different parts of the world, which are embedded in different social, institutional and cultural milieus. This implies that they operate in different selection environments (cf. Owen-Smith and Powell, 2002), which will result in different artistic expressions. This is very important for creative activities, since new cutting-edge expressions are constantly created but the locations of these creations are changing. Since the different artistic clusters are competing for attention, new cutting-edge creations in one cluster are significant stimuli for the generation of cutting-edge creations in other clusters.

It can as a consequence be hypothesized that both local 'buzz' and non-local networks offer special but different advantages for artists and other persons who engage in creative activities. Local 'buzz' is beneficial to learning and creative processes because it generates opportunities for a variety of spontaneous and unanticipated situations where artists interact and form interpretative and creative communities (cf. Nonaka et al., 2000). The advantages of non-local networks are instead associated with the integration of different selection environments. Such interaction may open up different potentials and feed local interpretation and the use of ideas, information and knowledge residing elsewhere. Some clusters are able to be creative just because some people in those clusters make connections with other clusters (cf. Malecki, 2000).

The use of existing non-local links and the establishment of new non-local links with other clusters and with individual artists in such clusters require planning, conscious efforts and specific investments. Flows of ideas, information and knowledge through non-local links are not automatic and participation is not free but instead involves a complex and costly process. Cost considerations will tend to make interaction in non-local links targeted towards certain predefined and planned goals. Information flowing through global pipelines has an intrinsic bias towards filtering out information about failures and mainly contains information about successes.

Interaction through global pipelines involves a selection of clusters and of individual artists to interact with – interaction here also includes migration for shorter or longer periods to another cluster. Such selection is not easy since information about the set of potential clusters and individual artists tends to be truncated and incomplete (cf. Malmgren, 1961). Furthermore, artists have to develop a joint interpretative context and a common language in order to engage in fruitful interaction and cooperation. Artists who want to participate in non-local interaction must learn to understand their different institutional regimes, interpretative schemes and artistic paradigms, which requires complex cognitive capabilities.

Since the interaction of artists in non-local networks can be interpreted as a conscious attempt to overcome identified weaknesses and shortcomings in one's own cluster in order to achieve certain creative goals, they are certainly prepared to make special efforts to bridge cultural, cognitive and other distances. Non-local interaction between artists from different clusters implies a mixing of partly different ideas, information, knowledge and artistic paradigms. When the overlap in these respects is large, we may assume that the extra creativity generated is minimal. However, when the overlap is small, there is, on the one hand, the risk that the lack of a common language will prohibit effective inter-action, but, on the other hand, the chance that the meeting between two very different artistic paradigms may stimulate the emergence of new artistic paradigms.

Identifying the value and location of external artistic ideas, information and knowl-edge as well as building links to access the external sources are only part of the challenge when attempting to boost creative capabilities. An equally important task is to develop the ability to interpret, understand, evaluate and integrate the external stimuli in creative processes, that is, to develop an absorptive capacity (cf. Cohen and Levinthal, 1990). It is important to observe that a cluster's absorptive capacity is larger than the sum of that of its individual artists and of other people interacting within the cluster. Instead, it is a function of the volume and the intensity of the local 'buzz' and non-local interaction. Internal gatekeepers and boundary-spanners become crucial for translating external ideas, information and knowledge into a form that can be understood by the individu-als for whom it is particularly valuable. The concept of absorptive capacity emphasizes both the role of diversity of expertise and its distribution within the cluster for creating new mental maps, which integrate the external stimuli in the local 'buzz'. The degree and distribution of expertise affect how external stimuli – which arrive through pipelines and are dispatched by the local gatekeepers – will be interpreted and absorbed by the artists in the cluster. If the existing expertise is too narrow, a cluster will not be able to take full advantage of its external stimuli. Cohen and Levinthal (1990, p. 134) state that 'while common knowledge improves communication, communality should not be carried so far that diversity across individuals is substantially diminished'.

CREATIVE REGIONAL ECONOMIC MILIEUS

Social scientists have for several decades pointed out that the developed economies have gone through fundamental changes during the post-war period. Different authors have used different concepts to characterize what they have seen as the most basic aspect of these changes. Concepts such as the information society, the service society, the post-industrial society, the knowledge society have thereby been introduced. Already in the 1980s the Swedish economist Åke E. Andersson started to describe the dynamics of long-term changes to Western societies by analysing the underlying driving forces (Andersson and Mantsinen, 1980; Andersson et al., 1984; Andersson, 1985a, 1985b, 1988, 1989; Andersson and Strömquist, 1989; Matthiessen and Andersson, 1993). According to him, the major driving force in the modern economy is creative activities and processes, which generate new knowledge that is spurred by culture and communication. The develop-ment, handling and presentation of new knowledge and information employ a steadily increasing share of the labour force. These activities are assumed to have strong spillover effects on industrial activities in manufacturing as well as in service production.

In the picture painted by Andersson, economic life is undergoing a process of change towards increasingly dynamic product competition. The resource base in developed economies is no longer mainly based on natural resources and energy but on education and assets that reflect creative activities. The development in these economies is based upon new complementary infrastructures. Traditional means of transport are complemented and sometimes substituted by the communication networks that have been created by modern information technology. Among the traditional means of transport, road and air transport is gradually becoming more dominant; access to material and non-material networks is becoming critical.

To be able to understand, predict and/or influence regional development in the creative society it is, according to Andersson (1985a), necessary to understand how the economic system can be divided into game or play and scene or arena. The economic and the political games with rapid and sudden changes are played on an arena where changes are slow. The arena consists of material infrastructures (for example, transport systems and buildings), non-material infrastructures (for example, knowledge stocks and knowledge networks) and institutions (such as formal and informal behavioural rules and property rights).

A fundamental difference between the creative knowledge society and earlier societies is that its infrastructure in a profound way consists of many interconnected layers. The material infrastructure not only consists of road, rail, air, and sea traffic networks. Rail, for example, serves local, regional, national as well as international transport demand. The rail traffic is complemented with successively more and more advanced information systems for traffic control as well as for planning and booking trips even in combination with other means of transport. The non-material arena consists of knowledge and information assets. What is typical for modern society is that knowledge and information flows are distributed over many different media and that electronic media increase their market share rapidly.

As regards institutions, the trends seem to go in different directions. On the one hand, there is an increasing focus on patents and copyrights to protect intellectual property rights. On the other hand, there are signs that intellectual property rights are becoming less interesting in a rapidly changing society, which is illustrated by the increased reliance on 'open innovation' (Chesbrough, 2003). What seems to matter more is the position of individuals, firms and regions in different networks and what access they have to relevant knowledge and essential information.

Andersson et al. (1990) demonstrate how industrial development and income growth in a region are positively influenced by a combination of universities and other research institutions,[17] which grow synergetically with telecommunications and good accessibility to rapid transport systems in the form of air and road transport. The creative society emerges and creates growth and prosperity in a number of regions which contain the appropriate synergetic potential. These regions tend to be centres of agglomeration and it is the diversity of knowledge, know-how, learning capabilities and resources found in these regions that enables them to become centres of creativity and innovation and which, in turn, contributes to their competitiveness (Johansson et al., 2009).

In earlier phases of development, the military played the most important role for stimulating creativity and innovation and for the generation of high-tech clusters (Hall, 1990). Other sources, such as experiences, entertainment, health, environment and food have in more recent phases become more important in generating a demand for creativity and innovation. Overall, a huge interest has in recent decades been devoted to, in particular, high-tech clusters among scientists, politicians and planners, as well as the media (Karlsson, 2008b). These clusters, which have been described as creative, innovative, and knowledge-intensive, contain one or several industries that are R&D-intensive and have a high share of university-trained employees.

Fujita and Thisse (1996) suggest against this background that human activities can be divided into two categories: production and creation, where the former represents routine methods of production. Creation, on the other hand, stands for the generation of new ideas, new knowledge, new technologies and new products. Andersson (1989) analyses what characterizes dynamic creative activities. Successful dynamic creative activities are large logistical networks of small, creative units. The creative units have a non-hierarchical structure and are often self-organized. This implies that economies of scale are combined with, and complemented by, economies of scope. These characteristics have strong implications for the development of the system of functional regions.[18]

The difference between knowledge-rich and knowledge-poor regions tends to grow. Regions with commercial R&D and research universities are centres for the development of fundamental research results, whether it occurs within the laboratories of universities or private firms. Such regions, which normally are large and dense, also offer deeper and more versatile knowledge, competence and supply of specialists as well as rich opportunities for personal contacts. The probability of 'spin-off growth' is simply greater if the regional milieu is information-rich (for example, through the mass media, the internet and inter-regional or international information networks) compared to information-poor milieus. It is also vital to have activities that demand scientific results within the region. With the existence of intra-regional demand, spin-off effects tend to occur, which stimulate further growth. There are breakaways from existing institutions and activities, since progressive inventors start their own business and become entrepreneurs. This is in line with the incubator or nursery-city model, which argues that those regions that are highly diversified and contain a broad spectrum of different types of industries and firm sizes will function as superior incubators for the development of new firms and the growth of small ones (Chinitz, 1961; Duranton and Puga, 2001). One major reason is that in this kind of economic milieu there will be a variety of local business services that support creativity in new and small firms.

For a creative region to grow and develop, it is important for the transport system to be of high quality and high capacity (Matthiessen and Andersson, 1993). Such a transport system allows contacts with and imports of new knowledge and innovations from other creative regions in the rest of the world. It is much better for a region to be an import centre than an export centre, even if exports also contribute to growth and prosperity. The reason is that the majority of ideas that generate new activities in a region get inspiration from other regions. Irrespective of how strong a region is in terms of R&D it will only produce a tiny share of all new knowledge in the world. Most new ideas inevitably come from other creative regions. The new ideas are imported; they are used; they are developed; they generate new production. The production of new goods or services places a firm among those firms that engage in product competition and that have a capacity to pay high wages and salaries.

General import activities and knowledge-importing organizations are concentrated in a limited number of urban regions in each country. Production that is based on imports is generally not a high-risk activity. The fact that something has been imported implies that it has been possible to produce and sell it somewhere else. Subsequently, the new products in the import regions spread to other (export) regions and thereby their exports are renewed (Jacobs, 1969, 1984).

There is disagreement in the literature as to whether diversified or specialized economic milieus offer the best conditions for creativity and innovation. Already Vernon and Hoover (1959) and Vernon (1960) have stressed the role of the diversity of the New York region for its economic development. Thus, diversity seems to be an important aspect of creative regions (Jacobs, 1961, 1969). Other important aspects of creative regions are, according to Andersson (1985a):

- flexibility in terms of social conditions, economic activities but also in terms of land use planning;
- willingness to overcome political, language, cultural and physical barriers; and
- a socio-cultural milieu marked by great openness and an atmosphere of tolerance.

Not least the last aspect enhances the attractiveness of creative regions for creative talent and makes them an inspiration for cultural producers. Social and cultural variety and openness, therefore, represents a specific type of cultural capital in a creative region, which makes it highly attractive for the actors in the creative economy. At the local level, this cultural capital of a creative region might also be characterized as a specific subcultural capital of particular districts within the region, because creative activities may in fact be highly localized within a creative region. These observations support Florida's (2002) contention that the economic growth of creative regions is driven by the location choices of creative people – the holders of creative capital – who prefer places that are diverse, tolerant and open to new ideas.

Andersson (1985a) summarizes the characteristics of creative milieus.[19] Many different factors work together in a creative milieu. The creative process can be seen as a form of dynamic synergy. To initiate a creative process many factors must be able to influence each other in a mutual ongoing interaction. This concurrence and interaction imply great demands on the regional milieu. It appears that the regional milieu must be of large scale but still culturally versatile, rich in deep original knowledge and competence and characterized by good communication possibilities internally and externally.

For intra-regional communication, physical proximity seems to be of great importance, since personal communication within groups of individuals sharing common interests seems to be a vital input to creativity (Jacobs, 1969; Lucas, 1988). To achieve considerable synergy effects there is a need for 'manifoldness' and variation. The different activities in a creative region are often of small scale as individual activities. Industries grow not by quantitative growth of the existing activities but through the emergence of new activities. The following seven factors seem to be fundamental conditions for creative processes, according to Andersson (1985a):

- Benevolent or tolerant attitudes towards experiments.
- A versatile composition of knowledge and competences.
- A versatile and relatively unregulated financial base for science, entrepreneurship and cultural life.

- Good possibilities for spontaneous and informal personal contacts between different parts of the region and with other regions.
- Heterogeneity rather than functional division of the social and physical environment.
- A feeling that needs are greater than existing resources or opportunities.
- A flexible social and economic organization that sometimes engenders structural instability.[20]

It seems, according to Andersson (1985a), as if structural instability is a necessary condition for creativity from both a micro and a macro perspective. During the major part of each research, design or development process, the activities are mainly routinized, which means that they proceed within a structurally stable equilibrium process. However, in a parallel process internal instability may develop. Logical inconsistencies become increasingly obvious concurrently with attempts to generalize the basic ideas. Exceptions from basic principles may be discovered. Now the process might stagnate and end, if there is a lack of people with original, deep and varied knowledge and competence. However, if there are enough people with the right background and with possibilities of active communication between each other, the process can turn into a powerful bifurcation or a phase of structural instability with great uncertainty about the future development path and thus a great potential for creative acts.

Such a structural instability may at the regional level be perceived as a period of fundamental uncertainty about future development. Trend extrapolations do not work. However, such uncertainty is both advantageous and risky. Due to the lack of stability within the system, smaller groups of people may be able to influence the system and choose a new stable course, which may create the subsequent possibility of several different stable courses. Of course, it is troublesome for regional planners and policy makers that creativity demands structural instability, manifoldness and uncertainty. In addition, it may be difficult to combine creativity with short-term productivity. On top of that, creativity at the regional level may be opposed to the maintenance of social stability.

CONCLUDING REMARKS

There is considerable interest in creativity among researchers in many disciplines, including psychology, pedagogy, management, economics and economic geography. The bulk of the research has focused on the creativity of individuals, but increasingly also on the creativity of teams and on the importance of the organizational context. Less interest has been devoted to the role of the wider context in terms of the characteristics of the local and regional economic milieu where the creative processes take place or to the connections of this economic milieu to other such milieus nationally and internationally. In this chapter, I argue that the clustering of creative agents and creative processes in specific locations generates creative advantages that stimulate creativity and the in-migration of creative agents. One further argument in this chapter is that the better connected an economic milieu is to other economic milieus via networks that transmit new ideas, information and knowledge, the higher will be the creative potential of that economic milieu. It is my hope that this chapter will stimulate researchers in different fields to consider more carefully the role of clustering and networks in stimulating creativity.

NOTES

1. According to Florida's ideas, the agglomeration of 'creative professions', that is, the 'creative class', is driven by the quality of life, tolerance and creative feel of cities (Florida, 2002). However, even if his book is rich in terms of data, he does not present any hard econometric data to support his theories (cf. Montgomery, 2005; Peck, 2005).
2. Amabile (1996) defines creativity as the development of new ideas that are potentially useful, that is, that can be embodied in products, practices, services or procedures. It is important to observe here that creativity also develops ideas such as nuclear bombs and cluster bombs!
3. This definition can be compared with the following earlier definitions: 'the process of bringing something new into birth' (May, 1959); 'in business, originality isn't enough. To be creative, an idea must also be appropriate – useful and actionable' (Amabile, 1998); 'is the ability to produce work that is both novel . . . and appropriate' (Sternberg and Lubart, 1999); 'a purposeful activity (or set of activities) that produces valuable products, services, processes, or ideas that are better or new (DeGraff and Lawrence, 2002); and 'the ability to understand, develop and express in a systematic fashion, novel orderly relationships' (Heilman et al., 2003).
4. Sternberg and Lubart (1999) also look upon entrepreneurship as a form of creativity. As remarked by Baumol (1990), not all entrepreneurship is productive. Some of it is pure rent-seeking and some of it is criminal.
5. This relates to the work by Schumpeter (1934) on innovation. He placed great emphasis on the fact that new ideas are rare, since most ideas are recombinations of existing ones.
6. 'Often, in common parlance, the words creativity and innovation are used interchangeably. They should not be, because while creativity implies coming up with ideas, it is the "bringing ideas to life" . . . that makes innovation the distinct undertaking it is' (Davila et al., 2005, p. xvii).
7. It should be observed that there is a fundamental difference between invention and innovation that has been lost in much of the literature, where the terms have been used more or less synonymously, without regard for the contrasting levels of risk and uncertainty or the very different kinds of work processes and creative processes that are involved in these two activities. 'Invention involves discoveries of new processes, products, or combinations that can lead to some practical application. Innovation involves the application of inventions, as a discovery or new product is refined and made suitable for marketing' (Suarez-Villa, 1996, p. 252).
8. According to Amiable (1996), intrinsic motivation is more important for creativity than extrinsic motivation. However, extrinsic motivation may support intrinsic motivation.
9. The capacity to combine core creative skills from both within and outside the organization is an organization's core competency (Prahalad, 1993).
10. Collins only finds three exceptions in the recorded history of man: Wang Chung (Taoist metaphysician), Bassui Tokusho (Zen spiritualist) and Ibn Khaldun (Arabic philosopher).
11. Much of the discussion dealing with clustering and creativity has dealt either with clustering of creative industries (Maskell and Lorenzen, 2004; Scott, 2006) or with the so-called creative class (Florida, 2002, 2005). I avoid using these concepts since I consider the definitions used in both these cases to be very arbitrary. For example, industries that are characterized as non-creative have to rely on creativity in processes such as marketing or product development (cf. Siedel et al., 2008). Thus, I prefer to focus on creative activities instead, which also can occur in industries that are not defined as creative industries as well as involve people who are not defined as belonging to the creative class.
12. Scherer (2001) claims that the demand for artistic products in (large) cities is important for the location and clustering of composers.
13. Other similar concepts used in the literature are 'local broadcasting' and 'noise' (Grabher, 2002b).
14. The paradigms change over time.
15. Unlike Florida, Scott is concerned with cultural production rather than consumption.
16. Kahn and Sokoloff (1993) make the interesting observation that there is evidence that great inventors in the United States during the early nineteenth century were both more likely to be born in counties with low-cost access to broad markets, and to migrate to (that is, cluster in) such counties. Thus, great inventors became highly concentrated in these clusters.
17. Karlsson and Andersson (2009) show that there is strong persistence or path dependence in the location of both industrial and university R&D. The location of industrial R&D seems to be quite sensitive to

the location of university R&D and there are indications that the location of university R&D is similarly sensitive to the location of industrial R&D.

18. A functional region is distinguished by its concentration of activities and its joint infrastructure, which facilitate high factor mobility within its interaction borders. In particular, a functional region has an integrated labour market, in which commuting as well as job search is intensive (Johansson, 1998).

19. The concept of creative milieu can be compared with the concept of 'milieu of innovation' introduced by Castells (1989, p. 82): 'By a milieu of innovation we understand a specific set of relationships of production . . . based on a social organisation that by and large shares a work culture and instrumental goals aimed at generating new knowledge, new processes and new products.'

20. It has been stressed in the literature that the social and organizational context often affects the level of creativity (Rasulzada, 2007).

REFERENCES

Allen, J. (1997), 'Economies of power and space', in R. Lee and J. Wills (eds), *Geographies of Economies*, London: Arnold, pp. 59–70.

Amabile, T.M. (1988), 'A model of creativity and innovation in organizations', in B.M. Staw and L.L. Cummings (eds), *Research in Organizational Behaviour*, Greenwich, CT: JAI Press, pp. 123–67.

Amabile, T.M. (1996), *Creativity in Context*, Boulder, CO: Westview.

Amabile, T.M. (1998), 'How to kill creativity', *Harvard Business Review*, **76** (September/October), 76–87.

Amabile, T.M., R. Conti, H. Coon, J. Lazenby and M. Herron (1996), 'Assessing the work environment for creativity', *Academy of Management Journal*, **39**, 1154–84.

Andersson, Å.E. (1985a), *Kreativitet – Storstadens framtid*, Stockholm: Prisma.

Andersson, Å.E. (1985b), 'Creativity and economic dynamic modelling', in D.F. Batten, J. Casti and B. Johansson (eds), *Economic Evolution and Structural Adjustment*, Berlin: Springer, pp. 27–45.

Andersson, Å.E. (1988), *Universitet – Regioners Framtid*, Stockholm: Regionplanekontoret.

Andersson, Å.E. (1989), *Sydsvensk framtid*, Södertälje: Moraberg Förlag.

Andersson, Å.E. and D.E. Andersson (2006), *The Economics of Experiences, the Arts and Entertainment*, Cheltenham, UK and Northampton, MA, USA: Edward Elgar Publishing.

Andersson, Å.E. and J. Mantsinen (1980), 'Mobility of resources: accessibility of knowledge and economic growth', *Behavioural Science*, **25**, 353–66.

Andersson, Å.E. and U. Strömqvist (1989), *K-samhällets framtid*, Stockholm: Prisma.

Andersson, Å.E., G. Törnqvist, F. Snickars and S. Öberg (1984), *Regional mångfald till rikets gagn*, Stockholm: Liber Förlag.

Andersson, Å.E., C. Anderstig and B. Hårsman (1990), 'Knowledge and communication infrastructures and regional economic change', *Regional Science and Urban Economics*, **20**, 359–76.

Argote, L. and E. Darr (2000), 'Repositories of knowledge in franchise organizations', in G. Dosi, R.R. Nelson and S.G. Winter (eds), *The Nature and Dynamics of Organisational Capabilities*, New York, NY: Oxford University Press, pp. 51–86.

Bain, A.L. (2003), 'Constructing contemporary artistic identities in Toronto neighbourhoods', *The Canadian Geographer*, **47**, 313–17.

Banaji, S., A. Burn and D. Buckingham (2007), *The Rhetorics of Creativity: A Review of the Literature*, London: Creative Partnership.

Bathelt, H. (2001), 'The rise of a new cultural products industry cluster in Germany: the case of the Leipzig media industry', *IWSG Working Papers 06-2001*, Frankfurt am Main.

Baumol, W.J. (1990), 'Entrepreneurship: productive, unproductive and destructive', *Journal of Political Economy*, **98**, 893–921.

Becker, H.S. (1982), *Art Worlds*, Berkeley, CA: University of California Press.

Bilton, C. (2007), *Management and Creativity: From Creative Industries to Creative Management*, Oxford: Blackwell.

Boden, M.A. (2004), *The Creative Mind: Myths and Mechanisms* (2nd edn), London: Routledge.

Brass, D.J. (1995), 'Creativity: it's all in your social network', in C.M. Ford and D.A. Gioia (eds), *Creative Action in Organizations*, Thousand Oaks, CA: Sage, pp. 94–9.

Bresnahan, T., A. Gambardella and A. Saxenian (2001), '"Old economy" inputs for "new economy" outputs: cluster formation in the Silicon Valleys', *Industrial and Corporate Change*, **10**, 835–60.

Burt, R.S. (1992), *Structural Holes: The Social Structure of Competition*, Cambridge, MA: Harvard University Press.

Burt, R.S. (2004), 'Structural holes and good ideas', *American Journal of Sociology*, **110**, 349–99.

Byron, K. (2007), 'Defining boundaries for creativity', keynote presentation at the Creativity or Conformity? Building Cultures of Creativity in Higher Education Conference, University of Wales Institute, Cardiff, 8–10 January.

Cappelin, R. (2003), 'Networks and technological change in regional clusters', in J. Bröcker, D. Dohse and R. Soltwedel (eds), *Innovation Clusters and Regional Competition*, Berlin: Springer-Verlag, pp. 52–78.

Castells, M. (1989), *The Informational City*, Oxford: Blackwell.

Cattani, G. and S. Ferriani (2008), 'A core/periphery perspective on individual creative performance: social networks and cinematic achievements in the Hollywood film industry', *Organization Science*, **19**, 824–44.

Caves, R. (2000), *Creative Industries*, Cambridge, MA: Harvard University Press.

Chesbrough, H. (2003), *Open Innovation*, Boston, MA: Harvard Business School Press.

Chinitz, B. (1961), 'Contrasts in agglomeration: New York and Pittsburgh', *American Economic Review*, **51**, 279–89.

Christensen, C.M., S.D. Anthony and E.A. Roth (2004), *Seeing What's Next: Using the Theories of Innovation to Predict Industry Change*, Boston, MA: Harvard Business School Press.

Cohen, W.M. and D.A. Levinthal (1990), 'Absorptive capacity: a new perspective on learning and innovation', *Administrative Science Quarterly*, **35**, 128–52.

Collins, R. (1998), *The Sociology of Philosophies: a Global Theory of Intellectual Change*, Cambridge, MA: Belknap Press.

Csikszentmihályi, M. (1999), 'Implications of a systems perspective for the study of creativity', in R. Sternberg (ed.), *Handbook of Creativity*, Cambridge: Cambridge University Press, pp. 313–35.

Davila, T., M. Epstein and R. Shelton (2005), *Making Innovation Work. How to Manage It, Measure It, and Profit from It*, Upper Saddle River, NJ: Wharton School Publishing.

DeGraff, J. and K.A. Lawrence (2002), *Creativity at Work. Developing the Right Practices to Make Innovation Happen*, San Francisco, CA: Jossey-Bass.

Desrochers, P. (2000), 'De l'influence d'une Ville Diversifiée sur la Combinasion de Techniques: Typologie et Analyse de Processus', dissertation, Montreal, QC: Univeristé de Montréal.

Desrochers, P. (2001), 'Local diversity, human creativity and technological innovation', *Growth and Change*, **32**, 369–94.

Drazin, R., M.A. Glynn and R.K. Kazanjian (1999), 'Multilevel theorizing about creativity in organizations: a sense-making perspective', *Academy of Management Review*, **24**, 286–307.

Duranton, G. and D. Puga (2001), 'Nursery cities: urban diversity, process innovation, and the life cycle of products', *American Economic Review*, **91**, 1454–77.

Ekboir, J.M. (2002), 'Developing no-till packages for small-scale farmers', in J. Ekboir (ed.), *World Wheat Overview and Outlook*, Mexico City: CIMMYT, available at http://www.betuco.be/CA/No-tillage%20 Cimmyt.pdf (accessed 10 March 2011).

Ellison, G. and E.L. Glaeser (1997), 'Geographic concentration in U.S. manufacturing industries: a dartboard approach', *Journal of Political Economy*, **105**, 889–927.

Fleming, L. and M. Marx (2006), 'Managing creativity in small worlds', *California Management Review*, **48**, 6–27.

Flew, T. (2002), 'Beyond *ad hocery*: defining creative industries', paper presented to Cultural Sites, Cultural Theory, Cultural Policy: The Second International Conference on Cultural Policy Research, Te Papa, Wellington, New Zealand, 23–26 January.

Florida, R. (2002), *The Rise of the Creative Class and How It's Transforming Work, Leisure, Community and Everyday Life*, New York, NY: Basic Books.

Florida, R. (2005), *The Flight of the Creative Class*, New York, NY: Harper Collins.

Ford, C. (1996), 'Theory of individual creative action in multiple social domains', *Academy of Management Review*, **21**, 1112–42.

Fuchs, M. (2001), *Von der lernenden Region zur lernenden Organisation*, INEF Report 52/2001, INEF, Duisburg.

Fujita, M. and J.-F. Thisse (1996), 'Economics of agglomeration', *Journal of the Japanese and International Economies*, **10**, 339–78.

Gertler, M.S. (1995), '"Being there": proximity, organization, and culture in the development and adoption of advanced manufacturing technologies', *Economic Geography*, **71**, 1–26.

Gertler, M.S. (2001), 'Local knowledge: tacitness and the geography of context', paper presented at the Annual Meeting of the Association of American Geographers in New York, NY.

Gibson, L. (1999), 'The arts as industry', *Media International Australia*, **90**, 107–22.

Glaeser, E.L, H.D. Kallal, J.A. Scheinkman and A. Schleifer (1992), 'Growth in cities', *Journal of Political Economy*, **100**, 1126–52.

Glynn, M.A. (1996), 'Innovative genius: a framework for relating individual and organizational intelligences to innovation', *Academy of Management Review*, **21**, 1081–111.

Grabher, G. (2001), 'Ecologies of creativity: the village, the group, and the heterarchic organisation of the British advertising industry', *Environment and Planning A*, **33**, 351–74.

Grabher, G. (2002a), 'The project ecology of advertising: tasks, talents and teams', *Regional Studies*, **36**, 245–62.

Grabher, G. (2002b), 'Cool projects, boring institutions: temporary collaboration in social context', *Regional Studies*, **36**, 205–14.

Granovetter, M. (1985), 'Economic action and economic structure: the problem of embeddedness', *American Journal of Sociology*, **91**, 481–510.

Grosenick, U. and R. Stange (2005), *International Art Galleries: Post-war to Post-millennium*, London: Thames & Hudson.

Hall, P. (1990), 'High-technology industry and the European scene', in *Urban Challenges*, Stockholm: Statens offentliga utredningar, (SOU 1990:33), pp. 117–33.

Hargadon, A.B. and B.A. Bechky (2006), 'When collections of creatives become creative collections', *Organization Science*, **17**, 484–500.

Harrison, B. (1992), 'Industrial districts: old wine in new bottles?', *Regional Studies*, **26**, 469–83.

Heilman, K.M., S.E. Nadeau and D.O. Beversdorf (2003), 'Creative innovation: possible brain mechanisms', *Neurocase*, **9**, 369–79.

Hellmanzik, C. (2009), 'Location matters: estimating cluster premiums for prominent modern artists', mimeo, Department of Economics, Trinity College, Dublin.

Howkins, J. (2001), *The Creative Economy: How People Make Money from Ideas*, London: Allen Lane.

Hutton, T.A. (2000), 'Reconstructed production landscapes in the postmodern city: applied design and creative services in the metropolitan core', *Urban Geography*, **21**, 285–317.

Im, S. (1999), 'The model of effect of creativity on new product success', dissertation, Kenan-Flagler Business School, University of North Carolina.

Jacobs, J. (1961), *The Death and Life of Great American Cities*, New York, NY: Random House.

Jacobs, J. (1969), *The Economy of Cities*, New York, NY: Random House.

Jacobs, J. (1984), *Cities and the Wealth of Nations*, New York, NY: Random House.

Johansson, B. (1998), 'Infrastructure, market potential and endogenous growth', mimeo, Jönköping International Business School, Jönköping.

Johansson, B., C. Karlsson and R.R. Stough (2009), 'Introduction: the rise of regions: innovation, agglomeration and regional competition', in B. Johansson, C. Karlsson and R.R. Stough (eds), *Innovation, Agglomeration and Regional Competition*, Cheltenham, UK and Northampton, MA, USA: Edward Elgar Publishing, pp. 1–15.

Kahn, B.Z. and K.L. Sokoloff (1993), 'Schemes of practical utility', *Journal of Economic History*, **53**, 289–307.

Kahn, B.Z. and K.L. Sokoloff (2004), 'Institutions and technological innovation during early economic growth: evidence from great inventors of the United States, 1790–1930', CESIFO working paper No. 1299.

Karlsson, C. (2008a), 'Introduction', in C. Karlsson (ed.), *Handbook of Research on Cluster Theory*, Cheltenham, UK and Northampton, MA, USA: Edward Elgar Publishing, pp. 1–19.

Karlsson, C. (2008b), 'Introduction', in C. Karlsson (ed.), *Handbook of Research on Innovation and Clusters*, Cheltenham, UK and Northampton, MA, USA: Edward Elgar Publishing, pp. 1–16.

Karlsson, C. and M. Andersson (2009), 'The location of industry R&D and the location of university R&D: how are they related?', in C. Karlsson, Å.E.Andersson, P.C. Cheshire and R.R. Stough (eds), *New Directions in Regional Economic Development*, Berlin: Springer, pp. 267–90.

Karlsson, C. and B. Johansson (2006), 'Dynamics and entrepreneurship in a knowledge-based economy', in C. Karlsson, B. Johansson and R.R. Stough (eds), *Entrepreneurship and Dynamics in a Knowledge Economy*, New York, NY: Routledge, pp. 12–46.

Karlsson, C. and A. Manduchi (2001), 'Knowledge spillovers in a spatial context – a critical review and assessment', in M.M. Fischer and J. Frölich (eds), *Knowledge, Complexity and Innovation Systems*, Berlin: Springer, pp. 101–23.

Karlsson, C., P. Flensburg and S.-Å. Hörte (2004), 'Introduction: knowledge spillovers and knowledge management', in C. Karlsson, P. Flensburg and S.-Å. Hörte (eds), *Knowledge Spillovers and Knowledge Management*, Cheltenham, UK and Northampton, MA, USA: Edward Elgar Publishing, pp. 3–31.

Karlsson, C., B. Johansson and R.R. Stough (2005), 'Industrial clusters and inter-firm networks: an introduction', in C. Karlsson, B. Johansson and R.R. Stough (eds), *Industrial Clusters and Inter-firm Networks*, Cheltenham, UK and Northampton, MA, USA: Edward Elgar Publishing, pp. 1–25.

Karlsson, C., R.R. Stough and B. Johansson (2009), 'Introduction: innovation and entrepreneurship in functional regions', in C. Karlsson, R.R. Stough and B. Johansson (eds), *Entrepreneurship and Innovations in Functional Regions*, Cheltenham, UK and Northampton, MA, USA: Edward Elgar Publishing, pp. 1–20.

Keeble, D. and F. Wilkinson (1999), 'Collective learning and knowledge development in the evolution of regional clusters of high-technology SMEs in Europe', *Regional Studies*, **33**, 295–303.

Kern, H. (1996), 'Vertrauensverlust und blindes Vertrauen: Integrationsprobleme im ökonomischen Handeln', *SOFI-Mitteilungen*, **24**, 7–14.

Kim, H. (2007), 'The creative economy of urban art clusters: locational characteristics of art galleries in Seoul', *Journal of the Korean Geographical Society*, **42**, 258–79.

Koestler, A. (1964), *The Act of Creation*, New York, NY: Macmillan.

Kostelanetz, R. (2003), *SoHo: The Rise and Fall of an Artists' Colony*, London: Routledge.

Krugman, P. (1991a), *Geography and Trade*, Cambridge, MA: MIT Press.

Krugman, P. (1991b), 'Increasing returns and economic geography', *Journal of Political Economy*, **99**, 483–99.

Kuhn, T.S. (1962), *The Structure of Scientific Revolutions*, Chicago, IL: University of Chicago Press.

Lamoreaux, N.R. and K.L. Sokoloff (1996), 'Long-term change in the organisation of inventive activity', *Proceedings of the National Academy of Sciences of the USA*, **93**, 12686–92.

Lamoreaux, N.R. and K.L. Sokoloff (1999a), 'Inventors, firms, and the market for technology in the late nineteenth and early twentieth centuries', in N.R. Lamoreaux, D.M.G. Raff and P. Temin (eds), *Learning By Doing in Markets, Firms, and Countries*, Chicago, IL: University of Chicago Press, pp. 19–57.

Lamoreaux, N.R. and K.L. Sokoloff (1999b), 'The geography of the market for technology in the late-nineteenth and early-twentieth century United States', in G.D. Libecap (ed.), *Advances in the Study of Entrepreneurship, Innovation, and Economic Growth*, Stamford, CA: JAI Press, pp. 67–121.

Latour, B. (1986), 'The powers of association', in J. Law (ed.), *Power, Action and Belief: A New Sociology of Knowledge?*, London: Routledge & Kegan Paul, pp. 264–80.

Laudel, G. (2001), 'Collaboration, creativity and rewards: why and how scientists collaborate', *International Journal of Technology Management*, **22**, 762–81.

Lawson, C. and E. Lorenz (1999), 'Collective learning, tacit knowledge and regional innovative capacity', *Regional Studies*, **33**, 305–17.

Lazzeretti, L., R. Boix and F. Capone (2008), 'Do creative industries cluster? Mapping creative local production systems in Italy and Spain', Document de Treball 08.05, Departament d'Economia Aplicada, Universitat Autònoma de Barcelona, Barcelona.

Leadbeater, C. (1999), *Living on Thin Air: The New Economy*, London: Penguin Group.

Ley, D. (2003), 'Artists, aestheticisation, and the field of gentrification', *Urban Studies*, **40**, 2527–44.

Lucas, R. (1988), 'On the mechanics of economic development', *Journal of Monetary Economics*, **22**, 3–42.

Lundin, R.A. and A. Söderholm (1998), 'Conceptualizing a projectified society – discussion of an eco-institutional approach to a theory of temporary organizations', in R.A. Lundin and C. Midler (eds), *Projects as Arenas for Renewal and Learning Processes*, Boston, MA: Kluwer, pp.13–23.

Maillat, D. (1998), '"Vom Industrial District" zum innovativen Milieu: Ein Beitrag zur Analyse der lokalen Produktionssysteme', *Geographische Zeitschrift*, **86**, 1–15.

Malecki, E.J. (2000), 'Knowledge and regional competitiveness', *Erdkunde*, **54**, 334–51.

Malecki, E.J. and P. Oinas (eds) (1999), *Making Connections. Technological Learning and Regional Economic Change*, Aldershot: Ashgate.

Malmgren, H.B. (1961), 'Information, expectations and the theory of the firm', *Quarterly Journal of Economics*, **75**, 399–421.

Manning, S. and J. Sydow (2007), 'Transforming creative potential in project networks: how TV movies are produced under network-based control', *Critical Sociology*, **33**, 19–42.

Marshall, A. (1920), *Principles of Economics* (8th edn), London: Macmillan.

Marshall, A. (1927), *Industry and Trade: A Study of Industrial Technique and Business Organization; and Their Influences on the Conditions of Various Classes and Nations* (3rd edn), London: Macmillan.

Martins, E.C. and F. Terblanche (2003), 'Building organisational culture that stimulates creativity and innovation', *European Journal of Innovation Management*, **6**, 64–74.

Maskell, P. and M. Lorenzen (2004), 'The cluster as market organization', *Urban Studies*, **41**, 991–1009.

Maskell, P. and A. Malmberg (1999a), 'The competitiveness of firms and regions: "ubiquitification" and the importance of localized learning', *European Urban and Regional Studies*, **6**, 9–25.

Maskell, P. and A. Malmberg (1999b), 'Localized learning and industrial competitiveness', *Cambridge Journal of Economics*, **23**, 167–85.

Matthiessen, C.W. and Å.E. Andersson (1993), *Øresundsregionen – Kreativitet, Integration, Vækst*, København: Munksgaard.

May, R. (1959), 'The nature of creativity', in H.H. Anderson (ed.), *Creativity and Its Cultivation*, New York, NY: Harper & Row, pp. 55–68.

McWilliam, E.L. (2007), 'Is creativity teachable? Conceptualising the creativity/pedagogy relationship in higher education', in *Proceedings of the 30th HERDSA Annual Conference: Enhancing Higher Education, Theory and Scholarship*, Adelaide, available at http://eprints.qut.edu.au/ (accessed 10 March 2011).

Milgram, S. (1967), 'The small world', *Psychology Today*, **2**, 60–7.

Mommaas, H. (2004), 'Cultural clusters and the post-industrial city: towards the remapping of urban cultural policy', *Urban Studies*, **41**, 507–32.

Montgomery, J. (2005), 'Beware of "the creative class". Creativity and wealth creation revisited', *Local Economy*, **20**, 337–43.

Montuori, A. and R. Purser (1996), *Social Creativity: Prospects and Possibilities*, Vol. 1, Cresskill, NJ: Hampton Press.

Mumford, M.D. (2000), 'Managing creative people: strategies and tactics for innovation', *Human Resource Management Review*, **10**, 313–51.

Mumford, M.D., G.M. Scott, B. Gaddis and J.M. Strange (2002), 'Leading creative people: orchestrating expertise and relationships', *Leadership Quarterly*, **13**, 705–50.

Murdoch, J. (1995), 'Actor-networks and the evolution of economic forms: combining description and explanation in theories of regulation, flexible specialization, and networks', *Environment and Planning A*, **27**, 731–57.

Myerscough, J. (1988), *The Economic Importance of the Arts in Britain*, London: Policy Studies Institute.

Naroll, R., E.D. Benjamin, F.K. Fohl, M.J. Fried, R.D. Hildreth and J.M. Schaefer (1971), 'Creativity: A cross-historical pilot study', *Journal of Cross-Cultural Psychology*, **2**, 181–88.

Negus, K. and M. Pickering (2004), *Creativity, Communication and Cultural Value*, London: Sage.

Nelson, R.R. and S.G. Winter (1982), *An Evolutionary Theory of Economic Change*, Cambridge, MA: Harvard University Press.

Nonaka, I., R. Toyama and A. Nagata (2000), 'A firm as a knowledge-creating entity: a new perspective on the theory of the firm', *Industrial and Corporate Change*, **9**, 1–20.

Norton, R.D. (2004), 'From Paris to New York: creativity and face-to-face networks in twentieth-century capitals', in C. Karlsson, P. Flensburg, S.-Å. Hörte (eds), *Knowledge Spillovers and Knowledge Management*, Cheltenham, UK and Northampton, MA, USA: Edward Elgar Publishing, pp. 171–203.

O'Connor, J. (2007), *The Cultural and Creative Industries: A Review of the Literature*, London: Arts Council England.

Oinas, P. (1999), 'Activity-specificity in organizational learning: implications for analyzing the role of proximity', *GeoJournal*, **49**, 363–72.

Owen-Smith, J. and W.W. Powell (2002), 'Knowledge networks in the Boston biotechnology community', paper presented at the Conference on Science as an Institution and the Institutions of Science in Siena.

Patel, P. and K. Pavitt (1991), 'Large firms in the production of the world's technology: an important case of "Non-Globalisation"', *Journal of International Business Studies*, **22**, 1–21.

Peck, J. (2005), 'Struggling with the creative class', *International Journal of Urban and Regional Research*, **29**, 740–70.

Perkins, D. (1981), *The Mind's Best Work*, Cambridge, MA: Harvard University Press.

Perry-Smith, J.E. (2006), 'Social yet creative: the role of social relationships in facilitating individual creativity', *Academy of Management Journal*, **49**, 85–101.

Perry-Smith, J.E. and C.E. Shalley (2003), 'The social side of creativity: a static and dynamic social network perspective', *Academy of Management Review*, **28**, 89–106.

Porter, M.E. (1998), *The Competitive Advantage of Nations*, London: Collier Macmillan.

Powell, W.W. and S. Grodal (2005), 'Networks of innovators', in J. Fagerberg, D.C. Mowery and R.R. Nelson (eds), *The Oxford Handbook of Innovation*, Oxford: Oxford University Press, pp. 56–85.

Prahalad, C.K. (1993), 'The role of core competencies in the corporation', *Research Technology Management*, **36**, 40–7.

Pratt, A. (2004), 'The cultural economy, a call for spatialised "production of culture" perspectives', *International Journal of Cultural Studies*, **7**, 117–28.

Quantas, P. (2002), 'Implications of the division of knowledge for innovation in networks', in J. De la Mothe and A.N. Link (eds), *Networks, Alliances and Partnerships in the Innovation Process*, Boston, MA: Kluwer, pp. 135–63.

Rank, O. [1932] (1989), *Art and Artist: Creative Urge and Personality Development*, New York, NY: W.W. Norton.

Rasulzada, F. (2007), 'Organisation, creativity and psychological well-being', dissertation, Department of Psychology, University of Lund, Lund.

Rhodes, M. (1961), 'An analysis of creativity', *Phi Delta Kappa*, **42**, 305–10.

Rifkin, J. (2000), *The Age of Access: How the Shift from Ownership to Access is Transforming Modern Life*, London: Penguin.

Robinson, K. (2000), *Out of Our Minds. Learning to Be Creative*, Oxford: Capstone.

Sassen, S. (1995), 'On concentration and centrality in the global city', in P.L. Knox and P.J. Taylor (eds), *World Cities in a World System*, Cambridge: Cambridge University Press pp. 63–78.

Scherer, F.M. (2001), 'Servility, freedom and magnet cities in classical music composers' occupation and locational choices', *The Musical Quarterly*, **85**, 718–34.

Schilling, M.A. (2005), 'A "small-world" network model of cognitive insight', *Creativity Research Journal*, **17**, 131–54.

Schumpeter, J.A. (1934), *The Theory of Economic Development*, Cambridge, MA: Harvard University Press.

Scott, A.J. (1997), 'The cultural economy of cities', *International Journal of Urban & Regional Research*, **2**, 323–39.

Scott, A.J. (1998a), *Regions and the World Economy: The Coming Shaping of Global Production, Competition and Political Order*, Oxford: Oxford University Press.

Scott, A.J. (1998b), 'From Silicon Valley to Hollywood: Growth and development of the multimedia industry in California', in H.J. Braczyk, P. Cooke and M. Heidenreich (eds), *Regional Innovation Systems: The Role of Governances in a Globalised World*, London: UCL Press, pp. 136–62.

Scott, A.J. (2000), *The Cultural Economy of Cities*, London: Sage.

Scott, A.J. (2001), 'Capitalism, cities and the production of symbolic forms', *Transactions of the Institute of British Geographers*, **26**, 11–23.

Scott, A.J. (2004), 'Cultural products industries and urban economic development: prospects for growth and market contestation in global context', *Urban Affairs Review*, **39**, 461–90.

Scott, A.J. (2006), 'Entrepreneurship, innovation and industrial development: geography and creative field revisited', *Small Business Economics*, **26**, 1–24.

Siedel, S., M. Rosemann and J. Becker (2008), 'How does creativity impact business processes?', in *Proceedings of the 16th European Conference on Information Systems*, Galway, Ireland, available at http://eprints.qut. edu.au/ (accessed 10 March 2011).

Simon, H.A. (1985), 'What do we know about the creative process', in R.L. Kuhn (ed.), *Frontiers in Creative and Innovative Management*, Cambridge, MA: Ballinger, pp. 3–20.

Simon, H.A. (1991), 'Beyond rationality and organizational learning', *Organization Science*, **2**, 125–34.

Simonton, D.K. (1976), 'Ideological diversity and creativity: a re-evaluation of a hypothesis', *Social Behaviour and Personality*, **4**, 203–7.

Simonton, D.K. (1984), 'Artistic creativity and interpersonal relations across and within generations', *Journal of Personality and Social Psychology*, **46**, 1273–86.

Simonton, D.K. (2000), 'Creativity: cognitive persona, developmental and social aspects', *American Psychologist*, **55**, 151–8.

Smith, A. (1776), *An Inquiry into the Nature and Causes of the Wealth of Nations*, London: W. Strahan and T. Cadell, reprinted 1937, New York: Modern Library.

Sokoloff, K.L. (1988), 'Inventive activity in early industrial America: evidence from patent records, 1790–1846', *Journal of Economic History*, **48**, 813–50.

Sternberg, R.J. (1985), *Beyond IQ: A Triarchic Theory of Intelligence*, New York, NY: Cambridge University Press.

Sternberg, R.J. (2007), 'Making creativity the centrepiece of higher education', paper presented at the Creativity or Conformity? Building Cultures of Creativity in Higher Education Conference, University of Wales Institute, Cardiff, 8–10 January.

Sternberg, R.J. and T.I. Lubart (1999), 'The concept of creativity: prospects and paradigms', in R.J. Sternberg (ed.), *Handbook of Creativity*, Cambridge: Cambridge University Press, pp. 3–15.

Storper, M. (1997), *The Regional World: Territorial Development in a Global Economy*, New York, NY: The Guildford Press.

Storper, M. and A.J. Venables (2002), 'Buzz: the economic force of the city', paper presented at the DRUID Summer Conference on Industrial Dynamics of the Old and the New Economy – Who Is Embracing Whom? in Copenhagen, Denmark.

Suarez-Villa, L. (1996), 'Innovative capacity, infrastructure and public policy', in D.F. Batten and C. Karlsson (eds), *Infrastructure and the Complexity of Economic Development*, Berlin: Springer, pp. 251–69.

Tardif, T.Z. and R.J. Sternberg (1988), 'What do we know about creativity?', in R.J. Sternberg (ed.), *The Nature of Creativity: Contemporary Psychological Perspectives*, Cambridge, MA: Cambridge University Press, pp. 429–40.

Tepper, S.J. (2002), 'Creative assets and the changing economy', *Journal of Arts Management, Law and Society*, **32**, 159–68.

Throsby, D. (2000), *Economics and Culture*, Sydney: Allen & Unwin.

Törnqvist, G. (1983), 'Creativity and the renewal of regional life', in A. Buttimer (ed.), *Creativity and Context: A Seminar Report*, Lund: Gleerup, pp. 91–112.

Tracey, P., G.L. Clark and H. Lawton-Smith (2002), 'Cognition, learning and European regional growth: an agent-centred perspective on the "new" economy', paper presented at the Annual Meeting of the Association of American Geographers in Los Angeles, CA.

Uzzi, B. (1996), 'The sources and consequences of embeddedness for the economic performance of organizations: the network effect', *American Sociological Review*, **61**, 674–98.

Uzzi, B. (1997), 'Social structure and competition in interfirm networks: the paradox of embeddedness', *Administrative Science Quarterly*, **42**, 35–67.

Uzzi, B. and S. Dunlap (2005), 'How to build your network', *Harvard Business Review*, 1–9 December.

Uzzi, B. and J. Spiro (2005), 'Collaboration and creativity: the small world problem', *American Journal of Sociology*, **111**, 447–505.

Uzzi, B., L.A.N. Amaral and F. Reed-Tsochas (2007), 'Small-world networks and management science research: a review', *European Management Review*, **4**, 77–91.

Vatne, E. (2001), 'Local versus extra-local relations: the importance of ties to information and the institutional and territorial structure of technological systems', paper presented at the Annual Residential Conference of the IGU Commission on the Dynamics of Economic Spaces in Turin, Italy.

Vaubel, R. (2005), 'The role of competition in the rise of baroque and renaissance music', *Journal of Cultural Economics*, **29**, 277–97.

Vernon, R. (1960), *Anatomy of Metropolis*, Cambridge, MA: Harvard University Press.

Vernon, R. and E.M. Hoover (1959), *Anatomy of Metropolis*, Cambridge, MA: Harvard University Press.

Wallas, G. (1926), *Art of Thought*, New York, NY: Harcourt Brace and World.

Watts, D.J. (1999), *Small World. The Dynamics of Networks Between Order and Randomness*, Princeton, NJ: Princeton University Press.

Wenger, E. (1998), *Communities of Practice: Learning, Meaning and Identity*, Cambridge: Cambridge University Press.

While, A. (2003), 'Locating art worlds: London and the making of young British art', *Area*, **35**, 251–63.

Woodman, R.W., J.E. Sawyer and R.W. Griffin (1993), 'Toward a theory of organizational creativity', *Academy of Management Review*, **18**, 293–321.

PART 2

PEOPLE

6   The open city
Peter Jason Rentfrow

The study of cities has historically taken a broad perspective and focused on an assortment of macro-level variables, from density, diversity and traffic, to human capital, crime and unemployment. Without a doubt, such variables are crucial to understanding cities and identifying the factors that set them apart. But cities are not merely repositories of buildings, schools, streets, businesses, town halls or jails. Cities are places where people live – where people work and play – and as such, they are fundamental to human existence. Yet research on cities rarely considers their psychological characteristics. This is curious considering that American folklore and popular culture are filled with images of what people in certain regions are like. For example, we stereotype New Yorkers as assertive, tense and impatient, Californians as relaxed, a bit creative and superficial, and Texans as slow talking, friendly and enthusiastic about guns. Considering that such beliefs are consensually shared and widespread (Berry et al., 2000; Schneider, 2007), it would certainly seem sensible for city scholars to consider the potential value that a psychological perspective can add to our understanding of cities. Do cities have a psychological dimension?

Although psychologists generally regard place as a variable that has no major effect on people's thoughts, feelings or behaviours, recent research is beginning to suggest otherwise. There is growing evidence for inter- and intra-national differences on several psychological constructs, from personality traits and values, to emotional expression and helping behaviour. That research suggests that the psychological characteristics common in a region are associated with a variety of social, political and economic indicators. Thus, if we are to develop a thorough understanding of cities – why some cities thrive while others struggle – we need to integrate the study of cities with the psychology of human behaviour.

The overarching goal of this chapter is to make the case that psychology can add a new dimension for conceptualizing, understanding and measuring cities. To develop that case, I draw from theory and research in psychology to argue that creative cities possess a certain mix of personality traits that sets them apart from other cities. But before we begin exploring the personalities of cities, there are some important questions that need to be addressed. First, are there psychological differences across regions? We may have stereotypes about the psychological characteristics of people in certain places, but is there any evidence for such differences? Second, what are the mechanisms that underlie regional differences? For there to be regional differences in personality, it is important to have some ideas about how those differences might have come about. And finally, how can psychology inform our understanding of creative cities? There is growing interest in creative cities, and because creativity is a psychological construct, it is important to investigate whether traits associated with psychological creativity are common in creative cities. Thus, this chapter is a first attempt at informing researchers about the connections between place and psychology with the aim of initiating further research in this area.

ARE THERE PSYCHOLOGICAL DIFFERENCES ACROSS GEOGRAPHICAL REGIONS?

In a very broad sense, research in social and personality psychology is concerned with understanding how variables in the immediate social environment influence inter- and intrapersonal processes. As such, attention is often given to how the actions of individuals or groups of individuals influence the thoughts, feelings and behaviours of other people, with little attention given to the broader contexts (for example, urban or rural) in which those interactions occur. Such research is concerned with identifying general patterns in human social behaviour, yet it is conceivable that our personal reactions to social events can vary depending on whether we live in a safe place where most people know each other or in an unpredictable environment where strangers cannot be trusted. With that in mind, it is important to consider that some aspects of social behaviour may be shaped by the broad social environments in which we live.

Recently, researchers have begun to broaden their conceptualizations of social contexts to include national and regional cultures. A considerable amount of research in this area has focused on national and cultural differences in personality. This interest stems largely from the establishment of the 'Big Five' personality dimensions as a framework for understanding the structure of personality (Goldberg, 1990, 1992; Costa and McCrae, 1992; John et al., 2008). Factor analyses of tens of thousands of trait ratings made by millions of people provided evidence for the existence of five broad personality factors. These so-called Big Five factors – extraversion, agreeableness, conscientiousness, neuroticism and openness – provide a basic model for conceptualizing and measuring personality. Extraversion comprises traits such as sociability, talkativeness and optimism. Agreeableness is defined by traits such as friendliness, kindness and generosity. Conscientiousness is composed of traits such as reliability, organization and efficiency. Neuroticism comprises traits such as anxiety, stress and irritability. And openness is marked by traits including creativity, curiosity and imagination.

To investigate the nature of these personality factors, researchers have collected data from several countries around the world to determine whether the Big Five are universal (for example, McCrae, 2001; Allik and McCrae, 2004; Hofstede and McCrae, 2004; McCrae et al., 2005; McCrae and Terracciano, 2007; Schmitt et al., 2007). This research indicates that there are greater concentrations of certain personality traits in particular nations than in others. For example, North American and European nations tend to be high in extraversion whereas Eastern European and East Asian nations tend to be low in extraversion (McCrae et al., 2005). Research on national personality also indicates that the personality traits common in nations are related to geographic social indicators, such as national rates of cancer, life expectancy, substance abuse, obesity and GDP. For instance, national levels of extraversion are positively associated with GDP and self-expression and national levels of openness are positively related to GDP, egalitarian values and human rights (McCrae et al., 2005).

While most research concerned with place and personality has focused on national differences, there is growing evidence that personality traits also vary within nations (Krug and Kulhavy, 1973; Plaut et al, 2002; Rentfrow et al., 2008, 2009a; Rentfrow, 2010). For example, results from investigations of regional personality differences in the USA indicate that rates of neuroticism tend to be high in the northeast and southeast and low in

Table 6.1   *Rankings of top and bottom ten metropolitan regions on the Big Five*
personality factors

Top ten metropolitan regions				
Extraversion	Agreeableness	Conscientiousness	Neuroticism	Openness
Columbus	Memphis	Memphis	New York	San Francisco
Cincinnati	Cincinnati	Indianapolis	Louisville	Los Angeles
Pittsburgh	Virginia Beach	Birmingham	Hartford	Austin
Chicago	Raleigh	Jacksonville	Boston	New York
Cleveland	Orlando	St Louis	New Orleans	San Diego
Milwaukee	Kansas City	Atlanta	Providence	San Antonio
Nashville	St Louis	Raleigh	Pittsburgh	Nashville
Orlando	Nashville	Buffalo	Oklahoma City	Las Vegas
Charlotte	Minneapolis	Providence	Las Vegas	Tampa
Phoenix	Tampa	Tampa	Philadelphia	Denver

Bottom ten metropolitan regions				
Las Vegas	Tucson	Boston	Richmond	Detroit
Tucson	Boston	Columbus	Miami	Minneapolis
Washington, DC	Rochester	Las Vegas	Tampa	Cleveland
Boston	Denver	Los Angeles	Charlotte	Columbus
Seattle	Los Angeles	Hartford	Salt Lake City	Pittsburgh
Portland	San Francisco	San Francisco	Birmingham	Indianapolis
Sacramento	New Orleans	Milwaukee	San Diego	Kansas City
San Jose	Hartford	New York	Atlanta	St Louis
Hartford	Las Vegas	San Jose	Orlando	Memphis
San Francisco	New York	New Orleans	Jacksonville	Cincinnati

Note: Metropolitan regions with populations $\geq$ 1 million ($N = 52$).

the midwest and west. Openness tends to be high in the New England, mid-Atlantic and
Pacific regions and comparatively lower in Great Plain, midwest and southeast states.
There is some consistency across studies for rates of agreeableness, which tend to be high
in the southern regions and low in the northeast, and for extraversion, which tend to be
high in the northeast and low in the west. Conscientiousness shows the least degree of
consistency across studies, but the evidence suggests that it tends to be high in the mountain and west north central regions, and low in the Pacific and west south central regions.
Moreover, recent work by Rentfrow et al. (2008) indicates that state-level personality is
related to a variety of important social indicators. For example, state levels of neuroticism were positively related to rates of cancer and heart disease, and state levels of openness were positively related to patent production, gay population and the creative class.
Just as personality varies at the broad state level, so too might it vary across cities. Using
a subset of the personality data reported in Rentfrow et al. (2008), I examined the distribution of personality traits across metropolitan regions. Table 6.1 presents rankings
of the top and bottom ten metropolitan regions with populations of at least one million
residents for each of the Big Five personality dimensions. The results indicate that the

metropolitan areas high in extraversion tend to be in the midwest (Columbus, Cincinnati, Pittsburgh) and southeast (Nashville, Orlando, Charlotte), whereas most of the metropolitan areas low in extraversion are in the west (Las Vegas, Tuscon, Seattle, Portland, Sacramento, San Jose, San Francisco). The metropolitan regions with high concentrations of agreeable individuals tend to be the south (Memphis, Virginia Beach, Raleigh) and midwest (Cincinnati, St Louis, Minneapolis), whereas regions with low proportions of agreeable individuals tend to be in the northeast (Boston, Rochester, New York) and west (Tuscon, Los Angeles, San Francisco, Las Vegas). Conscientiousness appears to be high in metropolitan regions in the southeast (Memphis, Birmingham, Jacksonville, Atlanta, Raleigh, Tampa), and comparatively lower in regions in the northeast (Boston, Hartford, New York) and west (Las Vegas, Los Angeles, San Francisco, San Jose). Neuroticism appears to be high in metropolitan areas in the northeast and midwest (New York, Hartford, Boston, Providence, Pittsburgh, Philadelphia) and low in metropolitan areas in the southeast (Richmond, Miami, Tampa, Charlotte, Birmingham, Atlanta, Orlando, Jacksonville). Openness appears to be high in cosmopolitan metropolitan areas (San Francisco, Los Angeles, New York) and low in areas in the midwest (Detroit, Minneapolis, Cleveland, Columbus, Pittsburgh, Indianapolis, Cincinnati).

Taken together, these results suggest that there are national as well as regional differences in personality. This means that people in a given area tend to think about, perceive and relate to their environment in similar ways. To illustrate, consider regions high in the personality trait agreeableness. In such regions, a disproportionately large number of residents are friendly, warm and trusting of one another; these are places with social capital. In contrast, where agreeableness is low, neighbours are distant with each other and reluctant to help each other out; these are competitive environments where people are struggling to get ahead of each other. Given that there are regional personality differences, it is necessary to consider how these differences come about.

HOW DO GEOGRAPHICAL DIFFERENCES IN PERSONALITY COME ABOUT?

The causes underlying geographical variation in psychological traits are complex and there are certainly multiple processes involved. One hypothesis is that regional differences are a result of selective migration – that people move to places that satisfy and reinforce their basic needs. A second hypothesis is that regional differences stem from social influence – the traditions and values common in an area create social norms that affect behaviour. A third hypothesis is that regional differences are a result of ecological influence – that aspects of the physical environment affect how people interact as well as the types of activities in which they can engage.

Selective Migration

The notion that people seek out environments that satisfy their needs is consistent with a long tradition of research in demography and economics (for example, Rossi, 1955; Tiebout, 1956; Roback, 1982). Traditionally, research on migration has focused on economic concerns as the driving factor of whether or not people move. Work by Tiebout

(1956) suggests that when people choose a place to live, they evaluate them in terms of how well the place satisfies their needs and preferences. According to Rossi (1955), when families' needs for space and local amenities are no longer met, they are likely to move into houses that are close to the amenities they desire. In fact, several researchers have argued that amenities are critical in determining migration decisions (Landale and Guest, 1985; Roback, 1982; Clark and Hunter, 1992; Glaeser et al., 2001; Clark et al., 2002; Florida, 2002). For instance, Roback (1982) posits that the availability of amenities leads to a sufficient increase in quality of life that people are willing to accept lower salaries, higher taxes and increased housing expenses. In a project concerned with place preferences, Florida (2008) found that people who lived in suburban areas placed considerable importance on safety, schools, local economy and career opportunities. People living in rural areas placed importance on their relationships with family and friends, the local environment and the natural beauty of their surroundings. And city dwellers placed importance on cultural diversity, access to museums, restaurants and live music.

Given that there are individual differences in place preferences, it is conceivable that such preferences have a psychological component. After all, research in psychology has revealed links between personality and a variety of preferences (Rentfrow and Gosling, 2003; Gosling, 2008; Naumann et al., 2009; Rentfrow and McDonald, 2009; Rentfrow et al., 2011). It is conceivable that people who are creative, curious and open, for instance, may try to escape the parochial small town in favour of a bustling cosmopolitan city where their interests in diversity and desires for varied experiences can be easily satisfied. In fact, there is evidence that people high, as compared to low, in openness and extraversion are more likely to move away from their hometowns (Jokela, 2009), whereas people high in agreeableness are less likely to move from their home region compared to people who are less agreeable (Boneva et al., 1998). Furthermore, research indicates that people who live in areas where they can easily pursue their hobbies are higher on measures of psychological wellbeing compared to people who live further from desired amenities (Rowles and Watkins, 1993; Frey et al., 2000; Barcus, 2004).

Social Influence

Social influence also contributes to regional psychological differences. There is a considerable amount of research in social psychology on attitude change and emotional contagion indicating that individuals' attitudes and emotions are affected by the attitudes, emotions and behaviours of the people in their immediate social environments (Hatfield et al,. 1993; Huckfeldt and Sprague, 1995; Joiner and Katz, 1999). For example, a classic study by Putnam (1966) showed that individuals' political attitudes are significantly affected by the attitudes of their neighbours. More recently, work by Fowler and Christakis (2008) showed that proximity to happy people significantly affects individuals' levels of happiness.

Where people live can also be a major source of psychological stimulation. Florida (2008) found that places with 'symbolic amenities', such as nature reserves and cultural centres, provide residents with visual and creative stimulation, which can yield fulfilment and satisfaction. There is also evidence that the degree of openness and tolerance in a region is associated with residents' levels of wellbeing. Several studies indicate that in nations and states where importance is placed on self-expression, human rights and discrimination, there are higher levels of psychological and physical wellbeing (Inglehart and Oyserman, 2004; Florida, 2008; Kuppens et al., 2008; Rentfrow et al., 2009b). In other words, where cultural diversity and alternative lifestyles are tolerated – where individuals are open and accepting of people from different cultures – residents are free to be themselves and pursue their own interests, which, in turn, foster fulfilment and life satisfaction. Thus, aspects of the social environment influence people's sense of mastery, satisfaction and wellbeing.

Ecological Influence

There are also good reasons to think that aspects of the physical environment contribute to regional psychological differences. As the preceding paragraphs make clear, the physical environment is related to the types of amenities that are available. So people sort themselves into environments where they can easily pursue their hobbies, and this could contribute to regional psychological differences. Additionally, aspects of the physical environment might also directly affect the psychological characteristics and behaviours of residents. For example, living in a warm and sunny area near a beach is going to allow people to spend ample amounts of time outside, which makes it easy to socialize with others and come into contact with strangers. In contrast, in cold and wet environments, people spend more time indoors and therefore have fewer encounters with strangers.

Most of the evidence for ecological influence is indirect. For example, research suggests that limited exposure to sunlight in the winter leads to symptoms of depression (Kasper et al., 1989), that depression is high in areas with poor quality housing and where basic necessities such as hospitals and markets are far away (Cutrona et al., 2006), and that heat is associated with high rates of violence (Anderson, 1989). Thus, it is conceivable that certain aspects of the environment attract and influence the expression and prevalence of certain personality dispositions.

In summary, geographical differences in personality traits could arise as a result of people selectively sorting themselves into regions that suit their psychological needs and preferences. To the extent that people with similar needs and preferences settle in the same places, homogeneity of values, attitudes and patterns of behaviours should emerge in those places. And such homogeneity, in turn, establishes social norms that reinforce certain psychological and behavioural characteristics in the region. It appears as though the personalities of places are dynamic, responding to changes in the social, political, cultural and ecological environment. But is personality related to city-level social indicators? Are the personalities of cities related to indicators of economic growth, creativity or innovation? If psychology has anything to contribute to the study of cities, especially the study of creative cities, it is necessary to determine how the personalities of cities relate to relevant social and economic indicators.

HOW CAN PSYCHOLOGY INFORM OUR UNDERSTANDING OF CREATIVE CITIES?

So far, I have discussed research showing that there are national and regional differences in personality and offered explanations for how geographical personality differences might come about. But how can research on personality and place inform our understanding of cities, and in particular creative cities?

As modern economies shift from industrial to post-industrial knowledge economies, creative industries have helped spawn new technologies, services and products that power economic growth. Over the past decade, researchers in geography and urban studies have become increasingly interested in the associations between creativity, place and economic growth. For example, Florida (2002) amassed compelling evidence indicating that creative capital fuels regional economic growth. Regions with high concentrations of scientists, artists, academics, designers, architects and other opinion-makers rank highly on measures of human capital, economic productivity, social and cultural diversity and innovation. In other words, regions with large proportions of creative workers are places where people are curious, intellectual and tolerant of different cultures and alternative lifestyles. These are progressive areas where individuality and self-expression are encouraged and where people are free to be themselves.

Florida's (2002) creative capital theory implies that there are links between occupations and personality. It turns out that there is a vast literature concerned with personality and occupational performance, success and satisfaction. Holland (1996) develops a framework for conceptualizing and categorizing occupations that comprises six broad occupational types. Two of those occupational types overlap considerably with Florida's creative capital jobs: investigative and artistic. Investigative occupations include scientists, engineers and researchers; artistic jobs include artists, designers and entertainers. Results from several studies indicate that people who seek out and prefer these professions score high on measures of openness, and possess traits such as creativity, curiosity, imagination and tolerance for ambiguity (Holland, 1996; Barrick et al., 2003; Ozer and Benet-Martinez, 2006).

The work described above reveals convergence between creative capital, regional economic growth and personality. Regions with high concentrations of creative jobs, technological innovation, human capital and social diversity should be places with large proportions of people high in openness. To examine that idea, I examined the correlations between metro-level openness and sets of education, economic, social diversity and creativity indicators among large metropolitan regions with at least one million residents.

As can be seen in the first data column of Table 6.2, the average level of openness in metropolitan regions is associated with several of the social indicators. City-level openness is positively related to the proportion of residents with college and post-graduate degrees, high incomes, foreign-born residents, gays and lesbians, artists and bohemians, and high-tech firms. These findings are consistent with the idea that creative regions have high concentrations of individuals who possess psychological traits associated with openness.

However, it is important to note that openness is related to education (Costa et al., 1986). Although the direction of causality is not entirely clear, there are good reasons to believe that people high in openness are more likely to graduate from college and attend post-graduate school than people low in openness, as educational environments are intellectually stimulating and challenging. It is therefore possible that the correlations between metro-level openness reflect education more than psychological proclivities. To investigate that idea, I ran another set of correlations, this time controlling for

Table 6.2   Correlations between city-level openness and social indicators for large metropolitan regions

	Openness	
	Bivariate	Partial[a]
Education		
Percentage with BA	0.32*	
Percentage with post-graduate degree	0.23[t]	0.01
Economic		
GDP per capita	0.19	−0.03
Average income	0.34*	0.20
Diversity		
Domestic migrants	−0.26*	−0.23
International migrants	0.43**	0.39**
Gay Index	0.69**	0.65**
Creative Innovation		
Bohemian Index	0.27*	0.15
Milken Institute Tech-Pole Index	0.46**	0.36**
Patent production	0.12	−0.05

Note: Metropolitan regions with populations ≥ 1 million ($N = 52$); BA = Bachelor of Arts; GDP = Gross Domestic Product; [a]controlling for percentage of residents with a BA.
$t < 0.1$, * < 0.05, ** < 0.01.

the proportion of city residents with college degrees. As can be seen in the second data column of Table 6.2, some of the variance in city-level openness overlaps with education, as the magnitude of a few of the correlations dropped substantially. Specifically, the correlations between openness and the proportion of residents with post-graduate degrees, GDP per capita and patent production all dropped to zero, and the correlations with income and the Bohemian Index remained moderate in size, but dropped below the threshold for statistical significance. However, the links between openness and the proportion of high-tech firms, gays, lesbians and foreign-born all remained quite large in magnitude.

These findings indicate that the average level of openness in regions is strongly related to social diversity, innovation and creativity. It makes sense that openness is related to the proportion of gays, lesbians and foreign-born because openness is related to having an interest in culture and negatively related to measures of prejudice and discrimination (McCrae and Sutin, 2009). For example, Flynn (2005) found that people high in openness had more positive perceptions and made more favourable evaluations of black interviewees than did people low in openness. Furthermore, openness is related to political ideology, such that people high in openness tend to endorse liberal political views, vote for liberal political leaders and support progressive political agendas, such as gay marriage, socialized medicine and marijuana legalization (Jost et al., 2008). It therefore appears that openness and diversity co-vary because open-minded people are socially tolerant of alternative lifestyles and cultures, which makes such places desirable to members of minority groups, and are concerned with creating an environment where people are free to be themselves.

The relationship between regional openness and creative innovation is consistent with research in psychology. The jobs at the centre of innovation, such as design, engineering, science, painting, music, software development, writing and acting appeal to individuals who are curious, creative, intellectual, imaginative, inventive and resourceful. These professions are primarily concerned with exploring, developing and communicating new ideas, methods and products. Several studies have shown that people in investigative and artistic professions score high on measures of openness (Holland, 1996; Barrick et al., 2003; Ozer and Benet-Martinez, 2006). Furthermore, people high in openness are prone to generating new perspectives on old issues, are comfortable with and able to adapt to change and are adventurous. They also value aesthetics, education, science, as well as independence and non-conformity (McCrae, 1996). It therefore makes sense that places with high concentrations of highly open individuals are also places with disproportionately large numbers of high-tech workers, artists, musicians and designers.

There appears to be a psychological dimension to cities that contributes to their ethos and character. Creative cities are places with large concentrations of open-minded people who are progressive, flexible and tolerant. And it is these characteristics that make creative cities what they are. This psychological dimension goes deeper than the social and cultural explanations provided by regional economists. It is not only that people sort themselves into places where they can find work, but people seek out environments where they can pursue their personal as well as professional interests. And when large concentrations of people with similar interests and needs congregate in the same region, their psychological dispositions become expressed at the macro social, political and economic levels.

CONCLUSION

The goal of this chapter was to make the case for including a psychological perspective in the study of cities. I presented evidence for regional personality differences, suggested ways in which those differences may have emerged, and provided evidence indicating that creative cities are homes to large concentrations of people with specific personality traits. The connection between psychological openness and creative cities confirms what city scholars have inferred about residents of creative cities (Florida, 2002). And in doing so, it helps lay the foundation on which to bridge research on cities with psychology. Including a psychological perspective in the study of cities will no doubt inform our understanding of regional economic growth, creativity, diversity and innovation. Furthermore, as researchers and policy makers consider questions about how to increase growth and creative capital, psychological theory and research can provide insight into why people may be attracted to certain environments and what might be done to attract more creative people.

As Jane Jacobs (1961) cogently argued in *The Death and Life of Great American Cities*, cities are for people. Indeed, if we are to understand why some cities flourish while others struggle, and what makes some cities great, it is crucial that we pay attention to the people who live and work in them.

REFERENCES

Allik, J. and R.R. McCrae (2004), 'Toward a geography of personality traits: patterns of profiles across 36 cultures', *Journal of Cross-Cultural Psychology*, **35**, 13–28.

Anderson, C.A. (1989), 'Temperature and aggression: ubiquitous effects of heat on occurrence of human violence', *Psychological Bulletin*, **106**, 74–96.

Barcus, H.R. (2004), 'Rural in-migration: migrant motivations and residential consequences', *Regional Studies*, **38**, 643–58.

Barrick, M.R., M.K. Mount and R. Gupta (2003), 'Meta-analysis of the relationship between the Five Factor model of personality and Holland's occupational types', *Personnel Psychology*, **56**, 45–74.

Berry, D.S., G.M. Jones and S.A. Kuczaj (2000), 'Differing states of mind: regional affiliation, personality judgement, and self-view', *Basic and Applied Social Psychology*, **22**, 43–56.

Boneva, B.S., I.H. Frieze, A. Ferligoj, E. Jarošová, D. Pauknerová and A. Orgocka (1998), 'Achievement, power, and affiliation motives as clues to (e)migration desires: a four-countries comparison', *European Psychologist*, **3**, 247–54.

Clark, D.E. and W.J. Hunter (1992), 'The impact of economic opportunity, amenities and fiscal factors on age-specific migration rates', *Journal of Regional Science*, **32**, 349–65.

Clark, T.N., R. Lloyd, K.K. Wong and P. Jain (2002), 'Amenities drive urban growth', *Journal of Urban Affairs*, **24**, 493–515.

Costa, P.T. Jr and R.R. McCrae (1992), *Revised NEO Personality Inventory (NEO-PI-R) and NEO Five-Factor Inventory (NEO-FFI) Professional Manual*, Odessa, FL: Psychological Assessment Resources.

Costa, P.T., R.R. McCrae, A.B. Zonderman, H.E. Barbano, B. Lebowitz and D.M. Larson (1986), 'Cross-sectional studies of personality in a national sample: II. Stability in neuroticism, extraversion, and openness', *Psychology and Aging*, **1**, 144–9.

Cutrona, C.E., G. Wallace and K.A. Wesner (2006), 'Neighborhood characteristics and depression: an examination of stress processes', *Current Directions in Psychological Science*, **15**, 188–92.

Florida, R. (2002), *The Rise of the Creative Class: And How It's Transforming Work, Leisure, Community, and Everyday Life*, New York, NY: Basic Books.

Florida, R. (2008), *Who's Your City?: How the Creative Economy Is Making Where to Live the Most Important Decision of Your Life*, New York, NY: Basic Books.

Flynn, F.J. (2005), 'Having an open mind: the impact of openness to experience on interracial attitudes and impression formation', *Journal of Personality and Social Psychology*, **88**, 816–26.

Fowler, J.H. and N.A. Christakis (2008), 'Dynamic spread of happiness in a large social network: longitudinal analysis over 20 years in the Framingham Heart Study', *British Medical Journal*, **337**, a2338.

Frey, W.H., K.-L. Liaw and G. Lin (2000), 'State magnets for different elderly migrant types in the United States', *International Journal of Population Geography*, **6**, 21–44.

Glaeser, E.L., J. Kolko and A. Saiz (2001), 'Consumer city', *Journal of Economic Geography*, **1**, 27–50.

Goldberg, L.R. (1990), 'An alternative "description of personality": the Big-Five factor structure', *Journal of Personality and Social Psychology*, **59**, 1216–29.

Goldberg, L.R. (1992), 'The development of markers for the Big-Five factor structure', *Psychological Assessment*, **4**, 26–42.

Gosling, S.D. (2008), *Snoop: What Your Stuff Says About You*, New York, NY: Basic Books.

Hatfield, E., J.T. Cacioppo and R.L. Rapson (1993), 'Emotional contagion', *Current Directions in Psychological Science*, **2**, 96–9.

Hofstede, G. and R.R. McCrae (2004), 'Personality and culture revisited: linking traits and dimensions of culture', *Cross-Cultural Research*, **38**, 52–88.

Holland, J.L. (1996), 'Exploring careers with a typology: what we have learned and some new directions', *American Psychologist*, **51**, 397–406.

Huckfeldt, R. and J. Sprague (1995), *Citizens, Politics, and Social Communication: Information and Influence in an Election Campaign*, New York, NY: Cambridge University Press.

Inglehart, R. and D. Oyserman (2004), 'Individualism, autonomy, and self-expression', in H. Vinken, J. Soeters and P. Ester (eds), *Comparing Cultures: Dimensions of Culture in a Comparative Perspective*, Leiden, Netherlands: Brill, pp. 77–96.

Jacobs, J. (1961), *The Death and Life of Great American Cities*, New York, NY: Random House.

John, O.P., L.P. Naumann and C.J. Soto (2008), 'Paradigm shift to the integrative Big Five trait taxonomy: history, measurement, and conceptual issues', in O.P. John, R.W. Robins and L.A. Pervin (eds), *Handbook of Personality: Theory and Research* (3rd edn.), New York, NY: Guilford, pp. 114–58.

Joiner, T.E. Jr and J. Katz (1999), 'Contagion of depressive symptoms and mood: meta-analytic review and explanations from cognitive, behavioral, and interpersonal viewpoints', *Clinical Psychology: Science & Practice*, **6**, 149–64.

Jokela, M. (2009), 'Personality predicts migration within and between U.S. states', *Journal of Research in Personality*, **43**, 79–83.

Jost, J.T., B.A. Nosek and S.D. Gosling (2008), 'Ideology: its resurgence in social, personality, and political psychology', *Perspectives on Psychological Science,* **3**, 126–36.

Kasper, S., T.A. Wehr, J.J. Bartko, P.A. Gaist and N.E. Rosenthal (1989), 'Epidemiological findings of seasonal changes in mood and behavior: a telephone survey of Montgomery County, Maryland', *Archives of General Psychiatry,* **46**, 832–3.

Krug, S.E. and R.W. Kulhavy (1973), 'Personality differences across regions of the United States', *Journal of Social Psychology*, **91**, 73–9.

Kuppens, P., A. Realo and E. Diener (2008), 'The role of positive and negative emotions in life satisfaction judgment across nations', *Journal of Personality and Social Psychology*, **95**, 66–75.

Landale, N.S. and A.M. Guest (1985), 'Constraints, satisfaction, and residential mobility: Speare's model reconsidered', *Demography*, **22**, 199–222.

McCrae, R.R. (1996), 'Social consequences of experiential openness', *Psychological Bulletin,* **120**, 323–37.

McCrae, R.R. (2001), 'Trait psychology and culture: exploring intercultural comparisons', *Journal of Personality*, **69**, 819–46.

McCrae, R.R. and A.R. Sutin (2009), 'Openness to experience', in M. Leary and R.H. Hoyle (eds), *Handbook of Individual Differences in Social Behavior*, New York, NY: Guilford, pp. 257–73.

McCrae, R.R. and A. Terracciano (2007), 'The Five-Factor Model and its correlates in individuals and cultures', in F.J.R. van de Vijver, D.A. van Hemert and Y. Poortinga (eds), *Individuals and Cultures in Multilevel Analysis*, Mahwah, NJ: Erlbaum, pp. 247–81.

McCrae, R.R., A. Terracciano and 79 Members of the Personality Profiles of Cultures Project (2005), 'Personality profiles of cultures: aggregate personality traits', *Journal of Personality and Social Psychology*, **89**, 407–25.

Naumann, L.P., S. Vazire, P.J. Rentfrow and S.D. Gosling (2009), 'Personality judgments based on physical appearance', *Personality and Social Psychology Bulletin*, **35**, 1661–71.

Ozer, D.J. and V. Benet-Martínez (2006), 'Personality and the prediction of consequential outcomes', *Annual Review of Psychology*, **57**, 8.1–8.21.

Plaut, V.C., H.R. Markus and M.E. Lachman (2002), 'Place matters: consensual features and regional variation in American well-being and self', *Journal of Personality and Social Psychology*, **83**, 160–84.

Putnam, R.D. (1966), 'Political attitudes and the local community', *American Political Science Review*, **60**, 640–54.

Rentfrow, P.J. (2010), 'Statewide differences in personality: toward a psychological geography of the United States', *American Psychologist*, **65**, 548–58.

Rentfrow, P.J. and S.D. Gosling (2003), 'The do-re-mi's of everyday life: the structure and personality correlates of music preferences', *Journal of Personality and Social Psychology*, **84**, 1236–56.

Rentfrow, P.J. and J.A. McDonald (2009), 'Music preferences and personality', in P.N. Juslin and J. Sloboda (eds), *Handbook of Music and Emotion*, Oxford: Oxford University Press, pp. 669–95.

Rentfrow, P.J., S.D. Gosling and J. Potter (2008), 'A theory of the emergence, persistence, and expression of regional variation in basic traits', *Perspectives on Psychological Science*, **3**, 339–69.

Rentfrow, P.J., J.T. Jost, S.D. Gosling and J. Potter (2009a), 'Statewide differences in personality predict voting patterns in 1996–2004 U.S. Presidential Elections', in J.T. Jost, A.C. Kay and H. Thorisdottir (eds), *Social and Psychological Bases of Ideology and System Justification*, Oxford: Oxford University Press, pp. 314–47.

Rentfrow, P.J., C. Mellander and R. Florida (2009b), 'Happy states of America: A state-level analysis of psychological, economic, and social well-being', *Journal of Research in Personality*, **43**, 1073–82.

Rentfrow, P.J., L.R. Goldberg and R. Zilca (2011), 'Listening, watching, and reading: the structure and correlates of entertainment preferences', *Journal of Personality*, **79**, 223–57.

Roback, J. (1982), 'Wages, rents, and the quality of life', *Journal of Political Economy*, **90**, 1257–78.

Rossi, P. (1955), *Why Families Move*, New York, NY: The Free Press.

Rowles, G.D. and J.F. Watkins (1993), 'Elderly migration and development in small communities', *Growth and Change*, **24**, 509–38.

Schmitt, D.P., J.A. Allik, R.R. McCrae and V. Benet-Martínez (2007), 'The geographic distribution of Big Five personality traits: patterns and profiles of human self-description across 56 nations', *Journal of Cross-Cultural Psychology*, **38**, 173–212.

Schneider, A. (2007), 'Politically correct stereotyping: the case of Texans', *International Journal of Contemporary Sociology*, **44**, 84–101.

Tiebout, C.M. (1956), 'A pure theory of local expenditures', *Journal of Political Economy*, **64**, 416–24.

7 The value of creativity
Todd M. Gabe

Some people are paid to work according to a set plan, while others earn a living from their creative ideas. Economists have a pretty good handle on the factors that influence the wages and salaries of those who 'work for a living'. It's all about productivity. Individuals who can produce a greater abundance of manufactured goods per hour or deliver services at a quicker pace typically earn more money than those who are less productive with their time. For this reason, plant-level investments in physical capital (for example, equipment and machinery that help automate routine and repetitive tasks) and information technology (for example, computers and digital networks that facilitate the management and transmission of information) typically enhance employee earnings. In addition, individual-level investments in human capital – actions like obtaining a college degree or learning a new skill – typically provide a productivity boost that is rewarded in the labour market.

But what about creativity? Does the act of creative thinking result in higher wages? Unlike the deliberate and often scripted job-related tasks of producing a manufactured good, selling a product or providing a service, the less tangible and more spontaneous process of creative thinking does not always directly result in 'stuff' that can be priced easily in a market.[1] Without prices, it is difficult to determine productivity and, thus, tricky to figure out how much money someone should be paid. Looking at the numbers, we can see that creative thinking appears to be well compensated in the labour market, as evidenced by the high wages earned by members of Richard Florida's so-called 'creative class'. As shown in Table 7.1, members of the creative class earn more than twice as much per year than members of the service class, the largest occupational category used by Florida (2002), and over US\$20 000 more per year than members of the working class. These figures certainly suggest that creative thinking provides a greater monetary reward than other types of job-related activities.

However, before we can conclude that creative thinking is responsible for the high earnings of those in the creative class, we need to rule out the possibility that this wage premium is not merely a reflection of the high educational demands of creative occupations. Edward Glaeser (2004), in a review of Florida's book *The Rise of the Creative Class*, presents the results from several basic regressions that attempt to isolate the effects of high creativity on regional population growth separate from the influence of human capital, represented by the share of the metropolitan area population with a four-year college degree. Glaeser finds that the college attainment variable generally has a positive and statistically significant effect on population growth, but that the share of the regional population in Florida's 'super-creative core' and related measures of creativity (for example, the Gay Index or the Bohemian Index) do not have a positive and significant effect on growth 'over and above the effect of human capital'. In a similar vein, it is possible that the high wages of those in the creative class could be associated with the steep educational requirements of many creative occupations

Table 7.1   Wages and salaries by broad occupational category, 1999

Category	Total workers	Average hourly wage($)	Average annual salary($)
Creative class	38 278 110	23.44	48 752
Super-creative core	14 932 420	20.54	42 752
Working class	33 238 810	13.36	27 799
Service class	55 293 720	10.61	22 059
Agriculture	463 360	8.65	18 000
Total US workforce	127 274 000	15.18	31 571

Source: Florida (2002, Table 4.1).

(such as 'computer and mathematical occupations' or 'life, physical, and social science occupations').[2]

The purpose of this study is to investigate the effects of creative thinking on the annual earnings of US workers. To do this, we use a wage regression model that allows us to isolate the returns to creative thinking as distinct from the well-established college wage premium.[3] A secondary set of goals is to determine how the returns to creative thinking are influenced by what a person makes and where he or she lives. More concretely, the 'what a person makes' is represented by a worker's industrial classification. Thus, I am interested in how the percentage of creative workers in an industry affects an individual's own return to creativity. A closely related question is how the creative thinking wage premium is related to the percentage of creative workers in a US metropolitan area ('where a person lives'). Previous studies (Rauch, 1993; Acemoglu and Angrist, 2000; Moretti, 2004) have looked at similar questions related to the externalities associated with human capital (such as receipt of a college degree) and generally find that 'an individual's education not only boosts his or her productivity, but also that of others' (Kolesnikova, 2010, p.12). Here, we look at whether the presence of other creative workers – either down the hall working for the same company, or across the street involved in another creative venture – affects the returns to creative thinking.

CREATIVE OCCUPATIONS, INDUSTRIES AND METROPOLITAN AREAS

In recent years, there has been growing interest in occupation-based approaches to urban and regional economic development (Feser, 2003; Markusen, 2004; Florida et al., 2008; Bacolod, et al., 2009a, 2009b; Gabe, 2009; Scott, 2009; Abel and Gabe, 2010). The basic idea is that we can use a person's occupation to determine the type of skills that he or she possesses. This approach has been used, among other applications, to look at differences in the skills composition across the urban hierarchy (Bacolod et al., 2009a; Scott, 2009) as well as the effects of knowledge on individual earnings and regional productivity (Gabe, 2009; Abel and Gabe, 2010). Florida's original characterization of the creative class has a very strong occupational orientation. In *The Rise of the Creative Class*, he assigned jobs within broad occupational categories into the classes shown in Table 7.1.

A. How <u>important</u> is THINKING CREATIVELY to the performance of *your current job*?

* If you marked Not Important, skip LEVEL below and go on to the next activity.

B. What <u>level</u> of THINKING CREATIVELY is needed to perform *your current job*?

Figure 7.1   Sample question from the O*NET survey

For instance, the super-creative core is made up of computer and mathematical occupations; architecture and engineering occupations; life, physical and social science occupations; education, training and library occupations; and arts, design, entertainment, sports and media occupations.

It this analysis, we take a slightly different tack to identifying activities that require high levels of creative thinking, but one that is related to occupations nonetheless. Following McGranahan and Wojan (2007) and Gabe et al., (2007), we use information from the US Department of Labor's Occupational Information Network (O*NET) to determine the importance (and level) of creative thinking required in a job.[4] This information is based on a survey question (Figure 7.1), posed to workers across a wide range of occupations, that asks the following question: 'How important is thinking creatively to the performance of your current job?' The survey prompts the respondent to rate the importance of creative thinking on a scale of 1 to 5, and then – if the respondent believes that creative thinking is at least 'somewhat important' (a rating of 2.0 or higher) to their job – they are asked to answer the question. 'What level of thinking creatively is needed to perform your current job?' For the follow-up, respondents are instructed to rate the level of creative thinking on a scale of 1 to 7, where 1 is similar to 'change the spacing on a printed report' and 6 is equivalent to 'create new computer software'.

Similar to the approach taken by Edward Feser (2003), who used O*NET data to group jobs into a set of knowledge-based occupational clusters, we calculated a creative thinking score that is the product of the importance and level of this occupational activity. With this information, we then used an individual's occupation to match a person to the amount of creativity required in his or her job. For this study, the individual-level data for US workers are from the 1 per cent sample of the 2008 US Census American Community Survey (Ruggles et al., 2009). After removing individuals from the sample who did not report an occupation, we arrived at a data set of 1.5 million people. From

Table 7.2   Twenty most creative US occupations, ranked by creativity index

Occupation	Creativity index
Astronomers and physicists	1.00
Actors	0.95
Writers and authors	0.95
Artists and related workers	0.89
Architects	0.84
Network systems and data communications analysts	0.83
Dancers and choreographers	0.81
Financial examiners	0.80
Public relations specialists	0.80
Clergy	0.79
Operations research analysts	0.77
Post-secondary teachers	0.77
Hairdressers, hairstylists and cosmetologists	0.77
Miscellaneous engineers	0.77
Miscellaneous social scientists	0.76
News analysts, reporters and correspondents	0.76
Database administrators	0.74
Producers and directors	0.74
Marine engineers and naval architects	0.73
Designers	0.72

Note: Occupational categories, which are shortened in some cases for brevity, are from the US Census Bureau. Information on occupational creativity is from the US Department of Labor, Occupational Information Network (O*NET).

here, we calculated an average and standard deviation of the creativity scores, and identified as 'high creativity' those jobs with a score that is at least one standard deviation above the mean.[5]

Table 7.2 shows the 20 most creative occupations, based on the O*NET information on the level and importance of thinking creatively. For ease of interpretation, we do not show the 'raw' creative thinking scores or a 'standardized' version that is based on the number of standard deviations above the mean, which we used to identify high-creativity occupations. Instead, we report values of an index that transform the creative thinking scores into a scale that ranges from zero to one. The scale is interpreted so that, for example, actors and clergy have job-related creative thinking activities that are 95 per cent and 79 per cent, respectively, as high as astronomers and physicists, the occupational category with the highest creative thinking score. Similar to the occupations frequently cited by Richard Florida as highly creative, the list presented in Table 7.2 includes several artistic-related jobs (for example, actors, writers and authors, dancers and choreographers), as well as 'techie' and computer-based occupations such as network systems and data communication analysts (miscellaneous), engineers and database administrators.

Table 7.3 presents a summary of the percentage of workers in high-creativity occupations by major Standard Occupational Classification (SOC), as well as information on

Table 7.3   High-creativity jobs by major occupational category, United States

Occupational category	% in high-creativity jobs	% with 4-year college degree
Arts, design, entertainment, sports and media	86.5	53.3
Education, training and library	85.9	74.7
Computer and mathematical	71.8	63.6
Legal	64.0	76.5
Architecture and engineering	61.5	61.4
Life, physical and social science	43.1	77.4
Management	33.8	50.6
Personal care and service	23.2	13.2
Community and social services	20.3	69.3
Business and financial operations	10.6	60.3
Sales and related	10.4	25.2
Installation, maintenance and repair	5.2	6.9
Healthcare practitioners and technical	4.6	53.7
Healthcare support	3.9	9.6
Food preparation and serving-related	3.4	6.5
Production	2.7	7.0
Protective service	0.7	20.2
Construction and extraction	0.3	6.0
Office and administrative support	0.1	16.6
Building, grounds cleaning and maintenance	0.0	5.6
Farming, fishing and forestry	0.0	6.1
Transportation and material moving	0.0	6.8

the percentage of those with at least a four-year college degree. These figures are based on individual-level data from the 1 per cent sample of the 2008 American Community Survey (Ruggles et al., 2009).[6] The top three major occupational categories, in terms of the percentage of employment in high-creativity jobs, are arts, design, entertainment, sports and media occupations; education and training occupations; and computer and mathematical occupations. These broad occupational categories all figure prominently in Florida's creative class; in fact, they are part of the super-creative core. Beyond these three examples, we see that the other broad occupational categories with the largest percentages of high-creativity workers (legal occupations; architecture and engineering occupations; life, physical and social science occupations) are included in Florida's creative class.

At the top end of the scale, our characterization of high-creativity jobs is generally similar to the broad occupation definition used by Florida (2002). All six of the occupational categories mentioned above as highly creative are included in Florida's creative class and five of them are in the super-creative core. Once we get beyond these broad occupational categories that are counted – both in our approach and Florida's definition – as highly creative, the two characterizations of creativity tend to diverge. Richard Florida counts management occupations; business and financial operations occupations; and healthcare practitioners among the ranks of creative professionals

– these groups are in the broadly defined creative class but outside the more restrictive super-creative core – whereas these categories do not rate highly (especially business and financial operations occupations; and healthcare practitioners and technical occupations) based on our measure of the percentage of jobs in high-creativity occupations.

Table 7.3 provides some evidence that diminishes the concerns raised by Glaeser (2004) and Markusen (2006) about the strong connection between creativity and human capital (such as the receipt of a college degree). Although it is the case that several of the broad occupational categories with the largest percentages of high-creativity jobs (for example, computer and mathematical occupations) are also characterized by steep educational requirements, the category of 'arts, design, entertainment, sport and media occupations' – which has the highest share of creative workers – is the ninth-ranked occupational group in terms of the percentage of workers with at least a four-year college degree. In addition, the occupational categories of business and financial operations occupations; community and social services occupations; healthcare practitioners and technical occupations; and management occupations have over one-half of their workers with at least a four-year college degree, but yet they have relatively low percentages of workers in high-creativity occupations.

Individual-level data from the 2008 American Community Survey suggest that 67.4 per cent of the workers in high-creativity occupations have a four-year college degree, whereas 22.8 per cent of those in non-high-creativity occupations have this amount of formal education.[7] Looking at it another way, we find that 40.2 per cent of individuals with a four-year college degree have a high-creativity occupation, while only 8.8 per cent of those without a college degree work in a job that requires high amounts of creative thinking. These figures suggest a weaker link between creativity and human capital than the estimates reported by Charlotta Mellander (2009), which are based on Florida's definition of the creative class. Mellander found that 88 per cent of the Swedish workers with a college degree had a creative occupation. Our results suggest that those with a college education are more likely than those without a degree to report a high-creativity occupation, but the evidence does not indicate that a four-year college degree and creative occupations always go hand in hand.[8]

After identifying the occupations that require the highest amounts of creative thinking, it is a relatively straightforward exercise to determine the most creative US industries and metropolitan areas. We returned to those occupations with creative thinking scores that are at least one standard deviation above the mean (the occupations shown in Table 7.2 as well as other high-creativity jobs outside the 'Top 20') and used individual-level US Census data from the 2008 American Community Survey to match people and their corresponding occupations to industries and places. This is the same general approach used by Currid and Stolarick (2010) in their study of the industries and occupations that make up the IT sector in Los Angeles.

Table 7.4 presents a list of the 20 most creative US industries, based on the percentage of employment in high-creativity occupations. It shows, for example, that almost 80 per cent of the individuals working in the beauty salons 'industry' are in high-creativity jobs. This ranking, however, is slightly different from the list we would have come up with using a constructed creativity index for each sector.[9] For example, three audio/video-related sectors (radio and television broadcasting and cable; motion pictures and

Table 7.4   Twenty most creative US industries, ranked by percentage of employment in high-creativity occupations

Industry	% high creativity in industry
Beauty salons	79.2
Specialized design services	76.2
Other schools, instruction and educational services	67.8
Elementary and secondary schools	63.3
Computer systems design and related services	59.7
Business, technical and trade schools and training	59.3
Independent artists, performing arts and spectator sports	57.9
Advertising and related services	53.9
Colleges, including junior colleges and universities	52.7
Software publishing	52.1
Architectural, engineering and related services	52.1
Publishing, except newspapers and software	52.0
Other information services	50.5
Florists	50.2
Offices of other health practitioners	49.7
Other professional, scientific and technical services	49.5
Religious organizations	48.3
Newspaper publishers	47.5
Electronic and precision equipment repair and maintenance	46.9
Legal services	46.3

Note: Industrial categories, which are shortened in some cases for brevity, are from the US Census Bureau. Percentages in the table are found by matching occupations to industries using individuals from the 1 per cent sample of the US Census 2008 American Community Survey (Ruggles et al., 2009).

video industries; and sound recording industries) are characterized by large creativity index values, but they are not counted among the most creative industries in terms of the percentage of workers in high-creativity jobs.

We can best think of Table 7.4 as a list of the industries with the largest concentrations of high-creativity workers. In the case of beauty salons, this likely means that about 80 per cent of the employees are hairdressers (or hairstylists or cosmetologists), which require high creativity. The other jobs sometimes found in beauty salons (for example, receptionists) are not in high-creativity occupations. As another example, we see that almost one-half of the workers in religious organizations require high creativity. This includes clergy as well as musicians, of which one-third in the USA are employed by religious organizations (Markusen and Schrock, 2006).[10]

Table 7.5 presents a list of the 20 most creative US metropolitan areas, also ranked in order of the percentage of employment in high-creativity occupations. Here, we see that the metropolitan areas with the highest concentrations of creative thinkers include places known for high technology (San Jose, Boston, Raleigh, Austin), the arts (Santa Fe) and several 'college towns' (Bloomington, Indiana; Auburn, Alabama; Iowa City, Iowa; and Gainesville, Florida). No surprises here . . . many of these metropolitan areas have been noted by Florida (2002) as places of high creativity. Looking at the top of the

Table 7.5   Twenty most creative US metropolitan areas, ranked by percentage of employment in high-creativity occupations

Metropolitan area	% high creativity in metropolitan area
Stamford, CT	32.7
San Jose, CA	30.6
Washington, DC/MD/VA	29.4
Danbury, CT	27.8
Gainesville, FL	27.0
Charlottesville, VA	26.8
Bloomington, IN	26.8
Auburn-Opekika, AL	26.5
Boston, MA-NH	26.5
Trenton, NJ	26.5
San Francisco-Oakland-Vallejo, CA	25.5
Raleigh-Durham, NC	25.4
Yolo, CA	25.3
Austin, TX	25.0
Santa Fe, NM	24.9
Santa Cruz, CA	24.9
Iowa City, IA	24.8
Seattle-Everett, WA	24.8
Huntsville, AL	24.8
Ann Arbor, MI	24.0

Note: Percentages in the table are found by matching occupations to metropolitan areas using individuals from the 1 per cent sample of the US Census 2008 American Community Survey (Ruggles et al., 2009).

list, we see that almost one-third of the workers in Stamford and San Jose are employed in high-creativity occupations.

EFFECTS OF CREATIVE THINKING ON EARNINGS

We use a wage regression model, shown below as equation (7.1), to estimate the effects of creative thinking on earnings.

$$\ln Earnings = \beta_0 + \beta_1 \, High \, Creativity + \beta_2 \, College \, Degree + \beta_3 \, Age + \beta_4 \, Age^2$$
$$+ \beta_5 \, Male + \beta_6 \, White + \beta_7 \, Married \tag{7.1}$$

This general approach has been used widely, with various modifications, to examine the monetary returns to a college degree (Mincer, 1974; Willis, 1986). Most relevant to our analysis, previous studies have used wage regression models to examine the returns to computer use and a variety of skills, knowledge and other job characteristics (Lucas, 1977; Krueger, 1993; DiNardo and Pischke, 1997; Dickerson and Green, 2004; Ingram and Neumann, 2006; Gabe, 2009). Lucas (1977) characterizes this framework as a 'hedonic wage equation', although it accounts for variables that describe people

Table 7.6   Summary statistics (n = 937 707)

Variable	Definition	Mean	Standard deviation
Income	Total income earned from wages or an individual's own business or farm, 2007	57 676	59 219
High Creativity	= 1 if individual works in an occupation that requires a high level of creative thinking, 0 otherwise	0.197	
College Degree	= 1 if individual's highest level of educational attainment is a bachelor's degree or higher; 0 otherwise	0.345	
Age	Individual's age in years	42.9	11.4
Male	= 1 if the individual is a male; 0 otherwise	0.577	
White	= 1 if individual reported a race of 'white', regardless of additional race(s) reported; 0 otherwise	0.816	
Married	= 1 if individual is married; 0 otherwise	0.642	

Note: Information is from the 1 per cent individual-level sample of the US Census 2008 American Community Survey (Ruggles et al., 2009).

(such as age) as well as their jobs (such as the amount of creative thinking required in a position).

In our analysis, we examine the annual earnings of a large sample of US workers (see Table 7.6 for summary statistics of the variables used in the regressions). Since the dependent variable is a measure of annual income – and not an hourly wage – the sample is restricted to full-time workers, defined as those who worked 36 or more hours per week for at least 50 weeks of the year. In addition, the analysis focuses on the 'working-age' population, that is, the population between the ages of 18 and 64. For these reasons, the empirical results cannot be generalized to the general US population or even those who are employed (full and part time).

Creativity is represented in the regression model by a dummy variable (*High Creativity*) that equals one if the individual is employed in an occupation that requires a high amount of creative thinking (a creativity score that is at least one standard deviation above the mean calculated for all US workers), and zero otherwise. As an important control variable, human capital enters into the analysis as a dummy variable that equals one if an individual has a four-year college degree (or more formal education), and zero otherwise. The regression model also includes an individual's age (and age-squared), which is commonly used to represent a worker's potential experience. The effects of the other demographic characteristics (*Male, White* and *Married*) on wages have been studied extensively in the literature (Price and Mills, 1985; Krumm, 1987; Fortin and Lemieux, 1998: Antonovics and Town, 2004).[11]

Table 7.7 presents regression results on the effects of creative thinking on the annual earnings of US full-time workers. Focusing on the first column of results, we see that, other things being equal, being heavily involved in creative thinking on the job has a positive and statistically significant effect on earnings. More specifically, working in a

Table 7.7   OLS regression results – effects of creative thinking on income of US full-time workers, 2007

Variable	Estimated coefficient		
	(*t*-statistic in parentheses)		
Constant	8.394*	8.409*	8.339*
High Creativity	(990.5)	(995.8)	(850.6)
	0.1618*	0.3524*	−0.4477*
	(94.81)	(124.0)	(−51.53)
(High Creativity) x (% in industry with High Creativity)		−0.5356* (−83.74)	
(High Creativity) x (% in metropolitan area with High Creativity)			3.028* (72.34)
College Degree	0.5218*	0.5352*	0.5146*
	(364.5)	(372.9)	(318.8)
Age	0.0754*	0.0748*	0.0786*
	(180.3)	(179.3)	(161.5)
Age C-squared	−0.0008*	−0.0008*	−0.0008*
	(−155.6)	(−154.7)	(−138.4)
Male	0.2814*	0.2730*	0.2608*
	(218.1)	(211.7)	(174.6)
White	0.1266*	0.1279*	0.1631*
	(76.98)	(78.05)	(91.09)
Married	0.1213*	0.1219*	0.1323*
	(87.09)	(87.85)	(82.70)
R-squared	0.2784	0.2837	0.3008
Number of observations	937707	937707	697481

Note: * indicates statistical significance at the 1 per cent level.

high-creativity occupation enhances earnings by about 16 per cent. This creativity wage premium is above and beyond the return to a college degree, which is estimated to bring about a 50 per cent boost to annual earnings.[12] Other findings shown in the left-hand column of results suggest that earnings increase with age (although they reach a peak and decline at 49 years old), and that gender, race and marital status affect the annual earnings of US full-time workers.

The middle and right-hand columns of Table 7.7 present results that are related to how the creative thinking wage premium is influenced by the percentage of high-creativity workers in an industry and metropolitan area, respectively. Looking at the centre column of results, we see a negative relationship between the return to high creativity and the percentage of workers in an industry who are involved in creative thinking. This suggests that a creative worker, who is isolated from people involved in similar activities on the job, tends to earn a more lucrative wage premium as compared to someone in a sector that abounds with others in high-creativity jobs. On the other hand, as shown in the right-hand column of results, we see that the high-creativity wage premium increases with the percentage of creative workers in a metropolitan area.[13] This suggests that a creative worker, who is surrounded by other similar thinkers in a geographic cluster of high creativity, receives a more lucrative wage premium than someone living in a creative 'wasteland'.

These regressions provide some interesting initial findings about how creative workers benefit from working and living around their peers. The well-known study by Glaeser et al. (1992), which examined the growth of industries in cities, may shed some light on these results. They found that industry specialization (a high geographic concentration of people in the same sector) has a negative effect on industry growth, whereas a high diversity of industries in a metropolitan area tends to enhance employment growth. Here – although we do not yet account for the types (that is, diversity) of creative workers in metropolitan areas – we find a similar pattern in that the higher productivity (as measured by individual wages) associated with creative thinking tends to increase when surrounded by a large group of creative workers in a metropolitan area. However, earnings are not enhanced (in fact, they fall) when surrounded by a large group of creative individuals working in the same industry (presumably involved in producing similar types of goods and services).

Our results related to the positive relationship between the creative thinking wage premium and the percentage of metropolitan area workers in high-creativity occupations are also very similar in spirit to those reported in a recent study by Knudsen et al. (2008). In a metropolitan-level regression framework that focused on the number of patents per 100 000 residents, they found that the interaction between urban population density and the percentage of workers in the creative economy has a positive effect on regional innovation. They used this finding to conclude that '[i]t is the geographic concentration of people with expertise, skills, and knowledge that powers the exchange and spillovers that precede innovation' (Knudsen et al., 2008, p. 474). Here, we find that a geographic concentration of high-creativity workers enhances an individual's return to creative thinking.

EXAMINING THE HIGH-CREATIVITY WAGE PREMIUM

To further investigate these ideas, we estimate some additional regressions that examine the high-creativity wage premium for each of the industries included in our study and then, as a separate analysis, for each of the metropolitan areas. The 1 per cent sample of the 2008 American Community Survey includes workers in 262 industrial sectors, as defined by the US Census Bureau. Thus, we re-estimated the equation (7.1) 262 separate times to estimate the high-creativity wage premium for each of the industrial sectors. We found that high creativity enhances earnings by more than 10 per cent in 220 sectors, lifts earnings between zero and 10 per cent in 31 industries, and has a negative effect on earnings in 11 industries. The average effect of high creativity, estimated across all 262 sectors, is a 24.7 per cent increase in earnings.

Figure 7.2 is a scatter plot showing the relationship between the creative thinking wage premiums and the percentages of high-creativity workers by industry. As expected, based on the regression results presented in Table 7.7, the figure reveals a negative correlation ($r = -0.41$) suggesting that the return to high creativity is lower in sectors with an abundance of creative workers than in industries where creative thinking is less prevalent. It is

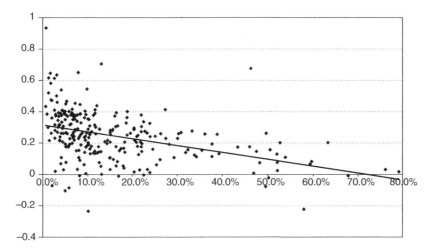

Figure 7.2   Relationship between wage premium (y-axis) and share of industry employment (x-axis) in high-creativity occupations

interesting to note that the return to creative thinking is less than 24.7 per cent, the mean value listed above, in 18 of the 20 high-creativity industries highlighted in Table 7.4. The two exceptions to this rule are the sectors of legal services (creativity wage premium of 67.5 per cent) and offices of other healthcare providers (creativity wage premium of 26.2 per cent), which are explained by the lucrative salaries earned by those in the high-creativity jobs of lawyers and selected healthcare occupations.

Perhaps the best example of the low (or negative) returns to creative thinking in high-creativity industries is found in the sector of 'independent artists, performing arts, spectator sports and related industries'. In this sector, the effect of high creativity is a 22 per cent reduction in earnings, other things being equal. This point is easy to identify (a combination of a large percentage of workers in high-creativity occupations and a substantial negative return to creative thinking) in the bottom right-side section of the scatter plot. The high-creativity jobs in this sector, as one might imagine, are occupations such as actors; writers and authors; artists and related workers; dancers and choreographers; and musicians, singers and related workers. The relatively lower-creativity occupations in this industry include financial managers; accountants and auditors; and agents and business managers of artists, performers and athletes. In this sector, the individuals involved in creative thinking – the actors, writers, musicians and dancers – well outnumber the people involved in their management and promotion – the agents, financial managers and accountants. Here, an abundance of creative talent leads to an artist's earnings penalty compared to those who manage and promote the artistic workers.[14]

At the other end of the spectrum is the industrial sector of taxi and limousine service, which is easy to pick out in the upper left-hand section of Figure 7.2. This sector has a very small share of workers in high-creativity occupations (less than 1 per cent), but yet the return to creativity is a 93.4 per cent increase in earnings. This is the largest high-creativity wage premium across all 262 industrial sectors. Looking at the individual-level data set, we see that the high-creativity occupations in this sector include mostly chief

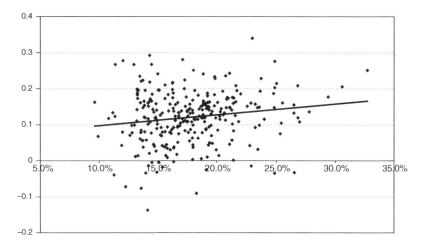

Figure 7.3   Relationship between wage premium (y-axis) and share of metropolitan employment in high-creativity occupations (x-axis)

executives, of which there are very few. The low-creativity jobs in this sector include dispatchers, automotive service technicians and mechanics, and – of course – taxi drivers and chauffeurs. In this sector, unlike the artists and related industries examined above, the high-creativity workers are in the minority and they – the chief executives – are involved in the management and promotion of those who do not use creativity in their jobs.

Figure 7.3 is a scatter plot showing the relationship between the creative thinking wage premiums and the percentages of high-creativity workers by region. Here, we use information on 284 US metropolitan areas that are included in the 2008 American Community Survey. By re-estimating equation (7.1) for each of these metropolitan areas, we found that high creativity enhances earnings by more than 10 per cent in 185 metropolitan areas, lifts earnings between zero and 10 per cent in 83 places, and has a negative effect on earnings in 16 regions. The average effect of high creativity, calculated across all 284 metropolitan areas, is a 12.1 per cent increase in earnings. Figure 7.3 reveals – although the pattern of relationship is not as strong as shown in Figure 7.2 – a slight positive correlation ($r = 0.158$) between the high-creativity wage premium in US metropolitan areas and the percentage of creative workers in the region.

Here, we find that the return to creative thinking exceeds 12.1 per cent, the mean value listed above, in 13 of the 20 high-creativity metropolitan areas shown in Table 7.5. The monetary return to creative thinking is quite substantial in places known for an abundance of creative workers such as Stamford (25.1 per cent wage premium), Austin (21.5 per cent wage premium), San Jose (20.5 per cent wage premium) and Santa Fe (20.2 per cent wage premium). The additional earnings associated with creative thinking ranges from a high of 34.0 per cent (Nashua, New Hampshire, which has 23.0 per cent of the working-age population in high-creativity occupations) to a low of –13.7 per cent (Waterbury, Connecticut, which has 14.2 per cent of its population in high-creativity jobs).

It is likely that several factors explain this positive relationship between the creative thinking wage premium and the share of the metropolitan area workforce in high-creativity jobs. First, it is possible that creativity generates positive externalities, in that a diverse group of creative workers in a region enhance the productivity of their peers (Florida, 2002). This explanation is in-sync with Jane Jacobs's (1969) ideas about cities and the importance of interaction among different types of workers (Glaeser et al., 1992). Likewise, as mentioned above, Knudsen et al. (2008) found that a high density of creative workers – although not necessarily in a diverse set of occupations – has a positive effect on regional innovation.

Another explanation for this finding is that metropolitan areas with a low percentage of workers in high-creativity occupations have creative economies that are dominated by teachers. McGranahan and Wojan (2007, p. 198) removed educators from their definition of the creative economy because these occupations, along with healthcare practitioners, 'are involved in economic reproduction and locate largely to provide essential services to a population'. Since all regions have some minimal percentage of the workforce involved in teaching, educators likely make up a larger portion of the creative economy in metropolitan areas with a small share of high-creativity workers. Compared to other technology-based occupations in the creative economy, teachers do not typically generate positive spillover effects that enhance the productivity of others outside of educational institutions (Florida et al., 2008; Gabe, 2009; Abel and Gabe, 2010).

To investigate these explanations, we look in more detail at the composition of the creative economy across the US metropolitan areas in our sample. A simple entropy index is used to measure the diversity of a region's creative economy. The entropy index is based on the percentage of metropolitan area employment in the broad occupational categories of arts, design, entertainment, sports and media occupations; education, training and library occupations; computer and mathematical occupations; legal occupations; architecture and engineering occupations; life, physical and social science occupations; and management occupations, which are the groups with the largest concentrations of high-creativity jobs. Low values of the entropy measure suggest that a region's creative economy employment is widely dispersed across these seven occupational categories, whereas values close to 1.0 suggest that employment is highly concentrated in a single category.

Looking at the 284 US metropolitan areas, we find a strong negative correlation ($r = -0.608$) between the percentage of employment in high-creativity jobs and the entropy measure of regional diversity across the seven occupational categories that are most prominent in the creative economy. This suggests that the metropolitan areas with the largest creative economies (in terms of the share of overall employment) also have the most diverse group of creative workers. Focusing on specific places, we see that the creative economies of Santa Fe, San Jose, Washington, DC, San Francisco and Austin are among the ten most diverse (as well as the largest, as shown in Table 7.5). Educators make up less than one-quarter of the creative economy (defined, in this case, to include the seven broad occupational categories listed above) in each of these five metropolitan areas.

We find a moderate negative correlation ($r = -0.288$) between the percentage of metropolitan area employment in high-creativity jobs and the share of creative economy employment (once again, defined to include the same seven broad occupational categories) that is made up by educators. This suggests, as speculated above, that metropolitan areas with a low percentage of workers in high-creativity occupations tend to have creative economies that are more heavily dominated by teachers. Pulling this information together, we can conclude that the positive relationship between the creative thinking wage premium and the share of metropolitan area workers in high-creativity jobs could be explained by the knowledge spillovers that take place among creative workers (Knudsen et al., 2008), the high diversity of creative work that takes place in creative clusters (Jacobs, 1969; Glaeser et al., 1992; Florida, 2002) or the relatively low prominence of educators in places with a large creative economy (McGranahan and Wojan, 2007; Gabe, 2009; Abel and Gabe, 2010).

SUMMARY AND CONCLUDING THOUGHTS

In *The Rise of the Creative Class*, Richard Florida examined the role that creativity plays in enhancing regional economic vitality. Florida's (2002, p. 249) 'creative capital theory' suggests that 'regional economic growth is powered by creative people' and '[g]reater and more diverse concentrations of creative capital in turn lead to higher rates of innovation, high-technology business formation, job generation and economic growth'. Building from these ideas, the current chapter investigates the monetary returns to working in an occupation that places a heavy emphasis on creative thinking. Controlling for an individual's receipt of a college degree, we analysed the effects of high creativity on earnings – an oft-used measure of productivity – and then looked at how the individual returns to creativity are influenced by what a person makes and where he or she lives.

Evaluating the measures of creative and human capital used in the analysis, we found that working in a high-creativity occupation and the receipt of a four-year college degree are not always one and the same. Workers in high-creativity occupations are substantially more likely than those in non-high-creativity jobs to have a college degree, but it is also the case that only 40 per cent of individuals with a college degree are in occupations that require high creativity. This means that almost 60 per cent of college-educated workers are in occupations that do not rely heavily on creative thinking.

Our empirical analysis of a large sample of full-time US workers shows that working in an occupation that relies heavily on creative thinking enhances annual earnings by about 16 per cent. This wage premium associated with high creativity is above and beyond the additional earnings connected with a college degree, suggesting that creativity is in some ways distinct from human capital (Florida, 2002). Interestingly, the high-creativity wage premiums estimated in the study varied widely across industrial sectors (from a 23.5 per cent penalty to a 93.4 per cent increase in wages) and US metropolitan areas (from a 13.7 per cent penalty to a 34.0 per cent increase in wages). Such a wide dispersion across industries and regions led us to wonder about the factors that influence the monetary returns to creativity. Is it working around other creative workers in the same industry? Is it interacting with other creative workers who reside in the same region? Or, is it being surrounded by a diverse group of others involved in different types of creative activities?

Focusing on the returns to creativity by industry, we found that the creative thinking wage premium is negatively associated with the share of creative workers in the same sector. This suggests that the productivity gains from creativity are not enhanced (in fact, they are diminished) by working around other creative workers that are involved in producing the same good or delivering a similar type of service. Looking at the returns to creativity by US metropolitan area, we found that the high-creativity wage premium is enhanced by the share of creative workers in the region. A metropolitan area's share of creative workers, however, is correlated with both the diversity of the region's creative economy and the percentage of metropolitan area creative workers who are teachers.

Thus, it appears that the positive relationship found between the creative thinking wage premium and the share of metropolitan area workers in high-creativity jobs could be explained by knowledge spillovers among creative workers, the high diversity of creative work that takes place in these regions or the relatively low prominence of educators in places with a large creative economy. It is likely a combination of all three. The first explanation is consistent with the study by Knudsen et al. (2008), which found that a high density of creative workers enhances regional productivity. The second explanation is squarely in line with Jacobs's (1969), Glaeser et al.'s (1992), and Florida's ideas, discussed above, about the importance of a 'diverse concentration of creative capital'. The final explanation is supported by other recent research on the effects of knowledge – namely, knowledge about education and training – on wages and regional productivity (Gabe, 2009; Abel and Gabe, 2010).

NOTES

1. Florida (2002, p. 8) makes a similar distinction among the occupational groups, suggesting that '[t]hose in the Working Class and the Service Class are primarily paid to execute according to plan, while those in the Creative Class are primarily paid to create and have considerably more autonomy and flexibility than the other two classes to do so'.
2. Markusen (2006) and Markusen et al. (2008, p. 27) raise the concern that 'in Florida's usage, the creative class boils down to those who have received higher education, whether or not they are actually doing creative work . . .'.
3. A rich literature exists on the monetary returns to human capital and the majority of studies reveal a positive relationship between earnings and educational attainment (Card, 1999).
4. See Peterson et al. (2001) for a detailed discussion of O*NET.
5. Using information from O*NET, we found an average creative thinking score (that is, importance of creative thinking multiplied by level of creative thinking required) of 10.16 across all occupations, with a standard deviation of 5.83. Thus, 'high-creativity' jobs are defined as those occupations with creative thinking scores that exceed 15.99.
6. The number of sample observations ranges from 14 990 for farming, fishing and forestry occupations to 259 541 for office and support occupations.
7. These estimates are based on the 1 per cent sample of the 2008 American Community Survey (Ruggles et al., 2009).
8. Along with the analysis described above, we also looked at the correlation between an individual's number of years of formal education and the raw creativity score of his or her occupation. Here, we found a moderate correlation ($r = 0.432$) between educational attainment and creative thinking.
9. Along with the rankings shown in Table 7.4, we also identified the 20 most creative industrial sectors according to creativity index values, based on the 'raw' creativity scores that we used to determine the high-creativity occupations.
10. If you have ever had your hair done before attending a religious ceremony, you would likely agree that the ratio of beauticians to all employees in a hair salon is slightly greater than the ratio of clergy and musicians to the total number of people employed at a place of worship.
11. For the most part, we found modest correlations among the explanatory variables. Aside from a correlation of 0.366 between the *High Creativity* and *College Degree* variables (and a high correlation between an individual's age and age-squared), we did not find a correlation greater than 0.25 among the other combinations of explanatory variables.
12. We also estimated a version of the model that included the number of years of formal education, instead of the receipt of a four-year college degree, as a measure of human capital. In this regression, we found

that working in a high-creativity occupation increases earnings by 15.0 per cent (*t*-value = 89.4, *p*-value = 0.000) – similar to our original findings – which, in this case, exceeds a 9.7 per cent (*t*-value = 406.3, *p*-value = 0.000) increase in earnings associated with an additional year of education.

13.   The sample size of 697 481 is smaller than in the other regressions because the far right-hand column of results is based solely on individuals living in US metropolitan areas.

14.   Using 1980 US Census data, Filer (1986) found that – controlling for education, experience and other personal characteristics – artists do not earn less money than other workers. In our analysis, the earnings of creative workers, in this case mostly artists and related workers, are compared to others in the sector of independent artists, performing arts, spectator sports and related industries; and not relative to all US workers.

REFERENCES

Abel, J.R. and T. Gabe (2010), 'Human capital and economic activity in urban America', *Regional Studies*, first published 5 July.

Acemoglu, D. and J. Angrist (2000), 'How large are human-capital externalities? Evidence from compulsory schooling laws', *NBER Macroeconomics Annual*, **15**, 9–59.

Antonovics, K. and R. Town (2004), 'Are all the good men married? Uncovering the sources of the marital wage premium', *American Economic Review*, **94**, 317–21.

Bacolod, M., B. Blum and W. Strange (2009a), 'Skills in the city', *Journal of Urban Economics*, **65**, 136–53.

Bacolod, M., B. Blum and W. Strange (2009b), 'Urban interactions: Soft skills vs. specialization', *Journal of Economic Geography*, **9**, 227–62.

Card, D. (1999), 'The causal effects of education on earnings', in O. Ashenfelter and D. Card (eds), *Handbook of Labor Economics*, Amsterdam: Elsevier, pp. 1801–63.

Currid, E. and K. Stolarick (2010), 'The occupation-industry mismatch: new trajectories for regional cluster analysis and economic development', *Urban Studies*, **47**, 337–62.

Dickerson, A. and F. Green (2004), 'The growth and valuation of computing and other generic skills', *Oxford Economic Papers*, **56**, 371–406.

DiNardo, J. and J.-S. Pischke (1997), 'The returns to computer use revisited: have pencils changed the wage structure too?', *Quarterly Journal of Economics*, **112**, 291–303.

Feser, E. (2003), 'What regions do rather than make: a proposed set of knowledge-based occupation clusters', *Urban Studies*, **40**, 1937–58.

Filer, R. (1986), 'The "starving artist" – myth or reality? Earnings of artists in the United States', *Journal of Political Economy*, **94**, 56–75.

Florida, R. (2002), *The Rise of the Creative Class*, New York, NY: Basic Books.

Florida, R.C. Mellander and Kevin Stolarick (2008), 'Inside the black box of regional development – human capital, the creative class and tolerance', *Journal of Economic Geography*, **8**, 615–49.

Fortin, N. and T. Lemieux (1998), 'Rank regressions, wage distributions, and the gender gap', *Journal of Human Resources*, **33**, 610–43.

Gabe, T. (2009), 'Knowledge and earnings', *Journal of Regional Science*, **49**, 439–57.

Gabe, T., K. Colby and K. Bell (2007), 'The effects of workforce creativity on earnings in U.S. counties', *Agricultural and Resource Economics Review*, **36**, 71–83.

Glaeser, E. (2004), 'Review of Richard Florida's *The Rise of the Creative Class*', available at http://post.economics.harvard.edu/faculty/glaeser/papers/Review_Florida.pdf (accessed 5 May 2010).

Glaeser, E., H. Kallal, J. Scheinkman and A. Shleifer (1992), 'Growth in cities', *Journal of Political Economy*, **100**, 1126–52.

Ingram, B. and G. Neumann (2006), 'The returns to skill', *Labour Economics*, **13**, 35–59.

Jacobs, J. (1969), *The Economy of Cities*, New York, NY: Vintage.

Knudsen, B., R. Florida, K. Stolarick and G. Gates (2008), 'Density and creativity in U.S. regions', *Annals of the Association of American Geographers*, **98**, 461–78.

Kolesnikova, N. (2010), 'The return to education isn't calculated easily', *The Regional Economist* (Federal Reserve Bank of St Louis), **18**, 12–13.

Krueger, A. (1993), 'How computers have changed the wage structure: evidence from microdata, 1984–1989', *Quarterly Journal of Economics*, **108**, 33–60.

Krumm, R. (1987), 'Regional wage differentials and race: 1973–1978', *Journal of Regional Science*, **27**, 119–28.

Lucas, R. (1977), 'Hedonic wage equations and psychic wages in the returns to schooling', *American Economic Review*, **67**, 549–58.

Markusen, A. (2004), 'Targeting occupations in regional and community economic development', *Journal of the American Planning Association*, **70**, 253–68.

Markusen, A. (2006), 'Urban development and the politics of a creative class: evidence from the study of artists', *Environment and Planning A*, **38**, 1921–40.

Markusen, A. and G. Schrock (2006), 'The artistic dividend: urban artistic specialization and economic development implications', *Urban Studies*, **43**, 1661–86.

Markusen, A., G. Wassall, D. DeNatale and R. Cohen (2008), 'Defining the creative economy: industry and occupational approaches', *Economic Development Quarterly*, **22**, 24–45.

McGranahan, D. and T. Wojan (2007), 'Recasting the creative class to examine growth processes in rural and urban counties', *Regional Studies*, **41**, 197–216.

Mellander, C. (2009), 'Creative and knowledge industries: an occupational distribution approach', *Economic Development Quarterly*, **23**, 294–305.

Mincer, J. (1974), *Schooling, Experience and Earnings*, New York, NY: NBER Press.

Moretti, E. (2004), 'Estimating the social return to higher education: evidence from longitudinal and repeated cross-sectional data', *Journal of Econometrics*, **121**, 175–212.

Peterson, N. M. Mumford, W. Borman et al. (2001), 'Understanding work using the Occupational Information Network (O*NET): implications for practice and research', *Personnel Psychology*, **54**, 451–92.

Price, R. and E. Mills (1985), 'Race and residence in earnings determination', *Journal of Urban Economics*, **17**, 1–18.

Rauch, J. (1993), 'Productivity gains from geographic concentration of human capital: evidence from the cities', *Journal of Urban Economics*, **34**, 380–400.

Ruggles, S., M. Sobek, T. Alexander et al. (2009), *Integrated Public Use Microdata Series: Version 4.0* (Machine-readable database), Minneapolis, MN: Minnesota Population Center (producer and distributor).

Scott, A. (2009) 'Human capital resources and requirements across the metropolitan hierarchy of the USA', *Journal of Economic Geography*, **9**, 207–26.

Willis, R. (1986), 'Wage determinants: a survey and reinterpretation of human capital earnings functions', in O. Ashenfelter and R. Layard (eds), *Handbook of Labor Economics*, Amsterdam: Elsevier, pp. 525–602.

8 Understanding Canada's evolving design economy
Tara Vinodrai

Over the past decade, there has been a flurry of attention paid to the emerging creative economy and its articulation across space: the creative city. Within this arena, designers are now viewed as central actors and design is celebrated as a critical factor contributing to the competitiveness and creativity of firms, cities, regions and nations. Yet, how prevalent is design work? How has design employment changed over time and space? What are the institutional conditions that support design employment in the so-called 'creative city'? To answer these questions, this chapter draws upon recent and ongoing research on design and the creative economy in Canadian cities.

The chapter begins by discussing why cities and metropolitan regions are critical to our understanding of creative and cultural activities. First, cities act as the ideal environment in which creative and cultural activities thrive. Second, places with strong institutions – particularly institutions of higher learning such as universities and colleges – can act as 'anchors of creativity' to support creative activity. Third, cities have unique social characteristics and spatial environments that act to attract and retain highly skilled workers. This chapter goes further to suggest that design can be viewed as a particularly unique form of creative activity that contributes to the urban milieu and creates both cultural and economic value through a 'design dividend' for the city-region (cf. Markusen and Schrock, 2006; Vinodrai, 2009). Following this discussion, the chapter introduces the methodological approach and data sources used in the analysis. The fourth section presents statistical evidence on how the design economy has evolved in Canadian cities over the past several decades. It uses employment data at the interurban level to examine the changing geography of design in Canada. Building on this discussion, the penultimate section focuses on Canada's two largest cities (Toronto and Montreal), where a significant proportion of Canada's design activity is concentrated. It draws upon a mix of quantitative data and recent qualitative case studies of design activity in these cities to demonstrate the path-dependent nature of the evolution of the creative city. Based on the findings and analysis, the chapter concludes by identifying the opportunities and challenges that face public policy in working towards a prosperous, inclusive and sustainable creative city through and by design.

CREATIVITY, DESIGN AND THE URBAN ECONOMY

Over the past decade, observers of contemporary economic development have highlighted the growing importance of creative and cultural activity, and the important role that cities play in incubating and fostering these activities (Hall, 1998; Florida, 2002; Scott, 2008). As noted by Scott (2007, 2008), there appears to be a broad shift underway in the economic base of cities in North America and across the globe towards what he refers to as 'cognitive-cultural' capitalism, in which production increasingly relies on symbolic and aesthetic considerations. The recent and growing literature on this topic suggests that there are a number of ways in which cities play a critical role as seedbeds of innovation and creativity. First, cities act as the ideal environment in which creative and cultural activities thrive. Second, and related to this first point, places with strong institutions and supportive policy environments that can act as 'anchors of creativity' are more likely to be successful in securing the presence of creative and cultural industries and the workers that participate in these industries (Gertler and Vinodrai, 2005). Third, cities have unique social and spatial characteristics that act to attract and retain highly skilled workers. Central to these ideas is the hypothesis that the economic performance of city-regions depends on a set of characteristics that define quality of place, including cultural dynamism, social diversity, openness and tolerance, social inclusion and cohesion. Each of these three dimensions of the 'creative city' is discussed briefly below.

Creative Cities and the Clustering of Economic Activity

The clustering of firms is a signature trait of many well-documented innovative sectors, including the biotechnology and the information and communication technology (ICT) sectors (Maskell and Malmberg, 1999; Wolfe and Gertler, 2004; Asheim et al., 2006; Braunerhjelm and Feldman, 2006). Such agglomeration facilitates collaboration, knowledge spillovers and learning – all of which are critical to the innovation process. Spatial proximity also allows firms to develop relationships with local customers and suppliers and draw upon shared resources such as pools of highly skilled labour and local institutional supports. There is now a growing body of research that suggests that these classic characteristics of innovation systems and cluster dynamics can also be observed in the creative and cultural industries (Brail and Gertler, 1999; Scott, 2001; Rantisi, 2002; Britton et al., 2009).

Scott (2001) and others argue that the urban environment provides an ideal setting for the formation of localized clusters of creative and cultural industries and the emergence of industrial districts that specialize in the production of particular cultural products. This research suggests, although far from universally, that such activities tend to agglomerate in major urban centres (often in downtown districts) and that these agglomerations not only contribute to economic growth, but can transform contemporary economies (Scott, 2001, 2008; Hutton, 2008).

Agglomeration is reinforced due to the nature of innovation in these industries, which place less emphasis on traditional innovation inputs and highlight the importance of other inputs, such as design. These creative and cultural industries are susceptible to rapid shifts in consumer demands and changing styles, necessitating higher rates of innovation, a constant search for novelty and easy access to information about changing tastes, all of which are best achieved through physical proximity. A critical mass of people doing cutting-edge work in the same and related fields generates and facilitates access to local 'buzz' about the latest trends and leading-edge practices (Bathelt et al., 2004; Storper and Venables, 2004).

Moreover, these industries rely on the unique identity and characteristics of places to bolster their competitiveness, which is often fostered by their locations in distinctive urban environments (Scott, 2001; Molotch, 2002; Rantisi, 2004). Other scholars have noted that the mode of production and innovation in these industries requires different organizational forms such as projects which are often temporary and that span across organizational and territorial boundaries, resulting in complex geographies and spatial patterns (Ekinsmyth, 2002; Grabher, 2002; Vinodrai, 2006). Feminist-inspired critiques of this emerging organizational form are quick to point out that cultural work is often precarious, exposing individual workers to high levels of personal risk, self-employment and other forms of 'flexible' work arrangements (McRobbie, 2009). Proximity and access to a wide range of supporting policies and institutions therefore becomes critical to overcoming the challenges and risks associated with this form of work.

Anchoring the 'Creative City'

As noted above, urban centres are often the locations for large concentrations of creative and cultural economic activity and supporting policies and institutions are necessary to mitigate risk and promote development. However, what institutions help to anchor creative, cultural and design-related activities in specific places? Within the literature on innovation systems, there is a well-established view that suggests that regions (and nations) support the growth of innovative and dynamic industries and clusters through the provision of both general and specialized infrastructure. An instrumental component of this knowledge infrastructure includes a well-developed education and research system that comprises universities, colleges and research institutes. A recent line of argument is that in addition to the important role that universities play in supporting the success and dynamism of locally based clusters and regional innovation systems, universities can also act as anchors of the creative economy (Gertler and Vinodrai, 2005). They do so in three mutually reinforcing ways. First, the university plays an important role in shaping the quality of place and fostering openness and tolerance through its creating a social environment that is open to difference. Second, the university acts as a talent magnet by making places attractive to highly skilled research talent from around the world. Third, universities can act to attract both domestic and foreign students, thereby acting as key conduits that link cities to other centres, both nationally and internationally. As we shall see below, these arguments resonate with arguments made elsewhere about the importance of openness and tolerance to the creative city.

However, given that innovation in creative and cultural industries is a highly interactive and social process that often requires an ongoing search for novelty, it should come as no surprise that in addition to these important institutions, a vast array of other organizations and actors are critical to supporting creative activity. Moreover, given that creative activities – especially activities such as design – blur the boundaries between the cultural and economic spheres (Leslie and Rantisi, 2006), the range of economic actors and policies that support creative activities is far more diverse. Recent research has shown that local policies that allow for mixed-use land development, as well as cultural policies and programmes that support local art and cultural initiatives are just as critical to anchoring the creative economy (Scott, 2001; Gertler et al., 2006). In other words, a vast array of institutions and actors are important for anchoring particular forms of creative activity in particular places. Yet, due to the local specificity of many of these policies and programmes – related to land use, innovation, arts and culture and economic development – it can be hypothesized that there are many development paths and trajectories towards the creative city.

Creative Cities and Talent Attraction

Some recent research suggests that firms are drawn to places that have a critical mass of creative workers. For example, in 2005, Sony opened its new design centre in Los Angeles to position itself as a design-led company and to 'take advantage of the diverse creative community in the Los Angeles area'.[1] Analysis by Richard Florida and others suggests that the most successful urban regions are those that develop tolerant and welcoming attitudes towards social diversity and offer a critical mass of cultural activity; it is these places that are most likely to attract and retain highly skilled creative workers, that is, 'talent' or the 'creative class' (Florida, 2002; Gertler et al., 2002; Florida et al., 2008). However, the ability of cities to generate and retain creative talent may also depend on quality of place and community characteristics that promote strong social cohesion (Gertler, 2001; Bradford, 2004; Markusen and Schrock, 2006). Beyond the simple presence of a vibrant arts and cultural scene, essential components of quality of place may also include affordable and liveable space; strong, socially cohesive neighbourhoods; access to employment and social services; access to childcare; and a host of concerns related to sustainability and the environment (Gertler, 2001; Donald and Morrow, 2003; Lewis and Donald, 2010).

As noted above, the work of Florida (2002) suggests that the most successful city-regions have a social environment that is open to creativity and diversity. Despite widespread interest in this topic from scholars and policymakers alike, this body of research has also been subject to pointed (and growing) criticism and debate on theoretical, methodological and ideological grounds (see Peck, 2005, 2009; Markusen, 2006; Scott, 2006; Donegan and Lowe, 2008; Sands and Reese, 2008; Storper and Scott, 2009; Lewis and Donald, 2010). For example, Donald and Morrow (2003) argue that key aspects of quality of life have been excluded from this analysis, and they raise important questions about the potentially exclusionary nature of talent-based strategies for developing city-regions. Others argue that some of the US cities that score highest on Florida's indicators of quality of place also exhibit signs of economic decay, instability and social polarization, suggesting that inequality may be an inevitable outcome (Peck, 2005; McCann, 2007). As Gertler (2010) notes, on this point, there may in fact be little disagreement, as Florida has similarly identified these troubling trends. In some places such as London, policymakers – who are actively pursuing a 'creative cities' strategy and where creative activity is an important driver of innovation and economic growth – have argued that policies must simultaneously address issues of social inclusion and the development of creative and cultural activity.

London is already Britain's most polarized region and needs to drastically reduce inequalities if it is to maintain social cohesion. The London Development Agency (2003, p. 15) writes that '[we] must ensure that growing employment and enterprise in the creative industries are reflected in jobs and opportunities for all Londoners. This means developing and linking initiatives that support large creative employers, as well as agencies actively involved in local and disadvantaged communities.'

In Canadian cities, Hulchanski (2007) documents trends that are related to growing social and income polarization. Such inequality is expressed through persistent patterns of poverty and social deprivation in particular neighbourhoods within large metropolitan areas. The dynamics of polarization may pose a serious threat to urban and regional economic prosperity. However, there is some (albeit limited) evidence that local strategies that simultaneously develop creative talent and work towards social inclusion are possible (see Gertler et al., 2006; Gertler, 2010).

One of the most worrisome issues raised by critics is related to creative city policymaking in action. A now standard claim in the literature is that many places have quickly and uncritically adopted the 'creative city' script as a form of 'fast policy' (Peck, 2005, 2009). While this may be the case in some places, it is important to dig a little more deeply into how the 'creative city' is being put into practice. In other words, rather than a wholesale rejection of the idea of a 'creative city', there is room to understand how the creative city is articulated, supported and enacted in various geographic contexts. Following lines of argument made by Markusen (2006), there is utility in exploring the underlying geography and dynamics of creative activity, and focusing more explicitly on particular aspects of work and production.

Design and the Creative City

In light of these recent debates, this chapter sheds light on these issues, through a consideration of the case of design. Designers figure prominently in Florida's concept of the 'creative class' (see above). Florida (2002, p. 69, emphasis added) defines the creative class as 'scientists and engineers, university professors, poets and novelists, artists, entertainers, actors, *designers and architects*, as well as . . . non-fiction writers, editors, cultural figures, think-tank researchers, analysts, and other opinion makers'. However, the 'creative class' is an incredibly diverse and heterogeneous group of workers. These workers may value different aspects of place and have very different patterns of employment and work practices, as well as being exposed to and influenced by different social and institutional dynamics that depend on their occupational identity and other factors. From this perspective, a focus on design and designers may enable us to better understand the development of the creative city.

Certainly, design has become a celebrated and central aspect of the contemporary economy. Academics, policymakers and business leaders increasingly recognize that design – an inherently creative activity that sits at the intersection of art, business and technology – is a critical input into the production of goods and services in both emerging and traditional sectors. Thus, design – in this context – must be understood broadly to encompass

> not just the aesthetic aspects of a product but also their overall technological performance and character. The act of design involves not just shaping a product's appearance but also involves a range of inputs into the creation of the form and function of a product and its production, marketing and appeal to the consumer. (Power, 2004, p. 7)

In much the same way that Markusen argues that places with a critical mass and concentration of artists can accrue an 'artistic dividend', my recent work on design activity in Canadian cities (Vinodrai, 2009) suggests that firms, communities, cities and regions can accrue a design dividend. Designers contribute to and enhance the local economy by:

1. Generating revenue from their own design practices which serve both local and global clients, require inputs and services from local suppliers, and create employment opportunities for other designers through the project-based nature of design.
2. Applying design skills and thinking to add value to and enhance the quality and sustainability of products and services in other sectors.
3. Acting as a source of new knowledge and innovation, often crossing disciplinary and sectoral boundaries.
4. Participating in activities that enhance community engagement and identity.
5. Contributing to the construction of quality of place and improving the aesthetic appeal and quality of the built environment.

Thus, through their very actions and practices designers help to construct – whether consciously or unconsciously – the 'creative city'. Designers are key animateurs of the creative economy and for this reason, it is instructive to critically examine the structure and dynamics of the design workforce and the institutional conditions that support design activity. Through the remainder of this chapter, we try to understand both in quantitative and qualitative terms how the design workforce has evolved over time and space. By focusing on the different policy and governance approaches that Canadian cities have used to support design work, as a particular form of creative activity, this chapter sheds light on how the development trajectory of the 'creative city' is highly context-specific and path-dependent.

DATA SOURCES AND METHODS

The chapter uses both quantitative and qualitative evidence to provide a detailed overview of the structure and institutional dynamics of the design economy in Canadian cities. In this chapter, the emphasis is on the design workforce defined in occupational terms. The distinction between studying industries and occupations is important (see Feser, 2003; Markusen, 2004); an occupational approach is useful for uncovering the talents that exist within the labour market and places the emphasis on the skills and capacities of a city-region's workforce. For the purposes of the quantitative analysis in this chapter, the design workforce is defined to include the following six design occupations as delineated using Statistics Canada's 2006 National Occupational Classification – Statistics (NOC-S): architects (C051); landscape architects (C052); industrial designers (C152); graphic designers (F141); interior designers (F142); theatre, fashion, exhibit and other creative designers (F143).

Statistical data have been extracted from the *Canadian Census of Population* covering the period from 1991 to 2006, as well as custom tabulations from the *Labour Force Survey* (LFS), 1987–2007. Combined, these datasets provide a window into how the design workforce has grown over the past decades. In Canada, a *Census of Population* is conducted every five years; since 1971, every fifth household is required to answer a longer mandatory survey which provides analysts with very detailed demographic and socio-economic information. The LFS is a monthly survey – using a rotating panel of approximately 54000 households – that covers the non-institutionalized civilian population that is 15 years of age or older. It provides estimates of a variety of labour force characteristics (for example, employment status, industry and occupation) at the national and provincial level, as well as for the largest cities. And while there are periodic changes to the survey instrument, as well as to the coding of industry and occupation variables due to modifications in the various classification schemes applied to the data Statistics Canada recodes the historical data to ensure compatibility over time. It should also be noted that there are some further limitations to using each of these data sources. While these cross-sectional datasets are quite comprehensive and can capture aggregate changes and trends over time, they tell us little about the historical evolution or dynamics of the labour force. In addition, to ensure confidentiality Statistics Canada applies random rounding rules to the Census (to the nearest 5 or 10) and LFS (to the nearest 100). In each case, data suppression rules are also applied to prevent either the direct or residual disclosure of information about individuals.

In addition to the statistical data described above, further insights have been drawn from several other sources. First, the research explicitly builds upon previous and ongoing research on Toronto's design community (see Gertler and Vinodrai, 2004; Vinodrai, 2005, 2006, 2009). This research uses insights from over 60 in-depth interviews with experts in the field, including practising designers, representatives from design schools, professional associations, policymakers and other government officials. Interviews were first conducted between 2004 and 2006; a second round of interviews was commenced in 2009. Interviewees were initially recruited through contacts with the Design Industry Advisory Committee (DIAC) as well as through other networks to allow for multiple entry points; a snowball sampling strategy was used. The interviews were semi-structured, recorded and transcribed. In analysing the interviews, points of agreements and divergence were noted. Second, this chapter uses findings from other recent studies that have examined the various dimensions of design and design-related activities in Canadian cities, conducted primarily – but not exclusively – under the auspices of the Innovation Systems Research Network (ISRN)[2] (cf. Gertler et al., 2007; Gertler and Geddie, 2008; Leslie and Brail, 2008; Rantisi and Leslie, 2008; Barnes and Hutton, 2009; Britton et al., 2009; Barnes et al., 2010).

CANADA'S EVOLVING DESIGN ECONOMY

Canada, like many advanced capitalist economies, has for the past several decades witnessed a transformation of the economy and labour market towards more knowledge-intensive, 'creative' and service-oriented forms of work (Gertler, 2001; Beckstead and Vinodrai, 2003; Vinodrai, 2010; Wolfe, 2010). As part of the transformation and evolution of the Canadian economy towards increasingly knowledge-intensive economic activities, design has become a more prominent activity. Table 8.1 shows the growth in the design workforce over the period between 1991 and 2006. Overall, Canada's design workforce grew from 60 000 workers in 1991 to almost 104 000 by 2006. This is the equivalent of a growth rate of 3.7 per cent per year, as compared to only 1.1 per cent for the labour force as a whole. However, even within the design workforce, not all design occupations grew at equal rates. The largest absolute increase was experienced amongst graphic designers, which includes individuals who work in areas such as web design and animation. In relative terms, industrial designers grew at the fastest rate (7.5 per cent

Table 8.1   Employment by design occupation in Canada, 1991 to 2006

Occupation	1991	1996	2001	2006	Mean annual growth (%)
Architects	9165	9400	12800	13960	2.8
Landscape architects	2125	1605	2410	1620	−1.8
Industrial designers	3455	5070	9795	10250	7.5
Graphic designers	28405	35310	44615	51890	4.1
Interior designers	7495	8175	11655	14355	4.4
Theatre, fashion and other designers	9090	9670	9825	11410	1.5
All design occupations	59735	69230	91100	103485	3.7
All occupations	14220230	14317545	15576565	16861185	1.1

Source: Statistics Canada, *Canadian Census of Population,* 1991–2006 (author's calculations).

per year) over the 15-year period between 1991 and 2006, followed by interior designers (4.4 per cent) and graphic designers (4.1 per cent). Overall, this confirms that design has become a more widespread activity within the Canadian economy.

Yet, unlike many other countries (especially Scandinavian countries such as Denmark, Norway and Sweden), Canada has not been known as a design nation – and this continues to be the case. There are several factors which may explain this, including Canada's position within the global manufacturing and production network as primarily a branch plant location for US and multinational companies. In addition, Canada has a long-standing role in the global economy as a key supplier of natural resources, leading to historical strengths in areas such as mining and forestry. Moreover, Canadian cultural policies have not focused on design in its various guises, instead focusing on other forms of artistic and cultural expression. Initiatives at the federal level have been limited in scope and success.

Similar to other advanced economies, design activity is heavily concentrated in urban centres (Power, 2004). Table 8.2 shows the growth in the size of the design workforce across Canada's 33 largest cities over the 1991–2006 period. Almost every city-region experienced an increase over this period. In fact, only two of the 33 cities experienced slight decreases in the size of their design workforce. However, these cities seem to be anomalies and must be understood in the context of the wider employment losses experienced in those cities, especially related to the continued decline of the manufacturing sector in these places. Certainly, the largest absolute increases in the design workforce were (not surprisingly) in Canada's three largest cities. In 1991, Toronto, Montreal and Vancouver collectively accounted for 33865 or 56.7 per cent of Canada's design workforce; by 2006, this had increased in absolute terms to 56455, but had decreased slightly in relative terms to 54.6 per cent.

While this relative shift could be interpreted as a decline in the design fortunes of Canada's largest cities, it is more apt to note the significant growth in design across the remaining cities. While the average rate of growth for the design workforce in Canada was 3.7 per cent per year, this was markedly higher across a number of Canadian cities, including Ottawa (5.0 per cent), Calgary (6.0 per cent), Hamilton (5.8 per cent),

Table 8.2   Design employment in Canadian cities, 1991 to 2006

City-region City	Province	1991		2006		1991–2006	
		Employed designers	Designers per 1000	Employed designers	Designers per 1000	Employed designers (change)	Annual growth (%)
Toronto	ON	16170	7.4	27960	10.1	11790	3.7
Montréal	QC	12345	6.1	17330	9.0	4985	2.3
Vancouver	BC	5350	6.1	11165	9.7	5815	5.0
Calgary	AB	2070	4.7	4975	7.6	2905	6.0
Ottawa-Gatineau	ON/QC	2940	5.6	3920	6.3	980	1.9
Edmonton	AB	1660	3.5	3185	5.3	1525	4.4
Québec	QC	2140	6.3	2505	6.3	365	1.1
Winnipeg	MB	1315	3.7	2240	5.9	925	3.6
Hamilton	ON	920	2.9	2135	5.9	1215	5.8
Kitchener	ON	620	3.1	1305	5.1	685	5.1
Victoria	BC	625	4.2	1230	6.8	605	4.6
London	ON	870	4.0	1145	4.6	275	1.8
Halifax	NS	600	3.3	1090	5.2	490	4.1
Oshawa	ON	445	3.4	920	5.1	475	5.0
St Catharines – Niagara	ON	620	3.4	865	4.3	245	2.2
Windsor	ON	390	2.9	840	5.2	450	5.2
Kelowna	BC	145	2.7	525	6.1	380	9.0
Regina	SK	255	2.5	470	4.2	215	4.2
Saskatoon	SK	240	2.2	470	3.6	230	4.6
Sherbrooke	QC	270	3.8	455	4.7	185	3.5
Guelph	ON	150	2.7	445	6.1	295	7.5
Barrie	ON	155	2.9	430	4.4	275	7.0
St John's	NL	185	2.1	335	3.5	150	4.0
Moncton	NB	115	2.1	325	4.6	210	7.2
Peterborough	ON	45	0.9	290	4.8	245	13.2
Abbotsford	BC	145	2.6	275	3.3	130	4.4
Saguenay	QC	320	4.4	270	3.7	−50	−1.1
Kingston	ON	230	3.1	265	3.4	35	0.9
Brantford	ON	145	3.5	250	3.8	105	3.7
Greater Sudbury Grand-Sudbury	ON	155	1.9	240	3.0	85	3.0
Trois-Rivières	QC	255	3.9	225	3.3	−30	−0.8
Saint John	NB	125	2.0	195	3.1	70	3.0
Thunder Bay	ON	120	1.8	140	2.2	20	1.0
Canada		59735	4.2	103485	6.1	43750	3.7

Source: Statistics Canada, *Canadian Census of Population,* 1991–2006 (author's calculations).

Kitchener (5.1 per cent), Oshawa (5.0 per cent), Windsor (5.2 per cent), Barrie (7.0 per cent), Guelph (7.5 per cent) and Kelowna (9.0 per cent). An extended discussion of these trends is beyond the scope of this chapter, however, it is worth noting that several of these cities are proximate to Toronto (for example, Hamilton, Brantford, Barrie and Kitchener). In some cases, it may also be the case that growth rates are

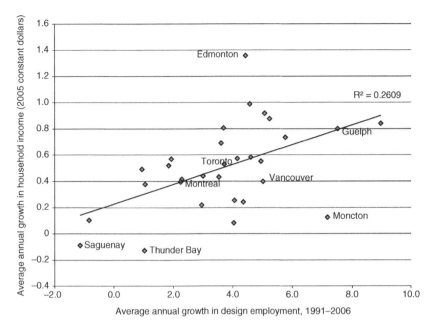

Note: Mean household income is adjusted to reflect constant 2005 Canadian dollars. Growth rates are calculated as average annual compound growth rates. Two outliers were removed (Calgary, Peterborough).

Source: Statistics Canada, *Census of Population* 1991 and 2006.

Figure 8.1 *Growth in design employment versus growth in household income in Canadian cities, 1991–2006*

slightly overstated due to small numbers (for example, Brantford saw an increase of only 105 designers over this 15-year period). However, growth in many of these city-regions may indicate industrial upgrading through an attempt to increase the design intensity of production; for example, Windsor, Kitchener and Oshawa are all centrally located in Canada's industrial heartland which has been the traditional manufacturing centre.

Recent research has shown that some Canadian manufacturing firms have been able to successfully gain competitive advantage in national and global markets through the use of design (Bathelt et al., 2010; Hatch, 2010). Finally, these data suggest the potential emergence of second-tier cities as centres of creative and design-related activity (see Vinodrai, 2009), a trend being observed in the United States as the most large and prominent centres for creative and artistic activity become increasingly costly places to live and work (Markusen, 2006). Nonetheless, Toronto, Montreal and Vancouver remain the most important design cities in Canada, accounting for more than half of all design employment.

There also appears to be a link between the presence and growth of a local design workforce and overall regional economic performance. Figure 8.1 shows a strong, positive relationship between the growth of the design workforce compared to the growth in average household incomes across Canada's largest city-regions.[3] Places that experience growth in this group of creative workers also experience growth in overall regional income levels, suggesting that a 'design dividend' does indeed accrue to places that invest in and nurture design talent.

DESIGN CITIES? TORONTO AND MONTREAL

The actual path to design success in Canadian cities varies substantially due to the mix of design occupations, the underlying industrial structure of the city, as well as other institutional, policy and historical factors that shape urban economic development. To underscore this point, two Canadian cities identified in the previous section as being leaders in terms of the size and growth of their design workforces (Toronto and Montreal) are examined in more detail and depth. As noted above, Toronto and Montreal are the largest centres of design activity in Canada, accounting for a substantial proportion of national design employment. Figure 8.2 shows the growth of design employment in each city over the 20-year period between 1987 and 2007 as compared with the performance of the overall regional labour market.

From the late 1980s to the early 1990s, Toronto's and Montreal's regional labour markets experienced stagnation and some decline. In Montreal, this decline was felt more acutely amongst designers, whereas in Toronto, there was growth followed by

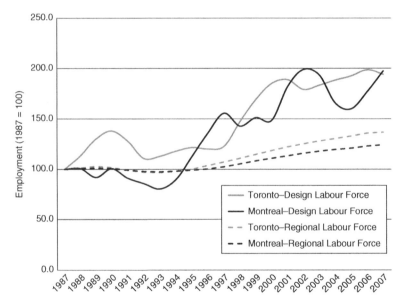

Note: Employment is indexed to facilitate comparisons (1987=100). Data represent three-year moving averages to overcome errors associated with sampling variability.

Source: Statistics Canada, *Labour Force Survey*, 1987–2007.

Figure 8.2   *Growth of the design labour force compared with growth of the total regional labour force, Toronto and Montreal, 1987–2007*

rapid decline in this period, which coincides with a significant economic recession in Canada (see below for futher discussion). Since the mid-1990s, both Toronto's and Montreal's regional labour markets have witnessed steady growth; however, growth of the design workforce has outpaced the regional labour market in both city-regions. It is also clear that design employment is susceptible to the business cycle and other external shocks, as is demonstrated by the volatility in the level of design employment throughout the period.

Despite sharing similar patterns of growth over the past two decades, the periods of growth and decline in the design labour force in each city are influenced by different local and contextual factors. This reflects the city-specific factors at work, which have influenced the local design milieu since 1990. The next sections of this chapter explore this in more detail to highlight the path-dependent and context-sensitive nature of the evolution of the creative city in Toronto and Montreal.[4]

The Diverse, Networked Design City: Toronto

Within the Canadian urban landscape, Toronto is the largest and most diverse city in both economic and cultural terms. While Toronto has gone through several waves of economic development (see Donald, 2002; Boudreau et al., 2009; Barnes et al., 2010), the city-region has in the early twenty-first century identified and nurtured strengths in a diverse range of knowledge-intensive economic clusters, including life sciences, ICT and financial services. In tandem with this focus on cluster development, the city has been explicitly pursuing a 'creative city' strategy since the early part of the millennium (City of Toronto, 2003; AuthentiCity, 2008; see also Gertler et al., 2006). However, despite these policy efforts, design has not been an explicit focus or target of the local and regional economic development agenda. It has only been more recently that design has become a more prominent element of Toronto's economic development strategy (City of Toronto, 2006; Mayor's Economic Competitiveness Advisory Committee, 2008). And it remains to be seen as to what influence this recent policy emphasis on design will have on the evolution of design activities in Toronto.

In addition to a historical lack of direct policy support for design at the local level, there is little evidence of coordination between various local institutional actors. While Toronto is the location of several design institutions including the Ontario College of Art and Design (OCAD), the Design Exchange (DX) and a host of other institutions of higher education engaged in design-related teaching and research, interviews with these actors indicated little coordinated and collective action. More recently, this has begun to change with the formation of the Design Industry Advisory Committee (DIAC), which includes participation by associations representing the various design professions, economic development officials from local and provincial government, as well as representation from the various higher education institutions that deliver design education. Additional collaborations between the OCAD and a host of other institutions resulting in innovative design thinking and design management programmes are only beginning to emerge at the time of writing (2010). It should, however, be noted that, when interviewed, designers consistently noted that many of the institutions and organizations involved in these and earlier initiatives have not always been viewed favourably by the design community itself. In addition, many practising designers do not hold

Table 8.3   Labour force status and median income by design occupation in Toronto, Montreal and Canada, 2006

			Median employment income (C$)		
	Self-employed (%)	Work at home (%)	Men	Women	All
Toronto					
All occupations	11.9	6.8	50 000	40 786	45 350
All design occupations	33.7	24.3	46 472	38 283	42 896
Architects	35.5	19.7	58 059	49 551	56 099
Landscape architects	27.4	21.7	–	–	57 362
Industrial designers	21.6	12.1	51 917	44 867	49 945
Graphic designers	32.2	25.7	42 049	39 091	40 123
Interior designers	43.0	33.2	44 839	37 779	39 898
Theatre, fashion and other	21.1	14.7	34 489	28 029	29 385
Montreal					
All occupations	10.9	6.1	43 858	34 869	39 419
All design occupations	29.5	20.8	44 007	33 656	39 227
Architects	33.6	14.7	60 925	42 380	57 368
Landscape architects	34.2	10.3	–	–	–
Industrial designers	20.3	13.9	45 694	35 714	42 701
Graphic designers	31.1	26.1	36 390	32 294	34 869
Interior designers	41.6	28.8	35 675	28 779	29 366
Theatre, fashion and other	21.1	14.7	35 871	34 567	34 667
Canada					
All occupations	11.8	7.7	46 778	35 830	41 401
All design occupations	22.6	23.8	45 336	34 679	40 535
Architects	34.6	17.4	59 982	46 664	57 102
Landscape architects	28.7	20.0	63 579	45 625	53 985
Industrial designers	20.8	15.6	53 675	40 243	50 001
Graphic designers	31.0	26.1	37 807	34 231	36 026
Interior designers	40.5	29.8	40 057	32 796	34 760
Theatre, fashion and other	31.4	21.5	36 156	29 114	30 941

Note: Some data suppressed due to small numbers.

Source: Statistics Canada, *Census of Population,* 2006 (author's calculations).

memberships with the professional associations that represent their respective disciplines (Vinodrai, 2005, 2006).

There are, however, several roles that professional associations or intermediary organizations could play – but historically have not played. For example, designers' work is often very individual, precarious and risky. This is borne out in Table 8.3 which shows median income by gender, the proportion of designers who work from home, and the proportion of designers who are self-employed by design occupation in Toronto, Montreal and nationally.[5] These data reveal that designers are far more likely to be self-

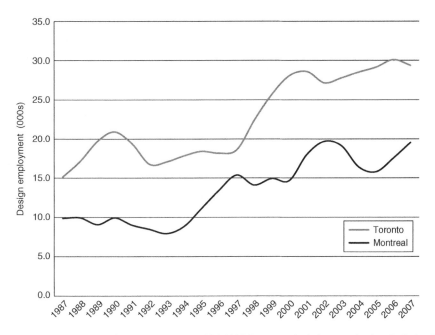

Source: Statistics Canada, *Labour Force Survey*, 1987–2007 (custom tabulations; author's calculations).

Figure 8.3 *Design employment (1000s) in Toronto and Montreal, 1987–2007*

employed and/or work from home compared to the overall labour force. Designers must often be on the lookout for their next project or contract and must take responsibility for their own skills upgrading and training. During interviews, many designers indicated they would benefit from support from formal institutions in these areas.

While there has been a minimal role for formal institutions, interviews with Toronto's community of practising designers indicated that designers rely heavily on a complex web of informal social and professional networks. The ability of designers to get work, access projects and learn about new, leading-edge practices rests very heavily on reputation (both in whom you have worked for and with) and in repeated social and professional interactions, usually in informal spaces and venues at the edges of downtown and in specific downtown neighbourhoods (Vinodrai, 2006; see also Gertler and Geddie, 2008; Leslie and Brail, 2008). Yet the very same neighbourhoods and spaces that house both the residences and workplaces of these creative workers are under constant market and land-use development pressures, which posit significant challenges to both the affordability and availability of space. Certainly, the data in Table 8.3 suggest that affordability challenges may be most acute for those working in the lower-paid design occupations, such as graphic and fashion design.

As briefly noted in the previous section, Toronto's design workforce has been susceptible to broader structural changes in the economy, as well as to changes in the business cycle (Figure 8.3). This is most evident when examining the period between 1987 and 1992, where Toronto experienced high growth and sudden decline. This development reflects the early 1990s recession in Canada, in which the manufacturing sector was hardest hit (Vinodrai, 2009). After a period of slow growth and recovery following the recession, Toronto's design workforce once again experienced high levels of growth in the late 1990s, which can be attributed to the growth of multimedia and new media activity in Toronto. This activity was supported by local demand from highly sophisticated customers such as the major Canadian banks (headquartered in Toronto's financial district) who required the development of online banking tools and other applications, as well as a range of other customers (Brail and Gertler, 1999; Britton et al., 2009). A small decline at the turn of the millennium can be attributed to the dot-com boom and bust, a further downturn at the end of the time period for which data are available reflects the most recent economic downturn in the economy, the broader outcomes and impacts of which are still to be fully determined.

In spite of this volatility and the lack of coordinated collective action and direct institutional and policy support, Toronto remains the largest centre of design employment in Canada. Despite its size, Toronto is not well known (with some exceptions) for design on the global stage. Yet design is a critical input into many other parts of Toronto's cognitive-cultural economy. There is a large and diverse base of local firms that hire designers. In other words, the industrial diversity of Toronto's economy and the existence of several dynamic clusters are reflected in the sectoral distribution of design work. Vinodrai (2006) found that more than half of designers worked for firms outside of the design industry. And, as Table 8.4 shows, in 2006 only 48.4 per cent of all designers worked in the architectural, engineering and design services industries. Notably, a high proportion of designers worked in manufacturing-related industries in which Toronto has historical strengths, particularly related to printing and publishing, as well as in the information and cultural industries (6.9 per cent) and the advertising industry (6.0 per cent). These industries have been consistently identified as an important element of Toronto's urban economy and – in contrast to design activity – have benefited from many years of direct public policy support at the local, provincial and national level. Overall, design success is rooted in the economic diversity of the city, as well as strong local social and professional networks that are supported by informal spaces rather than the presence of strong supporting institutions and public policies.

The Affordable, Supportive Design City: Montreal

Unlike Toronto, Montreal has a larger presence and reputation on the global design stage, best articulated through its status as a UNESCO City of Design and as the world headquarters of the International Design Alliance (IDA). However, the path to success has not been entirely easy. Returning to Figures 8.1 and 8.2 (above), we can see that Montreal experienced a slow and steady decline in design employment over the period between 1987 and 1993. This can be attributed to the ongoing decline of Montreal's traditional industrial base beginning in the 1980s. However, Montreal's design workforce has grown steadily since the mid-1990s. Similar to the experience in Toronto, the rapid increase and sudden decline in the early years of the twenty-first century parallels the years in which the economy experienced the dot-com boom and bust. The statistical data underscore the point made above regarding how design employment often reflects the broader characteristics of the local or regional economy. Table 8.5 shows the occupational breakdown amongst different types of designers. Looking at Montreal in par-

Table 8.4   Distribution of employment (%) by major industry in Toronto, Montreal and Canada, 2006

	Toronto		Montreal		Canada	
	Designers	Total	Designers	Total	Designers	Total
Primary, utilities, construction and transportation	2.3	11.7	2.7	10.9	2.9	16.5
Manufacturing	15.9	13.4	17.8	13.4	18.1	11.9
• Clothing and textile-related	2.4	0.7	6.6	1.7	2.7	0.7
• Printing and paper	5.4	1.2	2.4	1.3	5.3	1.1
• Other manufacturing	8.1	11.5	8.9	10.4	10.1	10.2
Wholesale trade	3.0	6.1	5.0	5.7	3.1	4.4
Retail trade	5.4	10.5	6.6	12.0	6.0	11.4
• Clothing-related retail	1.6	1.6	3.3	1.8	1.6	1.2
• Other retail	3.8	8.9	3.4	10.1	4.4	10.1
Information and cultural industries	6.9	3.7	7.4	3.6	7.7	2.5
Finance, insurance and real estate	1.5	9.8	1.0	8.3	1.3	6.7
Professional/scientific/technical	58.3	1.8	50.6	1.7	51.7	1.5
• Architecture, engineering, design[a]	48.4	–	42.6	–	–	–
• Advertising services[a]	6.0	–	3.8	–	–	–
• Other professional services[a]	3.8	–	4.2	–	–	–
Other services	6.6	35.3	8.6	39.5	9.3	40.8
All industries	100	100	100	100	100	100

Note: [a] Some data unavailable at time of writing.

Source: Statistics Canada, *Census of Population,* 2006 (custom tabulations; author's calculations).

ticular, it is evident that the occupational specializations within design are quite different compared with Toronto. Specifically, theatre, fashion and other designers account for roughly a fifth of the design workforce, almost double that of Toronto. And Table 8.4 shows that – outside of the architecture, engineering and design services industries – the highest proportions of designers can be found in clothing and textile-related manufacturing (6.6 per cent), clothing-related retail trade (3.3 per cent) as well as information and cultural industries (7.4 per cent). The specialization in fashion and clothing that emerges in both the overall occupational data and in the sectoral breakdown of design work speaks to both the historical strength of the city in textile manufacturing, but also to the reinvention, reorientation and industrial upgrading of that particular sector towards design throughout the value chain (Leslie and Rantisi, 2006, 2009; Rantisi and Leslie, 2008, 2010). In addition to the clear design strengths in fashion, the presence of a high proportion of designers in the information and cultural industries speaks to the development of a new media cluster rooted in old industrial neighbourhoods and the emergence of a set of internationally renowned video game producers located in the city (Britton et al., 2009).

In stark contrast to the Toronto case, city and provincial-level policies have played a critical role in directly supporting design in Montreal. Leslie and Rantisi (2006) note

*Table 8.5   Employment by design occupation in Toronto, Montreal and Canada,
1991 to 2006*

	1991		2006		1991–2006		
	Number	%	Number	%	Change (number)	Change %	% growth per year
Toronto							
All design occupations	16170	100.0	27960	100.0	11790	72.9	3.7
Architects	2375	14.7	3690	13.2	1315	55.4	3.0
Landscape architects	360	2.2	470	1.7	110	30.6	1.8
Industrial designers	830	5.1	2500	8.9	1670	201.2	7.6
Graphic designers	8195	50.7	14445	51.7	6250	76.3	3.9
Interior designers	2260	14.0	3735	13.4	1475	65.3	3.4
Theatre/fashion/other	2150	13.3	3120	11.2	970	45.1	2.5
Montreal							
All design occupations	12345	100.0	17330	100.0	4985	40.4	2.3
Architects	2010	16.3	2665	15.4	655	32.6	1.9
Landscape architects	630	5.1	195	1.1	−435	−69.0	−7.5
Industrial designers	700	5.7	2075	12.0	1375	196.4	7.5
Graphic designers	5145	41.7	6880	39.7	1735	33.7	2.0
Interior designers	1010	8.2	2090	12.1	1080	106.9	5.0
Theatre/fashion/other	2850	23.1	3425	19.8	575	20.2	1.2
Canada							
All design occupations	59735	100.0	103485	100.0	43750	73.2	3.7
Architects	9165	15.3	13960	13.5	4795	52.3	2.8
Landscape architects	2125	3.6	1620	1.6	−505	−23.8	−1.8
Industrial designers	3455	5.8	10250	9.9	6795	196.7	7.5
Graphic designers	28405	47.6	51890	50.1	23485	82.7	4.1
Interior designers	7495	12.5	14355	13.9	6860	91.5	4.4
Theatre/fashion/other	9090	15.2	11410	11.0	2320	25.5	1.5

Source: Statistics Canada, *Census of Population,* 1991–2006 (author's calculations).

that design has been an important part of policy discourse at the local and provincial level since the 1980s and that it is a fundamental element of both economic and cultural development policy. They identify several organizations and programmes that have been critical to Montreal's success in bolstering its position in the global design world, including Commerce Design Montréal, the Institute of Design Montréal (IDM), Société de Développement des Entreprises Culturelles (SODEC) and provincial tax credit programmes. For example, in order to embed design into the fabric of the city and in the minds of citizens, Commerce Design Montréal was a competition in which local merchants and businesses could participate and that required the procurement of local design expertise to upgrade their storefronts, thus stimulating the demand for local design while simultaneously becoming part of an urban revitalization and renewal strategy. In addition to this internationally well-regarded programme, the province has been one of the first jurisdictions to offer tax credits to firms that hire design expertise. As Leslie and Rantisi (2006, p. 322) note, 'the tax credit program is perceived to have been relatively successful in encouraging higher-value-added production in the furniture and fashion industries in particular'. This also appears in the official statistics both through higher proportions of industrial designers working in Quebec's cities (see Gertler and Vinodrai, 2004; Vinodrai, 2009), as well as in the proportion of designers working in particular industrial sectors.

However, these formal policies and programmes are complemented by an equally important array of informal sites and spaces within the city-region. According to Rantisi and Leslie (2010), particular neighbourhoods in Montreal, such as Montreal's Mile End, have played an important role in creating an open environment that is culturally diverse, having been the destination for successive waves of immigrants. The fabric of the built environment in this neighbourhood is also important. As a dense neighbourhood that once thrived during Montreal's industrial heyday, the spaces in the neighbourhood now offer more affordable housing for a range of creative workers (including designers) that provide opportunities for experimentation and collaboration (Rantisi and Leslie, 2010; see also Barnes et al., 2010).

As noted in earlier sections of this chapter, design work – like many forms of creative work – is often precarious, workers are exposed to high levels of risk, and remuneration is variable. Table 8.3 (above) shows several indicators that capture these dynamics, including levels of self-employment, the proportion of designers working from home and median income levels (overall and by gender). In the case of Montreal, the numbers are quite telling. While the levels of self-employment (29.5 per cent) and the proportion of the labour force working from home (20.8 per cent) are substantially higher for designers compared to the city-wide average (as noted, a trend observed in Toronto as well), these indicators are lower than in Toronto. In other words, designers appear to be exposed to less risk as compared with their counterparts in Toronto.

Overall, both the findings of other studies and the data presented here suggest a picture of affordability and of a supportive policy environment that mitigates individual risk to some extent and supports the development and evolution of the local design scene. Moreover, while the case of Toronto highlighted the importance of economic diversity, the Montreal case highlights the importance of specialization, significant institutional and public policy support (absent until recently in Toronto) and broader economic and structural conditions that support the ongoing liveability and affordability of the city for designers. In other words, the development of design in Montreal has been driven by several different local factors and policy interventions at the local and provincial level. Montreal's design activity is anchored by the availability of affordable housing and a broad set of strong local and provincial policy supports and initiatives.

DESIGN, THE CREATIVE CITY AND THE CHALLENGES FOR PUBLIC POLICY

As many scholars have noted, the response to external shocks such as major global recessions or the dot-com boom and bust at the turn of the millennium, is very much influenced by pre-existing conditions within each region. The development of urban and regional economies is often path-dependent and susceptible to the influence of a variety of factors, including their institutional and governance capacity, the particular configuration of regional business and associative networks, the presence (or absence) of public and private research infrastructure, regional culture, the distinct character of the local labour market (for example, skills and occupational mix), other territorial assets, as well as the underlying regional industrial structure, itself often a product of these same factors (Chapple and Lester, 2010; Wolfe, 2010).

Using the case of design employment in Canada's largest metropolitan regions, this chapter has shown that cities can pursue different pathways towards the development of the creative city. Toronto and Montreal have qualitatively and quantitatively different and distinctive forms of design activity that reflect the unique features of the local economy and the different industrial specializations that exist within each metropolitan regional economy. Each city has been differentially affected by broader macroeconomic circumstances and has followed different growth trajectories, supported by different local institutional configurations and local and provincial policy mixes.

This chapter began with the premise that designers are critical actors in the development of the creative economy and the creative city. Designers, through their grounded, material practices, contribute to the construction of quality of place and to the economic and innovation performance of firms and regions. Designers also rely on aspects of the urban fabric for inspiration in their work and to get work. Affordable spaces allow designers to live and work in close proximity to prospective clients and other practitioners in related fields. While the case of Toronto highlights the importance of strong clusters and economic diversity to generate opportunities for creative workers (designers) in the city, the Montreal case highlights the importance of a broad range of supportive institutions and policies to anchor creative activity and upgrade traditional activities in the city. It should also not go unnoticed that workers such as designers are often exposed to high levels of risk in their careers and work. Furthermore, there is significant variation in the levels of remuneration amongst designers by gender and occupation. In this sense, the shift towards policymaking that supports creativity-led economic development needs to be sensitive and attuned to the particular needs of workers operating in these fields.

Rather than a one-size-fits-all creative city strategy, policymakers need to pay close attention to the pre-existing industrial structure and other regional assets which may allow policymakers to intervene in the appropriate places. In the case of design, this means access to project opportunities and business/career networks, sophisticated and demanding clients, and access to affordable spaces in the city.

Given that the argument here is one that suggests that the evolution of the creative city is path-dependent and sensitive to local context, this raises the question: how can public policy support the development of a creative and inclusive city through and by design? First, based on the research presented and reviewed here, policymakers should build upon their existing industrial base and encourage firms to adopt a value-added strategy that incorporates design and design practices. As we saw in the Montreal case (and has been the case elsewhere in advanced, capitalist economies), tax credits and design promotion activities can lead to industrial upgrading, innovation and job retention in both traditional and emerging sectors.

Second, given that design work is risky, contingent, precarious and susceptible to shifts in the business cycle, it is important to ensure that designers remain on the leading edge of practice and are able to find work. Support for intermediary organizations and programmes that facilitate access to job-search and employment networks and that provide opportunities for professional training and skills upgrading are important in this regard. Such programmes would benefit designers and their employers alike, but remain all too rare.

Third, policymakers need to preserve and maintain access to informal and affordable spaces, even in the face of market forces. These spaces are essential for the (re)productive work of designers and other creative workers. This can be achieved through a variety of mechanisms, including land-use zoning and subsidies. Fourth, policymakers can lead by example, through including design criteria in their procurement strategies and consider ways to maintain the unique and authentic qualities of the local economy and the built environment. Certainly, this is not easily achieved and addressing these issues requires coordinated action across different levels of decision making (local, regional, provincial) and across traditionally separate policymaking arenas (for example, art and culture, education, industry and trade, innovation and economic development). However, rather than dismissing outright the potential for creative city-oriented strategies as a mechanism for urban economic development, this chapter has argued for a more nuanced consideration of the creative city. By showing that the evolution of the creative city is path-dependent, it illustrates the multiple paths to economic success and prosperity. From a policy perspective, this means that economic development strategy and policy attuned to local conditions and context, accompanied by coordinated action amongst economic actors, can lead to success in supporting creative work in cities in the contemporary period.

NOTES

1. L. Ozler (2005), 'Sony opens new U.S. design center in Los Angeles', available at http:// www.dexigner. com/news/3870 (accessed March 2011).
2. The Innovation Systems Research Network (ISRN) is a network of researchers examining the social dynamics of innovation, talent attraction and retention and governance across Canadian city-regions and is directed by Meric Gertler and David Wolfe at the University of Toronto. I have participated in this network since 2002.
3. Choosing a regional economic performance measure is not an easy task; total household income was chosen due to its availability in both Census years. Moreover, there is a myriad of other factors that influence individual earnings and household incomes. Fully isolating the effect of design on regional economic performance would require further research and is beyond the scope of this chapter.
4. Historically, Toronto and Montreal have battled for urban primacy within the Canadian urban landscape and while the two cities have many commonalities in terms of their economic development trajectories, there are many differences as well. A full account of their similarities and differences is beyond the scope of this chapter (see Barnes et al., 2010).
5. National averages are provided in Tables 8.3 to 8.5 for comparison purposes. However, it should be noted that the national averages are heavily influenced by Toronto and Montreal, since these two cities account for almost half of all designers in Canada.

REFERENCES

Asheim, B., P. Cooke and R. Martin (eds) (2006), *Clusters and Regional Development: Critical Reflections and Explorations*, New York, NY: Routledge.

AuthentiCity (2008), 'Creative city planning framework: a supporting document to the Agenda for Prosperity', report prepared for the City of Toronto, available at http://www.toronto.ca/culture/pdf/creative-city-planning-framework-feb08.pdf (accessed 7 March 2011).

Barnes, T. and T. Hutton (2009), 'Situating the new economy: contingencies of regeneration and dislocation in Vancouver's inner city', *Urban Studies*, **46**(5–6), 1247–69.

Barnes, T., T. Hutton, J.-L. Klein, D.-G. Tremblay and D.A. Wolfe (2010), 'A tale of three cities: innovation, creativity and governance in Montreal, Toronto and Vancouver', paper presented at the annual meeting of the Innovation Systems Research Network (ISRN), Toronto, Canada, 5–7 May.

Bathelt, H., A. Malmberg and A. Maskell (2004), 'Clusters and knowledge: local buzz, global pipelines and the process of knowledge creation', *Progress in Human Geography*, **28**, 31–56.

Bathelt, H., A.K. Munro and B. Spigel (2010), 'Challenges of transformation: Innovation, re-bundling and traditional manufacturing in Canada's Technology Triangle', paper presented at the Association of American Geographers Annual Conference, Washington, DC, 14–18 April.

Beckstead, D. and T. Vinodrai (2003), 'Dimensions of occupational change in Canada's knowledge economy, 1971–1996', *The Canadian Economy in Transition Series* (Catalogue No. 11-622-MIE2003004), Ottawa, ON: Analytical Studies Branch, Statistics Canada.

Boudreau, J., R. Keil and D. Young (2009), *Changing Toronto: Governing Urban Neoliberalism*, Toronto, ON: University of Toronto Press.

Bradford, N. (2004), *Creative Cities Structured Policy Dialogue Backgrounder*, Ottawa, ON: Canadian Policy Research Networks.

Brail, S. and M.S. Gertler (1999), 'The digital regional economy', in H.J. Braczyk, G. Fuchs and H.G.Wolf (eds), *Multimedia and Regional Economic Restructuring*, London: Routledge, pp. 97–130.

Braunerhjelm, P. and M. Feldman (eds) (2006), *Cluster Genesis: Technology-based Industrial Development*, Oxford: Oxford University Press.

Britton, J.N.H., D.-G.Tremblay and R. Smith (2009), 'Contrasts in clustering: the example of Canadian new media', *European Planning Studies*, **17**(2), 281–301.

Chapple, K. and T.W. Lester (2010), 'The resilient regional labour market? The US case', *Cambridge Journal of Regions, Economy and Society*, **3**, 139–52.

City of Toronto (2003), *Culture Plan for the Creative City*, Toronto, ON: Culture Division, City of Toronto.

City of Toronto (2006), *Drawing the Link: Advancing Design as a Vehicle for Innovation and Economic Development*, Toronto, ON: City of Toronto Economic Development Division.

Donald, B. (2002), 'The permeable city: Toronto's spatial shift at the turn of the millennium', *The Professional Geographer*, **54**(2), 190–203.

Donald, B. and D. Morrow (2003), 'Competing for talent: implications for social and cultural policy in Canadian city-regions', report prepared for Strategic Research and Analysis (SRA) Strategic Planning and Policy Coordination, Department of Canadian Heritage.

Donegan, M. and N. Lowe (2008), 'Inequality in the creative city: is there still a place for "old fashioned" institutions?', *Economic Development Quarterly*, **22**(1), 46–62.

Ekinsmyth, C. (2002), 'Project organization, embeddedness, and risk in magazine publishing', *Regional Studies*, **36**, 229–44.

Feser, E.J (2003), 'What regions do rather than make: a proposed set of knowledge-based occupation clusters', *Urban Studies*, **40**(10), 1937–58.

Florida, R. (2002), *The Rise of the Creative Class*, New York, NY: Basic Books.

Florida, R., C. Mellander and K. Stolarick (2008), 'Inside the black box of regional development: human capital, the creative class and tolerance', *Journal of Economic Geography*, **8**(5), 615–49.

Gertler, M.S. (2001), 'Urban economy and society in Canada: flows of people, capital and ideas', *ISUMA: The Canadian Journal of Policy Research*, **2**(3), 119–30.

Gertler, M.S. (2010), 'The rules of the game? The place of institutions in regional economic change', *Regional Studies*, **44**(1), 1–15.

Gertler, M.S. and K. Geddie (2008), 'Architectural talent: how does quality of place shape attraction and retention in Toronto?', paper presented at the Joint ONRIS/MRI Workshop, Toronto, ON, 6–7 November.

Gertler, M.S. and T. Vinodrai (2004), 'Designing the economy: a profile of Ontario's design workforce', report prepared for the Design Industry Advisory Committee.

Gertler, M.S. and T. Vinodrai (2005), 'Anchors of creativity: how do public universities create competitive and cohesive communities?', in F. Iaocobucci and C. Tuohy (eds), *Taking Public Universities Seriously*, Toronto, ON: University of Toronto Press, pp. 293–314.

Gertler, M.S., R. Florida, G. Gates and T. Vinodrai (2002), 'Competing on creativity: Ontario cities in North American context', report to the Institute for Competitiveness and Prosperity and the Ontario Ministry of Enterprise, Opportunity and Innovation, Toronto, ON.

Gertler, M.S., L. Tesolin, S. Weinstock et al., (2006), *Imagine a Toronto: Strategies for a Creative City*, Toronto, ON: Munk Centre for International Studies, University of Toronto.

Gertler, M.S., J. Rekers, K. Geddie and T. Vinodrai (2007), 'Architecture in Toronto: social foundations of talent and creativity', paper presented at the Innovation Systems Research Network, Vancouver, BC, 3–4 May.

Grabher, G. (2002), 'The project ecology of advertising: talents, tasks, and teams', *Regional Studies*, **36**, 245–62.

Hall, P. (1998), *Cities in Civilization*, New York, NY: Pantheon.

Hatch, C. (2010), 'Competitiveness by design: an institutional perspective on the resurgence of a "mature" industry in a high-wage economy', paper presented at the Association of American Geographers Annual Conference, Washington, DC, 14–18 April.

Hulchanski, J.D. (2007), 'The three cities within Toronto: income polarization among Toronto's neighbourhoods, 1970–2000', Research Bulletin No. 40, Centre for Urban and Community Studies, University of Toronto, Toronto, ON.

Hutton, T. (2008), *The New Economy of the Inner City: Restructuring, Regeneration, and Dislocation in the Twenty-first Century Metropolis*, New York, NY: Routledge.

Leslie, D. and S. Brail (2008), 'The role of quality of place in attracting and retaining fashion design talent', paper presented at the Joint ONRIS/MRI Workshop, Toronto, ON, 6–7 November.

Leslie, D. and N. Rantisi (2006), 'Governing the design economy of Montreal, Canada', *Urban Affairs Review*, **41**, 309–37.

Leslie, D. and N. Rantisi (2009), 'Fostering a culture of design: insights from the case of Montréal, Canada', in A. Pratt and P. Jeffcut (eds), *Creativity, Innovation and the Cultural Economy*, New York, NY: Routledge, pp. 181–99.

Lewis, N.M. and B. Donald (2010), 'A new rubric for "creative city" potential in Canada's smaller cities', *Urban Studies*, **47**(1), 29–54.

London Development Agency (2003), *Creative London: Vision and Plan*, London: London Development Agency.

Markusan, A. (2004), 'Targeting occupations in regional and community development', *Journal of the American Planning Association*, **70**(3), 253–68.

Markusen, A. (2006), 'Urban development and the politics of a creative class: evidence from the study of artists', *Environment and Planning A*, **38**, 1921–40.

Markusen, A. and G. Schrock (2006), 'The artistic dividend: urban artistic specialization and economic development implications', *Urban Studies*, **43**, 1661–86.

Maskell, P. and A. Malmberg (1999), 'Localised learning and industrial competitiveness', *Cambridge Journal of Economics*, **23**, 167–85.

Mayor's Economic Competitiveness Advisory Committee (2008), *Agenda for Prosperity*, Toronto, ON: City of Toronto.

McCann, E. (2007), 'Inequality and politics in the creative city-region: questions of livability and state strategy', *International Journal of Urban and Regional Research*, **31**, 188–96.

McRobbie, A. (2009), 'Reflections on precarious work in the cultural sector', in B. Lange, A. Kalandides, B. Stober and I. Wellmann (eds), *Governance der Kreativwirtschaft: Diagnosen und Handlungsoptionen*, Bielefeld: Transcript Verlag, pp. 123–39.

Molotch, H. (2002), 'Place in product', *International Journal of Urban and Regional Research*, **26**, 665–88.

Peck, J. (2005), 'Struggling with the creative class', *International Journal of Urban and Regional Research*, **29**(4), 740–70.

Peck, J. (2009), 'The cult of urban creativity', in R. Kiel and R. Mahon (eds), *Leviathan Undone? Towards a Political Economy of Scale*, Vancouver, BC: University of British Columbia Press, pp. 159–76.

Power, D. (2004), *The Future in Design: The Competitiveness and Industrial Dynamics of the Nordic Design Industry*, Uppsala: Centre for Research on Innovation and Industrial Dynamics.

Pratt, A.C. (1997), 'Employment in the cultural industries sector: a case study of Britain, 1984–91', *Environment and Planning A*, **29**(11), 1953–76.

Rantisi, N.M. (2002), 'The competitive foundations of localized learning and innovation: the case of the women's garment industry in New York City', *Economic Geography*, **78**, 441–61.

Rantisi, N.M. (2004), 'The designer in the city and the city in the designer', in D. Power and A.J. Scott (eds), *The Cultural Industries and the Production of Culture*, London: Routledge, pp. 91–109.

Rantisi, N.M. and D. Leslie (2008), 'Social and material foundations of creativity for Montreal design', paper presented at the Innovation Systems Research Network, Montreal, QC, 30 April–2 May.

Rantisi, N.M. and D. Leslie (2010), 'Creativity by design? The role of informal spaces in creative production', in T. Edensor, D. Leslie, S. Millington and N.M. Rantisi (eds), *Spaces of Vernacular Creativity: Rethinking the Cultural Economy*, New York, NY: Routledge, pp. 33–45.

Sands, G. and L.A. Reese (2008), 'Cultivating the creative class: and what about Nanaimo?', *Economic Development Quarterly*, **22**(1), 8–23.

Scott, A.J. (2001), *The Cultural Economy of Cities: Essays on the Geography of Image-producing Industries*, Oxford: Sage Publications.

Scott, A.J. (2006), 'Creative cities: conceptual issues and policy problems', *Journal of Urban Affairs*, **28**, 1–17.
Scott, A.J. (2007), 'Capitalism and urbanization in a new key? The cognitive-cultural dimension', *Social Forces*, **85**(4), 1466–82.
Scott, A.J. (2008), *Social Economy of the Metropolis: Cognitive-cultural Capitalism and the Global Resurgence of Cities*, Oxford and New York, NY: Oxford University Press.
Storper, M. and A.J. Scott (2009), 'Rethinking human capital, creativity and urban growth', *Journal of Economic Geography*, **9**, 1–21.
Storper, M. and A.J. Venables (2004), 'Buzz: face-to-face contact and the urban economy', *Journal of Economic Geography*, **4**, 351–70.
Vinodrai, T. (2005), 'Locating design work: innovation, institutions and local labour market dynamics', unpublished doctoral dissertation, Department of Geography, University of Toronto, 213 pp.
Vinodrai, T. (2006), 'Reproducing Toronto's design ecology: career paths, intermediaries, and local labor markets', *Economic Geography*, **82**(3), 237–63.
Vinodrai, T. (2009), 'The place of design: exploring Ontario's design economy', Ontario in the Creative Age Working Paper Series, Martin Prosperity Institute, University of Toronto.
Vinodrai, T. (2010), 'The dynamics of economic change in Canadian cities: innovation, culture and the emergence of a knowledge based economy', in T. Bunting, P. Filion and R. Walker (eds), *Canadian Cities in Transition* (4th edn), Toronto, ON: Oxford University Press Canada, pp. 87–109.
Wolfe, D. (2010), 'The strategic management of core cities: path dependence and economic adjustment in resilient regions', *Cambridge Journal of Regions, Economy and Society*, **3**, 139–52.
Wolfe, D.A. and M.S. Gertler (2004), 'Clusters from the inside and out: local dynamics and global linkages', *Urban Studies*, **4**, 1071–93.

9 Technology, talent and tolerance and inter-regional migration in Canada
Karen M. King

INTRODUCTION

In *The Rise of the Creative Class*, Richard Florida (2002) introduces the creative class theoretical framework and with it the occupational groupings of creative, service and working classes. Since its introduction, the creative class theory has been increasingly put into practice to encourage regional development and competitiveness. Florida (2002) argues that a region's ability to attract the creative class in turn encourages innovative development and knowledge-based economic growth. The creative class consists of individuals employed in occupations whose economic value is the creation of new ideas and forms and is comprised of two groups: the 'super-creative core' and 'creative professionals'. The concentration and diversity of the creative class and their creative capital can then be translated into innovations which drive economies forward. Therefore, those regions that are best able to attract and retain the creative class have the highest potential for economic growth in a knowledge economy. Florida (2002) found his 'high-tech index' to be strongly associated with the location of the creative class while his 'melting pot', 'gay' and 'bohemian' indices are strongly associated with the high-tech index for metropolitan areas in the United States in 2000, with similar findings in the Canadian context (Gertler et al., 2002). Although the majority of attention has focused on the creative class, the service and working classes also play important roles in the economy.

While traditional measures of human capital use education, creative capital attempts to improve on this by measuring how people employ their education, talents and skills through their occupations. Creative capital builds and expands on the more traditionally used 'human capital' concept (Schultz, 1961; Becker, 1964) and its relationship to economic development. The creative class theoretical framework and its relation to economic development have faced many criticisms (see, for example, Glaeser, 2004; Peck, 2005; Markusen, 2006; Scott, 2006). Malanga (2004) argues that Florida's indices are poor predictors of economic performance such as employment. Markusen (2006) argues that the creative class is a fuzzy concept that is defined by major occupational codes. That is, the use of major occupational codes is problematic due to the wide range in the types of occupations contained within each major occupational code. Glaeser (2004) argues that the creative capital theory of growth is a version of the human capital theory of growth. Another major criticism of the creative class theoretical framework is, as Baris (2003) argues, that the thesis does not consider inequality and poverty.

Although the creative class theoretical framework has faced several criticisms, there is empirical support of the importance of the presence of the 3Ts – technology, talent and tolerance and the creative class in relation to economic development and growth. In relation to new business formation and employment growth, the 3Ts and the creative class have been found to be positively correlated. For instance, start-up rates at the regional level in Finland, Germany, Norway and Sweden have been found to be positively correlated with measures of talent and the creative class (Boschma and Fritsch, 2009), while Lee et al. (2004) found the bohemian index to be strongly associated with new firm formation in the United States. The creative class share has a positive effect on employment growth both in Dutch cities (Stam et al., 2008), as well as in both non-metropolitan and metropolitan areas in the United States (Wojan et al., 2007).The 3Ts have also been found to influence productivity. While Rausch and Negrey (2006) found the share of the creative class to be unable to predict gross metropolitan product growth, tolerance and melting pot indices as well as high technology were found to be strong predictors in the United States. Ottaviano and Peri (2005a, 2005b) found that US-born citizens living in metropolitan areas with greater diversity were more productive as measured by increases in their wages.

Florida (2002) argues that a region's ability to attract and retain the creative class depends on a region's high 'quality of life', measured through the presence of a rich culture and diverse population. A region must have all the 3Ts of technology, talent and tolerance to attract the creative class, generate innovation and stimulate economic growth (Florida, 2002). However, there has been limited empirical examination of whether the presence of the 3Ts plays a role in the attraction or retention of the creative class. Indeed, the limited research thus far has found limited support of the importance of the 3Ts in internal migration propensities. Instead, results have found that traditional economic variables such as economic opportunities are more important than the 3Ts. Marlet and van Woerkens (2005) found that the aesthetic quality of cities and job opportunities are more important for the share and growth of the creative class in the Netherlands than four measures of tolerance: bohemian index, gay scene, ethnic diversity and pub closing hours. Hansen and Niedomsyl (2009) found life cycle effects to be important, as once individuals have attained their higher education they enter the job market in smaller cities which are ranked lower in 'people climate'. Similarly, in Scotland, Houston et al. (2008) found the creative class moving after obtaining an employment offer in another region. However, in the United States, Wojan et al. (2007) found that a larger share of creative class employment has a positive effect on net migration.

While the 3T measures of talent, tolerance and technology have been used to varying degrees in internal migration research, the importance of these regional characteristics in attracting and retaining the creative class as well as the service and working classes have yet to be undertaken. While migration research has paid some attention to the demographic profiles of regions, focusing on ethnicity or immigration, there has been less attention to tolerance, as measured by Florida's bohemian, gay and melting pot (or in the Canadian context 'mosaic') indices (2002). The creative class theoretical framework has received much less attention in Canada than in the United States or Europe (see, for exceptions, Gertler et al., 2002; Stolarick and Florida, 2006; Petrov, 2007; Florida, 2009; Florida et al., 2010). The available literature focuses on the theoretical framework at the macro level, with little examination on a micro level. Indeed, there has been little empirical analysis of whether higher levels of talent, technology and tolerance are indeed attractive to the creative class.

This chapter undertakes an exploratory analysis of the available talent, technology and tolerance of Canadian regions, and the influence of these factors on internal migration behaviour. More specifically, the chapter extends the creative class thesis by examining the attractiveness of regions in the context of the 3Ts not only for the creative class, but for the working and service classes as well. This chapter will add to our knowledge of internal migration behaviour in the context of the creative class framework as well as extend our knowledge about migration behaviours by occupation in the Canadian context.

OCCUPATION AND INTERNAL MIGRATION

While there has been limited empirical research on the migration patterns of the creative class in the context of the creative class theoretical framework, there has been even less attention to these patterns for the service and working classes, as the focus has been the retention and attraction of the creative class. Indeed, differentiation of internal migration patterns and behaviours by occupation has received much less attention than their international counterparts. International migration research has examined occupation groups with typically high levels of human capital such as researchers and scientists (Finn, 2007; Thorn and Holm-Nielsen, 2008), entrepreneurs (Saxenian, 2002, 2005, 2006, 2008; Desai, 2003; Saxenian and Li, 2003), technical talent (Docquier and Rapoport, 2004; Solimano and Pollack, 2004; D'Costa, 2006, 2008) and health professionals (ILO, 2004; Khadria, 2004; Bach, 2008) and their migration in relation to economic growth and development. High human capital occupations have been the focus as individuals with higher levels of human capital tend to be more migratory (Sjaastad, 1962; and see, for internal migration examples, Faggian et al., 2007; Faggian and McCann, 2009). However, unlike in the international context, recent internal migration research has more generally focused on labour force-aged individuals with less attention to differences between specific occupations.

Internal migration has been studied in several contexts, with the research examining migration patterns and behaviours focusing on both individual and place characteristics. The role of occupation in migration patterns and behaviours has largely been the focus of three streams of research (Ellis et al., 1993). The first stream which has received the most attention is occupation as a determinant of migration. Occupation, as with demographic and other socio-economic characteristics, has been used to explain differing migration behaviours. The second stream examines the importance of occupation credentials in the migration decision. Research in this stream has focused on credential recognition such as licensing that may hinder the movement of individuals. While this has been examined in the international migration context, there is a growing body of research on this in the case of recognition of occupational experience and credentials of immigrants. The third stream examines the migration patterns and behaviours by specific occupations. Thus far international migration research has examined occupations that typically require higher levels of education and skills such as engineering or computer science.

Internal migration differences by occupation garnered attention in the United States in the 1960s. Between 1949 and 1950, the occupations with the highest rates of inter-county migration included members of the armed forces, airplane pilots and navigators, athletes and clergymen (Tarver, 1964). From the 1960 Census, Ladinsky (1967a) found that male professional and technical workers had the highest lifetime mobility with 74 per cent having moved from their place of birth, while clergymen were the most and funeral directors the least migratory in the United States. Continuing this work using a stepwise regression, Ladinsky (1967b) found that, among professional workers and occupational groupings, age followed by income and education were the strongest factors in explaining migration variance. More specifically, Ladinsky (1967b, 1967c) found that of the professional occupations, the most mobile were salaried professionals while those self-employed, including professionals such as lawyers and dentists, were the least mobile. The self-employed tended to have lower rates of migration due to the location-specific investment, including capital investments and relationship with clients (Ladinsky, 1967b, 1967c). In comparing the 1960 Census of the United States with England, Japan and Canada, white-collar workers were found to have higher rates of long-distance migrations than blue-collar workers, which is likely due to the higher levels of human capital, while blue-collar workers had higher rates of short-distance moves (Sjaastad, 1962; Long, 1973). Moreover, of white-collar workers, professional and technical workers had the highest rates of migration in each of the four countries (Sjaastad, 1962; Long, 1973). Pashigian's (1979) study of interstate mobility in the United States found lower rates for men in occupations requiring licensing, likely due both to licensing differences across states and the financial and time costs of establishing a new practice. In line with this, from the 1950 Census, Holen (1965) found lawyers and dentists to have lower interstate migration rates than physicians.

Subsequent migration research in the United States has echoed earlier findings. According to the 1970 Census, professional and technical workers had higher interstate migration rates than labourers (Kleiner, 1982) and higher average probability of migration (Herzog and Schlottmann, 1984). Between 1975 and 1980, high-tech workers had an internal migration rate of 17.7 per cent with their likelihood of migration influenced by home prices, property taxes, educational quality and recreational opportunities (Herzog et al., 1986). In a study of engineers in the semi-conductor industry between 1980 and 1986, 34 per cent of job changes resulted in an interstate migration in the United States (Angel, 1989). Using the 1980 Census, Ellis et al. (1993) found that in both manufacturing and non-manufacturing industries, professionals, technicians and sales individuals have the highest inter-county migration rates. In addition, during this period there were lower inter-county migration rates in manufacturing industries for operators and labourers, skilled production workers, service workers and administrative support workers than among their counterparts in non-manufacturing industries (Ellis et al., 1993). Those employed in the manufacturing sector as professionals had the highest share of migrants that moved to a non-contiguous state while those in farming, services and administrative support had a larger share of intrastate migrants (Ellis et al., 1993).

In the Canadian context, there has been limited research on internal migration differentials between occupations and occupational groupings. Instead, the Canadian literature has focused on occupation as a determinant of internal migration, with this research primarily focusing on the provincial level. Earlier work by McInnis (1971) found that males in service occupations (followed by professional and managerial occupations) had the highest rates of inter-provincial migration in Canada between 1956 and 1961, with individuals in service and clerical occupations most responsive to earning differentials. Using the same dataset, Stone (1971) found a positive correlation between in-migration and out-migrations ratio of Census Metropolitan Areas (CMAs) with the highest coefficient for managers and the lowest for general labourers.

There has been less attention in recent years on the internal migration by occupational groupings in Canada. Among individuals laid off in computers and telecommunications in 2001 in the five CMAs of Toronto, Montreal, Vancouver, Calgary and Ottawa, on average one-third moved to another metropolitan area (Frenette, 2007). There has been some recent research on the migration behaviours of recent graduates in Canada. For example, of individuals who completed an apprenticeship between 2002 and 2004, 45 per cent who had moved settled in Alberta by 2007 (Paquin, 2009). From the National Graduates Survey, Class of 2005, 14 per cent of health graduates made an interprovincial migration within two years of graduation, with mobility the highest among medicine graduates (Statistics Canada, 2009).

DATA AND METHODOLOGY

The purpose of this chapter is to examine whether measures of talent, technology and tolerance in a region influence individual migration propensities. The 2001 Census of Canada Master File (20 per cent sample) provides detailed demographic and socio-economic information on individuals, with greater flexibility in sample size and geography as compared with the Public Use Microdata Files (PUMFs). Since 1991, the Census of Canada has collected mobility and residential data on place of residence on Census day as well as five years and one year prior to Census; specifically, there is information on whether the respondent lived in the same dwelling/address five and one years prior to the Census. The Census of Canada Master File provides residential information at a more refined spatial level that is unavailable in the Census of Canada PUMFs.

The analysis that I present in this chapter includes individuals aged from 25 to 64 years at the time of the Census who were residents of Canada throughout the 1996–2001 period. Individuals who are institutionalized were excluded from the sample, as were residents of the three northern territories. Migrants are defined as individuals who changed their CMA/region of residence between 1996 and 2001. Due to the nature of the migration data collected, it is expected that it underestimates the number of individuals who actually migrated between 1996 and 2001. In addition, due to issues with sample size, individuals who made single or multiple migrations are not differentiated between, nor are types of migration such as return or onward. Another limitation is the use of geographic boundaries to define whether a migration has occurred, as this may overestimate the number of migrants due to the potential occurrence of short-distance but boundary-crossing moves.

Unlike the Census of Canada PUMFs, the Master File allows for the examination of non-aggregated industry and occupation classifications. For the occupation data, the National Occupational Classification Statistics (NOCS) 2001 are used to categorize the occupations in the creative class. Occupations are classified into occupational classes which define the tasks and roles involved in each occupation: service, working, creative and 'fishing, farming and forestry'[1] as discussed by Florida (2002). These tasks and roles are classified according to two dimensions: autonomy and complexity. The level of autonomy of the occupation refers to the degree to which individuals have independence in their work. The level of complexity of the occupation refers to the degree to which those roles and tasks undertaken by the individual are complex.

Using the two dimensions of autonomy and complexity, each occupation is categorized into one of the four occupation classes. The service class includes occupations which have relatively low levels of autonomy and high levels of complexity. The service class consists of occupations which are generally routine-oriented such as hair stylist, wait staff, hotel cleaning staff and day care staff. The working class includes occupations which have relatively low levels of autonomy and complexity. The working class is typically comprised of occupations which are highly dependent on physical skills and repetitive tasks, including trade workers such as carpenters, plumbers and truck drivers. The creative class includes occupations which have relatively high levels of autonomy and complexity. The creative class consists of occupations whose economic value is the creation of new ideas and forms, and includes occupations such as engineers, programmers and managers.

In addition to the 27 CMAs defined by Statistics Canada in 2001, ten provincial regions are created to cover the residual areas (Figure 9.1). For example, the province of British Columbia contains three CMAs (Abbotsford, Vancouver and Victoria), with the 'Rest of British Columbia' containing all other areas in the province outside of these three CMAs. This process is continued for the other nine provinces (except for Prince Edward Island, which does not have a CMA), to create residual provincial regions. CMAs as defined by Statistics Canada (2010) are 'area(s) consisting of one or more adjacent municipalities situated around a major urban core' where 'the urban core must have a population of at least 100,000'. While this is a relatively large geographic scale, it is appropriate in the context of the regional characteristics of talent, tolerance and technology being examined. Generally, these measures have widespread influences which are embodied in large geographical regions and are best measured at the metropolitan level (see, for example, Florida, 2002; Gertler et al., 2002; Wojan et al., 2007). In the Canadian context, examination of internal migration and its relationship with creative capital and economic development would be the most appropriate at the CMA level. Canada has a small population in comparison with the United States, and examination at smaller geographic scales would render the residential characteristics less reliable due to small sample sizes.

The analysis utilizes binary logistic regression to measure the effect of individual and CMA/region characteristics on an individual's propensity to make an internal migration within Canada, defined as

$$P_i = 1/(1 + e^{\alpha + \beta X_i}) \tag{9.1}$$

where X is a vector of explanatory variables, and the dependent variable contrasts the population who has made an internal migration to those who did not change their CMA region. That is, how do these two groups differ in terms of covariates associated with making the choice whether to migrate?

Demographic and socio-economic characteristics which influence internal migration are drawn from existing research (Robinson and Tomes, 1982; Kritz and Nogel, 1994; Newbold, 1996, 2002; Gurak and Kritz, 2000). Demographic characteristics include age

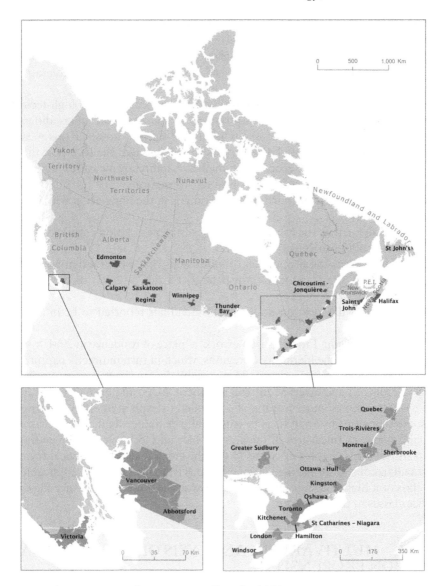

Figure 9.1   Census metropolitan areas in Canada, 2001

(25 to 34, 35 to 44, 45 to 54, 55 to 69, 70 and older); gender (female, male); ethnicity (British Isles, French, Other European (non-British Isles and non-French), Asian, all other ethnicities); household language (English only, French only, non-official language, official and non-official languages); marital status (married, single, divorced, separated, widowed); and immigration status (Canadian by birth, immigrant). Socio-economic characteristics include highest level of education (less than high school certificate, high school certificate, college, trades or some university, university degree or higher); household income (less than C$20 000, C$20 000 to C$39 999, C$40 000 to C$59 999, C$60 000

to C$79 999, C$80 000 to C$99 999, C$100 000 and higher); and labour force status (employed, unemployed, not in the labour force).

To examine the creative class theoretical framework, CMA characteristics are created to serve as proxies for Florida's measures of technology, talent and tolerance. The indices are defined as the following:

Tech-pole index: defined as the proportion of individuals employed in high-technology sectors in 2001 (Table 9.A1). This measurement of the tech-pole index differs from Florida (2002), as he uses high-technology industrial output; however this measure is similar to that used in Gertler et al. (2002). It is anticipated that the tech-pole index will have a positive association with economic growth as it indirectly measures regional high-technology intensity and high-technology business formation.

Talent index:[2] defined as the proportion of individuals in the population who had a university degree in 2001.

Bohemian index: defined as the location quotient of the population employed in artistic and creative occupations in 2001 (Table 9.A2).

Mosaic index: defined as the proportion of individuals that were foreign-born in 2001. The Mosaic Index is the Canadian equivalent to Florida's (2002) melting pot index (Gertler et al., 2002).

Gay index: defined as the location quotient of individuals reported to be in a same-sex partnership in 2001.

In addition to examining Florida's framework, a 'place of residence in 2001' variable is incorporated to capture the hierarchy of regions, which in turn indirectly captures other non-measured regional characteristics. This variable is constructed as comprising five categories: Toronto; Vancouver; Montreal; all other CMAs; all non-metropolitan areas.

While more traditional measures may be included to explain internal migration propensities, the scope of this analysis is to empirically examine whether the creative class theoretical framework (measures of talent, tolerance and technology) influences migration propensities. This chapter attempts to test the creative class theoretical framework in the Canadian context; in particular, whether this framework is only applicable to the creative class or if higher levels of talent, tolerance and technology influence the working and service classes in the same way.

RESULTS – MULTIVARIATE ANALYSIS OF THE INTERNAL MIGRATION PROPENSITY

Three binomial logit models were created: (1) individual characteristics; (2) individual and region characteristics; and the (3) full model, which includes individual and region characteristics as well as region of residence – which are examined on the creative, working and service classes. Region characteristics of talent, tolerance and technology are measured through the series of indices: talent, gay, mosaic, bohemian (or 'boho') and tech-pole. The discussion of the results will focus solely on Model 3.

As found in existing internal migration literatures, older individuals are less likely to make an internal migration than their younger counterparts (Tables 9.1, 9.2 and 9.3). In particular, the individuals in the age range of 55 to 69 years are the least likely to migrate, with the creative class having a smaller odds ratio (0.185) in comparison to the working

Table 9.1   Internal migration propensity of the creative class in Canada, 1996 to 2001

	Model 1		Model 2		Model 3	
	Coefficient	Odds Ratio	Coefficient	Odds Ratio	Coefficient	Odds Ratio
Intercept	−0.327		0.038		−1.201	
Age (25 to 34 reference)						
35 to 44 years	−0.895	0.409	−0.903	0.405	−0.905	0.404
45 to 54 years	−1.497	0.224	−1.515	0.220	−1.518	0.219
55 to 69 years	−1.663	0.190	−1.686	0.185	−1.690	0.185
Gender (male reference)						
Female	−0.173	0.841	−0.179	0.836	−0.180	0.835
Immigrant status (Canadian by birth reference)						
Immigrant	−0.104	0.901	−0.091	0.913	−0.092	0.912
Marital status (married reference)						
Divorced/widowed etc.	0.197	1.218	0.213	1.237	0.213	1.238
Single	−0.229	0.795	−0.213	0.808	−0.211	0.810
Ethnicity (British Isles reference)						
French	0.008*	1.008*	0.0158*	1.016	0.020	1.020
Other European	−0.214	0.808	−0.216	0.806	−0.208	0.812
Asian	−0.160	0.852	−0.154	0.857	−0.164	0.849
All Other Ethnicities	0.131	1.140	0.134	1.143	0.132	1.141
Home language (English reference)						
French	0.081	1.084	0.004*	1.004	0.112	1.118
Non-official	−0.203	0.816	−0.209	0.811	−0.188	0.829
Official/non-official	−0.033	0.968	−0.044	0.957	−0.0138*	0.986
Highest level of education (university degree reference)						
Less than high school	−0.435	0.648	−0.460	0.631	−0.470	0.625
High school diploma	−0.343	0.710	−0.357	0.700	−0.362	0.696
College, trades etc.	−0.225	0.798	−0.242	0.785	−0.245	0.783
Household income ($100 000 or higher reference)						
Less than $20 000	0.508	1.661	0.472	1.602	0.474	1.606
$20 000 to $39 999	0.429	1.536	0.395	1.484	0.399	1.491
$40 000 to $59 999	0.297	1.346	0.270	1.310	0.273	1.313
$60 000 to $79 999	0.196	1.217	0.175	1.192	0.177	1.193
$80 000 to $99 999	0.129	1.137	0.114	1.121	0.115	1.122
Region characteristics						
Talent index			−0.047	0.954	−0.034	0.967
Gay index			0.277	1.319	0.154	1.166
Mosaic index			0.006	1.006	0.012	1.012
Boho index			0.054	1.056	0.380	1.462
Tech-pole index			−0.0309*	0.970	0.769	2.158
Region of residence 2001 (Toronto reference)						
Vancouver					0.267	1.306
Other CMAs					0.634	1.885
Montreal					0.277	1.319
Non-CMAs					0.934	2.544
Per cent concordance	67.8		68.2		68.4	

Note: Weighted sample size migrants = 923 575; stayers = 3 607 210; * non-significant estimates ($p > 0.001$).

Source: Author's analysis of 2001 Census of Canada Master Files.

Table 9.2   Internal migration propensity of the service class in Canada, 1996 to 2001

	Model 1		Model 2		Model 3	
	Coefficient	Odds Ratio	Coefficient	Odds Ratio	Coefficient	Odds Ratio
Intercept	−0.415		−0.150		−1.448	
Age (25 to 34 reference)						
35 to 44 years	−0.727	0.483	−0.733	0.480	−0.734	0.480
45 to 54 years	−1.168	0.311	−1.178	0.308	−1.179	0.308
55 to 69 years	−1.407	0.245	−1.418	0.242	−1.421	0.241
Gender (male reference)						
Female	−0.153	0.858	−0.158	0.854	−0.161	0.851
Immigrant status (Canadian by birth reference)						
Immigrant	−0.185	0.831	−0.178	0.837	−0.175	0.839
Marital status (married reference)						
Divorced/widowed etc.	0.230	1.258	0.236	1.266	0.236	1.266
Single	−0.298	0.742	−0.293	0.746	−0.289	0.749
Ethnicity (British Isles reference)						
French	−0.003*	0.997*	0.007*	1.007*	0.008*	1.009*
Other European	−0.184	0.832	−0.186	0.830	−0.181	0.835
Asian	−0.153	0.859	−0.162	0.850	−0.174	0.840
All Other Ethnicities	0.074	1.076	0.080	1.083	0.081	1.084
Home language (English reference)						
French	0.081	1.084	−0.017	0.983	0.112	1.118
Non-official	−0.219	0.803	−0.242	0.785	−0.214	0.808
Official/non-official	−0.072	0.930	−0.103	0.902	−0.069	0.934
Highest level of education (university degree reference)						
Less than high school	−0.506	0.603	−0.521	0.594	−0.530	0.589
High school diploma	−0.414	0.661	−0.430	0.650	−0.435	0.647
College, trades etc.	−0.216	0.806	−0.232	0.793	−0.236	0.790
Household income ($100 000 or higher reference)						
Less than $20 000	0.397	1.487	0.380	1.462	0.384	1.468
$20 000 to $39 999	0.224	1.251	0.209	1.233	0.213	1.238
$40 000 to $59 999	0.127	1.135	0.116	1.123	0.118	1.126
$60 000 to $79 999	0.078	1.081	0.070	1.073	0.071	1.074
$80 000 to $99 999	0.054	1.055	0.047	1.048	0.047	1.049
Region characteristics						
Talent index			−0.051	0.950	−0.024	0.977
Gay index			0.348	1.417	0.077	1.080
Mosaic index			0.006	1.006	0.013	1.013
Boho index			0.135	1.144	0.320	1.377
Tech-pole index			0.0193*	1.019*	0.825	2.281
Region of residence 2001 (Toronto reference)						
Vancouver					0.442	1.556
Other CMAs					0.701	2.016
Montreal					0.481	1.617
Non-CMAs					1.001	2.722
Per cent concordance	65.4		65.7		65.9	

Note: Weighted sample size migrants = 990 105; stayers = 4 228 180; * non-significant estimates (*p* > 0.001).

Source: Author's analysis of 2001 Census of Canada Master Files.

Table 9.3   Internal migration propensity of the working class in Canada, 1996 to 2001

	Model 1		Model 2		Model 3	
	Coefficient	Odds Ratio	Coefficient	Odds Ratio	Coefficient	Odds Ratio
Intercept	−0.561		−0.398		−1.743	
Age (25 to 34 reference)						
35 to 44 years	−0.694	0.499	−0.697	0.498	−0.697	0.498
45 to 54 years	−1.200	0.301	−1.202	0.301	−1.201	0.301
55 to 69 years	−1.464	0.231	−1.471	0.230	−1.471	0.230
Gender (male reference)						
Female	−0.003*	0.997*	−0.009*	0.991*	−0.008*	0.992*
Immigrant status (Canadian by birth reference)						
Immigrant	−0.142	0.868	−0.201	0.818	−0.189	0.828
Marital status (married reference)						
Divorced/widowed etc.	0.367	1.443	0.356	1.428	0.354	1.425
Single	−0.191	0.826	−0.204	0.816	−0.203	0.816
Ethnicity (British Isles reference)						
French	−0.010*	0.990*	0.003*	1.003*	0.002*	1.002*
Other European	−0.165	0.848	−0.170	0.844	−0.171	0.843
Asian	−0.164	0.849	−0.179	0.837	−0.185	0.831
All Other Ethnicities	0.037	1.037	0.047	1.048	0.054	1.055
Home language (English reference)						
French	0.080	1.083	−0.014*	0.986*	0.107	1.113
Non-official	−0.249	0.780	−0.295	0.745	−0.269	0.764
Official/non-official	−0.093	0.911	−0.132	0.877	−0.105	0.900
Highest level of education (university degree reference)						
Less than high school	0.080	1.083	−0.014*	0.986*	0.107	1.113
High school diploma	−0.249	0.780	−0.295	0.745	−0.269	0.764
College, trades etc.	−0.093	0.911	−0.132	0.877	−0.105	0.900
Household income ($100 000 or higher reference)						
Less than $20 000	0.366	1.442	0.390	1.477	0.397	1.488
$20 000 to $39 999	0.258	1.294	0.285	1.330	0.292	1.340
$40 000 to $59 999	0.156	1.169	0.177	1.193	0.180	1.198
$60 000 to $79 999	0.077	1.080	0.091	1.095	0.092	1.096
$80 000 to $99 999	0.006	1.006*	0.012	1.012*	0.011	1.011*
Region characteristics						
Talent index			−0.050	0.951	−0.033	0.968
Gay index			0.363	1.438	−0.057	0.945
Mosaic index			0.009	1.009	0.015	1.015
Boho index			0.056	1.058	0.163	1.177
Tech-pole index			0.430	1.538	2.926	18.644
Region of residence 2001 (Toronto reference)						
Vancouver					0.946	2.575
Other CMAs					1.125	3.081
Montreal					0.598	1.819
Non-CMAs					1.230	3.421
Per cent concordance	65.2		65.6		65.7	

Note: Weighted sample size migrants = 482 735; stayers = 2 964 210; * non-significant estimates (*p* > 0.001).

Source: Author's analysis of 2001 Census of Canada Master Files.

(0.230) and service (0.241) classes. Females are less likely than their male counterparts to migrate; however, this result is only statistically significant for the service and creative classes. Immigrants are less likely than their Canadian-born counterparts to migrate for all three occupation classes. Individuals who are divorced, separated or widowed are more likely to have been migrants than their married counterparts; unexpectedly, individuals who are single are less likely to have migrated. In comparison to individuals with British Isles ethnicity, individuals who are Other European (non-British Isles and non-French) or Asian are less likely to migrate while those in the category 'all other ethnicities' are more likely. Creative class workers who are in the 'all other ethnicities' category are more likely to be migrants in comparison to their service and working-class counterparts (odds ratio 1.141 versus 1.084 and 1.055, respectively). Individuals reporting non-official languages as their home language are less likely to migrate than their English-speaking counterparts. Unexpectedly, those with a French home language are more likely to migrate, and this holds true across the three occupation classes. Generally, research in the Canadian context finds that individuals with French as their home language tend to be less mobile than their English-speaking counterparts due to the smaller number of French destinations.

As expected, individuals with lower levels of education are less likely to have migrated than their better educated counterparts, and individuals with less than a high school diploma are the least likely in comparison to individuals with a bachelor's degree. This trend holds for each of the three occupation classes, which is unexpected due to the occupational specification of the classes. With the creative class largely comprised of individuals with higher levels of education, it would have been expected that education would be more influential than for the service and working classes. In comparison to individuals in the highest household income range of C$100 000 or higher, individuals with lower household incomes are more likely to make an internal migration. Household income is more influential in the creative class model than the service or working class models, as the odds ratios are larger in each income range category. The household income odds ratios for the service and working classes increase more slowly than for their creative class counterparts. In comparison, those in the lowest income category, those with household incomes of less than C$20 000, have the highest odds of migration for the creative class (odds ratio of 1.606) in comparison to the service (1.468) and working (1.488) classes. Although it may have been expected that moves would be made for higher incomes, it may be the case that individuals in higher income employment may be tied to their region of residence due to higher-paying employment or barriers to migration such as capital investments that are related to their employment.

Region characteristics of talent, gay, mosaic, boho and tech-pole indices are all statistically significant. Individuals who resided in a region with higher measures of the talent index were slightly less likely to have been migrants. This finding is contrary to what would be expected for the creative class, as the creative class theory suggests places with higher levels of talent would be attractive. It is unclear why the talent index measure would not influence the migration decisions within the creative class. However, higher levels of talent may also serve as a retention mechanism or may create more employment competition for the creative class. If a higher level of talent creates more competition, individuals may choose to reside in places where their talents are more highly valued due to less competition. It would be expected that the talent index would be less important in the service and working class models; however, their results are similar to the creative class model.

Following the creative class theoretical framework, individuals who resided in regions in 2001 which have higher gay, mosaic and boho indices were generally more likely to have been a migrant than those residing in regions with lower levels. The gay index has the largest odds ratios for the creative class (1.462) as creative class individuals residing in areas with high gay index values are more likely to have been migrants. To a lesser extent the gay index influences the service class (1.08), but it has the opposite influence on the working class (0.945), as the working class is less likely to consist of migrants in those regions.

The creative class model has the largest odds ratio for the boho index (1.462) followed by the service class model (1.377) and the working class model (1.177). The odds ratio for the mosaic index has the value of approximately one across each of the three occupation classes, indicating that this index has little influence. However, this is surprising given the concentrated immigrant settlement patterns in Canada. While the creative class theory contends that tolerance measures are important to attract the creative class, these measures seem to be important for the working and service classes as well. Both the working and service class models are less influenced by the gay and boho indices than their creative class counterparts.

Each tolerance measure may capture a different attitude or level of openness; however, the weakness of the mosaic and boho indices may indicate overlap between these three measures. This is supported by the Pearson's correlation coefficient between the three tolerance indices: boho, gay and mosaic, which finds the indices positively correlated. This in part may explain the limited influence of the mosaic and boho indices in comparison to the gay index. In addition, there may be a hierarchy of tolerance indices such that regions with a higher gay index may inherently be the most tolerant.

The tech-pole index is statistically significant with a large influence on the migration decisions of the three classes. Individuals residing in regions with a higher tech-pole index are more likely to have made a migration than those living in regions with a lower tech-pole index. That is, for each unit increase in the tech-pole index for the region of residence, the individual is more than twice as likely to have been a migrant. The result suggests that the presence of a large high-technology industry sector is a strong attractor.

The region of residence variable is included to capture a hierarchy of regions, as individuals tend to migrate up the urban hierarchy. There is a hierarchy of regions as regions' characteristics differ widely. The analysis finds that in comparison to Toronto, individuals in all other regions are more likely to have been a migrant.

The strength of the region of residence variable is quite strong, ranging from an odds ratio of 1.306 for Vancouver to 2.544 for non-census metropolitan regions for the creative class. Therefore, creative class individuals who resided in non-census metropolitan regions are over 2.5 times more likely to have been a migrant than their counterparts residing in Toronto. This may in some way reflect the competition that is faced by the creative class when choosing to reside in the largest CMAs. In addition, this may reflect Toronto's ability to retain the creative class. The odds ratio for the working class ranges from 1.819 for Montreal to a high of 3.421 for non-census metropolitan regions while the odds ratios for the service class ranges from 1.556 in Vancouver to 2.722 for non-census metropolitan regions. Across each of the three models individuals residing in a non-census metropolitan area are more likely than their Toronto counterparts to have been migrants.

CONCLUSIONS

In the Canadian context, the creative class theoretical framework has received much less attention than in the United States or Europe. In particular, there has been limited empirical examination of whether the presence of the 3Ts – talent, tolerance and technology, as described by Florida (2002) – across Canada attracts the creative class, who in turn bring creative capital to a region, pushing innovation and driving economies forward. The scope of the analysis was to examine whether the measures of talent, tolerance and technology are statistically significant in explaining migration propensities in Canada. This chapter adds to the dearth of empirical research on the 3Ts and their influence on migration. In addition, it extends the creative class theory by not only examining the migration propensities of the creative class, but also those of the service and working classes. The central question in the chapter has been whether the 3Ts are statistically significant when examining the internal migration behaviour in Canada of the creative, service and working classes.

Much of the focus of Canadian internal migration research has examined the labour force by age or immigrant status, with less attention being paid to the migration behaviours and patterns of occupational groups (see, for example, Liaw, 1990; Newbold, 1994, 1996, 2002; Newbold and Liaw, 1994, 1995; Moore and Rosenberg, 1995; Hou and Bourne, 2004; Newbold and Cicchino, 2007). This chapter adds to the body of research which has examined internal migration differentials between occupations and occupational groupings. While place characteristics have been used in other research to analyse internal migration propensities, the focus has typically been on traditional economic variables such as unemployment and growth rates, housing prices and income levels, or other characteristics such as weather and crime rates. In addition, existing research has tended to include measures of population and ethnic diversity in light of Canada's large immigrant population. However, the Canadian research has yet to examine more explicitly tolerance as defined by Florida's boho and gay indices (2002). While much of the research on the creative class uses a macro approach, this analysis uses a micro approach to examine the importance of the 3Ts on individual migration behaviour.

Further research on the 3Ts and its influence on migration is needed. While this chapter represents a step towards further understanding the 3Ts in the context of complex internal migration dynamics, there are several limitations. First, due to the nature of the dataset used and migration definitions, different types of migration could not be differentiated from one another. Second, sample size limitations made it impossible to distinguish between long- and short-distance moves. Third, it may be argued that examining large aggregated occupational groups provides limited information. But the intention of the chapter has been to use a micro approach to empirically test the creative class theory and its relation to internal migration. Consequently, it offers insights into whether the creative class framework sheds light on the internal migration decisions of Canada's labour force.

The findings of the multivariate analysis corroborate the creative class thesis, which finds that creative class individuals are attracted by regions where there are high levels of tolerance and technology. However, the analysis does not support the argument that higher levels of talent are attractive to the creative class. In addition, the analysis finds that these 3T measures influence the working and service occupation classes similarly to how they influence the creative class. This is not surprising, since individuals regardless of occupation are likely to be attracted to regions that offer a good quality of place as well as a good quality of life as measured by the 3Ts. What may be surprising is that the odds ratios of the 3T measures are similar across the models for the creative, service and working classes. Moreover, the influence of the boho and gay indices are greater for the working and service classes than the creative class. The findings suggest that the 3Ts are important not only for the migration decision of the creative class but for other occupations as well.

ACKNOWLEDGEMENTS

I would like to thank the Martin Prosperity Institute in the Rotman School of Management at the University of Toronto for its support of the research.

NOTES

1. The occupation class of fishing, farming and forestry is not discussed in the chapter.
2. This analysis uses the traditional measure of human capital to estimate talent as discussed in Chapter 14 in *The Rise of the Creative Class*. While the creative class share has also been used to estimate the Talent Index, this measure has typically been used to measure creativity. The analysis presented in this chapter uses the more general measure of human capital as it is expected to be more appropriate, particularly for the service and working classes.

REFERENCES

Angel, D.P. (1989), 'The labor market for engineers in the U.S. semiconductor industry', *Economic Geography*, **65**(2), 99–112.
Bach, S. (2008), 'International mobility of health professionals: brain drain or brain exchange?', in A. Soliomano (ed.), *The International Mobility of Talent: Types, Causes, and Development Impact*, Oxford: Oxford University Press, pp. 202–35.
Baris, M. (2003), 'Review: Richard Florida, The Rise of the Creative Class (And How It's Transforming Work, Leisure, Community, and Everyday Life', *Next American City*, 1(February).
Becker, G. (1964), *Human Capital*, New York, NY: Columbia University Press.
Boschma, R.A. and M. Fritsch (2009), 'Creative class and regional growth: empirical evidence from seven European countries', *Economic Geography*, **85**(4), 391–423.
D'Costa, A.P. (2006), *The New Economic in Development: ICT Challenges and Opportunities*, Basingstoke: Palgrave Macmillan.
D'Costa, A.P. (2008), 'The international mobility of technical talent: trends and development implications', in A. Soliomano (ed.), *The International Mobility of Talent: Types, Causes, and Development Impact*, Oxford: Oxford University Press, pp. 44–83.
Desai, A.V. (2003), 'The dynamics of the Indian information technology industry', DRC Working Chapters, Centre For New and Emerging Markets, London Business School, London, available at http://www.Research4development.info/PDF/Outputs/CNEM/Drc20.Pdf (accessed 8 August 2010).
Docquier, F. and H. Rapoport (2004), *Skilled Migration: The Perspective of Sending Countries*, Washington, DC: World Bank.

Ellis, M., R. Barff and B. Renard (1993), 'Migration regions and interstate labor flows by occupation in the United States', *Growth and Change*, **24**, 166–90.

Faggian, A. and P. McCaan (2009), 'Human capital, graduate migration and innovation in British regions', *Cambridge Journal of Economics*, **33**, 317–33.

Faggian, A., P. McCaan and S. Sheppard (2007), 'Some evidence that women are more mobile than men: gender differences in U.K. graduate migration behaviour', *Journal of Regional Science*, **47**(3), 517–39.

Finn, M. G. (2007), 'Stay rates of foreign doctorate recipients from U.S. universities', 2005, working paper from the Oak Ridge Institute for Science and Education, available at http://orise.orau.gov/sep/files/stayrate07.pdf (accessed 8 August 2010).

Florida, R. (2002), *The Rise of the Creative Class*. New York, NY: Basic Books.

Florida, R. (2009), *Who's Your City?* (Canadian edn), Toronto, ON: Vintage Canada.

Florida, R., C. Mellander and K. Stolarick (2010), 'Talent, technology and tolerance in Canadian regional development', *The Canadian Geographer*, **54**(3), 277–304.

Frenette, M. (2007), 'Life after high tech', *Perspectives on Labour and Income*, **8**(7), 5–13, available at http://www.statcangc.ca/cgi-bin/af-fdr-cgi-l=eng&loc=../75-001-x2007107-eng.pdf (accessed 1 March 2010).

Gertler, M.S., R. Florida, G. Gates and T. Vinodrai (2002), 'Competing on creativity: placing Ontario's cities in North American context', working paper available at http://www.urban.org/publications/410889.html (accessed 8 August 2010).

Glaeser, E.L. (2004), 'Review of Richard Florida's the Rise of the Creative Class', paper available at http://www.creativeclass.com/Rfcgdb/Articles/Glaeserreview.pdf (accessed 8 August 2010).

Gurak, D.T. and. M. M. Kritz (2000), 'The interstate migration of U.S. immigrants: individual and contextual determinants', *Social Forces*, **78**(3), 1017–39.

Hansen, H.K. and T. Niedomysl (2009), 'Migration of the creative class: evidence from Sweden', *Journal of Economic Geography*, **9**, 191–206.

Herzog, H.W. Jr and A.M. Schlottmann (1984), 'Labor force mobility in the United States: migration, unemployment, and remigration', *International Regional Science Review*, **9**, 43–58.

Herzog, H.W. Jr, A.M. Schlottmann and D.L. Johnson (1986), 'High-technology jobs and worker mobility', *Journal of Regional Science*, **26**(3), 445–59.

Holen, A.S. (1965), 'Effects of professional licensing arrangements on interstate labor mobility and resource allocation', *Journal of Political Economy*, **73**(5), 492–8.

Hou, F. and L.S. Bourne (2004), 'Population movement into and out of Canada's immigrant gateway cities: a comparative study of Toronto, Montreal and Vancouver', Analytical Studies Branch Research Chapter Series No. 229, Ottawa, ON: Statistics Canada.

Houston, D., A. Findlay, R. Harrison and C. Mason (2008), 'Will attracting the "creative class" boost economic growth in old industrial regions? A case study of Scotland', *Geografiska Annaler: Series B, Human Geography*, **90**(2), 133–49.

ILO (2004), 'Towards a fair deal for migration workers in the global economy', paper presented at the International Labour Conference, 92nd Session, Geneva, Switzerland.

Khadria, B. (2004), 'Migration of highly skilled Indians: case studies of IT and health professionals', OECD Science, Technology and Industry Working Chapters, 2004/6, Paris: OECD Publishing.

Kleiner, M.M. (1982), 'Evidence on occupational migration', *Growth and Change*, **13**(3), 43–48.

Kritz, M.M. and J.M. Nogle (1994), 'Nativity concentration and internal migration among the foreign-born', *Demography*, **31**, 509–24.

Ladinsky, J. (1967a), 'Occupational determinants of geographic mobility among professional workers', *American Sociological Review*, **32**(2), 253–64.

Ladinsky, J. (1967b), 'Sources of geographic mobility among professional workers: a multivariate analysis', *Demography*, **4**(1), 293–309.

Ladinsky, J. (1967c), 'The geographic mobility of professional and technical manpower', *Journal of Human Resources*, **2**(4), 475–94.

Lee, S. Y., R. Florida and Z. Acs (2004), 'Creativity and entrepreneurship: a regional analysis of new firm formation', *Regional Studies*, **38**(8), 879–91.

Liaw, K.-L. (1990), 'Joint effects of personal factors and ecological variables on the interprovincial migration pattern of young adults in Canada: a nested logit analysis', *Geographical Analysis*, **22**, 189–208.

Long, L.H. (1973), 'Migration differentials by education and occupation: trends and variations', *Demography*, **10**(2), 243–58.

Malanga, S. (2004), 'The curse of the creative class', *City Journal*, Winter, 36–45.

Markusen, A. (2006), 'Urban development and the politics of a creative class: evidence from a study of artists', *Environment and Planning A*, **38**, 1921–40.

Marlet, G.A. and C.M. van Woerkens (2005), 'Tolerance, aesthetics, amenities or jobs? Dutch city attraction to the creative class', Discussion Chapter Series 05-33, Utrecht School of Economics, Utrecht.

McInnis, M. (1971), 'Age, education and occupation differentials in interregional migration: some evidence for Canada', *Demography*, **8**(2), 195–204.

Moore, E.G. and M.W. Rosenberg (1995), 'Modeling migration flows of immigrant groups in Canada', *Environment and Planning A*, **27**, 699–714.

Newbold, K.B. (1994), 'Changing patterns of primary, return and onward interprovincial migration in Canada: 1976 to 1986', *The Great Lakes Geographer*, **1**(1), 1–20.

Newbold, K.B. (1996), 'Internal migration of the foreign-born in Canada', *International Migration Review*, **30**, 728–47.

Newbold, K.B. (2002), 'Measuring internal migration among the foreign-born: insights from Canadian data', *Review of Regional Studies*, **33**(3), 370–89.

Newbold, K.B. and S. Cicchino (2007), 'Inter-regional return and onwards migration in Canada: evidence based on a micro-regional analysis', *Canadian Journal of Regional Science*, **30**(2), 211–30.

Newbold, K.B and K.L. Liaw (1994), 'Return and onward interprovincial migration through economic boom and bust in Canada: from 1976–81 to 1981–1986', *Geographical Analysis*, **26**(3), 228–45.

Newbold, K.B. and K.-L. Liaw (1995), 'Return and onward migrations in Canada, 1976–81: an explanation based on personal and ecological variables', *The Canadian Geographer*, **39**(1), 16–29.

Ottaviano, G.I.P. and G. Peri (2005a), 'The economic value of cultural diversity: evidence from US cities', *Journal of Economic Geography*, **6**(1), 9–44.

Ottaviano, G.I.P. and G. Peri (2005b), 'Cities and cultures', *Journal of Urban Economics*, **58**(2), 304–7.

Paquin, N. (2009), 'Mobility of apprenticeship completers in Canada from 2002 to 2007', in *Education Matters: Insights on Education, Learning and Training in Canada Vol. 6 No. 2*, Ottawa, ON: Statistics Canada.

Pashigian, P. (1979), 'Occupational licensing and the interstate mobility of professionals', *Journal of Law and Economics*, **22**(1), 1–25.

Peck, J. (2005), 'Struggling with the creative class', *International Journal of Urban and Regional Research*, **29**(4), 740–70.

Petrov, A. N. (2007), 'A look beyond metropolis: exploring creative class in the Canadian periphery', *Canadian Journal of Regional Science*, **30**(3), 451–78.

Rausch, S. and C. Negrey (2006), 'Does the creative engine run? A consideration of the effect of creative class on economic strength and growth', *Journal of Urban Affairs*, **28**(5), 473–89.

Robinson, C. and N. Tomes (1982), 'Self-selection and interprovincial migration in Canada', *Canadian Journal of Economics*, **15**, 474–502.

Saxenian, A L. (2002), 'Silicon Valley's new immigrant high-growth entrepreneurs', *Economic Development Quarterly*, **16**(1), 20–31.

Saxenian, A L. (2005), 'From brain drain to brain circulation: transnational communities and regional upgrading in India and China', *Studies in Comparative International Development*, **40**(2), 35–61.

Saxenian, A L. (2006), *The New Argonauts: Regional Advantage in a Global Economy*, Cambridge, MA: Harvard University Press.

Saxenian, A L. (2008), 'The international mobility of entrepreneurs and regional upgrading in India and China', in A. Soliomano (ed.), *The International Mobility of Talent: Types, Causes, and Development Impact*, Oxford: Oxford University Press, pp. 117–44.

Saxenian, A L. and C-Y Li (2003), 'Bay-to-bay strategic alliances: network linkages between Taiwan and U.S. venture capital industries', *International Journal of Technology and Management*, **25**(1–2), 136–50.

Schultz, T.W. (1961), 'Investment in human capital', *American Economic Review*, **51**, 1–17.

Scott, A.J. (2006), 'Creative cities: conceptual issues and policy questions', *Journal of Urban Affairs*, **28**(1), 1–17.

Sjaastad, L.A. (1962), 'The costs and returns of human migration', *Journal of Political Economy*, **70**(5), 80–93.

Solimano, A. and M. Pollack (2004), *International Mobility of the Highly Skilled: The Case Between Europe and Latin America*, Santiago: ECLAC.

Stam, E., J.P.J. De Jong and G. Marlet (2008), 'Creative industries in the Netherlands: structure, development, innovativeness and effects on urban growth', *Geografiska Annaler: Series B, Human Geography*, **90**(2), 119–32.

Statistics Canada (2009), 'Health human resources and education in Canada: where do health university graduates move after graduation?', Fact Sheet, Tourism and the Centre for Education Statistics Division, Catalogue No. 81-600-X, Issue No. 002, Ottawa, ON: Statistics Canada.

Statistics Canada (2010), *Geographic Units: Census Metropolitan Area (CMA) and Census Agglomeration (CA)*, Ottawa, ON: Statistics Canada.

Stolarick, K. and R. Florida (2006), 'Creativity, connections and innovation: a study of linkage in the Montreal region', *Environment and Planning A*, **38**(10), 1799–817.

Stone, L.O. (1971), 'On the correlation between metropolitan in- and out-migration by occupation', *Journal of the American Statistical Association*, **66**(336), 693–701.

Tarver, J.D. (1964), 'Occupational migration differentials', *Social Forces*, **43**(2), 231–41.

Thorn, K. and L.B. Holm-Nielsen (2008), 'International mobility of researchers and scientists: policy options for turning a drain into a gain', in A. Soliomano (ed.), *The International Mobility of Talent: Types, Causes, and Development Impact*, Oxford: Oxford University Press, pp. 144–67.

Wojan, T.R., D.M. Lambert and D. McGranahan (2007), 'Emoting with their feet: bohemian attraction to creative milieu', *Journal of Economic Geography*, **7**, 711–36.

APPENDIX

Table 9.A1   Definition of high-technology industries in Canada, 2001

SIC[a](3-digit)	Industry description
321	Aircraft and aircraft parts industry
335	Electronic equipment industries
374	Pharmaceutical and medicine industry
391	Scientific and professional equipment
482	Telecommunication carriers industry
483	Other telecommunication industries
772	Computer and related services
775	Architectural, engineering and other scientific and technical services
868	Medical and other health laboratories
961	Motion picture audio and video production and distribution

Note: [a] Standard Industrial Classification.

Source: Gertler et al. (2002).

Table 9.A2   Definition of bohemian occupations in Canada, 2001

SOC[a](4-digit)	Occupation description
F021	Writers
F031	Producers, directors, choreographers and related occupations
F032	Conductors, composers and arrangers
F033	Musicians and singers
F034	Dancers
F035	Actors
F036	Painters, sculptors and other visual artists
F121	Photographers
F141	Graphic designers and illustrating artists
F142	Interior designers
F143	Theatre, fashion, exhibit and other creative designers
F144	Artisans and craftspersons
F145	Patternmakers

Note: [a] Standard Occupation Classification.

Source: Gertler et al. (2002).

10 Higher education and the creative city
Roberta Comunian and Alessandra Faggian

The influence of higher education institutions (HEIs) on their local areas have been explored from a variety of perspectives. Whilst there is a general acknowledgement that the contribution of HEIs to the economic, social and cultural development of their own cities and regions is of paramount importance, describing and quantifying this contribution is a challenging task. Various attempts have been made by researchers in different disciplines including economists (Preston and Hammond, 2006), social scientists (Chatterton, 1999) and regional development specialists (Cramphorn and Woodlhouse, 1999: Charles, 2006). It is now clear that the picture is very complex because of the overlapping synergies, benefits and opportunities created by the HEIs in their local areas. Chatterton and Goddard (2000, p. 493) emphasize this by defining a HEI as a 'repository of knowledge about future technological, economic and social trends [that] can be harnessed to help the region understand itself, its position in the world and identify possible future directions'.

In this chapter we investigate the relevance of the interconnection between HEIs and their locale with specific reference to the creative economy literature and the concept of 'creative city'. Initial research in the United Kingdom shows that HEIs are key actors in developing sustainable creative economies. Wood and Taylor (2004), for example, looking at the case of Huddersfield, highlight the vital role played by the university in supporting the 'Creative Town Initiative'. More recently, the establishment of a new university centre in Folkestone – following the work of the Creative Foundation in promoting the local creative economy and attracting new creative industries – has further highlighted the potential of these local synergies (Noble and Barry, 2008; Arts Council of England, 2009). Examples of collaborations between creative industries, universities and local policy makers are becoming more common and, as a result, the 'triple helix' approach is now a reality also within the cultural and creative economy (Comunian et al., 2007).

Alongside this economic development perspective, further literature – mainly from the United States – underlines the role of HEIs in promoting the arts, particularly in relation to engaging students, exploring the practice and boundaries of creativity (Stanford Arts Initiative, 2007) and involving other local communities in creative activities on campus (Cantor, 2005). Tepper (2004) points out that while creativity has become a one-size-fits-all key to success for businesses, cities and regional economies, most American universities have not yet fully embraced the concept and do not consider it fundamental for their success. Some noticeable exceptions are Stanford, Princeton and Columbia which have established 'creative campus' initiatives and promoted the participation and engagement in arts and culture of students and members of staff (Tepper, 2004, 2006). Tepper also highlights that the involvement of American universities in the creative economy is growing, so much so that about 20 per cent of performing arts organizations claim some kind of involvement with American HEIs.

While there is common acknowledgement that this 'cultural provision' is part of the civic role played by HEIs in their local area (Chatterton and Goddard, 2000; Cantor, 2005), this can also be critically interpreted as the exploitation of 'loss leader' by HEIs (Garber, 2008a) where creative activities are used to attract students but do not support themselves either economically or academically as the 'arts [do] not seems to lend themselves easily to the "tenurable" standards of other university subjects' (Garber, 2008b).

Examples of collaborations between HEIs and the creative sector are not restricted to the United Kingdom and the United States. Matheson (2006), for instance, studying the case of New Zealand, points out how design education is now changing and a more holistic view of the subject has been introduced, which requires a substantial involvement of partners in the creative sector. Similarly, Cunningham et al. (2004), studying the case of the 'Creative Industries Precinct Project' within the Queensland Institute of Technology in Brisbane, Australia, show how HEIs can provide support for R&D activities in the creative economy. The initiative presents itself as 'Australia's first site dedicated to creative experimentation and commercial development in the creative industries'[1] led by a university.

However, while all these contributions recognize the importance of HEI spillovers and collaborations with private and public actors to foster the local creative economies, they seem to overlook the most important role of HEIs, that is, as a conduit for bringing potential creative practitioners into a region, educating them and producing high quality 'creative human capital', in other words, young graduates educated in creative and artistic subjects. As such, their primary role is in attracting and retaining students in creative disciplines.

In the present work we investigate the relationship between HEIs and the creative city by analysing the 'production' and retention of 'bohemian graduates' (individuals with high human capital who have obtained a degree in a 'bohemian' subject such as creative arts, performing arts and design). We explore in detail the location and migration choices of bohemian graduates and their connection with the creative economy and the creative city.

The chapter is organized in three sections. First, we present the literature and debate on the creative city and its relationship to higher education. Second, we introduce the concept of 'bohemian graduate' and detail the methodology and data used. Finally, in the result section we present the geography of higher education provision in creative disciplines in the United Kingdom, the location choices of bohemian graduates and the relationship between these and the creativity of cities. The chapter concludes with some preliminary conclusions and suggestions for further research.

THE CREATIVE CITY: FROM INFRASTRUCTURE TO PEOPLE

The concept of the 'creative city' has proved very appealing for academics and policy makers in the last 15 years. However, there is still confusion on the definition and interpretation of this concept.

The first coherent formulation of the concept of 'creative city' is to be attributed to the work by Bianchini and Landry (1995), later extended by Landry (2000). In their contributions, the concept of 'creativity' was presented in its broadest sense, as 'thinking outside the box' and solving everyday problems in 'innovative ways'. It was argued that creativity could assist in regenerating cities. In this sense, their work had links with the British urban development policy of the late 1980s and early 1990s, which underlined how cultural industries and cultural regeneration could play a fundamental role in improving the image of a city and eventually foster economic growth (O'Connor and Wynne, 1996). To support this idea of culture as an 'engine' of regeneration and growth, many researchers (Evans and Shaw, 2004; Cameron and Coaffee, 2005) pointed at successful collaborations between artists (and art organizations) and their locality with the aim of revitalizing communities.

This vision of using cultural industries and creativity to revitalize cities became even more popular in Britain following the European Capital of Culture (ECC) initiative, particularly after the title was awarded to Glasgow in 1990.[2] It was clear that the European initiative believed in the potential of culture and creativity to improve a city, its image and its economy. This idea of 'creative city' as a city where cultural activities and infrastructures lead to urban regeneration and growth remained dominant until the end of the 1990s (Griffiths, 2006).

However, as the word 'creative' gained popularity, it started being used in different contexts with slightly different meanings. Following the publication of the Department of Culture, Media and Sport (DCMS) document on 'creative industries' in 1998 and the work by Florida (2002b) on the 'creative class', the focus shifted from cultural infrastructures and consumption of cultural goods to creative production and people. Thereafter, the key to success for cities has been seen as the ability to attract and retain skilled labour as the driving force for the new 'knowledge-based and creative economy'.

Following the definition of 'creative industries' by the DCMS (1998), a new interpretation of the creative city emerged, now as the city where the work and production of the creative industries are concentrated and supported (Montgomery, 2005). There are elements of consumption, as when the creative industries and their cultural scenes are able to shape the image of a city and attract visitors, but these are only peripheral to the production perspective (O'Connor and Wynne, 1996; Pratt, 2004a).

The second, more recent and more powerful association is the one between the 'creative city' and the 'creative class' (Florida, 2002b). This has emerged from the success of Florida's 2002 book *The Rise of the Creative Class* and has added an extra connotation to the creative city term which, in many cases, has superseded the previous understanding. Florida (2002a, 2002b) suggests that the economic success of a city is determined by the presence of the 'creative class'. This 'creative class' encompasses a wide range of professionals, of which workers in the creative industries are only a small proportion.[3] As such, the term 'creative city' is now often interpreted as a city with a high presence of – or potential to attract – the creative class. There is still a small link with infrastructures, as Florida suggests that, in order to appeal to the creative class, cities should foster an appropriate cultural climate, promote diversity and offer cultural entertainment.[4]

The present chapter acknowledges the complementary role of these different interpretations of 'creative cities' and argues for a better understanding of the interconnections between infrastructure and image, between the 'cultural consumption-oriented' creative city with its human capital and creative communities and the 'creative production-oriented' creative city (Chapain and Comunian, 2009).

THE ROLE OF HIGHER EDUCATION IN THE CREATIVE CITY AND THE CREATIVE ECONOMY

From the discussion above it is clear that HEIs are important in building both the physical and human infrastructures for the creative city and that they do it in a variety of ways. Although it is impossible to provide a comprehensive list of the ways in which HEIs contribute to make a city more 'creative', we propose a classification which partially mirrors the definitions of the creative city as presented above.

If we take the view that a city is creative if it offers a wide array of cultural goods and opportunities (the cultural consumption-oriented view), then one of the roles of HEIs is to actively engage in the provision of cultural goods either directly or via collaborations and partnerships with the local cultural infrastructures and communities. Chatterton (1999) underlines that HEIs have traditionally been well positioned in providing the city with cultural facilities, such as art galleries and theatres, but more recently they have taken this role further, including a wider range of cultural facilities, such as media production facilities, recording studios or rehearsal spaces. The cultural opportunities offered by both the city and the HEIs are often interrelated and self-reinforcing. Also, the HEI infrastructures not only provide additional income for the city (hence favouring regeneration; see Robinson and Adams, 2008), but also strengthen the image of the city as a 'cultural' hub and provider of knowledge and innovation (Preston and Hammond, 2006), sometimes attracting tourists (for example, Oxford) and making the consumption of city-specific cultural goods more appealing.

If we take the view that a city is creative when its productive structure includes a strong creative sector (the creative production-oriented view), then we have to consider the role of the HEIs both as providers of knowledge and innovation (mainly in the form of knowledge spillovers) and providers of human capital (in the form of skilled creative workers). The production and transfer of knowledge to firms in the local area (and the related concept of knowledge spillovers) is probably the most recognized and cited contribution of HEIs to regional innovation systems (Fritsch and Schwirten, 1999; Etzkowitz and Leydesdorff, 2000). In the field of culture, arts and humanities, this innovation and knowledge transfer perspective has been overlooked and only recently have some contributions addressed, both on the academic (Cunningham, 2004; Taylor, 2005; Crossick, 2006) and policy side (NESTA, 2007). As Cunningham et al. (2004, p. 4) suggests, 'creative industries appear to be marginal within university-based research'. However, in the United Kingdom there are important examples of new emerging partnerships in this area – for example the Creative Industries Business Advisory Service (CIBAS), supported by the University of Portsmouth or the Institute for Creative Enterprise (ICE) at Coventry University.

There is also a lot of wishful planning on the potential of these collaborations, such as the Creative Convergence project drafted by Higher Education South East (HESE) to support the interaction between universities in southeast England and the regional creative economy.[5] As the high-profile *Lambert Review of Business-University Collaboration* (2003) suggests,

> there are many excellent examples of collaborations involving the creative industries and universities or colleges of art and design. Policy-makers must ensure that policies aimed at promot-

ing knowledge transfer are broad enough to allow initiatives such as these to grow and flourish, and that the focus is not entirely on science and engineering. (HM Treasury, 2003, p. 45)

Some specific cultural and creative clusters have benefited in the past from the interaction with HEIs. For example, Crewe and Beaverstock (1998) highlight the positive benefits of the involvement of Nottingham Trent University with the Lace Market cultural quarter and Rantisi (2002) considers the role of the Parsons School of Design in the development and growth of the New York garment district. Mould et al. (2009) also consider the involvement of Sheffield Hallam University in the Sheffield Cultural Quarter.

A relatively under-explored area so far is the role of HEIs in producing highly skilled creative workers. As Faggian and McCann (2006, 2009) contend, the primary role of the university system is being a conduit for bringing potential high quality undergraduate human capital into a region. The benefits of having a highly skilled labour pool far outweigh the benefits generated by knowledge spillovers. Hence, attracting and retaining higher human capital and creative individuals can be seen as a more effective and long-term strategy for local economic development (Mathur, 1999). The argument put forward by Florida (2002a, 2002b) suggests that this higher human capital level has connections also with the kind of urban environment and cultural setting that highly educated individuals look for when making a location choice.

Overall, it is clear that the relationship between HEIs and the creative city – and their contribution to the creativity of various locations – is a complex and multi-layered issue. In this chapter, we use the concept of 'bohemian graduate' as a key to better understand the connections between these dimensions. In particular, bohemian graduates are relevant to many of these theories and perspectives, as they are the means by which university knowledge can impact and be transferred to the local economy.

BETWEEN HUMAN CAPITAL AND CREATIVITY: THE ROLE OF BOHEMIAN GRADUATES AND THEIR LOCATION CHOICES

In light of the possible relations between HEIs and the creative city identified in the previous paragraph, this chapter explores the geography of creativity in the United Kingdom using the concept of 'bohemian graduates' (Comunian et al., 2010).

Bohemian graduates are graduates who obtained a degree in a 'bohemian' subject (creative arts, performing arts, design, mass communications, multimedia, software design and engineering, music recording and technology, architecture and landscape design). They can be considered as occupying the intersection between the creative class, creative industries and human capital (Figure 10.1).

In particular, we are concerned not only with the subjects that these bohemian graduates study but also their occupations and employment opportunities after graduation, including whether they find it difficult to enter a creative occupation. While it is clear that 'bohemian' graduates might find other career opportunities with economic benefits, it is assumed here that their first career choice is to enter a creative occupation, since they have specialized in specific creative skills at university. Creative occupations are defined in relation to the DCMS definition of creative industries and creative

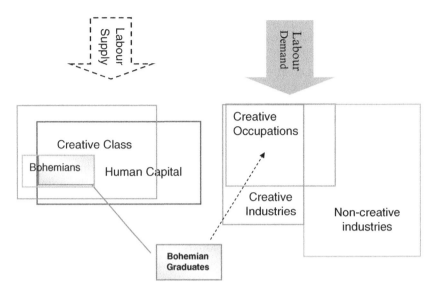

Figure 10.1   The 'bohemian' graduate

occupations.[6] The DCMS (1998, p. 4) defines them as 'those industries which have their origin in individual creativity, skill and talent and which have a potential for wealth and job creation through the generation and exploitation of intellectual property'. Included are advertising; architecture; arts and antique markets; crafts; design; designer fashion; film, video and photography; software, computer games and electronic publishing; music and the visual and performing arts; publishing; and television and radio. The DCMS framework (2009) is used to identify occupations within the creative industries (through Standard Industrial Classification codes) and creative occupations outside the creative industries (using Standard Occupation Classification codes).

Bohemians' location choices are important when studying the impact of HEIs on the creativity of cities, because of the embodied knowledge and skills they possess. Not only have they studied a 'creative' subject to a high level (investing consciously in their human capital), they often combine this with a passion and a natural innate ability in the creative disciplines (what some authors might call 'talent', while others simply include it in the human capital concept). As bohemian graduates combine creativity and human capital, their role in contributing to the local economy should be almost unanimously accepted by the advocates of the creative class theory as well as by the advocates of the human capital theory. Furthermore, because of their interest and passion for creative activities, they also exhibit 'sophisticated consumer demand' (Porter, 1998) for local cultural services and hence provide support for local cultural production.

The United Kingdom offers an array of opportunities for students who want to graduate in a 'bohemian' subject. Although the role of London as a creative city appears to be dominant, there are other creative British cities whose 'pull effect' on students should not be disregarded.

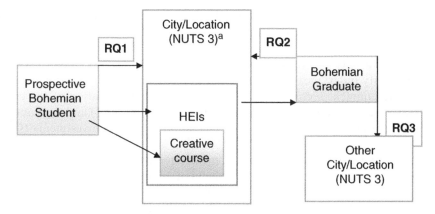

Note: ᵃ Nomenclature of Units for Territorial Statistics.

Figure 10.2   'Bohemian' graduates and their location choices

As Figure 10.2 shows, students are faced with two fundamental migration decisions, one upon 'entering' higher education, the second upon 'leaving' it. When prospective students decide that they want to enrol in a creative course, their first decision is whether to stay in the local area or to migrate to study in another city. This is obviously dependent on a series of considerations, including the provision of creative courses in their local area.

Upon graduation bohemian graduates are faced with a further location decision: staying in the city where they studied or moving elsewhere. One of the main determinants of this decision is the availability of creative jobs both locally and in other locations. The location choice for jobs should therefore reflect the geography of the creative economy; graduates should be attracted to cities and places that are able to offer them jobs in creative occupations. In this sense, 'creative cities' should have an advantage in attracting them and may thus benefit from a self-reinforcing virtuous cycle.

Our aim is to study the role that the 'creative city' plays in these location and migration dynamics by addressing the following research questions (RQs):

RQ1: Are 'Bohemian' courses mainly offered by HEIs located in 'creative cities', so that the likelihood of a student choosing to study a creative subject is influenced by living in a creative city to start with?
RQ2: How successful are the areas with the best provision of creative courses in retaining creative graduates?
RQ3: What places offer the best opportunities to enter a creative occupation? Are these creative occupations just restricted to a few creative cities?

In linking the location choices of students and graduates to the creativity of an area, we use the indices proposed by Clifton (2008) as measures of the 'creative city' phenomenon. Clifton (2008) critically applies a methodology à la Florida to provide insights into the creative class in the United Kingdom. He proposes three different indices. It is easy to see that these indices correspond to different interpretations of the creative city concept, thereby allowing us to test the relationship between the bohemian graduates' location choices and these interpretations. The three indices are as follows:

- The creative city as city of 'cultural consumption': Clifton's (2008) 'Cultural Opportunity Index' measures the level of employment in the recreational, cultural and entertainment sectors, which is linked to the interpretation of the creative city as a place of cultural consumption (Bell and Jayne, 2004) and the flourishing of tourism and entertainment economies around cultural investments (García, 2005).
- The creative city as city of 'cultural production': Clifton (2008) calculates the 'Bohemian Index' (based on the Bohemian Index by Florida, 2002a) as the level of employment in artistic and creative occupations using the Standard Occupational Classification 2000 and the DCMS guidelines (DCMS, 2009). This represents the view that a creative city is a place where production activities in the creative economy concentrates (Montgomery, 2005; Markusen, 2006; Pratt, 2008).
- The creative city as 'knowledge economy city': Clifton's (2008) 'Creative Professional Index' is closely related to the concept of 'creative class' (Florida, 2002b), and is linked to the interpretation of a creative city as a place that is able to attract creative workers and professionals. This interpretation is shared by Hospers (2003) and Musterd and Ostendorf (2004).

DATA AND METHODOLOGY

Our empirical analysis is based on data collected by the Higher Education Statistical Agency (HESA). Two different datasets are used. First, we employ the 'Students in Higher Education' data stream – which includes 1 723 260 student records for students enrolled in undergraduate courses in 2007 across the 166 British HEIs. This allows us to survey the provision of 'bohemian courses' in the United Kingdom. For each student, the survey includes information on personal characteristics (such as age, gender, ethnicity), course characteristics (including subject studied using the 4-digit JACS code,[7] mode of studying such as full-time or part-time, institution attended and the final grade achieved) and location of parental domicile (at unit postcode level). According to the Joint Academic Coding System (JACS) codes, 10.72 per cent (184 750) of the students in 2007 were registered for a 'creative' course either in 'media' (JACS code P)[8] or 'arts and design' (JACS code W).[9] To present the geography of 'creative' higher education provision in the United Kingdom, we analyse the student data at NUTS 1 level, as here the focus is on the critical mass and concentration of institutions and provision at the regional level. Considering that, as Charles (2003) suggests, the regional dimension is becoming more and more important in recent years in defining universities' missions, this geographical level seems the most appropriate.

Second, we combine the 'Students in Higher Education' data stream with the 'Destination of Leavers from Higher Education Institutions' (also known as DHLE) for students who graduated in the year 2007. The DHLE provides us with information on graduate employment between six and eighteen months after graduation. For the academic year 2006/07 information on 332 110 graduates was collected and it included not only the salary and location of their job, but also a brief description of their tasks and the SOC 4 and SIC 4 codes of their occupation. In the final combined database we had 242 470 'valid' cases (cases with no missing information). The location and migration decisions of graduates are presented at the NUTS 3 regional level. This allows a more detailed view of the local/urban dynamics and helps identifying more clearly where graduates tend to cluster. The analysis of the relationship between the concentration of students/graduates and the indices developed by Clifton (2008) is also carried out at the NUTS 3 regional level, since the focus is here on creative 'cities' and not larger regions.

THE GEOGRAPHY OF THE CREATIVE HIGHER EDUCATION PROVISION

The provision of higher education courses in the creative subjects is certainly not uniform across the United Kingdom, as is shown in Table 10.1. In absolute terms, Greater London and the South East attracted 37 per cent of the total number of students in these disciplines in 2007. Greater London on its own accounted for 24 per cent. The North West and Yorkshire follow with about 10 per cent, while the North East and Northern Ireland are last. However, it is clear that these percentages partly reflect the size of the population of each region.

A different geography emerges when looking at the concentration of bohemian students as a percentage of the number of students in the region (Table 10.1, column 5). Though Greater London still shows the highest 'specialization' in creative courses, the role of other regions emerges. The South West, perhaps unexpectedly, has over 13 per cent of students enrolled in bohemian courses and both the East Midlands and Wales

Table 10.1   General, student and bohemian student population by UK region (HESA, 2007), thousands

Region	Population 2010	Total students	Bohemian students	% bohemians in region	% bohemians of UK total
Greater London	7172	282	44	15.8	24.0
South East	8001	249	24	9.6	13.0
North West	6730	189	20	10.4	10.6
Yorkshire and the Humber	4965	164	17	10.3	9.1
South West	4928	121	16	13.2	8.6
East Midlands	4172	111	13	11.3	6.8
Scotland	5062	164	11	6.8	6.1
West Midlands	5267	128	11	8.6	5.9
Wales	2903	93	10	11.1	5.6
East	5388	106	11	9.8	5.7
North East	2515	78	7	8.4	3.6
Northern Ireland	1685	37	2	4.9	1.0
UK Total	58 789	1723	185	10.7	100.0

Table 10.2   Top ten 'creative' HEIs (absolute number of bohemian students and percentage of the 'bohemian' total)

Institution	Region	Total number of bohemian graduates	Percentage of bohemian students
University of the Arts, London	Greater London	12 470	6.8
University for the Creative Arts	South East	4795	2.6
Middlesex University	Greater London	3800	2.1
Southampton Solent University	South East	3610	2.0
Nottingham Trent University	East Midlands	3475	1.9
De Montfort University	East Midlands	3395	1.8
Manchester Metropolitan University	North West	3350	1.8
University of Central Lancashire	North West	3320	1.8
Birmingham City University	West Midlands	3120	1.7
University of Salford	North West	3075	1.7

have a percentage of bohemian students above the national average. Northern Ireland still has the lowest percentage.

It is important to notice that in certain regions some 'specialized' institutions dominate the scene. If we look at the geography of the most important HEIs in terms of the absolute number of bohemian students (Table 10.2), it is clear that the University of the Arts in London has a dominant role with over 12 000 students enrolled (almost 7 per cent of the national total). Previously known as the London Institute, this recently established university (it gained university status in 2004) comprises six separate colleges: the Camberwell College of Arts, Wimbledon College of Art, Central St Martin's College of Art & Design, Chelsea College of Art & Design, London College of Fashion and the London College of Communication. It claims to be the largest HEI in the field, not only in the United Kingdom but also in Europe. While their respective sizes may not be comparable with the University of the Arts, the other institutions in the top ten still educate a considerable number of bohemian students (more than 3000 each, which represents about 2 per cent of the total number of students educated in the United Kingdom). The geographical spread is also interesting. Although the top four HEIs are located either in Greater London or in the South East, the North West and the Midlands are also well represented (with three HEIs each and a total number of enrolled students around 10 000).

The role of Greater London is clear not only when we look at the absolute number of bohemian students, but also when we look at the location of smaller but highly specialized colleges. In the United Kingdom there are 21 HEIs whose percentage of students enrolled in bohemian subjects is above 50 per cent (Table 10.3); eight of them exclusively educate bohemian students. Of these 21 HEIs, ten are based in Greater London. Not only are there many more places in Greater London, but there is also a wider variety of options for students who want to study a creative subject, hence adding to the general feeling of London being a 'creative city'. It is therefore easier for Greater London to attract these students and, later on, to retain them after graduation.

Table 10.3   Top HEIs that specialize in 'bohemian' subjects

Institution	Region	Bohemian students total	% bohemian students
Norwich University College of the Arts	East	1165	100.0
Conservatoire for Dance and Drama	G. London	1095	100.0
Trinity Laban	G. London	830	100.0
Guildhall School of Music and Drama	G. London	705	100.0
Leeds College of Music	Yorkshire/ Humber	680	100.0
Royal Northern College of Music	North West	675	100.0
Royal College of Music	G. London	590	100.0
Dartington College of Arts	South West	585	100.0
Royal Academy of Music	G. London	670	97.6
Central School of Speech and Drama	G. London	805	96.5
University for the Creative Arts	South East	4795	95.5
Rose Bruford College	G. London	735	95.4
The Arts Institute at Bournemouth	South West	1835	93.5
Royal College of Art	G. London	795	89.7
University College Falmouth	South West	1950	88.3
Liverpool Institute for Performing Arts	North West	620	88.1
Royal Scottish Academy of Music/Drama	Scotland	665	87.9
University of the Arts, London	G. London	12470	83.3
Ravensbourne C. Design/Communication	G. London	840	75.9
Edinburgh College of Art	Scotland	1025	66.7
Glasgow School of Art	Scotland	1120	66.4

BOHEMIAN STUDENTS' AND GRADUATES' LOCATION CHOICES FOR STUDYING AND WORKING PURPOSES

Now that we have provided a brief description of the provision of 'bohemian' courses in the United Kingdom, it is interesting to turn our attention to the location choices of bohemian graduates. The DHLE HESA data provide us with information on graduates' job location between six and eighteen months after graduation. Although we recognize that this is a relatively short period, it still gives us insights into the ability of regions to retain their bohemian graduates in the short term. As the map shows (Figure 10.3), a high percentage of bohemian graduates choose – as expected – to work in the London area, followed by Greater Manchester and the South East. The urban environment with its 'buzz' is vital for artists. Such an environment offers a wider cultural infrastructure as well as creative networks and informal learning opportunities for artists and creative practitioners (Comunian, 2010). It also provides a wider range of job opportunities and potential contracts for bohemian graduates, which they can use to develop their portfolios and make a living. What is interesting, however, is the role of other 'regional' hubs such as Cardiff, Leeds and Newcastle. Newcastle – benefiting from the cultural investments that are mainly taking place in Gateshead – has been able to develop a strong profile as a 'creative city' (Minton, 2003), which can be clearly seen in its ability to attract

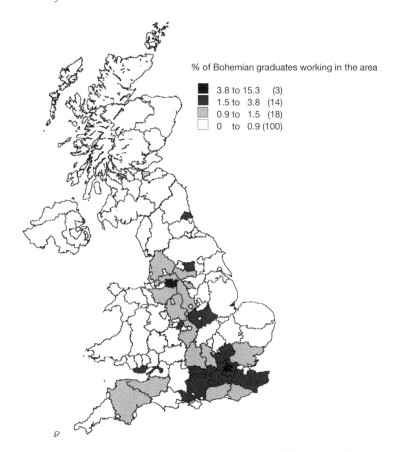

% of Bohemian graduates working in the area

■ 3.8 to 15.3   (3)
■ 1.5 to 3.8 (14)
▨ 0.9 to 1.5 (18)
□ 0 to 0.9 (100)

Figure 10.3   Map of bohemian graduates as a percentage of the regional population

students in this field. However, its lower profile in reference to creative occupations in general highlights the difficulty to create a stronger profile in the creative economy (Comunian, 2009), despite the policy rhetoric (One North East, 2007).

What this map does not show, however, is in what kind of professions these bohemians are employed in. The second map (Figure 10.4) shows the geographical distribution of graduates working in creative occupations (as defined by Comunian et al., 2010). When comparing the two maps, some similarities are clear. The role of London and the South East is confirmed, together with Manchester and Leeds. In their analysis of creative industries employment growth between 1991 and 2000, Fingleton et al. (2007) underline the high performance of districts in London and the South East, providing further evidence to this pattern of concentration. Similar results about the role of London are reached in the recent National Endowment for Science, Technology and the Arts (NESTA) (2009) report for all types of creative industries, although some regional clusters emerge in specific sub-sectors (for example, design and fashion in the East Midlands). Two main differences emerge when one compares the two maps. First, Cardiff has a lower concentration of creative occupations than bohemian graduates, while the opposite is true of Edinburgh, which benefits from being a recognized centre for performing arts and literature. Both cities are

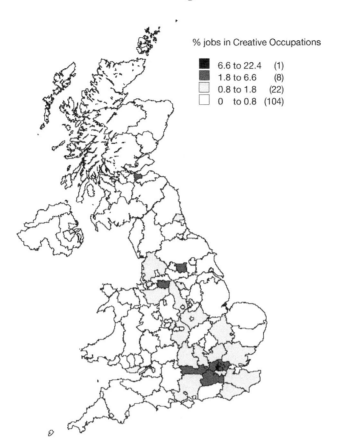

% jobs in Creative Occupations

■ 6.6 to 22.4   (1)
■ 1.8 to 6.6   (8)
□ 0.8 to 1.8   (22)
□ 0 to 0.8   (104)

Figure 10.4   Map of bohemian graduates working in creative professions

cultural capitals within their respective national boundaries and this emerges in the maps, as their surroundings do not present similar profiles. Second, creative occupations seem to be even more concentrated in the Greater London area than bohemian graduates.

To check this, Table 10.4 presents the top 20 areas in terms of percentage of bohemian students enrolled in local HEIs, percentage of bohemian graduates in the local labour force and percentage of graduates working locally in creative occupations.

Inner London-West tops all three rankings, even though the percentage (and hence absolute number) of graduates working in creative occupations is more than double the percentage of bohemian students. As such, this area of London appears to be the 'Mecca' for the creative economy and the best location to get a bohemian-type artistic job. The other half of Inner London fairs relatively well in terms of the creative job market (both the percentage of bohemian graduates working there and the percentage of graduates working in creative occupations are well above 5 per cent) despite not having nearly as many 'creative' HEIs located in the area.

In contrast, Greater Manchester ranks second in the percentage of bohemian students, but third in Bohemian graduates and only fourth regarding the percentage of graduates working in creative occupations. This seems to suggest that the local labour

Table 10.4　Top 20 areas for bohemian students, bohemian graduates and creative occupations

	Bohemian students	%	Bohemian graduates	%	Creative occupations	%
1	Inner London-West	10.4	Inner London-West	15.3	Inner London-West	22.4
2	Greater Manchester-South	4.4	Inner London-East	5.5	Inner London-East	6.6
3	Leeds	4.1	Greater Manchester-South	3.8	Outer London-West and North West	3.9
4	Outer London-West and North West	3.6	Outer London-West and North West	3.6	Greater Manchester-South	3.7
5	Inner London-East	3.6	Leeds	2.5	Surrey	2.0
6	North Somerset/South Gloucestershire	3.1	Outer London-East and North East	2.0	Leeds	2.0
7	Liverpool	3.0	Birmingham	2.0	Berkshire	1.9
8	Leicester	3.0	Hampshire County Council	1.9	Edinburgh, City of	1.9
9	Sheffield	2.8	Surrey	1.8	Outer London-East and North East	1.8
10	Southampton	2.6	Tyneside	1.8	Hampshire City Council	1.8
11	Bournemouth and Poole	2.4	Kent County Council	1.7	Oxfordshire	1.8
12	Nottingham	2.4	Bristol, City of	1.6	Tyneside	1.6
13	Birmingham	2.4	Outer London-South	1.6	Birmingham	1.6
14	Lancashire County Council	2.3	Cardiff and Vale of Glamorgan	1.5	Hertfordshire	1.6
15	Surrey	2.2	Hertfordshire	1.5	Glasgow City	1.5
16	Tyneside	2.2	Berkshire	1.5	Bristol, City of	1.5
17	Lincolnshire	2.1	Leicestershire County Council and Rutland	1.5	Kent County Council	1.4
18	Outer London-South	2.0	Glasgow City	1.5	Essex County Council	1.3
19	Brighton and Hove	2.0	Edinburgh, City of	1.4	Cardiff and Vale of Glamorgan	1.3
20	Cardiff and Vale of Glamorgan	1.9	Essex County Council	1.4	Leicestershire County Council and Rutland	1.1

market for creative jobs is not strong enough to retain all the bohemian graduates who were educated by local HEIs. This could also be linked to some potential occupational mismatch (Comunian et al., 2010) that could have further implications for the local creative economy. Previous studies have found that a very high percentage of bohemian graduates do enter a 'creative' occupation and that this is true not only in the short term (Comunian et al., 2010) but also in the medium-long term (Abreu et al., 2010).

The general impression from Table 10.4 is that creative occupations are a lot more concentrated in fewer areas – with Greater London accounting for over 34 per cent – while higher education provision of bohemian subjects, despite still being skewed towards Greater London, displays a lower concentration level.

It is interesting to highlight this connection between the place of study and the place of work. Knell and Oakley (2007) point out that London HEIs are a key part of the public infrastructure that supports London's creative economy. They suggest that HEIs (like publicly supported cultural institutions) function as an 'R&D lab, providing risk funding and an atmosphere of experimentation' (Knell and Oakley, 2007, p. 23) for the creative sector. They also see HEIs as vital for the development of – often exclusive – 'tightly bound social networks' (p. 18). This is also underlined in the different context of designers' careers in Toronto: Vinodrai (2006) finds that local design schools provide a shared institutional context that enables designers to work together as well as some of the leading designers to teach courses in the city. This can create further networks and interconnections: 'instructors use this teaching experience as an opportunity to assess students whom they may hire for themselves or recommend to others' (Vinodrai, 2006, p. 258). Therefore, higher education does not simply relate to student numbers but also to a more complex ecology of creative work. As other authors suggest (Gill, 2002; NESTA, 2008), one of the most common (second) occupations for creative workers is teaching in HEIs. According to one survey (Ball et al., 2010), one-third of creative graduates has had experience in teaching: 'when graduates changed from their initial career goal, it was most frequently towards teaching' (Ball et al., 2010, p. 6).

BOHEMIAN GRADUATES IN THE CREATIVE CITY

This section explores the relationship between students' and graduates' locations and the three measures of 'city creativity' à la Clifton (2008) introduced in the previous section: the Bohemian Index, the Creative Professionals Index and the Cultural Opportunities Index.

As Table 10.5 shows, there is a general positive correlation between students' location choices (both to study and to work) and the proxies that are used to identify the 'creative city'.

However, the size and significance of these correlations do differ. The creativity of a city is more highly correlated with the number of bohemian graduates and graduates

Table 10.5   Correlations between the locations of bohemian students/graduates and indices of city creativity

	Location of bohemians			Creative city indices		
	BS	BG	GCO	BI	CP	CO
Bohemian students (BS)	1.000					
Bohemian graduates (BG)	0.821*	1.000				
BG in creative jobs (GCO)	0.791*	0.987*	1.000			
Bohemian Index (BI)	0.691*	0.825*	0.822*	1.000		
Creative professionals (CP)	0.421*	0.616*	0.605*	0.706*	1.000	
Cultural opportunities (CO)	0.225	0.328*	0.347*	0.432*	0.377*	1.000

Note: * $p < 0.01$. The data used by Clifton (2008) are used as percentages of the national figures and refer to England and Wales, where complete data series were available.

in creative occupations than with the number of bohemian students. This suggests two things. First, 'city creativity' is more likely to influence labour market conditions than is the city's provision of higher education. Second, as seen before, the geographies of bohemian higher education and creative jobs do not completely coincide (and in fact the correlations between bohemian students (BS) and the other two measures, bohemian graduates (BG) and bohemian graduates in creative jobs (GCO) are 0.82 and 0.79, respectively; they are both lower that the correlation between the two labour market indexes involving bohemian graduates, BG and GCO, which equals 0.98). In other words, cities which have HEIs that specialize in bohemian courses do not necessarily have a job market that is dominated by the creative sector.

Another interesting result is that the Cultural Opportunities Index does not exhibit a very high correlation with any of the other indexes and especially as regards the location of bohemian students and graduates. The lowest correlation is between cultural opportunities and bohemian students at about 0.22 ($p = 0.02$). This seems to suggest that when students choose at which HEI to attend a bohemian course they tend to consider other factors (such as university quality) as more important. The consumption of cultural activities is not one of the main determinants of students' location choices. This could be linked to the fact that the cities with more prominent cultural and entertainment sectors are also the cities that are more attractive to tourists or outside visitors – which may influence house prices and the cost of living and thereby become unattractive to students. Perhaps more surprisingly, the correlations between the Cultural Opportunities Index and the location of graduates (either bohemians or people working in creative occupations) are also not that high. Without inferring any directional causality, this seems to imply that the concept of the creative city as a place for 'cultural consumption' (broadly speaking) is not what bohemian students and graduates are attracted to. Instead, they may view the 'creative city' as a place of 'cultural production' with a strong knowledge and creative sector.

CONCLUSIONS

This chapter presents a first investigation of the link between 'creative' higher education provision and 'creative cities'. This is an important issue because, as Murphy (2010) points out, there is 'no better place to support the creative triad of talent, technology and tolerance than an art classroom'.

Our results suggest a high degree of concentration in the spatial distribution of both the creative higher education and creative jobs. Especially for the latter, the role of London is dominant; this confirms the findings of recent research on clustering of creative industries (Pratt, 2004b; NESTA, 2009). Greater London and South East England have a leading role in Britain's creative economy thanks to a self-reinforcing and endogenous mechanism, which stems from the interaction between creative HEIs and the creative sector. Clearly these areas benefit from historical and infrastructural advantages in creative higher education provision, and these advantages are well exploited by the local creative production system, resulting in a long-lasting and embedded symbiosis. Törnqvist (2004, p. 241) contends that a milieu of creativity consists primarily of 'places and groupings that have attracted competencies within specialized disciplines', often over a long period of time. Hall (1998) and Scott (2006) also refer to agglomeration effects within the context of the creative city. This issue has numerous policy implications and deserves further research, especially in light of what Fingleton et al. (2007, p. 77) point out, which is that the science base of local universities is negatively correlated with the growth of employment in the creative industries, so that 'it appears that the arts and science do not mix. . . . [In] areas where the science base is strong, creative industries employment growth is weak'.

The fact that creative activities are highly concentrated in a few – usually urban – areas raises issues regarding the role of policy makers in sustaining more peripheral areas where the creative economy is more of an aspiration than a reality. To what degree this aspiration should be questioned or supported has already emerged as a critical issue (Oakley, 2006). While creating new courses and infrastructures for creative subjects in old and new HEIs appears to be an easy solution, the issue of long-term sustainability and real job opportunities should be considered (Heartfield, 2005). Furthermore, 'creative city' policies may play a role in increasing local inequality insofar as the need to attract the 'creative class' clashes with the needs of local residents and local artists (McCann, 2007). The literature also suggests that bohemian graduates are more likely to have temporary, part-time and poorly paid jobs (Abreu et al., 2010) than other graduates, which points to the central importance of the issue of sustainability and possible polarizations (McRobbie and Forkert, 2009).

The fact that the number of bohemian graduates and graduates working in creative occupations are more strongly correlated with the indices of 'cultural and creative production' than with 'cultural consumption' is yet another confirmation that creative HEIs and the local creative labour market work as an integrated system.

While this chapter represents a first attempt to highlight the issues surrounding HEIs in the creative city, our focus was specifically on the role of 'bohemian graduates' in the contribution of HEIs to local economies and creative cities. This is obviously a limited perspective as it does not take into account the role that other immigrants – such as low-paid international migrants in the non-creative sectors – play in the development and growth of cities (for an analysis of metropolitan areas in the United States, see, for example, Glaeser and Gottlieb, 2006).

Moreover, our analysis could be expanded and improved by considering the overall role of 'creative' HEIs in creative cities, including the role of research capacity and academic leadership and partnerships (Powell, 2007). Chatterton (1999, p. 177), referring to research in more artistic subjects, states that 'universities . . . are one of the few remaining places where artistic experimentation and integrity is financially viable . . . and their staff and student populations play a crucial role in sustaining the viability of many local cultural events and facilities'.

ACKNOWLEDGEMENT

We acknowledge the support of the 'Impact of Higher Education Institutions on Regional Economics Initiative' (ESCR grant number RES-171-25-0032 co-funded by HEFCE, Scottish Funding Council, HEFCW and DELNI). The authors also wish to thank HEFCE and HESA for providing access to the data used in this study and Nick

Clifton at University of Wales Institute Cardiff. Nevertheless, all views expressed are solely the responsibility of the authors.

NOTES

1. Details on the project and programmes offered are available on the Queensland Institute of Technology Creative Industries Precinct website: http://www.ciprecinct.qut.edu.au/about (accessed 8 March 2010).
2. Glasgow is the first city to be given the title that had not been a culturally recognized leading European city; previous hosts had been cities such as Florence and Paris. The choice of Glasgow was motivated specifically by Glasgow's potential ability to improve its image and regenerate the city.
3. In Florida's own words, at the core of the creative class there are 'people in science and engineering, architecture and design, education, arts, music and entertainment, whose economic function is to create new ideas, new technology, and/or new creative content', but also 'the creative professionals in business and finance, law, healthcare and related fields. These people engage in complex problem solving that involves a great deal of independent judgment and requires high levels of education or human capital' (Florida, 2002b, p. 8).
4. This is articulated further in the three Ts indices: technology, talent and tolerance are the proxies by which the ability of a city to attract the creative class can be measured and implemented.
5. The project remains for the moment in its final draft but has not been put into practice yet, see http://www.hese.ac.uk/documents/Creative-Convergence-final-report.pdf (accessed 8 March 2010).
6. We acknowledge that this definition has quite a few limitations (see Oakley, 2006) and might not be applicable to other countries, but considering that our analysis is set in the United Kingdom, this seems to be the most suitable definition to adopt. Therefore, it is important to clarify that 'creative occupations' are here not defined as occupations that are creative (this could include, for instance, scientific inventions and other creative jobs) but as occupation within the creative (and cultural) sector as defined by the DCMS.
7. For more information on the Joint Academic Coding System (or JACS), see http://www.hesa.ac.uk/index.php?option=com_content&task=view&id=158&Itemid=233 (accessed 8 March 2010).
8. These include: *Information Services*: P110 Information Management, P120 Librarianship, P121 Library Studies, P130 Curatorial Studies, P131 Museum Studies, P132 Archive Studies, P190 Information Services not elsewhere classified; *Publicity Studies*: P210 Public Relations, P290 Publicity Studies not elsewhere classified; *Media studies*: P301 Television Studies, P302 Radio Studies, P303 Film Studies, P304 Electronic Media Studies, P305 Paper-based Media Studies, P310 Media Production, P311 Television Production, P312 Radio Production, P313 Film Production, P390 Media Studies not elsewhere classified; *Publishing*: P410 Electronic Publishing, P411 Publishing on Audio/Video tape, P412 Publishing on CD-ROM, P413 Publishing via the World Wide Web, P420 Multimedia Publishing, P430 Interactive Publishing, P490 Publishing not elsewhere classified; *Journalism*: P510 Factual Reporting, P590 Journalism not elsewhere classified; *Others in Mass Communications and Documentation*: P990 Communications and Documentation not elsewhere classified.
9. These include: *Fine Arts*: W110 Drawing, W120 Painting, W130 Sculpture, W140 Printmaking, W150 Calligraphy, W160 Fine Art Conservation, W190 Fine Art not elsewhere classified; *Design*: W210 Graphic Design, W211 Typography, W212 Multimedia Design, W213 Visual Communication, W220 Illustration, W230 Clothing/Fashion Design, W231 Textile Design, W240 Industrial/Product Design, W250 Interior Design, W260 Furniture Design, W270 Ceramics Design, W280 Interactive and Electronic Design, W290 Design studies not elsewhere classified; *Music*: W310 Musicianship/Performance Studies, W330 History of Music, W340 Types of Music, W350 Musicology, W360 Musical Instrument History, W390 Music not elsewhere classified; *Drama*: W410 Acting, W420 Directing for Theatre, W430 Producing for Theatre, W440 Theatre Studies, W450 Stage Management, W451 Theatrical Wardrobe Design, W452 Theatrical Make-up, W460 Theatre Design, W461 Stage Design, W490 Drama not elsewhere classified; *Dance*: W510 Choreography, W520 Body Awareness, W530 History of Dance, W540 Types of Dance, W590 Dance not elsewhere classified; *Cinematics and Photography*: W610 Moving Image Techniques, W611 Directing Motion Pictures, W612 Producing Motion Pictures, W613 Film and Sound Recording, W614 Visual and Audio Effects, W615 Animation Techniques, W620 Cinematography, W630 History of Cinematics and Photography, W631 History of Cinematics, W632 History of Photography, W640 Photography, W690 Cinematics and Photography not elsewhere classified; *Crafts*: W710 Fabric and Leather Crafts, W711 Needlecraft, W712 Dressmaking, W713 Soft Furnishing, W714 Weaving, W715 Leatherwork, W720 Metal Crafts, W721 Silversmithing/Goldsmithing, W722 Blacksmithing, W723 Clock/Watchmaking, W730 Wood Crafts, W731 Carpentry/Joinery, W732 Cabinet Making, W733 Marquetry and Inlaying, W734 Veneering, W740 Surface Decoration, W750 Clay and Stone Crafts, W751 Pottery, W752 Tile

Making, W753 Stone Crafts, W760 Reed Crafts, W761 Basketry, W762 Thatching, W770 Glass Crafts, W771 Glassblowing, W780 Paper Crafts, W781 Bookbinding, W782 Origami, W790 Crafts not elsewhere classified; *Imaginative Writing*: W810 Scriptwriting, W820 Poetry Writing, W830 Prose Writing, W890 Imaginative Writing not elsewhere classified; *Others in Creative Arts and Design*: W990 Creative Arts and Design not elsewhere classified.

REFERENCES

Abreu, M., A. Faggian, R. Comunian and P. McCann (2010). '"Life is short, art is long", the persistent wage gap between Bohemian and non-Bohemian graduates', *Annals of Regional Science*, published online 11 January, doi:10.1007/00168-010-0422-4.

Arts Council of England (2009), *Capital Case Study: The Creative Foundation, Folkestone – Kent*, London: Arts Council of England.

Ball, L., E. Pollard and N. Stanley (2010), 'Creative graduates, creative future', London: Creative Graduates Creative Futures Higher Education Partnership and the Institute for Employment Studies.

Bell, D. and M. Jayne (2004), *City of Quarters: Urban Villages in the Contemporary City*, Aldershot: Ashgate.

Bianchini, F. and C. Landry (1995), *The Creative City*, London: Demos.

Cameron, S. and J. Coaffee (2005), 'Art, gentrification and regeneration – from artist as pioneer to public arts', *European Journal of Housing Policy*, **5**, 39–58.

Cantor, N. (2005), 'Collaborations on the creative "campus"', Conference on Campus-Community Art Connections and the Creative Economy of Upstate New York, Cornell University, Ithaca, NY.

Chapain, C.A. and R. Comunian (2009), 'Creative cities in England: researching realities and images', *Built Environment*, **35**, 212–29.

Charles, D. (2003), 'Universities and territorial development: reshaping the regional role of English universities', *Local Economy*, **18**, 7–20.

Charles D. (2006), 'Universities as key knowledge infrastructure in regional innovation systems', *Innovation*, **19**, 117–30.

Chatterton, P. (1999), 'The cultural role of universities in the community: revisiting the university – community debate', *Environment & Planning A*, **32**, 165–81.

Chatterton, P. and J. Goddard (2000), 'The response of higher education institutions to regional needs', *European Journal of Education*, **35**, 475–96.

Clifton, N. (2008), 'The "creative class" in the UK: an initial analysis', *Geografiska Annaler: Series B, Human Geography*, **90**, 63–82.

Comunian, R. (2009), 'Questioning creative work as driver of economic development: the case of Newcastle-Gateshead', *Creative Industries Journal*, **2**, 57–72.

Comunian, R. (2010), 'Rethinking the creative city: the role of complexity, networks and interactions in the urban creative economy', *Urban Studies*, published online 6 September, doi: 10.1177/0042098010370626.

Comunian, R., D. Smith and C.F. Taylor (2007), 'A new "Triple Helix"? Universities, creative industries and cultural policy', paper presented at the Triple Helix Conference VI, National University of Singapore, Singapore.

Comunian, R., A. Faggian and Q.C. Li (2010), 'Unrewarded careers in the creative class: the strange case of Bohemian graduates', *Papers in Regional Science*, **89**, 389–410.

Cramphorn, J. and J. Woodlhouse (1999), 'The role of education in economic development', *Industry & Higher Education*, **13**, 169–75.

Crewe, L. and J. Beaverstock (1998), 'Fashioning the city: cultures of consumption in contemporary urban spaces', *Geoforum*, **29**, 287–308.

Crossick, G. (2006), 'Knowledge transfer without widgets: the challenge of the creative economy', lecture given at the Royal Society of Arts, Goldsmiths University of London, London.

Cunningham, S. (2004), 'The humanities, creative arts, and international innovation agendas', in J. Kennaway, E. Bullen and S. Robb (eds), *Innovation & Tradition: The Arts, Humanities and the Knowledge Economy*, New York, NY: Peter Lang, pp. 221–32.

Cunningham, S., T. Cutler, G. Hearn, M. Ryan and M. Keane (2004), 'An innovation agenda for the creative industries: where is the R&D?', in *Media International Australia: Incorporating Culture & Policy*, **112**, 174–85.

DCMS (1998), *Creative Industries Mapping Document*, London: Department for Culture, Media and Sport.

DCMS (2009), *Creative Industries Economic Estimates*, London: Department of Culture, Media and Sport.

Etzkowitz, H. and L. Leydesdorff (2000), 'The dynamics of innovation: from national systems and "mode 2" to a triple helix of university-industry-government relations', *Research Policy*, **29**, 109–23.

Evans, G. and P. Shaw (2004), *The Contribution of Culture to Regeneration in UK: A Review of Evidence*, London: DCMS.

Faggian, A. and P. McCann (2006), 'Human capital flows and regional knowledge assets: a simultaneous equation approach', *Oxford Economic Papers*, **58**, 475–500.

Faggian, A. and P. McCann (2009), 'Human capital, graduate migration and innovation in British Regions', *Cambridge Journal of Economics*, **33**, 317–33.

Fingleton, B., D.C. Igliori, B. Moore and R. Odedra (2007), 'Employment growth and cluster dynamics in creative industries in Great Britain', in K. Polenske (ed.), *The Economic Geography of Innovation*, Cambridge: Cambridge University Press, pp. 61–84.

Florida, R. (2002a), 'Bohemia and economic geography', *Journal of Economic Geography*, **2**, 55–71.

Florida, R. (2002b), *The Rise of the Creative Class*, New York, NY: Basic Books.

Fritsch, M. and C. Schwirten (1999), 'Enterprise-university co-operation and the role of public research institutions in regional innovation systems', *Industry & Innovation*, **6**, 69–83.

Garber, M. (2008a), *Patronizing the Arts – The University as Patron*, Princeton, NJ: Princeton University Press.

Garber, M. (2008b), 'Higher art: universities should become society's great patrons of the arts', *Boston Globe*, 5 October, available at http://www.boston.com/bostonglobe/ideas/articles/2008/10/05/higher_art/ (accessed 8 March 2011).

Garcia, B. (2005), 'De-constructing the city of culture: the long term cultural legacies of Glasgow 1990', *Urban Studies* **42**, 1–28.

Gill, R. (2002), 'Cool, creative and egalitarian? Exploring gender in project-based new media work in Europe', *Information, Communication and Society*, **5**, 70–89.

Glaeser, E.L. and J.D. Gottlieb (2006), 'Urban resurgence and the consumer city', *Urban Studies*, **43**, 1275–99.

Griffiths, R. (2006), 'City/culture discourses: evidence from the competition to select the European capital of culture 2008', *European Planning Studies*, **14**, 415–30.

Hall, P. (1998), *Cities in Civilization: Culture, Innovation and Urban Order*, London: Weidenfeld & Wishart.

Heartfield, J. (2005), *The Creativity Gap*, London: Blueprint ETP.

HM Treasury (2003), *The Lambert Review of Business-University Collaboration*, London: The Stationery Office.

Hospers, G.-J. (2003), 'Creative cities in Europe: urban competitiveness in the knowledge economy', *Intereconomics*, September/October, 260–69.

Knell, J. and K. Oakley (2007), *London's Creative Economy: An Accidental Success?*, London: The Work Foundation.

Landry, C. (2000), *The Creative City: A Toolkit for Urban Innovators*, London: Earthscan Publications.

Markusen, A. (2006), 'Urban development and the politics of a creative class: evidence from the case study of artists', *Environment and Planning A*, **38**, 1921–40.

Matheson, B. (2006), 'A culture of creativity: design education and the creative industries', *Journal of Management Development*, **25**, 55–64.

Mathur, V.K. (1999), 'Human capital-based strategy for regional economic development', *Economic Development Quarterly*, **13**, 203–16.

McCann, E.J. (2007), 'Inequality and politics in the creative city-region: questions of livability and state strategy', *International Journal of Urban and Regional Research*, **31**, 188–96.

McRobbie, A. and K. Forkert (2009), 'Artists & art schools: for or against innovation? A reply to NESTA', *Variant*, Spring, available at http://www.variant.org.UK/pdfs/issue34/nesta34.pdf (accessed 8 March 2010).

Minton, A. (2003), *Northern Soul: Culture, Creativity and Quality of Place in Newcastle and Gateshead*, London: Demos & Rics.

Montgomery, J. (2005), 'Beware "the creative class". Creativity and wealth creation revisited', *Local Economy*, **20**, 337–43.

Mould, O., S. Roodhouse and T. Vorley (2009), 'Realising capabilities: academic creativity and the creative industries', *Creative Industries Journal*, **1**, 137–50.

Murphy, B. (2010), 'Growing up artistically in a creative city', 16 January, available at http://www.statesman.com/opinion/insight/growing-up-artistically-in-a-creative-city-182115.html (accessed 8 March 2010).

Musterd, S. and W. Ostendorf (2004), 'Creative cultural knowledge cities: perspectives and planning strategies', *Built Environment*, **30**, 189–93.

NESTA (2007), 'How linked are the UK's creative industries to the wider economy? An input-output analysis', Working Paper, London: NESTA.

NESTA (2008), *The Art of Innovation: How Fine Arts Graduates Contribute to Innovation*, London: NESTA.

NESTA (2009), *The Geography of Creativity*, London: NESTA.

Noble, M. and T. Barry (2008), 'Supporting regional regeneration and workforce development: establishing a new University Centre in Folkestone', paper presented at the UVAC Annual Conference Higher Education – Skills in the Workplace: Delivering Employer-led Higher Level Work-based Learning, Royal York Hotel, York.

O'Connor, J. and D. Wynne (eds) (1996), *From the Margins to the Centre: Cultural Production in the Post-industrial City*, Aldershot: Arena.

Oakley, K. (2006), 'Include us out: economic development and social policy in the creative industries', *Cultural Trends*, **15**, 255–73.

One North East (2007), *Commercial Creative Industries Sector*, Newcastle Upon Tyne: One North East and Culture North East.

Porter, M. (1998), *On Competition*, Boston, MA: Harvard Business School.

Powell, J. (2007), 'Creative universities and their creative city-regions', *Industry and Higher Education*, **21**, 323–35.

Pratt, A.C. (2004a), 'Creative clusters: towards the governance of the creative industries production system? ', *Media International Australia*, 50–66.

Pratt, A.C. (2004b), 'Mapping the cultural industries: regionalization; the example of South East England', in D. Power and A.J. Scott (eds), *Cultural Industries and the Production of Culture*, London: Routledge, pp. 19–36.

Pratt, A.C. (2008), 'Creative cities: the cultural industries and the creative class', *Geografiska Annaler: Series B, Human Geography*, **90**, 107–17.

Preston, J. and C. Hammond (2006), *The Economic Impact of UK Higher Education Institutions*, London: Universities UK.

Rantisi, N.M. (2002), 'The local innovation system as a source of variety: openness and adaptability in New York City's garment district', *Regional Studies*, **36**, 587–602.

Robinson, C. and N. Adams (2008), 'Unlocking the potential: the role of universities in pursuing regeneration and promoting sustainable communities', *Local Economy*, **23**(4), 277–89.

Scott, A.J. (2006), 'Creative cities: conceptual issues and policy questions', *Journal of Urban Affairs*, **28**, 1–17.

Stanford Arts Initiative (2007), 'Engaging the arts & creativity', available at http://arts.stanford.edu/assets/ArtsInitiative_L2.pdf (accessed 8 March 2010).

Taylor, J. (2005), 'Unweaving the rainbow: research, innovation and risk in a creative economy', AHRC Discussion Paper, London: AHRC.

Tepper, S. (2004), 'The creative campus: who's No.1?', *Chronicle of Higher Education*, **51**, B6.

Tepper, S. (2006), 'Taking the measure of the creative campus', *peerReview*, Spring.

Törnqvist, G. (2004), 'Creativity in time and space', *Geografiska Annaler: Series B, Human Geography*, **86**, 227–43.

Vinodrai, T. (2006), 'Reproducing Toronto's design ecology: career paths, intermediaries, and local labor markets', *Economic Geography*, **82**, 237–63.

Wood, P. and C. Taylor (2004), 'Big ideas for a small town: the Huddersfield creative town initiative', *Local Economy*, **19**, 380–95.

PART 3

NETWORKS

11 Research nodes and networks

Christian Wichmann Matthiessen, Annette Winkel Schwarz and Søren Find

Research is by definition an innovative and creative activity, and as such in itself a driver of urban growth. Interaction between researchers in different cities further enhances creativity as researchers work together to improve their performance. We claim that researchers from different cities work together to improve their output and that the result of collective work is greater than the sum of individual efforts. Research co-operation contributes to the status of a given city and, when added up, it demonstrates the nodal position of the centres in question. Co-authorships thus represent connectivity, and well-connected research cities are likely to be important cities in the global economy; nodality in research often corresponds to nodality in other parts of the local economy.

Based on earlier work (see, for example, Matthiessen and Andersson, 1992), this analysis is a continuation of our research on the global system of knowledge centres. Such centres are defined as urban regions as used in a number of earlier papers (Matthiessen and Schwarz, 1999; Matthiessen et al., 2000, 2002a, 2002b, 2006, 2010). Matthiessen and Andersson (1992) identified the major European research centres and analysed the composition of research for each city by classifying total research output by disciplines. Multivariate statistical methods made it possible to identify different types of research cities. Later papers (Matthiessen and Schwarz, 1999; Mathiessen et al., 2000, 2002a, 2002b) used a global approach, analysing the changing performance of the world's major research centres. In those papers, we identified the largest research centres of the world in terms of research output (number of bibliographic units in the Science Citation Index, see below), and we calculated growth rates. We also calculated collaborative links between large units in terms of co-authorship and citation patterns. The analysis of research co-operation consisted of two dimensions. One dimension represented total intercity relations, whereas the other represented the international parts of these links. We synthesized the analysis by providing a simple picture of the global system and by identifying research nodes. Matthiessen et al. (2006) summed up the pattern of global research centres and found winners and losers, while Mathiessen et al. (2010) discussed linkages and networks.

The present chapter is also linked to the well-known concept of cities as places of flows (Friedmann, 1986; Sassen, 1991; Castells [1996] 2000), and it has a particularly strong connection to the work of the Globalization and World Cities (GaWC) research network on the 'world cities' concept (Smith and Timberlake, 2001; Taylor, 2004, 2007; Derudder and Witlox, 2005; Taylor and Aranya, 2008; Taylor et al., 2010). The concept of world cities is based on the understanding that many cities are global service centres. Cities with world city status are metropolitan centres that have extensive transnational and global external links, and which assume a leading role in the organization of a number of significant networks.

Not only are the world's great cities important nodes in the world economy. They are command and control centres in a worldwide dominance hierarchy (Smith and

Timberlake, 2001). Cities are almost always also centres for a hinterland, which they more or less dominate, but cities are no longer only dependent on their hinterlands in the way Christaller (1933) conceives of a hierarchy of central places. Taylor et al. (2010) find that central place thinking represents one of two complementary generic processes, the other being described as a central flow theory through an interlocking network model. Central place theory takes reasonable care of hierarchical relations, but is deficient for understanding complex non-hierarchical relations. In central place theory, Taylor et al. (2010) claim that centrality of location is the basic building block upon which spaces of places are formally constructed. In contrast, in central flow theory it is flows that come to play a central role as the building blocks, generating a network: it is a space of flows that is formally constructed. In other words, it is a matter of what is considered most important: place or flow. The economic and social relations of cities are increasingly global and while national flows and connections are extensive and important, it is the transnational flows that are notable for their growth. The pattern of these transnational flows reflects the role of metropolitan centres as logistical and command centres in the global economy (Bayliss and Matthiessen, 2006).

It is generally acknowledged that world city status is obtained by relational data on what flows through cities (material, energy, people, information, knowledge and money) rather than on what is contained in them (Derudder and Witlox, 2005). But with the exception of flows of passengers between airports, data on intercity flows are inadequate. Taylor (2004, 2007) and the GaWC group consider cities in relational terms, as the product of networking activities. Their analyses of inter-urban flows and connectivity focus on cities as the organizing 'hubs' of globalization, interpreting cities as global service centres. They analyse data on multinational financial and business services co-operation across 315 cities worldwide by the use of standard multivariate statistical methods. The GaWC group identifies a hierarchy of world cities based on connectivity of business service networks. They state that it is the myriad of flows between offices in different metropolitan centres that forms the world city network. Through an analysis of leading global service firms – in terms of their overall network connectivity – they classify the network of world cities. In a later paper (Taylor and Aranya, 2008) they measure connectivity changes between 2000 and 2004 and identify an exceptional decrease in the connectivity of American cities (with the exception of New York) and a parallel rise of Chinese cities. In spite of these emergent trends, they also find a high degree of inertia and an overall stability over time in intercity relations. Figure 11.1 is based on Taylor (2004, 2007) and illustrates the concept of levels and bands. There are two cities that are truly global: New York and London. They are each in tight network connections with their own bands of cities, one in North America, the other in Europe. A third band is Asia-Pacific and comprises no global cities although Taylor and Aranya (2008) in a later paper mention Hong Kong as a city that is approaching the global city level.

Our study of the knowledge cities of the world is related to this research. We consider the system as not merely a subsystem of the 'world cities system' but as a combination of such a subsystem and a system in its own right. Knowledge production and distribution constitutes a significant network. Interaction between scientists is often an untraded relation, as described by Storper (1997), with benefits of a qualitative nature. Creativity flourishes in the co-operation between researchers; why else would they co-operate?

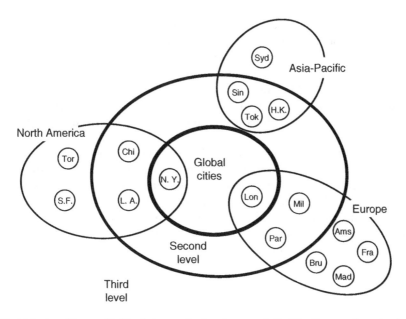

Note: The highest-ranking world cities in terms of network connectivity. The diagram shows levels and bands of the most important world cities, measured as intercity relations within major international financial and business service firms (see Taylor, 2004, 2005, 2007; Taylor et al., 2007).

Figure 11.1   World cities (based on Taylor, 2004, 2007)

In order to identify the upper-level network of research we isolate one type of non-material flow (co-authorship), which nevertheless reflects material flows of the individuals involved. They meet, talk with each other, work together and interact on the internet. Subsequently, they produce a result in the form of a research paper. Their actual interaction pattern is the consequence of a well-established and often long-lasting interaction network, and this in itself demonstrates one aspect of how cities are involved in the knowledge-producing parts of the world economy. The linking of cities that occurs in this way indicates that some cities host high-quality value-adding processes for the global knowledge economy. Research connectivity is an important feature for the status of a given city. The way in which the flows of ideas are structured and how these flows link various world cities of knowledge reflect patterns of interaction and dominance. For this reason, we analyse the overall patterns of the top-level global research system between 1996 and 2008, focusing on structure, growth, interaction and nodality.

THE DATA: THE SCIENCE CITATION INDEX AS REGISTERED IN FUNCTIONAL URBAN UNITS

The source of data is the Science Citation Index (SCI) from 1996 to 2008 (the time series was selected arbitrarily). The SCI comprises papers from leading international scientific journals and reports in natural science, medicine and technology (engineering). Papers are registered in the database with some delay and we have decided the time limit for inclusion to be the end of 2008; due to the nature of citations we only register citations to papers that were published before 2007. SCI database is produced by Thomson Reuters (previously the Institute for Scientific Information), along with a number of related products. It records – for over 6650 leading journals and numerous conference proceedings and other research publications – all contributions with full bibliographic description. The description includes all authors with their respective affiliations; subject codes for journals; all references (citations) to the research literature; and categorizes papers according to research disciplines.

When using the SCI, all the biases and problems inherent in this type of data affect the analysis. The international bibliographic databases are useful tools for studying many aspects of the international research system, but the data are not unproblematic. Among other things, the problems are due to various biases of coverage and to different publication patterns in different disciplines. The SCI measure exhibits an Anglophone bias and it presents technical intricacies such as the subject classification of articles and the handling of multiple authorships. Some analysts find it impossible to evaluate scientific productivity. We obviously do not share that opinion. Our conclusion is that analyses based on bibliographic data can give indications (but indications only) of a quantitative nature and that interpretations must be seen in the light of the biases and limitations that are inherent in the data.

The search methods that are applied to the SCI are combined with a spatial urban delimitation in order to elaborate a reasonably significant list of important research centres, as measured by research output according to the address of the institution of each author. There is also a need to focus on the problems associated with delimitating functional urban regions in a similar way for all locations. With a global view, it becomes inappropriate to use the Nomenclature of Units for Territorial Statistics (NUTS) system of the European Union or the Standard Metropolitan Area (SMA) concept as it is used in the United States. We have aimed at resolving delimitation inconsistencies by means of manual work and overbounding. In practice, we did this by delimiting our observation units – 'greater urban agglomerations' – according to a uniform logic: the objective was to identify each 'functional' unit in a way that included the city itself, its suburbs and its daily hinterland (that is, the labour market area). In addition, we combined neighbouring cities if the distance between the cities was less than 45 minutes by ground transport. We tested more than 100 urban regions in order to identify the largest centres and we are confident that our top 30 and top 40 lists really represent the 30 or 40 largest cities of the world in this respect (all cut-offs in this chapter are arbitrarily selected). We also present data analysis for a selection of 75 regions, but must then state that we cannot be certain that these city regions really are the 75 largest research centres, even if it comes close. Matthiessen et al. (2002a) present the method in detail.

STRUCTURE AND CHANGE

On a global scale, research efforts in medicine, science and technology resulted in 2 792 459 papers between 1996 and 1998, of which 922 888 or 33 per cent were produced in the 30 largest centres. From 2006 to 2008, there were 3 935 259 papers of which 1 421 422 or 36 per cent stemmed from the 30 largest centres. The total growth in research output between the two time periods was 41 per cent, while growth in the top 30 cities was 54 per cent, which amounts to a concentration process. Figure 11.2 presents the top 30 list of research cities for three periods of time. The giants of knowledge production are London and Tokyo-Yokohama. These two urban regions are in a league of their own. This is as true of the 1996–98 period as it is of the 2002–04 and the 2006–08 periods, which are the three periods of time that we analyse in this chapter. But the 'league rankings' have shifted in favour of Tokyo-Yokohama.

The two leading regions are followed by a group of nine cities, which comprises the second level of knowledge-producing centres. The second group is almost identical for the three time intervals. This group comprises the San Francisco Bay Area, Paris, Osaka-Kobe and Boston, together with New York, the Amsterdam Region (Amsterdam-Hague-Rotterdam-Utrecht) and Los Angeles. In 1996–98, Moscow was a member of the group, but this city subsequently suffered a dramatic decrease in its output of research papers and has fallen from sixth to twelfth place. Philadelphia was the lowest ranking city in this group in 1996–98 and had lost its member status by 2006–08. The new members of this group are Beijing and Seoul, which were not even on the top 30 list in 1996–98. In 1996–98 the two top levels consisted of five American, four European and two Japanese regions. In 2006–08 the same category included three American, three European and two Japanese regions, as well as a one new Chinese and one new Korean region.

The group of cities that ranked from 12th to 30th place included ten European and nine North American centres in 1996–98, but this had changed in 2006–08 to nine European, eight North American, one Asian and one South American centre. Although a high degree of inertia can be observed in the three top 30 lists there are still noticeable shifts: Beijing, Seoul and Shanghai all show dramatic advances in their rankings, and so do Madrid, Rome, Milan, Barcelona and Sao Paulo. Moscow, Copenhagen-Lund, Detroit-Ann Arbor, Stockholm-Uppsala, San Diego-La Jolla and Manchester-Liverpool account for similarly dramatic declines. Washington, DC, Edinburgh-Glasgow, Oxford-Reading and Cambridge likewise suffer dramatic falls in their respective rankings. Very few studies can be used to mirror our findings. One exception is Taylor (2005) who, on the basis of data published by Matthiessen et al. (2000), calculates high nodality for the same five cities that top our list for 1996–98. This is no surprise since the data used are identical, coming from our database.

Figure 11.3 sheds further light on the growth percentages. It is clear that some 11 cities have particularly high growth in this respect, but also that a few centres are in a losing mode. The 11 most rapidly growing cities (out of 75) consist of six Asian, two Latin American and two European urban regions plus one Australian city. St Petersburg and Moscow are the only cities that exhibit negative growth, while Washington, DC, Stuttgart, Osaka-Kobe and Jerusalem are in trouble with very low positive growth rates. Clearly the position of European and North American research centres is under challenge from new high-producing centres outside these continents. A new pattern in the knowledge world city system is evolving rapidly.

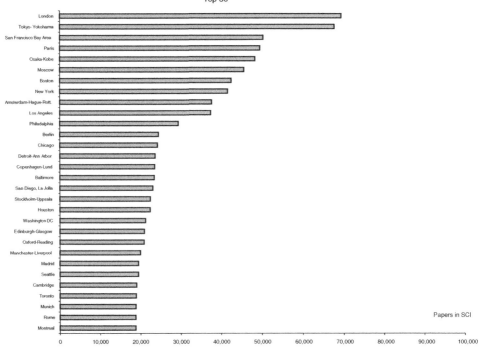

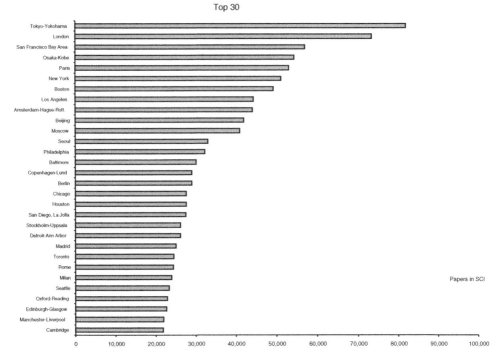

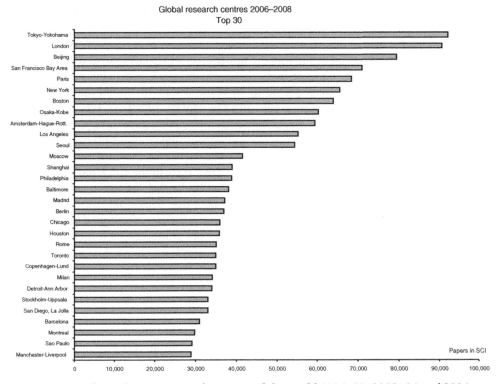

Figure 11.2   The 30 largest research centres of the world 1996–98, 2002–04 and 2006–08; measured by SCI output (papers) in medicine, science and technology

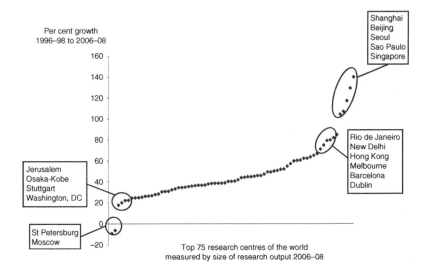

Figure 11.3   Growth of SCI output (papers) for 75 urban regions between 1996–98 and 2006–08

WINNERS AND LOSERS: RESEARCH OUTPUT VERSUS CITATIONS

With this basic understanding of the way the upper-level world city system of knowledge functions, we will now take a closer look at the general pattern of winners and losers between 1996 and 2006 (we were unable to survey citations to papers that were published after 2006 because of the time lag involved in citation statistics). We analysed the research performance of each of 75 analysed cities by relating growth in paper production to growth in citations per paper. It is our assessment that citations primarily indicate respect. Researchers often cite publications that were written by excellent and innovative colleagues; they want to relate to new findings or to the 'state of the art'. Citation patterns thus indicate leadership and nodality. We use a value-loaded terminology to indicate changes in the growth and reputations of individual cities. This is illustrated in Figure 11.4, while the map-like diagram in Figure 11.5 presents the classification of the cities.

Cities with high growth in output of research papers combined with high growth in citations per paper are labelled 'Hot spots'. The hot spots are located in southern and eastern Asia (Beijing, Seoul, New Delhi, Shanghai, Hong Kong and Singapore), in Australia (Sydney and Melbourne), in Latin America (Sao Paulo, Buenos Aires and Mexico City), and in southern and eastern Europe (Warsaw, Prague, Budapest, Milan, Barcelona, Madrid). Two European regions (Oslo and Dublin) and one North American region (Los Angeles) also belong to the group of research hot spots.

The second group is labelled 'Focus on success'. These are centres with a relative decline in total research output that is combined with high growth in citations per paper. The group presents a very distinct pattern. The two Japanese and the two Russian centres together with all British cities (except Birmingham) and Gothenburg, Jerusalem and Washington, DC constitute the group.

The third group, which comprises cities with high growth in their output volumes and decreasing citations per paper, is labelled 'Volume growth but loss in reputation'. The cities of this category are located in Europe (Helsinki, the Amsterdam Region, Zurich and Genève-Lausanne), North America (Toronto, New York, Baltimore and San Diego-La Jolla), and also includes Rio de Janeiro.

The fourth category is one of declining growth both as regards the total number of papers and citations per paper, and it is labelled 'Black holes'. These centres are the real losers and they are found in central Europe (Brussels, Paris, Mannheim-Heidelberg, Stuttgart and Basel-Mulhause-Freiburg) and in the United States (Chicago, St Louis, Denver, Dallas-Forth Worth, the San Francisco Bay Area and New Haven-Hartford).

The last category consists of cities that are close to average regarding paper production growth and increase in citations per paper. They are labelled 'Neutral' in Figure 11.5 and are located in Europe, North America and Israel. The total picture of success and failure clearly identify patterns. Extrapolating the results in order to identify which cities have the potential to be the future winners in the research world implies that one has to look outside the traditional research strongholds of Europe and North America. The places where one may look for future winners include the south-eastern quadrant of Asia, Australia and Latin America together with the southern and eastern halves of Europe.

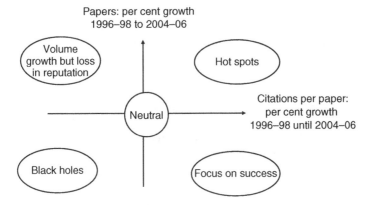

Figure 11.4   A typology of knowledge growth in the world's knowledge centres

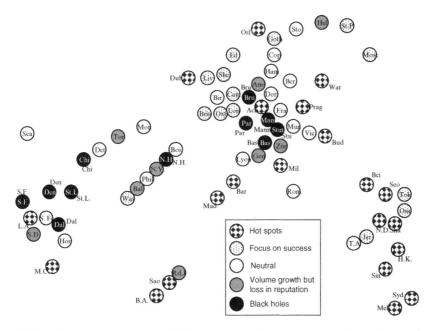

Figure 11.5   Growth trajectories of 75 large research centres; growth in volume of output by growth in citations per paper, 1996–98 to 2006–08

CO-OPERATION PATTERNS

Researchers work and publish with colleagues if they expect their own research to benefit. But the way researchers work together takes many paths and reflects co-operation at different levels and of different types. The interaction pattern of researchers mirrors the flows of ideas and reflects attraction patterns and traditions of co-operation. It is influenced by similarities and differences of many types, and it is also the consequence of different kinds of contact barriers. The pattern of co-operation reflects underlying structures such as distance, language, nationality, religion, culture, economic blocks, migration (expatriates), teacher-student relations and even friendship. Collaborative traditions are often very important and such traditions differ between disciplines, universities and between the university world and other producers of research results, such as private firms, organizations and public institutions.

The 40 largest research output centres range in size from 24 000 to 92 000 research papers in the 2006–08 period, and the size of the research environment obviously contributes to the potential level of interaction. Increasing the size of two research centres simultaneously raises the potential interaction volume. But size is only one aspect of the background factors that influence co-operation patterns, illustrated by Tables 11.1 and 11.2.

The strongest links between pairs of large research cities are listed in Table 11.1. For each of the city pairs we have counted the number of papers that were co-authored by researchers from the two cities in question (that is, a co-authored paper should have at least one author from each city). For example, there were 10 614 papers with at least one author from Tokyo-Yokohama and at least one author from Osaka-Kobe. The 20 links demonstrate an enormous flow of ideas and research co-operation between the included pairs of cities. The strength of the links partly reflects the combined size of the two cities. However, nationality exerts an even greater influence, and the most important links are within the same nation states. The two Japanese centres lead the list, which also includes American, British, Chinese, Spanish and Italian (but no German) city pairs. Only three of the top 20 links are international.

In Table 11.2 we have linked observed flows to expected flows and our assumption is that the total number of papers produced by the smallest urban region of a given city pair should decide the number of potential co-authorships. In this context, the strongest intercity links reflect greater numbers of co-authored papers than should be expected. Eighteen of the 20 links in Table 11.2 are national; only Stockholm-Uppsala with Copenhagen-Lund and Genève-Lausanne with Paris break the pattern. The highest level of co-operation is between Tokyo-Yokohama and Osaka-Kobe, followed by four British links. The top 20 list counts six British, six American and two Chinese links, as well as one link each from Japan, Spain, Italy and Germany. All non-US city pairs count at least one national capital region. Geographical distance clearly also plays a role, and there are no strong intercontinental links.

Figure 11.6 shows the level of co-authorship for each of the world's 40 largest centres of research. It is a relative measure for co-operation as the number of co-authors from the other 39 cities is related to the total output of the city in question. The English language is the dominant background factor. British followed by North American cities (with Washington,DC as the exception) stand for the highest degree of co-operation. The Anglophone cities are followed by non-British European centres, while the lowest level of co-operation is represented by the fast-growing Asian centres and by Sydney (who breaks the 'rule' about the importance of the English language) and Sao Paulo.

International research co-operation is high on many agendas and several structural relationships can be identified. International companies and organizations with research and development as part of their activities more or less ignore national boundaries, at least when they are able to protect their results. And although the vast majority of

Table 11.1 Top 20 research links by total number of co-authored SCI papers

Region (A)	Region (B)	Co-authored papers (A and B)
Tokyo-Yokohama	Osaka-Kobe	10 614
Beijing	Shanghai	4044
Los Angeles	San Francisco Bay Area	4008
London	Oxford-Reading	3810
Boston	New York	3604
London	Manchester-Liverpool	3373
Cambridge	London	3205
New York	San Francisco Bay Area	3188
Milan	Rome	3179
Los Angeles	New York	3094
Manchester-Liverpool	Oxford-Reading	3054
Boston	San Francisco Bay Area	3049
Barcelona	Madrid	2979
London	Amsterdam-Hague-Rotterdam	2736
London	Edinburgh-Glasgow	2542
London	Paris	2533
Stockholm-Uppsala	Copenhagen-Lund	2512
Beijing	Hong Kong	2478
San Francisco Bay Area	San Diego-La Jolla	2125
Baltimore	New York	2074

universities are allocated national funds, there are many incentives for co-operation. The European Union carries out series of research programmes that require multinational engagement. So does the United Nations and its many sub-organizations such as the United Nations Educational, Scientific and Cultural Organisation (UNESCO). Affiliated with the latter organization are the international associations of various scientific disciplines. These associations often do research on their own initiative and co-ordinate research activities at the international level. The Nordic and Association of South East Asian Nations (ASEAN) also have research co-operation as part of their respective programmes. In addition, international research co-operation is a feature of many non-governmental organizations.

In our analysis, observed co-authorships are linked to expected co-authorships between scientists of two cities. Expected co-authorships are estimated from statistical averages across all intercity links. The map-like diagrams that follow each identifies the strongest per cent of all possible links between the 40 largest centres according to SCI publication data. The diagrams of total intercity co-authorship are presented in Figure 11.7 and give national patterns in the United States a very clear and distinct appearance. The majority of all strong links are American. Another important system consists of Western Europe, in which two national subsystems can be identified: Britain and Germany. National systems of links are always important, and if there is more than one city from a nation in our database, it seems inevitable that each city will be strongly linked to the other national centres. Strong intercontinental links are very unusual.

Table 11.2   Twenty most over-represented links (observed/expected co-authorships), 2006 to 2008

Region (A)	Region (B)	% over-representation
Tokyo-Yokohama	Osaka-Kobe	1001
London	Oxford-Reading	758
Cambridge	London	710
London	Manchester-Liverpool	631
Manchester-Liverpool	Oxford-Reading	588
Beijing	Shanghai	548
Barcelona	Madrid	501
Edinburgh-Glasgow	London	491
London	Edinburgh-Glasgow	491
Milan	Rome	484
Beijing	Hong Kong	466
Stockholm-Uppsala	Copenhagen-Lund	376
San Francisco Bay Area	Seattle	358
Los Angeles	San Francisco Bay Area	353
San Diego-La Jolla	San Francisco Bay Area	303
Berlin	Munich	296
Baltimore	New York	291
Los Angeles	San Diego-La Jolla	287
Genève-Lausanne	Paris	280
San Francisco Bay Area	Detroit-Ann Arbor	263

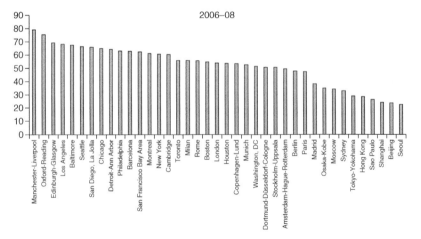

Figure 11.6   Co-authorships in 40 cities with the other 39 knowledge centres; total number of co-authors as percentage of output from centre

Nodality is identified by the number of strong links, and when such links are added up the centres of dominance emerge. London is therefore the world-leading research centre followed by four American centres: the San Francisco Bay Area, Los Angeles, Boston and New York.

Representing international co-authorship as in Figure 11.8 shows that the picture shifts by emphasizing European co-operation. North American cities do not co-operate much with the rest of the world, with the Canadian centres and the San Francisco Bay Area as exceptions. European co-operation is a patchwork of links although distance – but not language – plays a clear role. Intercontinental co-operation is of some importance in this picture of strong international links. Three cities play leading roles with each having almost exactly the same weight: London, Paris and the Amsterdam Region. They are followed by Genève-Lausanne (which is mainly due to the international high-energy physics research facility, CERN, with its international profile of co-operation), the San Francisco Bay Area and Rome. The general picture of nodality is one in which traditional European, and to a much lesser degree North American, centres play prominent roles. Asian cities are almost absent from this scene of co-operation and nodality.

Both Figures 11.7 and 11.8 demonstrate a very stable spatial pattern of research networks. Building up mutual acceptance and trust is a long-term process, and co-operation is consequently maintained once it has been established. The stability probably also reflects funding practices. When a network has been successful in obtaining research grants there will be an obvious incentive to keeping the network active.

THE SYSTEM OF WORLD CITIES OF KNOWLEDGE

The findings concerning research strength, links and nodality are rather similar to the findings of Taylor (2004, 2007) on the world system of service centres. We have therefore categorized the world cities of knowledge using a system that we have developed according to Taylor's method of hierarchical levels and bands of co-operation. The results are presented in Figure 11.9, where only cities at the upper two levels are indicated.

The uppermost level of the hierarchy consists of first-level global cities that are linked to cities all over the world. It includes London, the Amsterdam Region, Paris and the San Francisco Bay Area, which are all leaders of their own regional bands. Genève-Lausanne is also a true global first-level city, although it is a relatively small centre measured in output and does not have a band of its own but rather a global network. London has a band of British cities with Edinburgh on the second level of global centres. The Amsterdam Region plays a leading role within a northern European band with Copenhagen-Lund and Stockholm-Uppsala as second-level centres. The southern European band has Paris as the leader, with Milan, Rome and Barcelona on the second level. The North American band presents the San Francisco Bay Area on the first level, but has a series of urban regions as 'sub-leaders': Boston, Los Angeles and New York together with Montreal and Toronto. Germany, Japan and China have their own bands. The German band is well connected to the upper-level European cities, but the Asian bands are very isolated in respect of research connectivity.

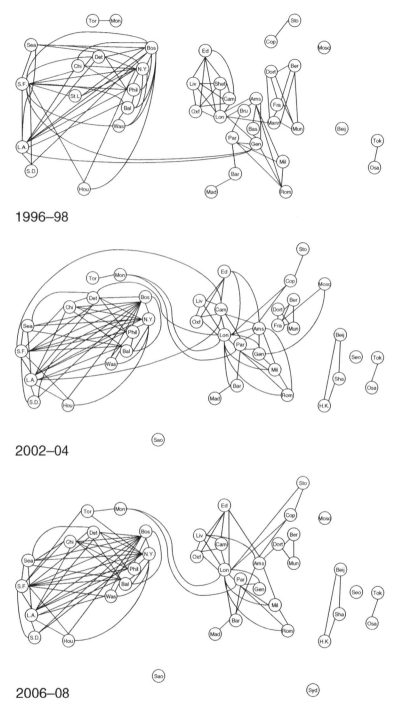

1996–98

2002–04

2006–08

Figure 11.7   Connectivity of 40 world cities of knowledge measured as strong co-authorship links, 1996–98, 2002–04 and 2006–08

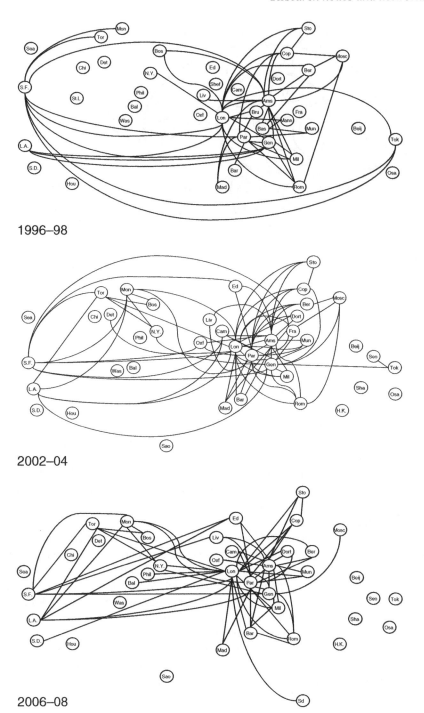

Figure 11.8   Strong international co-authorship links among the 40 leading research centres, 1996–98, 2002–04 and 2006–08

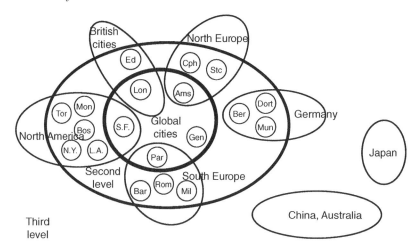

Figure 11.9   *Levels and bands of the world's knowledge cities based on volume and*
international nodality

SUMMARY

In this chapter we have demonstrated structure and nodality in the system of world cities of scientific knowledge. We have identified a high degree of inertia in the system but also a recent shift in location patterns. We find – in accordance with other findings – an extremely high and growing degree of concentration in the largest centres in combination with the development of a series of new urban research centres. The traditional strongholds in Europe, North America and Japan are rapidly being supplemented with new growth centres, especially in the south-eastern quadrant of Asia. Shanghai, Beijing, Seoul, Sao Paulo and Singapore are the big winners in the period from 1996–98 to 2006–08. Some centres are, however, losing status. Winning often turns out to be a faster process than losing, although the biggest losers – Moscow and St Petersburg – seem to contradict this observation.

Inspired by the work of the GaWC group on the system of world cities according to data on multinational financial and business services co-operation, we have tentatively constructed overviews of the world cities system of scientific knowledge in terms of levels and bands, using the GaWC approach as our model. We consider cities in relational terms, as the product of inter-urban networking activities, which also includes collaboration data and evaluations of dominance and subordinance within collaborative networks. A simple picture of the systemic structure of knowledge centres thereby emerges, and we obtain a more refined picture of the structure than is possible by simple measures of output volumes. The focus is on which scientific knowledge centres serve as the organizing 'hubs' of the globalization of scientific research. We consider the system of knowledge centres not merely as a subsystem of the world cities system, but as a combination of such a subsystem and a system in its own right.

Knowledge production and distribution constitutes a significant network. The upper level of the hierarchy consists of dominating first-level global cities that are linked to cities all over the world. It includes London, the Amsterdam Region, Paris and the San Francisco Bay Area, with each city functioning as a leader of its own regional band. Genève-Lausanne is also a true global first-level city, although it is a relatively small centre without a regional band of its own. When it comes to nodality, the traditional European and North American research strongholds still play the leading roles.

Regarding factors that influence research collaboration patterns, we find that the patterns are highly influenced by geographical proximity, and we find that this can be clearly identified in our results on research connectivity and in the levels and bands of the global city system of scientific knowledge. We do identify two cities which deviate from the rule of geographical proximity. The scientific co-operation pattern of the San Francisco Bay Area is pretty much emancipated from the distance factor and this is also true of Genève-Lausanne. San Francisco's SCI links probably reflect real inter-regional interactions, but Geneva's position could very well be the consequence of address confusion; the huge number of guest professors at the CERN facility perhaps report their home affiliations when they write together at CERN. We also identify language as a background factor that impacts co-operation patterns. It is clear that the English language plays an important role for co-authorship. Montreal plays an interesting role as the North American connector of Anglophone and Francophone research networks.

REFERENCES

Bayliss, D. and C.W. Matthiessen (2006), 'The European upper level urban system: a discussion paper', in R.C.L. Gonzáles (ed.),*Urban Changes in Different Scales: Systems and Structures*, Santiago de Compostela: Curses e Congresos da Universidade de Santiago de Compostela 169, pp. 449–62.

Castells, M. [1996] (2000), *The Rise of the Network Society*, Oxford: Blackwell.

Christaller, W. (1933), *Die Zentralen Orte in Süddeutschland*, Jena: Gustav Fischer Verlag.

Derudder, B. and F. Witlox (2005), 'An appraisal on the use of airline data in assessing the world city network: a research note on data', *Urban Studies*, 42(13), 2371–88.

Friedmann, J. (1986), 'The world city hypothesis', *Development and Change*, 17, 69–83.

Matthiessen, C.W. and Å.E. Andersson (1992), *Øresundsregionen. Kreativitet – integration – vækst*, København: Munksgaard.

Matthiessen, C.W. and A.W. Schwarz (1999), 'Scientific centres in Europe: an analysis of research strength and patterns of specialisation based on bibliometric indicators', *Urban Studies*, 36(3), 453–77.

Matthiessen, C.W., A.W. Schwarz and S. Find (2000), 'Research gateways of the world: an analysis based on bibliometric indicators', in Å.E. Andersson and D.E. Andersson (eds), *Gateways to the Global Economy*, Cheltenham, UK and Northampton, MA, USA: Edward Elgar Publishing, pp.17–30.

Matthiessen, C.W., A.W. Schwarz and S. Find (2002a), 'The top-level global research system, 1997–99: centres, networks and nodality. An analysis based on bibliometric indicators', *Urban Studies*, 39(5–6), 903–27.

Matthiessen, C.W., A.W. Schwarz and S. Find (2002b), 'The ups and downs of global research centers', *Science Magazine*, 297(5586), 1476–7.

Matthiessen, C.W., A.W. Schwarz and S. Find (2006), 'World cities of knowledge – research strength, networks and nodality', *Journal of Knowledge Management*, 10(5), 14–25.

Matthiessen, C.W., A.W. Schwarz and S. Find (2010), 'World cities of scientific knowledge: systems, networks and potential dynamics. An analysis based on bibliometric indicators', *Urban Studies*, 47(9), 1879–97.

Sassen, S. (1991), *The Global City: New York, London, Tokyo*, Princeton, NJ: Princeton University Press.

Smith, D.A. and M. Timberlake (2001), 'World city networks and hierarchies 1977–97: an empirical analysis of global air travel links', *American Behavioral Scientist*, 44(10), 1656–78.

Storper, M. (1997), *The Regional World: Territorial Development in a Global Economy*, New York, NY: The Guilford Press.

Taylor, P.J. (2004), *World City Network: A Global Urban Analysis*, London and New York, NY: Routledge.

Taylor, P.J. (2005), 'Leading world cities: empirical evaluations of urban nodes in multiple networks', *Urban Studies*, 42(9), 1593–608.

Taylor, P.J. (2007), *World City Network. A Global Urban Analysis*, London and New York, NY: Routledge.
Taylor, P.J. and R. Aranya (2008), 'A global "urban roller coaster"? Connectivity changes in the world city network 2000–2004', *Regional Studies*, **42**(1), 1–16.
Taylor, P.J., B. Derudder, P. Saey and F. Witlox (2007), *Cities in Globalization. Practices, Policies and Theories*, London and New York, NY: Routledge.
Taylor, P.J., M. Hoylor and R. Verbruggen (2010), 'External urban relational process: introducing central flow theory to complement central place theory', *Urban Studies*, **47**(13), 2803–18.

12 Scenes, innovation, and urban development
Daniel Silver, Terry Nichols Clark and Christopher Graziul

This chapter investigates the consequences of local 'scenes' for urban development. It treats the particular constellation of amenities in a place – cafes, galleries, pubs, music venues, fashion houses, dance clubs, antique shops, restaurants, fruit stands, convenience stores and the like – as constituting the local scene. These constellations of amenities define the scene by making available an array of meaningful experiences to residents and visitors. Scenes give a sense of drama, authenticity and ethical significance to a city's streets and strips. Depending on its particular configuration of amenities, a vibrant scene can transform an urban area into a theatrical place to see and be seen (glamorously, transgressively or in other ways), an authentic place to explore and affirm local, ethnic or national identities (among others), an ethical place to share and debate common values and ideals (such as tradition or self-expression). The availability of these experiences varies substantially across and even within cities and regions. These variations have significant consequences for urban economies and populations.

This chapter proposes several hypotheses and analyses about scenes as one factor that contributes to 'creative cities'. It situates these propositions within a broader universe of ideas about the significance of creativity. First, it offers a brief overview of the processes involved in what we call the institutionalization and internalization of creativity. This is a process whereby creativity moves from the margins to the centre of basic conceptions of human action, bringing with it special attention to the specific mechanisms through which creative activity is more likely to occur in one place and moment rather than another. Second, we briefly review some classic and contemporary hypotheses about what these multiple mechanisms might be, such as education, technology, density and the like. Third, we propose adding scenes as a distinctly important factor of creativity. We offer a brief introduction to our scenes perspective on urban development, before proposing and testing several hypotheses about how scenes drive urban development.

In sum, this chapter aims to systematically unpack the importance of 'scenes' to urban development. While work on this topic has been done theoretically and ethnographically (for example, Lloyd, 2006; Currid, 2007), we aim to pinpoint the variables that create scenes and specify how scenes influence particular attributes of economic development. We seek to connect how and where people consume with how and where they produce. Typically, there has been a disparity between consumption and production models of culture. This chapter proposes a set of mechanisms and causal linkages that join the two.

THE INSTITUTIONALIZATION AND INTERNALIZATION OF CREATIVITY

To provide context, we begin our analysis with what has come to be known as the 'creative cities thesis' – largely because this topic has attracted much recent attention, both among academics and policy-makers (Romein and Trip, 2009 review key aspects of this literature). Spurred by the decline and outsourcing of manufacturing in Western economies since the 1970s, many cities have sought alternative sources of vitality. Cities have cheated 'the death of distance' (Cairncross, 1997) through developing themselves, as in New York and London, into hubs for business and financial services (Sassen, 2001); into centres for tourism, consumption and leisure activities as in Bilbao, the Boston waterfront and Chicago's Millennium Park (Clark, 2004); or into focal points for gathering the talented, creative individuals ('human capital') crucial to success in 'knowledge economies', as in Silicon Valley, Seattle, Barcelona and the North Carolina research triangle (Reich, 1992; Becker, 1993; Florida, 2002). Human performance has come to count for economists as one of the key factors of production (Parsons, 2006). This, it is claimed, is 'an economy where a person's ideas, not land or capital, are the most important input and output' (as cited in Peters and Besley, 2008). Economic geographers have stressed that locations able to harness the means of cognition are as significant as those that harness the means of production (cf. Polensky, 2007). Indeed, this anthology attests to the ascendance of creativity as an economically vital cognitive skill.

This recent focus on 'creative cities' builds on deeper social and cultural changes. To be sure, creativity is not a new value; it is as at least as old as Genesis 1, after all. But beginning especially in the nineteenth century, a number of intellectual movements made creativity increasingly internal to their understanding of human action as such (Joas, 1996): Herder on expression; Marx on revolution and praxis; Schopenhauer, Nietzsche and Simmel on life; Weber on charisma; Durkheim on collective effervescence; and James, Dewey and Mead on intelligence and pragmatic improvisation. Schumpeter's 'creative destruction' built innovation and not just cost-effective production into the core of economic activity, and Jane Jacobs made surprise and disorder the very stuff of urban development (Jacobs, 1961, 1969; see also Sennett, 1970). These movements congeal in what Howard Rosenberg called the historically novel 'tradition of the new' (Rosenberg, 1959).

In the twentieth century, and especially since the 1960s, this tradition – formerly more exclusive to an intellectual and artistic 'avant-garde' – diffused to the broader public (Parsons, 1978; Clark and Hoffmann-Martinot, 1998; Taylor, 2007). Key social drivers include mass education, mass communication, increased geographic mobility and – in some theories – the need of capitalism to generate new needs (Bell, 1973). At an existential level, some authors have highlighted an increasing awareness of life's fragility, unsettledness and alterability, made unavoidable by two world wars (Joas, 2004). Others have stressed 'expressive' reactions against a stifling, bureaucratic, overly rational culture (Marcuse, 1964); while still others have sought to understand the conditions under which such an 'expressive revolution' could be integrated into basic societal functions, such as production, domestic relations and politics (Parsons, 1978). A related stream of thought points to internal value pressures within Western culture towards individuality and spontaneity, both as 'inner-worldly' activism as well as an 'expressive individualism' already implicit in early Christian notions of the personal experience of love (Bellah et al., 1996). As this expressive dimension rose in social salience, personalities formed on the basis of the disciplined Protestant work ethic made room for the bohemian and romantic quest for authenticity and personal meaningfulness, unsettling distinctions between productive work and unproductive play (Campbell, 1989; Bell, 1996; Brooks, 2000; Taylor, 2007).

Given this intellectual, cultural and historical context, questions about how to institutionalize and internalize the value of creativity in cities and individuals have naturally become central. Municipal cultural policy has grown, together with investment in cultural infrastructure, artist support and arts incubators. Quebec, for instance, has seen a 14-fold increase in the number of cities with official municipal cultural policies between 1992 and 2002 (De La Durantaye, 2002). In 1975, Saul Bellow wrote that 'there were beautiful and moving things in Chicago, but culture was not one of them' (p. 69). By 2009, the director of the National Endowment of the Arts could say that 'Mayor Daley should be the No. 1 hero to everyone in this country who cares about art.'[1] The number of individuals employed as artists and in the cultural industries has risen dramatically in many countries, as has the number of and participation in cultural organizations and amenities (most dramatically in the United States, Canada and the Netherlands; see Clark and da Silva, 2009).

New questions arise: what infrastructure, education, work environments, public policy and political culture best harness the human creative potential? How can artistic, entrepreneurial and scientific endeavour be instituted as activities unto themselves, and combined with one another in ways that enhance development, innovation and the broader public good? With questions like these, 'the creative class' seems on its way to self-consciousness.

Factors of Creativity

Given the long historical narrative connecting creativity, innovation and production, the 'new' creative cities thesis has provided ample opportunities for derision (cf. Chatterton, 2000). One popular Youtube video, 'Juicing the Creatives',[2] depicts 'creativity fields' where an old English farmer grows various assortments of hipsters and artists, before distilling their essence into a creativity juice to be sold on the open market.

Much of this response is sensible. Many advocates have promoted one-dimensional, one-size-fits-all quick fixes that generalize from single cases or single dimensions of creativity. A Bilbao for every city! Bike paths for all! Bohemias everywhere! Attract the gays and the rest will follow!

Such unilateral and rigid approaches defy the very fluidity, situation specificity and nuance so central to successful creative endeavour. Thus, in this chapter, we stress the multiple overlapping factors that may contribute to the creativity and growth of cities, and investigate what happens when we add scenes to the mix. We test our hypotheses about scenes in reference to classic and contemporary factors thought to drive urban development and innovation: education, technology, social climate, social density, artist concentrations and natural environment. Because these have received considerable attention, we briefly highlight them before beginning our discussion of scenes.

Education

Urban development has been linked with the consequences of the explosion of higher education in the United States and globally. Universities, not factories, are increasingly at the centres of successful cities. Berkeley, Stanford and Silicon Valley provide perhaps the most famous examples. The relative success of Columbus, Ohio as compared with

Cleveland, Ohio – the former with Ohio State University at its centre, the latter struggling after the decline of steel – speaks to a more general significance.

The mechanisms driving this connection between education, innovation and urban developments are diverse. Talcott Parsons (1971) considered the 'educational revolution' as important as the industrial revolution. It bound productivity more explicitly to cultural factors such as scientific research, organization and managerial intelligence. Daniel Bell (1973) linked 'the coming of post-industrial society' to the rising social power of university-educated professional groups. Robert Reich (1992) ties success in the new, global economy to 'mind workers' especially trained in the manipulation of symbols. Richard Florida (2002) connects the 'means migration' of educated, skilled persons to a relatively small number of densely populated regions with success in the creative economy. Glaeser (2004) argues that 'skilled' people are the key to urban success because such high human capital people tend to increase 'new idea production'. His primary measure of 'human capital' is years of schooling. We follow these authors and include in our analyses measures of the proportion of the population with bachelor's degrees and post-graduate degrees.[3]

Technology
Technology may well be a significant driver of urban growth in its own right, operating with its own distinct social processes above and beyond education. Florida (2002), for example, links creative cities not only to 'talent' but also to 'technology'. Acs (2002) ties high technology employment to urban success, and economists such as Robert Solow and Paul Romer have long argued that technology is central to economic growth. Technology, however, is more than machines and enhanced craft-tools, as authors such as Heidegger (1977) and Parsons (1991) among others have argued. Technology may make cities into centres for innovation by promoting a certain outlook on existence: the world can be altered and transformed in new ways. Nature – including human nature – is not fixed once and for all.[4] To crudely summarize, according to this line of thought, where there is more technological work, we would expect there to be more creative production and more growth. We therefore include in our analysis a measure of the local concentration of technological jobs, relative to the United States as a whole.

Social climate
Education and technology indicate the presence of skilled workers engaged in work that is especially concerned with innovation. Nurturing and attracting such persons, however, may depend on a city's broader social climate. Indeed, many authors posit a link between, on the one hand, diversity, openness and tolerance, and, on the other, innovation (Florida, 2002; Kotkin, 2001; Romein and Trip, 2009). Tolerant residents, they argue, support an environment in which alternative styles, unconventional ideas, and diversity in thought and practice can flourish. New ideas are more likely to be brought to fruition and reach the public, and innovative persons are likely to be attracted to such opportunities for experimentation. Florida (2002) treat the percentage of the population that is gay as an indicator of this sort of climate, not because gays are or are not particularly creative, but because their presence may indicate a tolerant city. Even if the specific link between gays and tolerance is spurious (Clark, 2004), other more direct

indicators of a generally open social climate may well vindicate the link between tolerance, creativity and development.[5]

Social density

Social climate indicates the value system in which new ideas are nurtured or repressed. But the ability to communicate those ideas efficiently may also influence urban development. Jane Jacobs famously linked the creativity and development potential of a city to its transport and communication potentials. Much work in the geography of innovation has shown that spillover effects are central to innovation (as summarized by Hoekman et al., 2008). Knowledge is not easily contained in one firm, and when knowledgeable individuals change jobs (Almeida and Kogut, 1999), start their own firms (Klepper, 2001) or exchange knowledge informally with others (Lissoni, 2001), ideas spread rapidly. Such exchanges are known to be highly geographically concentrated (Breschi and Lissoni, 2001; Egeln et al., 2004). Glaeser et al., (2004) suggest that places with high transport costs will suffer as time becomes more valuable.[6]

Artist concentrations

The presence of a critical mass of working artists in a city may be a further factor driving its growth and innovativeness, not reducible to these others.[7] Most straightforwardly, concentrations of artists indicate concentrations of individuals devoted to creative endeavour as a primary value governing their activity, even if that ideal is rarely realized. Not only does artistic endeavour lead by itself to creative outputs like paintings, novels and musical works, but artistic work is embedded within 'art worlds' (Becker, 1984) that employ many others in creative work – from stage managers to museum staff to art dealers. Post-industrial workplaces increasingly resemble artists' studios in many ways, not least in that they require many artists for services, such as graphic designers, web designers, product designers, marketers, voice-overs or advertising copy editors (Markusen and King, 2003). Artists sell their work to local firms, creating a more stimulating and interesting work environment, and sometimes lead workshops for employees. High concentrations of artists contribute to high quality of place, attracting skilled workers and new businesses to interesting artist neighbourhoods and cities (Florida, 2002; Markusen and King, 2003; Lloyd, 2006). The widespread increased use of 'design' as a term in even traditional industries shows the rise in sensitivity to aesthetic concerns (for example, Daniel Pink's *A Whole New Mind* (2006)). To assess the impact of artists, we include in our models the number of local arts jobs and the local concentration of arts jobs relative to the national average.

Natural environment

A long cultural tradition holds that nature inspires creativity.[8] Such cultural and intellectual traditions suggest that cities with natural assets may foster distinct forms of creative work. For example, Van Ulzen (2007) suggests that many architects and designers choose to live in more industrial Rotterdam over more tourist-oriented and cultural Amsterdam because of Rotterdam's port and the inspiration from 'the rhythm of the river'. Kotkin (2001), by contrast, suggests that natural assets are less attractive to creative persons, who prefer the action of central cities. Certainly natural amenities like warm weather and opportunities for outdoor recreation, such as mountain climbing or swimming, influence migration, even if the consequences of such migration for innovation and development are mixed (Brooks, 2000; Clark, 2004; Glaeser et al., 2004).[9]

THE SCENES PERSPECTIVE: A (VERY) BRIEF INTRODUCTION

The scenes perspective adds another key consideration to these drivers of urban development. It focuses attention on different types of amenities and consumption opportunities, asking how variations in these influence the development and creativity of a place. Since this perspective is new, we first outline its main principles.

The first principle of the scenes perspective is that local amenities make vital contributions to the qualities that constitute the urban scene. Cafes, theatres, parks, music venues, restaurants, markets, shops and other amenities define a range of possible experiential qualities that give meaning and value to a given place. The value is derived from the fact that relating to cities as collections of amenities defines urban spaces in a way that makes such spaces more than places for living and working. They become affective arenas for sharing, affirming or rejecting feelings, sensibilities and values; they become scenes. And the particular character of a city's scenes, as we shall see, strongly influences its patterns of development and levels of innovation.

Consistent with much past research, the scenes perspective holds that the particular configuration of amenities indicates a place's particular local scene (Clark, 2004; Currid, 2007; Florida, 2008). Drawing on both classical social theory and philosophy (from Weber and Bellah to Heidegger and Habermas) and contemporary research into many scenes (from Latin Salsa to Hardcore to Chicago Blues), our scenes perspective specifies a range of symbolic meanings that collections of amenities may make available to participants (Silver et al. (2010) summarizes several research streams from urban studies, cultural studies and youth studies that converge on the notion of a scene). Film festivals, high fashion and movie stars may, for example, indicate the presence of a glamorous scene that enables experiences of glamorous theatricality; tattoo parlours, punk music venues, body art studios and piercing salons may indicate the presence of a more transgressive scene that enables experiences of transgressive theatricality; local crafts stores, farmers markets, community centres and arts festivals may indicate the presence of a local scene, enabling the experience of local authenticity. These issues are further articulated elsewhere (Silver et al., 2006, 2010).

We arrange the meaningful experiences enabled by amenities into three analytic categories: legitimacy, theatricality and authenticity. Each corresponds to a category of meaningfulness affirmed or resisted through various types of consumption. Roughly, the legitimacy of a scene is the extent to which its activities enable participants to feel right, to feel that the experience is normatively good. By contrast, authenticity promotes the sense of being real, being rooted in some genuine identity. Finally, theatricality is the extent to which a scene's activities promote styles of social dramatics, offering occasions for mutual self-display.

These three forms of symbolic meaning form a schema for understanding variation in different types of scenes. Each category is further specified in terms of the specific type of legitimacy, theatricality or authenticity the scene affirms or resists, such as traditional, charismatic or self-expressive legitimacy; glamorous, transgressive or neighbourly theatricality; and local, ethnic or national authenticity. The symbolic qualities of a given scene may be determined by the way collections of amenities combine positive, neutral or negative valuations of various aspects of legitimacy, theatricality and authenticity. Any set of amenities may be 'translated' into this grammar of scenes by scoring them in terms of these dimensions. Systematic comparative analysis of the local scene is thus possible by analysing variations in the mix of experiential qualities projected by local amenities. Table 12.1 summarizes this theoretical approach to the 'internal environment' of scenes. It also includes some illustrative samplings of amenities from our national database that we use as indicators for each of these dimensions.

SCENES AS FACTORS OF CREATIVE CITIES

Scenes have their own internal logics and dramas that unfold, for instance, around how to express original feelings rather than conform to pale imitations, stay true to rather than do violence to a tradition, shine glamorously rather than fade into anonymity, project warmth and intimacy rather than distance and aloofness, and maintain an authentically real life rather than a phony existence. Our present concern, however, is less with this internal 'life in scenes' (Hitzler et. al., 2005) than with the consequences of scenes for urban development.[10]

Many authors posit a link between aspects of a scene and its development impacts. Some see their value in their attractiveness to skilled workers. Kotkin (2001) distinguishes between the different built environments attractive to 'nerds' versus young childless couples, linking the relative fortunes of different cities to their ability to attract these different groups. Central city cultural areas are attractive to creative workers because 'that is where the action is' (Kotkin, 2001). Florida (2002) suggests that experiential and participatory amenities like bike paths attract the creative class. Glaeser (2004) suggests that cities grow by providing 'the basic commodities desired by those with skills'. Though he does not find any connection between art museums and county population growth, he does find that amenities appealing to 'high human capital workers' – for example, live performance venues and restaurants – significantly predict population growth, while 'amenities appealing to low human capital workers – such as bowling alleys and movie theatres – are both negatively associated with later county population growth' (Glaeser et al., 2004, p. 181). Clark (2004) contends that the attractiveness of different amenities varies across subcultures. Though population in general grows in amenity-rich places, college graduates are more numerous where there are more constructed amenities like brew pubs, operas, juice bars, Starbucks, whole foods, bicycle events and museums; they are less numerous where there are more natural amenities. For the elderly, the situation is reversed: their numbers are rising in places with more natural amenities and fewer constructed amenities. Residents who file high technology patents, he finds, live in places with more natural and constructed amenities.

Others have analysed scenes as more direct engines of urban growth, hypothesizing mechanisms through which scenes add value to the production process beyond attracting skilled workers who would *ex hypothesi* be just as productive somewhere else. Landry (2000) writes of the importance of 'third spaces' such as cafes, restaurants, clubs, bars, record shops and bookstores for 'creative cities' in that such spaces foster stimulating

Table 12.1   The symbolic dimensions of scenes

Theatricality

Scenes generate a chance to see and be seen, shaping the bearing and manners of their members. Participants can enjoy the essentially social pleasure of beautifully performing a role or a part, or of watching others do so. This is the pleasure of appearances, the way we display ourselves to others and see their images in turn.

Sub-dimension	Example	Sample Amenity Indicators
Glamour	Standing on the red carpet at Cannes gazing at the stars going by	Fashion Shows & Designers; Designer Clothes & Accessories; Beauty Salons; Nail Salons; Motion Picture & Video Exhibition; Motion Picture & Sound Recording Studios; Agents, Managers for Artists & Other Public Figures; Film Festivals; Night Clubs; Jewellery Stores; Casinos
Formality	Going to the opera in a gown or white tie and tails	Formal Wear & Costume Rental; Opera Companies; Fine Dining; Private Clubs; Dance Companies; Night Clubs; Golf Courses & Country Clubs; Theatre Companies & Dinner Theatre; Religious Organizations; Offices of Lawyers; Professional Organizations
Transgressive	Watching a performance artist pierce his skin	Body Piercing Studios; Tattoo Parlours; Adult Entertainment: Nightclubs; Adult Entertainment: Comedy and Dance Clubs; Leather Clothing Stores; Skateboard Parks; Casinos; Beer, Wine & Liquor Stores; Gambling Industries
Neighbourliness	Attending a performance by the community orchestra	Bed & Breakfast Inns; Civic & Social Organizations; Religious Organizations; Golf Courses & Country Clubs; Sports Teams & Clubs; Playgrounds; Elementary & Secondary Schools; Fruit & Vegetable Markets; Coffee Houses; Pubs; Baked Goods Stores
Exhibitionism	Watching weightlifters at Muscle Beach	Adult Entertainment: Night Clubs; Fashion Shows & Designers; Body Piercing; Tattoo Studios; Health Clubs; Fashion Shows & Designers; Beauty Salons; Nail Salons; Discotheques

Authenticity

The human possibility to be realized in a scene, even where it is highly theatrical, may also be defined by the extent to which a scene affirms a sense of rootedness, confirming or reshaping the primordial identity of their members. Participants may seek the pleasure of having a common sense of what makes for a real or genuine experience. This is the pleasure of identity, the affirmation of who we are at bottom and what it means to be genuine and real rather than fake and phony.

Sub-dimension	Example	Sample Amenity Indicators
Local	Listening to the blues in the Checkerboard Lounge, landmark of the Chicago blues	Bed & Breakfast Inns; Historical Sites; Fishing Lakes & Ponds; Marinas; Book Dealers: Used & Rare; Antique Dealers; Scenic & Sightseeing Services; Nature Parks & Other Similar Institutions; Spectator Sports; Sports Teams and Clubs; Microbreweries; Fruit & Vegetable Markets; Meat Markets

Theatricality

Ethnic	Recognizing the twang of Appalachia in the Stanley Bros.' Voices	Ethnic Restaurants (approximately 40 cuisines); Ethnic Music; Ethnic Dance; Folk Arts; Cultural and Ethnic Awareness Programmes; Language Schools; Gospel Singing Groups; Martial Arts Instruction
Corporate	Reviling a Britney Spears show because she is a corporate creation	Marketing Research; Management Consulting Services; Warehouse Clubs & Superstores; Designer Clothes & Accessories; Fast Food Restaurants; Business & Secretarial Schools; Department Stores; Convention & Trade Shows; Public Relations Agencies; Spectator Sports; Amusement & Theme Parks; Advertising & Related Services
State	Visiting the Gettysburg Battlefield	Political Organizations; Embassies and Delegations; Historical Sites; American Restaurants
Rational	Revelling in the cosmic scope of human reason at a planetarium	R&D in Physical, Engineering and Life Sciences; Scientific R&D Services; Colleges, Universities and Professional Schools; Planeteria; Aquariums; Human Rights Organizations; Management, Scientific & Technical Consulting; Exam Preparation and Tutoring; Libraries & Archives; Computer Training; Offices of Lawyers

Legitimacy

In addition to their theatricality and authenticity, scenes may be defined by a judgement about what is right and wrong, how one ought to live, structuring the legitimacy of social consumption, shaping the beliefs and intentions of their members. Participants can seek the pleasure of a common sense of being in the right or rejecting those in the wrong. This is the pleasure of a good will, intending to act on what one takes to be valid beliefs.

Sub-dimension	Example	Sample Amenity Indicators
Traditional	Sharing in the stability and assurance of hearing Mozart performed in the Vienna State Opera as you believe it was earlier	Genealogy Societies; Historical Sites; Opera Companies; Antique Dealers; Fine Arts Schools; Libraries & Archives; Family Restaurants; Family Clothing Stores; Religious Organizations; Dance Companies; Museums
Utilitarian	Attending a benefit concert because it contributes to positive outcomes or savouring the value of efficient production at a museum of industry	Fast Food Restaurants; Technical & Trade Schools; Warehouse Clubs & Superstores; Business & Secretarial Schools; Management Consulting Services; Convenience Stores; Business Associations; Junior Colleges; Computer Systems Design; Database & Directory Publishers; Exam Preparation & Tutoring; Educational Exhibits

Table 12.1   (continued)

Theatricality		
Egalitarian	Enjoying the democratic implications of a crafts fair	Human Rights Organizations; Salvation Army; Public Libraries: Elementary & Secondary Schools (Public); Environment & Wildlife Organizations; Junior Colleges; Services for Elderly & Disabled Persons; Social Advocacy Organizations; Individual & Family Services; Religious Organizations
Self-expressive	Enjoying hearing a jazz musician play something that could only be improvised spontaneously at that particular moment	Dance Companies; Fashion Shows/Designers; Yoga Studios; Art Dealers; Comedy Clubs; Body Piercing; Tattoo Parlors; Recorded Music Stores; Vintage & Used Clothing; Custom Printed T-Shirts; Music Festivals: Fine Arts Schools; Graphic Design Services; Independent Artists, Writers & Performers; Musical Groups & Artists; Performing Arts Companies; Sound Recording Industries; Hobby, Toy, & Game Stores; Interior Design Services; Karaoke Clubs
Charismatic	Watching a Chicago Bulls game because of the charismatic aura of Michael Jordan rather than because one is a Chicagoan	Designer Clothes & Accessories; Fashion Shows/ Designers; Motion Picture & Video Exhibition; Art Dealers; Dance Companies; Historical Sites; Motion Picture & Sound Recording Industries; Musical Groups & Artists; Performing Arts Companies; Promoters of Entertainment Events; Spectator Sports; Fine Arts Schools; Sports Bars; Sound Recording Studios

communication between people (Landry, 2000, p. xxiii). Some scenes may facilitate the sorts of 'buzzing' face-to-face interactions and vibrant milieus that Storper and Venables (2004) show are crucial to success in co-ordinating, sustaining and enhancing creative work (see also Bathelt et al., 2004; Bahlmann et al., 2009). The glamour of the fashion scene in New York and the film scene in Los Angeles heightens demand for the products they produce, generating independent economic value (Currid, 2007). Persons not only move to places because there are certain amenities there; participation in those amenities enables them to live out and actually become the types of persons they wish to be (Silver et al., 2006). Being in a place with many self-expressive or glamorous or traditionalistic amenities makes it more likely that one will meet self-expressive or glamorous or traditionalistic people, have experiences of the majesty of glamour, the uniqueness of the expressions of a self or the power of a tradition, and commit to making the lifestyles associated with those experiences a part of one's identity and social connections. People can abstractly value glamour while living in many places; but in Los Angeles, for example, it is uniquely possible to exist in a glamorous way and become a glamorous person. Thus, even if many talented people move to cities in part because of their amenities and consumption spaces, participation in those amenities may generate independent consequences.

Another strand of research focuses specifically on bohemian scenes. What kind of connection might join bohemian neighbourhoods and urban development? Bohemias are more than artistic enclaves. Most bohemians are not themselves artists, but dress, speak and consume in an 'artsy' way (Grāna, 1964). From the beginning, bohemian neigh-bourhoods were significant not only for the art they produce; they spatially concentrate individuals against the Establishment, producing a common mood of transgressing the rules in a quest for unusual, exotic experiences. Bad is Good: crime, marginal groups and drugs may all be positively valued. Silver et al., (2010) indeed find that bohemian amenities are more common in high-crime areas, though the impacts of such scenes vary a great detail in different contexts. Bohemias crystallize in a place the spirit of trans-gression, but they need not be revolutionary – Marx, Benjamin and Sartre criticized bohemians for being more concerned with etiquette, manners and experiences than with transforming the economic bases of society.

All of this makes bohemian neighbourhoods – filled with used clothing boutiques, late night bars, tattoo parlours, smoke shops, galleries, ethnic restaurants and marginal individuals – highly suitable as laboratories for generating new consumption styles. Analogous on the consumption side to scientific research and development on the pro-duction side, they are integrally connected to, and not necessarily in combat with, a creative economy that expands by generating new demands (Campbell, 1989). Where it is important for firms to be on the cutting edge and to appeal to youth, edginess, differ-ence, otherness and retro style, then the presence of a bohemia could provide vital inputs. Bohemias provide growing cultural economies with 'useful labour' (Lloyd, 2006) – not only in the form of artists and designers, but also in all the highly educated support staff, marketers and executives who can go to the bars and find out what is (about to be) hip (Currid, 2007). They can consume on the edge of accepted conventions, without them-selves having to be artists or revolutionaries. Thus, the presence of thriving bohemian communities could add to the creative workplace by providing relatively safe spaces for a more educated workforce that has internalized avant-garde culture.

The above discussion of scenes focuses largely on their direct consequences for urban development. Yet it also suggests added attention to the ecological context within which scenes operate and how scenes define the context within which other variables shift their dynamics. Bohemia is a case in point. For bohemias are highly contextual phenomena. Typically, the wider metropolitan areas of which bohemian neighbourhoods are a part are not very bohemian. The Latin Quarter in the 1840s stood out because the rest of Paris provided very few opportunities for concentrated and public experiences of self-actualization (as defined by the bohemians). Wicker Park in the 1990s existed within a Chicago that until very recently was dominated by the social life of ethnic churches and neighbourhoods as well as the political machine. Yorkville in the late 1960s and early 1970s existed within a moralistic Toronto where one was not legally permitted to bring an alcoholic drink from one table to another without supervision by licensed staff. The bohemian breakthrough often occurs in and celebrates such transitional, liminal moments in the life of a city. Social connections and individual identity based on tradi-tion, ethnicity, residence, occupation and formal conventions are suddenly joined and redefined by those based on personal style, sensibility and affect. Bohemias therefore thrive in particular contexts: when the 'expressive revolution' is diffusing to the general populace but is still relatively rare, fragile and new.

Though it is possible to imagine numerous other ways beyond bohemia in which scenes are contextually salient, here we limit our discussion to three others. One is the intersection of scenes and neighbourhood walkability. A neighbourhood may be walkable in that many people walk to work or take public transport and are therefore more likely to move about among many amenities in close proximity. But that alone does not convey the feel of the neighbourhood – an equally high Walk Score can be achieved on walk.com, for example, via many McDonalds or many local bakeries. A scene of local authenticity, by contrast, may create a distinctive environment in which walking is more likely to connect persons to place and build a sense of community involvement and investment.

A second contextual effect we propose joins scenes and technology industry clusters. A city may contain large concentrations of technological work, but without diverse scenes, the spillover effects noted by geographers may not occur. People need places to interact informally, places whose experiential qualities heighten those interactions. Amenities promoting the value of spontaneous self-expression may better facilitate the informal interactions that add value to technology firms.

A third contextual hypothesis concerns nature and scenes. Though proximity to mountains and beaches may provide advantages to some cities, others with fewer natural amenities may compensate via amenities generating a sense of rootedness in an authentic place. Jim Brainard, Mayor of Carmel, Indiana, puts this proposition clearly: 'We have something La Jolla doesn't have. It's called "diversity of weather". But we have to be able to compete with those places. We don't have the Pacific Ocean, we don't have the Rocky Mountains. So we have to work harder on our cultural amenities and in our built environment to make it beautiful – and to make it a place where people want to choose, to spend their lives, raise their families, and retire. . .'.[11] Scenes of local authenticity may become more salient for urban development in places with fewer natural amenities.

EMPIRICAL PROPOSITIONS

From these ideas about the economic consequences of scenes it is possible to derive numerous testable hypotheses. Many more are possible, but those below connect clearly to existing urban development discussions. Testing them serves to demonstrate the utility of the scenes concepts for such discussions.

We start at the most general level:

Variations in local amenity mix lead to differential urban development outcomes.

Specifying the proposition for concrete types of scenes yields the following:

Urbane scenes facilitate innovation and attract highly skilled workers.

Stressing specific scene dimensions typically considered crucial suggests:

- *Highly glamorous and individually self-expressive scenes add value to urban places over and above their general urbanity.*
- *Scenes that stress communitarian values attract socially integrated sub-populations and generate patterns of urban development hospitable to them.*

If we focus on the proposed economic consequences of bohemian scenes, the following propositions should hold:

- *Bohemian scenes promote novel ideas, attract young college graduates and generate more employment in the broader economy.*
- *The impact of bohemias is contextual; it is greater when bohemias contrast more sharply with alternatives.*

Other propositions about how scenes create distinctive ecological contexts for urban development could include:

- *Walkable neighbourhoods experience distinctive development outcomes when they feature scenes of local authenticity.*
- *Technology industry clusters are more likely to lead to growth and innovation when they are located amidst amenities that promote experiences of self-expression.*
- *Amenities that highlight local authenticity are more likely to impact urban development in places with fewer natural amenities.*

Data and Methodology

We tested these propositions using our national database of urban amenities, controlling for other factors known to affect urban economic development.

The theory of scenes, we saw, includes a matrix to identify specific types of meanings, starting with theatricality, legitimacy and authenticity. To 'translate' amenities into the 'grammar' of scenes, all amenities (some 600) in our database were coded on a five-point scale for each of the 15 sub-dimensions of scenes in Table 12.1. Lower scores indicate a negative (not weak) relation to that sub-dimension, as in rejecting tradition or opposing transgressiveness; positive scores indicate a positive relation, as in actively affirming equality or rationality. Based on these codes, a 'performance score' was computed for each scene dimension at the zip code level (details on index construction are available at http://scenes.uchicago.edu/cch/cchAppendix.docx). This score is the salience of each dimension (for example, self-expressiveness or neighbourliness) indicated by the amenities in that zip code. Other measures are of course possible and potentially useful, but the performance scores have demonstrated considerable face validity (Silver et al., 2010) and construct validity (Navarro, 2010). These measures provide a powerful way to capture the range and combinations of cultural meanings present in various places, as embedded in and projected by the amenities of daily life.

The 15 sub-dimensions summarize the huge amounts of cultural information from the amenities database into a manageable set of indices. These capture facets of a scene to help analyse its 'internal' environment. Or they can be used as we do below: as independent variables to explain other phenomena, like economic productivity, innovation, population changes, social trust political affiliation and activism.

In addition to these measures of scenes, we also utilize composite indicators of the array of dimensions of meanings in a given place – that is, combinations of all the 15 dimensions of meaning. We use two strategies. The first is more inductive, the second more deductive. The inductive strategy led to our measure of urbanity. It is based

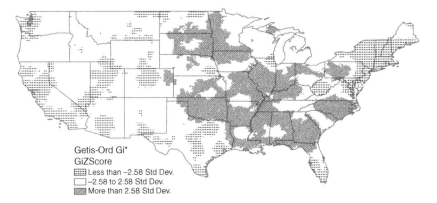

Note: Areas with diagonal lines are more 'communitarian' scenes, small towns and rural counties with higher scores on neighbourliness and tradition (where there are more churches, parks, family restaurants, etc., and people say they know their neighbours, participate in civic meetings with them, and invite them to dinner, etc.) and are adjacent to other counties with similar characteristics. We see a band of such hot spots that runs from Mississippi up the centre of the USA to Minnesota and North Dakota. Blue areas are not small-town neighbourly, but more often urbane in scoring higher on self-expressive, exhibitionist, transgressive and glamorous dimensions.

The Coolest locations on the map have considerable face validity: they are California, especially Southern California along the coast, as well as Colorado, and the New York to Washington DC corridor. These are interestingly distinct from the more commonly discussed Red /Blue map of Republican/Democratic voting. Our Hot and Cold spots seem to capture more the social/cultural dimensions that dovetail more with 'social liberalism' as discussed in the New Political Culture (and by Ronald Inglehart, David Brooks and others). We focused on them as social life, migration decisions and debates among political candidates – much research suggests – increasingly stress these social/cultural lifestyle elements (complementing the material, job and fiscal dimensions of life).

Note that this map of our scenes dimensions is similar to maps of the 'big five' personality types, such as conscientiousness and agreeableness in the South and Midwest, and openness to experience on the two coasts (Florida, 2008, p. 196).

Figure 12.1   The American scenescape

on a principal component analysis of all 15 sub-dimensions, the first factor of which accounted for approximately 44 per cent of the total variance. This factor score permits us to measure where any location falls along the spectrum that most powerfully divides the American scenescape as a whole. The loadings for each sub-dimension suggest a consistent interpretation: it embodies the classic contrast between *Gemeinschaft* and *Gesellschaft*. On one end of the spectrum are 'urbane' scenes of glamorous and transgressive theatricality, utilitarian and self-expressive legitimacy, and rational, state and corporate authenticity. On the other are 'communitarian' scenes of traditional and charismatic legitimacy, formal and neighbourly theatricality, and local authenticity. Figure 12.1 shows a map of this factor score across all US zip codes.

We generate our measure of bohemian scenes with a more deductive strategy. Using a sub-dimensional profile of an ideal-typical bohemia, we assign every US zip code a score indicating how well it matches this abstract concept. Our construction of the ideal-typical bohemia draws on past and recent discussions of the nature of bohemia to determine how a bohemian scene combines the 15 sub-dimensions of scenes. Table 12.2 summarizes this profile.

Defined thus, a scene is more bohemian if it exhibits resistance to traditional legiti-

Table 12.2   Ideal typical Bohemian scene

Sub-dimension	Score	Sub-dimension	Score	Sub-dimension	Score
Traditionalistic	2	Neighbourly	2	Local	4
Self-expressive	5	Formal	3	Ethnic	4
Utilitarian	1	Glamorous	3	State	2
Charismatic	4	Exhibitionistic	4	Corporate	1
Egalitarian	2	Transgressive	5	Rational	2

Source: Silver, Clark and Navano (2010).

Note: One (1) is negative, three (3) is neutral and five (5) is positive.

macy, affirms individual self-expression, eschews utilitarianism, values charisma, promotes a form of elitism (Baudelaire's 'aristocracy of dandies'), encourages members to keep their distance, promotes transforming oneself into an exhibition, values fighting the mainstream, affirms attending to the local (Balzac's intense interest in Parisian neighbourhoods), promotes ethnicity as a source of authenticity (cf. Lloyd, 2006, p. 76), attacks the distant, abstract state, discourages corporate culture and attacks the authenticity of reason (Rimbaud's 'systematic derangement of all the senses'). Scenes whose amenities generate profiles that are closer to this ideal-type receive a higher score on our Bohemian Index (measured as the value distance from the 'bliss point' defined by Table 12.2). This measurement from a bliss point is analogous to policy distance analyses in voting (for example, Riker and Ordeshook, 1973, Chapter 11). Operationally, we subtract the distance of each zip code on each of the 15 dimensions from the bohemian 'bliss point' defined in Table 12.2. We then aggregate these 15 distances and take the reciprocal score. Yes, there is room for debate on this and any characterization of bohemia. In practice, the index identifies many neighbourhoods which others cite as distinctly bohemian: in Chicago, the highest scoring neighbourhoods in 2000 include Bucktown, Wicker Park, Humboldt Park and Logan Square, all commonly perceived as bohemian at the time (Lloyd, 2006), even if they may have changed subsequently.

Other variables
To consider how our scenes operate alongside widely discussed past approaches, we chose our main dependent variables as the most widely used in the social sciences: changes in per capita income, population, gross rent, employment, college graduates and post-graduates. We also add the classic measure of innovation: the per capita rates at which three different types of patents were filed with the US Patents Office – technology patents, entertainment patents and other patents from 1975 to 1999. We refer to these dependent variables collectively as Creative City Dependent Variables (CCDVs), but also discuss them separately.

Our general strategy is to include a set of independent variables drawn from past research that we term 'the Core'. These are basic measures used by leading researchers in the subfield studying each dependent variable. The Core includes population size, per cent of population who are non-white, median gross rent, per cent college graduates, per cent Democratic vote in presidential elections, crime rate and the location quotient of a broad measure of artistically related jobs. Finally, the Core includes the factor score mapped above. All impacts reported below are net of the above Core group of independent variables. More details about our data sources, variable definition and variable construction methods can be found at http://scenes.uchicago.edu/cch/cchAppendix.docx.

In performing our research we discovered that some items were either not available in a consistent manner nationally, or were too strongly intercorrelated with other items to permit including them all in the model. We typically omitted independent variables which had Pearson correlations with each other that exceeded ± 0.5, but also relied on variance inflation factors (VIFs) to detect problematic multicollinearity. For most models the VIF of independent variables does not exceed four, and in no case ten. After resolving these issues, our analyses all begin with Core models for each estimated dependent variable, using multiple regression and related methods. To these models we add 'other variables', one or a few at a time, depending on the substantive proposition. These were added to assess both direct effects and the possible suppression of Core items by the other variables. This method of beginning with a set of Core variables and adding other measures to the analysis as needed has been robust in past works (cf. Clark, 2004). It allows us to maintain a consistent frame of reference across propositions by testing each with respect to a widely acknowledged set of predictors. Thus we are agnostic towards debates about which of the Core may be most important for any given dependent variable, but remain sensitive to the relative impact of including our variables of interest.

Our units of analysis are multiple. This is unavoidable given the availability of patents, crime rate and voting data. None of these three variables were reliably available at the zip code level for the entire United States. Our main scenes data were collected for individual street addresses (from sources such as the electronic yellow pages) or zip codes (from the County Business Patterns (CBP) data). Statistical analyses involving scenes included other zip code level items, but due to issues such as varying catchment areas for different scenes we experimented with different unit sizes, especially counties and metropolitan areas. For instance, a coffee shop's catchment area is normally less than a zip code, but a sports stadium or opera may serve a metropolitan area; both could attract college graduates or interact with other factors of creativity. We thus merged zip code level variables into files with variables measured at the county, municipal or metropolitan levels.

In this way we often combined several levels in a single regression analysis, especially if we posit cross-effects between levels (for instance, migrants to a zip code can be attracted by the metropolitan area stadium as well as by the zip code cafe). The typical approach to assessing multi-level effects is to employ Hierarchical Linear Modelling (HLM) and related methods. Initial explorations of these methods yielded generally consistent results to those we report below. For our purposes here, however, the violation of independence introduced by adding county-level measures as predictors/outcomes is in addition to the violation of independence introduced by the spatial autocorrelation of zip codes (which are either adjacent or in proximity). To fully address these issues we would have had to use a combined HLM and spatial dependence approach that is currently being developed and applied (see Savitz and Raudenbush, 2009) and therefore exceeds the scope of an initial analysis. Obviously such methods will provide substantial opportunities for future research and testing of our findings.

We analyse both direct and interaction effects. Direct effects are most simply measured by coefficients of independent variables in a multiple regression. Interaction effects are present when direct effects shift across contexts – such as when glamour is more important for job growth in Los Angeles than Chicago – and are investigated here mainly by performing separate regressions on different quintiles of a key variable. Local culture and scenes can operate both ways: first by exerting their own direct effects, second by defining a context (such as glamorous) which shifts the effects of other variables. Sharp (2005) and DeLeon and Naff (2004) have stressed that local political cultures can be detected in such interactions.

Missing data was substantial in some instances, especially when we combined various data sources. For instance, the Census population data are not reported fully for zip codes when reporting could violate confidentiality (that is, zip codes with very small populations). Hence some 10000 of the roughly 40000 zip codes omit data for income, education and similar items from the Census of Population. Another reason for this discrepancy is that many zip codes are merely post boxes for mailing purposes (that is, corporate offices).[12]

We do not include tables showing detailed regression outputs, opting instead to report substantively interesting results and representative summary figures.

Results

Figure 12.2 reports a series of regression results designed to assess some of the direct impacts of scenes outlined in the propositions above. The bars represent standardized regression coefficients (plotted with their 95 per cent confidence intervals) for five of the 15 sub-dimensions of scenes especially germane to the above propositions: self-expressive legitimacy, traditional legitimacy, glamorous theatricality, neighbourly theatricality and local authenticity. Figure 12.2 also reports results for our measure of urbanity, derived from a principal component analysis of all 15 scenes dimensions as outlined above. The results were powerful. We discuss those significant above the 0.05 level of probability.

The general feeling of urbanity captured by our factor index of amenities was positively associated with job growth, income growth, gains in post-graduate degree holders (weak), gains in college graduate growth and declining rents, but unrelated to patents and population growth. This most general dimension of the American scenescape – *Gemeinschaft* versus *Gesellschaft* – is thus clearly linked to urban development trajectories. Nevertheless, as Talcott Parsons pointed out (Parsons, 1951), there is significant room for variation within and between these forms of association. The weak relationship between urbanity and change in college graduates, for instance, might suggest that this group is sensitive to distinctions among different types of urbanity; the insignificant relation to patents of all types might suggest that urbanism as such is less important than specific types of experiences (for example, self-expressive or glamorous) for facilitating interactions likely to generate innovative products.

Scenes that promote experiences of individual self-expression were significantly and positively associated with all CCDVs except for high tech patents, which were nearly significant (associated at the $\alpha = 0.1$ level). Self-expression is the only variable we tested – including such urban development staples as growth and level of human capital, arts jobs, technology jobs, population density, commute times – associated with six of our seven dependent variables: patents of all kinds, increasing population, rents, income, total jobs and human capital.

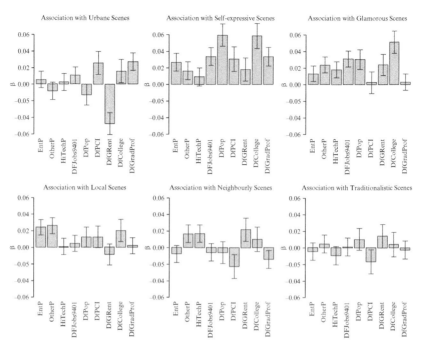

Note: In these and other figures, bars show the impact via the standardized regression coefficients for each independent variable (like self-expressive scenes here) on nine dependent variables (EntP etc.). Whiskers indicate the 95 per cent confidence interval for each coefficient. Thus if the whiskers do not cross the horizontal line at zero, the results are statistically significant. From left to right, dependent variables are log entertainment patents per capita, log other patents per capita, log high tech patents per capita, log proportional change in total employment (1994–2001), log proportional change in population (1990–2000), proportional change in per capita income (1990–2000), proportional change in gross rent (1990–2000), difference in proportion of college graduates (1990–2000) and difference in proportion of individuals with post-graduate degrees (1990–2000). These are classic least squares multiple regression point estimates. Unless otherwise noted, the Core variables are included as controls. Basic descriptive statistics are reported at http://scenes.uchicago.edu/cch/cchAppendix.docx Subsequent analysis of an expanded model that included all variables created to measure the various factors of creative cities (available at http://scenes.uchicago.edu/cch/cchExtendedAnalysis.docx) revealed basically similar results.

Figure 12.2   Scenes hypotheses

Glamorous amenities were positively linked with all CCDVs except for change in total jobs and post-graduates. In fact, both glamour and self-expression suppress the impact of college graduates on population growth. They also suppress the impact of urbanity on change in college graduates, suggesting that such persons are responsive to exceptionally glamorous and self-expressive areas more than the general urbanity found in many places. Post-graduate degree holders, by contrast, rose in urbane but not glamorous places, what we could label 'square urban development'. These seem to be separable effects: putting glamour and self-expression in the same model does not significantly alter any of the above relations. For some outcomes, that is, glamour and self-expression each generate value all their own.

The results for the more communitarian dimensions of scenes reported in Figure 12.2 – traditional legitimacy, neighbourly theatricality and local authenticity – were surprising. These are the places filled with the amenities that Glaeser et al. label 'low human capital'. Traditional amenities are linked with declines in per capita incomes, as are neighbourly amenities, which also have modestly larger declines in post-graduate degree holders. And yet: amenities of local authenticity are positively and significantly – if weakly – associated with gains in college graduates, while neighbourly amenities are significantly associated with rising rents. Not only theatres and restaurants but also bed and breakfasts, golf courses and local bakeries appeal to skilled persons. Still, for the most part, the communitarian dimensions do not exhibit statistically significant relationships with most of our economic development variables. The most surprising exception is patents: neighbourly zip codes predict more high tech and other patents, while those with more locally authentic amenities have more entertainment and other patents. Cities producing the most patents contain highly neighbourly and locally oriented communities.

This finding contrasts so much with the standard story of edgy creative class domination that we investigated it further to see if the result was spurious. It seems not. Rather, it seems that the standard picture is overwhelmed by the strong relationship between rents and patents. When we exclude rents from the model, the associations of neighbourly and local amenities are negative with patents. Yet when we add rents (as a cost of living indicator), the relationship reverses: local and neighbourly amenities are significantly associated with higher concentrations of patents. We performed many tests to check whether this result is mere statistical noise or whether it carries substantive meaning. It appears to be the latter.

Interpretation? Many urban economists have noticed the strong positive relationship between high rent districts and creative industry clusters. Silicon Valley has very high rents, and many firms and individuals continue to move there, even when rents would be cheaper in Nevada. Why? They typically point to spillover effects, where locating near other innovating firms and individuals increases the productivity of everybody; the whole is greater than the parts. Others have posited a signalling process, whereby high rents signal to firms and workers that productive, talented workers are located there; a sorting effect (Berliant and Yu, 2009). Some, as we saw, suggest a premium on certain amenities, like theatres and restaurants (Glaeser et al., 2004). High human capital workers are willing to pay higher rents to gain access to these sorts of amenities and the other high human capital people likely to frequent them; low human capital amenities are correlated with lower rents and less skilled people.

Our finding complicates these stories. If we only look at the simple bivariate correlation between, on the one hand, our measures of local authenticity and neighbourly theatricality, and, on the other, patents, we find a negative relationship for both. There is less patent production in places with more amenities such as historical sites, family restaurants, parks, civic and social organizations, bakeries, fruit and vegetable markets, libraries and archives, playgrounds, coffee houses, pubs, cemeteries, antique dealers, churches and historical societies. However, once we control for rents, the relationship reverses: places that provide connection to and express the value of a tradition and neighbourliness have more patents. That places which foster neighbourly styles of theatricality have lower rents biases our view of such places (the correlation is −0.2). If we take out the effect of high rents – whether due to sorting, spillover or high-priced amenities – then we can see that a lifestyle rooted in the local and committed to the community via scenes

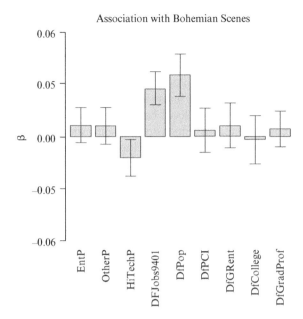

Note: See Figure 12.2 for more detailed information regarding the models presented.

Figure 12.3   Generic effect of bohemia

composed of amenities that express and enact the values of local authenticity and neighbourly theatricality is perfectly consistent with innovative work.

What specific mechanisms are here? Consider two. One proposes indirect and another direct mechanisms through which such scenes encourage novel ideas. First, the promise of a local community lifestyle may attract high-skilled workers to more rural or neighbourhood settings, 'compensating' for the loss of the high-rent prestige of Silicon Valley, Los Angeles or New York City with a lifestyle full of neighbourly and locally authentic amenities. In fact, some land-grant universities like the University of Wisconsin-Madison and Virginia Tech have been actively pursuing this strategy with their local governments. The presence of such workers could then lead to more innovation. Yet interacting with this first process is a second, more directly connecting local roots and neighbourly interaction to innovation, cultivating sensibilities for certain sorts of creative work. The security of a life connected organically and intimately to a community of neighbours who 'know your name' provides a firmer backdrop and support for the inevitable failures and risks of all creative endeavours. The best new knowledge can be like the best food: it comes slow, not fast, and is organically connected with local practice. It finds nourishment in extended conversations that unfold over years, working out of (not against) its history to find insight not in abstract, disembodied universal processes but in the particular dynamics of a concrete place. The availability of life in neighbourly and local scenes may enable these sorts of ideals to form the basis of everyday personal and social experience.[13]

What about bohemia (Figure 12.3)? An equally complicated picture emerges. At the national level, patents are not more likely to be filed by residents of cities with strong

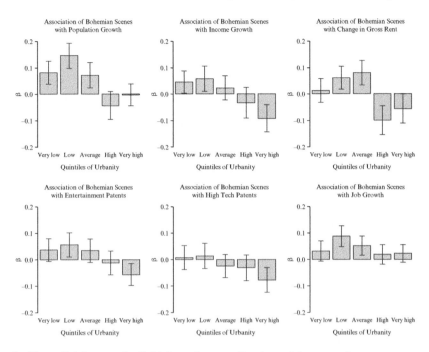

Note: See Figure 12.2 for more detailed information regarding the models presented.

Figure 12.4   Differential effect of bohemia, via urbanity

bohemian scenes. Nor are bohemian scenes attracting college graduates or experiencing rising rents or incomes. They are, however, showing increased jobs and population. Moreover, the Bohemian Index suppresses the impact of our measure of general urbanity on population growth. These results again complicate the simple stories of gentrification and Red State versus Blue State.

Above, we underscored the highly contextual nature of bohemia. This led us to go beyond traditional national analyses to look for how bohemian scenes vary in specific local contexts. If bohemias are liminal spaces between the passing of an old world and the emergence of a new, our propositions suggest that their impact should be greater when embedded in more communitarian contexts. We tested this idea by creating a variable using the county mean of our scenes factor score, which we treat here as a single variable measure of the degree of urbanity or communitarianism of the county as a whole. Places with lower scores are thus more communitarian on this measure.[14] The key was then to split our national file into quintile groups based on this measure (Figure 12.4). This reveals how the impact of bohemian amenities shifts across places which are more or less urbane.

The results are highly suggestive. Bohemias are not significantly linked with entertainment patent filing nationally; however, they are in its less urbane segments, and they are associated with lower concentrations of entertainment patents (and high tech patents) in, and only in, the most urbane areas. Moreover, though nationally bohemias predict increases in total employment, this effect is almost entirely contained within the middle

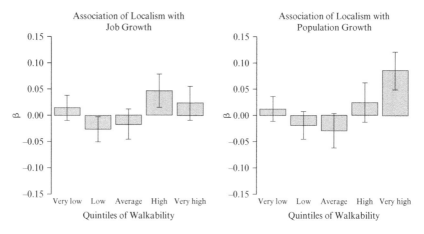

Note: See Figure 12.2 for more detailed information regarding the models presented.

Figure 12.5   Differential effect of localism, via walkability

and second-most communitarian group of counties in the country. And though nationally bohemias are experiencing population growth, this growth is mostly within the most communitarian quintiles and is absent in the most urbane segments of the country. A similar pattern emerges for the relationship between bohemias and income growth: while bohemias do not predict increasing incomes nationally, they do in the lower quintiles, and their impact declines in linear fashion until, in the most urbane parts of the country, they are associated with declining incomes. The relationship between bohemias and rents shows a similar, if less linear, pattern.

These results offer strong confirmation of the notion that, for example, Lloyd's observations of Wicker Park's rise in the 1990s are not unique to Chicago but may instantiate a general phenomenon. Bohemias play a pivotal role in the early phases of a city's 'expressive revolution', where formerly blue-collar and bourgeois cities or neighbourhoods experience their first, transitional reverberations of the tradition of the new. But as that revolution becomes institutionalized and thereby moderated, the contrast between 'establishment' and 'radical' is reduced, and specifically bohemian neighborhoods stand out less. One potential indication of this developmental sequence is given by the fact that post-graduate degree holders – harbingers of the establishment – actually increase in bohemias located within the more urbane parts of the country.

Analysis by quintiles also yielded some intriguing findings for our other hypotheses about the contextual aspects of scenes' consequences for urban development. We report here on the strongest patterns, but caution that many other relationships are not so clear or coherent.

Scenes and neighbourhood walkability powerfully interact, as Figure 12.5 shows. At the national level, local authenticity is unrelated to job growth and weakly to population growth. However, within the zip codes with the largest shares of residents who walk to work, local authenticity is positively related to both job and population growth. Local authenticity has no effect in the places where fewer people walk to work.

Self-expressive scenes seem to enhance the gains associated with technology clusters.

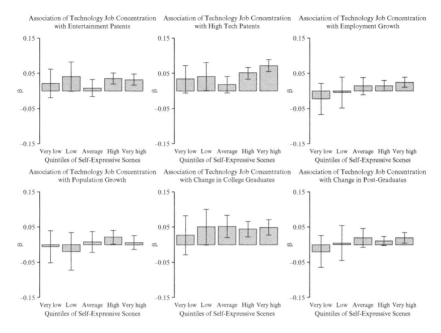

Note: See Figure 12.2 for more detailed information regarding the models presented.

Figure 12.6 Differential effect of technology job concentration, via self-expressive scenes

As we saw, in national analysis clusters of technology jobs are positively related to patent concentration, job growth, population growth and human capital gains, while they are negatively related to rents and incomes. However, these effects are strongly mediated by the self-expressiveness of the amenities that are near technology jobs, as is shown in Figure 12.6.

The relationship between technology industry clusters and two types of patents (entertainment and technology) is mostly found within only the two most self-expressive segments of the country. The association of technology clusters with job growth is significant only within the most self-expressive quintile, their association with population growth is significant only in the second-most self-expressive quintile, and their association with post-graduate gains is significant only in the most self-expressive quintile. The association between technology clusters and change in college graduates shows a similar pattern: a positive relationship between technology jobs and increasing college graduates exists in the parts of the country with scenes less legitimized by individual self-expression. But that association grows stronger through the two top quintiles. Technology clusters may play a part in the new urban economy, but that role seems to significantly depend on such clusters locating in scenes that provide occasions for spontaneity, improvisation and unique expression.

Scenes of local authenticity are related to different urban development outcomes depending on their proximity to natural amenities, as shown in Figure 12.7.

Nationally, locally authenticated amenities are associated with higher concentrations of entertainment and other patents, rising college graduates, population and income,

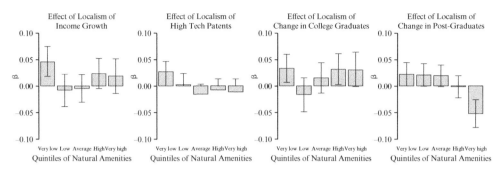

Note: See Figure 12.2 for more detailed information regarding the models presented.

Figure 12.7   Differential effect of localism, via natural amenities

and unrelated to our other dependent variables. However, local authenticity shifts in impact with the natural amenity context. The positive impact of local authenticity on both income growth and high tech patents is significant only in the 20 per cent of the country with the fewest natural amenities. The positive association of local authenticity with gains in post-graduate degree holders is only (barely) significant in the quintiles with the fewest natural amenities. It is insignificant or negative in areas with the most natural amenities. Local authenticity is tied to growing numbers of college graduates in the places with the least and most natural amenities, not the ones in between. There might be something to Mayor Brainard's intuition. Amenities can both enhance a natural setting, and compensate for limited access to natural amenities. Scenes transform the dynamics of other urban development variables.

While not conclusive, these analyses of amenities and scenes illustrate, as several authors above argued, an independent 'scene effect' generated by the experiential opportunities indexed by local amenities. The economic effect of scenes runs partly through scenes attracting skilled workers, by providing them with occasions to experience distinctive styles of life. But human capital attraction does not exhaust the impact of the scene. For example, when we include change in college graduates in the model with self-expressive and neighbourly scenes, it should be noted that neither the self-expressive nor the neighbourly scene effect on the CCDVs is suppressed. Scenes add independent value to urban economies. They invest products made by their participants with the charge of glamour and more. They expose residents to interactions devoted to the search for new ways of thinking and being; they connect them to community, and to a sense of place.

REFLECTIONS

Max Weber was fond of using the phrase 'every man a monk' to characterize the world-historical implications of the Protestant Reformation. It threw open the walls of the monastery, injected its ascetic element into everyday life and offered positive religious backing for the focused, disciplined and rational exercise of mundane activities like work and household management. Normative ideals formerly restricted to religious virtuosi were extended to a wider population, tremendously expanding and deepening the personal religious commitments and experiences available to them. Heightened expectations of disciplined performance as an everyday occurrence, outside of specialized settings, generated new anxieties and conflicts. And, most fatefully, the productivity gains for which the 'disciplinary revolution' (Taylor, 2007) was partly responsible placed the rest of the world in its steel shell. If Calvinists pursued work with the ascetic zeal of a religious calling, others for whom worldly toil was a burden were forced to work harder or move aside.

Our investigation of the conditions most likely to lead to urban growth in the contemporary world might be interpreted as suggesting that the process Weber identified has moved to a new level. 'Every man a musician' could describe it in general, if not the most accurate, terms. The walls of the lab, lecture hall and Latin Quarter have been thrown open, injecting the expressive and creative element into everyday life. Practices and sensibilities formerly restricted to creative virtuosi have been extended from the garret, studio and study to boardrooms, city halls, office cubicles and main streets nationwide. This marks a great upgrading of the expressive and creative possibilities available to the general populace. It also subjects more individuals to previously more exclusive anxieties oriented around the quest for authenticity and the demand to construct meaning for oneself.

And, perhaps just as the rise of the Protestant ethic did before it, the current institutionalization and internalization of creativity, as the present chapter documents, has transformed the economic playing field. That process has put a premium on the ability to generate new ideas and styles. Places that best facilitate idea and style-generation are succeeding, though success cannot be attributed to any single factor. Education is important, but so are basic research, technology and artistic work. Tolerant social climates create environments more open to experimentation and attractive to the most skilled workers. Hierarchical social climates often stifle innovation and growth; they are losing college graduates and generating fewer patents. Workaholic social climates leave their residents little psychological space to reach beyond the analytical mind into modes of experiences not accessible to rationalism. And finally, the places that have filled their streets and strips with opportunities for unique expressions of individuality and glamorous theatricality are not only attracting the most educated and talented, they are adding value to that talent. This is a world that Weber would have hardly recognized.

Has it thrown up an iron cage of creativity? Innovate or Die? Bohemia or Bust? There is no one, clear answer in these analyses. We can say that places that encourage residents to express and glamorously display themselves may be at the leading edge of the creative economy, yet they do not have a monopoly on innovation or growth. Other places with neighbourly social climates that encourage a sense of place are also growing and innovating; they may create networks of continuity, support, security and trust that make tolerable the unavoidable uncertainties of creation. Some places that root residents in the local or put them in contact with nature are growing, innovating and attracting people with education and skills. Nashville's country music industry rivals music industries in New York and Los Angeles. Yet each city's musical genres feed on the strikingly different amenities and scenes in which they are embedded: three of the five most abundant types of amenities in Los Angeles are jewellers, bakeries and commercial artists; in New York the top categories include jewellers, delicatessens and art dealers. Some of the most numerous amenities in Nashville are automobile customizing services, Methodist churches and the Church of Christ. God and cars can fuel cultural production as much as bling, art and lunch on the go.

CONCLUSION

Both analysts and policy-makers, we suggest, may advance by paying more attention to scenes. We show several powerful impacts of scene components in this chapter, some simple, others complex. We have shown here too how to measure and analyse scene dimensions in terms almost as precise and concrete as education or income and other classic variables that we include in our 'Core' analyses, building on previous studies. In the new economy where consumption and production more often join, we have shown how the components of specific scenes can generate synergistic results. We have done so by using the same widely studied basic policy variables as in the best recent work: changes in population and jobs, increases in income and rents, the rise of college-educated and post-graduate populations, and patents.

But we have dug deeper into many dynamics by modelling these processes using all the US zip codes – some 40000 – as well as combining zip code processes with those in larger units such as counties where appropriate. Our probing more deeply reveals more subtle processes, just as does a microscope or cyclotron. Both national and more scene-specific results emerge in a rather dramatic way: glamour and tradition can generate innovation and growth, just as can bohemia. Bohemian processes do not work everywhere: they are strongest in areas that are breaking with tradition and taking off in artistic and economic activity, as measured by our scenes factor score. Bohemian impacts are nil in many other places. Localism and walking can shift how other processes operate. Some places that seem left out of the 'creative economy' still manage to build successfully on their distinctive assets and lifestyles. Localism is most powerful in its positive effects precisely in those locations that have less of other things, for example, grand mountains or urbane nightlife. There are many contrasting ways to be creative. Analysts and policy-makers who attend to these more subtle combinations of classic processes can make more informed decisions.

NOTES

1. http://leisureblogs.chicagotribune.com/the_theater_loop/2009/10/new-nea-chief-lauds-daley-arts-policy-says-model-for-nation.html#at (accessed 13 March 2011).
2. http://www.youtube.com/watch?v=hgYwTELj-fs (accessed 13 March 2011).
3. A number of specific mechanisms have been posited that connect education and creativity. Increased education means that decisions are increasingly based on symbols and cultural meanings, rather than tradition or custom. Symbols are infinitely more malleable and manipulable than 'stuff'; they can be combined in limitless ways, and can harness and control vast quantities of energy. The scientific method presses relentlessly towards new discoveries. Theories are born to be surpassed. Education opens persons to alternative ways of living and thinking, breeding a more critical stance on life that is less willing to accept the world as given. Through training engineers, computer scientists and other more technical professionals, scientific innovation and values diffuse from universities into firms and cities more widely. Through the humanities and some social sciences, values of critique, aesthetic novelty and 'paradigm-shifting' spread (Lipset and Altbach, 1969). Mass higher education institutionalizes innovation in more organizations and internalizes it in more individuals (Clark and Seymour, 2001). Concentrations of human capital may con-

tribute to urban development directly though the productivity gains created by increased idea-generation by talented workers, or indirectly through spillover effects and their tendency to raise quality of life by minimizing social problems and encouraging better schools (Glaeser et al., 2004).

4. Critics treat technological innovation as 'domination', leading to environmental disaster, the decline of craftsmanship (Sennett, 1998; Crawford, 2009) and impoverished personal connection to Mother Nature. Others claim that the 'technological understanding of being' goes deeper than satisfying a range of given human wants and needs. It involves a life oriented around expanding and continually transforming our possibilities (Dreyfus and Spinosa, 1997). Its 'instrumental-activist' value-pattern means that it is never finished; we are continuously on the move to a new understanding of self and world (Parsons, 1951).

5. We created a more direct index of how tolerant a city's social climate is. Our index compiles questions drawn from the DDB Lifestyle Survey about, for instance, beliefs that the father is not the natural boss of a household, that a woman's place is not necessarily in the home, that men are not by nature more intelligent than women, about the desire to learn about other cultures and about interest in visiting places different from one's home. We also investigated other social climates: a workaholic social climate, indicated by belief that one works late, works very hard most of the time and spends very little time in leisure pursuits; a hierarchical social climate was measured by responses that, for example, indicate patriarchal beliefs, being disturbed by changes in routine, feeling that the world is changing too quickly, pining for the good old days and opposing pre-marital cohabitation; a localistic social climate was indicated by responses such as being content to live in the same town for one's whole life, not expecting to move in the coming years and favouring government restrictions on imported products; and a neighbourly social climate was indicated by frequently attending club meetings, working on community projects, often visiting friends and feeling influential in one's neighbourhood. However, we do not include these and other indices of social climate in the analyses reported here. They are in the expanded model that is described in Table 7 at http://scenes.uchicago.edu/cch/cchAppendix.docx. Results of our analyses of social climate are available for download at http://scenes.uchicago.edu/cch/cchExtendedAnalysis.docx.

6. We created several measures of social density: travel time to work, percentage of the population working at home and walking to work, public transport use and population density. However, as with social climate, we do not include these in the analyses reported here but provide more detail at http://scenes. uchicago.edu/cch/cchAppendix.docx. Suffice it to say that subsequent analyses suggest that social density and social climate do not seem to seriously modify the scenes analysis, which is our primary concern here.

7. Artists deserve extra attention as they are quintessential creatives, masters at taking material from the world – stone, colour, sound, and so on – and refashioning it into a new perspective on the human experience. Beyond this broader notion of artistic creativity, the more narrow avant-garde sensibilities of novelty and contingency, as Daniel Bell has argued (1996), have in the past century come to dominate the cultural sphere in general and artistic work in particular, though there are exceptions.

8. For instance, Kant argued that aesthetic appreciation of nature's beauty provokes a spontaneous play among our faculties that cannot be reduced to rules. He also wrote of the sublime experience of awesome mountains and oceanic depths as shattering our sense of stability and settledness. Romantics celebrated the wilds of nature, seeing in its unpredictability a source of creativity beyond rational calculation and aesthetic harmony. Transcendentalists saw in nature an expression of the divine whole that could be mixed with human will in the production of art.

9. To capture some of the role of natural amenities in urban development, we created measures of average January temperature, average July temperature and the United States Department of Agriculture (USDA) index of natural amenities as general indicators. We complement these with an index of waterfront amenities from our amenities database, using places with lakes, rivers and oceans as well as marinas, beach accessories, boat charters, river trips and tours and waterfront food service. These are included in the expanded models and results reported at http://scenes.uchicago.edu/cch/cchExtendedAnalysis.docx.

10. In focusing here on the links between scenes and economic growth, we in no way endorse the proposition that economic standards are the only or primary measure of the value of scenes. Scenes have their own autonomous standards of value that evaluate economic standards; scenes also contribute to arenas beyond the economic, such as neighbourhood cohesion or political mobilization. For a study of scenes as one symbolic resource among others, see Silver and Clark (2009).

11. http://www.urbanophile.com/2010/01/29/midwest-miscellany-26/ (accessed 13 March 2011).

12. Thus the US Post Office lists these post boxes as 'zip codes', but the Census Bureau drops these and uninhabited areas like forests. One consequence of this, and the fact that actual zip codes are not static nor bounded within a single county or state, is that the Census Bureau uses the label 'Zip Code Tabulation Areas (ZCTAs)' to contrast with the US Postal Service's official Zone Improvement Plan (ZIP) code. At the same time, the branch of the Census Bureau responsible for reporting data on the type and number of businesses in a given location (that is, the CBP data) includes about 10 000 more ZCTAs than the Census of Population. This is a major case of a partially 'truncated' data file that we had to address, generated by the disparity between the Census Bizzip data (N = nearly 35 000) and Census of Population data

(N = 28 000). While many of our zip code items are from the Census, we retain the term zip code rather than ZCTA to ease communication with those unfamiliar with the distinction. Officially the Census Bureau claims there is no relationship between the two, but in practice the fact that we use only ZCTAs eliminates possible confusion regarding overlapping geographies.

13. This scenes' formulation dovetails with the two sorts of innovation identified by Galenson (2007): youthful brilliance and elderly synthesis. Similarly, we are more sensitive to these personalistic elements embedded even in large cities from the nearby strong case of Chicago. The Catholic (especially Irish) tradition legitimating such local ties makes Chicago and theorists exposed to it more sensitive to these neighbourly elements than those in other cities (such as New York, Los Angeles or Paris) where advocates of other urban theories are more numerous. See the debates involving Michael Dear, Michael Moore, John Mollenkopf, Dennis Judd, Terry Clark and others in Clark (2009).

14. Our earlier discussion of more communitarian scenes analysed differential effects of separate dimensions of communitarian scenes, such as local authenticity, neighbourly theatricality and traditional legitimacy. The present discussion analyses the single factor score that combines these.

REFERENCES

Acs, Z.J. (2002), *Innovation and the Growth of Cities*, Cheltenham, UK and Northampton, MA, USA: Edward Elgar Publishing.

Almeida, P. and B. Kogut (1999), 'Localization of knowledge and the mobility of engineers in regional networks', *Management Science*, **45**(7), 905–17.

Bahlmann, M.D., M.H. Huysman and T. Elfring (2009), 'Global pipelines or global buzz?: a micro-level approach towards the knowledge-based view of clusters', Series Research Memoranda 0002, Faculty of Economics, Business Administration and Econometrics, VU University Amsterdam.

Bathelt, H., A. Malmberg and P. Maskell (2004), 'Clusters and knowledge: local buzz, global pipelines and the process of knowledge creation', *Progress in Human Geography*, **28**(1), 31–56.

Becker, G.S. (1993), *Human Capital: A Theoretical and Empirical Analysis, with Special Reference to Education*, Chicago, IL: University of Chicago Press.

Becker, H. (1984), *Art Worlds*, Berkeley, CA: University of California Press.

Bell, D. (1973), *The Coming of Post-industrial Society: A Venture in Social Forecasting*, New York, NY: Basic Books.

Bell, D. (1996), *The Cultural Contradictions of Capitalism*, New York, NY: Basic Books.

Bellah, R., Madsen, W.M. Sullivan, A. Swidler and S.M Tipton (1996), *Habits of the Heart*, Berkeley, CA: University of California Press.

Bellow, S. (1975), *Humboldt's Gift*, New York, NY: Penguin.

Berliant, M. and Ch-M. Yu (2009), 'Rational expectations in urban economics', MPRA Paper 12709, University Library of Munich, Germany.

Breschi, S. and F. Lissoni (2001), 'Knowledge spillovers and local innovation systems: a critical survey', *LIUC Papers in Economics*, **84**, 905–17.

Brooks, D. (2000), *Bobos in Paradise: The New Upper Class and How They Got There*, New York, NY: Simon and Schuster.

Campbell, Colin (1989), *The Romantic Ethic and the Spirit of Modern Consumerism*, Oxford and Cambridge, MA: Blackwell.

Chatterton, P. (2000), 'Will the real creative city please stand up', *City*, 4(3), 390–7.

Clark, T.N. (ed.) (2004), *The City as an Entertainment Machine*, Boston, MA and Amsterdam: Elsevier.

Clark, T.N. (2009), 'The new Chicago School – not New York or L.A., and why it matters for urban social science', available at http://www.uic.edu/depts/pols/ChicagoPolitics/NewChicagoSchool.pdf (accessed 13 March 2011).

Clark, T.N. and F.C. da Silva (2009), 'Revisiting Tocqueville: citizenship norms, political repertoires, and cultural participation', in M. Cherkaoui, P. Hamilton and A. Frenod (eds), *Raymond Boudon: A Life in Sociology*, Oxford and Paris: Bardwell Press/GEMAS, pp. 247–78.

Clark, T.N. and V. Hoffmann-Martinot (eds) (1998), *The New Political Culture*, Boulder, CO: Westview Press.

Clark, T.N. and M.L. Seymour (2001), *The Breakdown of Class Politics: A Debate on Post-industrial Stratification*, Washington, DC and Baltimore, MD: Woodrow Wilson Center Press and Johns Hopkins University Press.

Craincross, F. (1997), *The Death of Distance: How the Communications Revolution Will Change Our Lives*, Cambridge, MA: Harvard Business School Press.

Crawford, M.B. (2009), *Shop Class as Soulcraft: An Inquiry Into the Value of Work*, New York, NY: Penguin.

Currid, E. (2007), *The Warhol Economy: How Fashion, Art and Music Drive New York City*, Princeton, NJ: Princeton University Press.

De La Durantaye, M. (2002), 'Municipal cultural policies in Quebec', *Canadian Journal of Communication*, **27**(2), 305–13.

DeLeon, R. and K.C. Naff (2004), 'Identity politics and local political culture', *Urban Affairs Review*, **39**(July), 689–719.

Dreyfus, H. and C. Spinosa (1997), 'Highway bridges and feasts: Heidegger and Borgmann on how to affirm technology', available at http://www.focusing.org/apm_papers/dreyfus.html (accessed 13 March 2011).

Egeln, J., S. Gottschalk and C. Rammer (2004), 'Location decisions of spin-offs from public research institutions, *Industry and Innovation*, **11**(3), 207–23.

Florida, R. (2002), *The Rise of the Creative Class: And How It's Transforming Work, Leisure, Community and Everyday Life*, New York, NY: Basic Books/Perseus.

Florida, R. (2008), *Who's Your City?: How the Creative Economy is Making Where to Live the Most Important Decision of Your Life*, New York, NY: Basic Books.

Galenson, D. (2007), 'Artists and the market: from Leonardo and Titian to Andy Warhol and Damien Hirst', NBER Working Papers 13377, National Bureau of Economic Research.

Glaeser, E.L. (2004), 'Review of Richard Florida's The Rise of the Creative Class', available at http://www.creativeclass.com/rfcgbd/articles/GlaeserReview.pdf (accessed 15 March 2011).

Glaeser, E.L., J. Kolko and A. Saiz (2004), 'Consumers and cities', in T.N. Clark (ed.), *The City as an Entertainment Machine*, Boston, MA and Amsterdam: Elsevier, pp. 177–84.

Goffman, E. (1974), *Frame Analysis: An Essay on the Organization of Experience*, New York, NY: Harper & Row.

Gräna, C. (1964), *Bohemian Versus Bourgeois; French Society and the French Man of Letters in the Nineteenth Century*, New York, NY: Basic Books.

Heidegger, M. (1977), *The Question Concerning Technology, and Other Essays*, New York, NY: Garland Publishing.

Hitzler, R., T. Bucher and A. Niederbacher (2005), *Leben in Szenen. Formen jugendlicher Vergemeinschaftung heute*, Wiesbaden: VS Verlag für Sozialwissenschaften.

Hoekman, J., K. Frenken and F.G. Van Oort (2008), 'The geography of collaborative knowledge production in Europe', KiTES Working Papers No. 214, Universita' Bocconi, Milan, Italy.

Howkins, J. (2002), *The Creative Economy: How People Make Money from Ideas*, New York, NY: Penguin.

Jacobs, J. (1961), *The Death and Life of Great American Cities*, New York, NY: Vintage Books.

Jacobs, J. (1969), *The Economy of Cities*, New York, NY: Vintage Books.

Joas, H. (1996), *The Creativity of Action*, Chicago, IL: University of Chicago Press.

Joas, H. (2004), 'Morality in an age of contingency', *Acta Sociologica*, **47**, 392–99.

Klepper, S. (2001), 'Employee startups in high-tech industries', *Industrial & Corporate Change*, **10**(3), 639–74.

Kotkin, J. (2001), *The New Geography: How the Digital Revolution is Reshaping the American Landscape*, New York, NY: Random House.

Landry, Charles (2000), *The Creative City: A Toolkit for Urban Innovators*, New Stroud: Earthscan.

Lipset, S.M. and P. Altbach (1969), *Students in Revolt*, Boston, MA: Houghton Mifflin.

Lissoni, F. (2001), 'Knowledge codification and the geography of innovation: the case of Brescia mechanical cluster', *Research Policy*, **30**(9), 1479–500.

Lloyd, R. (2006), *Neo-bohemia: Art and Commerce in the Postindustrial City*, New York, NY and London: Routledge.

Marcuse, H. (1964), *One-dimensional Man; Studies in the Ideology of Advanced Industrial Society*, Boston, MA: Beacon Press.

Markusen, A. and D. King (2003), *The Artistic Dividend: The Arts' Hidden Contributions to Regional Development*, Minneapolis, MN: Project on Regional and Industrial Economics, Humphrey Institute of Public Affairs, University of Minnesota.

Navarro, C.J. (2010), 'The cultural dimensions of cities (Scenes Project in Spain)', paper presented at the International Sociological Association World Congress, Gotheburg, Sweden, RC03.

Parsons, T. (1951), *The Social System*, Glencoe, IL: The Free Press.

Parsons, T. (1971), *The System of Modern Societies*. Englewood Cliffs, NJ: Prentice-Hall.

Parsons, T. (1978), *Action Theory and the Human Condition*, New York, NY: Free Press.

Parsons, T. (1991), *The Social System*, London: Routledge.

Parsons, T. (2006), *American Society: Toward a Theory of Societal Community*, Boulder, CO: Paradigm.

Peters, M.A. and T. Besley (2008), 'Academic entrepreneurship and the creative economy', *Thesis Eleven*, **94**(1), 88–105.

Pink, D.H. (2006), *A Whole New Mind: Why Right-brainers Will Rule the Future*, New York, NY: Riverhead Trade.

Polensky, K.S. (ed.) (2007), *The Economic Geography of Innovation*, Cambridge, MA: Cambridge University Press.

Reich, R.B. (1992), *The Work of Nations: Preparing Ourselves for 21st Century Capitalism*, New York, NY: First Vintage Books.

Riker, W. and P. Ordeshook (1973), *An Introduction to Positive Political Theory*, Englewood Cliffs, NJ: Prentice-Hall.

Romein, A. and J.J. Trip (2009), 'Key elements of creative city development: an assessment of local policies in Amsterdam and Rotterdam', paper presented at the City Futures Conference, Madrid, Spain, 4–6 June.

Rosenberg, H. (1959), *The Tradition of the New*, New York, NY: Horizon Press.

Sassen, S. (2001), *The Global City: New York, London, Tokyo*, Princeton, NJ: Princeton University Press.

Savitz, N.V. and S.W. Raudenbush (2009), 'Exploiting spatial dependence to improve measurement of neighborhood social processes', *Sociological Methodology*, **39**(1), 151–83.

Sennett, R. (1970), *The Uses of Disorder: Personal Identity & City Life*, New York, NY: Knopf.

Sennett, R. (1998), *The Corrosion of Character: The Personal Consequences of Work in the New Capitalism*, New York, NY: Norton.

Sharp, E.B. (2005), *Morality Politics in American Cities*, Lawrence, KS: University Press of Kansas.

Silver, D. and T.N. Clark (2009), 'Buzz as a social resource', paper presented at the American Political Science Association Annual Meeting, Toronto, ON.

Silver, D., T.N. Clark and L. Rothfield (2006), *A Theory of Scenes*, Working Group on Scenes, University of Chicago, IL, available at http://scenes.uchicago.edu/book.html (accessed 15 March 2011).

Silver, D., T.N. Clark and J.C. Navarro (2010), 'Scenes: social context in an age of contingency', *Social Forces*, **88**(5), 2293–324.

Storper, M. and A.J. Venables (2004), 'Buzz: face-to-face contact and the urban economy', *Journal of Economic Geography*, **4**(4), 351–70.

Taylor, C. (2007), *A Secular Age*, Cambridge, MA: Belknap Press of Harvard University Press.

Van Ulzen, P. (2007), 'Waar blijft dat Rotterdamse designhotel?', *KAAT kunst & economie in Rotterdam*, **1**, 30–1.

13 The arts: not just artists (and vice versa)
Elizabeth Currid-Halkett and Kevin M. Stolarick

Since the early 1990s, the arts have been seriously considered in scholarship and practice for their role in the economic development of the regions and cities in which they concentrate. There is no question that the arts, and more broadly cultural production, have been an important field of study in the social sciences since the turn of the nineteenth century (Veblen [1899] 1994; Simmel, 1904; Robinson, 1961; Blumer, 1969). However, in more recent years, the arts have been looked at for their practical application in the development of place (Molotch, 1996, 2002; Scott, 2000, 2005; Currid, 2006, 2007b; Markusen and Schrock, 2006b; Markusen et al., 2008). In the face of the globalization and homogenization of the urban experience, a regional arts economic base is significant in establishing a region or city identity or what Markusen and Schrock (2006a) call 'distinction'.

The insertion of the arts into economic development has resulted in large-scale tourism developments (Judd and Fainstein, 1999; Strom, 2002), efforts to use the arts as redevelopment (Zukin, 1989; Plaza, 2006; Grodach and Loukaitou-Sideris, 2007) and as a part of larger amenity schemes (Glaeser et al., 2001; Florida, 2002a; Clark, 2004). Other types of arts-oriented economic development have tended to invest in large-scale tourism and cultural 'hard branding' (Evans, 2003), using museums and corporate investments as a means to create a cultural milieu to lure visitors and new desirable residents (Sassen and Roost, 1999; Strom, 2002; Plaza, 2006). Additionally, developers have sought to create the smaller art districts that are viewed as important means for preserving local heritage and authenticity that are attractive to high-skilled workers (Florida, 2002b; Lloyd, 2005; Carr and Servon, 2007). Non-profit and advocacy organizations have made the case that the arts generate jobs and revenue in their own right (Wassell and DeNatale, 1997; Americans for the Arts, 2004; Keegan et al., 2005; Alliance for the Arts, 2007; NESTA, 2008, among others).

Yet efforts to capture the full contribution of the arts to regional economies prove difficult. First, from both a practitioner and scholarly approach, there are vast differences in the definition of the arts and what occupational and industrial categories ought to be included. Studies of the arts or 'creative economy' range from including media (Markusen and Schrock, 2006b; NESTA, 2008), religion (Markusen et al., 2008), 'taste-driven' industries (Currid, 2007a); or grouping the arts as a part of the larger 'creative class' (Florida, 2002a). In addition, researchers tend to look at either industry or occupation data in their study of the arts. Some research focuses on the arts industries (Keegan et al., 2005; Scott, 2005; Alliance for the Arts, 2007; Otis Gollege and LAEDC, 2007; Currid and Williams, 2010).

Other scholars have started using occupational categories as a measure of a region's artistic composition, an approach originally put forth by Thompson and Thompson (1985). Leading this effort are the studies by Markusen et al. (see Markusen and King, 2003; Markusen et al., 2004; Markusen and Schrock, 2006a, 2006b, among others) whereby both Census and Bureau of Labor Statistics (BLS) data at the occupational level have been employed to analyse the distribution of different types of artistic workers across various metropolitan areas. Currid (2006) also incorporates the use of BLS occupational level data to test regional competitive advantage by artistic occupational cluster. However, by picking either occupation or industry, scholars and practitioners limit their assessment of the full composition of a region's artistic economy.

As Barbour and Markusen (2007) have pointed out, occupational and industrial structures do not 'imply' one another. Markusen et al. (2008) conclude in their analysis of three arts advocacy institutions that policy agendas often drive data selection and analysis as well as choices between industry and occupational data, thus leading to different research outcomes. As the authors remark, '. . . differing cultural industrial and cultural occupational definitions produce different aggregate snapshots of the regional creative economy' (Markusen et al., 2008 p. 35). Renski et al.'s (2007) study of different datasets (value chain versus labour-based) produce remarkably different results, which they conclude should be taken into account in policy-making. They remark that their 'findings strongly suggest that a narrowly defined cluster analysis . . . may overlook important regional interindustry synergies, industry specializations and strengths and that may be the legitimate focus of cluster oriented economic development strategies' (Renski et al., 2007, p. 382).

Despite the significant differences in approaches towards studying the arts, important findings remain consistent. First, the arts are producing viable contributions to their local and regional economies. Second, art composition is extraordinarily place-specific, and thus understanding the arts' impact requires regional and city-specific data. We argue that in order to measure the complex role of the arts in a regional economy, an integration of the methodological approaches must be employed, enabling a deeper understanding of the arts as industries, skill sets as well as artists' skill linkages with other industries. Because cultural workers also tend to cross-fertilize with other non-artistic industries, providing skills on an ad hoc basis (Markusen et al., 2004; Currid, 2007a), and producing 'spill-crosses' (Stolarick and Florida, 2007) or 'crossover' contributions to more commercial sectors (Markusen et al., 2008), measuring the arts' contribution requires a many-tiered approach. Additionally, non-artistic occupations are also important to culture industries, and often artists are employed in cultural industries providing non-artistic work (for example: the actor desperate to get a foot in the door who works as an usher for a theatre company).

The consensus, pioneered by Markusen et al., has been that both occupations and industries must be analysed and incorporated in order to fully grasp a region's artistic economic base and cultivate competitive advantage. In this chapter, we extend these earlier contributions studying the intermix between occupations and industries by undertaking a regional comparative analysis. As previous scholars have noted, occupations contribute by industry and this contribution can be place-specific (Thompson and Thompson, 1985; Barbour and Markusen, 2007).

We believe this observation is particularly acute in arts industries and analyse the interplay between arts and artists. We observe that the occupation-industry interplay occurs both within artistic and non-artistic sectors of the economy. We employ a multi-data approach across the national and regional level in the United States to understand the interaction between industry and occupation. Our aim is to further contribute to the growing body of work evidencing the importance of looking at both skills and industries simultaneously. By looking at a number of regions and national level data we hope to demonstrate on an aggregate level the unique interplay between these two aspects of economic composition and how this relationship is of particular significance to the artistic economy. We both reaffirm what scholars have observed with a macro-level research approach and introduce new methods for this analysis.

In this chapter, we establish a three-tiered methodological approach using 2005 BLS Occupational Employment Statistics, 2005 County Business Patterns and 2000 Census Public Use Micro Sample (PUMS) national-level data. We looked at the relationship between artistic occupations and artistic industries on both the national and regional level. Because artistic industries and occupations tend to be located in metropolitan areas, we compare the 30 largest such areas. We found that over 50 per cent of artists do not work in arts-related industries, and that artistic industries tend to rely on a dense and complicated network of labour pools, many of which do not rely on artistic contributions. We further found that particular metropolitan regions, especially Los Angeles and New York, drive artistic occupational clustering in cities. We also performed a series of correlation and variance tests using the Herfindahl Index as well as correlation analysis looking at linkages between presence of artistic industries and occupations. Our research points to the other industries in which artists tend to contribute their skills. We believe that such findings have significant implications for researchers and practitioners engaged in economic development for the arts. We argue that this more in-depth and all-encompassing approach will lend insight to research and practice directed towards 'the arts' and artists – which are, as it turns out, not necessarily the same thing.

DATA LIMITATIONS IN STUDYING THE ARTS

The arts are complicated to study due to how artists and art skills are employed both in art industries and non-artistic industries. Artists are often freelance and thus are not always picked up in firm data, they are also employed as much in non-artistic industries as in artistic sectors. Art firms need a diversity of non-artistic occupational skills in the production of cultural goods and services. Below we briefly discuss the benefits and limitations to the various data available to study the arts.

Industry Data

Industry-level data, as reported by the BLS North American Industrial Classification System (NAICS), is widely used to document firm size, total wages, concentration and location; it is a good measure of those workers and firms that are 'economically viable'. In other words, if a firm is able to employ workers and must report earnings to the BLS, it is by extension a legitimate participant in the region's economic base. There are, however, several limitations in using this approach, particularly as it pertains to art and culture. First, industry data does not give us composition of firm type and in this respect undercounts the role of cultural workers in 'non-artistic' industries. For example, NAICS code 511 130 (book publishers) tells us nothing about the various types of workers involved in this type of firm. On one level this limitation is ubiquitous across industries: the financial services category does not tell us about the administrative assistants, public relations and other such skills that are involved in that industrial category. But for artists this chasm is particularly pronounced: because artists are often hired on an ad hoc basis, are often hired as 'independent contractors' and because their skills are widely used outside of 'cultural industries', using industry data fails to capture their contribution to other industrial sectors.

By way of example, financial analysts generally work for financial service firms and thus industry data provides a fairly accurate account of the financial industry, in the sense that there is a general alignment between occupation and industry. But because artists 'cross over', they tend to work for a multitude of industries ranging from finance to book publishing to record labels to public relations. Industry data alone thus tells very little about artistic contributions to a regional economy (Markusen et al., 2006).

Moreover, industry data tells us nothing about the internal dynamics of an industry within a particular place. For development and policy, understanding baseline skills within a region is central. As Massey (1984) documented in her study of the automobile industry, industries distribute their various parts of the production process in different spatial locations, a finding that Audretsch and Feldman (1996) corroborate in their study of high technology industry. More generally, industry data only tells us what industry is located there, but it does not tell us which specific part, or parts of that industry's production process, is in a specific location. This latter information is critical to understanding place-based regional development.

Occupational Data

Industry data demonstrates limitations in its scope of understanding local economic dynamics and competitive advantage (Thompson and Thompson, 1985; Markusen, 2004). As Thompson and Thompson (1985) argue, figuring out which occupational strengths a region possesses determines both local needs and advantage. Several different theoretical and methodological approaches have been argued for in making the case for occupational analysis. Markusen (2004) posits that occupational analysis gives a much clearer picture of local economic dynamics, aiding in more effective economic development policy. Barbour and Markusen (2007) point out that innovative industries cannot be predicted by their industry alone, as occupations are more geographically divided, with research and development locating in one part of the country and production in another, a point that Massey (1984) and Nelson (2003) also argue. As such, occupations for the same industry can be different for different geographies. Similarly, Feser (2003, p. 1937) argues in favour of a distinction between 'the kinds of work the local economy does [versus] the kinds of products it makes' – largely a function of the education and skills that a region possesses. Workers may move between jobs and industries within the same region, often without having to attain significant new skills, because 'many skills and knowledge-bases are common to multiple occupations' (Feser, 2003, p. 1940).

Current empirical research has emphasized the use of occupational data as measured by both the Census and the BLS Occupational Employment Statistics (OES). Markusen's extensive work on the 'artistic dividend' argues that because artists tend to be footloose and thus not tied to an industry, the best gauge of cultural worker concentration is through self-reported Census data. Currid (2006) incorporates industry-reported OES data in her analysis of artistic competitive advantage, making the point that artists affiliated with firms is a measure of them making tangible economic contributions as opposed to being 'starving artists', whose skills in the latter case would not be providing any meaningful or quantifiable value to the local economic base. These occupational approaches do, however, exhibit some drawbacks.

While these data sources get to exactly which type of cultural workers are present within a regional economy, their drawbacks are the converse of industry data: they do not tell us which industries are benefiting from these skills (as measured by occupation). In other words, there may be a high concentration of graphic designers in San Francisco (either reported through the Census or OES), but this observation alone does not tell us which industries demand these skills or if these skills are even needed by local firms and industry. If the OES data is employed, we will know that graphic designers are employed in the region but we will not know by which industrial sector. Further, as cultural workers have a greater tendency towards freelance work than other occupational groups, OES data may not capture these workers if they are not full-time employees. If self-reported Census data is used, this only tells us that there are a lot of individuals who define themselves as graphic designers, but that does not necessarily mean that they are working as such or that their local region needs these skills.

While the earlier work of Thompson and Thompson used a very generic categorization for occupational clusters, both Feser (2003) and Koo (2005) base their definitions of occupational clusters on the knowledge requirements of approximately 600 occupational categories as defined in the (Occupational Network, O*Net) ONET system. In his study of the Cleveland metropolitan area, Koo (2005) argues for a three-tier approach in analysing the regional economy, targeting both occupations and industries. Both in Feser's and Koo's studies, the result was to consolidate the ONET-defined occupational categories into around 20 clusters. Rather than using the widely used and recognized framework developed by Porter, Koo uses a model that directly incorporates both occupations and industries. Recently Barbour and Markusen (2007) have investigated the relationship between regional occupational and industry structure. They conclude that industry is not always sufficient on its own as a way to understand regional economic activity. Their result adds further support to the argument that both industry and occupational viewpoints are needed.

Occupational strengths can often act as leverage to attract industries seeking out particular skills – not the other way around. Occupational analysis indicates what specific type of human capital a region possesses, thus giving a more place-sensitive analysis of productivity and growth. Further, occupational analysis captures those individuals engaged in economically valuable work that may not have a bachelor's degree or above. This analysis has become an important component of contemporary economic development analysis, as it allows for greater nuance and a deeper understanding of regional growth, and how it differs across geographies.

There is both strong theoretical and empirical evidence that occupational analysis has become an effective method of understanding regional advantage and productivity. Economic development policy can be aided significantly by capitalizing on local strengths, best measured through the occupational or skill-based mix a region possesses. A solely industrial-based analysis neglects the role of human capital in understanding clustering. Industry may set the stage, but tacit knowledge, network structure and capital exchanges involve people. Industries may demonstrate their own physical economies of scale and scope, but industries also benefit from the external economies that concentration of human capital and skills produces.

In this respect, the Porter (1998) industry-clustering model only tells us partly what is going on. It shows the demand side: where the industries are and what they are producing. But occupational analysis explains why the industries are geographically located where they are – for the specific skills that particular regions possess. Occupational analysis informs the supply side of regional productivity and growth. It gives a deeper understanding of what types of work are going on and how these types of work are engaging one another and the potential for those skills to contribute to various industries. In other words, occupational analysis gets inside the black box of what types of human capital and skills are more or less important to regional productivity.

RESEARCH APPROACH

Overall, the research and methodological approaches using occupational data begin to get at the regional skill base of each region, giving a greater understanding of regional advantages than just looking at industries. But our understanding of a region is still limited because we are not able to link occupational skills to particular industries and thus do not have an understanding of the interplay between industries and workers. Because cultural workers contribute to a regional economy in many and often complicated ways (for example, dancers working as Starbucks baristas waiting for their 'big break' (which might or might not come)), occupational data alone does not tell us enough. For the purposes of regional economic development, both industrial and occupational data only enable carpet-bombing policy approaches because neither provides enough nuances to target artists and cultural workers in a specific way.

In this chapter, we argue that the most effective way to measure the arts' contribution to the regional economy is to look at the interplay between industries and occupations. Current occupational research accounts for these dynamics partially, but we argue that occupational and industrial analysis is not an either/or approach. Occupational analysis only provides a partial lens to understand regional dynamics. To be useful, any model of occupational clusters needs to be much more finely grained, and the industry side of the equation should be addressed by those methods that are already generally accepted and most widely used. Regional dynamics must be understood on two levels: first, the industries, industry mix and clusters. Second, the occupations, occupation mix and clusters. And, finally, the specific relationship of occupations within each industry or industry cluster.

Using national and regional data allows us to make some aggregate and comparative assessments of the state of the arts and how they engage across various industrial sectors. Regions that have similar employment across an industry can have very different occupational profiles, reflective of vastly different locations on that industry's value chain or significant differences in the education, skills and talent available in the regional labour market. Along with using this broad analysis to demonstrate the place specificity of artistic composition, we show to which industries artists are most likely to contribute their skills and which skills are most significant to cultural industries. We find that industry or occupational data alone tells us very little about the relationship between the arts and the regional economy, and future work on art and culture must consider the crucial link between industry and occupation in order to be truly effective in understanding local and national economic bases. Understanding these differences will allow for a much more nuanced and complete understanding of a regional economy.

DATA, VARIABLES AND METHODS

Using detailed Census and BLS data, we aim to attain deeper understanding of the role of human capital and skills and their interaction with local industry with a focus on the arts. Details about our occupational and industry selection can be found in the endnotes. The data needed to investigate these relationships is divided into three different categories: occupational (OES from the BLS); industry by employment and firm (County Business Patterns, NAICS); and data showing linkages between the industry and occupation distributions (Census PUMS). We will go into each data source in more detail below.

Occupational Employment Statistics (OES)

Individual occupation and employment data is from the US Bureau of the Census and the BLS Occupational Employment Statistics (OES). We picked the OES because it provides two important aspects of our analysis: data at the occupational level and industry reported, thus capturing people gainfully employed in artistic work. While we are aware this data excludes freelancers, it is a good proxy for capturing artists working for firms. Later, we use PUMS data which does include freelance workers. The Standard Occupation Classification (SOC) forms the basis for the OES. Occupational data reports on individuals currently working in the specified occupation. In addition, we looked at linkages between occupations and industries using 2000 Census PUMS. OES data (unlike PUMS) is specifically occupational data.

Detailed information, statistics and correlations are reported for each occupation separately so the reader is free to limit or expand their definition of what should be included in 'the arts' as they see fit. In order to get a comprehensive view of artistic occupations on the national level, we have included a consolidated list of summary statistics for some key artistic occupations and their location quotients. We provide summary statistics for all datasets as an overview before undertaking more specific analysis. These summary statistics (Table 13.1) demonstrate that nationally the arts are not equally represented: almost all location quotients (LQs) are below one. The standard deviation reveals considerable inter-regional variation, a finding we will discuss in more detail later in our analysis. Because some cities are disproportionately overrepresented (as demonstrated by the maximum metropolitan region LQ results) and others not at all (as the minimum metropolitan LQ reveals), the results below indicate that on the whole most US regions tend to be underrepresented in arts occupations. The mean LQ for most occupations is significantly under one.

*Table 13.1   Summary statistics for national occupation data (*n = *core-based statistical area)*

Variable	N (metro-politan regions)	Mean employ-ment	Stan-dard devi-ation	Min. metro-politan region employ-ment	Max. metro-politan region employ-ment	Mean LQ	LQ stan-dard devia-tion	Min. metro-politan region LQ	Max. metro-politan region LQ
Total Employment	406	366467	767835	15700	8110630				
Arts, design, entertain-ment, sports, and media occupations (GROUP)	406	5464	17417	30	181290	0.35	0.64	0.00	3.98
Actors	406	121	1491	0	21620	0.42	0.62	0.00	5.12
Archivists	406	11	67	0	1070	0.25	0.71	0.00	7.68
Art directors	406	99	412	0	5210	0.06	0.53	0.00	10.04
Choreo-graphers	406	24	101	0	1160	0.20	1.05	0.00	15.57
Commercial and industrial designers	406	91	366	0	4410	0.15	0.95	0.00	12.37
Craft artists	406	2	12	0	130	0.18	0.75	0.00	11.19
Curators	406	17	64	0	760	0.22	0.86	0.00	9.92
Dancers	406	25	152	0	1560	0.22	0.79	0.00	7.55
Editors	406	303	1187	0	16260	0.54	0.93	0.00	5.60
Fashion designers	406	52	476	0	6530	0.84	0.66	0.00	3.22
Fine artists, including painters, sculptors and illustrators	406	16	81	0	1050	0.25	0.67	0.00	6.05
Multi-media artists and animators	406	74	368	0	4560	0.10	0.41	0.00	3.72
Music directors and composers	406	15	104	0	1520	0.21	0.60	0.00	4.83
Musicians and singers	406	129	691	0	9040	0.09	1.23	0.00	24.52
Photographers	406	75	223	0	2050	0.15	0.55	0.00	4.35
Producers and directors	406	202	967	0	10130	0.37	0.82	0.00	5.39
Writers and authors	406	116	423	0	4460	0.14	0.52	0.00	5.09

Table 13.2   *Summary statistics for industry establishment data (n = core-based statistical area)*

Variable	N (metro-politan regions)	Mean metro-politan estab.	Stan-dard devia-tion	Min. metro-politan estab.	Max. metro-politan estab.	Mean metro-politan estab. LQ	Stan-dard devia-tion	Min. metro-politan estab. LQ	Max. metro-politan estab. LQ
TOT_EST	382	18 357.1	41 801	792	536 845				
Publishing industries (except Internet)	382	80.7	206	1	2533	0.71	0.51	0.01	3.75
Motion picture and video industries	382	60.9	335	0	5607	0.47	0.50	0.00	7.97
Broadcasting (except Internet)	382	23.2	42	0	452	0.87	0.64	0.00	3.54
Performing arts, spectator sports and related industries	382	107.4	567	0	9344	0.64	0.92	0.00	9.21
Museums, historical sites and similar institutions	382	15.8	31	0	396	0.69	0.88	0.00	6.02
Amusement, gambling and recreation industries	382	173.5	340	2	4360	0.99	0.70	0.08	6.53

County Business Patterns NAICS industry data

The second category is industry data, which was taken from the Census Bureau's 2005 County Business Patterns. We chose this data source because it captures industry employment and firm-level data. This data allows us another lens into the economic composition of a region. Industry data is reported at the firm or establishment level and is reported for firms that have employees or sales. The industries that were selected include those most often associated with the 'cultural industries' (for example, publishing, broadcasting and motion pictures). Tables 13.2 and 13.3 show summary statistics for selected industries by establishment and employment, respectively. The industry data demonstrates slightly more overall concentration than artistic occupations. Like the occupational results, the data in these tables demonstrates again that some metropolitan regions are significantly concentrated while others lack artistic industry completely (as the maximum and minimum LQ results indicate). In both

Table 13.3   Summary statistics for industry employment data (n = core-based statistical area)

Variable	N (metro-politan regions)	Mean metro-politan emp.	Stan-dard devia-tion	Min. metro-politan emp.	Max. metro-politan emp.	Mean metro-politan estab. LQ	Stan-dard devia-tion	Min. metro-politan estab. LQ	Max. metro-politan estab. LQ
TOT_EMP	382	291 146.2	646 973	10 806	7 558 206				
Publishing industries (except Internet)	382	2836.2	8527	2	108 361	0.80	0.40	0.07	2.46
Motion picture and video industries	382	765.5	5899	0	110 145	0.57	0.38	0.00	5.08
Broadcasting (except Internet)	382	728.8	2214	0	32 719	1.32	0.78	0.00	4.05
Performing arts, spectator sports and related industries	382	1065.1	3785	0	51 062	0.63	0.41	0.00	4.80
Museums, historical sites and similar institutions	382	310.9	922	0	12 880	1.21	0.74	0.00	4.63
Amusement, gambling and recreation industries	382	3381.5	7527	41	70 955	1.14	0.36	0.27	3.42

firm and employment data, artistic industries tend to have very high LQ maximums but below average mean LQs. For example, museums and broadcasting firms demonstrate some overrepresentation in employment (mean LQ 1.21 and 1.32, respectively), which may reflect their ubiquity. However, like the occupational data, some industries are clearly overwhelmingly concentrated as witnessed by the maximum LQ results. The motion picture industry, for example, has a maximum LQ of 7.97 in firm concentration, while having only a mean of 0.47. Similarly, employment in motion pictures has a maximum LQ of 5.08, while only a mean LQ of 0.57. Performing arts firm concentration has a maximum LQ of 9.21 and a mean LQ of 0.64 (Tables 13.2 and 13.3).

PUMS Variables

The final category is data on individuals that includes both occupation and industry information. All data is from the 2000 US Census 5 Per Cent Public Use Micro Sample (PUMS). While the previous two sources report separate information on occupations or industries, this final source allows for reporting of occupations within an industry or for the reporting of all industries for a given occupation. This data gives us insight into the interplay between industry and skills on a national and regional level. Again, we chose those industries and occupations most aligned with the arts. For occupations this included musicians, dancers and entertainers. Our industries included broadcasting, recording industry and artists. Below we will discuss our analysis using these three data-sets and the lenses they provide into our national and regional economies. Because the arts tend to concentrate in big cities we also analysed the 30 largest metropolitan regions separately. We performed a series of correlation and variance tests using the Herfindahl Index to analyse the linkages between presence of artistic industries and occupations.

RESULTS

The most salient result of our analysis has been the vast diversity of industries in which artistic skills are employed, and the great variety of occupations comprising artistic industries, corroborating earlier work by Barbour and Markusen (2007) and Wassell and DeNatale (1997). Understanding the arts and artists requires a comprehensive look at many different intermingling industries and skill sets. Through the use of all aforementioned datasets we demonstrate our findings below.

First, we look at PUMS data on the distribution of occupations within the three broadly identified artistic industries: artists, broadcasting and recording. Overall, the arts industries are comprised of vastly different occupational skills. We find that while artistic occupations are dominant, it is nevertheless the case that less than 50 per cent of the employment of even the 'artists' industrial category is made up of people in occupations classified as 'artistic' (Table 13.4). In broadcasting and recording the artistic composition is significantly smaller. For example, only 12 per cent of workers in the recording industry are musicians, singers and related workers. On one level, this is no surprise: industries require a wide variety of inter-related but different skills in order to produce their goods and services. Accountants, computer technicians and managers are still necessary to produce albums and music concerts, even if musicians are the necessary but insufficient initial input. Yet that the most artistic industries are significantly composed of 'non-artistic' occupations demonstrates the heterogeneity and diversity of skills that is needed in the production of artistic goods and services.

Conversely, we found that there is a great degree of diversity among the industries employing artists. Cultural workers, or artists, tend to seek out employment in very diverse industrial categories. While the three PUMS artistic occupational categories are all primarily employed within the 'independent artists' industrial category, less than 50 per cent of each artistic occupation is employed in artistic industries. For 'dancers, entertainers and musicians' their secondary industrial sector is different but tends to explain (along with the 'artists' industry) over 60 per cent of employment (Table 13.5). For

Table 13.4   Top five occupations within artistic industries (United States)

Industry	% of industry total	Occupation titles
Artists	14.38	Artists and related workers
	12.10	Musicians, singers and related workers
	9.60	Writers and authors
	4.75	Athletes, coaches, umpires and related workers
	3.77	Actors
Broadcasting	8.06	Advertising sales agents
	7.86	Telecommunications line installers and repairers
	7.43	Producers and directors
	6.16	Customer service representatives
	5.71	Announcers
Recording	18.26	Broadcast and sound engineering technicians and radio operators
	11.90	Musicians, singers and related workers
	7.29	Managers, all other
	5.39	Producers and directors
	3.35	Marketing and sales managers

Table 13.5   Top five industries for artistic occupations (United States)

Occupation	% of occupation total	Industry titles
Dancers	42.72	Independent artists, performing arts, spectator sports and related industries
	31.55	Drinking places, alcoholic beverages
	11.17	Other amusement, gambling and recreation industries
	2.68	Restaurants and other food services
	2.36	Other schools, instruction and educational services
Entertainers	40.37	Independent artists, performing arts, spectator sports and related industries
	19.62	Other amusement, gambling and recreation industries
	8.91	Drinking places, alcoholic beverages
	5.11	Motion pictures and video industries
	4.54	Other personal services
Musicians	46.44	Independent artists, performing arts, spectator sports and related industries
	31.18	Religious organizations
	3.10	Restaurants and other food services
	2.51	Sound recording industries
	1.98	Drinking places, alcoholic beverages

Table 13.6   Herfindahl Index for variation of occupations across industry

Industry	Herfindahl Index
Artists	543.59
Broadcasting	357.96
Recording	632.88

Table 13.7   Herfindahl Index for variation of industries across occupation

Occupation	Herfindahl Index
Dancers	2965.33
Entertainers	2182.68
Musicians	3159.32

example, almost 80 per cent of musicians are employed in either the artistic or religious industrial sectors, with the remaining three top five industries accounting for less than 8 per cent of employment. Dancers and entertainers are more diverse than musicians in their employment, yet still 75 per cent and 61 per cent of their employment is attributed to just two industrial sectors, respectively. Entertainers are the most diverse occupational category with almost 20 per cent of their employment being in the third-placed to fifth-placed industries.

The Herfindahl Index

In the previous section, we demonstrated that artistic industries are driven by non-artistic skills as much as artistic skills and that artists seek out work in non-artistic industries. To what extent do artistic industries vary in their occupational structure and how diverse are the industries in which artists are employed? In order to get a sense of the overall variation of industry and occupational composition, we employed the standard Herfindahl Index, which allows us to see variation of occupations across each industry, and second, the variation of industries across the occupations. The Herfindahl Index is simply the sum of squared percentages. If, for example, an entire industry had people in only one occupation, the index would be 10 000. The closer the value is to zero, the greater is the variation within the industry.[1]

The Herfindahl Index results show that there is significant variation of occupations across the entire sample and that there is also variation in occupations across the broadcasting, artists and recording industries (Table 13.6). The broadcasting industry has the greatest variation of occupations and the recording industry has the least variation (though it exhibits a significant amount of variation, nonetheless). Table 13.7 shows that, again, there is significant variation in industry within occupations.

There is, *per force*, less variation across industries than there is across occupations because there are only 264 industries but as many as 475 occupations. However, the difference in the Herfindahl Index for the three culturally creative occupations reveals that these occupations are generally much more concentrated in a small number of industries than the corresponding concentration of occupations among culturally creative industries. Overall, these results indicate that cultural occupations as a whole tend to show up in many industries and thus industry or occupational data alone gives us a very small lens of a much more diverse and complicated dynamic. While some occupations, such as dancers, musicians and entertainers have a less variable industrial make-up, they still are not linked directly to one particular industry. Taken together, these results strongly suggest that investigating artistic clusters by industry is much more error-prone than simply using occupations. We maintain that analysis from both perspectives is the best approach. Thus far, these results indicate that industrial policy versus skill-targeting are distinctly different, and we think that these approaches would produce significantly different results.

Correlations Between Industries and Occupations (LQs)

We were interested in seeing if the regional concentration of artistic occupations begets a concentration of artistic industries and vice versa. Thus, we ran correlations between the LQs of occupations and industries. Overall, our results demonstrate that occupations are not a good predictor of industry location. Among all analysed industries and occupations, there is only a strong correlation (at the metropolitan area level) between the employment location quotients of one occupation and industry pair – 27-2011 (actors) and 512 (the motion picture industry) at 0.76. While the co-location of these groups is to be expected, we were surprised that there were not more pairs of occupations and industries that have stronger correlations.[2] The next largest correlations ranged between 0.47 and 0.49:

Correlation Occupation and Industry Employment
0.493   27-0000 (overall arts, design, entertainment) and 511 (publishing)
0.488   27-0000 (overall arts, design, entertainment) and 512 (motion pictures)
0.484   27-4012 (broadcast technicians) and 515 (broadcasting)
0.476   27-1014 (multimedia artists and animators) and 512 (motion pictures)

While industry establishment has a stronger link with occupations than industry employment, in general there are not many strong correlations between occupations and industry establishments. The largest correlations are:

Correlation Occupation and Industry Establishments
0.632   27-2011 (actors) and 512 (motion pictures)
0.585   27-0000 (overall arts, design, entertainment) and 512 (motion pictures)
0.578   27-3041 (editors) and 511 (publishing)

Overall, these correlation results clearly show that the concentration of artistic occupations and industries are generally different from each other. Generally, locations with high (or low) concentrations of employment in artistic industries do not necessarily have high (or low) concentrations of artistic occupations. There are no pairs of industries and occupations that are significant with large negative correlations, so a high concentration of one is generally not associated with a low concentration of the other. In general, the

Table 13.8   Correlations among industries (LQs)

		Artistic establishments					Artistic employment					
		712	713	511	512	515	711	712	713	511	512	515
Artistic establish- ments (by code number)	Performing arts, spectator sports (711)	0.13	−0.02	0.41	**0.77**	−0.09	0.30	0.27	0.25	0.30	**0.59**	0.04
	Museums, historical sites (712)		0.39	0.14	0.00	0.11	0.05	0.44	0.18	0.03	−0.06	0.08
	Amusement, gambling and recreation (713)			−0.07	−0.10	−0.01	0.07	0.15	0.24	−0.11	−0.18	−0.07
	Publishing (511)				0.40	−0.16	0.07	0.25	0.12	**0.72**	0.19	−0.03
	Motion picture and video (512)					−0.09	0.18	0.20	0.17	0.31	**0.75**	0.08
	Broadcasting (515)						−0.08	−0.09	−0.13	−0.15	−0.07	**0.58**
Artistic employ- ment (by code number)	Performing arts, spectator sports (711)							0.14	0.09	0.07	0.16	0.06
	Museums, historical sites (712)								0.18	0.15	0.10	0.00
	Amusement, gambling and recreation (713)									0.07	0.11	−0.05
	Publishing (511)										0.16	0.00
	Motion picture and video (512)											0.10

correlations are positive and significant but not that strong. Table 13.8 provides general correlations across industries by industrial code.

Again, within the culturally creative industries, there are few strong correlations between concentrations of employment at the metropolitan area level among the various industries. In essence, the results above show that there is not clustering of these industries on a higher level. Between establishment and employment location quotients, there are (not surprisingly) strong positive correlations between the concentration of establishments and the concentration of employment. Although positive significant correlations are shown for all six, they are only notably strong for publishing (511), motion pictures (512) and broadcasting (515). Publishing and broadcasting have higher average employment per establishment which would help to explain the large correlation, and motion pictures are already known to be concentrated in a small number of regions (Scott, 2005). The only other strong correlations are between performing arts, spectator sports

Table 13.9   Location quotient (LQ) correlations among artistic occupations

Correlation	Occupations
0.771	27-2011 (actors) and 27-2099 (entertainers and performers, all other)
0.683	27-1011 (art directors) and 27-1014 (multi-media artists and animators)
0.673	27-0000 (overall arts, design, entertainment) and 27-2012 (producers and directors)
0.628	27-1014 (multi-media artists and animators) and 27-2012 (producers and directors)
0.618	27-0000 (overall arts, design, entertainment) and 27-1024 (graphic designers)
0.604	27-0000 (overall arts, design, entertainment) and 27-1014 (multi-media artists/animators)
0.584	27-0000 (overall arts, design, entertainment) and 27-3031 (public relations specialists)
0.584	27-0000 (overall arts, design, entertainment) and 27-3041 (editors)
0.575	27-1014 (multi-media artists and animators) and 27-2011 (actors)
0.560	27-1011 (art directors) and 27-2012 (producers and directors)

and related industry (711) establishments and motion picture and video (512) industry establishments and employment.

Correlations Among Occupations (LQs)

We also undertook correlation analysis between concentrations of occupations and industries to see if there was a relationship between being overly represented in an industry and being overly represented in artistic occupations, and vice versa. Location quotients are a measure of a region's representation in a particular industry or occupation vis-à-vis a larger geographical area.[3] In this case, we looked at the US metropolitan concentrations compared to the United States as a whole. We then studied whether concentration in an artistic occupation was closely correlated to artistic occupation concentration overall. In other words, if a metropolitan region is concentrated in musicians does that indicate a concentration in other types of artistic occupations? We undertook the same analysis on the industry level as well. In general, these correlations, like the industry correlations show that there is not a lot of occupational clustering of artistic occupations in US metropolitan areas (Table 13.9). There are not many that are negatively correlated with each other either. So, while there are some relationships, they are generally not that strongly related with each other. Table 13.9 reports the highest correlations between the LQs for the occupations.

This table shows that concentrations of artistic industries do not give us a good measure of artistic skill concentration, and conversely a strong presence of artists or cultural workers is not an indication of possessing great advantages in cultural industries. The higher correlation between some occupations and the 27-0000 category, which is the LQ for all arts, design and entertainment employment in the region, does show some general clustering across the entire gamut of artistic occupations. For example, the high correlation for producers and directors indicates a wide variety of other artistic occupations occur in regions with higher concentrations of producers and directors, but the specific occupations vary across regions – some regions might have more actors, other regions more dancers or musicians. On the whole, these results suggest that while artistic occupations do not seem to geographically co-locate, they do not deter one another either. Generally, these findings suggest neutral linkages across artistic occupations, and affirm that artistic industries and occupations do not inform one another. We speculate that this is due to the way in which metropolitan regions tend to specialize in particular artistic strengths rather than possessing a strong advantage in cultural industries and skills overall. This finding corroborates our earlier PUMS analysis. Artistic industries are associated with non-artistic occupations as much as with artistic occupations and vice versa. Overall, this lack of correlation may be a deterrent to a region's ability to establish an arts-based economy. Recent research does, however, indicate that there is reason to believe that a region's ability to cultivate a diverse artistic mix may be important in the production of artistic innovation and competitive advantage (Currid, 2006, 2007b).

Undoubtedly, there are particular artistic hubs that challenge these results, but these cities are rare, and may drive many of the outlining results presented (particularly our results on the maximum LQs). Only exceptionally concentrated and dense metropolitan regions tend to exhibit denser and more diverse correlation results. Los Angeles and New York have long been documented for having strong concentrations of various artistic industries and cultural workers that tend to feed off one another, sharing skills and cross-fertilizing (Currid, 2006; 2007a; Scott, 2000, 2005; Alliance for the Arts, 2007; LAEDC, 2007; Markusen and Schrock, 2009). That said, we believe that Los Angeles and New York are exceptions rather than the rule. As previous work has noted, lots of smaller cities have become significant specialized artistic hubs by cultivating distinct types of painting, writing or music (Markusen, 2004). In other words, Los Angeles and New York act as large global cultural and artistic hubs, while smaller locales around the country tend to contribute more specialized artistic production and skills. Thus, such niche tendencies must be taken into account in forming arts-oriented policy at the local level.

THIRTY LARGEST REGIONS

Artists and big cultural firms have long demonstrated a desire to locate in big cities. Due to the tendency for artistic industries and workers to disproportionately concentrate in big cities, we narrowed our analysis to look at just the top 30 metropolitan regions. We looked at the interplay between artistic occupations and industry as well as their interaction with non-artistic firms and skills. We used a similar approach with this more limited sample as that which we undertook for our general analysis. Below we discuss our results. In Tables 13.10 and 13.11 we present the summary statistics which demonstrate that overall the top 30 metropolitan regions are not significantly more concentrated as a whole in artistic occupations demonstrating that artists are not wholly a big city phenomenon. The industry results do, however, demonstrate a slightly greater concentration of arts industries in the biggest metropolitan regions. On the whole, the top 30 metropolitan regions are not significantly more represented in the arts than the nation as a whole, with the exception of New York and Los Angeles (Currid, 2006). As the standard deviations

Table 13.10   Summary statistics for national occupation data (n = 30 largest core-based statistical area)

Variable	N (metropolitan regions)	Mean employment	Standard deviation	Mean LQ	LQ standard deviation
Total employment	30	2 007 506	1 585 186		
Arts, design, entertainment, sports and media occupations (GROUP)	30	32 414	41 199	1.08	0.38
Actors	30	831	3937	0.43	1.58
Archivists	30	101	208	0.79	0.88
Art directors	30	677	1010	1.18	0.69
Choreographers	30	163	277	0.54	0.84
Commercial and industrial designers	30	600	940	1.14	1.68
Craft artists	30	20	36	0.33	0.56
Curators	30	122	155	0.84	0.82
Dancers	30	184	387	0.58	1.02
Editors	30	1946	3047	1.04	0.67
Fashion designers	30	376	1259	0.79	1.72
Fine artists, including painters, sculptors and illustrators	30	117	204	0.70	0.73
Multi-media artists and animators	30	569	923	1.20	1.03
Music directors and composers	30	114	285	0.70	1.10
Musicians and singers	30	855	1817	0.79	0.73
Photographers	30	397	577	0.42	0.54
Producers and directors	30	1311	2396	1.00	0.76
Writers and authors	30	854	1096	1.19	0.97

for LQ and mean employment demonstrate, there is significant variation across the 30 largest US metropolitan regions, which is reflected in the disproportionate concentration of film in Los Angeles, authors in San Francisco and art in New York City. With the exception of a few metropolitan regions, US cities are not all art-centric, but are instead driven by a few critical creative hubs.

What does the composition of metropolitan arts industries look like? The results are somewhat unsurprising. Overall, the arts industries in the top 30 metropolitan regions are comprised of the same occupations as that of the nation as a whole. The top five occupations in the arts are the same as those for the nation, with the exception of agents which are 3.32 per cent of arts jobs in the top metropolitan regions but are not in the top five for the nation. However, the representation of these occupations within the arts industries is distributed differently: artists are more prominently employed in arts industries in the nation overall (14.32 per cent, see Table 13.5 for national results) than in the top 30 metros (10 per cent, Table 13.12). Musicians are distributed almost exactly the same in the nation and top 30 metropolitan regions (13.11 per cent versus 12.10 per cent nationally). Actors and agents are more prominently employed in the arts in the

Table 13.11   *Summary statistics for industry employment data (*n = *30 largest core-based statistical area)*

Variable	N (metropolitan regions)	Mean metropolitan emp.	Standard deviation	Mean metropolitan estab. LQ	Standard deviation
Total employment	30	1 943 381	1 449 764		
Publishing industries (except Internet)	30	22 749	21 328	1.17	0.64
Motion picture and video industries	30	7412	20 159	0.94	1.35
Broadcasting (except Internet)	30	4942	6314	0.89	0.39
Performing arts, spectator sports and related industries	30	8745	10 770	1.11	0.52
Museums, historical sites and similar institutions	30	2384	2367	1.10	0.43
Amusement, gambling and recreation industries	30	23 334	15 512	1.15	0.72

Table 13.12   *Top five occupations within artistic industries (30 largest metropolitan regions)*

Industry	% of industry total	Occupation titles
Artists	13.11	Musicians, singers and related workers
	10.88	Writers and authors
	10.10	Artists and related workers
	8.54	Actors
	3.32	Agents and business managers of artists, performers and athletes
Broadcasting	10.48	Producers and directors
	6.21	Advertising sales agents
	5.12	Telecommunications line installers and repairers
	4.39	Broadcast and sound engineering technicians and radio operators
	4.37	Customer service representatives
Recording	14.77	Broadcast and sound engineering technicians and radio operators
	11.72	Musicians, singers and related workers
	8.12	Managers, all other
	4.62	Marketing and sales managers
	4.62	Producers and directors

biggest metropolitan regions, which may be a reflection of the disproportionate concentration of these workers in Los Angeles and New York (Scott, 2005; Currid, 2007b). The broadcasting industry's occupational composition is roughly the same across the metropolitan regions and nation, demonstrative of the ubiquity of the industry across

Table 13.13   Top five industries for artistic occupations (30 largest metropolitan regions)

Occupation	% of occupation total	Industry titles
Dancers	62.58	Independent artists, performing arts, spectator sports and related industries
	15.48	Drinking places, alcoholic beverages
	6.77	Other amusement, gambling and recreation industries
	3.23	Motion pictures and video industries
	2.90	Other schools, instruction and educational services
Entertainers	48.08	Independent artists, performing arts, spectator sports and related industries
	16.73	Other amusement, gambling and recreation industries
	11.54	Motion pictures and video industries
	4.62	Restaurants and other food services
	3.46	Other personal services
Musicians	59.77	Independent artists, performing arts, spectator sports and related industries
	17.06	Religious organizations
	4.77	Sound recording industries
	3.35	Restaurants and other food services
	1.93	Drinking places, alcoholic beverages

the United States. The recording industry is almost mirrored identically in rank and representation nationally and in the top 30 metropolitan regions, a surprising finding given the concentration of the music industry in major metropolitan areas. We speculate that these results are indicative of the basic occupational skills necessary in the recording industry regardless of place. The conclusion is similar for the broadcasting industry. Contrast these findings to arts industries which tend to specialize (art, fashion music and so forth) by locale, thus allowing for differences across place and population size of metropolitan region.

Industry data on the top 30 metropolitan regions reveals a different pattern than what is observed on the national level. Likely due to the greater representation of arts industries in top metropolitan regions, dancers are more likely to be employed in arts industries in the biggest cities than in the nation as a whole – 62.6 per cent (Table 13.13) versus 42.7 per cent. Musicians are also more likely to be employed by art industries in metropolitan regions than in the nation as a whole (59 per cent versus 46 per cent) and are much less likely to be employed by religious organizations in the biggest cities (17 per cent versus 31 per cent nationally). While the largest metropolitan areas are not more concentrated in artistic workers, as the summary statistics demonstrate, they are more likely to be centres of artistic industry. As mentioned earlier, the arts industries tend to be comprised of a multitude of occupational categories that are 'non-artistic' as well as artistic. Yet, the concentration of the arts industry in the top 30 metropolitan regions may enable artistic workers who are located in these places to have greater opportunity to work in an art industry.

IMPLICATIONS FOR RESEARCH AND PRACTICE

Economic development practice and research has become increasingly focused on the arts as an important part of local and regional growth. But both our research and development have been limited somewhat by our lack of understanding as regards the interaction of the arts and the composition of the arts in regional, national and local economies. We do not aim to recommend particular strategies for development; our intention has simply been to articulate the multiple ways in which the arts show up in the economy. We hope this helps inform practitioners in their efforts to employ and support the arts in development. We hope this chapter has conveyed that supporting the arts and employing them in development is far more nuanced than targeting arts industries and hoping that a rising tide raises all boats. Most fundamentally, what we have demonstrated is that artistic industries are not the same thing as an artistic skill base. Art industries need non-artists and artists work for non-artistic industries. These findings have implications for how to target development towards the arts along with how to cultivate the skill base and resources necessary for art industries to thrive.

Equally important is that these findings are not universal. While art industries do tend to have a general composition that appears consistent across various levels of aggregation, particular cities tend to have specializations and some metropolitan regions have greater concentrations of artistic employment opportunities. Thus, while the arts industries are primarily comprised by artists, musicians and writers across different geographies, certain hubs of artistic industrial activity are simply able to employ more of these workers than other locales and thus within these cities there are more artists working within the arts industries (Currid, 2007b).

Overall, there are four important findings in our analysis. First, current data analysis and collection approaches capture only one aspect of artistic and cultural economic distributions both locally and nationally. Second, there is wide variance in the types of industries that cultural occupations are present in and cultural workers tend to use their skills in many more industries than just those that would obviously require their skills (musicians, are for example, not all singing at the opera or at rock venues). Third, geographical concentration of industry is not an indication of occupation composition and vice versa. In fact, artistic industry and occupational concentrations do not in general co-locate. Fourth, particular cities, especially Los Angeles and New York, do act as artistic hubs for a wide variety of industries and occupations. These cities may drive some of the overall metropolitan results. Below we outline what we hope are important practical and research implications of this analysis.

Three-tier Data Collection and Analysis

As we discussed data limitations in depth earlier in this chapter, we will only briefly address our perspective here. As we have found, by collecting more data from a variety of sources we have not created redundancy but rather a more comprehensive and nuanced understanding of the arts. Further, the unique contribution that each dataset gives allows us to assess the linkages between skills and industries. In other words, a concentration of artists as found through OES data does not mean that these workers work in art industries but it takes looking at County Business Pattern and Census PUMS data to discover this finding and to figure out which sectors are employing them. Corroborating Barbour and Markusen's (2007) and Markusen's (2004) work, OES data may tell us about those artists working for firms that report to the BLS, but this data does not tell us anything about freelance artists, which are only captured through Census PUMS data. Thus, using datasets together allows both researchers and practitioners greater ability to study economic dynamics and in turn to inform local development.

Arts are Extraordinarily Place-specific

The national and 30 metropolitan regions analysis is useful in telling us some general skills and occupations that arts industries are comprised of and also something about the industries where artists find work. But when we look at specific case studies we find that cities are much more specialized. Actors thrive in Los Angeles but are less likely to find work in Cleveland. When we look at musicians nationally they are often employed by religious organizations, while in New York City many more work in the arts. Data on the local level gives us a much more meaningful perspective on what drives the local artistic economy and the industries and occupations of which it is comprised. Silicon Valley, initially a bastion of computer scientists and technology, has evolved into a centre of new media and video game production, largely using the same skills that pioneered its initial competitive advantage. Los Angeles has also become a leading centre for video game and new media technology, but this advantage is fuelled by its initial skills in film-making and animation. Thus development approaches for Silicon Valley and Los Angeles would require engaging different base industries and skills in each place in order to produce a similar end product. From an occupational perspective, particular types of workers with the same skills apply them to different industries depending on their locale. Writers in Los Angeles are essential to Hollywood films, while writers in New York may work in publishing. Artists in San Francisco contribute to new media; artists in New York work in the fine arts or in public relations. More to the point, skills (of all sorts) are applied to many different industries, and industry composition is different depending on where the industry and skills are located.

Industry Does Not Beget Skills and Vice Versa

Our LQ correlation analysis indicates that not only are industries and occupations diverse in their composition and inter-linkages, but that artistic industrial concentration is not synonymous with artistic skill concentration and vice versa. In other words, our LQ analysis suggests that, bar Los Angeles and New York, there is overall little evidence that artistic industries or artistic occupations cluster together. Particular places have niche specializations in particular types of artistic skills and/or industries, but skills and industries are not strongly correlated or predictive of one another. Santa Fe may possess sculptors or fine artists but that does not imply that the region also has a strong representation in actors or musicians. The cross-fertilization and overall artistic economy tends to be in Los Angeles and New York City (Scott, 1996; Currid, 2007a). These two cities possess a great preponderance of artistic industries and occupations, but these locales are the exception, not the rule. On the whole, having a strong concentration in a particular artistic sector or skill does not imply an overarching concentration of artistic activity or specialization in another cultural industry.

Similarly, the Herfindahl indices show that the variance across industries in which artists participate is vast and diverse. The skill composition of cultural industries is driven by a variety of artistic and non-artistic occupations. Thus, efforts to promote artists may involve supporting non-artistic industries that employ them. Artistic industries tend to be extremely varied in their skill sets, and artistic skills are used for many different industries.

Overall, we hope this analysis informs research and by extension practical approaches to studying and developing the arts. Art and culture are some of the most complicated occupations and industries to study, partially because artistic skills are needed in many different industrial sectors. Equally important, despite art's reputation as being wildly creative and organic, fundamentally it depends on a wide industrial and skill infrastructure to distribute itself to a larger marketplace. Thus, in our efforts to understand the arts in national, regional and local economies, we must recognize that not only are the arts and artists not the same, but that both also require 'non-artistic' skills and industries in order to realize their creative and economic potential.

NOTES

1. The Herfindahl Index:

$$H = \sum_{i=1}^{N} S_i^2$$

s_i = percentage of occupation or industry i and N = the number of occupations/industries.
2. Because our results here were rather underwhelming, we only briefly discuss some of the results in the text. The full correlation results are available from the authors upon request.
3. $LQ = (OR/TER)/(ON/TEN)$ where OR = regional occupational employment; TER = total regional employment; ON = national occupational employment; TEN = total national employment.

REFERENCES

Alliance for the Arts (2007), *Arts as an Industry: Their Economic Impact on New York City and New York State*, New York, NY: Alliance for the Arts.
Americans for the Arts (2004), *Creative Industries Study*, Washington, DC.
Audretsch, D.B. and M.P. Feldman (1996), 'Knowledge spillovers and the geography of innovation and production', *American Economic Review*, **86**, 630–40.
Barbour, E. and A. Markusen (2007), 'Regional occupational and industrial structure: does one imply the other?', *International Regional Science Review*, **30**(1),72–90.
Blumer, H. (1969), 'Fashion: from class differentiation to collective selection', *Sociological Quarterly*, **10**, 275–91.
Carr, J. and L.Servon (2007), 'Cultural authenticity and urban economic development', presentation at the ACSP Annual Meeting, Milwaukee, WI, October.
Castells, M. (2000), *The Rise of the Network Society* (2nd edn), New York, NY: Blackwell.
Clark, T.N. (2004), *The City as an Entertainment Machine*, Oxford: Elsevier.
Currid, E. (2006), 'New York as a global creative hub: a competitive analysis of four theories on world cities', *Economic Development Quarterly*, **20**(4), 330–50.
Currid, E. (2007a), *The Warhol Economy: How Fashion, Art and Music Drive New York City*, Princeton, NJ: Princeton University Press.

Currid, E. (2007b), 'How art and culture happen in New York: implications for urban economic development', *Journal of the American Planning Association*, **73**(4), 454–67.

Currid, E. and S. Williams (2010), 'Two cities, five industries: similarities and differences within and between cultural industries in New York and Los Angeles', *Journal of Planning Education and Research*, **29**, 322–35.

Evans, G. (2003), 'Hard-branding the cultural city – from Prado to Prada', *International Journal of Urban and Regional Research*, **27**(2), 417–40.

Feser, E.J. (2003), 'What regions do rather than make: a proposed set of knowledge-based occupation clusters', *Urban Studies*, **40**(10), 1937–58.

Florida, R. (2002a), *The Rise of the Creative Class: And How It's Transforming Work, Leisure, Community and Everyday Life*, New York, NY: Basic Books.

Florida, R. (2002b), 'Bohemia and economic geography', *Journal of Economic Geography*, **2**(1), 55–71.

Glaeser, E., J. Kolko and A. Saiz (2001), 'Consumer city', *Journal of Economic Geography*, **1**(1), 27–50.

Grodach, C. and A. Loukaitou-Sideris (2007), 'Cultural development strategies and urban revitalization', *International Journal of Cultural Policy*, **13**(4), 349, doi:10.1080/10286630701683235.

Judd, D.R and S.S Fainstein (1999), *The Tourist City*, New Haven, CT: Yale University Press.

Keegan, R., N. Kleiman, B. Seigel and M. Kane (2005), *Creative New York*, New York, NY: Center for an Urban Future.

Koo, J. (2005), 'How to analyze the regional economy with occupation data', *Economic Development Quarterly*, **19**(4), 356.

LAEDC (2007), *Report on the Creative Economy of the Los Angeles Region*, Los Angeles County Economic Development Corporation, Prepared for Otis College of Art and Design, Los Angeles, CA, 1 March.

Lloyd, R. (2005), *Neo-bohemia: Art and Commerce in the Postindustrial City*, New York, NY: Routledge.

Markusen, A. (2004), 'The distinctive city: evidence from artists and occupational profiles', Project on Regional and Industrial Economics, University of Minnesota.

Markusen, A. and D. King (2003), 'The artistic dividend: the arts' hidden contributions to regional development', Project on Regional and Industrial Economics, Humphrey Institute of Public Affairs, University of Minnesota, July.

Markusen, A. and G. Schrock (2006a), 'The distinctive city: divergent patterns in growth, hierarchy and specialization', *Urban Studies*, **43**(8), 1301–23.

Markusen, A. and G. Schrock (2006b), 'The artistic dividend: urban specialization and economic development implications', *Urban Studies*, **43**(10), 1661–86.

Markusen, A. and G. Schrock (2009), 'Consumption-driven urban development', *Urban Geography*, **30**(4), 344–67.

Markusen, A., G. Schrock and M. Cameron (2004), 'The artistic dividend revisited', Project on Regional and Industrial Economics, Humphrey Institute of Public Affairs, University of Minnesota, March.

Markusen, A., S. Gilmore, A. Johnson, T. Levi and A. Martinez (2006), 'Crossover: how artists build careers across commercial, nonprofit and community work', Project on Regional and Industrial Economics, Humphrey Institute of Public Affairs, University of Minnesota.

Markusen, A., G.H. Wassall, D. DeNatale and R. Cohen (2008), 'Defining the creative economy: industry and occupational approaches', *Economic Development Quarterly*, **22**(1), 24–45.

Massey, D. (1984), *Spatial Divisions of Labor*, New York, NY: Metheun.

Molotch, H. (1996), 'L.A. as design product: how art works in a regional economy', in A.J. Scott and E.W. Soja (eds), *The City: Los Angeles and Urban Theory at the End of the Twentieth Century*, Los Angeles: University of California Press, pp. 225–75.

Molotch, H. (2002), 'Place in product', *International Journal of Urban and Regional Research*, **26**, 665–88.

National Endowment for Science, Technology and the Arts (NESTA) (2008), *Beyond the Creative Industries*, London: NESTA.

Nelson, M.K. (2003), 'Producer services, agglomeration economies and intra-metropolitan location: the public accounting industry in the Chicago and Minneapolis-St. Paul regions', PhD dissertation, Rutgers University.

Otis College and LAEDC (2007), *Report on the Creative Economy of the Los Angeles Region*, prepared by the Los Angeles Economic Development Corporation for the Otis College of Art and Design.

Plaza, B. (2006), 'The return on investment of the Guggenheim Museum Bilbao', *International Journal of Urban and Regional Research*, **30**(2), 452–67.

Porter, M.E. (1998), 'Clusters and the new economics of competition', *Harvard Business Review*, **76**(6), 77–90.

Renski, H., J. Koo and E. Feser (2007), 'Differences in labor versus value chain industry clusters: an empirical investigation', *Growth and Change*, **38**(3), 364–95.

Robinson, D. (1961), 'The economics of fashion demand', *Quarterly Journal of Economics*, **75**, 376–98.

Sassen, S. and F. Roost (1999), 'The city: strategic site for the global entertainment industry', in D. Judd and S. Fainstein (eds), *The Tourist City*, New Haven, CT: Yale University Press, pp. 143–54.

Scott, A. (1996), 'The craft, fashion and cultural products industries of Los Angeles', *Annals of the Association of American Geographers*, **86**, 306–23.

Scott, A. (2000), *The Cultural Economy of Cities*, London: Sage.

Scott, A. (2005), *Hollywood: The Place, the Industry*, Princeton, NJ: Princeton University Press.

Simmel, G. (1904), 'Fashion', *American Journal of Sociology*, **52,** 541–8.

Stolarick, K. and R. Florida (2007), 'Creativity, connections and innovation: a study of linkages in the Montréal region', *Environment and Planning A*, **38**(10), 1799–817.

Strom, E. (2002), 'Converting pork into porcelain: cultural institutions and downtown development', *Urban Affairs Review*, **38**(1), 3–21.

Thompson, W.R. and P.R. Thompson (1985), 'From industries to occupations: rethinking local economic development', *Economic Development Commentary*, **9**(3), 12–18.

Veblen, T. [1899] (1994), *The Theory of the Leisure Class,* New York: Penguin Classics.

Wassell, G.H. and D. DeNatale (1997), *Arts, Cultural and Humanities in the New England Economy*, 1996, Boston, MA: New England Foundation for the Arts.

Zukin, S. (1989), *Loft Living: Culture and Capital in Urban Change*, New Brunswick, NJ: Rutgers University Press.

14 The creative potential of network cities
David F. Batten

Some creative regions in the world consist of a functionally cohesive web of not-too-distant settlements. Classic examples are Randstad Holland and the Kansai region of Japan (Figure 14.1). Other polycentric urban agglomerations are appearing in North America, such as New Mexico's Technology Triangle (T2) clustered around Albuquerque, Santa Fe and Los Alamos. Have these urban agglomerations formed because the suburban boundaries of nearby cities and towns have simply spread outwards and almost bumped into each other? Do the more creative ones possess unique economic, cultural and infrastructural properties that provide them with key comparative advantages over their monocentric rivals? Does each settlement in these urban networks gain from dynamic synergies, such as reciprocal growth (through co-operative knowledge exchange) and the shared benefits of complementarity and creativity. Perhaps there are other explanations?

In some earlier papers, I referred to these phenomena as 'network cities' because of the dynamic, networking process by which their polycentric structure evolved.[1] To a large extent, this process was one of concentrated deconcentration. I called them network cities to avoid using the term 'polycentric'. The problem with 'polycentric' is that it can refer to intra-urban clusters of population and economic activity – such as in London, Paris or Los Angeles, for example – or to interurban patterns – as in the Dutch Randstad or Japan's Kansai region (for more a more detailed discussion, see Davidi, 2003; Parr, 2004). Most large cities are polycentric. Since my focus was only on interurban patterns of reciprocal co-operation and complementarity between historically independent cities and towns, to avoid any confusion I chose the term 'network city' to distinguish this specific class of polycentric urban settlements.[2]

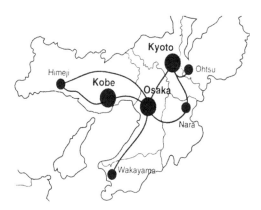

Figure 14.1   The Kansai region

In earlier papers, I considered the dynamic potential of network cities in comparison with cites displaying monocentricity (sometimes known as the central place model). Interest in the former has increased recently, partly because certain configurations of network cities may generate less congestion and pollution and offer greater accessibility, diversity and creativity than monocentric cities of a similar size. Also, several recent contributions to urban economics have supplied valuable modelling frameworks that (eventually) could provide a stronger economic rationale for network cities from an analytical viewpoint – especially in a carbon-driven economy (cf. Fujita and Mori, 1997; Mun, 1997; Tabuchi, 1998).

Noting the advantages of concentrated deconcentration several decades ago, Peter Hall (1984, pp. 114–15) claimed that many of the world cities of our time may be at a disadvantage in comparison with a network city like Randstad Holland. Does the Dutch experience carry a message for the citizens and planners of world cities such as New York, London, Paris or Tokyo? It is unlikely that a network city can derive creative advantages purely from its polycentric form. As Hall noted, the British thought that the answer to the problem of metropolitan growth was the green belt. Yet the green belt is well suited only to a city with a static population. When placed within a rapidly growing population, such a belt creates and suffers from many problems. Because of the need to plan for growth, the Dutch rejected the green belt in favour of the corridor extension and the green heart. For most of the still-growing world cities of our time, it seems likely that adaptive solutions could be very worthwhile. Thus the network city model warrants closer scrutiny.

This chapter begins by discussing some creative urban regions in Europe. Interestingly, about half of these regions seem to be evolving into network cities. Part of the rationale for this may be improved international access to the creative arts, higher education, Research and development (R&D) activities and high-technology industries. Better access also comes from more efficient transport networks: air, fast rail and road. Then I summarize the evolutionary development of a classical network city: Randstad Holland. My historical analysis reveals a dual rationale for its polycentric structure. The twin forces of chance and necessity have intermingled over time. Other factors which turn out to be highly relevant in our analysis of network cities include the conflicting forces of spatial agglomeration and dispersion, geographical proximity and commuting time, transport costs, diversity and complementarity of functions, land prices and access to quality green space. This chapter concludes with a brief and speculative assessment of prospects for the development of a creative European system of transnational network cities in the future.

EUROPE'S CREATIVE NETWORK CITIES

Previous studies of evolving European regions have shown that knowledge-intensive activities are important for a regional economy, and that these activities tend to grow faster in regions with a university and good accessibility by fast transport – air, rail and road. Urban regions that have a very strong commitment to R&D and creativity, together with efficient access to modern communications and air transport, often lead the way in terms of economic performance indicators such as regional productivity

Table 14.1   The ten most important creative regions of Europe

Metropolitan region	Scientific creativity	Air transport capacity
1. London-Cambridge	100	100
2. Paris	70	69
3. Randstad Holland	33	25
4. Bonn-Dusseldorf-Cologne	33	21
5. Stockholm-Uppsala	26	23
6. Brussels-Leuven-Ghent	24	12
7. Frankfurt-Mainz-Giessen	22	42
8. Munich	22	17
9. Heidelberg-Karlsruhe-Stuttgart	22	17
10. Copenhagen	19	21

Source: Adapted from Andersson and Persson (1993).

(Anderstig and Hårsman, 1986; Andersson et al., 1990; Andersson and Persson, 1993). Some outperform classical cities that rely predominantly on manufacturing activity.

Table 14.1 suggests that five of these creative urban regions have a settlement structure that is polycentric. Also, London and Stockholm are strategically linked to nearby towns with high R&D capabilities. Despite the fact that the initial nodes (towns and cities) developed independently, today they are more or less partners. Efficient corridors of transport and communications infrastructure link the larger metropolises to each other, to smaller human settlements and to green space. In most cases, transport infrastructure is enhanced by the presence of an airport of international standing. Some smaller settlements may be university towns or centres of knowledge-intensive activity (such as R&D or high-tech manufacturing). Network cities of this kind include Randstad Holland, Bonn-Dusseldorf-Cologne, Brussels-Leuven-Ghent, Frankfurt-Mainz-Giessen and Karlsruhe-Heidelberg-Stuttgart. London-Cambridge and Stockholm-Uppsala may be thought of as corridor cities. Several old university towns – Cambridge, Heidelberg, Leiden and Uppsala – have been incorporated into these modern urban networks of creative activity.

At each of these locations, network cities have reached different stages of development.[3] The close geographical proximity of the settlements involved allows them to benefit from the dynamic synergies of interactive growth via reciprocity, knowledge exchange and unexpected innovations. Moreover, they can achieve significant scope economies, aided by fast and reliable corridors of transport and communications infrastructure. Each of these regions places a relatively high priority on knowledge-based activities: research, education and the creative arts. It is noteworthy that a majority of these creative regions are corridor or network cities. In each such agglomeration, closely co-operative links have been forged between places of complementary function or knowledge creation, not simply on the basis of demand thresholds.

How did these particular regions develop their creative, networking relationships? To what extent was their polycentric structure planned in advance or triggered by chance events, such as the vagaries of political decision-making? Or was it inevitable that they would evolve into network cities because they fulfil some key social, cultural, spatial and economic conditions? Before we try to answer these questions, there is much to be learnt by taking a closer look at the evolutionary history of the most mature network city listed in Table 14.1. This is the task of the next section.

THE EVOLUTION OF A NETWORK CITY: RANDSTAD HOLLAND

The classical European network city is Randstad Holland, meaning 'rim' or 'edge' city according to the Dutch translation. This designates an urban area at the edge of a circle with empty space in the middle. Shaped like a giant horseshoe, this complex urban region runs from Dordrecht (south-east of Rotterdam) via Rotterdam to the coast at the Hook of Holland. Then it turns right, taking in The Hague and Delft. A coastal belt incorporates the towns of Leiden and Haarlem, as well as many small seaside resorts. To the north of Haarlem, it turns right again and runs inland to Amsterdam. Then it traverses the high ground to Hilversum and finally converges on Utrecht and the surrounding hill area (Figure 14.2).[4]

As late as 1795, only Amsterdam could boast more than 200 000 people. No other city in the Netherlands had reached even 60 000. How, then, did all these towns and cities grow and change to form such a remarkable network city? Historically speaking, the seeds of a network city may have been sown with revolutions in transport, trade and industry during the nineteenth century. A decade or so after the first Dutch steamship arrived in 1825, the first Dutch railway line was built between Amsterdam and Haarlem. When the German empire became a reality in 1871, the Ruhr began its period of prodigious growth into the greatest industrial area of Europe (Hall, 1984, pp. 91–2). As Germany rose to industrial might, the Netherlands rose with it to commercial power.

Thus began an urban transformation of an unusual kind. The first town to challenge Amsterdam's primacy was Rotterdam, which benefited greatly from the building of a sea canal known as the New Waterway in 1872. As its population rose four-fold between

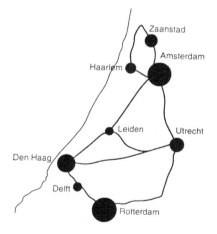

Figure 14.2   The Randstad region

Table 14.2   Growth and decline within Randstad Holland, c.1650–1995

City or town	Population (thousands)					
	c. 1650	*c.* 1795	1850	1900	1947	1995
Amsterdam	115	201	225	510	804	720
Rotterdam	30	58	112	368	646	595
The Hague	17	41	65	236	533	443
Leiden	45	31	36	54	87	116
Haarlem	39	21	26	65	157	212
Utrecht	22	32	49	104	185	548

Source: Hall (1984, p. 92) and Statistics Netherlands.

1850 and 1913, it replaced Amsterdam as the first port of the Netherlands in about 1900. At the same time, The Hague benefited from an unprecedented growth of power in terms of the functions of central government, to such an extent that its population also increased four-fold between 1850 and 1913. The evolutionary progress of the six largest Randstad settlements is recorded in Table 14.2. Rotterdam and The Hague grew respectively from 29 per cent and 20 per cent of Amsterdam's size in 1795, to 83 per cent and 62 per cent in 1995. More significantly, the distance between the boundaries of each urban agglomeration shortened appreciably. Today the cities and towns have converged so closely to each other that we may speak of the Randstad as a mature network city. With Schiphol airport located near its centre, it has evolved into one of the most accessible urban regions in the world. As such, it may be viewed as the earliest agglomeration to possess both network city and world city characteristics (Shachar, 1994).

As Peter Hall has stressed, this is a metropolitan region of a different nature and order from other world cities such as New York, London, Paris or Tokyo. The Dutch themselves stress the essential difference which, they claim, gives them a real advantage in planning for continued growth. It is that the traditional functions of an urban centre – government, trading and financial institutions – are not all concentrated in one centre but are dispersed into several, which still remain physically separate despite their proximity to each other. Specifically, the government function is fixed in The Hague; the port and wholesaling function – along with the heavy industry that accompanies it – are located in Rotterdam; and the financial functions, along with many cultural and retail functions and a wide range of port industries and light manufacturing, are in Amsterdam. This is the basis of the network city model: functional (non-hierarchical) complementarity between nodes.

Amsterdam is the capital city, but it is not the seat of government. There is a contrast between the entrepôt functions of Rotterdam and Amsterdam, on the one hand, and the orientations towards the government (The Hague) and the national economy (Utrecht), on the other. Enormous expansion of the lighter manufacturing industries, characteristic of all urban development in the twentieth century, has not been channelled into an amorphous ring around a single city. Instead it has gone mostly into towns that are quite separate from the big three but within easy reach of them. Prominent among these are Leiden, Haarlem and the area known as Het Gooi around Hilversum.

Can Randstad Holland claim to be a truly creative network city? One thing it can claim is to be a seat of learning. Throughout the seventeenth and eighteenth centuries, most continental scholars viewed Leiden as the greatest of the European universities (Grafton, 1988). The influential French *Encyclopédie* called Leiden 'the first Academy in all of Europe'. Students from the entire Protestant world – England and Scotland, Sweden and Prussia – used to crowd into Leiden's few lecture halls and cramped lodging houses. Historians have drawn attention to the development of new subjects with a bearing on Holland's commercial expansion – above all, Oriental languages and international law. They emphasized that Leiden's university helped Holland become the greatest intellectual intermediary between Northern and Southern, Eastern and Western Europe.

At about the same time, the city of Amsterdam was responding to the need for reliable banks to protect the growing transactions associated with trade. At the start of the seventeenth century, the governors of Amsterdam made a spectacular innovation by establishing an officially guaranteed central bank. Merchants could deposit silver coins in the bank in exchange for officially guaranteed bank notes which could be used in international trade. This innovation led to other banks following Amsterdam's example, and confirmation that Amsterdam was Europe's leading financial centre. Thus the seed of a creative and innovative Dutch network of nearby cities was planted initially in the city of Amsterdam and the university town of Leiden.

Today, Amsterdam is the creative driving hub of the Randstad with its 24-hour economy, liberalization of cannabis, sexual freedom, unusual artists and a vibrant music scene. A multitude of cultures and languages are spoken there. Beginning in 2002, researchers at the University of Amsterdam used random sampling to chart where knowledge workers employed in Amsterdam live (Arnoldus and Musterd, 2002; Groenemeijer, 2002; Lukey and van der Steenhoven, 2004). A striking feature of the results was the large groups extending well outside Amsterdam, with a clear concentration within the northern wing of the Randstad. This wing stretches from Zandvoort to Almere and from Castricum to Blaricum. Other Amsterdam knowledge workers live in the city itself, concentrated in the north–south axis that runs from the banks of the river Ij via the centre and south Amsterdam to Amstelveen. This is the traditional high-status axis that established itself in Amsterdam during the twentieth century.

Over the last few decades, a major topic in the Randstad is the conflict between the cities and the nearby towns. These towns are known as the *Groene Hart* (Green Heart) and are mostly much greener than the cities. The tendency has been to expand westwards to the Old West and Westerpark districts, where many commuters who work in the cities are housed. There are further concentrations in the Gooi and Kennemerland, as well as in cities like Zaanstad and Almere. Artists and architects are over-represented in areas close to the city centre of Amsterdam, while university professors live in the centre or outside the city. Those working in the information and communications technology (ICT) sector display a strong preference for the suburbs or other parts of the Randstad when it comes to housing.

When the main centre of knowledge and creativity (Amsterdam) is compared with other Dutch cities as a place for the creative class to live, the capital does not outshine them in all respects. In the *Atlas voor Gemeenten* (Atlas for local authorities), Amsterdam is only eighth when the size of its creative class is measured as a percentage of its population. This is probably true of many world cities, including New York, London,

Paris or Tokyo. In the case of the Randstad, Utrecht has the highest percentage of creative knowledge workers, closely followed by Leiden and Nijmegen. The Hague and Rotterdam are well behind Amsterdam, Utrecht and many medium-sized cities when it comes to attracting the creative class and its subgroups. This suggests that many creative knowledge workers prefer to live in or near places where there are many creative and knowledge-intensive jobs (Amsterdam and Utrecht) or outside the bigger cities in the smaller, greener towns. Many of the creative class prove to be ordinary people in other respects: they too want to avoid traffic jams, live in qualitatively nice homes, and be able to enjoy both nature and culture without having to travel very far to reach them. Thus the diversity of the Randstad appeals in different ways to different members of its creative class.

Historically, the Randstad also has a history of competition. Rotterdam and Amsterdam compete on many levels, from football to art. Lately, the cultural sector has tried to limit this rivalry and search for mutual strengths. Two of the main cultural organizations in Amsterdam, the Concertgebouw and Holland Festival, have joined forces with similar organizations in Rotterdam, by way of *ARdam*.[5] In 2007, these organizations published a manifesto with plans for co-operation. One of their goals is to strengthen the international position of culture and art in the Netherlands in the international context. Taken together, Amsterdam and Rotterdam can boast the leading cultural repertoire in the country, with a variety of creative disciplines of international quality, such as architecture, design, music and theatre. By cultural co-operation and joint investments, they aim to strengthen the power of the reciprocal combination of the two centres, and thereby play a leading role in the strengthening of the cultural and creative infrastructure within the Randstad.

However, the Randstad faces several daunting problems. Perhaps the worst of these is growing traffic congestion. Despite a strong belief (by all the agencies responsible for policy initiatives) that travel times between agglomerations in the Randstad can be lower than those in the mononuclear prototypes of London and Paris, congestion has increased steadily since 1965. One would expect better, given the tripling of the length of national roads since that time. But the Randstad has the largest share of congested roads in the Netherlands – having 41 of 2001's 50 most problematic congestion spots in their national road network (see Meijers et al., 2003, pp. 38–9).

Notwithstanding this congestion, the quality of infrastructure within the Randstad is of a higher standard than most of Europe. A dense network of motorways is coupled with a dense network of fast trains with frequent connections. This is supported by second-to-none accessibility to the rest of the world, through the world's biggest port and one of the major European hub airports, as well as plenty of inland water transport.

A DUAL RATIONALE FOR NETWORK CITY FORMATION

Let us now return to the questions posed earlier. There we asked how a network city's constituent settlements initiate co-operation and develop complementary relationships. Are they purely the outcome of chance events or is it inevitable that such not-too-distant places will evolve towards a network city if they satisfy some key (yet to be determined) preconditions?

With the hindsight of Randstad Holland's developmental history at our fingertips, we can rephrase the above question as follows: if certain key events in European history had been different, would the network structure of the Randstad differ in a significant way? More specifically, if the Ruhr had not grown so prodigiously as an industrial area in the nineteenth century, thereby enabling the Rhine to become Europe's major waterway for commercial trade, could different 'chance events' have created a different set of Dutch settlements to the ones that we have today? This amounts to asking if Randstad Holland's deconcentrated pattern of industrial and residential location (as described in the previous section) follows a path that depends purely upon history.

As Brian Arthur (1987, 1994; see also Batten, 2000a) notes, two profoundly different views on this issue prevailed among the great German school of industry location theorists in the early part of the twentieth century. The first – which we can associate with the names of Johann Heinrich von Thünen, (the early) Alfred Weber, Andread Predöhl, Walter Christaller, August Lösch and Walter Isard – regarded any geographical assignment of industry as preordained, by geographical endowments, transport possibilities, firms' needs and the spatial distribution of rents and prices that these induced. In this view, the resulting locational pattern was a natural equilibrium and history did not matter. Since the equilibrium outcome was unique, it was inevitable. The observed locational pattern of industry was seen as a predictable solution to a well-defined spatial economic problem.

The second view, which threaded its way less explicitly through the writings of (the later) Weber, Oskar Engländer, Hans Ritschl and Tord Palander, saw industry location as being path-dependent. Thus it was more like a living organism or ecosystem. New industry was laid down upon, and strongly influenced by, inherited locational patterns and assets already set in place. Spatial endowments and transport possibilities were still important, especially for Weber, but the main driving forces here were agglomeration economies – the benefits of being close to other firms or to concentrations of industry. In this view, the early firms arriving by 'historical accident' might establish themselves in locations that were attractive for geographical reasons. Later firms were then attracted to those same places by the very presence of the early locators, rather than the geography. Industry ends up clustered in the early-chosen places. But this outcome is never unique. A different set of early pioneers might have steered the chosen pattern into a different outcome. Thus settlement history is crucial.

Two viewpoints thus prevailed – one dependent on history, the other preordained. We could call them 'chance' and 'necessity' (Table 14.3). These two views would explain Randstad Holland's emergent pattern somewhat differently. Necessity (also called the determinism school) would argue that the Randstad's polycentric structure is a result of geographical proximity, transport efficiencies and improved accessibility to the rest of the world. By way of contrast, chance (or historical dependence) would see the Randstad as the outcome of a set of unexpected events – like the transport revolution and an emerging dominance of the Rhine as Europe's principal waterway for commercial traffic. Such key events combined to fuel the rapid growth of Rotterdam and The Hague (as administrative centre) during the nineteenth century. Adopting this stance, it could be argued that chance events gave Rotterdam the edge over Amsterdam as the key Dutch port.[6] From there on, perceived opportunities for functional complementarity among the closely spaced Dutch towns and cities triggered a self-reinforcing pattern of concentrated deconcentration.

Table 14.3   Chance and necessity in urban development

Necessity	Chance
Stasis	Morphogenesis
Deterministic	Stochastic or path-dependent
Mechanistic (Newtonian)	Organic (Darwinian)
Unique outcome (equilibrium)	Multiple possible outcomes
Predictable	Unpredictable
Diminishing returns	Increasing returns
Convex	Non-convex
Easy to model	Difficult to model
A SIMPLE WORLD	A COMPLEX WORLD

Source: Batten (2000a, p. 39).

Which view is correct? Both are to some extent, but they are intertwined together. It is likely that a complex system like a network city is only partly the result of spatial and economic factors such as intercity distances, transport costs, land prices and green space. It will also be the result of what kings or emperors decreed, or where politicians dictated that canals, roads and airports be built, or where some creative people decided to settle (cf. Florida, 2002). Recent insights provided by non-linear dynamic systems theory have confirmed that any human settlement's future path of development cannot be predicted in advance.[7] At the end of the eighteenth century, for example, who could have predicted that Rotterdam's population would double in the first half of the nineteenth century, while Amsterdam's would hardly change at all? If a settlement's future development cannot be predicted, no compact, law-like description of its evolution can be found.[8] Thus it is unlikely to reach or remain at the kind of stable equilibrium that determinism often implies. There are too many other possible pathways and attractor states.

Sometimes, one of these two viewpoints – chance or necessity – appears to outweigh the other. For example, a highly creative network city has been developing over the last few decades in the Kansai region of Japan. The key driving forces behind this new network city initiative do not appear to be any chance events in history, but a shared desire on the part of a powerful group of the leading residents of this historically powerful region of Japan to see it compete more effectively with its larger rival, Tokyo. The chosen strategy is to transform the Osaka Bay Area into a 'cosmo-creative metropolis' (Yoshikawa, 1993) that is to be qualitatively different from its key rival. Clearly, the Osaka Bay Area is gaining more confidence in its ability to offer a more attractive suite of creative activities and amenities of global significance than its larger rival.

Like the Dutch Randstad, the Kansai region is shaped like a giant horseshoe – in this case encircling Osaka Bay. It is made up of the six prefectures of Osaka, Hyogo, Kyoto, Nara, Wakayama and Shiga. Each prefecture adds to the rich diversity of the Kansai region in that each possesses its own distinctive cultural and historical identity. Although this may have caused a lack of cohesion in the decades when Tokyo was growing dominant, today this cultural diversity might unlock the key to a more prosperous future.

The core cities of the Kansai region are depicted in Figure 14.1. Fast and efficient transport links ensure that the smaller cities of Himeji, Nara, Otsu and Wakayama are integrated within easy reach of the larger trio – Osaka, Kyoto and Kobe. The cultural richness and creative diversity of the region can be gauged from the fact that it contains two former imperial capitals of Japan: Nara and Kyoto. It is some 12 centuries since Nara, then known as Heijō, was the imperial capital. Although it remained so for only 74 years, many temples, historical buildings and the ancient plan still remain in central Nara. It has become a pilgrimage city, with millions of visitors attracted annually to the great temples that once dominated local politics and religion and still dominate the visual scene today. Fascinatingly, it remains as a key example of China's strictly geometrical approach to city planning (a rectangular grid pattern), fostered in Japan during the Yin dynasty.

Being far more fortunate than Nara, Kyoto remained Japan's capital for 11 centuries. Kyoto's influence peaked during the Tokugawa period (1568–1867), stemming mostly from the fact that it was the only metropolis in Japan prior to the seventeenth century. During this time, the great cities of Kyoto, Osaka and Edo (Tokyo) became known collectively as the 'Three Metropolises' (*santo*). They had large, highly developed communication systems for disseminating new information – political, economic and cultural. According to Moriya (1990), all three cities played roles of great importance to Japan at that time, but advanced culture and creativity developed earlier in western Japan, principally in Kyoto.

Kyoto was not only the seat of imperial government (from the eighth century), but also the greatest industrial city in the early modern period. This was mainly because of its high-quality textile production – spinning, dyeing and weaving – which made up the largest and finest handicraft industry in Japan. Kyoto was also advanced in the field of design, in which the accumulation of knowledge had been continuous from ancient times (Moriya, 1990). Thus the city enjoyed overwhelming superiority, with its advanced understanding of textiles and design spreading nationwide during the eighteenth century, raising the quality of both. Also, Kyoto was the cultural centre, being the hub of Japan's scholarship, letters and religious thought. This great concentration of scholars, writers and artists forms an impressive accumulated legacy, still attracting numerous scholars and artists from other parts of the nation. Given the proximity of Kyoto to Osaka and Nara, one is tempted to speculate on whether the seeds of Kansai's creative network city of today might have been sown as far back as the seventeenth century.[9]

It is interesting to consider the growth and change of Japan's national system of cities over the last four centuries. As the largest city in Japan, Kyoto was first surpassed by Osaka and then by Tokyo towards the end of the sixteenth century (Table 14.4). In the pre-war years, Kyoto traded places with Kobe and Nagoya for the positions of fourth and fifth largest cites. In 1947, it revived to be the third largest, but its population has declined ever since. By 1960 it had fallen to fifth again and by 2000 it had dropped to seventh. Meanwhile, Yokohama moved past Osaka to become the second largest Japanese city in 1980.

This juxtaposition of city rankings might leave the impression that both Osaka and Kyoto have declined in national importance, possibly at the hands of Tokyo and Yokohama. But the truth of the transition is more subtle. By declaring and striving for Kansai to become a 'cosmo-creative' network city, people in Osaka, Kyoto and Kobe are intending to combine their two great assets to attract more foreign visitors and international attention: (1) their historically unique endowment in heritage buildings and the

Table 14.4   Nighttime population in Japanese cities and major metropolitan areas (MMAs)

City/MMA	Population (thousands)		
	c. 1600	1800	2000
Osaka	360	383	2595
Kyoto	300	377	1454
Kobe	N/A	N/A	1492
Nara	N/A	N/A	365
Keihanshin	N/A	N/A	18644
Tokyo (Edo)	60	685	12060
Keihin'yo	N/A	N/A	34493

Source: Statistics Bureau of Japan and Wikipedia.

creative arts, and (2) their highly efficient roads, airports, seaports and teleports. For example, it is often said that the Kansai area has a better road network than Tokyo-Yokohama.

A 'cosmo-creative network city' is defined in terms of its suite of creative skills, activities and functional characteristics. In Kansai's case, the historical centres of Kyoto and Nara serve as key attractors for many artists and international events such as exhibitions, conventions and conferences. Also, they provide a cultural heritage to complement the seaport cities of Kobe and Osaka. Osaka is also the region's centre of commerce and industrial activity. The striking contrasts between this complementary system of cultural, trading, commercial and industrial centres, combined with their enthusiastic willingness to work together towards a unified vision of the future, could transform the Kansai region into one of the most exciting and creative network cities of the twenty-first century.

Although we suggested earlier that chance events did not seem to play a part in Kansai's evolution towards a network city, this was an oversimplification. If Nara and Kyoto had not served as the national capital, thereby accumulating a rich legacy of historically important buildings, temples, artifacts and creative skills, such a rich vein of cultural capital on which to build a network city of the future would never have materialized. So, once again, we see that history does matter. Those chance events that led to Nara and Kyoto becoming the imperial capitals of Japan, and those that led to the retention of much of their cultural capital after their demise, have combined to provide a foothold for the later development of the Kansai region as a creative network city. Just as the twin forces of chance and necessity helped to shape Randstad Holland, so have they combined to forge the Kansai region of Japan.

WHAT MAKES OR BREAKS A CREATIVE NETWORK CITY?

The creative capacity of any city rests heavily on the creative potential of its population. In a book about the recent rise of the creative class in the United States, Florida (2002) associates this rise with powerful and significant shifts in human values, norms and attitudes. Some key values that he discerns from his field research to be of growing importance to the creative class are:

- Individuality – always valued by creative people, but becoming more pervasive.
- Meritocracy – the creative class values hard work, challenge and stimulation.
- Diversity and openness – valued in its older and newer manifestations.

Although these values have always been important to more highly educated and creative people, and thus do not break with the past, Florida believes that they are becoming more pervasive and may represent a merging of traditional values and newer ones. Could a network city nurture these values better than a monocentric city? One argument for this is that we may expect to find more diversity and openness in a network city, because of the visible diversity of options and choices that are realizable in a system of settlements that are attractively close to one another but identifiably different in function, amenity and green space. For example, the opportunities for anyone to fit in and live comfortably in one community, and commute to and work in another that is qualitatively different from the first, would seem to be greater in a multi-nodal network city.

Creative people are mobile. They move to different locations. Thus they value highly the diversity afforded by mobility in its various forms. Some of this mobility is over longer distances, based on the perceived utility of interactions with people or amenities in more distant locations. Some mobility is over shorter distances, easily achievable within a developing network city like Kansai. In fact, Kansai's 'Grand Vision' envisages the following specific preconditions among others (see Yoshikawa, 1993):

- the creation of a creatively diversified atmosphere for citizens by amalgamating various urban functions for living, working, learning and playing;
- the formation of cultural and knowledge corridors which bring about synergistic interactions among creative minds;
- the provision of nature-rich amenities for the citizens;
- the sophistication of a multi-polar metropolitan structure

In the following sections, we discuss four key factors that may be important when it comes to comparing network cities and monocentric cities.

SPATIAL DISPERSION AND THE COST OF MOVEMENT

In the 1940s, George Kingsley Zipf (1949, especially Chapter 9) suggested that man's dual roles – as both a producer and a consumer – introduced a profound conflict in the economy of his location. Two extreme courses of action may result. One involved moving people close to sources of raw materials, to save on transport costs. The effect of this action, which he called the 'force of diversification', would be to split the population into many small, scattered communities. We shall refer to this action as 'dispersion'. The other extreme course of action, called the 'force of unification' by Zipf, would move all the raw materials to the people. Thus all production and consumption would take place in one big city, where the entire population would live. We shall refer to this action as 'agglomeration'.

Urban theories of historical path-dependence suggest that the existence of modern urban areas can be explained in terms of scale/agglomeration economies.[10] Many cities enjoy increasing returns to scale. By agglomerating in a city, for example, the producers and consumers can exchange products and information on a face-to-face basis, thus reducing the transaction costs between them. However, as cities grow in size, other forces tend to erode the benefits of agglomeration. Eventually, excessive concentration in larger cities generates negative externalities such as higher congestion, pollution, greenhouse gas emissions and land prices. These externalities encourage urban dispersion. An acceptable level of urban concentration can only be achieved by finding a suitable balance between the centripetal forces of agglomeration and the centrifugal forces of dispersion.

Several factors exert an influence on the relative importance of these two forces. I would argue that the most important factor is transport costs – in other words, the oil price. There are two aspects of this. First, intercity transportation costs have decreased over time relative to changes in other costs and prices, due to technological progress and improvements in transport facilities. Second, the true costs of intra-city commuting have increased, because population growth in cities and rising levels of car ownership have caused higher levels of congestion, pollution, greenhouse gas emissions, noise and traffic accidents. As a monocentric city grows, it can reach a point where negative externalities begin to outweigh positive ones. Since creative people are sensitive to positive amenities and negative externalities, they may vote with their feet and elect to disperse. For several reasons, creative people tend to be more footloose than others in a modern workforce. If those forces favouring dispersion overpower those favouring agglomeration in the aggregate, a city (like an enterprise) can suffer a transition from increasing to decreasing returns to scale.

The outcome of this is a U-shaped relationship between the level of spatial dispersion and the cost of movement.[11] Dispersion is favoured by both firms and footloose workers when movement costs are relatively low or relatively high, but agglomeration is favoured at intermediate cost levels. The explanation for such a relationship is as follows. When movement costs are very low, agglomeration is unnecessary because access to other firms and consumers is easy. As movement costs rise to intermediate levels, firms agglomerate to enjoy the forward-backward linkages of Marshallian externalities.[12] If movement costs become excessive, however, some firms find it more efficient to disperse and meet each node's demand locally.

Depending on the shape and distances between nodes of a network city, a configuration may be found that is superior to a monocentric city of a similar size – when movement costs are at relatively extreme values, either very low or very high. At intermediate levels between these two extremes, agglomeration economies will encourage firms and workers to locate in the same place. Precise cost levels that favour one configuration over another await more detailed analysis in the future.

DIVERSITY THROUGH FUNCTIONAL DISPERSION

The argument put forward by the Dutch in favour of a network city is that the traditional economic functions of a metropolis – namely, government, trading and financial functions – should not be concentrated in one centre, but spread out in several.[13] This argument extends to all cultural, educational, retail and manufacturing developments that follow from the above basic functions.

Why is functional dispersion so important? According to the Dutch urban planners, it is because dispersion caters for unexpected growth and change more effectively. Not only does it offer a more diverse set of choices, but it also provides greater insurance against any unforeseen developments in the future. The key rationale for functional dispersion is that greater diversity improves the adaptive capabilities of a settlement system, just as it improves the adaptive resilience of ecosystems. This is an evolutionary argument.

Earlier in this chapter, we mentioned that the Dutch planners recognized that there was no need for the expansion of lighter manufacturing industries – so characteristic of development in all the world cities of the last century – to be channelled into an amorphous ring around one city. In a network city, such industries can be dispersed conveniently among a number of smaller nodes that are not the biggest, but are still within easy reach of the biggest. This allows the larger nodes to remain physically separate from each other and it ensures that they retain the unique elements of their own cultural and economic structure.

Another key strategy in the pursuit of functional dispersion is to encourage certain public good activities, such as government, education and research, to decentralize as well. For example, improved access to high-quality educational and scientific services can emerge from strengthening links between larger commercial settlements and smaller university towns. Older university towns – for example, Cambridge, Heidelberg and Uppsala – are excellent examples of this corridor development strategy. Six of the largest creative network cities in Europe (see Table 14.1) feature knowledge-oriented corridors of this type. Agglomeration of educational and scientific activities in corridors of creativity is a strategy that can reap the benefits of spatial and functional dispersion. As mentioned earlier, synergies between high-speed transport capacity and university capacity may be at the heart of some potential benefits of the polycentric network city structure.[14]

GEOGRAPHICAL PROXIMITY AND COMMUTING TIME

There will be upper and lower bounds on the dimensions of a successful network city. These follow from the desired trade-offs between commuting time, congestion and improved access to services and a cleaner environment. For example, the peripheral areas of constituent cities and towns should not be so close that they bump into each other. Each city should be separated from its neighbours by buffer zones of green space. On the other hand, commuting distances between different nodal centres should not be excessive.

What distance between nodes would be acceptable? One answer is based on day-to-day mobility patterns. Swedish studies have shown that daily mobility increased from an average of 0.5 kilometre in 1900 to almost 40 kilometres in 1990 (Westin and Östhol, 1990). Despite stretching the distance covered by a factor of 80 times in only 90 years, the average time spent in motion did not change appreciably. It still averages about one hour per day. Only the speed of travel has grown enormously, fuelled by the well-known sequence of improvements to transport systems.

This 'one-hour rule' serves as a dual constraint. First, it sets a limit on the size and density of a monocentric city. Second, it constrains the shape and dimensions of a network city. However, the lengthening distance afforded by advances in transport technology means that an ever-increasing number of network city configurations may be able to compete favourably with monocentric cities of a similar population size. More importantly, networking with nearby towns and cities can improve the internal state of the very largest world cities, by easing some of the pressure on their traditional transport arteries. The one-hour rule has been adopted by Kansai planners. This approach may be crucial for the future survival of world cities such as London, Paris and Tokyo.

ACCESS TO LOW-DENSITY HOUSING AND GREEN SPACE

Because of a large tract of arable land inside its vast horseshoe of development, Randstad can be thought of as a 'greenheart' metropolis. Yet, intrusions into this green space have been increasing over the last few decades. While the population in the urban ring has been falling, the greenheart population has been growing rapidly. Such intrusions seem to be unintended and unplanned. Prevailing spatial policy in the Netherlands may make sufficient allowance for the locational preferences of its population.

A challenge for all cities lies in the desire by urban households (especially families) to have access to low-density, affordable housing and access to high-quality green space. Experiences in the United States, Britain and Australia have confirmed that the 'green belt' approach to this planning problem cannot satisfy the needs of a growing population. An alternative solution is required. The flexibility inherent in the network city model does offer some hope in this respect. But explicit policy measures must be introduced in order to protect high-quality green areas from invasion by potential businesses and residents. In other words, a policy of ecological balance must prevail over green space in order to build on the perceived advantages of the network city model.

Without explicit policy measures of this type, there is always a danger that a network city could lose its unique appeal to the creative classes and deteriorate into another vast urban sprawl. At the same time, variations of the network city model may represent a way out of some of the problems faced by several major urban regions around the world. In the next section, we shall briefly examine the development prospects for a creative system of transnational network cities in the future.

WHERE NEXT – A TRANSNATIONAL CONSTELLATION?

What are the chances of a transnational system of creative network cities developing during this current age of globalization? Given the existence of the European Union as a co-operative force for European nations, together with the fact that about half of its most creative urban regions have a settlement structure that are polycentric or corridor-like (see Table 14.1), I would rate Europe as the most likely location for a creative constellation of cross-national network cities to form in the future. Some developments in this direction are underway already. As they progress, sustainability is becoming a more important attribute for cities and towns striving to partner and (in doing so) grow greener.

According to Florida's Euro-creativity index, the most creative European nations are in the Nordic area – Sweden, Finland and Denmark – followed by Western Europe – the Netherlands, Germany and Belgium (Florida and Tinagli, 2004). If we look closely at these two macro-regions, some interesting possibilities emerge. Two creative urban systems in the Nordic region are of interest: (1) the Stockholm-Uppsala corridor, and (2) the system linking Copenhagen to Malmö, Lund and Helsingborg. As both of these regions were included in Table 14.1 (our list of Europe's most creative regions), we know that each has significant creative capital. But are their respective centres complementary in intention and function so that they could all benefit from closer co-operation with one another or with other 'not too distant' centres?

POTENTIALLY CREATIVE NETWORK CITIES IN THE NORDIC REGION

Taking the Stockholm-Uppsala corridor first, some research co-operation exists already. Six major institutions – Stockholm University, Uppsala University, the Royal Institute of Technology, Karolinska Institute, the Swedish University of Agricultural Sciences and the Stockholm School of Economics – are collaborating to create a corridor for research in Sweden that can benefit from their collective expertise. Because these six institutions make up nearly half of the country's doctoral students and professors, and receive 46 per cent of the country's science funding, this corridor will compete for the world's best researchers. With Arlanda airport close to halfway between these two centres, and with a large cluster of high-tech companies along the 70-kilometre corridor, it could become very competitive with other established knowledge centres – including Boston and the San Francisco Bay Area. For example, more than half of Sweden's biotech firms are located in the corridor.

It is tempting to contemplate transnational extensions of this knowledge corridor to form a larger network city, but to do so risks being premature and overly simplistic. Although part of the Nordic world are only 30 minutes flight time from Arlanda, the creative class in Helsinki speaks a vastly different language from Swedes. Or do they? In most creative pursuits, language is rarely a problem. Most scientists, artists and musicians prefer to let their work speak for them. Greater Helsinki is similar to the Stockholm-Uppsala region in various respects and both countries share parts of the same history. Recently, Helsinki adopted some innovative solutions that have resulted in a thriving business and research region and the new Aalto University – a unique merger between the Helsinki School of Economics, the University of Art and Design Helsinki and the Helsinki University of Technology. Finland has some of the best performing students in the world, teaching being considered a high-status profession. Also, Finland has acted on the importance of collaboration between politics, business and academia, and both the Stockholm and Helsinki regions have a high-tech specialization – more than 60 per cent above the Nordic average. Be that as it may, the Gulf of Finland and the cultural/language differences still do represent huge challenges to the formation of a truly functional network city linking the Stockholm-Uppsala corridor to Helsinki and Turku.

As for the network linking the Danish capital of Copenhagen to Sweden's Malmö, Lund and Helsinborg, the completion of a combined two-track rail and four-lane road bridge-tunnel across the Øresund strait has improved the accessibility between these important centres considerably.[15] It is the longest combined road-and-rail bridge in Europe. This region may develop into the first creative, transnational network city in the world. Some reasons for suggesting this are that: (1) Sweden and Denmark rank first and fifth on Florida's Euro-creativity index; (2) Copenhagen is among the ten most creative regions in Europe (see Table 14.1); (3) Swedes and Danes have a close, co-operative relationship; (4) the international European route E20 runs across the bridge and through the tunnel via the two-lane motorway (as does the Øresund railway line), so travel times between all of the centres are modest; (5) the bridge crosses the border between Denmark and Sweden, but thanks to the Schengen Agreement there are no passport controls and few customs stops and (6) the bridge symbolizes a common cultural identity for the region, with many people in the region calling themselves 'Øresund citizens'.[16]

But are these four centres sufficiently complementary in function to develop significant co-operative links and shared activities that are mutually beneficial to each? To gain a clearer picture of their potential, let's look at each in turn.

As the third most populous city in Sweden (after Stockholm and Gothenburg), Malmö was an early industrial town in Scandinavia. Until the turn of the millennium, it struggled with the adaptation to post-industrialism. Since then, it has renewed itself with impressive architectural developments, new biotech and information technology (IT) companies and greening in various ways. Known for its extensive parks and green space, it is now a model of sustainable urban development. By 2020, it plans to be climate neutral and, by 2030, the municipality will run on 100 per cent renewable energy. At present, solar, wind and water sources are being used in Malmö's western harbour. Its claim to being eco-friendly was confirmed in 2007, when it was ranked fourth of *Grist Magazine's* 15 Green Cities. During the last few years, there has been an influx of students attending the university college (Malmö University) and much of the town's planning is focused on education, arts and culture. Also, it is very open to the outside world, with 38 per cent of its inhabitants being of foreign backgrounds (including a large Muslim community). Thus Malmö possesses the diversity and openness that Florida and others have earmarked for a creative city.

Along with Uppsala, Lund is one of the oldest cities in Sweden. Lund University was established in 1666, and is one of Scandinavia's largest with 42 000 full-time or part-time students. This figure includes Lund Institute of Technology, which is to some extent independent of the old university. As late as the 1940s, Lund was a relatively small city with few large-scale industries, covering only about a fourth of the current urban area. It was dominated by the cathedral and the university. Since then, the student population has increased about 12-fold and many companies in creative industries such as the medical, electronics and information management industries have set up in the city. This has helped to transform the town's population, architecture and pulse. From the top of Lund's Sankt Hans Hill, it is possible to see Copenhagen, and Malmö is only about 15 kilometres away.

Helsingborg is one of the oldest towns in Sweden, having been settled officially since

1085. The town is Sweden's closest point to Denmark and is relatively small, with 95 000 inhabitants in 2008. But it is growing by around 2 per cent per year, partly due to a favourable location in the Øresund region and its scenic beauty. With many old buildings, it is both a historic and a scenic coastal town. Today's buildings are a blend of old-style, stone-built churches and modern commercial buildings, with a mediaeval fortress in the town centre. *Kullagatan*, the main shopping street in the city, was the first pedestrian-only street in Sweden. Nowadays, Helsingborg is a major regional centre of trade, transport and business. In terms of connectivity to Denmark, in 1892 a train ferry was put in service, connecting Helsingborg with its Danish sister town, Helsingør. Nowadays, European route E55 traverses the two cities, with ferries connecting the two sides.

Copenhagen (København) is the largest city in Denmark, with an urban population of almost 1.2 million (or 1.9 million in the metropolitan 'Capital City Region'). It is a major regional centre of culture, business, media and science, as indicated by several international surveys and rankings.[17] Life science, IT and shipping are important sectors, and R&D plays a major role in the city's economy. Its strategic location and excellent infrastructure, with the largest airport in Scandinavia located 14 minutes by train from the city centre, has made it a regional hub and a popular location for regional headquarters as well as conventions. It is also considered one of the world's most environmentally friendly cities, having repeatedly been recognized as one of the cities with the best quality of life. It was ranked sixth among *Grist Magazine's* 15 Green Cities in 2007, making it the greenest capital in Europe. The water in the inner harbour is so clean that it can be swum in, and 36 per cent of all residents commute to work by bicycle every day. Since the turn of the millennium, Copenhagen has seen strong urban and cultural development and has been described as a boomtown. This is partly due to massive investments in cultural facilities and infrastructure, and a new wave of successful designers, chefs and architects.

Except for the Øresundsbron bridge-tunnel project, I have, however, not found any evidence of an attempt by all or some of these four centres to work together in the premeditated way that centres involved in the Randstad and Kansai network cities are doing. It is not clear if the main functions of the smaller settlements in Sweden are sufficiently complementary to those in Copenhagen to warrant broader co-operation. Thus any answer is uncertain if we return to the question of whether this important part of the Nordic landscape may develop into the first creative, transnational network city in the world.

TOWARDS A LEAGUE OF CREATIVE NETWORK CITIES IN WESTERN EUROPE

The other part of Europe that could develop a transnational network city structure extends from Randstad Holland to the Flemish Diamond and the Rhine-Ruhr region of Germany. This is a larger area in population terms than the Nordic ones discussed above, having the highest density of development in Europe. Each of the component regions has a network city structure to a greater or lesser extent, as has been discussed in the literature (Dieleman and Faludi, 1998). There are numerous medium-sized cities and smaller towns in this region of deconcentrated urban concentration. The designated areas in the Netherlands, Belgium and Germany possess two important attributes that are important for our present discussion: (1) they all show highly dispersed patterns of urbanization; and (2) they all score highly on Florida's Euro-creativity index (as discussed earlier). Thus this densely populated area of network cities is another candidate for the world's first creative, transnational network city.[18]

The creative potential of this megalopolis stems partly from the fact that it has one of the world's highest concentrations of people, money, industry and infrastructure networks. Although its infrastructure is more industrial than IT in character, it is above average in quality and speed throughout the area. Thus the region is of interest to multinational companies, not only for its good transport infrastructure, but also for its convenience as a central hub of European operations. The impressive transport infrastructure includes key airports such as Amsterdam, the ports of Rotterdam and Antwerp, as well as plenty of roads and fast rail. Also, the region contains the main offices of international organizations, including the International Court in The Hague and the North Atlantic Treaty Organization (NATO) headquarters in Brussels.

Having already discussed the creative capacity of the Randstad, in this section we shall look briefly at the other two network cities. The Flemish Diamond refers to an area in the central provinces of Flanders in Belgium. Its corner markers are the agglomerations of Brussels, Ghent, Antwerp and Leuven and about 5.5 million people live in the area. In the Middle Ages, it was one of the most highly urbanized areas in Europe, and it has been a centre of economic innovation for centuries. It is believed that a strongly bound, urban network has existed between the separate cities since the twelfth century (see Stabel, 1997). Thus the seeds of this prosperous Belgian network city of today may have been sown many centuries ago. Fernand Braudel noted that Antwerp was 'the center of the entire international economy' in the sixteenth century – a centre of international trade and a staple market for all Portuguese spices and exotic products from the New World and East Asia. In the nineteenth century, the first railway on the European continent was built in the Flemish Diamond, between Brussels and Mechelen. Today, the Flemish Diamond is one of the most productive and wealthiest regions in Europe.[19]

The distance from Brussels to Antwerp is approximately 51 kilometres. Antwerp is 70 kilometres from Dordrecht (the southernmost part of the Randstad) and about 82 kilometres from Rotterdam. So, these two network cities are relatively close to one another and are connected by several rapid transport links (air, rail and road). Thus the potential for closer co-operation exists, supported by the fact that Belgium and the Netherlands are members of the Benelux, a customs and economic union that links them to each other and Luxembourg. This union promotes the free movement of workers, capital, services and goods in the region, and could therefore underpin an even closer relationship between Randstad and the Flemish Diamond. Rather than pursuing this possibility further at this point, we shall turn instead to the Rhine-Ruhr complex.

The Rhine-Ruhr metropolitan region is the largest metropolitan region in Germany with about ten million inhabitants.[20] It has a network city structure and covers an area of 7110 square kilometres, lying entirely within the federal state of North Rhine-Westphalia. The region spreads from the Dortmund-Bochum-Essen-Duisburg (Ruhr Area) megalopolis in the north, to the urban areas of the cities of Mönchengladbach, Dusseldorf, Wuppertal, Cologne (the region's largest and Germany's fourth largest city) and Bonn in the south. Its location at the heart of Europe makes it well connected to other major European cities and to the Randstad and the Flemish Diamond. Also, many parts of it are not far from Frankfurt, Germany's principal international airport.

Germany's federal government took the initiative of conceptualizing the Rhine axes and the industrial Ruhr as one functional metropolitan region. The background was similar to the Dutch: concern for the competitive position of German regions in a wider European context. Several planning documents expressed a preference for sustaining the existing dispersed pattern of urban settlements. A number of 'European metropolitan areas' were identified in Germany, the Rhine-Ruhr being one of them. Nevertheless, several authors have expressed doubts about the combination (see, for example, Dieleman and Faludi, 1998). The Rhineland is staunchly Catholic, includes several very old cities, and the old mining and steel industries still make it difficult for the region to shake off its 'rustbelt' image. Thus it is hard to see a sustainable feeling of togetherness and co-operation emerging between the Rhine and the Ruhr. As it seems to be more of a top-down planning concept than an intrinsic process of self-organization, a true nexus seems unlikely to take root.

So we are left with the question of whether the Randstad and the Flemish Diamond will join forces to form the first creative and international network city of our time. While it is too early to make a definitive statement on this, many factors (including the proximity of the two regions and their union via the Benelux Parliament) do suggest that, among all the existing and potential network cities to be found in Europe, these two areas stand out as the leading candidates for transformation into a creative, transnational network city at some point in the future.

CONCLUDING REMARKS

This chapter began by drawing attention to several of the more creative urban regions in Europe. Interestingly, about half of them seem to be evolving into network cities. A key part of the rationale for this trend may be improved local and international access to the creative arts, higher education, R&D activities and high-technology industries. Another key factor of interest to the creative class is ease of movement. Better access between the respective nodes of a network city comes only from more efficient transport links: air, fast rail and road. Further criteria stem from the fact that the creative class tends to prefer cities that offer both diversity and openness in a cultural sense.

In my summary of the evolutionary development of a classical and creative network city – Randstad Holland – my historical analysis revealed a dual rationale for its polycentric structure. The twin forces of chance and necessity had intermingled over time. A similar rationale was found to apply to the Kansai region of Japan, but the element of chance was found much further back in that region's history and the key driving force for the Kansai of today was seen to be current competition from Tokyo. Other factors which proved to be relevant in our analysis of network cities included: conflicting forces of agglomeration and dispersion; geographical proximity and commuting time; local transport costs; diversity and complementarity of function; land prices; and access to quality green space. The chapter concluded with a brief, speculative assessment of prospects for the emergence of a creative European system of transnational network cities in the future. Although there is a cultural divide by language, and it is far too early to say with certainty, such a co-operative nexus may eventuate in time between two well-established network cities in the Benelux, namely, the Dutch Randstad and the Flemish Diamond.

Many spatial planners like to identify particular spatial patterns. Their ingenuity in this respect knows few bounds, and has led to the 'discovery' of many other spatial entities in Europe, such as the European Pentagon, the Saxon Triangle, France's Hedonic Growth Crescent, the Munich-Bologna Growth Archipelago, the Southern European Growth Belt and various others.[21] The main problem with all these entities is that the spatial form tends to become reified, to the neglect of its functional and economic bases. Without a solid, functional underpinning for each entity (allowing a possible validation or rejection of the supposed spatial form) and some research into its history, economic structure and the composition of creative classes that inhabit the entity, it is very difficult to claim that any such region possesses more or less creative potential than any other.

The work I have described and cited in this chapter remains primitive and unfinished in many respects and speculative in others. Nevertheless, it is clear that a suite of creative, polycentric urban agglomerations are developing at some key locations around the world. These places offer a mix of characteristics: an attractive, culturally diverse environment, advanced R&D and educational facilities, a flexible and creative workforce, improving accessibility both locally and internationally, and a dynamic vision of their future. It is hardly surprising to learn that, within the most creative European nations of today, cities and towns are forging closer links based on functional complementarity and other forms of synergistic co-operation, rather than on the basis of distance or demand thresholds. Welcome to the interactive age of networking and creative network cities!

NOTES

1. For an introduction to the network city concept, and brief discussions of Randstad Holland and the Kansai region of Japan, see Batten (1993, 1995). Network cities have been discussed in the literature under various guises, such as 'city networks' (Westin and Östhol, 1992; Camagni and Salone, 1993) and 'polycentric urban regions' (Parr, 2004). Shachar (1994) calls the Randstad a 'regional world city'. Other authors to have discussed the advantages and disadvantages of network cities include Hall (1984, Chapter 4), Sabel (1989), Rietveld and Stam (1992), Clark and Kuypers-Linde (1994) and Curtis (2006).
2. It is gratifying to learn that, in the late 1990s, spatial concepts based on the networking metaphor began to dominate the Dutch planning debate, leading to a conceptual switch from the *compact* city to the *complete* city and then to the *network* city (see Meijers et al., 2003, p. 42).
3. The Swedish economist, Åke Andersson, refers to them as 'C-regions', where C stands for competence, culture, communication and creativity. He also claims that they are part of a slowly emerging, new global network, which is replacing the old industrial cities such as those facing the North Atlantic.
4. Recently, Dutch planners have started to refer to the Randstad as *Deltametropool*, consisting of two large metropolitan areas: the *Noordvleugel* (North Wing) with a population of around 4.5 million people, and the *Zuidvleugel* (South Wing) with a population of around 3.5 million people.
5. See http://www.inspiringcities.org/index.php?id=1&page_type=Article&id_article=18253 (accessed 5 March 2011).
6. The parallel example in North America was the catapulting of New York ahead of Philadelphia as the leading port on the eastern seaboard, after the opening of the Erie Canal.
7. Arthur claims that we cannot explain the observed pattern of cities by economic determinism alone, without reference to chance events, coincidences and circumstances in the past. Without knowledge of chance events, coincidences and circumstances yet to come, we cannot predict with accuracy the shape of urban systems in the future. For a fuller discussion, see Arthur (1987, 1994).

8. Urban development has some features in common with the evolution of the human brain. Both develop from a small centre, growing and changing discontinuously based on networking patterns. Innovative replacement of defective parts is selective, since the system as a whole must continue to function during such repairs. The functions of many old parts are too vital for them to be replaced altogether. They possess vintage properties, in the sense that some parts are older and less reliable than others. Nonetheless, these older parts must struggle on, mostly out of date and sometimes even counterproductive, an inevitable consequence of ageing and evolution. For a discussion of the analogy between cities and brains, together with a discussion of the self-organizing nature of human settlements, see Batten (2000b).
9. To date, the author has not found any concrete evidence of this.
10. Urban agglomeration economies are typically positive externalities which induce concentrations of firms, consumers and workers (especially knowledge workers). For an interesting discussion of factors causing urban agglomeration and dispersion, see Tabuchi (1998).
11. Movement costs are the sum of freight transportation and commuting costs.
12. When the cost or difficulty of movement between two locations passes through certain critical values, sudden agglomeration or dispersion can occur. Among the authors to have stressed such bifurcation possibilities are Mees (1975), Krugman (1991) and Tabuchi (1998).
13. London is another excellent example of polycentric dispersion of economic functions.
14. The study undertaken by Andersson et al. (1990) provides more concrete evidence of this relationship than do other general studies which have focused mostly on the link between infrastructure and productivity (such as the work of David Aschauer).
15. The reason for incurring the additional cost and complexity of building a tunnel instead of another section of bridge is to avoid obstructing aircraft from nearby Copenhagen airport and to provide a clear path for shipping.
16. In Sweden and Denmark, the bridge is referred to as *Öresundsbron* and *Øresundsbroen*, respectively. The bridge company insists on *Øresundsbron*, a compromise between the two languages. Because the crossing comprises a bridge, an island and a tunnel, it is sometimes called the 'Øresund Link' or 'Øresund Connection' (Danish: *Øresundsforbindelsen*, Swedish: *Öresundsförbindelsen*).
17. For a full list of these awards, see http://en.wikipedia.org/wiki/Copenhagen (accessed 5 March 2011).
18. The Randstad, Flemish Diamond and Rhine-Ruhr are part of a discontinuous corridor of urbanization in Europe with a population of around 90 million people which has been dubbed various names, such as the Blue Banana, the Hot Banana, European Megalopolis or European Backbone. It stretches from North West England in the north to Italy's Milan in the south. The curved corridor includes at least six creative network cities mentioned in Table 14.1: London-Cambridge, Randstad Holland, Brussels-Leuven-Ghent, Bonn-Dusseldorf-Cologne, Frankfurt-Mainz-Giessen and Heidelberg-Karlsruhe-Stuttgart.
19. The term itself is mainly an infrastructural concept of the Flemish government, denoting one of the larger European metropolitan areas.
20. The area is named after the Rhine and Ruhr rivers, which are the region's defining geographical features and (historically) its economic backbone.
21. I am grateful to John Parr for drawing my attention to these spatial constructions and providing thoughts on their usefulness. For further perspectives on these and other spatial entities in Europe, see Parr (2005).

REFERENCES

Andersson, Å.E. and O. Persson (1993), 'Networking scientists', *Annals of Regional Science*, **27**, 11–21.

Andersson, Å.E., C. Anderstig and B. Hårsman (1990), 'Knowledge and communication infrastructure and regional economic change', *Regional Science and Urban Economics*, **20**, 359–76.

Anderstig, C. and B. Hårsman (1986), 'On occupation structure and location pattern in the Stockholm region', *Regional Science and Urban Economics*, **16**, 97–122.

Arnoldus, M and S. Musterd (2002), "Wonen in de regionale kennisstad. Wonen in de ambitieuze stadverdieping', working paper, University of Amsterdam.

Arthur, B. (1987), 'Urban systems and historical path dependence', in J.H. Ausubel and R. Herman (eds), *Cities and their Vital Systems – Infrastructure: Past, Present and Future*, Washington, DC: National Academy Press, pp. 85–97.

Arthur, B. (1994), *Increasing Returns and Path Dependence in the Economy*, Ann Arbor, MI: University of Michigan Press.

Batten, D.F (1993), 'Network cities versus central place cities: building a cosmo-creative constellation', in Å.E. Andersson, D.F. Batten, K. Kobayashi and K. Yoshikawa (eds), *The Cosmo-creative Society*, Berlin: Springer-Verlag, pp. 137–50.

Batten, D.F. (1995), 'Network cities: creative urban agglomerations for the 21st century', *Urban Studies*, **32**, 313–27.

Batten, D. (2000a), *Discovering Artificial Economics: How Agents Learn and Economies Evolve*, New York, NY: Westview Press.

Batten, D.F (2000b), 'Emergence and co-evolutionary learning in self-organised urban development', in D.F. Batten, C.S. Bertuglia, D. Martellato and S. Occelli (eds), *Learning, Innovation and Urban Evolution*, Boston, MA: Kluwer, pp. 45–74.

Camagni, R. and C. Salone (1993), 'Network urban structures in northern Italy: elements for a theoretical framework', *Urban Studies*, **30**, 1053–64.

Clark, W.A.V. and M. Kuypers-Linde (1994), 'Commuting in restructuring regions', *Urban Studies*, **31**, 465–83.

Curtis, C. (2006), 'Network city: retrofitting the Perth metropolitan region to facilitate sustainable travel', *Urban Policy and Research*, **24**, 159–80.

Davidi, S. (2003), 'Polycentricity in European spatial planning: from an analytical tool to a formal agenda', *European Planning Studies*, **11**, 979–99.

Dieleman, F. and A. Faludi (1998), 'Randstad, Rhine-Ruhr and Flemish Diamond as one polynucleated macroregion?', *Tijdschrift voor Economische en Sociale Geografie*, **89**, 320–7.

Florida, R. (2002), *The Rise of the Creative Class*, New York, NY: Basic Books.

Florida, R. and I. Tinagli (2004), *Europe in the Creative Age*, Pittsburgh, PA: Carnegie-Mellon Software.

Fujita, M. and T. Mori (1997), 'Structural stability and the evolution of urban systems', *Regional Science and Urban Economics*, **27**, 399–42.

Grafton, A. (1988), 'Civic humanism and scientific scholarship at Leiden', in T. Bender (ed.), *The University and the City*, New York, NY: Oxford University Press, pp. 59–78.

Groenemeijer, L. (2002), 'Woonpatronen van Amsterdamse kenniswerkers', mimeo, Delft.

Hall, P. (1984), *The World Cities* (3rd edn), London: Weidenfeld and Nicolson.

Henderson, J.V. (1974), 'The sizes and types of cities', *American Economic Review*, **64**, 640–56.

Krugman, P. (1991), 'Increasing returns and economic geography', *Journal of Political Economy*, **99**, 483–99.

Lukey, R. and P. van der Steenhoven (2004), 'Indicatoren Amsterdamse kenniseconomie 2004', working paper, Amsterdam.

Mees, A. (1975), 'The revival of cities in medieval Europe', *Regional Science and Urban Economics*, **5**, 403–25.

Meijers, E.J., A. Romein and E.C. Hoppenbrouwer (2003), *Planning Polycentric Urban Regions in North-west Europe: Value, Feasibility and Design*, Housing and Urban Policy Studies 25, DUP Science, 210pp.

Moriya, K. (1990), 'Urban networks and information networks', in C. Nakane and S. Oishi (eds), *Tokugawa Japan: The Social and Economic Antecedents of Modern Japan*, Tokyo: Tokyo University Press, pp. 97–123.

Mun, S. (1997), 'Transport network and system of cities', *Journal of Urban Economics*, **42**, 205–21.

Parr, J. (2004), 'The polycentric urban region: a closer inspection', *Regional Studies*, **38**, 231–40.

Parr, J. (2005), 'Spatial planning: too little or too much', *Scienze Regionali*, **4**, 113–29.

Priemus, H. (1994), 'Planning Randstad: between economic growth and sustainability', *Urban Studies*, **31**, 509–34.

Rietveld, P. and W. Stam (1992), ''Randstad infrastructure: its use and its deficiencies', in M. Dieleman and S. Musterd (eds), *The Randstad: A Research and Policy Laboratory*, Dordrecht: Kluwer.

Sabel, C.F. (1989), 'Flexible specialisation and the re-emergence of regional economies', in P. Hirst and J. Zeitlin (eds), *Reversing Industrial Decline*, Oxford: Berg, pp. 17–70.

Shachar, A. (1994), 'Randstad Holland: a 'World City', *Urban Studies*, **31**, 381–400.

Stabel, P. (1997), *Dwarfs Among Giants: The Flemish Urban Network in the late Middle Ages*, Leuven: Garant.

Tahuchi, T. (1998), 'Urban agglomeration and dispersion', *Journal of Urban Economics*, **44**, 333–51.

Westin, L. and A. Östhol (1992), 'City networks and the search for regional potential', CERUM Working Paper 1992:13, University of Umeå.

Yoshikawa, K. (1993), 'Creative renaissance of the Osaka Bay area: towards a cosmo-creative region in the 21st century', in Å.E. Andersson, D.F. Batten, K. Kobayashi and K. Yoshikawa (eds), *The Cosmo-Creative Society*, Berlin: Springer-Verlag, pp. 281–94.

Zipf, G. (1949), *Human Behaviour and the Principle of Least Effort*, New York, NY: Hafner.

15 Why being there matters: Finnish professionals in Silicon Valley
Carol Marie Kiriakos

With 'distances no longer meaning anything', localities, separated by distances, also lose their meanings. . .. (Bauman, 1998, p. 18)

Creative people, in turn, don't just cluster where the jobs are. They cluster in places that are centers of creativity and also where they like to live. From classical Athens and Rome, to the Florence of the Medici and Elizabethan London, to Greenwich Village and the San Francisco Bay Area, creativity has always gravitated to specific locations. (Florida, 2002, p. 7)

Why does being in a location matter for high-tech professionals in a global age? The question is relevant across academic disciplines and bodies of literature. It is one of the fundamental topics related to globalization and has been addressed, in different ways, in social and cultural theory, sociology, economic geography, and innovation and management studies. There seem to be, roughly, two kinds of perspectives on the issue, illustrated in the quotes above: the 'distance – and therefore location – is dead' view and the 'location continues to be crucial' view. The first emphasizes that virtual technologies make information access and collaboration possible regardless of where one is located. Some authors have declared distance dead (Cairncross, 1997) or meaningless (Bauman, 1998) and, in a similar vein, the world flat (Friedman, 2005). Different theoretical conceptualizations aim to capture this phenomenon, for example, 'time-space distanciation and the "disembedding" of social relations from local contexts' (Giddens, 1990); the 'deterritorialization of the social' and 'collapse of distance' (Beck, 2000); the 'annulment of temporal/spatial distances' (Bauman, 1998); and the 'space of flows' and 'timeless time' substituting the space of places (Castells, 2000).

Furthermore, many authors claim that privileged people in particular have become detached from places. For example, Arjun Appadurai (1996, pp. 9–10) and Manuel Castells (2004, p. 11) argue that globalization has diminished distance and the meaning of place, especially for elites who inhabit the 'timeless space of flows of global networks and their ancillary locales' (Castells, 2004, p. 11). Zygmunt Bauman (2007, p. 75) goes as far to suggest that the virtual world is the real home of the privileged and the place where they physically live is 'just one locality among many'.

The second perspective, location is still crucial, can be found especially in empirical studies on the economic clustering of firms and industries, innovation and work across distances and the transnational mobility of people. Innovation studies indicate that geographical clustering is still the best way to stay competitive in the global market, particularly when it comes to accessing complex, tacit knowledge and important networks (see, for example, Porter, 2000; Leamer and Storper, 2001; Sorenson, 2004). Studies of virtual communication and distant collaboration report challenges in reaching mutual understanding, building trust, and achieving smooth long-distance interactions (Hinds and Bailey, 2003; see also Hinds and Kiesler, 2002). Annalee Saxenian's (2006) study of global entrepreneurs – the 'new Argonauts' – shows how important it is to have individuals with intimate knowledge of local culture and language to build successful collaboration between Silicon Valley and distant, emerging locations in China, India, Taiwan and Israel. Finally, Richard Florida (2002, 2005, 2008) unequivocally rejects the idea of the death of place: his body of work emphasizes how choosing a location is one of the most important decisions in creative professionals' lives. In particular, Florida (2002) maintains that the values of the creative class are about seeking overall meaning and happiness in life, which makes the qualities of localities even more crucial. According to Florida (2002), today's professionals often select the location first and then look for work in that location. They do not merely move for jobs anymore, but look for localities that allow them to be creative in the community.

Therefore, the point of departure and background motivation for this chapter comes from the above-mentioned tension between these conflicting perspectives on the relative importance of geographical space. Many things indeed seem to have changed. Yet the best questions to ask for social scientists may not be so much about whether location matters anymore but about how exactly, considering that virtual technologies have certainly brought more connectedness between different, perhaps previously unconnected, places in the world.

This chapter offers a qualitative, human perspective on the issue of why location matters in the global age. Thus, the viewpoint is not primarily that of a location: here we do not discuss directly what makes locations attractive or prosperous, although this is a crucial issue in itself and indeed closely related. Instead, my emphasis is on how people experience and find places meaningful and what exactly locations can mean to them. Highly skilled, elite professionals (also called knowledge workers or the creative class) are a curious case at the heart of the 'distance is dead versus location is crucial' debate. On the one hand, skilled knowledge professionals are assumed to be those for whom, at least, distance should be dead because they have the access and the ability to use the latest information and communication technologies that are supposed to make the world smaller. Then again, they are also the ones who are expected to be more mobile and seek places where they find true meaning in life and they are also those that locations will want to attract (Landry, 2008).

As previously mentioned, Florida's work in particular (2002, 2008) discusses the values and characteristics of creative professionals from the viewpoint of locations. Yet deeper insight into their experiences is useful in order to understand the dynamics between locations and the choices presumably available to mobile people. I will offer a complementary perspective to Florida's core argument that technology, talent and tolerance (the three Ts) are crucial to attract global talent. However, from the perspective of the people themselves, what they seek and how they experience being in the right or ideal location is perhaps best summed up by three Is: information, interaction and inspiration. That is, these are the things they look for and get, at best, when they are in a location where they can lead meaningful, fulfilling working lives and make the most of themselves as innovators, entrepreneurs or creators.

In this chapter, then, the emphasis is on personal experiences and the meanings the professionals themselves give to them. I will discuss these through an empirical case study and illustrate how location matters for highly skilled Finns in Silicon Valley. This chapter offers insight into the experiences of important players in the global economy and their locational choices. By focusing on individual knowledge workers, this study also contributes to the understanding of the micro-foundations of knowledge spillovers, which have been mostly ignored so far (for an exception, see Fornahl et al., 2004). As such, of course, this study contributes to the current literature in two ways: it provides useful information both for those who are interested in the experiences, values and choices of today's globally mobile, highly skilled professionals and for those who wish to understand why some locations thrive and others do not.

EMPIRICS: FINNS IN SILICON VALLEY

Informant B19: It seemed that there are lots of stimuli here. And there was a kind of maybe glamour too. Like, California, wow! Like Boston, well, that may not sound so cool, but California sounds nice.[1]

Silicon Valley continues to be one of the most important regions in the world when it comes to innovation and high technology. The curious thing is that, as Brown and Duguid (2002) note, it is the very place where the technologies that are supposed to have diminished the need for meeting face to face were created – and still are. Nevertheless, it continues to be a place where global highly skilled professionals gather from different parts of the world, to be in closer contact and to interact with their colleagues (Brown and Duguid, 2002). While it is one of the places where the meaning of location was supposedly erased, its existence seems to prove that place still matters. In sum, it is perhaps the place where the contemporary dynamics and tensions concerning the importance of place/locality are most obvious.

Finnish highly skilled people are an appealing case for studying the meaning of location and distance, because in terms of global innovation activity and a talented workforce, their country of origin can be seen at the same time as both relevant and marginal. During the past decade or so, Finland has consistently been placed among the top countries in global rankings of competitiveness, innovation and education (World Economic Forum, 2005; Dahlman et al., 2006). Finland is therefore a technologically advanced, innovative and successful national economy. It can in some ways be considered as an important locality for global high-technology markets and innovation. However, with its population of about 5.4 million, it is also small and geographically peripheral, and certainly not in itself one of the key locations for attracting global talent. Migration both to and from Finland is relatively low; unlike many other nationalities or ethnic groups, Finns do not have significant diasporas that would clearly facilitate the global connections of today's innovators.

Finns relocating to Silicon Valley represents a case of West–West migration (from one Western, successful location to another). Favell et al. (2006) have pointed out that highly skilled global mobility remains insufficiently understood and empirically little studied. Migration studies typically focus on unskilled migration from the 'global South or East' to the 'global North or West', or make no distinction between the highly skilled and the unskilled. Because of this, there are many assumptions regarding global 'elites' and their relationship to place that remain empirically questionable. As mentioned, some authors suggest that these people appear to be the most detached from place. Their work is also typical for the global era in that a crucial part of their everyday activities involves the use of information and communication technology, and they also tend to be frequent travellers. Another essential part of their work is being in contact or collaborating with people who are located in other – often geographically distant – places.

This study is qualitative and ethnographic in nature. The main observations consist of semi-structured, in-depth interviews with Finns who were working in Silicon Valley[2] at the time of the fieldwork or had been working there in the past ten years. The great strength of this method is that it produces a fair amount of textual data that is close to the informants' world, language and vocabulary, instead of data where what is important or relevant has been decided in advance by the researcher(s), as is the case for surveys. In addition, observations from the approximately 12 months I spent in the area between August 2006 and December 2008 (as a visiting researcher at the University of California at Berkeley) as well as other relevant data (documents, reports, newspaper articles) are used. I also conducted interviews in Helsinki between February and May 2007 with professionals who had lived in Silicon Valley but had returned to Finland.

There is no official record of Finns or Finnish firms in Silicon Valley, therefore I found the informants using a snowball method. The basic criteria for selecting informants were: Finnish nationality; working and being based in Silicon Valley either currently (at the time of the data collection) or at some point during the past decade; and working in a position relevant for innovation. In practice, this meant Finns working in the broad field of information and communication technologies and related professions: entrepreneurs, employees, academic researchers, public officials whose purpose was to promote Finnish innovation and entrepreneurship, venture capitalists and other experts. This criterion excludes other types of Finnish migrants to the region, for example, school teachers, housewives, au pairs, undergraduate students and craftsmen.[3]

I conducted in-depth face-to-face interviews with 50 Finnish professionals; some of them were interviewed more than once. With few exceptions, the informants were born, raised and educated in Finland, and only left Finland for Silicon Valley as adults because of their work (the exceptions are as follows: one informant had lived for some time outside Finland as a child, a few had completed their university studies or undertaken a significant part of them outside Finland). The vast majority of the informants had advanced degrees (Master's or PhD) in engineering or a related area from a Finnish university, although I was not specifically looking for engineers. Other educational backgrounds included degrees in economics, management, computer science and physics.[4]

Practically all of the informants claimed that work was the reason for moving to Silicon Valley. It was typically discussed first and apparently easiest to mention as a reason for the move. Yet it became clear in the interviews that personal motivations intertwined closely with more rational and work-related reasons. Many informants had a desire to go abroad and experience another location. They saw the relocation as a chance to develop and challenge themselves both personally and professionally, or as a chance to pursue their dreams. They were curious about what life would be like in a distant place and how they would survive. Many had also taken the initiative themselves and actively sought opportunities to relocate: the first initiative did not always come from the employer. Thus, although there were clear rational and objective reasons to move to

Silicon Valley – such as closer collaboration with partners there or establishing a firm's new office – more subtle, personal motivations clearly mattered too.

The rest of the chapter will examine their experiences further, focusing on the above-mentioned three Is; information, interaction and inspiration.

INFORMATION

Information is a key ingredient for innovation. There is so much information available today that no single individual or organization can keep up on their own: interaction with others is needed. Furthermore, the pace of innovation is so fast that interaction is crucial – it is hard to be innovative alone (Chesbrough, 2003; Chesbrough et al., 2006). As the complexity of the information/knowledge increases, social networks become ever more important for knowledge sharing (Sorenson, 2004), which is probably one of the main reasons why high-technology industries still cluster (Porter, 2000; Storper, 2000). Michael Porter (2000, p. 260) argues that access to information and knowledge is one of the mechanisms through which location contributes to the competitiveness of firms.

Yet there is a tension between the observation that, on one hand, today's communication technologies have made information available anywhere and, on the other, that organizations and individuals still need to be in close physical proximity to other relevant actors. In Michael Storper's (2000, p. 151) words, '. . . firms suggest that they use proximity to help with the flow of ideas or negotiations, even though – as we know – information is cheap and easy to transport. What are we to make, analytically speaking, of this evidence?'

In the experiences of Finns in Silicon Valley, two main aspects are highlighted when it comes to information access. First, when you are located in Silicon Valley you get information that you would not otherwise get; you get the very latest information and you are on the cutting edge of what is happening. Second, when in Silicon Valley you are able to make sense of what is relevant and what individual pieces of information mean.

The importance of locality, being present and face-to-face interaction becomes highlighted when one distinguishes between information and knowledge. Information is something that is relatively simple to codify, store in databases and share or access by virtual means. The nature of information is such that it does not require extensive interpretation and that it is relatively simple to understand, once a basic expertise is acquired (for example, the ability to understand technical information). Knowledge – or tacit knowledge – is more subtle in nature and difficult to codify, store in databases or share over long distances. It is commonly understood that tacit knowledge requires a shared context and understanding and often face-to-face interaction to be transferred. Thus, it appears that while information is not dependent on location and travels effortlessly across space, knowledge is closely tied to humans and locations and does not travel easily (see Nonaka, 1994; Brown and Duguid, 2000; Storper, 2000; Leamer and Storper, 2001; Audretsch et al., 2004).

The experiences of the Finnish professionals are in line with previous literature, in that certain kinds of easily codified information do seem to travel in an unimpeded way across space, being easily accessed through virtual networks. So for this kind of information location is not crucial: the information is available on the Internet, or easily accessed via email or phone. Second, also in line with existing literature, the findings show that knowledge does not travel easily: the kind of tacit, context-specific, non-codifiable know-how that is necessary for innovation. As has been found in previous studies, shared context, repeated face-to-face interaction, trust and common understandings are needed for accessing and acquiring knowledge.

My research sheds further light on some of the nuances of this. The experiences of Finns suggest some reasons why it is important to be present in a locality to access certain information/knowledge, which may not have only to do with the nature of the information as such (how difficult it is to codify), but also with the nature of the social interaction locally and from afar. Thus, it is not just a question of codifiability but also of the nature of the social relationships that matters for whether information travels effectively.

This is based on the finding that there seems to be certain kinds of information that could in principle easily be codified and transferred across space, but that for some reason these kinds do not travel well. There is nothing in the nature of the information as such that would make it difficult to codify and then, for example, sent by email or shared in phone conversations. This information is neither highly specified knowledge nor technical information that would require extensive background information or prior knowledge or expertise; it is also not closely tied to people and places in the sense that only locals would understand it or that it could only be understood through face-to-face interaction (where there are visual cues present, not only words). It is indeed local knowledge in the sense that it can at first only be observed and accessed locally. Yet it consists of easily codifiable, simple messages and thus in theory this information may be passed on in a straightforward manner by phone or email. Specifically, the information that does not seem to travel easily, even if it should be easy to codify, is information on what is relevant and informal information.

> A6: And of course afterwards we have discovered that it is clear that nowadays you get all the information on the Internet immediately so that is not the issue. But then whether something is important or not important. The feeling that you just can't get only by reading on the internet. You just sort of sense it when you are there in the locality.

Informant A6 describes the difficulty of making sense of what is relevant and what is noise and argues that for this one has to be in the locality. This is in line with existing understanding of knowledge: it is local and tacit. However, if we consider the example here further, we see that the information as such is not complex; once it is observed, it is not particularly challenging to codify it and say, for instance, that 'here everyone believes that mobile phone games are the next big thing and everyone is working on them' or that 'people (here) say that Conference X will be much more useful than Seminar Y'. Instead of the informants having to be there, a known local person could in theory pass on that information to them. Yet this informant maintains that you have to be there yourself.

In the following quotation, the informant B18 answers my question, whether he or she would get all the same information if he or she were in Finland and had access to the Internet rather than being present in Silicon Valley:

> B18: I would, yeah yeah. But here *in addition to that* I can participate in various events. And then comes the, like the unofficial information that does not travel electronically. Now, about

three weeks ago we had a beer bash, we just invited all the people we know in this quite modest pub to drink beer together. And it was really fun. You always hear something then. And you see from the behaviour of people how they are doing and what's in right now and what's out. And so on. But quite a lot does happen electronically.

Informant B18 maintains that although a lot of information is easily accessible on the Internet, there is the unofficial information that you can only get locally, face to face. Again, the information is not particularly complex as such (how people are doing, what is in and what is out), yet there seems to be something in its nature that makes it difficult to access from a distance. Even if in principle it could be mentioned in an email by a local colleague ('I was at this beer bash yesterday and heard that the lead engineer in Company X is going to quit'), for some reason this does not seem to happen easily. Therefore, it seems that although a lot of relevant information is accessible virtually, local presence is important for sense-making and understanding what is relevant and for accessing certain information that is not codified and disseminated to other parts of the world even if in principle it could be.

The reason why certain information does not travel although it does not appear to be difficult to codify may have to do with the nature of the social relationship and, in particular, trust. Trust may be one of the factors that facilitate the sharing of information, including long-distance sharing. According to many accounts, however, trust and proximity seem to go hand in hand. Trust relationships are close relationships, with closeness referring not only to emotional aspects but often to physical proximity as well.

A4: The face has to be familiar and the body language has to be familiar. Simply, you have to be able to recognize the person. That is really what has to be working. If you wouldn't recognize a person when they walk by in the street, there is no, there is absolutely no chance of creating the trust electronically.

Indeed, trust seems notoriously difficult to build in any other way than through face-to-face meetings. Leamer and Storper (2001, p. 643) argue that face-to-face contact leads to trust that, in turn, leads to tacit knowledge transfer. These authors refer to 'complex uncodifiable messages' which can be understood as tacit knowledge. They maintain that 'many messages can be communicated effectively only if the parties "know" each other'. Leamer and Storper (2001, p. 653) further note that 'it is the complex, context-dependent messages that require the greatest investments in relationships'. While this is undoubtedly true, what the case of Finns in Silicon Valley suggests is that it is not only complex messages that require trust, but also certain kinds of simpler information, such as informal information or rumours – which are, nevertheless, important for innovation and business activity. Brian Uzzi's (1997) research on entrepreneurs in the fashion industry also found that the nature of the social tie (in particular, trust) played a role in what kind of information (and how much of it) was exchanged.

Thus, my findings suggest that while the distinction between information and knowledge is useful in understanding why proximity is essential for certain kinds of knowledge access, the importance of local presence and face-to-face interaction is not only due to the complexity of the information as such but the fact that even simple, codifiable messages do not travel well in professional relationships that are weaker and do not include trust. Next, we will look at the dynamics of local and distant interaction, which further highlight how some things seem to travel well while others do not.

INTERACTION

Local interaction in knowledge work cannot be fully understood without contrasting it with virtual interaction, in particular interaction over long distances. These are not mutually exclusive; both are a necessary and inevitable part of today's micro-level innovation activity. However, there are some limitations and challenges related to virtual, distant interaction and collaboration that shed light on why local face-to-face interaction still matters. Virtual interaction, crucial as it is, is particular in nature. As seen in the previous section, not all information is disseminated across long distances even if in theory it could.

Generally, and perhaps somewhat surprisingly, the global professionals are very conscious of geographical distances when communicating and collaborating virtually. The implicit assumption inherent in the 'world is flat' perspective – that there are no distances in the virtual world – appears to be largely a myth. In the following quote, informant B29 considers whether Finland feels close or far from Silicon Valley:

> B29: When you are here, whether it feels close or far . . . you are aware, you are conscious of the physical distance. And the fact that often people are not awake at the same time. So in that sense [it feels] far, a little far. If I could choose so that everything else would stay the same, if you could keep everything else the same but move to Europe that would be better.

One informant described vividly how he used to work in Silicon Valley with a local partner while he was still himself based in Finland. He used to visit Silicon Valley for important meetings, but mainly they communicated from a distance, on the phone or email. Whenever the partner had been in an important meeting in Silicon Valley, he would call this informant in Finland to report the latest news. The informant described the challenge of getting on the same wavelength and mood as the partner, of understanding what was going on, if, for instance, the meeting had gone well and the partner was excited about it. The challenge was to be able to communicate while being in entirely different physical contexts. The time difference is ten hours. When it is day in Silicon Valley, it is night in Finland. The informant said that sometimes it was difficult for the partner to get him to listen in Finland, in the middle of the night, and understand what was going on in Silicon Valley or to agree on a specific course of action. The informant described how the partner developed a method to help get him in the same frame of mind over the phone: the partner in Silicon Valley would tell the informant in Finland to 'close your eyes, think about when you were here the last time, remember the client's office, the sunshine, sitting in the car after the meeting drinking Starbucks coffee, imagine you are here'. This, he said, would help make the communication on the phone about business decisions between them easier.

The same informant further described why he himself moved to Silicon Valley. He had to spend about two weeks every month in Silicon Valley for business already when based in Finland. He said that each time the plane took off he could feel how he immediately started to lose touch on what was happening in Silicon Valley, how he couldn't 'feel its pulse anymore'.

The other informants' accounts support this. Many talked about how it can be difficult to convince colleagues in Finland how a certain strategy or decision would be necessary for smooth progress in Silicon Valley. They said that the distance is often palpable; the colleagues in Finland are in a very different context and what makes sense in Silicon Valley does not always seem sensible or intelligible in Finland. This is not only about cultural differences, it is clearly about the physical environment, because when these same people are in Silicon Valley and meet the clients or local contacts face to face they understand why some decisions and strategies make sense and some do not.

There is also an 'out of sight, out of mind' effect that increases with increasing distance. In the following passage, the informants talk about the challenges related to distance when the colleagues are located in Finland and the informant is in Silicon Valley:

B19: There are difficulties, because if you are not active yourself, they will not remember you, you are not there to get a cup of coffee with them, chitchatting and telling them what movie you went to see at the weekend. So it is very easy to forget that there is someone on the other side of the globe who you should be in contact with. It requires being active in being in contact with Finland from the part of the one who is here [in Silicon Valley], especially in an organization like this where the major part of the operations are in Finland.

A6: In these collaboration projects because this is a long distance, ten-hour time difference, it is like a really big thing. So of course we used email to communicate but then you meet every now and then, that brings a certain vigour to it.

Besides direct, face-to-face interaction with other people in a location, there is also another kind of interaction that is only possible by physically being there: the interaction with the environment or indirect contact with other people there. The environment contains messages that cannot be received without being there. These messages are received when following the local media, overhearing pieces of conversations, seeing people, reading the flyers on the message boards in coffee shops, listening to the radio while driving, or even seeing what physical buildings and places look like – in sum, being part of the local buzz.

B30: Well, [it's just] that you get into the *physical* place. You live here like the locals live here. So I don't know if I can say it better but. That way you like *suck in* the information, the way of thinking, the model of thinking, the culture, like automatically. And just the face-to-face communication in creating social ties. It's not the same if you send email to some researcher here like, how's it going. But if you go to *lunch* with them here and chat about how are things now, there is easily, there is a chance for a chain of events then. 'Oh, you have this kind of a thing going on, well who is in it, oh those people are, well could we work together or could we have some common interests to do together?' So I at least think that it is considerably more difficult to do it from a distance, for example, via email. In Finland it would be like, well, here you are basically 24/7. You are here and you are taking in the information. But you can't be at the computer 24/7 in Finland and think now I'm going to find out what's happening in Silicon Valley.

Furthermore, as the quote above also implies, local presence appears to be crucial for accessing important global networks. Networks are often studied either from a local perspective (focusing on the networks of a specific location) or, alternatively, as if they are not tied to places at all but flowing in spaces outside physical ones (Castells, 2000). Yet it is clear that some locations, such as Silicon Valley (in the case of people working in innovation) offer better opportunities to access global networks.

> A6: And then also as an ecosystem it [Silicon Valley] is an extremely interesting place. The way you get access to what happens, in Silicon Valley, because there are a lot of these venture capitalists that attract business start-ups from different parts of the world. So in Silicon Valley you get in touch with what happens in Israel and what happens in India or what happens in China.

Therefore, some locations seem to offer gateways into other locations' networks – and curiously, this does not seem to have much to do with actual physical distances or locations, but more with the social and economic ties connecting the locations (Saxenian, 2006). Although the people in networks may be geographically mobile, local face-to-face contact is often needed to access networks. When one is already part of a network, this membership is not necessarily bound to one place and members can maintain and perhaps expand global and virtual networks – although we should not forget the principle of 'out of sight, out of mind', which still seems to apply to some extent. But often the initial access to certain networks happens through first contacts, which require at the very least a superficial level of trust, which then allows people to move ahead in the networks. Creating this trust, in turn, typically involves at least one face-to-face contact where a potential new member is assessed before making further references to other contacts in the network. Furthermore, it is still a reality that the people who form networks are tied to places and move in and between physical places.

Finally, my informants also pointed out that location sends an important message to others: competitors, customers, potential collaborators and such. When you are located in Silicon Valley, you show that you are dedicated and people will take you seriously. When you introduce yourself to new people and are able to give a local address and phone number, it is more likely that you will be contacted. Interestingly, many informants mention that a local phone number may be vital in creating first contact with important people: since there is so much competition, people will not bother to make an effort to dial a phone number with a foreign area code they may not understand. This observation is also related to trust: it is harder to trust someone who is non-local, 'far away' and 'distant' than someone who is geographically close and whose behaviour you can observe in a familiar environment, where it is perhaps even possible to ask other people in the professional network what they know about the person in question. Thus, a local address and phone number is a matter of accessibility, accountability, reputation and trust, which are all vital when creating first contacts and building networks.

INSPIRATION

> B18: One thing is fearlessness.
> CK: Hm, whose fearlessness?
> B18: Everyone's.
> CK: So it's like a general atmosphere?
> B18: Yeah, here you just do it. You don't fear that you don't know enough, you don't fear that you will fail or that you will succeed. You just go for it.

The last of the three Is, inspiration, builds on the first two, information and interaction; it derives from these yet it is clearly analytically independent and adds to them. It is also perhaps the most difficult to access or capture in research (let alone measure). Even in qualitative in-depth interviews, inspiration is typically not something explicitly discussed, but it emerges from the way the informants talk about their work and everyday activities in Silicon Valley. This section summarizes the aspects related to inspiration, such as effortlessness, energy, being in the centre of things and the feeling of fitting in. Despite all the possibilities that are offered by virtual connectedness, the basic fact that people seem to want to be in certain places and not others remains. Even if technologies in principle could do many things such as resolve issues considered as problems – for example, make possible the inexpensive sharing of information and knowledge from afar – we may happily ignore some of these and still prefer specific places, both for personal and work-related reasons. The present research on Finns highlights how locations – both the origin and the destination – play a part in people's personal motivations, aspirations and identities. Locations may represent ways to fulfil personal or professional goals, to pursue dreams and to develop or challenge oneself as an individual. These kinds of reasons constitute the inspirational element of the importance of place or location: place plays an important part in fostering personal motivation and inspiration. What does the inspirational element include and how does it manifest itself?

In the following, informant B16, who was a visiting scholar at a prestigious university in the Silicon Valley area, describes the experience of being inspired and the feeling of being in the right place, at the centre of things:

> B16: This is quite a unique place. You even develop a kind of an emotional relationship to it. I am experiencing this for the first time, I have never had that with any place . . . the kind of emotional relationship I have with this place.
> CK: Well, what would you say, like . . . can you describe it at all, what is it about, what do you get from here or what is it that is so great here?
> B16: Well. . . . It's on so many levels. First . . . this is very inspiring as a milieu. It is good, easy to be here and this place gives freedom and air for your thoughts. But also every day so many interesting things are happening here, the best researchers, the best artists in the world visit here. You have very inspiring guest lectures, very inspiring courses and this is altogether a very active community, the students, the visiting researchers. . . . There is the extra [aspect] that any day the Dalai Lama might come and give a talk or a world-leading politician or the leading researcher in your field. . . . And then if you think of Silicon Valley more broadly and combine the amenities of San Francisco, you get a cornucopia where you have the feeling all the time that you are in the centre of everything essential and that this is *the* Place where things happen. And also here the future is being created every day. So this is the Florence of our time.

Meeting Fascinating People

An important part of inspiration is face-to-face encounters with interesting people. Who is interesting is naturally highly subjective: what matters is that you are in a place where there are people that you find fascinating and admire. Meeting brilliant people means that you can learn from them, and seeing how they do things helps you to develop yourself. It is therefore also inspiring to have role models and to be in close proximity to them: to be able to attend when they give public talks, or even to get the chance to arrange individual meetings with them. Being in the right place thus means being closer to your 'idols', which is highly motivating.

Being in the Centre of Things

Many informants speak of how in Silicon Valley they feel that they are at the centre of things. They are in the very place where the most important events take place, where the most brilliant people (from each individual's perspective) come to from all over the world. When you are in the centre of things you do not have to move or travel so much in order to catch the important people and events: they come to where you are. It also means being able to participate fully, not merely following the developments in your field from a distance, but contributing actively, participating in discussions and innovation activities. Being in the centre of things means being on the cutting edge – you can be sure of doing the most relevant, meaningful things.

Chance Encounters

The possibility of crucial, influential chance encounters is also a vital aspect of being in the centre of things, and, in turn, of inspiration. When one is in the right location, anything interesting can happen at any moment, and one can run into crucial people, or pieces of information, by accident. Silicon Valley represents such a concentration of relevant talent that you never know who might sit next to you. One informant described how he was sitting on a plane from San Francisco to Seattle, and a young man sat next to him. They started talking, and it turned out that the man was the assistant to the chief technology officer of Company X, which is a global leader in its field and highly relevant for this informant's business. The informant said that if he had sat on a plane from Helsinki to Jyväskylä (a small university town in central Finland), something like this would never have happened. It was highly inspiring – and potentially fruitful for business – to be able to have an informal conversation with someone so influential (or someone so close to someone so influential).

Energy

Inspiration manifests itself as enhanced energy and creativity. One informant told me, when we met in Silicon Valley, that he had just got three weeks' worth of work done in one week: he said he was just so inspired and energized by everything there and that he had come up with so many ideas to develop. He also added that he had never had this energy in Finland: it was due to the surroundings. There seems to be an optimistic element in the environment, which is perhaps specific to Silicon Valley: people are encouraged and allowed to try anything. Many informants mention how failure is not frowned upon, and how motivating it is (for someone coming from the Finnish entrepreneurial culture) that the attitude is more one of '(s)he who does not try is a loser but (s)he who tries and fails is an entrepreneur'.

> B30: Here things happen by themselves a lot so you don't necessarily need to work for everything, it happens by itself.

Effortlessness

The informants describe how some things require less effort when working in Silicon Valley: things seem to happen almost by themselves, to fall into place when one is in the locality. This is obviously a stark contrast to the cruel competitiveness that is also typical to Silicon Valley. Yet the positive side of this competitiveness is that it takes place in a location with a high concentration of brilliant people, and when you interact with those people it is inspiring.

Using One's Capacities More Fully

An inspiring location offers the chance to use one's talents and capacities more fully, to express and test one's ideas in discussions with other successful, intriguing people and to develop oneself professionally (and personally). It seems that the physical environment, the location, plays an important part in fostering inspiration. Certain places have the culture and other elements that encourage individuals to express themselves and fulfil their dreams. Again, where such a place is depends on a person's work and interests.

The Feeling of Fitting In: Diversity

An important aspect of Silicon Valley is the diversity of its population and their backgrounds. The Finnish informants say that in Silicon Valley, it does not matter who you are or what your background is, people are only interested in what ideas you have, what you have to say and what you can create. Many informants mention that in Silicon Valley there is the feeling that everyone is welcome, that everyone fits in. As it is such a mixture of ethnic, social and cultural backgrounds, nobody is different or stands out. This can be very liberating. This is also emphasized by Florida (2002): diversity is one factor that makes a location attractive to the highly skilled creative class. According to Florida, members of the creative class seek to live in places where diverse ideas and perspectives can coexist. Diversity in ideas and backgrounds is also understood to be beneficial for innovation, because truly novel things come from combining different kinds of existing knowledge and perspectives in a new way. People with different backgrounds can learn from each other. This seems to form a part of the inspiring culture of Silicon Valley: the freedom to be oneself and learn from people with different backgrounds.

CONCLUDING REFLECTIONS

Sean Ó Riain (2006) observes that for neoclassical economists, the global workplace is essentially a virtual place where the limitations of space, social organization and local institutional arrangements have largely lost their meaning. In this situation, the boundaries between the virtual and the real are blurred; virtual ties are as real as 'actual' ones and knowledge is created and shared in interaction in the virtual space.

There is also contradictory evidence: the more that activities become global or virtual, the more physical proximity and time are emphasized. Beunza and Stark (2003) found in their study of a Wall Street trading room that the organization of the physical surroundings and the opportunity for quick, immediate face-to-face communication between traders were crucial to the successful carrying out of work. Indeed, in his ethnographic work Ó Riain (2000, 2006) found a phenomenon of 'time-space intensification': in global work, instead of losing their meaning, time and space actually become more important, emphasized and immediate. Ó Riain (2006) concludes that 'global competitiveness is . . . dependent on increased spatial embeddedness'. His ethnographic empirical evidence shows that the knowledge economy is deeply embedded in social relations and social spaces. Thus, it is far from disembedded, and distance has not lost its meaning. 'The intensification of space is not just a matter of the increased importance of face-to-face interaction or of competition between places but of the increasing importance of the ability to mobilize space as a resource in social relations . . .' (Ó Riain, 2006, p. 510).

However, Ron Boschma (2005) argues that physical (geographical) proximity as such is neither necessary nor sufficient for learning and innovation: other forms of proximity, such as cognitive, social or institutional, may act as substitutes for physical proximity. So, simply being in a place is not enough: this was also pointed out often in my interviews with Finns. While we have seen that being in a location matters, the mere presence in a place, or physical closeness to other relevant actors, is not enough in itself for things to happen (for knowledge access, collaboration, learning, innovation and so on). While proximity clearly helps to gain access to many important things, one must make use of proximity and take the initiative in order to achieve the desired outcomes.

Nevertheless, it is crucial to note that geographical proximity may be vital where other forms of proximity are missing or do not yet exist. Thus, being physically close may be fundamental in order to create other forms of proximity. The professionals needed to relocate to Silicon Valley in order to construct networks (social proximity), to learn the rules of the game (institutional proximity) and to deepen their knowledge base (cognitive proximity). Although Boschma (2005) maintains geographical proximity to be neither a necessary nor a sufficient condition, in practice geographical proximity may be the most essential one, especially when other kinds of proximity are lacking. I agree that geographical proximity is not alone sufficient for innovation, but to create other kinds of proximity it may be necessary – at least at certain phases of the process – since not everything can be planned.

Indeed, informant A4 talked about how the main purposes for going to Silicon Valley in the first place is to expect the unexpected, to give a chance to all those things that cannot be defined or anticipated beforehand. This informant had lived in Silicon Valley himself, and had later created important forms of collaboration between local universities and his Finnish organization. He was now sending young Finnish professionals to Silicon Valley within the framework of this programme, and emphasized how important it was (1) to go there and (2) to go there for a sufficiently long period of time.

> A4: . . . it is better that they are there a little longer and have time to settle and on the other hand build the network. And learn something that we *didn't* send them for. So that there would be unexpected added value. We expect the unexpected, in a way.

Thus, one advantage of being located in a place is that you learn and experience things you did not expect. From a distance, you can access what you know you are looking for, but when living in the locality, you can access what you did not know you needed. It is well documented in the current literature that the process of innovation is by definition unpredictable: what kind of information is needed or what you are looking for is not known at the outset (Chesbrough, 2003; Chesbrough et al., 2006). When the purpose is to arrive at an end product or idea that cannot be defined at the outset, it becomes impossible to define in advance what information to look for or what questions to ask. From this perspective, it is wise to expect the unexpected: the manager who sends young professionals to Silicon Valley says that it requires a certain amount of time for them to get anything out of it; a few months is not enough for someone who is in Silicon Valley for the first time. This manager believes that it is a time-consuming process to gain access to subtle, tacit knowledge and to the people who embody it.

Although the particular location (Silicon Valley) and people (professionals from Finland) undoubtedly bring their distinctive flavours to the present research, the results can be assumed to hold across other innovative locations as well. That is, the three Is could be expected to be experienced in other places too, not only Silicon Valley. What matters is what the most relevant place for specific people and professional fields is. Some empirical studies on skilled migrants have reported similar findings on the importance of being 'where things happen' for accessing information, having interaction with key people and motivation. Examples include workers in the headquarters of multinational companies (Bozkurt, 2006), British financial professionals in Singapore and New York City (Beaverstock, 2002, 2005) and skilled people from New Zealand in London (Conradson and Latham, 2005, 2007). What seems important is that the city or location is relevant for your particular field, personal goals and aspirations and that there is enough diversity and dynamism to give room for creativity. Geographical interconnectedness (for example, major airports) is essential too.

To conclude, the findings discussed in this chapter are in line with previous studies that suggest that it may be a bit too hasty to declare distance and locality dead. Many of the assumptions related to this idea do not seem to find support in empirical reality. For example, Peter Dicken (2000) has noted that the truly global corporation is a myth; both the places of origin and the places where firms operate play a role in how they behave. In a similar vein, I wonder whether perhaps truly global people are a myth too: even the most privileged ones are always tied to specific places, and although connectedness across great distances has become an everyday reality, we are always physically present somewhere while connected to other people who are, likewise, located in a physical place. Thus, it seems to be more fruitful to approach issues related to the contemporary world without the assumption that distance is dead or that location does not matter. This does not imply that nothing has changed. The actual realities of people, firms and locations are lived somewhere in between the extremes. Many things have changed. But, as this chapter has illustrated, many of the things that used to matter to us about locations still continue to make a difference.

NOTES

1. The quotations from interviews are labelled according to the following system: the first letter (A or B) indicates whether the interview was carried out in Finland (A) or in Silicon Valley (B). Thus, the informants labelled with the letter A are those who were at the time of the fieldwork based in Finland but had

been based in Silicon Valley at some point in the past ten years. Accordingly, the informants labelled with the letter B are those based in Silicon Valley at the time of the fieldwork. The number indicates the order in which the interviews were carried out. Thus, interview B11 took place in Silicon Valley with an informant currently based there and was the 11th of all the interviews. I translated the interview quotations from Finnish to English. Furthermore, where necessary I have slightly cleaned up speech (both mine and informants) in the quotations, because speech as it actually occurs is sometimes messy and may be difficult to follow. Thus I have edited the quotations in such a way that they still include word for word what was said and stay true to the style of the speaker, but are easier for the reader to follow. In the interview quotations an *italicized* word or phrase means that the speaker stressed that word in his or her speech (tone of voice). Words or phrases in square brackets are my added explanations or comments if, for instance, names of individuals or companies have been changed to protect the anonymity of those involved, or some part of the quotation refers to something said earlier which is not directly clear from the immediate context.

2. Silicon Valley is not a location with specific, official boundaries; it typically refers to the southern part of the San Francisco Bay Area in northern California known as Santa Clara Valley. There are several cities and towns in this area, for example, Palo Alto, Santa Clara, Mountain View and San Jose (see Saxenian, 1994). For the purposes of my research, a rigid geographical delimitation of the area was not required. The idea was to study Finns who work in the most important high-technology region in the world. Thus, in addition to Santa Clara Valley, I understand Silicon Valley in a rather broad sense as consisting of the San Francisco Bay Area, including the city of San Francisco. Brown and Duguid (2002) characterize Silicon Valley as the 'ill-defined area that stretches from north of San Francisco to south of San Jose, California'. They further note that '[S]ilicon Valley is still, if not the absolute center, then one of the most significant nodes in the "wired," the "digital," the "networked," or most simply the "new" economy – a concentration of inspired ideas, astounding wealth, and the means to turn the former into the latter'.

3. No exact record of the number of Finns relevant for this research exists. Based on the estimates of various informants, it seems that the number is between 100 and 200; thus, not a significant number considering how the Silicon Valley innovation ecosystem consists of large networks of diverse ethnic and national backgrounds (for example, Indian, Chinese, Russian, Israeli). However, there are more numerous 'older-generation' Finns: people who moved to northern California several decades ago. These early migrants are not the focus of the present research. It also seems that there is no significant interaction between these two groups of Finns in Silicon Valley

4. I did not specifically ask the informants for their age, but some mentioned it. A large majority of the informants were men in their 30s and 40s: the youngest appeared to be in their late 20s, and the most senior was 62. Of the 50 main informants – those who were interviewed face to face at least once – six were women and 44 were men. Nineteen were entrepreneurs managing their own businesses (including venture capital firms) or other independent actors; 16 were employees in firms; ten were academics or scientists; and five worked at one of the Finnish public offices. However, it is important to note that about half of the informants had multiple roles, a combination of two or even three of the above categories. The classification mentioned is based on their primary activity at the time the fieldwork was carried out. Those with multiple roles worked, for example, for a public office, but with prior or additional careers as entrepreneurs, or the other way around: former public officers who had started their own firms in Silicon Valley; academics who had started their own firm; academics employed by large firms because of their expertise and so on. In general, many of the informants had wide-ranging career paths (or perhaps a career in the traditional sense is not the appropriate way to describe the work paths of these professionals). They were clearly in many ways 'the best and the brightest' of their home country, in the sense that Saxenian (2006) describes the new Argonauts in her research. More than half of the informants went to Silicon Valley with their spouses and many of those with spouses also had children. About half of the informants had lived abroad (either in the United States or elsewhere) at some point in their lives before moving to Silicon Valley.

REFERENCES

Appadurai, A. (1996), *Modernity at Large: Cultural Dimensions of Globalization*, Minneapolis, MN and London: University of Minnesota Press.

Audretsch, D.B., D. Fornahl and C. Zellner (2004), 'Introduction: structuring informal mechanisms of knowledge transfer', in D. Fornahl, C. Zellner and D.B. Audrersch (eds), *The Role of Labour Mobility and Informal Networks for Knowledge Transfer*, Heidelberg: Springer, pp. 1–7.

Bauman, Z. (1998), *Globalization: The Human Consequences*, Cambridge: Polity Press.

Bauman, Z. (2007), *Liquid Times: Living in an Age of Uncertainty*, Cambridge: Polity Press.

Beaverstock, J.V. (2002), 'Transnational elites in global cities: British expatriates in Singapore's financial district', *Geoforum*, **33**, 525–38.
Beaverstock, J.V. (2005), 'Transnational elites in the city: British highly-skilled inter-company transferees in New York City's financial district', *Journal of Ethnic and Migration Studies*, **31**(2), 245–68.
Beck, U. (2000), *The Brave New World of Work*, Cambridge: Polity Press.
Beunza, D. and D. Stark (2003), 'The organization of responsiveness: innovation and recovery in the trading rooms of Lower Manhattan', *Socioeconomic Review*, **1**(2), 135–64.
Boschma, R.A. (2005), 'Proximity and innovation: a critical assessment', *Regional Studies*, **39**, 61–74.
Bozkurt, O. (2006), 'Wired for work: highly skilled employment and global mobility in mobile telecommunications multinationals', in M.P. Smith and A. Favell (eds), *The Human Face of Global Mobility: International Highly Skilled Migration in Europe, North America and the Asia-Pacific*, New Brunswick, NJ and London: Transaction Publishers, pp. 211–46.
Brown, J.S. and P. Duguid (2000), *The Social Life of Information*, Boston, MA: Harvard Business School Press.
Brown, J.S. and P. Duguid (2002), 'Local knowledge: innovation in the networked age', *Management Learning*, **33**(4), 427–37.
Cairncross, F. (1997). *The Death of Distance: How the Communications Revolution Will Change Our Lives*, London: Orion Publishing.
Castells, M. (2000), *The Rise of the Network Society* (2nd edn), Malden, MA: Blackwell.
Castells, M. (2004), 'Informationalism, networks, and the network society: a theoretical blueprint', in M. Castells (ed.), *The Network Society: A Cross-cultural Perspective*, Cheltenham, UK and Northampton, MA, USA: Edward Elgar Publishing, pp. 3–45.
Chesbrough, H.W. (2003), *Open Innovation: The New Imperative for Creating and Profiting from Technology*, Boston, MA: Harvard Business School Press.
Chesbrough, H.W., W. Vanhaverbeke and J. West (eds) (2006), *Open Innovation: Researching a New Paradigm*, Oxford: Oxford University Press.
Conradson, D. and A. Latham (2005), 'Friendship, networks and transnationality in a world city: antipodean transmigrants in London', *Journal of Ethnic and Migration Studies*, **31**(2), 287–305.
Conradson, D. and A. Latham (2007), 'The affective possibilities of London: antipodean transnationals and the overseas experience', *Mobilities*, **2**(2), 231–54.
Dahlman, C., J. Routti and P. Ylä-Anttila (eds) (2006), *Finland as a Knowledge Economy: Elements of Success and Lessons Learned*, Washington, DC: The World Bank.
Dicken, P. (2000), 'Places and flows: situating international investment', in G.L. Clark, M.P. Feldman and M.S. Gertler (eds), *The Oxford Handbook of Economic Geography*, Oxford: Oxford University Press, pp. 275–91.
Favell, A., M. Feldblum and M.P. Smith (2006), 'The human face of global mobility: A research agenda', In M.P. Smith and A. Favell (eds), *The Human Face of Global Mobility: International Highly Skilled Migration in Europe, North America and the Asia-Pacific*, New Brunswick, NJ and London: Transaction Publishers, pp. 1–25.
Florida, R. (2002), *The Rise of the Creative Class: And How It's Transforming Work, Leisure, Community and Everyday Life*, New York, NY: Basic Books.
Florida, R. (2005), *Cities and the Creative Class*, London: Routledge.
Florida, R. (2008), *Who's Your City? How the Creative Economy is Making Where to Live the Most Important Decision of Your Life*, New York, NY: Basic Books.
Fornahl, D., C. Zellner and D.B. Audretsch (eds) (2004), *The Role of Labour Mobility and Informal Networks for Knowledge Transfer*, Heidelberg: Springer.
Friedman, T. (2005), *The World is Flat*, London: Penguin.
Giddens, A. (1990), *The Consequences of Modernity*, Cambridge: Polity Press.
Hinds, P.J. and D.E. Bailey (2003), 'Out of sight, out of sync: understanding conflict in distributed teams', *Organization Science*, **14**(6), 615–32.
Hinds, P.J. and S. Kiesler (eds) (2002), *Distributed Work*, Cambridge, MA: MIT Press.
Landry, C. (2008), *The Creative City: A Toolkit for Urban Innovators*, London and Sterling, VA: Earthscan.
Leamer, E.E. and M. Storper (2001), 'The economic geography of the internet age', *Journal of International Business Studies*, **32**(4), 641–65.
Nonaka, I. (1994), 'A dynamic theory of organizational knowledge creation', *Organization Science*, **5**(1), 14–37.
Ó Riain, S. (2000), 'Net-working for a living: Irish software developers in the global workplace', in M. Burawoy, J.A. Blum, S. George, et al. (eds), *Global Ethnography: Forces, Connections and Imaginations in a Postmodern World*, Berkeley, CA: University of California Press, pp. 175–202.
Ó Riain, S. (2006), 'Time-space intensification: Karl Polanyi, the double movement, and global informational capitalism', *Theory & Society*, **35**, 507–28.

Porter, M.E. (2000), 'Locations, clusters, and company strategy', in G.L. Clark, M.P. Feldman and M.S. Gertler (eds), *The Oxford Handbook of Economic Geography*, Oxford: Oxford University Press, pp. 253–274.

Saxenian, A. (1994), *Regional Advantage: Culture and Competition in Silicon Valley and Route 128*, Cambridge, MA: Harvard University Press.

Saxenian, A. (2006), *The New Argonauts: Regional Advantage in a Global Economy*, Cambridge, MA: Harvard University Press.

Sorenson, O. (2004), 'Social networks, informational complexity and industrial geography', in D. Fornahl, C. Zellner and D.B. Audrersch (eds), *The Role of Labour Mobility and Informal Networks for Knowledge Transfer*, Heidelberg: Springer, pp. 79–96.

Storper, M. (2000), 'Globalization, localization and trade', in G.L. Clark, M.P. Feldman and M.S. Gertler (eds), *The Oxford Handbook of Economic Geography*, Oxford: Oxford University Press, pp. 146–65.

Uzzi, B. (1997), 'Social structure and competition in interfirm networks: the paradox of embeddeddness', *Administrative Science Quarterly*, **42**(1), 35–67.

World Economic Forum (2005), *Global Competitiveness Report 2005–2006*.

PART 4

PLANNING

16 Creative cities need less government
David Emanuel Andersson

Over the past 40 years, creative cities have come to embody traits that reflect the ongoing transformation of the world's most developed regions into an emergent post-industrial and postmodern society. This transformation is affecting almost all aspects of life: manufacturing is being outsourced, production strategies are being increasingly focused on the creation of knowledge and values are becoming postmodern. Creative cities are the centres of gravity of this new society in the making.

A statistical analysis of creative cities would reveal many structural commonalities. Some of these commonalities represent a continuation of established roles in the spatial division of labour. Like the urban foci of merchant and industrial capitalism, interregional trade volumes attain their greatest volumes in the stock, real estate and merchandise markets of the largest creative cities. These cities are also the most multicultural cities; ethnic diversity indices reach their highest levels in New York and Toronto. But the unprecedented concentrations of creative workers such as scientists, artists and entertainers are even more emblematic of post-industrialism (Lakshmanan et al., 2000). Richard Florida (2002) describes this phenomenon as the emergence of a new creative class.

NEW VALUES AND THE DIVISION OF KNOWLEDGE

Less familiar is the change in values that is taking place in the world's most post-industrial regions. Ronald Inglehart (1997) calls this change 'postmodernization'. The postmodern value system refers to a cluster of values that exhibits significant positive correlations among individual responses to interview surveys. This cluster includes giving priority to freedom of expression and quality of life as well as tolerance of various minority groups and lifestyles.

The increasing importance of knowledge creation, multifaceted diversity and post-modern values reflects more complex social structures as well as widespread adoption of life-long learning. Complex economies reward the acquisition of connoisseurship (Earl, 1983), which denotes greater individual specialization. Individuals benefit from this greater specialization both as producers and as consumers. Specialization implies a greater division of knowledge, which makes a population more diverse in their priorities and preferences. There is thus a knowledge-derived increase in preference diversity that parallels increasing ethnic, religious, language and sexual diversity.

In agrarian societies, most people live in small villages with a limited division of labour. Such villagers tend to share many aspirations in life. Agrarianism is therefore – relatively speaking – compatible with the imposition of joint small-area plans and regulations, since typical leaders such as village elders are able to form reasonably accurate interpretations of widely shared concerns. While all top-down planning must confront its inability to make use of detailed individual knowledge (Hayek, 1945), the attendant knowledge losses are more limited in agrarian than in more complex societies. Industrialization – with its thoroughgoing division of labour and new opportunities for upward mobility – gives rise to substantial knowledge losses in those cases where political leaders attempt to impose a planned economy. In his refutation of central planning, Friedrich Hayek (1988) contrasts the anonymity and diversity of modern economies with the tribal and village economies of the distant past, where economic interactions occurred in small face-to-face networks.

In the creative cities of postmodern society, population diversity reaches a new level. There are several reasons for expecting large-scale planning to cause more severe knowledge problems in postmodern than in modern society. If this is indeed so, it reinforces the case for polycentric planning.

The expected increase in the problems associated with top-down planning rests on two empirical observations. The first observation is the tendency towards greater population diversity. This diversity is multidimensional and includes individual attributes such as ethnicity, lifestyle, knowledge and aesthetic preference. The second observation is the increasing preoccupation with self-expression and quality-of-life aspirations, which replaces the earlier priority given to material and existential security.

POSTMODERNIZATION

Ronald Inglehart has spent the past 40 years analysing people's basic values around the world. On the basis of patterns that he first identified in Western Europe and North America in the 1970s, Inglehart has developed a theory of value change dubbed 'postmodernization theory' (Inglehart, 1997). Inglehart's argument is three-fold. First, people establish their core values before they reach the age of 20. Second, the value system that they develop tends to reflect perceived childhood conditions. Third, the values of a population change as a result of cohort replacement: as old people die, young people with new values enter society.

Inglehart has focused on the typical values of modern industrial and postmodern postindustrial societies. In modern societies, people have 'scarcity values', which reflect their material insecurities. These insecurities make them give priority to social goals that aim at ensuring material provisions and existential security. In contrast, people who grow up under more affluent conditions tend to take their material security for granted, and give top priority to objectives that are only partly satiated. Examples include self-expression, quality of life and freedom of choice. Material security also engenders confidence: people with postmodern values do not feel as threatened by non-conforming behaviour as modernists. Thus, they tend to be more tolerant of minorities and alternative lifestyles.

Inglehart's 'postmodernization process' is most similar to theories where consumers engage in lexicographic choice. Such an understanding has precedents both within economics (Pasinetti, 1981; Earl, 1983) and cognitive psychology (Gigerenzer, 2007). In Luigi Pasinetti's (1981) theory of consumer choice, consumers satiate what they perceive as their most important needs first, typically food and shelter. Only with greater incomes can they afford to consume goods that they perceive as less essential for their survival.

If we adopt the concept of satiation, it becomes clear that Inglehart's theory posits that individuals give priority to values that are not fully satiated or are perceived as being in danger of not being fully satiated. The focus of the individual's priorities is neither on societal attributes that are taken for granted, nor on those attributes that she perceives as being beyond her reach; it is on attributes that are at the margin of consumption. As an example, a middle-income individual may focus on buying a car, rather than on buying staples such as rice or bread – for which satiation is taken for granted – or on buying a yacht – which she is likely to view as an unattainable goal.

For social values, the reasoning would be similar, although the individual should according to Inglehart (1997) exhibit greater intertemporal stability. An individual who has grown up in an affluent society presupposes satiation of food and shelter, and gives priority to values that are associated with those social attributes that are expected to be consumed but not fully satiated. Young affluent citizens of a newly industrialized and somewhat authoritarian society may therefore focus on the social attributes of democracy and freedom of speech, while we may expect young people in the mature democracies to focus on what they perceive as the partially satiated attributes of aesthetic quality of place and social tolerance of non-conforming lifestyles.

The postmodern value structure includes the values that are tapped by Inglehart's Postmaterialism Index, as well as various measures of tolerance vis-à-vis groups that have historically been discriminated against. Studied tolerance measures include attitudes towards immigrants, gays and religious minorities. Simple and partial correlation analyses reveal that the best single predictor of socio-economic development[1] at the level of the nation state is the average justification of homosexuality (measured on a Likert scale), with the percentage of respondents who do not want homosexual neighbours a close second. These two measures are also the most robust by being least sensitive to business cycle effects. People who are tolerant of homosexuality as teenagers tend to remain tolerant during economic crises. Conversely, a lot of people tend to reassess the importance of economic growth and their acceptance of immigrants during recessions (immigrants may be perceived as competitors for scarce jobs).

Richard Florida (2002) draws attention to the importance of tolerance of homosexuality with his 'gay index' for cities in the United States. Florida's contention is that cities with the greatest representation of gays also tend to have the greatest concentration of creative people and high-technology industry. According to Florida (2002), creative cities combine 'the three Ts' of talent, technology and tolerance. The people who make up the talent pool are referred to as the creative class, which encompasses workers ranging from scientists to dancers. While gay people are not necessarily more likely to belong to the creative class, Florida argues that the acceptance of gays by the general population signals a broader array of tolerant values that are conducive to creative endeavours and individual lifestyle choices.

Florida (2002) uses a number of indicators of talent, technology and tolerance to derive a 'creativity score' for individual American cities. The top four cities on this creativity measure are San Francisco, Austin, San Diego and Boston – all cities that specialize in the production of new knowledge. These creative cities share a number of features: they tend to add economic value by specializing in creativity and innovation; they tend to be multicultural places where a variety of ethnicities, languages, religions and sexual orientations have substantial constituencies; and they have the most complex economies by hosting the greatest division of knowledge.

INCREASING COMPLEXITY LEADS TO DIVERGENT PREFERENCES

Economic development is the process of attaining increasingly complex capital structures. One way of understanding the relative complexity of a city is as the minimum length of the 'recipe' that describes its economy. Another definition involves the number of nodes and links between the resources that make up the production system of the urban economy. As economies grow more complex, material and human resources become more heterogeneous as a result of increasing resource differentiation. Both production and consumption goods come to embody a greater number of attributes that are perceived as distinct from one another (Andersson, 2008).

Ludwig Lachmann ([1956]1978) explains how our understanding of capital is distorted when it is defined as a homogeneous capital stock. The stock concept is misleading because it only applies to hypothetical end-state equilibria, rather than to the ongoing entrepreneurial process of innovation and speculation. While the set of productive activities in an industrial economy includes a small subset of innovative activities, post-industrial society has been described as having an economy where leading firms specialize in continuous innovation.

The capital structure – unlike the capital stock – consists of a variety of multi-attribute resources, each with a different level of 'specificity'. The specificity of a capital good refers to the number of production processes in which the good is a valued input, with greater specificity implying a smaller number. The agglomeration of human capital that is embodied in the population of a city is also a capital structure; a human capital structure (Lewin, 1999). Creative cities have human capital structures that are exceptionally heterogeneous. This heterogeneity derives from the complexity of production processes and the far-reaching division of knowledge brought about by high levels of specialization.

Individuals learn explicit and tacit knowledge, increasing their connoisseurship both as producers and consumers. As producers, this implies that they can distinguish an increasingly fine-grained division of production attributes. For example, a specialist interior decorator is able to distinguish more shades of the colour green and a greater variety of leather textures than the average person. As consumers, individuals develop certain skills that make them better able to distinguish between attributes in their favoured consumption activities. A sophisticated consumer of music may be able to perceive subtle rhythmic changes and a variety of complex chords, which alludes to a greater level of connoisseurship than the average listener (Andersson and Andersson, 2006).

The development of productive connoisseurship for the most part relies on formal education and work experience. Consumptive connoisseurship reflects both formal education and leisure activities. Such activities give rise to informal learning.

For the analysis of consumer choice, it is consumptive connoisseurship that is most relevant. In creative cities, it is quite common for people to have 16 or more years of combined general-purpose and specialized formal education. Formal education imparts knowledge that people can benefit from in their role as consumers: literacy may promote connoisseurship in the consumption of literature and physical education may lead to more skilful consumption of basketball games for participants and spectators alike.

But leisure activities may be more important for consumption, since leisure time other than time devoted to eating or sleeping accounts for about half of the average person's lifetime in the most developed parts of the world (Maddison, 1988; Andersson, 2008, p. 158). The combination of high formal levels of education and plenty of leisure time means that it is common for consumers to become quite skilled in their favourite activities. The individual consumption experience therefore reflects individual learning trajectories as well as influences from other people. Higher levels of connoisseurship imply that we can expect increasing preference heterogeneity, both within groups with shared interests and between groups representing different leisure time pursuits.

The combined effect of increasing material security (Inglehart, 1997), increasing formal education (Andersson, 2008, p. 92) and increasing leisure time is a more widespread preoccupation with quality-of-life concerns. For this reason, aesthetic choices may come to be seen as more relevant to one's overall life situation than in the past. Empirically, this tendency is demonstrated by the high average income elasticity of demand for art and entertainment goods throughout Europe and North America (Andersson and Andersson, 2006). The higher priority given to the aesthetic dimension of life has also been the subject of a number of popular books (for example, Postrel, 2004).

WHO'S YOUR CITY?

Florida (2008) argues that people have three really important choices in their lives: what (job), who (spouse) and where (location)? With increasing mobility – due in part to falling transport costs and the removal of some barriers to migration – there are increasing opportunities for individual location choices. For some people, particularly members of the creative class, the set of feasible locations encompasses cities and regions in many different parts of the world. Examples of employers that take advantage of global labour markets include multinational corporations and research universities.

But there are still barriers that limit the individual freedom of choosing one's location. Immigration laws are an obvious example. There are also numerous other cultural and regulatory hurdles. I will limit my discussion to two such hurdles: language regulations in the education system and floor-area ratios as an urban planning tool, both of which illustrate the inadequacies of top-down planning, particularly in a postmodern setting.

LANGUAGE POLICIES

When people choose where to live, it is inevitable that language is one of many considerations. This is not always conscious; entire countries or continents may be unconsciously excluded from the set of feasible options because of the perceived need for proficiency in a difficult or unusual language. Most of these required languages are consequences of conquest and domination. The Yiddish-speaking linguist Max Weinreich (1945) aptly used the Yiddish formulation[2] '*a shprakh iz a dialekt mit an armey un flot*', or 'a language is a dialect with an army and a navy'.

For the prospective resident in a city with an official language that is different from her mother tongue, the problem is not only limited to shopping for groceries or filing tax returns. Frequently, governments demand fluency in an official language as a formal graduation requirement at all levels of education. In addition, there is often a de facto language requirement for contacts with civil servants and for participation in local organizations of various types.

The typical situation need, however, not be so constraining. The world of science – which is a supranational community without formal language laws – is interesting because it has developed as a spontaneous order (Hayek, 1979) beyond the reach of any individual political jurisdiction. The spontaneous order of scientific language conventions is evident in the gradual evolution of standards, rather than their being subject to a planned order of top-down language dictates. Of particular interest are those scientists with other native languages than English. If we look at the language choices of scientists outside the English-speaking world, an interesting pattern emerges: English has evolved into the increasingly accepted medium of scholarly interaction, thereby reducing the overall transaction cost level. At the same time, most of these scientists choose to speak their own native language when interacting with family and their local friends.

Hong Kong constitutes another clue to the workings of what a general spontaneous order of languages might look like. The British colonial administration adopted a policy of linguistic tolerance towards their local subjects. The effect was similar to the world of science: local residents with substantial multicultural business activities became increasingly fluent in English, while virtually all Cantonese residents of Hong Kong preserved their fluency in the Cantonese language (misleadingly called the Cantonese dialect since it has never been backed by the coercive apparatus of the state). In fact, Cantonese is the only Sinic language that has developed a number of Chinese characters that are not used by speakers of Mandarin. Tellingly, when one crosses the border to neighbouring Guangdong province, proficiency levels in both Cantonese and English drop, while proficiency in army-and-navy-backed Mandarin improves.

A deregulation of language use would mean that there would be no legal requirement to learn government-imposed languages, with the effect that the schools in a city could teach in a variety of languages according to the diverse preferences of both established and newly arrived residents. The set of feasible location choices would grow, and a possible scenario is both greater language standardization (if the spontaneous language order results in global rather than national standards) and greater preservation of minority mother tongues.

FLOOR-AREA RATIOS

The effect of top-down language planning has many parallels in top-down urban planning, although the psychological effects on residents with contrary preferences are unlikely to be as dramatic. A common planning instrument is the imposition of maximum floor-area ratios (FARs), which most planners interpret as being more compatible with market-led urban development than more detailed land-use plans. Many urban planning authorities use maximum FARs as one of their main planning tools, particularly in the United States and Japan. But top-down standardization of FARs gives rise to problems that in many ways are analogous to language laws.

For the most part, urban planning is ostensibly concerned with provision of public goods, promotion of positive externalities and abatement of negative externalities. These public goods are not the pure public goods of pure non-spatial economics but rather territorial goods, so that it is costly rather than impossible to exclude non-payers, while consumption rivalry mounts with increasing congestion. Positive externalities arise when the costs of establishing and maintaining property rights over resources are perceived as being greater than their marginal value. Negative externalities exist for analogous reasons: the transaction costs of administering liabilities are perceived as being greater than the added value associated with establishing and maintaining the corresponding property rights (Barzel, 1989; Webster and Lai, 2003). Both territorial 'public' goods and externalities tend to influence land prices. A public park, friendly neighbours, and a noisy street are all reflected in site values to the extent that buyers and sellers perceive these attributes and have preferences that are important enough to influence their willingness to pay.

The conventional distinction between public goods and different types of externalities hides the fact that they refer to different descriptions of what is in essence the same phenomenon (Buchanan and Tullock, 1962). The persistence of the distinction is perhaps due to the theoretical predilection for distinguishing between pure public goods and distance-attenuated externalities. But most instances of what is commonly referred to as public goods are in fact also subject to distance effects or geographical delimitations; location specificity even applies to military defence, which is a common but erroneous example of a pure public good. Consequently, it is possible to analyse a park as a generator of positive externalities (the spillover effects of an amenity that is not explicitly traded). It is also possible to construe traffic congestion as a 'negative territorial public good' or, equivalently, a 'public bad'. In the latter case, a public good interpretation gives rise to a description of congestion couched in public good terminology. Congestion could then be characterized as a situation where it is costly to exclude people who do not pay for their marginal contribution to congestion levels, and where consumption of the congestion attribute is non-rival and associated with shared utility losses.

In this context, it is important to remember that whether a resource or attribute is a territorial public good/externality varies according to the open-ended subjective values and preferences of individual consumers. The sight of a gay couple holding hands in one's neighbourhood may constitute a positive externality to individuals who value a tolerant and inclusive neighbourhood, while it may be a negative externality to traditionalists. Others may be indifferent about the sexual orientations of others, but the gay couple may still have an indirect impact which might make these indifferent others care for economic rather than cultural or religious reasons. The indirect impact derives from the effects of market transactions on land values. Increasing the 'gayness' of a neighbourhood may raise the relative price of land in a city where most people have postmodern values even though an identical increase might have reduced the price in modernist cities of the industrial era.

Maximum FARs are usually presented as a type of regulation that reduces negative externalities – 'public bads' – such as traffic and electricity grid congestion, unpleasant views, noise and fire hazards. The stated rationale behind FAR policies is that they aim to ensure a pleasant living environment. The aim supposedly justifies government regulations, owing to the high transaction costs and potential free-riding problems that could arise if residents were left to their own devices.

There are at least three problems with this line of reasoning. First, it ignores the subjectivity and heterogeneity of consumer preferences. Second, it ignores the problem of discovering what those preferences are. Third, it ignores the existence of a market for club goods where amenities and disamenities are capitalized in real estate prices.

Many urban planners assume that FARs above a certain threshold are unattractive to people in general. It is never really clear what ratio corresponds to this threshold – which is presumably where marginal agglomeration economies equal marginal agglomeration diseconomies. One may surmise that the desired threshold rose among planners who were persuaded by the high-density advocacy of Jane Jacobs (1961): the low FAR of the garden city yielded to the higher FAR of the new urbanist city. But is there any ratio that is 'naturally' appropriate?

The simple answer is that there is no fixed ratio that optimizes density. The insurmountable problem is that one person's congestion may be another person's lively and bustling urban neighbourhood. The Chinese have an expression for high-density urban spaces: they say that it is *renao*, which connotes approval and attractiveness. The expression is often used for some of the world's most crowded urban neighbourhoods. And the preference for high-density neighbourhoods seems to be widespread: a hedonic study of seven metropolitan regions in Taiwan revealed strong negative correlations – the correlation coefficients ranged from –0.35 to –0.75 – between geographical distance to the urban core and neighbourhood income and education levels (Andersson et al., forthcoming). Likewise, the most prestigious neighbourhood in Hong Kong (Mid-levels) is a cluster of skyscrapers that abuts the central business district. Many Chinese parents express a preference for inner-city living 'because it's better for children'.

These Chinese observations do not invalidate the many parents who claim that they want to live in the suburbs because they think children benefit from single family homes and open spaces. But it shows that it is not inevitable that parents make up a homogeneous group with the same location preferences. Such preference heterogeneity is to be expected, especially in knowledge societies where aesthetic and environmental preferences play an increasing role in location decisions.

DIVERSITY AND EXPERIMENTS

Land-use preferences are neither given nor homogeneous. They are impossible to survey in their entirety by urban planners. Land-use regulations make up an open-ended set; there will always be room for experiments and entrepreneurial innovation. And the difficulties of planners are compounded by the fact that individuals know their own preferences best, owing to the cognitive limitations of the human mind (Hayek, 1952).

Decentralized experimentation, on the other hand, gives rise to new attribute combinations that will gradually be capitalized in the price of land. The price thereby disseminates distilled information about the attractiveness of the experiment in the judgement of consumers according to their own preferences (Hayek, 1945). Such composite market prices are more difficult to interpret than the prices of more homogeneous goods (for example, crude oil or tap water). But a system with decentralized entrepreneurial land-use planners will nevertheless disseminate knowledge of consumer preferences more effectively than top-down planners. It will also be able to satisfy a greater variety of preferences.

As a hypothetical example, consider the situation of a family that wants to choose their city. In this case, the family consists of two women and one child. One of the two women is an artist who is a native speaker of Mongolian, while the other is a musician who is a native speaker of Kurdish. Together, they are raising their adopted daughter.

The socio-economic description of this family does not fall neatly into any of the standard categories devised by government statisticians; it is an example of the type of previously unusual household that is becoming increasingly common in creative cities around the world. Let us further assume that the two parents want their daughter to learn both of her mother tongues as well as English, and that they prefer to live in a newly built housing unit in a high-energy place with high densities and FARs. This is based on their perception that high-density cities are more likely to have lively art and music scenes.

In the present situation with mostly top-down government regulations, they may find that Mongolian is only taught in Mongolia, that Kurdish is only taught in what is today known as northern Iraq, while English is offered in a variety of locations. They may also discover that the formal and informal institutions of both Asian regions make them unattractive for lesbian couples, while tolerant English-speaking locations with relevant agglomeration economies (in art and music) only offer affordable new housing in low-density neighbourhoods. In these neighbourhoods, neither Kurdish nor Mongolian is part of any school curriculum.

Decentralized language and land-use planning does not guarantee that any location meets all preferences of our hypothetical Kurdish-Mongolian artist-musician lesbian family. But decentralized planning improves the odds for each unusual consumer preference. It would, for example, be possible for a group of tolerant creative-class Mongolians to get together, start their own neighbourhood with their own preferred land-use regulations anywhere in the world and invest in a bilingual Mongolian-English school.

The couple may find that their daughter can only receive formal education in English and Mongolian while Kurdish remains unavailable; that the neighbourhood is embedded in a conurbation with an appropriate music scene but without a relevant art cluster; and that the neighbourhood that was initiated by a group of Mongolian-speakers (and their metaphorical 'fellow travellers') is of medium rather than high density. Still, the existence of a neighbourhood that allows FARs greater than one, that hosts a bilingual Mongolian-English school and which welcomes lesbian couples and their adopted children represents a much better matching of supply and demand than would be possible in cities with one-size-fits-all language, land-use, marriage and adoption policies.

Standardization, whether of language policies, FARs or interpretations of what constitutes a family are but three instances of top-down planning that share systemic features. The next section provides some general guidelines that deal with the choice between unitary and diverse standards.

UNITARY OR DIVERSE STANDARDS?

Most political regulations have the purpose of standardizing goods and services. Such standardization reduces the transaction costs that are associated with information search: if there is only one combination of languages or one FAR that is offered to consumers, the search for attractive language bundles or FARs is eliminated and the attendant search costs disappear. But there are opportunity costs that may be substantial; in this case, a lack of variety that may result in most consumers being unable to match their location with a reasonably attractive mix of languages and FARs.

As a general principle, however, standardization results in lower transaction costs which may offset the loss of variety, but only if the regulator is the lower-cost processor of information. A regulatory authority may have such cost advantages if its time costs are low or if there are scale economies in information processing. For such standardization to be attractive to consumers, potential scale economies and low time costs must, however, also be sufficiently large to offset two intrinsic problems that regulatory authorities cannot avoid.

The first problem is that supra-individual regulators have an information-processing handicap. The handicap stems from the difficulty of eliciting information that represents the heterogeneity of consumer preferences; it is sometimes referred to as the Hayekian knowledge problem. The problem increases with increasing heterogeneity and instability of preferences in the affected population.

The second problem is that opportunistic tendencies on the part of the regulator may offset its possibly superior ability to identify and measure the objects of standardization; corrupt regulators tend to be unreliable. The potential transaction cost savings must therefore exceed the transaction cost losses that result from inferior knowledge of consumer preferences and potential rent-seeking behaviour.

A way of ameliorating the handicaps of both consumers and regulators is through a competitive market for regulators. Such competition can preserve variety and suppress opportunism, since regulators with a good reputation can sell their services at a premium. Regulatory organizations that are more responsive than others to various niches of consumers with similar preferences will see an appreciation in the capital value of organizational resources. Examples of such resources include the ability to inspire trust, the degree of fit with consumer preferences in one or more market segments and lack of variability in relevant output attributes. The development of corporate brand names thus fulfils the same economic function as regulatory agencies. Unlike regulatory agencies, variability may be preserved through the co-existence of several brand names, and the co-existence of several organizations that compete with one another over non-captive consumers keeps rent-seeking in check.

Fred Foldvary (1994) explains how private territorial organizations provide a variety of territorial public goods that are often associated with public sector activity. Examples include roads, parks and land-use regulations. Such territorial public goods amount to goods without an explicit price (that is, externalities) that nonetheless enter the price system as they become capitalized in the market value of the affected land. If the supplier of a park also owns the territory that it affects, it becomes possible to recoup the investment cost: a profitable park then implies park-derived aggregate land value increments that more than offset the investment cost. Foldvary (1994) shows how organizations such as Disneyworld and various hotel and condominium developments are able to supply public goods and regulations in the absence of both taxation and political assemblies. Both material infrastructure investments and local institutions such as regulations may thus be subjected to market feedback, which comes into being through a combination of land transactions and short-term rentals.

Hotel brands constitute one example of using short-term territorial clubs to supply land-use regulations and public goods. A hotel is a type of micro-neighbourhood that offers territorial public goods such as swimming pools, parking lots and elevators, as well as land-use regulations such as aesthetic guidelines, a property-specific FAR, and explicit or implicit language requirements for customers' interactions with agents of the organization.

Hotel brands divide naturally into niches, offering local environments that range from basic tenements to elaborate beach resorts or mountain retreats. For example, in the popular 'three-star' niche, consumers can choose between the regulations and public goods of several brands such as Ibis, Holiday Inn Express and Comfort Inn. They can also opt for an independent hotel (an unbranded bundle of location attributes), which sometimes offers lower rates in exchange for the lack of brand name predictability. Conversely, some hotels have chosen not to affiliate with chains because they cater to specific niches. Examples include hotels that can be rented by the hour, hotels for observant Muslim businessmen and hotels that cater to gay couples.

There is also a second level of regulation in the market for regulators. Michelin, Fodor's, Frommer's and Lonely Planet are examples of brand names that compete in a higher-order regulation market, by rating hotel brands as well as individual hotels. They serve as a guide for consumers in their choice between different location options. The rating organizations are imperfect substitutes that target different or partially overlapping subsets of potential consumers; they both compete with and complement one another. These higher-order regulators offer an additional source of knowledge that is disseminated as market feedback. The feedback has two main consequences. First, price-rating combinations affect consumer demand, to the extent that consumers read and believe the reports. Second, producers receive third-party expert assessments of their perceived strengths and weaknesses.

The great number of rating organizations has even induced various guides to the rating organizations themselves. These guides amount to an even higher-order regulatory level. In the market for quality regulations, the opportunities for infinite regress are only limited by the perceived opportunity cost of prospective participants at each successive level.

Hotels amount to small neighbourhoods with short-term residents. Residential neighbourhoods only differ in degree, not in kind. They tend to be somewhat larger in square acreage and have residents that stay for longer time periods. None of these differences makes it more difficult to supply shared infrastructure in the form of physical facilities or institutional regulations. As the size of a private neighbourhood increases, the upper limit of the largest park and longest street will also tend to increase, reflecting the spatial enlargement of the area from which land-value gains accrue to the investor.

By noting the economic commonalities between residential neighbourhoods, hotels and amusement parks, it becomes a straightforward exercise to envision an analogous market for neighbourhood brands within different market segments, as well as independent neighbourhoods that sometimes serve small minority niches. Apart from noise regulations and shared elevators – which are already common in most private multi-family housing – brands may compete by offering distinct and sometimes idiosyncratic entrepreneurial combinations of neighbourhood attributes. Different brands could offer different combinations of shared attributes such as building codes, land-use zoning principles, fire codes, smoking regulations and speed limits within their respective spatial domains.

While a diversity of neighbourhood types would facilitate the matching of supply and demand, it still does not address the spatial extent of a competitive neighbourhood. While a small neighbourhood may encompass the 'market area' of the local FAR and a few one-way residential streets, it will tend to be too large for deciding on the interior design of individual dwellings, and too small for engaging in airport development. What is then the appropriate aggregation level of various types of plan? The subsidiarity rule addresses this question.

THE SUBSIDIARITY RULE

Yoram Barzel (1989) explains the subsidiarity rule: the tendency of a property right over a resource to end up in the possession of the individual or organization most able to influence the value of the resource.[3] This tendency comes about because individuals who perceive that they are capable of adding value – compared with the existing use of a resource – will tend to out-bid competitors in the market. If a market participant judges that she has greater ability to add value to the use of a resource than its current owner, then this will imply a higher reservation price than the current market price. The higher reservation price is caused by the owner's status as the residual claimant to variations in resource value. In other words, the residual claimant earns profits and suffers losses as a result of changes in the market price of the resource; this makes her assume the uncertainty-bearing function of the entrepreneur (Knight, 1921; Foss et al., 2007, Andersson, 2008, pp. 99–106).

Incorrect perceptions are common, but tend to be weeded out by market losses. The adjustment process will be especially effective for entrepreneurial ventures with a short time horizon, but even long-term projects will have to exit the market in the face of long-term persistent losses.

The reason for the tendency of competitive markets to promote higher-valued resource use is not that the future is in any way predetermined; the reason is that society is not made up of an undecipherable collection of random events. All relevant factors may change, but they change on different time scales. Stable rules (institutions) are particularly important among the slowly changing factors that make convergent expectations possible (Koppl, 2002). Such institutions not only stabilize expectations of market prices but also make human behaviour intelligible and – as regards the habitual as opposed to entrepreneurial components of behaviour – predictable.

The subsidiarity rule relies on the operation of competitive producers and consumers. When a centralized state monopolizes the use of a resource, there is no such tendency for resource control and residual claims to flow to the party with the greatest ability to influence value. The common underperformance of state organizations in their role as supplier of consumer goods and services (Mueller, 1989) derives from an intrinsic feature of all protected monopolies: many errors remain undetected because market feedback about consumer preferences has been eliminated. Monopolies become hotbeds of ignorance about consumers (the knowledge problem), not merely hotbeds of listless neglect (the incentive problem).

As competition increases, subsidiarity rule effects increase as well. For example, competitive contracting for the production of tax-funded goods implies that the control of production will tend to flow in the direction of the most cost-efficient producer, to the extent that such contracting operates in a system without widespread corruption. Decentralized political jurisdictions imply that mobile resources (people and some capital goods) will tend to flow to those jurisdictions with the most attractive mixture of policies and access to resources. The balance of inflows and outflows will gradually come to be incorporated in land values and the tax base.

The subsidiarity rule applied to language use implies that organizations such as schools and regular firms will tend to adopt those languages that add most value to their output. This ultimately depends on the consumer preferences of affected parties such as potential students and parents (for schools) and potential employees and exchange partners (for regular firms). Consumers might value knowledge of a global language – which might lower transaction cost levels – and a local language – which could reflect subjective valuations of cultural heritage preservation. Some may value languages other than their mother tongue or a global communication language, for example, Latin because of a subjective valuation of historical knowledge or Italian because of a subjective interest in Italian food, architecture or opera. A market for languages has the potential of both promoting global standardization and those minority languages that have not been adopted as the preferred tongue of some ruling political elite. Examples of widely spoken non-official languages include Cantonese, Kurdish and Yiddish as well as stigmatized varieties of official languages.

The subsidiarity rule applies with equal force to the production of FAR regulations. Those most able to influence the FAR effects of a specific neighbourhood correspond to the individual or organization that controls the closest approximation of the market area of the regulation. The market area corresponds to the geographical extent of land-value effects attributable to the specific FAR, which in this case may coincide with an existing neighbourhood, or be smaller or larger depending on the exact configuration of utility spillovers between neighbourhoods.

In practice, most empirical studies of neighbourhood attributes – including both land-use regulations and the socio-economic attributes of residents – imply that such attribute effects tend to have steep price-distance gradients. Thus, land-value effects are for the most part limited to small neighbourhoods of less than one square kilometre. By way of example, a hedonic study of Singapore's condominium market showed that the socio-economic character of individual condominiums had a greater effect on land prices that the socio-economic character of the postal district in which the condominium was located (Andersson, 2000).

WHAT SHOULD GOVERNMENTS DO?

Although many territorial public goods only have small-area effects, there are important exceptions. Particularly for one category of territorial public goods, it is not likely that a sufficient supply will be forthcoming if one relies exclusively on decentralized market processes. James Buchanan and Gordon Tullock (1962) explain that in the case of a public good that affects an area with widely dispersed land ownership, it is likely that high transaction costs will preclude agreements that make beneficiaries pay for large-area goods according to their respective shares of the expected benefit. Market transactions depend on the principle of unanimous consent: only those transactions that are in an *ex ante* sense perceived as representing a utility gain will be embarked upon by market participants. For some transactions, however, costs associated with search, contracting, monitoring and enforcement may be such that they dwarf otherwise substantial utility gains.

An airport is a good example of an investment that would often fall prey to free-riding problems in a pure free market setting, resulting in high transaction costs. Buchanan and Tullock (1962) therefore propose that it would be in the individual's interest to accept political decision-making for goods that affect a large number of land owners. Unfortunately, large-area public goods are also more susceptible to political opportunistic behaviour (rent-seeking) than smaller-area goods, since the cost of the exit option increases with the spatial extent of the jurisdiction, other things being equal. Entry and exit of residents or capital functions as a signal of institutional performance by becoming capitalized in aggregate land values, and serves to limit opportunities for political rent-seeking. Still, the accessibility effects of airports may be important enough to imply a preference for majority voting over unanimity rules in most cities.

Other examples of where we may expect the benefits of tax-funded supply to exceed its costs are all those widely used infrastructures that affect an area with a large number of land owners. It goes without saying that this category includes the soft infrastructure of delineating, cataloguing and enforcing property rights. It also includes hard infrastructures such as utility networks, transit systems and major roads. Like the legal system, basic scientific research arguably also belongs to the type of soft infrastructure where spatially delimited governments may add more than they subtract. However, even potentially beneficial government investments may be perverted if governments not only organize their funding but also their production (Mueller, 1989) or if they outlaw competing private infrastructures (Hayek, 1960).

CONCLUSION: THE PRIVATE DEFAULT

For many neighbourhood attributes it will be private governance organizations rather than political governments that will be most able to influence attribute value. Such organizations will have an incentive to add value as long as it remains the residual claimant: the measure of the attractiveness of a land-use regulation or a shared facility is its ability to elicit an additional aggregate willingness to pay in excess of costs. The subsidiarity rule also implies that the market will sustain present owners as long as they at least break even and have an implicit or explicit willingness to pay that exceeds the bids of all other market participants. Thus, the idea of profit-seeking neighbourhoods that control those facilities and regulations that are in joint use within their respective spatial domains is consistent with the workings of the subsidiarity rule.

The subsidiarity rule is general in that it can be applied to all areas of social life. A seemingly remote example is from the sociology of religion, where Rodney Stark and Roger Finke (2000) reach conclusions that are virtually identical from an empirical investigation of the dynamics of competitive churches. They find that churches attract most donations and participation if the individual congregation has to compete for patronage with other congregations, both within and across denominations. Priests, ministers or rabbis whose incomes and utility levels depend on voluntary contributions and attendance are more likely to respond to consumer feedback than religious workers within a monopoly church with tax-funded revenue. On the basis of this finding, Stark and Finke (2000) argue for the separation of church and state. But their conclusion is not limited to religion, since a religious service is a typical example of a territorial public good with potential free-riding problems. They could with equal justification be arguing for the separation of language and state or FARs and state. Indeed, they could extend their conclusion to encompass the separation of education and state or neighbourhood land-use planning and state.

NOTES

1. Analyses of partial correlations (controlling for Inglehart's 4-item or 12-item Postmaterialism Index) reveal that justification of homosexuality or acceptance of gay neighbours exhibit consistently significant correlations with a host of indicators of national socio-economic development, unlike the Postmaterialism Index, tolerance of other minorities or justification of other controversial lifestyles (controlling for justification or tolerance of homosexuality). The simple correlation between justification of homosexuality and development is 0.79 where development is measured as a composite socio-economic index comprising the Human Development Index (weight: 50 per cent), the Corruption Perception Index (weight: 25 per cent) and the Press Freedom Index (weight: 25 per cent). This is based on my own calculations, using the most recent data from the 81 countries that carried out interview surveys between 1990 and 2008 (data available at http://www.worldvaluessurvey.org) and the most recent data (in 2009) from Transparency International (data available at http://www.transparency.org), Freedom House (data available at http://www.freedomhouse.org) and the United Nations Development Programme (data available at http://www.undp.org) (websites accessed 15 May 2009). The partial correlation between justification of homosexuality and development (controlling for the Postmaterialism Index) is 0.58 while the partial correlation of the Postmaterialism Index and development (controlling for justification of homosexuality) is 0.19.
2. The original Yiddish reference is 'טאַלף װאָ יימאַראָ נאַ טימ טקעלאַריַ א זיא ָ ראַרפשַ א'.
3. See also Webster and Lai (2003) for applications of the subsidiarity rule that are explicitly spatial and urban.

REFERENCES

Andersson, D.E. (2000), 'Hypothesis testing in hedonic price estimation: on the selection of independent variables', *Annals of Regional Science*, **34** (2), 21–34.
Andersson, D.E. (2008), *Property Rights, Consumption and the Market Process*, Cheltenham, UK and Northampton, MA, USA: Edward Elgar publishing.
Andersson, Å.E. and D.E. Andersson (2006), *The Economics of Experiences, the Arts, and Entertainment*, Cheltenham, UK and Northampton, MA, USA: Edward Elgar Publishing.
Andersson, D.E., Oliver F. Shyr and A. Lee (forthcoming), 'The successes and failures of a key transportation link: accessibility effects of Taiwan's high-speed rail', *Annals of Regional Science*, doi: 10.1007/s00168-010-0405-5.
Barzel, Y. (1989), *Economic Analysis of Property Rights*, New York, NY: Cambridge University Press.
Buchanan, J.M. and G. Tullock (1962), *The Calculus of Consent: Logical Foundations of Constitutional Democracy*, Ann Arbor, MI: University of Michigan Press.
Earl, P.E. (1983), *The Economic Imagination: Towards a Behavioural Theory of Choice*, Brighton: Wheatsheaf.
Florida, R. (2002), *The Rise of the Creative Class and How It's Transforming Work, Leisure, Community, and Everyday Life*, New York, NY: Basic Books.
Florida, R. (2008), *Who's Your City? How the Creative Economy is Making Where to Live the Most Important Decision of Your Life*, New York, NY: Basic Books.

Foldvary, F. (1994), *Public Goods and Private Communities: The Market Provision of Social Services*, Aldershot, UK and Brookfield, VT, USA: Edward Elgar Publishing.

Foss, K., N.J. Foss, P.G. Klein and S.K. Klein (2007), 'The entrepreneurial organization of heterogeneous capital', *Journal of Management Studies*, **44** (7), 1165–86.

Gigerenzer, G. (2007), *Gut Feeling: The Intelligence of the Unconscious*, New York, NY: Viking Press.

Hayek, F.A. (1945), 'The use of knowledge in society', *American Economic Review*, **35** (4), 519–30.

Hayek, F.A. (1952), *The Sensory Order*, Chicago, IL: University of Chicago Press.

Hayek, F.A. (1960), *The Constitution of Liberty*, Chicago, IL: University of Chicago Press.

Hayek, F.A. (1979), *Law, Legislation, and Liberty*, Chicago, IL: University of Chicago Press.

Hayek, F.A. (1988), *The Fatal Conceit: The Errors of Socialism*, Chicago, IL: University of Chicago Press.

Inglehart, R. (1997), *Modernization and Postmodernization: Cultural, Economic, and Political Change in 43 Societies*, Princeton, NJ: Princeton University Press.

Jacobs, J. (1961), *The Death and Life of Great American Cities*, New York, NY: Random House.

Knight, F.H. (1921), *Risk, Uncertainty, and Profit*, Boston, MA: Houghton Mifflin.

Koppl, R. (2002), *Big Players and the Economic Theory of Expectations*, Basingstoke: Palgrave Macmillan.

Lachmann, L.M. [1956] (1978), *Capital and Its Structure*, Kansas City, MO: Sheed Andrews and McMeel.

Lakshmanan, T.R., D.E. Andersson, L. Chatterjee and K. Sasaki (2000), 'Three global cities: New York, London, and Tokyo', in Å.E. Andersson and D.E. Andersson (eds), *Gateways to the Global Economy*, Cheltenham, UK and Northampton, MA, USA: Edward Elgar Publishing, pp. 49–80.

Lewin, P. (1999), *Capital in Disequilibrium: The Role of Capital in a Changing World*, London: Routledge.

Maddison, A. (1988), *Phases of Capitalist Development*, Oxford: Oxford University Press.

Mueller, D.C. (1989), *Public Choice II*, Cambridge: Cambridge University Press.

Pasinetti, L.L. (1981), *Structural Change and Economic Growth*, Cambridge: Cambridge University Press.

Postrel, V. (2004), *The Substance of Style: How the Rise of Aesthetic Value is Remaking Commerce, Culture, and Consciousness*, New York, NY: Harper Perennial.

Stark, R. and R. Finke (2000), *Acts of Faith: Explaining the Human Side of Religion*, Berkeley, CA, Los Angeles, CA and London: University of California Press.

Webster, C. and L.W.-C. Lai (2003), *Cities, Planning, and Markets: Managing Spontaneous Cities*, Cheltenham, UK and Northampton, MA, USA: Edward Elgar Publishing.

Weinreich, M. (1945), 'The YIVO faces the post-war world', *YIVO Bletter*, **25** (1), 3–18.

17 Land-use regulation for the creative city
Stefano Moroni

As is well known, over half of the world's population live in cities; the figure in Europe is over 75 per cent. Cities have become our standard environment worldwide and a template for human life on earth. Our postmodern cities are characterized by radical pluralism (that is, a strong diversification and differentiation of citizens' ideas of the good, lifestyles and preferences) and extreme dynamism (a continuous flow and change of processes and events).

Cities have always been wealth-creating entities, but recently this fact has become even more accentuated. Today's cities account for over 80 per cent of wealth in developed nations: cities have become the true engines of economic growth and development. 'Despite all the hype over globalization . . ., place is actually more important in the global economy than ever before' (Florida, 2008, p. 9).[1]

Consequently, the way in which we regulate land use in cities must *per force* have a strong influence on our way of life, our welfare and our prosperity. The central focus of this chapter is how we can regulate land use in our contemporary cities in a manner that is both effective and legitimate. After discussing these two aspects of the issue, and demonstrating how the traditional and, in many respects, current approach to land-use planning[2] is in this regard inadequate and open to critique (second section), I will suggest where and how we might look for an answer (third section), that will also contribute to making today's cities more creative (fourth section).

It is worth outlining what I mean here by the term 'creative cities'. The concept of 'creativity' has gained critical traction, primarily in reference to so-called 'creative economics', that is, economics that pivot on knowledge and innovation (Howkins, 2001). In this perspective, we can apply the expression 'creative cities' to denote cities in which the economy and community are actively involved in generating knowledge and innovation. In this sense the expression 'creative cities' is purely descriptive and empirical. I hold that this is the pertinent application of the expression, given how the idea has been unacceptably diluted over time,[3] to the point of absorbing local administration activity, and even assuming an undesirable and immediate normative implication. As I will try to show, the passage from the analytical concept of the creative city to a certain kind of (creative) policy-making has been too simplistic.

THE PROBLEM: FACTS AND VALUES SHAPING THE ISSUE OF EFFECTIVE AND LEGITIMATE LAND-USE REGULATION

The first aspect mentioned above – effectiveness – points to a question of facts (first subsection); while the second – legitimacy – points to a question of values (second subsection).

Facts: Complexity and Self-organization

With regard to effectiveness, we could begin by observing that it is commonplace today to acknowledge that the world is complex, as so many sophisticated theories indicate.[4] A complex system is a system having a very large number of components; it is polycentric; it exhibits stable emergent patterns; it is self-organizing and dynamic (that is, adaptive and evolutionary).[5]

Let us now reconsider each of the above-mentioned characteristics with specific reference to that fundamental social system that the market system is or – as I prefer to call it, interpreting it broadly as the totality of voluntary exchange relations – the 'catallactic system'.[6] With regard to cities, we may speak of the 'catallactic urban system' as being part of a more inclusive catallactic order. Five observations are relevant in this context.

First, the market system is clearly a system with many components, in this case individuals, each of whom is trying to implement his or her conception of 'the good life' according to individual preferences, ideas and aspirations. Individuals are not necessarily selfish, but they do focus on their own personal notions of what constitutes a good life (Kirzner, 1992).

Second, the market system is a polycentric one, that is, a decentralized system of decisions and actions in which individuals interact continuously. Each individual adjusts his or her actions to the state of affairs that results from the actions of other individuals.

Third, a social system such as the market presents emergent patterns of behaviour. The orderliness of the pattern of actions that emerges is in no sense part of the aim of any single individual. The orderliness manifests itself in the fact that the actions of the various independent individuals adjust reciprocally to one another. It is interesting to note that the greater the diversity of the individuals in a system is, the richer the emergent global patterns will be. We must be careful here to distinguish clearly between the 'set of rules' and the 'order of actions': the former governs the behaviour of the individual members of the group, while the latter is the global socio-economic pattern that results for the collective as a whole. The spontaneous order of actions does not coincide with the systems of rules of conduct that are followed by individuals.[7]

Fourth, the market system is a self-organizing and self-sustaining one. Here, self-organization is of great benefit to individuals: the market system is the most efficient, productive and creative economic mechanism yet discovered. The reason that the market system is so efficient and productive is because it is able to spontaneously activate and make use of dispersed knowledge. Thanks to a decentralized self-adapting mechanism – which we could label 'division of knowledge', echoing the term 'division of labour' – we are able to make use of more knowledge; in one sense we may state that 'knowledge grows by division' (Loasby, 1999). To be able to interact in a collectively advantageous way, individuals need a 'telecommunications' system, which in this case is the price system. The price system enables individuals to exchange abstract information even when they are remote from one another.[8] It is worth noting that the gains that individuals receive in the market do not reflect their skills and efforts alone, but also their luck; and it is for the very reason that chance comes into play in the market mechanism that new and unexpected outcomes may ensue.

Fifth, the market system is highly dynamic and in constant evolution. In particular, competition is a procedure of discovery; it is not simply a mechanism for handling scarcity, but most importantly a process for activating and testing new knowledge, new means and new wants.[9] Competition is the most important creative trigger: from this it follows that creativity has both an individual and a social dimension.[10] The market, therefore, is clearly not a zero-sum game. To this end it is worth defining the question of resources. Resources do not exist in their own right, independently from us. They are not a fixed quantity – a stock – whose contours are predefined (Kebir and Crevoisier, 2008). Resources depend on human desires, perceptions, knowledge and technological skills. Strictly speaking, they are not so much discovered as invented.[11] Resources are therefore not absolute, but relative; not natural, but created (Simon, 1996).

If we accept this interpretation of the market – namely, the one taken by the Austrian school,[12] which has always focused on human creativity as the ultimate source of economic growth and social development – it transpires that knowledge and innovation are always an integral part of the complex market mechanism.[13] Consequently, what is nowadays dubbed 'the creative economy' is not an entirely novel form of organization and production of goods and services, but simply a form that accentuates a feature that was already present earlier. We may therefore assert that the 'traditional economy' and 'creative economy' are not actually two distinct genera, but two distinct species of the same genus.

So, strictly speaking, I do not think that 'knowledge and creativity have *replaced* natural resources and the efficiency of physical labor as the sources of wealth-creation and economic growth' (Florida, 2005, p. 49, emphasis added); instead, knowledge and human creativity have *always* been the source of economic growth.

Elsewhere, Richard Florida (2007, p. 26) distances himself from the idea of the absolute novelty of the creative economy, and accepts that it is more likely a question of degree:

> I call the age we are entering the creative age because the key factor propelling us forward is the rise of creativity as the prime mover of our economy. . . . In a larger sense, it's always been this way: People think of something new – farming instead of hunting and gathering, building a steam engine instead of harnessing a horse – and the material and social realities follow. What's happened in recent times is that the pace and intensity of all forms of creative work have exploded. (Florida, 2007, p. 26)

Coming back to our central issue, the point that needs stressing is that if we recognize the market as a complex creative structure, it is clear that it is not possible to plan the economic system, that is, to achieve order in it by directly employing a method for putting such order into place. Here it is useful to briefly recall the two main criticisms made of central (economic) planning by the Austrian school of economics (Hayek, 1948).

First, it is impossible to concentrate the dispersed knowledge that enables complex economic systems to function, since this knowledge is both 'situated' (spatio-temporally specific) and 'tacit'. Tacit knowledge refers to know-how that is acquired through a process of 'learning by doing'. It is therefore a type of knowledge that is internalized in the mind of the individual, who makes use of it without deliberate, explicit reflection. Consequently, it is therefore impossible to make such knowledge 'public', regardless of whether individuals are motivated or not.

Second, an attempt to do so – that is, to centralize knowledge and guide the economy

– would result in a drop in productivity and efficiency, due to the fact that we would be forcing the system to use less than the knowledge that is actually available in society.

Underestimating complexity and ignoring self-organization
This new way of understanding the world – through the paradigm of complexity – has had very little impact on the field of land-use regulation. Although the phenomenon of self-organization, for example, garnered attention some years ago among researchers in urban and regional studies (Pumain et al., 1989; Allen, 1997; Portugali, 1999), this did not have a significant impact on either land-use planning theory or – in particular – on land-use planning practice; or perhaps I should say that its impact was much less than could have been expected, given the salience of the issue to the field of (land-use) regulation and control.[14] This is likely due to people's difficulty in accepting the very notion of self-organization in complex systems.

Land-use planning practice, in particular, continues for the most part to be based on the assumption that it is possible to guide and manage urban development in a top-down and detailed manner – whether it be through some sort of general, more or less flexible plan, or thanks to case-by-case evaluations and decisions, where public administrators retain the power to contract with private parties as they please. In such cases, public administrators and planners are convinced that they possess the knowledge, information and skills required to deliberately superintend the evolution of urban growth. The idea is that a conscious ordering process is the only possible ordering process for our cities.

Many land-use planning systems are still modelled on an orthodox notion of planning and government, based on the conviction that socio-spatial systems are simple – or at least easy to understand by way of simple models – and controllable and manageable by way of a set of concrete, specific rules and directives. The assumption seems to be that there is only a small difference, a mere difference in scale, between micro-orders (for example, organizations) and macro-orders (for example, society), and that we may therefore use similar approaches and tools for guiding and controlling both.

It is hardly necessary to note that there are differences between land-use planning systems and practices in different Western countries (Thomas et al., 1983; Cullingworth, 1993; Newman and Thornley, 1996; Needham, 2006). What is significant in this regard, however, is the fact that, even so, there are important analogies among these systems in terms of some of their basic underlying characteristics – characteristics that contribute to their underestimating the problem of complexity (as we see here), and the substantive requirements entailed by the liberal-democratic ideal (as we shall see hereafter).

The crucial point here is that the (Austrian) critiques of central economic planning can also be made of land-use planning. It is a mistake to think – as urban planners generally do[15] – that these criticisms hold only for central economic planning but not also for more circumscribed forms of planning, such as land-use planning.[16]

As Mark Pennington (1999, p. 48) writes, it is an error to think that planning 'can improve on the apparently haphazard operation of markets in order to achieve an integrated land-use policy, because planners may not have the information to know what they are supposed to be integrating'. In the words of E.C. Pasour:

> What data are required to determine efficient land use? The same data . . . required for central planning in general – data on preferences, resources and production opportunities. These data

are, of course, not given; and the land-use planner who attempts to obtain the relevant statistical data faces similar problems to those identified by Hayek [for central economic planning]. (Pasour, 1991, p. 6)

Pasour continues:

> A crucial implication of the economic calculation debate is that prices are necessary for rational land-use planning. Yet, this fact is ignored in most land-use planning literature where land classification is presented as an alternative to market prices in allocating land to various uses. ... [usually] land classification is assumed to be a scientific or technical skill. ... [but] land classification contains no mechanism to utilize the dispersed bits of incomplete knowledge that all separate individuals possess about the demand and supply of land. ... The land-classification approach fails to take into account the fact that technical information – such as soil type, which is readily obtainable – is likely to be of trivial importance when compared with the information required to carry out the ordinary processes of economic activity – knowledge of the particular circumstances of time and place. (Pasour, 1991, p. 7)[17]

It should be noted that the fundamental 'knowledge of the particular circumstances of time and place' is, as regards our present postmodern cities, more dispersed, fleeting and dynamic than ever.

Moreover, economic problems are intrinsically rooted in change: in a dynamic economic process, such as that which characterizes today's postmodern and post-industrial cities, any land-use pattern will quickly and inevitable become obsolete. Planning through zoning therefore inhibits innovation in land use and organization (Siegan, 1977; Sommer, 1982; Corkindale, 2004),[18] and with the introduction of arbitrary connections between demand and supply, it raises house prices (Glaeser and Gyourko, 2002; Downs, 2005; Pennington, 2005; O'Toole, 2009). Note that zoning is not simply one of the instruments of traditional land-use planning, but is at its core: 'directional' systems of rules demand zoning.

Briefly put, all-embracing land-use planning tends to impede the efficient activation and use of fundamental 'dispersed and dynamic' knowledge. And this seems all the more true for today's polymorphic, multi-centred and pluralistic postmodern cities.

In conclusion, contrary to the traditional idea that the more complex a system becomes, the more we need planning (Mumford, 1938), it would seem that the more complex a system becomes, the less we need planning.

Values: The Liberal-Democratic Ideal

We could break down the term 'liberal-democratic state' by saying that the liberal component is concerned principally with granting every individual a private, protected sphere of action and with limiting the power of the state (by establishing barriers and institutional mechanisms to prevent public bodies from indiscriminately interfering in the private sphere of individuals),[19] while the democratic component is concerned principally with the functioning of public power and the decision-making procedures it must follow.

It is important not to forget that a liberal democracy is not simply a 'democracy' but, more precisely, a '*liberal* democracy'. Seen from this perspective, a liberal institutional framework is the indispensable prerequisite of an acceptable and viable form of democracy. In other words, democratic decision procedures can start only after a liberal framework has been established, and only within the limits it sets. In this perspective, the state acts both *per leges* and *sub lege*. The liberal-democratic ideal strongly points in the direction of 'politics by principle', and not 'politics by interest':

> *Politics by principle* is that which modern politics is not. What we observe is *politics by interest*, whether in the form of explicitly discriminatory treatment . . . of particular groupings of citizens or of some elitist-dirigiste classification of citizens into the deserving and non-deserving on the basis of a presumed superior wisdom about what is really good for us all. The proper principle for politics is [on the contrary] . . . that of generalization or generality. This standard is met when political actions apply to all persons independent of membership in a dominant coalition or an effective interest group. (Buchanan and Congleton, 2003, p. xix, emphasis added)

Thus liberal democracy is exactly the oppose of what (after Lowi, 1979) is known as 'interest-group liberalism', that is, a situation in which the public interest is equated simply and solely with the equilibrium among organized interest groups (Lindblom, 1990).

I am emphasizing these concepts because I think that the term 'liberal democracy' is frequently used in a far too vague and generic sense. Moreover, I don't believe that the idea of liberal democracy is an exclusively Western phenomenon; various elements that form part of it have been identified independently – and often in a pioneering sense – in Eastern traditions.

As regards legitimacy – and assuming that we accept the specified version of a liberal-democratic state – we need thus to focus attention on the following ethical issues.

First, we need to focus on the centrality of specific individual rights and freedoms that protect each individual's private sphere from external intrusion, so that each individual can pursue his personal idea of the good life, and freely apply his talents and knowledge to that end.

The second focus is on the need for some form of equal treatment, the idea being that the law should apply equally to all under certain predetermined circumstances.

The third focus is on the importance of some kind of predictability of state actions, to ensure a certain degree of certainty and stability of the legal framework.

These are not the only prerequisites of a liberal-democratic paradigm, but they are surely among the most important. Strictly speaking, they are meta-requisites for every kind of public rule and intervention. It is interesting to note that all of them imply a shift away from a strictly 'consequentialist' ethics towards a primarily 'deontological' ethics: the former valuing actions that 'do good' (with the focus exclusively on the consequences of those actions), while the latter those that 'are right' (with the focus on the actions themselves).[20] And they imply a shift away from the 'administrative state' towards the 'rule of law' (Moroni, 2007b).

If we agree to the aforementioned prerequisites, it is clear that we cannot accept any kind of central economic planning whatsoever. Let us recall here the main ethical criticism of this form of planning, once again a criticism anticipated by the Austrian tradition, together with the other critiques already mentioned (Mises, 1927, 1929; Hayek, 1944, 1948). This criticism holds that planning unacceptably reduces individual freedom, greatly interfering with the possibility of individuals to use their means and knowledge to pursue their own ends. This happens largely because planning fails to respect the rule of law by treating various individuals, groups and economic units unequally, since each component of the social system must perform its own specific role in order to achieve a concrete predefined end-state, or a concrete preferred trajectory. Moreover, planning jeopardizes the ideal of the certainty of the law due to the unavoidable fact that each plan is unpredictable, since such plans in practice must adapt to the circumstances of place and time as understood by the planning authorities. It is important to note here that the possibility of unequal treatment also has the undesirable consequence of opening the door to corruption.

Undervaluing and undermining the liberal-democratic ideal

Current land-use planning practices do not always demonstrate much respect for the aforementioned liberal-democratic requirements, which I think must be acknowledged in a forceful and substantive manner if we aim to avoid undermining the liberal-democratic ideal. Indeed, in many countries the manner in which planning practices have evolved has meant that only formal, superficial attention has been given to liberal-democratic values. This situation has frequently involved forms of marked unequal treatment and highly unpredictable modes of public intervention. In many cases, contextual discretion and the 'inventive' use of rules are seen as forms of active and dynamic planning – planning that is able to adapt to the variable conditions of the socio-economic world – while often they are instead actually infringements of fundamental liberal-democratic principles.

The point is that the ethical critiques of central economic planning hold for land-use planning as well: in both cases the rule of law fails to be respected, and individual liberty is put at risk.

In orthodox land-use planning centred on zoning, the public administration seeks to channel the use of resources and means towards particular predefined end-states – particular urban configurations – or, at the very least, development along some kind of preferred trajectory. In this case, planning decisions can neither be deduced from formal stable principles, nor clearly worked out far in advance. In fact they are greatly – and inevitably – dependent on the circumstances of the moment, as interpreted by the planning authority that holds the power to decide. It is impossible, then, for a land owner to predict whether his or her land may be designated by the plan for one use or another, or to what particular restrictions and obligations the use of the land will be subjected. Remarking upon some well-known US Supreme Court decisions that authorized the use of zoning by local governments at the beginning of the twentieth century,[21] Bernard Siegan (1997, pp. 75–6) writes: 'The ordinary and normal use of property was rendered insecure after these decisions.'

To this could be added the fact that imperative planning centred on zoning leads to strongly differentiated and highly unequal treatment among individuals: this becomes inevitable once we establish an end-state, and try to assign to each piece of land its own 'peculiar' function in order to help reach that end-state. As Anthony Sorensen and Martin Auser (1989, p. 36) write: 'Planning, or rather zoning . . ., deliberately sets out to be discriminatory.' The main point here is that 'nonuniform regulation by local government is almost inevitably unfair regulation' (Ellickson, 1973, p. 711). Note that nothing changes if we adopt forms of flexible planning: if what is flexible is still planning, the same problems will arise, even in a more evident manner.

Clearly, in this case too the inequality of treatment leaves room for corruption.

Indeed, it is where there is the greatest possibility of differentiating between the positions of single individuals (land owners, developers and so forth) by way of public decisions that we find increased levels of corruption. The point is not that developers and land-use officials are especially prone to corruption, but that the traditional legal-administrative land-use systems intrinsically instigate action in that direction: 'The amounts of money at stake in switching parcels of land from one zone to another assure that zoning will continue to be an arbitrary and largely corrupt system' (Ellickson, 1973, p. 711).

PERSPECTIVES: TOWARDS A NEW OUTLOOK

Ultimately, I think that we need to look for forms of regulating land use in our contemporary postmodern cities that take more seriously both the fact of complexity (connected with the crucial phenomenon of self-organization), and the values of the liberal-democratic ideal (interpreted in the strict manner that I think is indispensable); the former being a challenge regarding what we can do, and the latter regarding what we ought to do.[22] These issues call for a more radical and critical scrutiny of current land-use planning theories and practices, and perhaps also a definitive abandonment of some of them. More in general, they demand that we rethink the idea of law itself, and its role in contemporary cities and societies. While I am convinced that accepting the general values of the liberal-democratic ideal correctly interpreted – as well as accepting the fact of complexity – is sufficient to make evident the drawbacks of certain land-use planning approaches, looking for an answer to the problem of effective and legitimate land-use regulation requires that we adopt a more specific approach. My personal step in this direction entails a more specific, substantive articulation of the liberal-democratic ideal – something that I define as 'active liberalism' (Moroni, 2007a) – and which is the basis of what I will discuss in the following paragraphs. In other words, it seems to me that the *pars destruens* of the argument can be widely accepted, while the *pars construens* obviously implies a more substantive stance.

A brief but fundamental digression is needed before we continue. Most surprisingly, it has become a common attitude to attribute the 2008 economic and financial crisis to a lack of regulations – when actually the number of regulations has increased exponentially in the last few decades, in all sectors of the economy as well as in the financial sector itself. Furthermore, the central governments in the West, who until the day before the crisis started had not foreseen nor grasped the imminent economic collapse, are convinced they now have the right recipe to solve the crisis (which implies the creation of further rules – usually another layer identical to those that already exist – while jacking up government spending). It is far more convincing – although counter-intuitive and unpopular – to identify erroneous public regulations and inadequate public policies as the main causal factors of the economic crisis that started in 2008. It was the American housing bubble that triggered the financial crisis of 2008. That housing bubble derived partly from local land-use plans and policies that distorted supply (O'Toole, 2009) and favoured certain land owners and certain forms of land speculation (Gaffney, 2009); and, partly, the bubble derived from national regulations and policies that distorted demand. The demand for housing was distorted by regulations and policies that encouraged banks to offer high-risk loans to low-income families and that required government-sponsored enterprises such as Fannie Mae and Freddy Mac to buy more loans from low- and moderate-income families (Dowd, 2008; Paul, 2008; Taylor, 2009; White, 2009; Woods, 2009). To this we can add the state-mandated deposit insurance of the banking system itself, and the volatile, unstable and discretionary intervention of the Federal Reserve (Dowd, 2008; O'Driscoll, 2008; Taylor, 2009; Thornton, 2009). National and local policies and regulations have, in the case of the United States (and in many other countries), therefore led to a drastic distortion of the situation. As a result, the line to take is not to pass from an unregulated system to a regulated one, but from a badly regulated system to one that is adequately regulated. Similarly, the point is not to pass from an excess of competition to one that is confined and delimited, but from a thwarted type of competition to true competition. This applies in general terms as well as for the more specific issues under discussion here, to which we will return forthwith.

Relational Sets of Rules

Clearly, rules are needed for us to be able to live together in our complex and dynamic postmodern societies, while each achieving our own personal objectives through the application of our talents and knowledge; but not any kind of rule is able to fulfil this purpose. In other words, not just any kind of sets of rules of conduct will turn out effective and legitimate. Certain types of rules may have undesirable consequences for freedom and general welfare. In the end, then, the question concerns which type of set of rules is preferable. What I am focusing on here – to resume my central question – is that part of rules which is represented by law, namely, the systems of rules that are formally recognized and granted by the state (at both central and local levels).

I think that the kind of rules that are required by a complex socio-economic system that accepts the values of the liberal-democratic ideal must satisfy at least four fundamental requirements: they must be impersonal, simple, robust and stable. These requirements could be interpreted as meta-legal prerequisites for ensuring viable sets of rules; and it is my belief that in the field of land-use regulation we have failed to recognize their importance for a long time now. I characterize the systems of rules that present these requirements as 'relational', in contrast with the 'directional' systems of rules that are more typical of the planning approach.

First, we need rules that are impersonal. Impersonal rules are primarily abstract and general: in other words, they contain no reference to particular individuals, objects and so forth, and they regard cases that are as yet unknown (that is, they refer to general 'types' of situations or actions, not to specific ones). These rules are predominately negative: they prohibit individuals from interfering with the private domain of other individuals, rather than imposing some positive action. Rules of this kind apply equally to everyone, and guarantee that the actions of individuals are co-ordinated only as regards their typical features (that is, their repeatable, time-independent and situation-independent aspects), not as regards their specific features (their unrepeatable, time-dependent and situation-dependent aspects). The main point here is that we need rules not in order to achieve certain predetermined, specific common ends, but to enable the peaceful co-existence of various individuals pursuing totally different ends.

Second, we need rules that are simple. In other words, we must dismiss complex rules and seek out simple rules for a complex world (Epstein, 1995). In many countries during the nineteenth century, important attempts were made to simplify the legal rules in order to make rule compliance easier and cheaper for the individuals and groups, and equally to reduce the costs of operating the law itself. Since then, however, the law has been made more and more complex, accepting the odd idea that law has to mirror the growing complexity of our societies (Kasper and Streit, 1998).[23] Both theory and practice have demonstrated that complex rules do not work well 'because they overtax human cognition and impose unnecessarily high compliance costs' (Kasper and Streit, 1998, p. 123). To have simple rules – which avoid technicality, density, differentiation and indeterminacy – is not a utopian dream but a workable alternative, and not least a real necessity: 'The more complex the system, the greater the need for simple rules to achieve order' (Webster and Lai, 2003, p. 211).[24]

Third, we need rules that are robust. Robust rules are rules that have been shaped by long-term human experience and trial; they are rules that have developed through a long evolutionary process of gradual and incremental feedback and adjustment (Hayek, 1982). The important thing is not to 'invent' rules, but to discover and implement those rules that have evolved spontaneously over time and have proven to work well (Moroni, 2010b).

Finally, we need rules that are stable. Such rules enable citizens to have dependable expectations – in general terms and over long periods of time – with regard to the actions of others, and in particular to the actions of the state itself. It is difficult to know, abide by and respect rules that constantly change; if legal rules are continually subject to change, the information they provide becomes negligible and useless. On the other hand, stability improves reliability, with the consequence of facilitating human interaction. Stability – permanence – is the cardinal virtue of a system of legal rules that make private innovation and progress possible. Stability can be achieved by adopting a series of devices; for example, by avoiding 'legislative inflation' (the over-production of laws, regulations instructions and so on); by pursuing a gradual evolution of the system of laws and keeping away from continuous change (a piecemeal improvement of the systems of laws can be undertaken as long as we keep in mind the need to maintain the consistency and compatibility of its parts); and by reducing as far as possible the discretion of public power (and, in particular, of administrative levels).

All of this points in the direction of an out-and-out rejection of a strictly 'instrumental' notion of the law.[25] The law must be interpreted not as an instrument for achieving some sort of specific outcome (that is, to maximize or minimize some parameter[26]), but rather as an abstract and stable meta-framework for the peaceful co-existence of many different individuals with incommensurable and continuously changing goals.[27] Rules define the private spheres within which each of us can freely and legitimately carry on our own activities. As Hayek (1982, Vol. II, pp. 20–1) writes: 'Man has developed rules of conduct not because he knows, but because he does not know what all the consequences of a particular action will be.' The rules of conduct cannot then be designed to produce particular foreseen benefits, but must be interpreted as multi-purpose devices 'developed as adaptations to certain kinds of environment because they help to deal with certain kinds of situation' (Hayek, 1982, Vol. II, p. 4). In this perspective, law serves no concrete specific purpose; it simply provides the means for the realization of the incommensurable separate purposes of separate individuals.[28] In sum, there are certain requirements that are in some sense intrinsic to law, that have to do with its 'internal' integrity and real possibilities of functioning (Fuller, 1964). Law is thus not entirely subject to our whims and will.[29]

This perspective entails a rediscovery of the fundamental ideal of the 'certainty of the law'. It seems to me that the traditional critiques of the latter – from the more simplistic critiques levelled by those who defended the conventional welfare state (Friedmann, 1949, 1951), to the more sophisticated ones subsequently made by theorists from the Critical Legal Studies Movement (starting from texts such as Unger's (1975)) – are too easily accepted as conclusive, while they simply point to previously acknowledged problems that we could easily resolve if we really wished to.[30]

Towards Effective and Legitimate Land-use Regulation: Two Separate Tasks for the Local State

Getting back to the problems of present-day pluralist and dynamic cities, I think that relational systems of rules are of fundamental importance. More precisely, and according to 'active liberalism' (Moroni, 2007a), the idea is that local governments have two different and clearly distinct tasks.

The first task, which is of vital importance, is to guarantee impersonal, simple, robust and stable rules of the game for private urban activities. These rules must be gathered within a durable 'urban code' (something totally different from an 'urban plan'),[31] and must be adopted by a qualified majority, that is, a supermajority that is constrained by strong institutional bonds and restrictions. The rules of an urban code concern the relationships between and among individuals with regard to their use of the land. They can be applied in a quasi-automatic fashion, without any marked discretionary features. These rules of the game are 'locationally generic' rather than 'locationally specific' (to use Needham's (2006) terminology). They are locationally-generic within the territory on which the local government introducing them has legitimate power. They refer to typical situations and are based on knowledge of typical facts; and are for the most part negative rules that impede certain kinds of externalities in the construction and use of buildings – that is, external effects that stem from development, and which directly and tangibly affect someone.[32]

The externalities we have to deal with are not those presumed to lower social efficiency (as occurs in the consequentialist utilitarian perspective as well as in welfare economics), but those that infringe upon what we consider individual rights (as occurs in liberal rights theories). The point here is not market failures, but the institutional requirements required to minimize interpersonal conflict (Cordato, 2004). The problem is not to prohibit certain activities in certain places of the city, but to directly prohibit certain externalities everywhere. As Benjamin Rogge (1979, p. 231) writes: 'If a firm can find a way to make bricks in the centre of an affluent suburb in such a way as to produce no externalities, no damage to surrounding properties, and if this is what it believes to be the appropriate site for the activity, the state should not intervene – as it now does with its zoning laws.'

As regards 'development rights',[33] we can imagine that these rights are allocated – in compliance with an identical index or parameter of conversion applicable to the surface area of land – to land owners in all places; land owners can either exercise those rights, or sell them to others to do so – or, obviously, do nothing at all (Corkindale, 1998, 2004).

Note that here I suggest tradable development rights, not as a way of compensating restricted land owners in order to make zoning more acceptable for them (Renard, 2007), but as a way of uniformly regulating development without traditional zoning – and as a way of assigning to market exchanges the choice of appropriate places to develop. In my opinion, the fundamental ratio of tradable development right must be, strictly speaking, equal treatment.[34]

Observe how relational, impersonal rules strongly diminish the problem of corruption involving land-use issues, due to the fact that they do not differentiate among individual positions. The only way to stamp out corruption and pressures on public officials is to construct a legal system in which government officials 'do not have the power to create or destroy fortunes with a stroke of the pen' (Epstein, 1995, p. 130). In other words, 'good games depend on good rules more than they depend on good players' (Brennan and Buchanan, 2000, p. 167).

The second task of the local governments, which is secondary and complementary – and depends on the resources upon which public administrations can effectively rely – is to provide a circumscribed range of services and infrastructures on public lands via a form of limited planning. This kind of planning is necessarily based on the ascertainment of specific circumstances, with all the discretionary powers that are required so as to employ public resources efficiently in this direction, and in line with the political programme of the simple majority. It directly regards the actions of the public sector and the land owned by the public sector, not the actions of private parties regarding private land. The directives introduced in this second case are obviously location-specific. In such instances, public planning is not a strategic comprehensive activity, but a modest complementary activity, the use of which is circumscribed to very particular circumstances – regarding the public actor itself, not the private actors.[35]

In summary, I think that local governments must regulate the actions of the private actors (allowing land owners and developers to make use of their land, as suggested by their particular knowledge of circumstances of time and place, within a framework of relational rules that apply equally to everyone, and as long as such land use does not create a serious nuisance for others), and plan their own actions (co-ordinating the use of public resources at their disposal in a responsible and efficient manner, to guarantee infrastructures and furnish services).[36]

Ultimately, the idea is not to achieve a flexible system of land-use regulation in order to follow social dynamics, but to have a certain set of rules that enables society to be flexible. In this perspective one can envisage that a broad space will be taken by voluntary, private forms of land-use organization and service provision (Foldvary, 1994; Nelson, 2005).

Some Specifications and Clarifications

In my perspective, the 'good city' or the 'desirable city' cannot be defined in terms of certain characteristics and features, but only in terms of the aptness of the framework of rules within which it will emerge and function. The 'good city' will be whatever arrangement of things and activities emerges from the decisions and transactions of individuals when such decisions are made within a framework of appropriate rules (Rogge, 1979). The point is thus not to structure the overall configuration of a city, but to guarantee the relational rules regarding (uniformly and universally permitted, or prohibited) land uses.

And the aim is not to have a comprehensive vision of the 'good' urban life or lifestyle, but to set up the rules within which many different notions of the good life can flourish. A spontaneous social order is beneficial, not despite the existence of several different conceptions of the good, but exactly because of that variety (Hayek, 1982, 1988). The idea that diversity is crucial for growth and prosperity has always been pivotal in classical liberalism. Richard Florida (2005, 2007, 2008) must, however, be credited with having directed attention to the importance of diversity to city life and to the gains to be had for all citizens: as he observes, 'diversity is not merely enjoyable; it is essential' (Florida, 2007, p. 35).[37]

To avoid any misunderstanding, I should emphasize that I am not asserting the need for a 'high' level of urban government that formulates general and abstract rules, and a 'lower' one that transforms them into specific and particular rules. What I wish to say is that many abstract and general rules, once they have been formulated, are operative just so. They can be applied nearly automatically: there is no need for them to be 'contextualized' through ad hoc public acts. I should also clarify that when I talk about abstract and general rules I do not so much or only mean procedural rules (rules for the production of rules meant for the administrators themselves), but instead, and above all, rules of conduct. Rules of conduct are behavioural rules meant for all citizens and in this case concerns the ways in which they may use or modify real estate.

It has sometimes been observed, when questioning approaches such as my own (Cusinato, 2009), that because places are different – and there is something important in having differentiated places – we need to use location-specific public rules to regulate them. However, we could turn this observation on its head by observing that it is precisely because places are not intrinsically different, but become different in the unpredictable and creative flow of socio-economic relations, that we need location-generic rules to allow this process to occur. If the socio-economic process were not prone to cause the differentiation of places, different rules could, on the contrary, be more helpful.

Others might observe, as Barry Needham (2007) does, again in opposition to approaches like mine, that not everything citizens might desire can be realized through a system of relational rules. Needham is correct in stating that one cannot achieve everything with a system of relational rules; but the point is that the law cannot and should not be thought of as a tool for achieving anything. The law is not a tool like others, which can be adapted for any use or goal; it is a public framework, imposed and maintained authoritatively, within which citizens may freely seek to reach their own objectives, either as individuals or together. And it is precisely because law, correctly understood, cannot be bent to achieve any and all results, that it is able to serve as a universal reference point. The point here is that – within a liberal-democratic vision – citizens cannot decide whatever they wish; in particular, the forms and types of laws that can be introduced must be set – blocked – a priori, precisely in order to defend all citizens.

All of this clearly has nothing to do with the idea that 'anything goes'. The market system, including the land market, requires a legal framework that guarantees individuals' protected spheres, reciprocal restrictions and the enforcement of contracts – as has always been clear in classical liberal thinking. With regard to the market system, we can therefore speak of a kind of a spontaneity that is shaped by institutions and which favours a kind of self-organization among a plurality of individuals. The point is not rules versus laissez-faire, but rules of one kind versus rules of another kind.

Consequently, this has nothing to do with any kind of deregulation either; on the contrary, what I am proposing here is a form of strong re-regulation. Indeed, I believe that law must once again take on the central role that it has regrettably lost over time – a predicament in which we now find ourselves thanks also to the inappropriate way in which we envisioned law for too long (that is, instrumentally, whereby planning – by no accident – became the main tool of urban government).[38] Genuine cohesion in a great, complex society will be rediscovered only once law – correctly interpreted – has again become central.[39]

Eric Corijn notes how living with differences, with strangers, is the most characteristic element of cities, and how this characteristic is accentuated in our postmodern cities:

> The dense mix of functions, the proximity of difference and the spaces of flows all determine the dominance of distinction. In that sense, the city is an exception to the 'normal' ways of building human societies. These have been founded on sense of commonality, and have been based on what people shared. Social bond has been derived from common characteristics. Cities were states of exception. . . . We are now going to a passage where that kind of living together with strangers shifts from the exceptions to the norm. (Corijn, 2009, p. 200)

However, this situation by no means requires that local government produces a substantive vision for all, that it works for the recovery of the polis (as many seem to think), but that it invests in the crucial role of law as a relational system of impersonal, simple, robust and stable rules.

It is my belief that if we wish to act in a way that is both effective and legitimate, it is fundamental that we learn this lesson, also within the field of land-use regulation. Clearly, many of the problems that I have touched upon have also been acknowledged by land-use planning theorists, as well as by land-use planning practitioners, yet not in the radical manner that I believe is necessary. In my opinion, the point is not to try for the umpteenth time to invent a new, more sophisticated form of (land-use) planning, but to recognize that we can continue to use a quite traditional form of planning for certain quite limited purposes (in particular, providing certain kinds of infrastructure), and rely on something completely different – urban codes as relational systems of rules – to indirectly generate orders of actions.

CONCLUSION: A NON-CREATIVE INSTITUTIONAL FRAMEWORK FOR CREATIVE HUMAN LANDSCAPES

Liberty Under the Rule of Law as the Fundamental Condition for Creativity

A form of regulation of land use that takes seriously the problem of complexity and the value of liberal democracy is also the one that fosters the creative city in a strong and radical way. It is interesting that in recognizing the complexity of the world as an inevitable fact, and by embracing liberal-democratic values, we reach a conclusion that points towards a certain type of regulation, and it is interesting to note that this approach is also the one that is most consonant with a creative society.

There have been many attempts to pinpoint the conditions for creativity, but too many appear to forget the most important condition, namely, liberty under the rule of law. In his celebrated book on the creative city, Charles Landry (2008, p. xxxiii) asks: 'How do we create conditions for people to become curious or imaginative?', 'What atmosphere encourages people to give of their best?' To my mind, the answer is this:

> A human being gives the best of himself when he is free. Given freedom, he makes the most of his ability to create, work, dream, live, serve others in the marketplace, which is to say, he makes the most of his profound human potential. . . . The freer he is, the more these traits come to the fore. (Stewart, 2000)

Richard Florida (2007) rightly turns the focus on the need to educate people for the creative age. I believe that, above all, this implies re-educating people for freedom itself. The pivotal issue is that, in everything, the human being is the crucial resource. As Julian Simon (1996, p. 589) writes, 'the ultimate resource is people – skilled, spirited, and hopeful people who will exert their wills and imaginations for their own benefit, and inevitably they will benefit not only themselves but the rest of us as well'.[40]

The fundamental question is therefore not to attract a fluctuating predefined creative class, but to generate the conditions of certainty regarding individual freedoms so that everyone can become creative, in a perpetually experimental urban environment that involves all. Richard Florida has recently claimed that only a reductive and simplistic reading of his earlier works can have led people to believe that he was focusing only on one sector of society, namely, the creative class as exclusive elite. Irrespective of the correct interpretation of his earlier works, it is interesting to note that Florida himself later kept underscoring that '[c]reativity is as biologically and intellectually innate a characteristic to all human beings as thought itself' (Florida, 2005, p. 4) and that '[e]very single person is creative in some way' (Florida, 2005, p. 22).[41]

In this perspective, I would like to state that while the cultural sector can without doubt contribute to a creative city, to reduce creativity to culture alone (or predominantly to culture) in its narrowest sense – as unfortunately has been done in many works on the subject – is an unacceptable diminution of a concept with a more far-reaching and fertile scope.

In the end, a vital observation needs to be made. Many believe that 'a necessary component of a creative city are governance systems that are creative, imaginative, flexible and accommodating' (Smith and Warfield, 2008, p. 287). But the crucial point is that it is the city – its citizens – who must be creative, not the urban policies. Hence, in order to achieve the creative city, the policies do not themselves necessarily need to be creative. It is not the policy-maker's job to become creative, but the job of ordinary citizens. The policy-makers must not develop so much a 'civic creativity' (Landry, 2008),[42] as a 'civic modesty'.

The system of rules that favours the creative city must actually be impersonal, simple, robust and stable. The public administration does not always need to do something positive in order to attain the creative city;[43] it must more often simply refrain from doing too much, from perpetually interfering. The aim is not, in my opinion, to pass from 'government' to 'governance', from 'welfare policies' to 'enabling policies', from 'technocratic planning' to 'collaborative-communicative-relational planning' (Healey, 1997, 2007), from 'land-use planning' to 'urban strategy making' (Landry, 2008), but from 'teleocracy' to 'nomocracy' (Moroni, 2010a).

The Problem of Poverty in the Creative City

Before closing, there is one further key issue to consider: it has often been noted that the idea of the creative city overlooks the weaker elements of the community – namely, the poorest – or it may even worsen their conditions, increasing the disparity.[44] In my personal approach to the creative society and the creative city – which hinges on a classical form of liberalism – there are three critical observations to be made in this respect.

First, liberty under the rule of law – that is, the type of liberty guaranteed by a liberal-democratic state – defends the weakest above all (Sartori, 1957). Ensuring that the state can only issue relational, impersonal laws principally defends society's weakest members, rather than the strongest (who can and will take advantage of discretionary political power).

Second, dismantling the traditional forms of land-use planning and many of the traditional 'constructivist' economic policies (Hayek, 1982) will also favour the weakest. The point is that poverty is in part caused by mistaken government attempts at guiding the market (Holcombe and Powell, 2009). A really competitive catallactic system is as important for the poor as it is for everyone: this becomes clear if we abandon the reductionist outlook that sees the market merely as an allocative mechanism, and recognize instead its fundamental role as a mechanism of discovery, driven by the boundless human imagination – whereby creativity is not seen merely as the province of certain segments of society or sectors of the economy (for instance, the cultural industries), but as a universal engine.

Third, I do not rule out in an approach such as my own the possibility of complementary forms of direct support to the weak, as long as these are semi-automatic (that is, in strict accordance with the rule of law; see Hayes, 2001, pp. 182–5) and are aimed exclusively at combating absolute poverty (Chiappero-Martinetti and Moroni, 2007).[45]

Summing Up

To sum up, in this chapter I have upheld three principal arguments regarding the creative city.

First, that creativity is not a feature of the contemporary economy alone, but of the market economy (or better, of catallaxis) as such: no resource can be useful to man independently from human creativity. Second, in a complex world, the core condition for creativity is liberty under the rule of law. Third, to achieve a creative city it is not necessary that the policies likewise are continually creative, but that the basic regulatory system is impersonal, simple, stable and robust, so as to favour the beneficial self-organization of the socio-economic system, and a constant state of experimentation.

NOTES

1. 'Perhaps the greatest of all modern myths about cities is that geography is dead. . . . Never has a myth been easier to deflate. Not only do people remain highly concentrated, but the economy itself . . . continues to concentrate in specific places . . .' (Florida, 2005, p. 28).
2. In this chapter I will use the term 'planning' to indicate a (public) control device. What I have in mind is a future-oriented, forward-looking and purpose-dependent control device that is typically presumed to

be rational and information-based as regards the situation at hand; but it is planning exactly because it imposes some sort of plan, that is, a directional system of rules that tries to define the preferable configuration of a system, and to co-ordinate the various activities in light of that (Moroni, 2010a).

3. 'The term creativity is so . . . overused that it is rendered meaningless' (Chatterton, 2000, p. 393).

4. This includes chaos theory, generalized thermodynamics, synergetics, the theory of autopoietic systems and others.

5. My discussion of complexity is based on the assumption that it is a quality/property of the world, not simply something beheld by the observer.

6. It was Hayek (1982, Vol. II, p. 108) who suggested that we abandon the term 'economy' and adopt the term 'catallaxy' instead in order to describe the system of inter-related actions that constitute the market order; the term 'catallaxy' derives from the Greek *katallattein* which means not only 'to exchange' but also 'to admit into the community' and 'to change from enemy into friend'.

7. In a 'made order', on the contrary, the system of rules of conduct and the order and configuration of actions tend to coincide, since the rules are set out precisely in order to achieve a particular kind of order and a particular configuration.

8. The price system does not simply 'convey' information but generates flashing green lights that alert actors of the possibility of entrepreneurial profit: prices are therefore not merely indicators, but also the catalysts of a competitive system of discovery (Kirzner, 1992; Thomsen, 1992).

9. The market is therefore not merely an allocative mechanism that aims at the maximization of certain outcomes, but a more far-reaching and inclusive process of continuous discovery and mutual aid. As Buchanan (1979) observes, the simplistic notion that the market is a mere allocative mechanism (and that the economic problem is simply that of allocating scarce means among alternative ends) is a recent one, having originated in the work of Lord Robbins; it partly subverted the previous, broader and more convincing classical conception.

10. As Hayek (1988, p. 19) observes, one revealing indication of how poorly the market mechanism is understood is the common idea that co-operation is always better than competition. But co-operation presupposes a considerable and substantial measure of agreement on goals as well as on methods employed in reaching them; it works in a small group whose members share particular information and aims. But it makes no sense when the central problem is to adapt to unknown circumstances. In this second case, it is competition that works better; it is a procedure of discovery that leads men unwittingly and creatively to respond to novel situations. And it is through further (regulated) competition, not through (large-scale) agreement, that we increase opportunities and efficiency.

11. The properties of a 'material' are irrelevant if we do not know how to take advantage of them.

12. See the theory of the market as a spontaneous order as conceived by Hayek (1948, 1967, 1982) and developed by authors such as O'Driscoll and Rizzo (1985) and Kirzner (1992, 2000).

13. It is worth noting that the Austrian school of economics emphasizes the role of the entrepreneur, who had all but vanished from neoclassical economic theory. Israel Kirzner (1973) distinguishes the Austrian entrepreneur from the neoclassical economizer: entrepreneurship is not mere calculating and maximizing within a situation of given means and ends, but rather alertness to new potential means and ends. The central issue that applies to the present argument is the 'essentially creative nature' of entrepreneurship.

14. There has been some impact on approaches and techniques for analysing and comprehending cities (Batty, 2005), but little in terms of reflection regarding how to control and intervene in cities.

15. 'Despite the almost universal recognition that the market system works better than central [economic] planning for the production of goods and services, in other areas, including land-use planning, people continue to make the argument that central planning is needed to overcome the shortcomings of the market' (Holcombe, 2001, p. 144).

16. 'The drawbacks of central planning apply to cities as well as countries' (Hoppe and Block, 2002, p. 233).

17. See also Gordon et al. (2005, p. 197): 'Top-down planners of all stripes are fatally hobbled by their inability to tap local knowledge. . . . Just as many people presume the inevitability of top-down planning because of external effect and information problems, events show the opposite. . . . It takes decentralized markets to generate the required information through trial-and-error learning.' See also Holcombe and Staley (2001), Holcombe (2004), Staley (2004) and O'Toole (2007).

18. As John Sommer (1982, p. 520) observes, the ability – for instance – of a firm to re-establish its activities at a new site is a benefit both for the producer and for the consumers (as is the improvement of this ability). But, against this mechanism of market-responsive movement, policies are adopted which attempt to maintain routine patterns and habits: 'on an urban scale, land use plans, zoning laws, rent controls, and other dislocative non-market forces forestall the emergence of imaginative city forms and functions because they constrain spontaneous combinations'.

19. In this chapter I use the term 'liberal/liberalism' in the classical European sense. This idea of liberalism is different from the 'new-right liberalism' that many authors critique today under the (what I consider) quite erroneous label 'liberalism/neo-liberalism' (see Touraine, 1999; Amin, 2004; Harvey, 2005).

20. The consequentialist ethical approach is that which traditionally characterizes planning theory and practice (Sillince, 1986, pp. 121–162).
21. For example, *Village of Euclid v Ambler Realty Co.*, 1926.
22. We could also reject the liberal-democratic ideal (or at least a certain version of it), but we must be clear about what exactly we are rejecting, something that superficial critics of the ideal seem not always to understand. As regards complexity (and self-organization), on the contrary, I believe that we cannot avoid some consequences that derive from acknowledging these phenomena.
23. Systems of complex rules – peculiar to the traditional and current land-use planning systems – are sets of rules that present the following features (Epstein, 1995, pp. 23–5): 'technicality', that is, the trait of those rules that request a high level of expertise to understand and apply them (this means that ordinary citizens are not able to directly know whether they are in compliance with the rules, and therefore need professional help); 'density', in reference to those rules that try to cover in minute details all aspects of certain actions or activities; 'differentiation', which regards the plurality of different overlapping sources of law concerning a given situation; 'indeterminacy', referring to the fact that to be able to decide whether a given action is illegal, it is necessary to deal with several factors provided for, none of which is decisive (the rules fail to give a clear yes/no answer).
24. Obviously, as Richard Epstein (1995, p. 53) observes, no set of rules will be totally perfect: 'indeed, knowing when to quit is one of the driving forces behind a set of simple rules'; on the contrary, 'complex rules are for those who have an unattainable vision of perfection' (p. 39).
25. The instrumental notion of law became widespread and broadly accepted in the twentieth century – it is not by chance that planning also was accorded growing importance – and is still taken for granted today. In an instrumental perspective, law is intended primarily as a tool or means for achieving desired objectives; it can be shaped in any way necessary to reach our ends. The supply of possible ends is intended to be totally open and without limits of any sort. In other words, law is 'an empty vessel to be filled as desired, and to be manipulated, invoked, and utilized in the furtherance of ends' (Tamanaha, 2006, p. 1); it is an empty box 'devoid of any inherent principle or binding content or integrity unto itself' (Tamanaha, 2006, p. 7). This notion of law was clearly influenced strongly by Enlightenment thinkers' illusions regarding the power of human reason: 'The Enlightenment confidence that humans can shape and improve the conditions of their existence encouraged the instrumental view of law' (Tamanaha, 2006, p. 23).
26. See Hirsch (1988, p. 4): 'Rule formulation seeks to maximize or minimize some specified goal.'
27. 'Rules do not . . . lead to the best results in particular cases, but they serve a number of other values. General rules foster the virtues of reliance, predictability and stability: by reducing variance in individual cases, they allow individuals and associations to plan their lives' (Macedo, 1994, p. 154).
28. 'Law . . . provides a framework within which persons carry on their own separate private purposes. . . . In this conception, there is no social purpose to the law. Law . . . is not specifically designed to further explicitly defined social goals' (Buchanan and Congleton, 2003, p. 13).
29. We can accept this without necessarily coming back to natural law doctrines but (for instance) accepting a more sophisticated evolutionary idea of the law (Hayek, 1982).
30. I am thinking here of the well-known 'indeterminacy thesis' which asserts that the law – because of the 'open texture' of the language – does not always produce a single (right) answer, a fact that seems to seriously undermine the certainty of the law and the predictability of outcomes. As Tamanaha (2004, p. 87) writes: 'The main response put forth by opponents of the indeterminacy thesis was to point out the substantial degree of predictability in law. There are many easy cases, cases in which lawyers can reliably anticipate the likely outcome, in which there will be little or no disagreement among judges. . . . Claims about rampant indeterminacy were exaggerated because critical theorists overemphasized appellate cases . . . which indeed showed a greater proportion of disagreement, but represented a small, misleading sampling of the totality of cases.' In brief: 'Despite the unavoidable open texture of language and rules . . ., experience demonstrates that people reliably communicate through language and routinely understand and follow rules. . . . When ambiguities and doubts exist in a given situation of rule application, they are resolved through reasoned analysis. Hence indeterminacies, given that they exist, do not inevitably defeat the determinacy of a legal system' (Tamanaha, 2004, p. 88). And this is all true, particularly if we create rules in an appropriate manner.
31. The term 'urban code' (or 'spatial code') is used in a similar way by Alfasi and Portugali (2007).
32. Rules such as: 'Every building project or modification must, in whatever place, avoid generating the externalities A, B and C'; 'Buildings of Type M must not be constructed within X metres of buildings of Type N' and so forth.
33. A 'development right' is a legal entitlement to develop a piece of land.
34. The reallocation of development rights through market exchanges can be restricted by a 'ceiling' uniformly applied to all places. No-building areas – the areas where no one can build but which some people still have the right to trade – must not be defined at the local level via orthodox, incidental and particular

zoning ordinances, but via abstract and general supra-local rules (for example, 'It is not permitted to build within X metres from a river' or 'within Y metres from the sea').

35. For this reason, it is not challenged by the critiques that I mentioned earlier.

36. And all of this should take place without any kind of bargaining or partnership whatsoever between private and public parties. I believe that the private actor and the public actor must perform their separate roles independently from each other; each time that one of the two fails to achieve something without bargaining with the other means that whatever it was should not be carried out.

37. He must also be credited for having aptly insisted on the centrality of the pioneering (and still greatly underestimated) teaching of Jane Jacobs in this regard.

38. 'In industrialized democracies, the culture of playing by the rules has been weakened. . . . Much of this weakening has resulted from misguided social engineering. The weakening of property rights . . . and the abandonment of the fault basis of liability through numerous legislative interventions and discretionary powers have not only distorted rules of justice directly but have also led to a general decline of the culture of responsibility for one's own conduct' (Ratnapala, 2006, p. 116).

39. 'What makes men members of the same civilization and enables them to live and work together in peace is that in the pursuit of their individual ends the particular . . . impulses which impel their efforts towards concrete results are guided and restrained by the same abstract rules. . . . What reconciles the individuals and knits them into a common and enduring pattern of a society is that to . . . different particular situations they respond in accordance with the same abstract rules' (Hayek, 1982, Vol. II, p. 12).

40. As Landry (2008, p. xxxiii) observes, people are the 'real assets': 'Seen in this way, people and how they feel are highlighted as the crucial resource.'

41. See also Florida (2005, pp. 3–4): 'Perhaps the single most overlooked – and single most important – element of my theory is the idea that every human being is creative'. And Florida (2007, p. 35): 'By our very nature, each and every person is endowed with an incredible capacity for innovation, a by-product of the innate human capability to evolve and adapt. Creative capital is thus a virtually limitless resource.'

42. 'Civic creativity is defined as imaginative problem-solving applied to public good objectives. The aim is to generate a continual flow of innovative solutions to problems which have an impact on the public realm. Civic creativity is the capacity for public officials and others oriented to the public good to effectively and instrumentally apply their imaginative faculties to achieving higher value within a framework of social and political values' (Landry, 2008, p. 190).

43. As Hospers (2003a, p. 149) observes, it is an illusion to think that we can force creativity and directly construct a knowledge-intensive city: 'The unpredictability surrounding creativity and innovation means that a tailor-made, unambiguous creative competitive strategy for urban environment is not available.' In brief: 'Creative cities cannot be constructed from the ground up. . . . In their enthusiasm, local authorities sometimes tend to forget this' (Hospers, 2003b, p. 266). See also Florida (2007, pp. 245–6): 'It's impossible – and undesirable – to outline a ten-, fifty-, or one-hundred point plan for building the creative society; this cannot be a top-down or centralized endeavor.' 'We can't legislate urban creativity any more easily than we can legislate economic growth' (Florida, 2007, p. 259).

44. This is an objection that is frequently made to Florida's original position (see Peck, 2005; McCann, 2007; Zimmerman, 2008; Catungal and Leslie, 2009; Catungal et al., 2009; Oakley, 2009) and which Florida (2005, pp. 171ff., 2007) countered with only some brief cursory observations.

45. Such as vouchers for certain basic services.

REFERENCES

Alfasi, N. and J. Portugali (2007), 'Planning rules for a self-planned city', *Planning Theory*, **6**, 164–82.
Allen, P.M. (1997), *Cities and Regions as Self-organizing Systems*, Amsterdam: Gordon and Breach.
Amin, S. (2004), *The Liberal Virus*, London: Pluto Press.
Batty, M. (2005), *Cities and Complexity*, Cambridge, MA: MIT Press.
Brennan, G. and J.M. Buchanan (2000), *The Reason of Rules*, Indianapolis, IN: Liberty Fund.
Buchanan, J. (1979), *What Should Economists Do?*, Indianapolis, IN: Liberty Fund.
Buchanan, J.M. and R.D. Congleton (2003), *Politics by Principle, Not Interest*, Indianapolis, IN: Liberty Fund.
Catungal, J.P. and D. Leslie (2009), 'Contesting the creative city', *Geoforum*, **40**, 701–4.
Catungal, J.P., D. Leslie and Y. Hii (2009), 'Geographies of displacement in the creative city', *Urban Studies*, **46**(5/6), 1095–114.
Chatterton, P. (2000), 'Will the real creative city please stand up?', *City*, **4**(3), 390–7.
Chiappero-Martinetti, E. and S. Moroni (2007), 'An analytical framework for conceptualizing poverty and re-examining the capability approach', *Journal of Socio-Economics*, **36**, 360–75.

Cordato, R.E. (2004), 'Toward an Austrian theory of environmental economics', *Quarterly Journal of Austrian Economics*, **7**, 3–16.
Corijn, E. (2009), 'Urbanity as a political project', in L. Kong and J. O'Connor (eds), *Creative Economies, Creative Cities*, Dordrecht: Springer, pp. 197–206.
Corkindale, J. (1998), *Reforming Land-Use Planning*, London: Institute of Economic Affairs.
Corkindale, J. (2004), *The Land Use Planning System*, London: Institute of Economic Affairs.
Cullingworth, J.B. (1993), *The Political Culture of Planning*, London: Routledge.
Cusinato, A. (2009), 'Le ragioni del piano, tra ideologia e storia', *Scienze regionali*, **2**, 121–30.
Dowd, K. (2008), 'Moral hazard and the financial crisis', paper presented at the Cato Institute 26th Annual Monetary Conference Lessons from the Subprime Crisis, Cato Institute, Washington, DC, 19 November.
Downs, A. (2005), 'Local regulations and housing affordability', in E. Ben-Joseph and T.S. Szold (eds), *Regulating Place*, London: Routledge, pp. 103–12.
Ellickson, R. (1973), 'Alternatives to zoning', *University of Chicago Law Review*, **40**(4), 681–781.
Epstein, R.A. (1995), *Simple Rules for a Complex World*, Cambridge, MA: Harvard University Press.
Florida, R. (2005), *Cities and the Creative Class*, London: Routledge.
Florida, R. (2007), *The Flight of the Creative Class*, New York, NY: Collins.
Florida, R. (2008), *Who's Your City?*, New York, NY: Basic Books.
Foldvary, F. (1994), *Public Goods and Private Communities*, Aldershot, UK and Brookfield, VT, USA: Edward Elgar Publishing.
Friedmann, W. (1949), *Legal Theory*, London: Stevens & Sons.
Friedmann, W. (1951), *Law and Social Change*, London: Stevens & Sons.
Fuller, L.L. (1964), *The Morality of Law*, New Haven, CT: Yale University Press.
Gaffney, M. (2009), *After the Crash*, Chichester: Wiley-Blackwell.
Glaeser, E. and J. Gyourko (2002), 'Zoning's steep price', *Regulation*, **25**, 24–30.
Gordon, P., D.T. Beito and A. Tabarrok (2005), 'The voluntary city', in E. Ben-Joseph and T.S. Szold (eds), *Regulating Place*, London: Routledge, pp. 189–202.
Harvey, D. (2005), *A Brief History of Neoliberalism*, Oxford: Oxford University Press.
Hayek, F.A. (1944), *The Road to Serfdom*, London: Routledge.
Hayek, F.A. (1948), *Individualism and Economic Order*, Chicago, IL: University of Chicago Press.
Hayek, F.A. (1967), *Studies in Philosophy, Politics and Economics*, London: Routledge.
Hayek, F.A. (1982), *Law, Legislation and Liberty*, London: Routledge.
Hayek, F.A. (1988), *The Fatal Conceit*, London: Routledge.
Hayes, M.T. (2001), *The Limits of Policy Change*, Washington, DC: Georgetown University Press.
Healey, P. (1997), *Collaborative Planning*, London: Macmillan.
Healey, P. (2007), *Urban Complexity and Spatial Strategies*, London: Routledge.
Hirsch, W.Z. (1988), *Law and Economics*, London: Academic Press.
Holcombe, R.G. (2001), 'Growth management in action', in R.G. Holcombe and S.R. Staley (eds), *Smarter Growth*, Westport, CT: Greenwood Press, pp. 131–54.
Holcombe, R.G. (2004), 'The new urbanism versus the market process', *Review of Austrian Economics*, **17**, 285–300.
Holcombe, R.G. and B. Powell (eds) (2009), *Housing America*, New Brunswick, NJ: Transaction Publishers.
Holcombe, R.G. and S.R. Staley (eds) (2001), *Smarter Growth*, Westport, CT: Greenwood Press.
Hoppe H.-H. and W. Block (2002), 'On property and exploitation', *International Journal of Value-Based Management*, **15**, 225–36.
Hospers, G.-J. (2003a), 'Creative cities: breeding places in the knowledge economy', *Knowledge, Technology and Policy*, **16**, 143–62.
Hospers, G.-J. (2003b), 'Creative cities in Europe: urban competitiveness in the knowledge economy', *Intereconomics*, September/October, 260–9.
Howkins, J. (2001), *The Creative Economy*, London: Penguin.
Kasper, W. and M.E. Streit (1998), *Institutional Economics*, Cheltenham, UK and Lyme, NH, USA: Edward Elgar Publishing.
Kebir, L. and O. Crevoisier (2008), 'Cultural resources and regional development', in P. Cooke and L. Lazzaretti (eds), *Creative Cities, Cultural Clusters and Local Economic Development*, Cheltenham, UK and Northampton, MA, USA: Edward Elgar Publishing, pp. 48–69.
Kirzner, I.M. (1973), *Competition and Entrepreneurship*, Chicago, IL: University of Chicago Press.
Kirzner, I.M. (1992), *The Meaning of Market Process*, London: Routledge.
Kirzner, I.M. (2000), *The Driving Force of the Market*, London: Routledge.
Landry, C. (2008), *The Creative City*, London: Earthscan.
Lindblom, C.E. (1990), *Inquiry and Change*, New Haven, CT: Yale University Press.
Loasby, B.J. (1999), *Knowledge, Institutions and Evolution in Economics*, London: Routledge.
Lowi, T. (1979), *The End of Liberalism*, New York, NY: Norton.

Macedo, S. (1994), 'The rule of law, justice and the politics of moderation', in I. Shapiro (ed.), *The Rule of Law*, New York, NY: New York University Press, pp. 148–77.

McCann, E.J. (2007), 'Inequality and politics in the creative city-region', *International Journal of Urban and Regional Research*, **31**(1), 188–96.

Mises, L. von (1927), *Liberalismus*, Jena: Gustav Fischer.

Mises, L. von (1929), *Kritik des Interventionismus*, Jena: Gutav Fischer.

Moroni, S. (2007a) *La città del liberalismo attivo*, Torino: CittàStudi.

Moroni, S. (2007b), 'Planning, liberty and the rule of law', *Planning Theory*, **6**(2), 146–63.

Moroni, S. (2010a), 'Rethinking the theory and practice of land-use regulation: towards nomocracy', *Planning Theory*, **9**(2), 137–55.

Moroni, S. (2010b), 'An evolutionary theory of institutions and a dynamic approach to reform', *Planning Theory*, **9**(4), 275–97.

Mumford, L. (1938), *The Culture of Cities*, San Diego, CA: Harcourt Brace & Co.

Needham, B. (2006), *Planning, Law and Economics*, London: Routledge.

Needham, B. (2007), 'Final comment: land-use planning and the law', *Planning Theory*, **6**, 183–9.

Nelson, R.H. (2005), *Private Neighborhoods*, Washington, DC: Urban Institute Press.

Newman, P. and A. Thornley (1996), *Urban Planning in Europe*, London: Routledge.

Oakley, K. (2009), 'Getting out of place: the mobile creative class takes on the local', in L. Kong and J. O'Connor (eds), *Creative Economies, Creative Cities*, Dordrecht: Springer, pp. 121–34.

O'Driscoll, G.P. (2008), 'Asset bubbles and their consequences', Cato Institute Briefing Paper No. 103, Washington, DC: Cato Institute.

O'Driscoll, G.P. and M.J. Rizzo (1985), *The Economics of Time and Ignorance*, London: Routledge.

O'Toole, R. (2007), *The Best-laid Plans*, Washington, DC: Cato Institute.

O'Toole, R. (2009), 'How urban planners caused the housing bubble', *Policy Analysis*, **646**, 2–27.

Pasour, E.C. (1991), 'Land-use planning: implications of the economic calculation debate', in J.C. Wood and R.N. Woods (eds), *Friedrich A. Hayek*, Vol. IV, London: Routledge, pp. 1–15.

Paul, R. (2008), *The Revolution*, New York, NY: Grand Central Publishing.

Peck, J. (2005), 'Struggling with the creative class', *International Journal of Urban and Regional Research*, **29**(4), 740–70.

Pennington, M. (1999), 'Free market environmentalism and the limits of land-use planning', *Journal of Environmental Policy and Planning*, **1**, 43–59.

Pennington, M. (2005), 'The dynamics of interventionism: a case study of British land use regulation', in P. Kurrild-Klitgaard (ed.), *The Dynamics of Intervention*, Oxford: Elsevier, pp. 335–56.

Portugali, J. (1999), *Self-organization and the City*, Berlin: Springer.

Pumain, D., L. Sanders and T. Saint-Julien (1989), *Ville et Auto-organisation*, Paris: Economica.

Ratnapala, S. (2006), 'Moral capital and commercial society', in R. Higgs and C.P. Close (eds), *The Challenge of Liberty*, Oakland, CA: The Independent Institute, pp. 97–119.

Renard, V. (2007), 'Property rights and the transfer of development rights', *Town Planning Review*, **78**(1), 41–60.

Rogge, B.A. (1979), *Can Capitalism Survive?* Indianapolis, IN: Liberty Fund.

Sartori, G. (1957), *Democrazia e definizioni*, Bologna: Il Mulino.

Siegan, B.H. (1997), *Property and Freedom*, New Brunswick, NJ: Transaction Publishers.

Sillince, J. (1986), *A Theory of Planning*, Aldershot: Gower.

Simon, J.L. (1996), *The Ultimate Resource 2*, Princeton, NJ: Princeton University Press.

Smith, R. and K. Warfield (2008), 'The creative city: a matter of values', in P. Cooke and L. Lazzaretti (eds), *Creative Cities, Cultural Clusters and Local Economic Development*, Cheltenham, UK and Northampton, MA, USA: Edward Elgar Publishing, pp. 287–312.

Sommer, J.W. (1982), 'The post-interventionist city', *Cato Journal*, **2**, 501–41.

Sorensen, A.D. and M.L. Auser (1989), 'Fatal remedies: the sources of ineffectiveness in planning', *Town Planning Review*, **60**, 29–44.

Staley, S.R. (2004), 'Urban planning, smart growth, and economic calculation', *Review of Austrian Economics*, **17**, 265–83.

Stewart, R. (2000), *Limón Real: A Free and Autonomous Region*, Tonopah, NV: Heather Foundation.

Tamanaha, B.Z. (2004), *On the Rule of Law*, Cambridge: Cambridge University Press.

Tamanaha, B.Z. (2006), *Law as a Mean to an End*, Cambridge: Cambridge University Press.

Taylor, J.B. (2009), *Getting Off Track*, Stanford, CA: Hoover Institution Press.

Thomas, D., J. Minett, S. Hopkins, S. Hamnett, A. Faludi and D. Barrell (1983), *Flexibility and Commitment in Planning*, The Hague: Martinus Nijhoff.

Thomsen, E.F. (1992), *Prices and Knowledge*, London: Routledge.

Thornton, M. (2009), 'The economics of housing bubbles', in R.G. Holcombe and B. Powell (eds), *Housing America*, New Brunswick, NJ: Transaction Publishers, pp. 237–62.

Touraine, A. (1999), *Comment sortir du libéralisme?*, Paris: Librairie Arthème Fayard.
Unger, R.M. (1975), *Knowledge and Politics*, New York, NY: The Free Press.
Webster, C. and L.W.-C. Lai (2003), *Property Rights, Planning and Markets*, Cheltenham, UK and Northampton, MA, USA: Edward Elgar Publishing.
White, L.J. (2009), 'Fannie Mae, Freddie Mac, and housing: good intentions gone awry', in R.G. Holcombe and B. Powell (eds), *Housing America*, New Brunswick, NJ: Transaction Publishers, pp. 263–86.
Woods, T.E. (2009), *Meltdown*, Washington, DC: Regnery Publishing.
Zimmerman, J. (2008), 'From brew town to cool town: neoliberalism and the creative city development strategy in Milwaukee', *Cities*, **25**, 230–42.

18 The emergence of Vancouver as a creative city
Gus diZerega and David F. Hardwick

Cities are incubators for creativity. They attract creative citizens and enable them to form the subtle and intricate networks required to pursue their dreams, to the benefit of us all. But not all cities are equal in this respect. This chapter explores how insights arising from the study of emergent processes shed light on what enables a city to become a magnet for creative people, a lasting incubator for their dreams and their accomplishments.

Our understanding of modern cities often becomes dominated by economic and prescriptive models of what makes a community viable. While important insights have arisen from these approaches, equally important blind spots accompany them. This is because cities are far more complex than markets co-ordinated through financial feedback can encompass. In addition, they are also far more uncertain and dynamic than traditional planning could successfully handle. Both economic and prescriptive approaches towards understanding and governing cities reflect an engineering understanding of urban processes. In our current reality these social processes are too varied and uncertain in their details for a traditional planning perspective such as this to be satisfactory over many issues or for a long period of time.

This is certainly the case with social environments able to attract culturally creative residents into an urban area. People are motivated by a number of basic values, important among them being money, power and recognition by their peers. All contribute to the basic goal of personal growth and survival. A good urban environment will address all these needs.

A great many creative people do not rate economic success or power and influence as highly on their priorities as the opportunity to be part of an interesting and stimulating culturally creative community. Even when they do, they are more likely to make choices to live for a time making considerably less money than they might otherwise, the better to pursue their dream. But those dreams not only enliven a city, they contribute heavily to its cultural and often indirectly to its economic well-being.

Affordable housing located close to socially important amenities and opportunities to network with other creative persons ranks high on a creative minority's criteria for a destination community, our term for a community able to attract people who have various other viable options before them. So also is the availability of facilities able to exhibit creative work at a variety of levels, from small venues to large public auditoriums and galleries. The 'micro level' is particularly important in this respect, for it encourages communities of creative innovators only some of whom will 'make it big' but all of whom seek the potential recognition of the social interactive matrix from which stars may emerge (Florida, 2002, pp. 258–61). These creative communities cannot be constructed, they must be encouraged (for examples of planning failures, see Scott, 1998). However they tend to be under-appreciated within the dominant market-oriented standards for community planning and growth typically emphasizing the economic growth of downtown.

Tolerance of diversity in lifestyles is an obvious plus as well, as it implies security for creative persons. Pressures to live in accord with a single hierarchy of values, no matter how composed, discourages creative residents. Attracting such residents requires varied and welcoming neighbourhoods close to major amenities. Again, these values tend to be under-emphasized by contemporary economically dominant models of urban planning, with their focus on 'downtown' land values.

Vancouver, British Columbia, has explored an alternative approach to urban growth and development with its roots in the widespread 1960s objections to these one-dimensional bureaucratic approaches to human life. The result some 40 years later has been an extraordinary success. Vancouver is not only a city attracting visitors world-wide, it has also become one of Canada's scientific and creative centres. A part of the reason for its success rests in Vancouver's profound divergence in development strategies beginning in the late 1960s compared to its more orthodox trajectory before that time.

We argue for a focus on cities as complex adaptive systems containing powerful tensions between different urban social networks as well as between the networks and the organizations that arise within them. Such a focus on 'emergent order' and directed but not controlled change sheds important light not only on Vancouver's success; it also offers guidance as to how other communities might learn from Vancouver's experience. Vancouver's success in integrating a variety of emergent (or as F.A. Hayek put it: 'self-organizing') social processes within a dynamic process cannot be grasped with either a one-dimensional market-focused analysis nor through the framework of traditional urban planning models.[1]

COMPLEXITY

When we use the term 'complexity' we are referring to social phenomena where individual participants do not and cannot have a picture of the process as a whole, nor specific knowledge of its outcome (Hayek, 1967). The world is complex in this sense, but so are many other phenomena, such as language, culture, the market and a city. In all these examples complexity should not be confused with chaos or confusion. They are examples of ordered complexity.

The kinds of social complexities crucial for our argument have another characteristic: they are adaptive systems as well as complex ones. This means that while no participant has a complete overview or control, the results of participating within the system generates feedback useful not only for the actor but also for other unknown actors to better achieve their goals, whatever they may be. The market is a well-known example, relying on price signals to co-ordinate otherwise independently conceived actions. The rules of grammar and intelligibility accomplish the same end for language. The all-inclusive term for this kind of process is 'complex adaptive system'.

Unlike markets and language, however, cities are characterized by many feedback systems produced by people acting within many networks shaped by different contexts and values. A city can be legitimately influenced by any resident acting within any urban network seeking to achieve any value compatible with its democratic structure. This includes the use of language and markets, of course, so cities are more complex than either. Cities are multi-purpose entities whose residents seek employment, entertainment, social ties and the fulfilment of many other values within their boundaries.

This complexity is all the greater because no single set of values or standards can satisfactorily balance them, nor will any particular hierarchy of values meet the needs of a city's residents all the time. Some of these values can be represented adequately through monetary feedback, but others cannot. Values change over time, as does their relative importance in residents' lives. Ideally a democratic city will be responsive to as many values as possible while retaining the ability to harmonize many of them in viable public policy. But what these values are and their attributed importance will vary over time, and must be discovered and rediscovered rather than taken for granted.

This is particularly true for creative minorities attracted to cities by the prospect of finding a destination community of kindred spirits. Cities with diversity encourage respect for different perspectives that generates creative work. But just how these values will manifest, and who will do the manifesting is intrinsically unpredictable.

Certain attractive amenities are obvious. The presence of a four-year college or even better, a university is a valuable asset in drawing creative people to a community by providing abundant opportunities for them to learn and explore. So is a hall for the performing arts. But many cities have these amenities without becoming vital creative destinations. In both cases a depth of community interaction within relevant fields is necessary, a depth often not immediately obvious when looking at a great auditorium or university campus.

This depth cannot be constructed, but it can be cultivated. For example, creative communities often depend on individual 'spark plugs' that cannot be predicted. We cannot identify innovative people by their social status or income or level of education, but to an important degree the personal characteristics of key actors, especially in less financially oriented networks, play an important role in the patterns of association and choice that emerge. For example, in one study a neighbourhood salmon restoration group in Seattle, Washington, was sparked by a long-time resident, housewife and home owner who lived next to a creek, whereas in neighbouring Tacoma the equivalent spark came from a young expert on the local ecology who lived in part on federal Supplemental Security Income (SSI) in a beat-up trailer. Superficially he resembled a social drop-out and it is difficult to imagine the two being selected from a random sample of citizens as the crucial innovators in restoring their community's salmon runs, which they did.

All that can be done to encourage such outcomes is providing a social environment where such 'different' people have an opportunity to make the connections they need to help initiate a creative and secure community in the arts or sciences or business. This makes a city a destination city not so much for tourists as for a wide variety of people who desire to live there, particularly creative ones.

CONTRADICTION IN COMPLEXITY

Cities are networks of networks. These different networks respond to different values mediated through feedback signals no one fully controls or even completely understands. The market is an obvious example of such a co-ordinating network, but a complex reality lies even within this simple one-dimensional statement. Even from a purely market-oriented perspective a city is a complex network of businesses providing employment, services and commodities both for its residents and for export outside its boundaries and, in addition, a network of market-oriented property owners who seek increasing value in their land. Both of these networks are mediated through the price system and its signals of profit or loss, real or anticipated. However, unless a business owns its property, the interest of the two networks often clash.

These economic networks are only two of many networks whose interests are even less easily harmonized. This is especially the case with cities able to attract and retain a wide range of culturally creative citizens, who are not strongly money oriented (Florida, 2002, pp. 77–82). To appreciate these other networks we need to look with a finer lens to see the varied and shifting networks that comprise civil society.

Like 'complex', the term 'civil society' has been used in a number of different ways. We use it to refer to those voluntary face-to-face relationships citizens have with one another as interdependent equals who are not intimates (Hardwick, 2008). We differentiate the market economy considered as a whole from civil society because so much of it is impersonal and guided by only financial criteria. However, face-to-face businesses are a part of civil society (diZerega, 2004). We also exclude family relationships because they are unique enough (due to their intimacy and child rearing) to be considered separately in their own right (Horwitz, 2008).

Civil society includes the educational, artistic and cultural networks that add immensely to a community's desirability and cultural richness as a creative destination in which to live. Here also are the social networks of clubs, associations and religions that make up much of the rest of social life, operate with only tangential concern for prices and often have little interest in extensive political involvement. Finally we include the informal networks existing within neighbourhoods and other places where people have become familiar with one another.

Neighbourhood relationships help keep order, provide the broader environment where children are raised and are concerned with the city as home rather than an investment. The point is not that home owners are uninterested in the value of their home. They normally are. Our point is that its monetary value is usually secondary to its status as their home. What makes the home something more than an investment is in no small part due to the networks of neighbourliness and mutual aid that can characterize an urban neighbourhood (Jacobs, 1961). It is not surprising that Richard Florida observes how Jane Jacobs's work on neighbourhoods illustrates conditions both reflecting and nurturing creativity (Florida, 2002, pp. 42–3).

Even more than in the economy, all these networks are dynamic structures whose details elude general models. They are complex, responding in different ways to the universal human motivations of power, recognition, wealth and ultimately survival and growth.

ORGANIZATIONS, NETWORKS AND LEVELS OF COMPLEXITY

Organizations emerge in networks when people come together to accomplish specific projects. Organizations are difficult to form, but once formed it is common for members to find the organization's continued existence useful for their own purposes, over and above whatever may have initially led to its creation. As a result, once they exist organizations often begin to take on a life of their own, putting their institutional survival ahead of most or all other goals. All significant networks have organizations within them seeking to pursue their own ends.

The networks within which they exist make these organizations possible and also potentially can lead to their dissolution. So organizations are both dependent on networks and threatened by them. As a consequence successful organizations will often seek to control the networks on which they depend. To do so, if necessary, they may go outside this network and import resources from elsewhere to exercise that control. This is most obvious in the case of businesses seeking political favours from city officials and bureaucrats and to that degree freeing themselves from purely economic forces, but the tendency is ubiquitous. Indeed, it would be strange were it not so.

This means cities have at least two levels of irreducible complexity that can be neither predicted in detail nor harmonized by any formula or institution. First, different networks essential for a successful community respond to different values, and so can and do clash. Second, organizations will seek control to safeguard their existence within particular networks and to the degree they succeed, they rigidify an area of city life or colonize it with resources obtained from outside.

A successful city handles this dynamic complexity by enabling all networks to have a voice when it matters, without deferring to any one of them all the time, and not letting any organized subset of a network dominate the network's voice as a whole. The contradictions and tensions within and between networks means a complete laissez-faire approach to urban life defined only through market forces cannot lead to a city optimally conducive to developing creative communities. The delicate social networks these communities require would be continually disrupted by purely economic criteria because the near universality of money as a means enables it to colonize other networks, subordinating their dominant organizations to narrowly financial criteria (diZerega, 2004). Again we emphasize that no single feedback mechanism gives adequate weight to all the complexities of urban life.

URBAN DEMOCRACY

The political network of cliques, parties and the organized interests that seek to influence them make up a city's democratic structure. An urban democracy is a network of networks within which everyone seeks to influence the quality of urban life through deliberate decisions binding on all residents. The ultimate feedback that matters to political networks is votes leading to political power, and often votes can be obtained by spending money or by organizing popular participation. The political network potentially includes representatives of every other major urban network because its decision making can help or hinder their own concerns. But a democracy cannot be reduced to or defined simply by the presence of elections. The networks creating the ongoing adaptive context within which voting occurs are as important (Kingdon, 1995).

Politics provides the forum where city-wide issues are addressed and acted upon, and also where smaller networks within a city can seek to have their interests protected and promoted. It is inevitably conflictual because the interests of legitimate urban networks often clash, as we noted above. Democratic politics is a shifting mixture of people promoting what they believe is in the public good and what they believe benefits themselves without reference to the community as a whole. The second element is the price paid for being able to address the first. Voting temporarily settles the issue of who makes a final decision, but vital as voting is, it clearly constitutes only a small part of the political process as a whole.

To 'take the politics out' of city life through establishing largely independent planning bureaucracies simply excludes networks that do not have ready access to urban decision makers. Political influence is not taken out; it is only narrowed to a small number of well-placed interests. Such interests have little in common with the messy diversity that nurtures creative communities. They traditionally focus on competing proposals to serve dominant or downtown business concerns whereas neighbourhoods are typically the incubators of cultural creativity.

DEMOCRATIC GOVERNANCE

From this perspective a democratic city government provides a means where these networks can mutually influence one another and consequently city policy. The problem that arises is that government becomes a prize to be captured at two levels. First, because of government's prescriptive power, if dominated by one set of interests they can give themselves privileges at the expense of the rest of the community. In such cases politics tends to become zero-sum. Second, those in office, particularly bureaucratic office, can seek to free themselves from political control and run the government as they personally see fit. At best this results in competent technocratic planning and at worst in incompetent technocratic planning, neither of which easily responds to or encourages civic diversity.

Within a democratic framework the results of such technocratic domination are not necessarily disastrous or exploitative in the short run, but the advantages an open political system can bring to a community are reduced to approving one set of experts over another at election time. A largely passive citizenry selects one group over another to be its rulers until the next election (Schumpeter, 1942, is the classic statement of this view of democracy). Sensitivity to currents of urban life that are not easily bundled into one platform or another is lost. Distortions emerge without anyone necessarily intending them, as the complexities of real urban life are submerged under simple dichotomies of choice that exclude input and perspectives from smaller networks.

These distortions of the political process often create dysfunctional rigidities. Distortions honouring only a small number of elements within a successful city, usually part of the business community, can undermine the vitality and quality of life of the city as a whole, even while some favoured interests prosper and make money. Isolated and independent planners become captive to their models, which may not fit the community to which they are applied, and so become divorced from popular sentiment.

Vancouver provides an alternative model, one that replaced prescriptive planning with planning based on facilitating and cultivating unpredictable developments combined with effective urban fiscal management that would contribute to the expression of all the basic networks making up a modern city.

VANCOUVER, BRITISH COLUMBIA

Vancouver started with important advantages in becoming the city it is today. Situated in a setting of unsurpassed beauty, enjoying a mild climate (even an occasional palm tree can be found there, tough ones, but still palm trees), and serving as Canada's gateway to the growing economies of Asia, Vancouver has major advantages when evaluated by that favourite formula for realtors: location, location and location. In many ways Vancouver would be an attractive location regardless of how it developed.

Vancouver's first years, around the turn of the last century, were politically and culturally dominated by commercial interests lasting until a depression shortly before the First World War. Public institutions were largely undeveloped. There was not even a publicly owned city hall. The utilitarian views of those times are preserved today in the grid pattern of the city's streets.

However, Progressive visions of urban planning found receptive minds in Vancouver, and by the first decade of the twentieth century initiatives were afloat to create efficiently managed municipal government based on the principles of Taylorist scientific management that were being applied to corporations (Taylor, 1911). Planning was considered primarily as an engineering problem, focusing on the physical infrastructure of roads, bridges, sewers and street lights. These ideals could be harmonized with older elites' concern that growth was shifting the city centre towards the west, lowering older property values. Zoning promised a means to safeguard those values.

Even so, the Progressive planning ideal took time to become established. Only after substantial growth occurred in the 1920s did planning become a central feature of Vancouver governance. This outcome arose from an important convergence of views that emerged among business leaders, city beautiful advocates and people ideologically committed to active city planning.

Vancouver's adoption of planning was dominated by the best ideas in urban design of the time. Urban planner Harald Bartholomew focused on the street system and transit, industrial, transport and port facilities, public recreation, land-use zoning and 'civic art' (Bottomley, 1977). His vision of the city was that of the core-focused radially organized city, a product of the market forces of the nineteenth century. Beyond the infrastructure bias, he also had a sense of the importance of neighbourhoods, seeking to juxtapose schools, parks and retail ribbon commercial services. During the 1930s Vancouver's boundaries came to resemble those of today and the earlier governance structure that was based on elections in 12 wards was replaced by aldermen that were elected at large. The intent was to bring the city under the direct control of the political 'Non Partisan Association' (NPA) party, which largely represented the West Side affluent community. This corporate reform succeeded in its goals.

During the next three and a half decades city politics was characterized by the growth of the civil service to a dominant position within civic government. The planning process took place with only indirect oversight by the NPA-dominated city council, whose members were convinced that planning was the domain of professionals dedicated to maximizing the efficient use of space, thereby maximizing property values. The mayor and aldermen considered themselves as a part-time 'Board' and the professional civil service the source of expertise and a larger view. Under this arrangement leadership flowed increasingly into the hands of the senior officials. Vancouver thereby participated in a natural development seen around much of North America at that time, one reflecting the basically harmonious relationships between the downtown business community, major civic organizations, the press and planning experts. It was to last into the 1960s.

By the late 1960s the Engineering Department had become the primary agent for transforming Vancouver's material infrastructure. The civic landscape had been transformed with some high-rise apartment towers rising in the city's West End and two viaducts extending into the core – the beginnings of an unannounced through-city freeway. In addition, suburban roads were macadamized (black-topped) and ornamental street lighting was established throughout the city. In the 1950s trolley buses replaced streetcars as they did in many other cities, a fascinating story in itself (Kwitney, 1981). These had been popular transformations as Canadians settled into enjoying a sustained postwar prosperity after years of depression and conflict.

But in terms of becoming a destination for creative citizens, Vancouver was not very far along. The University of British Columbia had become an integral part of the city, but was not yet a major education and research centre. The arts community was not prominent. The smaller and more intricate networks of a vital creative civil society were not well represented or, for that matter, listened to.

These cultural shortcomings were not due to corruption or incompetence. The city budget was handled responsibly. Income obtained from the sale of city land for economic development went into an increasingly large urban endowment, largely freeing the city from depending on market rates of interest in financing major urban improvements. Vancouver could borrow money much more cheaply due to this collateral, and pay the principal back in time through tax revenues. This endowment lasted intact until the recent spending over the 2010 Winter Olympics, which will deplete it until property values return to those prevailing in 2008.

As the 1960s began, Vancouver served as a well-run example of orthodox urban management. The 'at large' city council continued to under-represent its neighbourhoods and over-represent the downtown business community, as it had been designed to do. The council tended to go along with the city manager's proposals because his recommendations served their interest as well as the relative independence of the city's bureaucracy. However, and this is important, these biases were popular ones in harmony with the preferences of many Vancouverites.

During those years most of the city's political and developmental initiatives originated within the bureaucracy were filtered by senior administrators, and then recommended to council. It was rare that the council did not endorse the recommendations of its city managers. It seldom had a practical opportunity to do so. In the late 1960s when a reform party, The Electors Action Movement (TEAM), first won seats on the council, they discovered that the manager's normal approach was to put a thick pile of papers in front of every council member for them to decide upon that evening. There was no time to really study those reports and documents, and so the normal procedure was to passively accept the manager's recommendations.[2]

As Walter Hardwick, a TEAM alderman at that time, observed, 'even in the turf of the

Parks Board the bureaucracy seemed more interested in culverts and drainage tiles than the uses of parks'. In the language of current social science discourse, the political and administrative structure was a formal representation of high modernism (Scott, 1998, pp. 103–45).

However, and this is one of our major points, the centres around which urban agreement coalesces can and will shift. When it does, entrenched systems that are not responsive to these changes can exacerbate social conflict. Undemocratic political systems are obvious examples, but democratic systems too dominated by an ingrown established power structure can become problematic as well. Vancouver was such a system. As the cultural ferment of the 1960s led to new demands and expectations from its citizens, the city manager and planners initially set up 'hearings to learn what the public wanted'. These hearings, however, proved to be limited in their capacity to comprehend the enormous complexity of citizen concerns.

The city, however, proved able to transit from one relatively stable pattern of governance to another. The political system was open and adaptable enough that old elites could be balanced by new political forces with a different vision of urban possibilities. Yet this otherwise accurate description misleads in an important detail. A closer look reveals that the 'new blood' was different in kind from the old. It was far less monolithic than the old elites it replaced. The TEAM party's members and interests were diverse, and as a result so was the city that emerged from their efforts – the vibrant and creative city we see in Vancouver today.

In his account of Vancouver's politics from 1929 to 1980, Paul Tennant writes:

> In retrospect it is clear that by the mid-sixties groups were emerging in Vancouver which, although unorganized and without spokesmen in the beginning, would come to form the opposition to the established order. One of these groups consisted of younger downtown business and professional people . . . another consisted of volunteer and professional community workers together with lower income neighbourhood and youth groups; another consisted of planners and architects; another consisted of ratepayer groups in more affluent areas; and yet another consisted of school teachers and UBC academics. . . . From these groups emerged the reform leaders and under their leadership some of the groups began to take positive action to oppose the NPA and the civic bureaucracy. (Tennant, 1980, p. 13)

Walter Hardwick, a University of British Columbia (UBC) Geography professor who became a TEAM alderman, described what was beginning to emerge in terms sensitive to the new understanding of emergent order. Vancouver, he wrote, was 'a good example of what [Ilya] Prigogine (1984) calls a bifurcation: a period in which information in the city and city life held by myriad individuals began to diverge. The amplitude of the sine waves of information grew until it became unstable.'[3]

SETTING THE STAGE

A triggering event precipitating movement towards a new pattern was sparked during the late 1950s, when Canada experienced a recession, with declining economic activity within Vancouver's core downtown. In a diagnosis standard for the time, American consulting firms invited in for advice recommended that shoppers be enticed downtown with enhanced parking and ease of access. Subsidized parking and a new freeway system would rescue a faltering downtown economy.

One of these revitalization projects was to be a freeway built through several less prosperous neighbourhoods, including an ethnic Chinese neighbourhood considered 'blighted'. The intent was to provide better connection between growing suburbs and downtown business. The primary beneficiaries were to be downtown businesses and property owners and the primary losers were the neighbourhoods that stood in the path of 'progress'.

In typical fashion for the time, like its American equivalent, this Canadian 'urban renewal' was planned without meaningful input from the neighbourhoods intended to pay the brunt of the price for the freeway's construction. Their interests were considered too myopic compared to the more expansive vision offered by 'downtown'. The first stage of freeway development proceeded smoothly enough. An old Sikh neighbourhood was destroyed, the residents submitting to their eviction without serious complaint, and an expensive elevated freeway link to downtown Vancouver was constructed. Next to be targeted was the largely Chinese community of Strathcona.

From a North American perspective this approach was not unusual. From one end of the continent to the other, neighbourhoods were repeatedly sacrificed in order to 'revitalize' or further 'enhance' the economic well-being of downtowns. Neighbourhoods were considered centres of selfish short-sightedness, divorced from the city's 'real' downtown economic interests. But in Vancouver the complacent plans of even the most public spirited urban planners were to go awry as the city began taking a very different approach to urban governance.

The cultural ferment of the 1960s created a new appreciation for the role viable neighbourhood cultures played in contributing to urban environments. Jane Jacobs's then newly published *Death and Life of Great American Cities* (1961) provided a trenchant critique of traditional models of urban planning that ignored the intricate and uncontrollable networks making up real city life. However, her ideas, and similar outlooks, were initially popular only in academic circles and areas influenced by the counterculture. As it turned out, friends and colleagues of Jacobs were to be instrumental in why Vancouver took its different approach, enabling the city to diverge sharply from the North American norm.

Strathcona was dilapidated not because the residents were poor, but because the neighbourhood had been redlined on recommendation of the city planners. As a result residents were unable to get bank loans to improve their dwellings. Buildings looked increasingly run-down. The council could then justify its demolition because the neighbourhood was dilapidated, presenting its residents with an urban version of *Catch-22*.

Strathcona's problems were externally created. Internally, as a neighbourhood network Strathcona was close-knit, and its residents inclined to defend themselves given the right leadership. The neighbourhood's reaction to the proposed freeway that would destroy it in the name of 'progress' and 'efficiency' was one major factor that led to the creation of the reform TEAM party, which responded to the demand that people most affected by political decisions have a significant voice in the content of those decisions. This meant reversing a pattern of passive acceptance to whatever the city manager and his bureaucrats proposed. Traditionally, private developers had made their proposals public, supported by the city bureaucracy, only at a very late stage of planning, when plenty of momentum was working in their favour. In most cases citizens did not know what was up until too late to challenge it effectively. This approach was destroying neighbourhoods as the city's freeway land purchases made their way north. Strathcona would have suffered the same fate if it had not had effective local organizers along with key legal help (Harcourt et al., 2007).

With TEAM's victories, politics in the traditional sense of citizens seeking, debating and deciding the good of their communities began to take over the driver's seat. The Progressive ideal of experts managing passive citizens was abandoned. Technocratic expertise was to be the public's servant, not its master. Vancouver was not a business corporation and according to TEAM should not be run as one.

After dramatic public forums including the 'Great Freeway Debate', freeway development was stopped. To this day Vancouver's inner neighbourhoods have not been sliced apart by the mammoth freeways characteristic of so many American cities. Strathcona remains a vital and cohesive neighbourhood, very far from being an area of urban blight. Its older houses are in good repair while its residents provide essential economic support to Vancouver's neighbouring Chinatown. But back in the 1970s still more was to come than the successful defence of a neighbourhood.

The defeat of the freeway proposal was proof that the old way of managing Vancouver's affairs was no longer viable. The TEAM party ran for office, winning two aldermanic seats in 1968 and winning a dominant majority of the council along with the mayoralty in 1972. The 1972 election also gave TEAM seats on the Board of the Greater Vancouver Regional District, which enabled many of their projects and procedures to impact the region as a whole. Their goals were ambitious. Partly intuitive and partly deliberate, they sought to change Vancouver's political culture from a prescriptive and corporate model to one that was enabling and consultative.

The city's new governors encouraged public meetings attended by a wide variety of interested parties and organizations. Citizens were urged to get involved in city governance. From the very beginning the TEAM ticket argued first for more openness for council members and then, as they became a majority, instituted these same principles between the city government and the citizenry.

In the process, a deeper appreciation for the requirements of a vital urban environment emerged. As noted, many of these requirements would have once been dismissed as purely aesthetic or a waste of scarce money, but their collective impact was to open governance in Vancouver to meaningful input from the many networks that, taken collectively, make a city great.

Among the adjustments to traditional planning that emerged were improvements in the city's pedestrian environment. Public plazas required building setbacks and downtown street level parking was discouraged. Infill was encouraged because it contributed to a more enriched pedestrian experience.

Some downtown businesses argued for and got downtown residences constructed. Until then they had been banned. Instead of being distributed to suburbs connected by freeways, permanent residents now enlivened the urban centre and encouraged a greater diversity of businesses. The continual human presence they created increased the safety as well as the diversity of life downtown.

But TEAM's attention was not directed only towards the downtown. Vancouver had long been diverse in its population, a diversity that has continued to grow to the present.

Even in the 1960s it had become a city of neighbourhoods reflecting different lifestyles among its residents. Openness to public input meant that city policies were increasingly sensitive to the significant differences in how different groups and ethnic communities liked to live.

The transformations of beliefs, values and attitudes among socially and ecologically aware citizens were taken seriously, not only in the area of participation but also in the design of a number of neighbourhoods and the urban core as well. Forty years ago a vision for cities and suburbs – only highlighted in the 1990s by Andres Duany in Seaside (Florida) and Peter Calthorpe in Sacramento (California) – were not simply proposed, but studied and actually being implemented in Vancouver.

DIRECTING CHANGE AND ENHANCING URBAN EMERGENCE

In 1974, two citizens who had been deeply involved in the reform movement wrote an article entitled 'Civic governance, corporate, consultative, or participatory?' (Hardwick and Hardwick, 1974). They rejected the Progressive corporate model but did not argue for creating a completely participatory/plebiscite-driven model in its place. Instead they developed an argument that the best in urban self-governance required both active and informed citizen involvement and clear delegation of responsibility for final decision making.

Vancouver's traditional governance reflected Progressive values from early in the twentieth century. Government was to be an efficient provider of services to citizens conceived of as consumers of expert decisions, and rewarding the successful with continued political support at the polls. Based on idealizations of corporate governance, it was well suited to a world of large-scale neighbourhoods from which residents commuted to and from work, shopping and play. Roads and lighting should be good, access easy, and public amenities should be of high quality and inexpensive.

This model could not easily adapt to the rapidly growing complexity in the public's desires. It tended to foster isolated bureaucracies relatively disconnected from specific neighbourhoods and citizens as well as 'at large' elections designed to keep them that way. As demands grew for greater attention to neighbourhoods, the limitations to an intrinsically managerial approach to governance became increasingly evident.

On the other hand, seeking a plebiscitary/participatory model as the alternative led to a practical inability to get needed decisions implemented. Winnipeg, Manitoba, had tried such an approach, with unpleasant results. Most residents did not want to constantly participate, and those that did were not necessarily the community's wisest or best endowed with good judgement. Even New England's famed small town direct democracies met only annually.

The logic of representative democracy, the authors insisted, would provide better governance than either the Progressive or the participatory models if and when the elected truly represented their constituents' diversity. To accomplish this, constituents needed as much access to information as did their representatives. This is a vital insight from the participatory perspective. On the other hand, while central to any creative and adaptive system, the local meetings this openness entailed possessed weaknesses of their own.

They tended to over-emphasize more parochial interests and had all the disadvantages as well as advantages of amateurism. In an unpublished manuscript, Walter Hardwick wrote that

> we valued this type of input, however, we believe that in many issues there was a broader public good that had to be taken into account, and inputs too that often came from professionals, or broad civic groups with a strong sense of memory. Memory is important, because long term residents with a continuity of view can often provide better perspective and detached judgment, than those most closely affected. (Hardwick, undated, p. 7)

The authors of *Community Participation* contrasted managing change with directing (Hardwick et al., 1987), or in a relevant neologism, 'directoring' change (Hardwick, 1998). The applicable metaphor shifted from being an engineer who designed and built to a farmer who planted and cultivated. An engineer looks upon the land and its residents as raw material. The farmer (a good one anyway) looks upon the land and soil as partners whose well-being are essential to his own purposes. Cultivating a pattern that was not unilaterally determined by the cultivator replaces engineering a solution to a problem understood and solved by an expert. The cultivator encourages; the engineer controls.

In this vein, many of the changes adopted by the TEAM reform council were procedural rather than prescriptive. Key reforms directed how things were to be done without always proclaiming what was to be done. They were designed to supply more information to the public, ensure that representatives of civic departments appeared before the city council to support their initiatives, and guarantee that citizens had more opportunity to appear before the council. For example, council meetings were shifted from daytime business hours on Tuesdays to evening meetings, when people could attend without sacrificing work time. Later, developers were required to post their properties with large signs on sheets of plywood providing passers-by with information on proposed redevelopments or re-zonings. The purpose of these changes was to ensure the public at large would know well in advance when changes were proposed in either policy or its implementation. They enhanced the city's capacity as a complex adaptive system.

A profound change in Vancouver's political culture took place, a change that has lasted to this day. Rather than being decided quietly in meetings attended by few, with most citizens learning about decisions after they had been made, city business was subject to newspaper, radio and television coverage and discussion. Interested citizens could find a public forum for airing their views. With the appointment of Ray Spaxman, an extraordinary planner from Toronto, even the city's bureaucracy was transformed towards a less prescriptive approach (Punter, 2003, pp. 28–9).

In all cases the elected council made the final decisions. Lines of ultimate responsibility were clear while the city's culture transformed to make sure those in responsible positions had ample input from a broad range of city groups. The culture of public decision making and responsibilities was changed.

Subsequently, although council members have been elected under various party labels, on most major issues differing coalitions were put together to defeat or support particular issues. While, as always, there is some correspondence among individual voting preferences, there was also considerable diversity. Decisions are sometimes delayed when groups bring information to light that had been unknown or under-appreciated.

Sometimes even more input was sought. Beginning in the 1970s, unprecedented transparency prevailed in city affairs. This is as we would expect when political processes are established within a complex entity that enable the full range of community networks access to knowledge and later, if they wish, influence over city decisions. In his study of Vancouver during this time, Paul Tennant concludes:

> citizen participation implied at least three major elements; (1) vigorous public discussion during election campaigns and the use of campaign methods resting on active participation of candidates and supporters (as opposed to the bland uninformative media campaigns of the NPA), (2) full provision of information to the public by developers and the civic administration about development projects, (3) participation, through public hearings and such devices as planning committees, by representatives of all affected groups in the formation and final approval of particular projects. (Tennant, 1980, p. 15)

One result of this was a definitive change in how the city approached its neighbourhoods. The story of the False Creek area, now one of Vancouver's gems, is illustrative.

NEIGHBOURHOOD PLANNING: FALSE CREEK

By the 1960s False Creek was a seriously polluted and deteriorating small ocean inlet and industrial area located almost in the city's centre. It had been slated for eventual redevelopment into an industrial park before the TEAM reform party won control of city government.

In 1965 students in Geography and Architecture at the UBC had recommended that these long-established but never acted upon plans be laid aside. Instead the False Creek area should be incorporated more directly into urban life and become primarily residential. The students were ignored by city planners and the council, all used to viewing issues from their persisting early twentieth-century corporate perspective.

With the TEAM reformers' victory these proposals received a more sympathetic ear, and the city allocated six months for more extensive meetings with concerned interest groups. The meetings succeeded in helping to clarify what would be best for the city as a whole. Out of these hearings several principles emerged to govern False Creek's redevelopment. It should be residential rather than industrial, and housing should be mixed. The neighbourhoods that developed should consist of different socio-economic groups and ages. Social housing should be available offering subsidized rents to guarantee this diversity. They should also be pedestrian-friendly with the automobile de-emphasized. Their vision was that the neighbourhoods eventually arising should be vital and lively urban environments every day of the week.

To this end neighbourhood enclaves were planned to be approximately 500 feet across, each with between 100 and 400 dwellings. As Jane Jacobs (1961, pp. 120, 333) and others have shown, a pedestrian-friendly environment needed to be on a pedestrian-friendly scale. No long blocks need apply.

The city's intent was not to micro-manage or prescribe the kinds of neighbourhoods that would appear, but to cultivate conditions favourable to neighbourhoods in general, and then let the natural dynamics of people moving and working establish the content within the framework. Neighbourhood blocks were separated by parks, pedestrian walkways, schools, businesses and a hospital rather than by a grid of streets. According to Walter Hardwick (1994), '[e]ach enclave was then free to take on its own lifestyle, and in the process assure the diversity within the development as a whole, as required by the city council's goals'.

It succeeded. Today, 40 years after the processes that created the False Creek area as a residential centre were first implemented, the neighbourhood is one of Vancouver's biggest success stories. Its homes and apartments serve people both wealthy and of limited means, and every gradation between them. Its residences are linked with land-scaped walkways and parks, offering a beautiful, peaceful and safe environment for families and singles alike. In the process, the False Creek neighbourhood has become a major centre for people involved in the arts. Again, we refer to how this vision has turned out to exemplify conditions encouraging urban creativity (Florida, 2002, pp. 42–3).

ZONING IN VANCOUVER COMPARED TO TRADITIONAL ZONING

The False Creek example shows how zoning can encourage creativity and diversity through providing options rather than limiting people's choices, as has usually been the case. As noted above, zoning traditionally had normally been a top-down affair by professional planners usually with input from well-placed members of the West Side social elite. The intricate networks existing within a city but operating independently from financial values tended to be slighted, destroyed or prevented from arising.

Large independent zoning boards frequently become powers unto themselves, squelching innovation and often forcing a cookie-cutter approach to a city's development. One of the authors will never forget the pride with which a councilman in a town within which he lived showed him the proposed new map of the community, once 'better zoning' had gotten rid of so much 'non-conforming' land uses. And the map was truly prettier, with more attractive and less 'busy' patches of colour. However, that visual busy-ness on the old map actually was a sign of the vitality of local activity and businesses that the planners wanted to simplify. For example, the councilman seemed surprised that streets might involve more than the efficient movement of cars. Setting zoning aside because of these problems would lead to a different set of winners based on purely economic criteria, but again do little to enrich the non-economic networks within a city.

In Vancouver zoning was not abolished. Far from it. But zoning was made subject to the preferences and visions of the citizens who lived in the city and in the neighbourhoods that were to be affected. An example of how this was accomplished is a neighbourhood called Champlain Heights. It was one of the last pieces of undeveloped land in Vancouver and was slated to be an extension of the adjacent grid neighbourhoods outlined earlier in the century. The reformers' critics complained that the processes of community forums would delay zoning by being 'burdened with the intricacies of community agreement' (Seley, 1974, p. 109). The critics proved mistaken and a plan evolved similar to the 'False Creek model'. It included social amenities, a school location, park spaces and streets friendly to pedestrian interaction. A vital and successful zoning-based development was the result.

When only market forces and values shape how a city develops, non-monetary values are slighted. For example, on a lot-by-lot basis, parks would bring in more money to developers if housing was built on them. But the quality of the area as a place for human habitation would be lessened. People do not live by bread alone, and neither do great cities. Our point is not anti-market, quite the contrary. Without the market a city such as Vancouver could not exist. But its success requires more than that.

Another example of balancing social agendas with economic realities was the development of city blocks at the West End, which opened on to Stanley Park. This land was adjacent to downtown Vancouver. Initially owned as railway land-grant property by the property firm of the Canadian Pacific Railway, Marathon Realty, it was ultimately transferred to hotel ownership, now the Westin Bayshore Hotel. After extensive public debate and two civic referenda, the block adjacent to the park continued to be undeveloped land, as it remains, while the block immediately to the east has additional high-density, high-rise residential and hotel development. This solution responded to the wishes of the West End population for open sightlines and pedestrian waterfront access while enabling appropriate high-density residential high-rises, hotels and corporate offices. Again, citizen input helped define the values zoning was supposed to achieve. The authorities, elected and bureaucratic alike, were then responsible for seeing as best they could that these popular visions were implemented effectively. And they did.

A great city able to attract and nurture creative citizens is one that offers not just a good physical infrastructure or recreational amenities. It must offer a suitable micro environment, a human scale that facilitates communities of similarly minded creative citizens, places they can congregate and live and work closely enough to foster those unexpected encounters that spawn new developments. When a university is more than a commuter campus and has intellectually active neighbourhoods, unexpected breakthroughs can emerge in the arts and sciences and business. For example, Stanford and Palo Alto provided such conditions in the late 1960s and the 1970s, which shaped the creation of the personal computer that has utterly transformed lives worldwide (Markoff, 2005).

There as well were the artistic communities that contributed disproportionately to the music of that period and also many of the philosophical and spiritual currents that arose then and still flow today. It could not happen on 'the Peninsula' today. The place is far too expensive. Only attention to maintaining a diverse community with housing available to many different income groups would make that possible.

THE DOWNTOWN EAST SIDE

The bulk of this discussion about neighbourhoods has focused on the process of creating a balance of inputs into creative design for a city and outlining how Vancouver became an attractive destination to many creative individuals. As described, it sounds idyllic. But Vancouver is not heaven, however much it might seem like it on a good day. It has its rough sides. On a less positive note, one part of the city of Vancouver – the 'downtown east side' – is a destination for drug users, alcoholics and others who are attracted to the opportunity to live an unfettered existence with freedom to pursue their choice of lifestyle, as well as being a destination for the genuinely homeless and poor.

Many people in other parts of the city view this community simply as a result of people's 'homelessness'. They believe nobody in their right mind would want to live that way. To be sure, some residents are poor and homeless, but due to personal issues many appear to choose this lifestyle and urban setting. Thus Vancouver, like most other cities, has this area that is not a destination of choice for the majority of its population. But as it happens, even the downtown east side and its character fits our model of cities and their neighbourhoods as destinations, and our contention that neighbourhoods be able to develop their own character within reason.

A government-sanctioned 'self-injection centre' accommodates the needs of some who choose this destination. The drug-addicted population overlaps with those homeless for other reasons. It is in the downtown east side that charitable food services are concentrated, as are shelters. Given that no city has solved the problems of drug addiction and the mental injuries that can lead to homelessness, Vancouver's approach has considerable merit. These problems are concentrated rather than being more widely spread throughout the city. People attracted to the area learn 'the ropes' and how to navigate within the particular subculture represented there.

VANCOUVER AND ITS REGION

TEAM's political victories influenced more than the city itself. They also shaped development in the entire lower mainland region of British Columbia. Vancouver exists in partnership with several co-adjacent cities and municipalities. The regional area shares a number of programmes such as the water system, sewage and waste system, transit and highways. The regional planning is facilitated by the existence of a Greater Vancouver Liveable Region Planning process which was led by Walter Hardwick in the early 1990s. Additionally, two of Vancouver's mayors have subsequently been elected as premiers of British Columbia. Both former mayors facilitated the regionalization process and emphasized the need for consensus among partner cities. This balance of financial integrity and socio-political input has been fostered at the regional level as well as within the city of Vancouver to everyone's benefit.

PLANNING AS ENABLING A BALANCE

What emerges here is a dynamic balance between citizens' input and planning expertise. The former establishes the values and priorities to be pursued while the planners' expertise creates the rules and land-use layouts that encourage these goals to develop. This kind of planning encourages and balances spontaneous growth in harmony with the broad public values arising from consultative processes with the city's citizens. This approach stands in sharp contrast to planners imposing their latest theories or one-sided political pressure doing the same, in either case treating the residents as passive raw material for implementing their vision.

Planning has not been abandoned. A democratic model open to the intricate flows of urban life has replaced a corporatist one that was intrinsically prescriptive and hierarchical. A hierarchical operational structure remained, but was subordinated to the democratic governance structure. In the process a means was created by which all significant urban networks were enabled to influence urban policy while benefiting from the expertise of skilled professionals.

A city is composed of the dreams and hopes of hundreds of thousands or sometimes millions of citizens, but it is more than the sum total of those dreams. A city also shapes the hopes and dreams that are possible and those that are not. Our approach defines democratic cities as complex adaptive and transformative systems comprising diverse and not entirely predictable networks that must be actively encouraged and consulted. In the case of Vancouver the result is one of the world's most impressive urban successes.

VANCOUVER'S CULTURAL TAKE-OFF

Vancouver's cultural take-off was embryonic in the 1950s, even after the creation of the Vancouver Opera and modest enhancements of the Vancouver Symphony Orchestra. At the time a Vancouver Arts School existed but was also small. There was a small but active artistic community. The reconfiguration of Vancouver in 1970 and particularly Granville Island's change from an industrial slum into an arts and crafts/market/theatre gathering centre as part of the False Creek development created a magnet that drew artistic talent to the area. The Emily Carr Arts School was located on Granville Island, and has grown to become Emily Carr University. The Vancouver Art Gallery is located downtown in a central location, in what was previously the Central Law Courts.

Somewhat later, the province of British Columbia provided a support system for making movies in 'Hollywood North'. Vancouver had been a location for movie-making since the 1930s, but it has now become North America's third largest film production centre. Vancouver now is home to a number of important film studios, including Bridge Studios, Canadian Motion Picture Park, Eagle Creek Studios, Mammoth Studios, MJA Studios, North Shore Studios, Vancouver Film Studios and Washington Studios. The proximity of so many studios as well as a number of universities has in turn made the city one of North America's best places to study film, video, music, animation-making and production, screen writing and the media in general.

Vancouver's artistic and cultural creativity has been accompanied by economic creativity. Microsoft's location in Puget Sound has encouraged an information technology (IT) spillover to British Columbia. That in turned encouraged local IT companies, the most successful of which has been MacDonald/Dettwiler. Vancouver's many amenities are building on and reinforcing one another. What we are witnessing here, as well as in so many other areas, is a growing synergistic effect where 'those that have get more'. This is a good illustration of Richard Florida's (2002, pp. 261–3) argument about the symbiotic relationship between creativity in the arts and technological innovation.

DESTINATION CITIES

We have proposed the term 'destination city' as a means of evaluating the success of a city's responsiveness to its citizens' priorities. The emphasis here is not on becoming a destination for tourism, it is on becoming a destination for people seeking a good place to live and to pursue their chosen dreams and opportunities. The tourists will follow.

The basic qualities defining a destination are comfort, security, opportunity and choice, as well as a shared social network of similarly motivated people (Hardwick, 1990). For over four decades Vancouver has proven a success by these criteria. Vancouver has provided a choice of the various innovative and creative activities that attract creative citizens. Once there they have the opportunity to enter existing cultural networks at every level from the neighbourhood to downtown. The facilities are there. Security exists because with mixed integrated urban neighbourhoods most of Vancouver enjoys low crime rates, and while a part of this simply reflects Canadian's greater law-abidingness compared to their southern neighbour, the presence of vital and racially diverse neighbourhoods with a healthy street life helps to maintain and augment that safety. Vancouver offers physical, social and economic comfort as well. This is not entirely due to its means of governance of course. The beauty of its location and its position as Canada's westernmost major city would make this the case regardless, as would its temperate climate moderated by the Japanese Current. But this is not the whole picture. Nor perhaps is it even most of it. Vancouver today has many features that attract the creative, and are the direct result of this change in city governance. First, and perhaps most importantly, it is a city of extremely diverse and vibrant neighbourhoods. These neighbourhoods did not simply arise. They were not spontaneous creations generated by the market any more than they were testimonies to enlightened technocratic planning.

Crucial for those neighbourhoods that were planned after the TEAM reforms was the requirement to have a variety of kinds of housing and that housing be available to a wide range of socio-economic groups, from the very wealthy to those requiring subsidized 'social housing'. Granville Island in False Creek was designed to be a centre of cultural and artistic creativity, as the UBC has become a major academic institution. Vancouver's downtown has many permanent residents, a radical change from more orthodox theories of planning and zoning which forbade downtown residents and encouraged suburban living. These people disproportionately provide the nightlife, diverse economic wants and population density that make a vibrant arts community possible. Deliberate encouragement of a pedestrian-friendly environment further attracts people downtown. Vancouver is a city primarily for all its residents rather than existing to serve its suburbs and downtown business interests.

Social housing makes housing available to artists and other creative citizens who have chosen values other than economic success as primary in their lives. Because these values contribute to the city's well-being, it benefits from their presence, and in turn their presence makes for the density needed for creative neighbourhoods to arise. We are observing a complex urban ecology far too intricate for anyone to grasp in detail. But the conditions making for a healthy urban ecology can be cultivated. For this reason the reformers and the principles of governance they helped to institutionalize played a vital role in making Vancouver a true destination city both for Canadians and immigrants.

The term 'destination city' reminds us that a city is first and foremost home for a multitude of human beings. A good city attracts additional residents, and a city able to attract creative citizens must offer more than employment opportunities. It must offer the kind of urban environment that makes a city home. To do so it must remain always open to and seek to enrich the intricate networks of relationships that develop in human communities.

NOTES

1. The term 'spontaneous order' describes certain kinds of complex adaptive systems. F.A. Hayek first developed its implications with primary reference to market economies and Michael Polanyi at about the same time with reference to science. Both emphasized that these examples did not limit instances of spontaneous order, and Hayek in particular went on to explore its implications in common law. For an account of Hayek's work in this area see Bruce Caldwell (2004, especially pp. 261–319). Michael Polanyi's most detailed description is in Polanyi (1951).
2. This is based on personal conversations with Walter Hardwick.
3. From an unpublished manuscript by Walter Hardwick, p. 7. Hardwick was referring to Prigogine and Stengers (1984, pp. 160–70).

REFERENCES

Bottomley, J. (1977), 'Ideology, planning and landscape: the business community, urban reform and the establishment of town planning in Vancouver, British Columbia, 1900–1940', PhD thesis, University of British Columbia, Vancouver, BC.
Caldwell, B. (2004), *Hayek's Challenge: An Intellectual Biography of F.A. Hayek*, Chicago, IL: University of Chicago Press.
diZerega, G. (2004), 'Toward a Hayekian theory of commodification and systemic contradiction: citizens, consumers and the media', *Review of Politics*, **66**(3), 445–68.
Florida, R. (2002), *The Rise of the Creative Class and How It's Transforming Work, Leisure, Community, and Everyday Life*, New York, NY: Basic Books.
Harcourt, M., K. Cameron and S. Rossiter (2007), *City Making in Paradise: Nine Decisions that Saved Vancouver*, Vancouver, BC: Douglas & McIntyre.
Hardwick, D.F. (1990), 'Destinations in pathology', *Modern Pathology*, **2**, 551.
Hardwick, D.F. (1998), '"Directoring" and managing in a professional system', *Modern Pathology*, **2**, 585–92.
Hardwick, D.F. (2008), 'Medical science is a self organizing social environment', *Studies in Emergent Order*, **1**, 119–34.
Hardwick, D.F., W.G. Hardwick and G. diZerega (1987), 'Directing change: a contemporary administrative challenge', *Modern Pathology*, **10**, 380–3.
Hardwick, W.G. (undated), 'Directing Change in Vanconver', unpublished manuscript.
Hardwick, W.G. (1994), 'Responding to the 1960s: designing adaptable communities in Vancouver', *Environment and Behavior*, **28**(3), 338–62.
Hardwick, W.G. and D.F. Hardwick (1974), 'Civic governance, corporate, consultative, or participatory?', *BC Geographical Series*, **19**, 89–95.
Hayek, F.A. (1967), 'The theory of complex phenomena', *Studies in Philosophy, Politics and Economics*, Chicago, IL: University of Chicago Press, pp. 22–42.
Horwitz, S. (2008), 'Is the family a spontaneous order?', *Studies in Emergent Order*, **1**, 163–85.
Jacobs, J. (1961), *The Death and Life of Great American Cities*, New York, NY: Random House.
Kingdon, J.W. (1995), *Agendas, Alternatives, and Public Policies* (2nd edn), New York, NY: Addison Wesley Longman.
Kwitney, J. (1981), 'The great transportation conspiracy: a juggernaut named desire', *Harpers*, February.
Markoff, J. (2005), *What the Dormouse Said: How the Sixties Counter-culture Shaped the Personal Computer Industry*, New York, NY: Penguin.
Polanyi, M. (1951), *The Logic of Liberty*, Chicago, IL: University of Chicago Press.
Prigogine, I. and I. Stengers (1984), *Order Out of Chaos*, Boston, MA: Shambhala.
Punter, J. (2003), *The Vancouver Achievement: Urban Planning and Design*, Vancouver, BC: University of British Columbia Press.
Schumpeter, J.A. (1942), *Capitalism, Socialism and Democracy*, New York, NY and London: Harper & Brothers.
Scott, J.C. (1998), *Seeing Like a State: How Certain Schemes to Improve the Human Condition Have Failed*, New Haven, CT: Yale University Press.
Seley, J. (1974), 'Towards a paradigm of community based planning', *BC Geographical Series*, **19**, 109–26.
Taylor, F.W. (1911), *The Principles of Scientific Management*, New York, NY: Harper & Row.
Tennant, P. (1980), 'Vancouver civic politics, 1929–1980', *B.C. Studies*, **46**, 3–27.

PART 5

MARKETS

19 Cultivating creativity: market creation of agglomeration economies
Randall G. Holcombe*

Creativity is contagious. That contagion gives rise to agglomeration economies, and is the reason why policy makers want to implement policies that cultivate creativity in their jurisdictions. Richard Florida (2002, 2005a) has given a good account of the role of cities in cultivating the creative class, because creative people want to be where there are 'vibrant urban districts, abundant natural amenities, and comfortable suburban "nerdistans" for techies so inclined' (Florida, 2002, p. 11). There are two related but separate issues involved in cultivating creativity in a particular location: what attracts creative people to a particular location; and what makes people creative? A general theme in this chapter is that the first question has been overemphasized in analyses of the creative class, while the second has been relatively neglected. Beyond a doubt creative individuals desire certain lifestyle amenities where they are living, but those amenities will be attracted to locations where creative people live, so policy makers do not need to focus on the amenities. Rather, public policy should focus on implementing policies that make people creative.

WHAT MAKES PEOPLE CREATIVE?

Florida (2005a, pp. 3–4, emphasis in original) observes that '. . . the single most overlooked – and single most important – element of my theory is that *every human being is creative*. . . . Tapping and stoking the creative furnace inside every human being is the great challenge of our time.' But while every person is creative, not everyone is a part of the creative class. Florida (2005a, p. 3) says that in 1950 less than 15 per cent of the workforce could be characterized as 'creative workers', and this rose to more than 30 per cent by 2005. Florida (2005a, p. 4) says that the '"Creative Class" is the shorthand I use to describe the roughly one-third of U.S. and global workers who have the good fortune to be compensated monetarily for their creative output'.

What puts people in the creative class, then, is determined by the market forces of supply and demand. Everyone is creative, but only some people have the 'good fortune' to be paid for their creativity. Some people undoubtedly have stronger preferences than others to engage in creative work – that is the supply side of the creative class – but for people to be compensated for their creativity there must also be a demand for workers in the creative class. One can see that Florida's conception of the creative class is market-driven and depends on market forces to produce opportunities for creative activity to be profitable.

Florida (2005a, pp. 3–4) divides employment into creative workers, manufacturing workers and service workers. Creative workers are those 'engaged in science and engineering, research and development, and the technology-based industries, in arts, music, culture, and aesthetic and design work, or in the knowledge-based professions of health care, finance, and law'. One can quibble with Florida's taxonomy, and surely the divisions here are imprecise. For example, a nurse is classified as part of the creative class, even though many nurses only follow the instructions of others. Meanwhile, many in manufacturing and service jobs may have substantial opportunities for creativity. As Adam Smith ([1776] 1937, p. 9) noted, a 'great part of the machines made use of in those manufactures in which labour is most subdivided, were originally the inventions of common workmen, who, being each of them employed in some very simple operation, naturally turned their thoughts towards finding out easier and readier methods of performing it'.

Echoing Smith's observation, Florida says that:

> Japanese manufacturing firms leaped ahead of ours with their 'creative factory' methods, which tap the intelligence of every worker on the factory floor to make continuous small improvements in the production process. U.S. firms – stuck in the Fordist system, whereby the engineers and top managers do all the thinking while the masses are paid to execute – nearly had their doors blown off. Many of our firms have now caught on to the new way. (Florida, 2005b, p. 194)

Today, the creative class is not as segmented by occupational category as Florida's empirical definition would make it appear. Furthermore, it is not uncommon for tradespeople to begin their careers working for others, but eventually to set up their own companies to build on what they learned from their earlier employment.

F.A. Hayek (1945) emphasizes the specific knowledge of time and place possessed by every individual, and the role that a market economy has in enabling everyone to make the most productive use of that knowledge. Everybody has specific knowledge that others do not, and often it is difficult to share this knowledge because it is difficult to articulate knowledge that is accumulated through experience. Good management always listens to all workers' ideas on how they can more effectively accomplish their assignments. There is not an unambiguous line that divides the creative class from other income earners.

While one might critically analyse the specific empirical implementation Florida gives to define members of the creative class, the idea behind Florida's concept of creativity makes a clear and important distinction between people who are compensated for their creativity and those who have little room for creative input in their work. Furthermore, Florida notes that everybody is creative, and what separates the creative class from others is their being compensated for their creativity. By this definition, creativity is market-driven. Cultivating the creative class is not about making more people creative – everyone is creative – it is about encouraging people to market their creativity (supply) and making it attractive for people to purchase the creative output of others (demand).

CREATIVITY IN MARKETS

While Florida (2002) has a market-based definition of the creative class, he emphasizes the importance of cultural amenities that at first glance might strike people as better indicators of creativity: music, arts, restaurants, museums and so forth. But these amenities will be available only if there is a market for them. They are the result, not the cause, of market-based activity. Similarly, Florida emphasizes tolerance of others with cultural and lifestyle choices outside the mainstream, but tolerance is also market-driven, as will be discussed in more detail below. To understand how all these factors reinforce the creative class, one must first understand how markets encourage creativity.

Economic theory can be misleading if taken too literally when analysing the creativity of markets. Throughout the twentieth century economic theory developed increasingly refined models of economic equilibrium in which the quantity supplied equals the quantity demanded in all markets, all profit opportunities have been competed away, and profit-maximizing behaviour is depicted as choosing the appropriate quantities of inputs to produce output at lowest cost, and managing a firm's production to ensure that no resources are wasted (for example, labour is working at maximum productivity and not shirking).[1] When economists talk about competitive markets, they assume that firms produce homogeneous output, which by assumption eliminates a major source of creativity: the product differentiation that improves the features of goods and services firms offer for sale.[2] Economic equilibrium depicts a situation in which creative activity in an economy has ceased, and people continue to do the same things in the future they have been doing in the past, because they are maximizing their profits, and their utility, at that equilibrium. Things could not be any better than they are at equilibrium, because if they could, the economy would not be at an equilibrium.[3]

In fact, things can always be better, and as Joseph Schumpeter (1954, p. 82) says, '[t]he essential point to grasp is that in dealing with capitalism we are dealing with an evolutionary process. . . . Capitalism, then, is by nature a form or method of economic change and not only never is but never can be stationary.' While the equilibrium models of economics are useful for many purposes, they misrepresent the creative and continually evolving nature of a market economy. Indeed, Schumpeter's term 'creative destruction' is more descriptive. Entrepreneurs are constantly introducing new products into markets, improving the characteristics of old ones and developing new production processes that can produce the same products at lower cost. The creativity of some people in markets forces everyone to be innovative, for if they are not, they will constantly be losing ground to those who are. That creativity is the engine of economic progress.

Creativity in markets is entrepreneurship. Israel Kirzner (1973) identifies entrepreneurship as spotting and acting on a previously unexploited profit opportunity.[4] When someone discovers a way to manufacture a product at lower cost, that creative activity improves welfare because the resources that are saved in its manufacture can then be used for other purposes. When someone alters a product's characteristics so that consumers prefer the newly altered product to the old design, that creative activity improves welfare by bringing better products to consumers. When someone invents a new good, or develops a new service that people prefer to what was available before, people's welfare is enhanced by its availability. Entrepreneurship is the way creativity is manifested in markets. The musical group that markets a new song, or the chef who puts a new recipe on the restaurant menu, is being creative and entrepreneurial, as is the manufacturer who offers an improved version of a product, or the bookkeeper who offers clients a new service.

PROFIT AND LOSS MEASURES THE VALUE OF CREATIVITY

Profit and loss provide the test regarding whether the creative activity is welfare-enhancing. If an entrepreneur takes resources that have a certain value in the market and combines them to produce an output that is more valuable than the inputs used up, the entrepreneur adds value to the economy. That entrepreneur produces something more valuable than the cost of producing it, and should be rewarded for that value-enhancing activity, and in fact in a market economy the entrepreneur is rewarded, with profits. Conversely, if an entrepreneur combines resources of a certain value and produces an output that is worth less than the resources used to produce it, that entrepreneur reduces the well-being of the economy and should be penalized for the value-reducing activity. In a market economy, the penalty is assessed in the form of losses. Profit and loss are essential for measuring whether entrepreneurial activity adds to society's welfare or detracts from it.

This same profit and loss criterion determines whether people are members of Florida's creative class, because people will have the good fortune to be compensated monetarily for their creative output only if the revenue they receive exceeds the costs they incur to engage in their creative activities. If their creative efforts do not return profits, their careers will be pushed in other directions by economic forces.

When contemplating entrepreneurship there is a tendency to focus on the great entrepreneurial successes of people like Henry Ford and Steve Jobs. The failures tend to slide into obscurity, so it is easy to overlook the fact that many entrepreneurs have tried unsuccessfully to bring innovations to market. New products fail, musicians are unable to cover their living costs and go back to their day jobs, and diners reject some new menu items. The profit and loss system is at work here, limiting the resources available to unsuccessful entrepreneurs, because their losses mean they have fewer and fewer resources to work with over time. Meanwhile, the profits of successful entrepreneurs provide them with additional resources as a reward for effectively bringing innovations to market, as an indicator of what types of innovations the market will reward, and as a way to supply them with additional resources to continue their creative activities.

People will join the creative class to the extent that it is profitable for them to do so. As Richard Florida notes, everybody is creative, but not everybody is able to market their creativity and be compensated for it. So, expanding the creative class means creating an environment in which creativity is rewarded, in which impediments to engaging in creative activity are low, and in which activity that impedes creativity is discouraged. Cultivating creativity means cultivating entrepreneurship.

PRODUCTIVE AND DESTRUCTIVE ENTREPRENEURSHIP

William Baumol (1990, 1993) emphasizes the importance of an economy's institutional structure in determining the role that entrepreneurship plays in that economy. Much as Florida argues that everybody is creative, Baumol argues that the propensity toward entrepreneurship is relatively constant across societies. However, a society's institutional structure affects the way that people's entrepreneurial impulses are channelled. When an economy has institutions that encourage market activity, people will channel their entrepreneurial impulses toward improving production processes and producing innovative goods and services. When institutions discourage market activity, entrepreneurial impulses will be channelled toward predatory activities that limit the opportunities for economic progress.

Entrepreneurship is inherently risky. When an entrepreneur spots a profit opportunity that has not yet been acted on by others, there is no firm evidence on whether that profit opportunity will pay off, because nobody has tried it before. When Steve Jobs and Steve Wozniak started Apple Computer, management in existing computer companies – the industry experts – thought that there would not be a sufficient market for personal computers to make the enterprise profitable. Jobs and Wozniak took a risk which paid off, and their entrepreneurship was rewarded by profits. But there were many entrepreneurs in the young personal computer market in the 1980s, most of whom failed and went out of business. Companies had slightly different business models and slightly different products. The entrepreneurs who had the most accurate assessment of the market were rewarded with profits, while losses signalled to the others that their innovation and creativity did not add value for consumers, and they closed up shop.

For potential entrepreneurs to be enticed to take the risks involved in acting on their insights and exploiting the profit opportunities they see, they must anticipate that if they are correct their ventures will be profitable. This requires an institutional structure that protects property rights and enforces the rule of law. Those institutions are described in detail by Gwartney and Lawson (2005). Berggren (2003) and Gwartney et al. (2004) provide evidence that the characteristics cited by Gwartney and Lawson (2005) enhance income and income growth, and more generally, Landes (1998) and Mokyr (1990) argue that throughout history, countries with market institutions have prospered while those without market institutions have been left behind in poverty.

Protection of property rights is crucial to productive entrepreneurship, because potential entrepreneurs need to be assured that if the risks they take pay off, they will be able to reap and retain the rewards from their creativity and innovation. Otherwise, there is a disincentive to taking a risk that exposes them to potential losses, if any profits they might make are not secure. Similarly, rule of law means that there is an objective body of law that applies to everybody, and everyone is treated the same under the law. Without rule of law, entrepreneurs – if they take risks and earn profits – have no assurance that other parties who are more favoured by the legal system will not use the force of government to confiscate their wealth. This is an obvious disincentive to risk-taking. Other factors are important too. Market activity is encouraged when there are low tax and regulatory barriers. Taxes impose obvious costs on entrepreneurs by taking some of their profits. Similarly, regulations can stand in the way of entrepreneurial activity, or make entrepreneurship more costly. Rule of law and protection of property rights are especially important for the promotion of productive entrepreneurship.

People can increase their wealth in two ways: they can engage in productive activity, or they can take wealth from others. If property rights are not securely protected, this opens up the opportunity for people to engage in predatory rather than productive activity to enhance their well-being.[5] Similarly, without rule of law some people are favoured over others by the legal system, and people have an incentive to work toward being included in the favoured group, so that they can use their favoured position for predatory activities to enhance their wealth. Thus, when market institutions are absent, the entrepreneurial impulses that would have been channelled toward productive activity are instead channelled toward predatory activity. Entrepreneurial individuals find it more advantageous to use the political system to take wealth from others than to produce it themselves. Market institutions are essential for the cultivation of entrepreneurship and creativity, rather than destruction and predation.

INSTITUTIONS, ENTREPRENEURSHIP AND CREATIVITY

The creative class is a product of market activity, and market activity must be supported by institutions that reward production and innovation, and that stand in the way of predation. Following the outline of Gwartney and Lawson (2005), those institutions are rule of law, protection of property rights, limited government, a stable monetary system and freedom of trade both domestically and internationally. Limited government means low taxes and government spending, and low regulatory barriers to market activity. When these features are present an economy will be entrepreneurial and creative; when they are absent an economy will be destructive and predatory.

One must be impressed by the creativity of the market economy, although those living in one may tend to take the benefits of innovation for granted. At the beginning of the twentieth century electricity and telephones were rare, horses were used for short-distance transportation and railroads for longer hauls. There were no movies, or television, and the internet wasn't widely available until the end of the century. By the end of the twentieth century people lived in air-conditioned accommodation, travelled by automobile and aircraft, and communicated by mobile phone and email. Products such as microwave ovens, flat-panel televisions and laptop computers, which were unimaginable at the beginning of the twentieth century, were commonplace by the end.

The creativity of the market economy has brought a huge increase in people's living standards, and at the same time provided unprecedented access to the creativity of others. Whereas at the beginning of the twentieth century dramas or musical performances had to be experienced in person, at the beginning of the twenty-first century people could watch recorded dramas in movie theatres, at home on television or over the internet, and through the magic of technology could watch these dramas when they wanted to, rather than when the performers are performing. At the beginning of the twentieth century people could see live performances by the best musicians in the local area, when they were performing. By the end of the century people could have a library of performances by the world's best musicians, to enjoy whenever they wanted. The old options are still available, along with remarkable new opportunities. Meanwhile, creative individuals in the arts, like actors and musicians, can share their performances with the whole world, and for the most popular among them, earn incomes beyond the wildest dreams of those in the same occupations a century earlier.

People are part of the creative class if they have the good fortune to be compensated for their creativity, and the economic progress that has occurred since the beginning of the Industrial Revolution has enabled people to more effectively market their creativity to increasingly larger audiences. Musicians can sell recorded music to people all over the world, and even for live performances the development of amplification allows larger audiences, and advancement in transportation technology allows them to travel to perform for audiences in more distant locations. Likewise, the development of transportation and communication technology allows people to market goods and services throughout the world. An MRI can be sent via the internet to be read by a specialist on a different continent, and producers of specialty crafts, foods or other products can market them on the internet and ship them via FedEx. With a larger market, people can engage in creative activities that would not have been feasible without these developments. A larger market increases demand, which causes the creative class to grow.

THE CRUCIAL ROLE OF MARKET INSTITUTIONS AND MARKET REWARDS

While the preceding discussion has focused on the market creation of goods and services, in his discussion of the creative class Florida (2002) emphasizes the role of amenities and tolerance in attracting the creative class. These features of creativity are the result of market institutions, so amenities preferred by the creative class come from the entrepreneurial creativity fostered by markets. Before considering how these same market institutions that produce ever-improving goods and services also produce amenities, tolerance and the social structure that cultivates the creative class, it is crucial to see why all of this depends on, and requires, market institutions.

The emphasis to this point has been on the creation of goods and services, such as automobiles and personal computers. The same arguments apply to restaurant menus, housing, clothing, home furnishings and so forth. What about the creativity that produces art and cultural amenities? Those too require markets for their production, because markets determine what cultural amenities are valuable. Consider an example. Would one consider smashing tubes of toothpaste, computer keyboards, cartons of milk and watermelons with a sledgehammer to be creative? Many people will recognize that this describes the act of stand-up comedian Gallagher, who sells out performances whacking such objects with his 'Sledge-O-Matic'. Why does this pass the creativity test? Because, using Florida's criterion, Gallagher is able to command compensation for his activity.

Gallagher is able to be compensated for his creativity because (1) there are market institutions that allow him to be entrepreneurial; (2) those institutions are structured such that not only can he be entrepreneurial, if he is successful he can keep the profits from his activities; and (3) he lives in a society prosperous enough that some people find his antics entertaining enough that they are willing to pay to watch him smash things. Gallagher's creativity is enabled by market institutions that direct resources toward creativity others find valuable.

To see why markets are crucial to this process, consider two examples. First, seeing Gallagher's success, what would you imagine would be the result if you asked people to compensate you for smashing things with a sledgehammer? Gallagher has a special talent for turning this activity into something marketable, and not everybody could receive the same compensation (or any compensation) from imitating Gallagher. The market mechanism has revealed that when Gallagher does this, it is entertainment people value, whereas when other people do this, it is merely destructive activity. When Gallagher does it, it is creative; when other people do it, it is destructive.

The market mechanism is what reveals creative activity to be creative in Florida's (2002) sense. Many people engage in creative activities as recreation. People are amateur painters, photographers and musicians. They are not members of the creative class, however, unless they receive monetary compensation for their creative activities. While the Gallagher example might at first seem trivial or irrelevant, it shows the importance of market demand and supply, and illustrates the principles that determine whether someone can join the creative class as a photographer, musician or chef, or as an inventor or business owner.

Not everybody can market the same skills that Gallagher does, but Florida's point is that everybody has the potential to be creative in some way. The law of comparative advantage still holds. Some people are more creative musically; others may lack musical ability, but have a talent for computer programming. The market mechanism cannot transform every aspiring novelist into a successful author. The market provides the opportunity for people who want to try, and offers the promise of financial reward to those who are successful. It encourages creativity, and through its reward structure determines how much that creativity is worth to other members of society.

As a second example, some readers may recall the wildly successful Palm Pilot from the 1990s. How many remember that Apple beat them to market with their own hand-held computer, featuring handwriting recognition? The Apple Newton was introduced in 1993, prior to the Palm Pilot's 1996 introduction, but the Newton failed the market test, whereas the market showed the Palm Pilot to be valuable.

While Apple's other products like the Apple II, Macintosh, iPhone and iPad pass Florida's creative test because they were profitable, the Newton fails this test because it could not earn compensation sufficient to pay its costs. From the standpoint of creativity, the Newton was like the amateur artist who cannot sell paintings for enough to cover the cost of the materials, or the amateur musician who enjoys playing but cannot earn enough to cover the cost of the musical instruments. What elevates such activities into the creative class is compensation: passing the market test.

There is more of a similarity than might at first be apparent between the successful manufacture of an automobile or computer and the activities of the creative class. Creativity, defined as Florida defines it, is entrepreneurship, and for creative activity to qualify its creator for entry into the creative class, the creator must pass the market test. This is what distinguishes Gallagher, a member of the creative class, from other people who smash items with sledgehammers but are not members.

AMENITIES FOR THE CREATIVE CLASS

Creative cities need to have amenities that attract creative individuals. Some amenities are purely a matter of geography. A city's climate and proximity to beaches or mountains are beyond the reach of policy makers. Other amenities, such as the availability of parks and recreational opportunities, professional sports franchises and transportation networks (including mass transit and the road network) are the products of public policies. Still others, such as the nightlife, bars, restaurants and diversity in population and lifestyle are market-driven rather than policy-driven. Policy makers can make it easier or harder for restaurants to open, but they cannot keep them open in the absence of clientele to support them. Similarly, policy makers can make a city attractive to people with diverse lifestyles and cultural backgrounds, but cannot force people to move in or keep them from moving out.[6] Florida (2005a, pp. 83–4) notes that market-driven amenities, such as entertainment, nightlife, arts and culture, and the demographic characteristics of the population, tend to rank very high in attracting members of the creative class.

Florida (2005a, p. 86) writes that in order '[t]o gain competitive advantage, regions need to create mechanisms for harnessing the knowledge and ideas of all citizens at the neighborhood, local, and regional levels for improving their quality of place'. How can this be done? Hayek (1945) emphasizes the decentralized nature of knowledge, noting that each individual has some specific knowledge that not only is not shared with others, but that would be difficult to share because it is difficult to articulate. The challenge is to develop a system in which all individuals have an incentive to use their knowledge – and especially their tacit knowledge – in a way that produces the greatest benefit to the group.

The market economy is that system. Florida (2005b) opens his book by describing how movie director Peter Jackson started his movie studio in a former New Zealand paint factory, attracting creative individuals to join him. In hindsight one can see that this was a successful venture, but how could one determine beforehand that the building was better suited for a movie studio than a paint factory? Through the market mechanism entrepreneurs take risks to acquire resources, which they will do only if the risk they take up front is balanced by the lure of profit they can reap if they are right about their creative judgements. What might have stood in the way of Jackson's creativity? Some possibilities are zoning laws, building codes, workplace regulations and taxes. The payoff to creativity is always uncertain, because creativity means doing things differently from what has been done before. Regulations that restrict people's options, that make it more costly for them to take risks, and taxes that limit the return they can get if the risks pay off, all are impediments to creativity.

The way to encourage arts, entertainment, nightlife, a variety of restaurants and cultural opportunities more generally is to reduce the cost of acting entrepreneurially. Everybody is creative, but not everybody is willing to take that chance to give up a more secure but less creative job to act entrepreneurially and join the creative class. Cities that want to encourage creativity can lower the barriers to entrepreneurship so that joining the creative class appears potentially rewarding. Starting a restaurant or an art gallery is a risky undertaking, and entrepreneurs who start them must have the confidence that they have correctly gauged the market along with the confidence that if they are right, they will be able to profit from their entrepreneurship. Government policy can impose barriers to entrepreneurship, or remove them.

The market determines what activities are, in fact, amenities for the creative class. Profitable restaurants are amenities; unprofitable restaurants use up more resources than they return in value. Profitable nightclubs, art galleries and specialty stores are amenities; unprofitable ones use up more resources than they return in value. Government policy encourages creativity by lowering the cost of engaging in creative activity.

Florida (2002) argues that cultural amenities attract members of the creative class, but from a market perspective, it is really the other way around. The creative class attracts cultural amenities, because they are the people who consume those amenities. A community of creative people who enjoy restaurants, nightlife, art galleries and specialty stores will attract those types of activities. They have the demand for creative amenities, and creative people will supply those amenities, as long as restrictive regulations and taxes do not stand in their way.

In developed economies government regulation and taxation are impediments to creative activity, and public policy designed to reduce taxation and regulation will cultivate creativity. Sometimes residents of developed economies take for granted the government's protection of property rights and enforcement of rule of law, but these activities are also fundamental to cultivating creativity. From a public policy standpoint, cultivating creativity means protecting property and other rights, enforcing rule of law and removing tax and regulatory barriers to entrepreneurial activity. This creates an environment in which the market mechanism can reward people for their creative activity. This is an environment that produces the amenities that attract the creative class.

ENABLING TOLERANCE, DIVERSITY AND A BOHEMIAN LIFESTYLE

Tolerance, diversity and the ability to live a more bohemian lifestyle are factors Florida (2005a) argues attract the creative class. Bohemians 'prefer more libertine lifestyles, and favor enjoyment and self-actualization over work' (Florida, 2005a, p. 115). While one might question the degree to which people who favour enjoyment over work are able to make creative contributions, Florida argues that integrating such people into the economic fabric can enhance creativity, and that creative people prefer less regimentation and a more bohemian cultural atmosphere. Market institutions support tolerance, diversity and all types of lifestyle choices, not so much because they encourage these things but because they penalize people who discriminate against others for non-economic reasons.

If people in markets discriminate against others based on race, lifestyle choices or other reasons, those who discriminate pay a price, as Thomas Sowell (1981, 1983) argues. If employers decide they do not want to hire women, or minorities, or gays, they give up opportunities to hire productive workers, and those who are discriminated against by some employers can work for non-discriminatory employers for the mutual benefit of both the employees and the employers. Non-discriminating firms will be more profitable, because they hire based only on the productivity of their employees, not on other characteristics unrelated to productivity.

This is not to say that people in markets never discriminate; rather, it is to say that those who discriminate pay a price for doing so, while those who make decisions in government organizations, financed by taxes, do not bear a cost should they discriminate. That is why, as Jonathan Bean (2009) notes, segregation and discrimination in the United States and elsewhere has been enabled by government intervention, in the form of Jim Crow laws, 'separate but equal' educational facilities, and other more subtle forms of discrimination. Someone hiring for government positions, for example, can discriminate based on any criteria without bearing any personal cost for not hiring the person best qualified for the job. In markets, if some people discriminate in hiring, they sacrifice profits from not hiring the most productive workers. Meanwhile, others can profit from hiring the group being discriminated against, providing some protection against the negative consequences of discrimination. If some people discriminate against some customers, other businesses can profit by serving those customers. Market incentives work against discrimination; government planning allows people to indulge in discrimination without having costs imposed on them.

Another factor that makes markets more tolerant than government is that in markets people only deal with others in areas where they have mutual interests. If someone shows up at a convenience store to buy gas, the purchaser wants the gas while the store clerk wants the money, and on that basis they get along perfectly, with no conflict. The two people could have different political views, different religious views, they may live different lifestyles, and have different cultural backgrounds, yet they are able to co-operate without any tension or friction between them because in that one area where they interact – the market transaction they are undertaking – they have desires that are completely consistent with each other.

In politics, in contrast, even slight differences among people who mostly agree brings out frictions and creates conflict, because in politics a large number of decisions are made by some political body, and political outcomes are forced on everybody regardless of whether they agree. So, if two interest groups, or legislators, agree on 90 per cent of all issues, their focus will be on that other 10 per cent, and each will be trying to score a victory over the other, creating conflict. In markets, people only deal with each other when they have mutually agreeable goals, so conflict never arises. Market transactions are voluntary, and people do not have to buy products they do not want or deal with sellers they prefer to avoid; government transactions are mandatory, and all taxpayers – even those who mostly agree with their political leaders – end up paying taxes for some things they would prefer not to buy, and end up being governed by regulations they believe are counterproductive. The force of government creates conflict, whereas the voluntary nature of market exchange encourages co-operation.

The creative class is cultivated by tolerance, diversity and the possibility of indulging in a more bohemian lifestyle, and all of these lifestyle elements are supported by market institutions but are interfered with by government. Suppose that the creative class is attracted to arts, music and other cultural amenities. If government designs a plan to provide these amenities, those empowered by government will choose who to hire to further these goals, and ultimately will choose the types of art, the nature of the venues and everything else about the amenities. Discrimination is almost certain to occur regardless of the intentions of those doing the planning, because those in charge have a vision of what they want to accomplish and so will hire others with a similar vision to support their work.

This type of top-down planning stifles creativity because the plans are made by the planners and people below them carry out those plans. In a decentralized market environment everybody makes their own plans, resulting in a spontaneous order more creative than any planned order, because everybody exercises their creativity. Market mechanisms are guided by consumer choice; government plans are run by force.

If these cultural amenities are provided by markets, then individuals will decide what types of galleries to open, what types of musical venues to create, what kind of restaurants to open and so forth, and ultimately it will be the consumers of the art, the music and the food who determine which amenities survive and thrive. In a market, those who sell the products of their creativity have an incentive to target their efforts toward the preferences of potential buyers. With government in charge, 'experts' are in a position to produce what they think the public should want rather than what consumers actually do want. People who might object to placing an individual who wants to promote Indian or Chinese culture on a city board to provide cultural amenities to a city, because it would slant the city's programmes, are happy to eat at Indian or Chinese restaurants, which are products of Indian and Chinese culture, because the only transaction involved is the meal. If people want more Indian or Chinese culture, they can buy Indian or Chinese art, or listen to Indian or Chinese music, but the market does not force them to. Markets support tolerance and diversity; government works the other way.

A common characterization is to say that markets are based on competition and politics on co-operation, but in fact the opposite is true. In markets, people only deal with each other when they have a mutual coincidence of wants, and they do so voluntarily. Thus, it is easy for diverse individuals to get along with each other without conflict. When people go to a store to buy a product, their thoughts are focused on that product and whether it is worth the purchase price. Meanwhile, the seller's thoughts are focused on making the sale, and convincing potential buyers that the product is a good value. The seller is focused on doing something the buyer wants, and the buyer is focused on doing something the seller wants, because unless both want the transaction to occur, it will not. Market transactions are based on voluntary agreement and co-operation. Thus, it pays both parties to be tolerant of any differences they may have in other areas of their life, and in fact they tend not even to notice them, because they are irrelevant to the goals of both the buyer and seller. How many people even know the political, religious and social views of those they deal with in a market setting? And, of those who know, few care.

In politics, competition is the rule, because political decisions force everyone to go along with them. If a law is passed, a regulation imposed or a tax levied, it applies to those who support the measure as well as to those who are opposed. Thus, people's differences are naturally pulled to the forefront and political decisions naturally create conflict. It makes sense, then, that in a political environment people will be less tolerant of those different from them, because the force of government can be used to impose the views of those with differences – even when they are in the minority – on the rest of the group. Government operates by force and people have no choice but to abide by its mandates. In politics, people have good reason to be less tolerant, because those who have different views have the potential to use the force of government to implement them as public policy. Markets create a cultural environment that enables tolerance, diversity and a variety of lifestyles, because market activities occur only by mutual consent. Government, because it forces everyone to abide by its mandates, is by its nature intolerant.

WHY CITIES?

The policy aspects of the discussion to this point have dealt with government policy generally, rather than the more narrow topic of creative cities. Why should the focus be on cities? The answer is that there are agglomeration economies that result from creative people being in close proximity to each other. The implications of agglomeration economies have been dealt with by others, and Pierre Desrochers (2001) provides an especially readable and insightful treatment. Rather than reviewing the reasons agglomeration economies exist, this analysis accepts that they do in order to emphasize the role of market mechanisms, market price signals and the role of market-generated profit and loss in identifying, attracting and rewarding the creative class to produce creative cities.

Agglomeration economies are important because they suggest that even if a nation or a state or a region has completely homogeneous policies, the creative class will not be uniformly distributed across the area. Agglomeration economies imply that creative people benefit from clustering together, so two cities might be identical from the public policy standpoint and yet one is able to attract the creative class while the other sees an out-migration of creative individuals. Why? Because creative people want to cluster, so creative cities start with an advantage in attracting more of the creative class. One cannot hope to replicate Boston or Silicon Valley by replicating the public policies of those areas and hoping to attract the creative class. Agglomeration economies mean that one needs a nucleus of creative activity in place to cultivate creativity. But, as Florida notes, everybody is creative, so the cultivation of creativity starts with reinforcing the creative aspects of an area's existing population. It then continues by making it easy and attractive for others in the creative class to migrate in.

Florida emphasizes cities as places that have cultural amenities that attract the creative class, but the reason the creative class clusters in cities to begin with is the agglomeration economies that increase productivity. Creative people are more creative, and productive people are more productive, when they are in an environment with other creative and productive people. Agglomeration economies result in a clustering of creative people, and that clustering of the creative produces the demand for the cultural amenities the creative class enjoys. Those amenities follow the creative class more than they attract the creative class. Creative individuals migrate to places where they can put their creativity to productive use, not necessarily to places that have the best restaurants and art galleries. The amenities follow the creative class because the creative class generates the demand for those amenities.

URBAN PLANNING, OR SPONTANEOUS ORDER?

When one looks more specifically at policies cities can undertake to cultivate creativity, they tend to fall along a continuum running from urban planning to spontaneous order. There is a continuum, because all cities use some planning, and all rely to some degree on spontaneous order.

Planning consists of elements like roadway network design, parks and public spaces, mass transit options and other aspects of the physical infrastructure. In the twentieth century zoning became an integral part of local planning in most areas, and more comprehensive land-use planning has become common since the 1970s. Planning will also often use some existing local nodes of creativity as a springboard for attracting more of the creative class. Universities, medical centres and recreational amenities like ski slopes, lakes and golf courses are some examples. Planners then develop their plans for leveraging these features to attract the creative class. One aspect of planning is that the plan is created by the planner, and everyone else conforms to the plan. For that reason, planning stifles creativity.

Reliance on spontaneous order means creating conditions that make it inexpensive and easy for people to act on their creative impulses. If someone wants to start a restaurant or an art gallery or a software company, what impediments will they run into as they proceed? Local governments can step out of the way by lowering regulatory and tax barriers, and can even facilitate finding a location and getting started. Governments often do this in the name of economic development to attract big corporations and big facilities, effectively trying to select which elements of the creative class they want to attract, but often the same governments create impediments to smaller and start-up enterprises, which could produce creativity in unexpected ways. Creating an advantage for some automatically means creating a disadvantage for others who are not in that favoured group.

Creativity, by its very definition, provides unexpected results. Thus, creativity and planning seem at odds with one another, at least if one goes so far as to plan out the results one hopes to achieve. Consider some basic examples. Zoning restricts the way that people can use their property. If someone wants to redevelop an old house into an art gallery or a restaurant, zoning laws cannot help and may stand in the way. Zoning was designed to prevent incompatible uses of land, but as Bernard Siegan (1970, 1972) insightfully explains, market forces are sufficient to mitigate incompatible land uses, and have other advantages as well. For example, art galleries and restaurants will be more successful on busy thoroughfares and heavily travelled locations than in quiet residential neighbourhoods, so it is unlikely that someone would locate such a business, or a gas station or convenience store, next to somebody's home in a subdivision.[7] As urban areas develop and grow, the best uses for land will change, and in a dynamic community the rigidity of zoning is an impediment to creativity. Yet rather than backing away from such regulatory impediments, state and local governments are enacting more in the name of comprehensive planning, which goes well beyond land-use planning. Holcombe and Staley (2001) and Holcombe and Powell (2009) offer a critical analysis of the smart growth and new urbanism movements that, in the name of planning, stand in the way of creativity.

Florida (2005b) emphasizes the barriers that immigration policy places on creativity by preventing the most creative individuals from in-migrating. At a local level, smart growth policies do the same thing by restricting new development, locking in the status quo and preventing the entrepreneurship that generates creativity. The constructed order of planning crowds out the spontaneous order that cultivates creativity. Local communities have a limited ability to prohibit people from entering, but through zoning ordinances, building codes and restrictions on development they can discourage in-migration, which stands in the way of cultivating creativity.

Economic planning is another impediment to cultivating creativity. After the collapse of the Berlin Wall in 1989, there has been widespread acknowledgement that the market mechanism works better to allocate resources than central economic planning. Yet despite this recognition, economic planning is common at all levels of government. At the local level, many cities offer tax breaks, industrial development grants and other enticements to attract specific businesses to their area. The benefits provided to specific employers must be paid for by everyone else, so what appears to be a creativity-enhancing policy instead stifles creativity. In some cases such enticements are aimed specifically at what Richard Florida called the creative class, to entice medical research centres, software design firms and similar creative employers. Along the lines of Frédéric Bastiat's (1995) observations, what is seen is the new facility locating in a community; what is not seen is what that new economic activity has crowded out, and that would have occurred but for the costs imposed by the new facility. Creativity is crowded out by planning.

At the national level economic planning goes by the name of industrial policy, which was used by Japan and South Korea as their economies displayed very high rates of growth. The government picked and supported particular firms, giving them economic assistance to be competitive in world markets. Through the 1980s the apparent success of Japanese industrial policy prompted many in the United States to advocate similar policies, but as the Japanese economy stagnated in the 1990s explicit calls for industrial policy waned, although support for policies that would benefit specific firms at a cost imposed on the rest of the economy did not.

In Japan and Korea, favoured firms were picked because they were already competitive. Sony in Japan and Samsung in Korea were successful because of the entrepreneurs behind those firms, so when the government stepped in behind them it gave the illusion of successful industrial policy. The real success was the entrepreneurship of the firms' management. But no firm stays on top forever, and industrial policy stifles the creativity of emerging firms – of the ever-changing creative class – that keeps the creativity in creative cities. Had policies like that been in effect in the United States in the 1960s, industrial policy would have supported and given special privileges to firms such as IBM, which would have hindered and perhaps prevented the creation of firms such as Apple and Microsoft. Because of its focus on successful firms over start-ups, industrial policy helps to lock in the old economy and prevent the creative destruction that generates economic progress.

The alternative to planning is the spontaneous order of the market. The creative class is market-generated, in that it exists because people are able to supply their creative talents in the market for compensation, and others have the means to demand those talents. Free markets allow entrepreneurial individuals to supply amenities that the creative class demands, and because market transactions are voluntary they encourage tolerance and diversity. People interact with each other only when their interests are compatible. Because creativity by its definition produces unforeseen results, planning stifles rather than cultivates creativity. The spontaneous order of the market cultivates creativity.

The challenge any economy faces, whether we are talking about a city or a nation or the global economy, is co-ordinating the economic activities of all its participants. As Hayek (1945) notes, everybody has some specific knowledge that others not only do not know, but cannot know. People have tacit knowledge which allows them to know how to accomplish particular tasks, even though they may not be able to articulate that knowledge to pass it on to others. A market economy makes best use of that knowledge and co-ordinates the activities of everyone, for the benefit of everyone.

Cities are concentrations of knowledge. Because much knowledge is tacit, being in close proximity with those in the creative class can enable people to observe and learn from them, as Desrochers (2001) explains. A concentration of creativity allows more movement of creative workers to more suitable employment. A creative worker is more likely to move to a better job in the same city than in a different one because, first, it is easier to change jobs, and second, it is more likely that information about the job match will be available because of the proximity. This enables creative cities to become more creative, making them more attractive for others of the creative class. Because of agglomeration economies, creative cities have an advantage in maintaining their creative edge, and it is difficult for other cities to join the ranks of creative cities.

Some planners look to earlier success stories for inspiration. 'Let's see how Austin did it!' But imitation is not creativity, and is unlikely to work because agglomeration economies and the existing creative class gives Austin an advantage over other cities that want to be like Austin. Rather, planners should provide an environment that facilitates entrepreneurship, keeps the cost of creativity low and allows creative individuals to keep the rewards of their creativity. That is, in fact, how Austin did it. Lower tax and regulatory barriers, and provide infrastructure and support where the creative class wants it rather than where the planners think it should go. Austin did not join the ranks of creative cities by trying to become the next Boston or San Francisco.

New concentrations of creativity will emerge partly because the success of creative cities makes small-scale creativity more costly. Rents and real estate prices rise, making start-up operations more costly, and more significantly, as creative enterprises grow they lose some of their agility. They also gain more political clout, and as local governments turn their attention toward maintaining the goodwill of their larger taxpayers, a local industrial policy emerges that makes small-scale entrepreneurship more difficult. That opens opportunities for new areas that have low tax and regulatory barriers, and that are receptive to the spontaneous order of the market, to join the ranks of creative cities.

Agglomeration economies give creative cities such as New York and San Francisco an edge, but not necessarily a permanent one. Fifty years ago Detroit was a creative city, and it would have taken quite a visionary to foresee not only the rise of other creative cities as Detroit fell, but also to foresee the computer industry overtaking the auto industry as the anchor of many creative cities. The best way to join the next wave of creative cities is to provide an environment conducive to entrepreneurial activity, and reap the rewards that will be the result of an unplanned order. Cities can create an environment that will cultivate creativity, but they cannot plan out an outcome that is of necessity the result of bottom-up individual activity.

CONCLUSION

Florida (2005b, chapter 3) emphasizes openness as an essential ingredient to economic progress. He emphasizes the mobility of people, to allow the creative class to migrate to locations where their talents can be used most productively, and this analysis supports that idea. Florida (2005b, pp. 74–8) downplays economic incentives, noting that creative impulses are 'beyond greed'. But economic incentives are better viewed as opportunities for creativity than as greed. The economic incentives must be there for people to be compensated for their creativity, and that compensation provides the evidence of the value that others place on the activities of the creative class.

People often associate markets and materialism, but markets are essential to the cultivation of the creative class. Not only does Florida's definition of the creative class rely on market compensation, markets also provide the social environment that the creative lifestyle seeks. Creative individuals demand cultural amenities like restaurants, art galleries and an active nightlife, which the market supplies. Cities that make it easy to establish these amenities cultivate creativity. The market mechanism also generates tolerance and acceptance of lifestyle differences, because with market transactions people only interact with each other when it is in their mutual interest to do so.

A market economy cultivates creativity; government planning stifles it, almost by definition. Creativity produces unexpected outcomes whereas planning works to generate the outcome designed by the plan. To cultivate creativity cities should create an environment in which it is easy for people to be entrepreneurial, where tax and regulatory barriers are low, where property rights are protected and where everyone is treated the same under the law. Barriers to migration should be minimal, to encourage the in-migration of the creative class. This applies at the national level, but also at the local level where smart growth policies have limited in-migration. The creative class exists because the individuals in it are able to market their creativity. The creative class is a decentralized organization of people, not the product of a plan.

The idea of planning a creative city misses the whole concept of creativity. The creative class is cultivated by establishing an environment within which all individuals have the freedom to act on their creative potential. Creativity is cultivated in an environment within which individuals can reap the rewards of acting entrepreneurially to market their creativity, not planning out creativity as a result. Creativity is a process, not an outcome, and the status quo of the creative class today cannot be the status quo of the creative class in the future. If it were, there would have been no creativity.

NOTES

*   The author gratefully acknowledges helpful comments from two anonymous reviewers.
1. Kohn (2004) offers an insightful critique of this framework, along with an alternative.
2. Economists make the assumption that competitive firms produce homogeneous products to enable the output of firms to be added up to find the output in the market. One cannot add apples and oranges. Despite the assumption of homogeneous products, product differentiation is one of the most effective competitive strategies available to firms. Holcombe (2009) discusses this in more detail.
3. This conclusion relies on a commonly held but not universal view of economic equilibrium. See Holcombe (1999, 2006) for a more detailed discussion.
4. This extends slightly Kirzner's definition of entrepreneurship, as Kirzner identifies the entrepreneurial act as noticing a profit opportunity that has previously gone unnoticed. Acting on the opportunity applies other factors of production (labour, capital) to realize the profit. The extended definition fits present purposes better, because simply observing something does not place the observer in the creative class. The compensation for the creativity comes from acting on the profit opportunity that the individual observes.
5. Florida (2002) puts attorneys in the creative class, and because they are knowledge workers, with good reason. Attorneys do help people protect their rights, but the legal system also creates opportunities for the creativity of attorneys to be used in predatory ways. For example, patent laws create the opportunity for firms to obtain patents not for the purpose of producing anything, but to sue productive firms to win a monetary settlement. The intent of this creative activity is purely predatory.
6. Florida (2005b) notes that nations can keep people from moving in, which repels the creative class, in contrast to cities, which have minimal control over who crosses their borders once they are in the country.
7. Also, the long-standing common law doctrine of nuisance would stand in the way of incompatible land uses, and indeed this is how the issue was dealt with prior to zoning.

REFERENCES

Bastiat, F. (1995), 'What is seen and what is not seen', *Selected Essays on Political Economy*, Irving-on-Hudson, NY: Foundation for Economic Education, Chapter 1.

Baumol, W.J. (1990), 'Entrepreneurship: productive, unproductive, and destructive', *Journal of Political Economy*, **98**(5), 893–921.

Baumol, W.J. (1993), *Entrepreneurship, Management, and the Structure of Payoffs*, Cambridge, MA: MIT Press.

Bean, J. (ed.) (2009), *Race & Liberty in America*, Lexington, KY: University Press of Kentucky.

Berggren, N. (2003), 'The benefits of economic freedom: a survey', *Independent Review*, **8**(2), 193–211.

Desrochers, P. (2001), 'Geographical proximity and the transmission of tacit knowledge', *Review of Austrian Economics*, **14**(1), 25–46.

Florida, R. (2002), *The Rise of the Creative Class: And How It's Transforming Work, Leisure, Community, & Everyday Life*, New York, NY: Basic Books.

Florida, R. (2005a), *Cities and the Creative Class*, New York, NY: Routledge.

Florida, R. (2005b), *The Flight of the Creative Class*, New York, NY: HarperCollins.

Gwartney, J. and R. Lawson (2005), *The Economic Freedom of the World: 2005 Annual Report*, Vancouver, BC: Fraser Institute.

Gwartney, J., R. Holcombe and R. Lawson (2004), 'Economic freedom, institutional quality and cross-country differences in income and growth', *Cato Journal*, **24**(3), 205–33.

Hayek, F.A. (1945), 'The use of knowledge in society', *American Economic Review*, **35**(4), 519–30.

Holcombe, R.G. (1999), 'Equilibrium versus the invisible hand', *Review of Austrian Economics*, **12**(2), 227–43.

Holcombe, R.G. (2006), 'Does the invisible hand hold or lead? Market adjustment in an entrepreneurial economy', *Review of Austrian Economics*, **19**(2–3), 189–201.

Holcombe, R.G. (2009), 'Product differentiation and economic progress', *Quarterly Journal of Austrian Economics*, **12**(1), 17–35.

Holcombe, R.G. and B. Powell (2009), *Housing America: Building Out of a Crisis*, New Brunswick, NJ: Transaction Publishers.

Holcombe, R.G. and S.R. Staley (2001), *Smarter Growth: Market-based Strategies for Land-use Planning in the 21st Century*, Westport, CT: Greenwood.

Kirzner, I. (1973), *Competition and Entrepreneurship*, Chicago, IL: University of Chicago Press.

Kohn, M. (2004), 'Value and exchange', *Cato Journal*, **24**(3), 303–39.

Landes, D.S. (1998), *The Wealth and Poverty of Nations: Why Some Are So Rich, and Some So Poor*, New York, NY: W.W. Norton.

Mokyr, J. (1990), *The Lever of Riches*, Oxford: Oxford University Press.

Schumpeter, J.A. (1954), *Capitalism, Socialism, and Democracy* (4th edn), London: George Allen & Unwin.

Siegan, B.H. (1970), 'Non-zoning in Houston', *Journal of Law & Economics*, **13**(1), 71–147.

Siegan, B.H. (1972), *Land Use Without Zoning*, Lexington, MA: D.C. Heath.

Smith, A. [1776] (1937), *The Wealth of Nations*, New York, NY: Modern Library.

Sowell, T. (1981), *Discrimination, Affirmative Action, and Equal Opportunity: An Economic and Social Perspective*, Vancouver, BC: Fraser Institute.

Sowell, T. (1983), *The Economics and Politics of Race: An International Perspective*, New York, NY: W. Morrow.

20 The sociability and morality of market settlements
Arielle John and Virgil Henry Storr

Since at least Max Weber, social scientists have looked closely at the nexus between markets and cities. Weber believed that cities and markets were inextricably linked. In his seminal work *Economy & Society,* for instance, Weber ([1921] 1978, p. 1213) describes the city as a market settlement. As he writes, 'a city . . . is always a market centre. It has a local market which forms the economic centre of the settlement and on which both the non-urban population and the townsmen satisfy their wants for craft products or trade articles by means of exchange.' The difference between a city and other settlements, then, is the existence of a market rather than the size of the population, or the type of dwellings, or the nature of the social activities that occur, or any other criteria that we might use. Although Weber's centrally located marketplaces have long since been replaced by malls and shopping plazas and high-rise business districts and swanky shopping streets, market activity is still at the centre of city life.

Weber went on to describe three ideal-typical cites: (1) the consumer city, (2) the producer city and (3) the merchant city. The consumer city is one where the market depends on the spending of wealthy consumers. In producer cities, on the other hand, the market depends on the existence of industries within the city. Finally, the market in the merchant city depends on profits derived from foreign goods sold locally, local goods sold abroad or from brokering the sale of foreign goods in foreign markets. Of course, no city falls purely in any of the three categories. As he (Weber, [1921] (1978) p. 1217) writes, 'actual cities almost always represent mixed types'. Indeed, the modern creative city is arguably a combination of all three. Regardless of type, however, Weber consistently maintained that the existence of a market (of some type) was the critical feature of every city.

A burgeoning literature now exists that examines this market-city nexus. This literature clearly demonstrates that markets thrive in cities and cities thrive because of markets. Murray Bookchin (1986, p. 68), for instance, has also argued that 'whatever else may be the principal functions of the early city, certainly in advanced urban society the authentic nexus of the city is the marketplace – the arena in which necessities of life are exchanged and in which urban contact has its workaday center'. Although different kinds of markets and the prevalence of different modes of work give rise to different types of cities, the link between markets and cities is an indelible one.

Jane Jacobs (1969, 1984) has also consistently stressed that the market is essential to the existence of the city. For her, cities are centres of and are necessary for entrepreneurship, innovation and economic prosperity. Similarly, Edward Glaeser (Glaeser et al., 1992) found support for Jacobs's contention that the economic diversity that exists within cities leads to knowledge spillovers across industries and so to economic growth. Additionally, Glaeser and Mare (2001) focus on knowledge spillovers when explaining why cities are so conducive to the growth of markets. Although urban workers command higher nominal wages than rural workers, they argue, it is not necessarily because they are more productive or possess higher levels of human capital. Instead, Glaeser and Mare (2001, p. 322) insist that 'even if cities are no better educated than the hinterland, urban density will increase interactions and intellectual spillovers'. And these interactions and intellectual spillovers will generate wealth.

Additionally, Pierre Desrochers (2001) concludes that the geographic proximity offered by cities facilitates the transmission of tacit knowledge and so promotes innovation. Duranton and Puga (2001) offer similar insights. With innovation as their focus, Duranton and Puga (2001, p. 1455) argue that abundant and diverse local knowledge concerning production techniques exists within cities, and that entrepreneurs learn this knowledge and use it to experiment with and develop new techniques. This accessibility of knowledge, which they describe as one of the 'dynamic advantages to urban diversity', represents a cost saving to urban firms that are in their learning stage (Duranton and Puge, 2001, p. 1455). This cost saving translates into firm growth, and the increasing employment requirements of innovating firms fuels the population growth of cities.

Markets, then, thrive in cities relative to non-urban settings because different types of people with different kinds of experiences are more likely to interact within cities than elsewhere. These interactions lead to innovations, these innovations lead to firm growth, and this firm growth attracts resources and workers to the city. As such, markets thrive within cities because there are economic advantages to being in an urban environment. Likewise, cities thrive because market activity attracts people and possessions.

So the economic prosperity generated in markets is essential for the growth of cities, and the interactions and knowledge spillovers that occur within cities are critical to the development of thriving markets. However, the sociability that occurs within and because of markets as well as the trust and civility market interactions engender both also play important roles in the development of cities, particularly modern, diverse, creative cities. Markets are social as well as moral spaces and these properties of markets are critical for the sustainability of creative cities (Storr, 2008, 2009). Moreover, while social distance can be higher in cities than in non-urban settings, opportunities for meaningful social interactions, especially among members of small social groups, are arguably higher within market settlements than in more rural communities. Markets sustain subcultures and, as a result, city dwellers are more likely to find the kinds of groups and activities that they desire than rural residents (Fischer, 1975, 1995).

Unfortunately, with a few exceptions, not much attention has been paid to how the social capital that develops within markets supports and sustains cities. This chapter is an effort to explore this role of markets. The next section discusses the sociability that occurs within as well as because of markets and describes how markets promote virtuous behaviour. The sociability and morality encouraged by markets, we argue, aids in the development of creative cities. The third, then, discusses how markets extend the opportunities for meaningful and civil social interactions and so mitigate the problems associated with the high levels of social distance found within cities. The positive extra-economic aspects of markets (that is, the potential for sociability and morality), we argue, should complicate if not counter any discussion of the 'necessary' social ills that plague urban centres. The final offers concluding remarks.

FROM MARKETS AS SOCIAL AND MORAL SPACES TO CREATIVE CITIES

As Virgil Storr (2009) argues, the market is both a social and a moral space. Rather than being a space that grows at the expense of the community, the market is an arena where communities can and often do flourish. The market is a space where meaningful conversations occur and meaningful social bonds develop. Storr (2008, p. 141) writes that 'markets . . . are vibrant, colorful social spaces where real relationships and meaningful contacts are developed and nurtured'. In addition to being spaces where we can meet our friends and cultivate our friendships, markets are also arenas where we can become more virtuous. Instead of being primarily an arena where only vices (such as greed) are encouraged, the market is arguably also a space where a number of the virtues (especially prudence, honesty and courage) are fostered and rewarded. As Deirdre McCloskey (2006, p. 13, emphasis in original) argues, the expansion of markets has made us 'ethically *better*'.

Voltaire was one of the first scholars to praise the market for its ability to enhance virtues such as tolerance. In his *Philosophical Letters* ([1733] 2003), Voltaire observes that English society displays a higher degree of tolerance than France, tolerance being a virtue highly esteemed by Voltaire. This tolerance, Voltaire explains, exists because Englishmen actually respect commerce. At the level of governance, both England and France exhibited religious intolerance at the time. That is, the governments of both countries sought to compel religious conformity and homogeneity. So why did English society generally become more tolerant? As Voltaire theorized, only in France were those engaged in commerce made to feel embarrassed by their trade. He claims that French society encouraged the 'well-powdered lord . . . who gives himself airs of grandeur while playing the role of slave in a minister's antechamber' but simultaneously denigrated the 'great merchant who enriches his country . . . and contributes to the well-being of the world' (Voltaire, [1733] 2003, p. 40). Why then did France privilege the 'well-powdered lord' over 'the great merchant'? He claimed that English merchants, operating in an arena in which they were free to act in their economic self-interest, found it desirable to cast aside their religious and class prejudices in order to maximize economic benefits. In order to transact profitable business, Voltaire recognized, one had to be tolerant. As Voltaire explains,

> go into the Exchange in London, that place more venerable than many a court, and you will see representatives of all the nations assembled there for the profit of mankind. There the Jew, the Mahometan, and the Christian deal with one another as if they were of the same religion, and reserve the name of infidel for those who go bankrupt. (Voltaire [1733] 2003, p. 26)

Voltaire thus hailed the market as contributing to the tolerance, peace and harmony that differentiated English society from that of France. In his view, divided and conflict-ridden societies were much more likely to result from limitations on market freedom. This is a point we return to later.

Adam Smith also highlighted the community-enhancing aspects of markets. 'The necessity or conveniency of mutual accommodation', Smith ([1759] 1976a, pp. 223–4) argues, 'very frequently produces a friendship not unlike that which takes place among those who are born to live in the same family. Colleagues in office, partners in trade, call one another brothers; and frequently feel towards one another as if they really were so.'

Coworkers will frequently come to care quite deeply for one another. Although these are sometimes unlikely pairings and had they met outside of work they might never have become friends, the trust that must exist between coworkers if they are to succeed at their jobs and the hours that they spend working with and relying on one another makes the development of a true friendship (or at least true tolerance) between them quite natural. Smith believed that commercial friendships often developed into actual friendships and could even develop into brotherhoods. While he did not believe that these friendships of necessity or convenience were superior to friendships 'founded altogether upon . . . esteem and approbation', he did nonetheless believe that these workplace friendships were meaningful and quite normal. That they were friendships of necessity or conven- ience did not mean that they were not true friendships.[1]

Murray Rothbard (1993) similarly argues that friendships and even civility are made possible because of markets. As he writes,

> it is far more likely that feelings of friendship and communion are the effects of a regime of (contractual) social co-operation rather than the cause . . . in a world of voluntary social co- operation through mutually beneficial exchanges, where one man's gain is another man's gain, it is obvious that great scope is provided for the development of social sympathy and human friendships. (Rothbard, 1993, p. 85)

Rothbard is underscoring a crucial aspect of markets here. The existence of markets makes peaceful social co-operation and so the development of friendships possible. In order to benefit from the desirable, recurring transactions that markets make possible, people willingly adopt respectful, friendly and even kind demeanours toward each other. Eventually these behaviours become automatic, unthinking responses when dealing with others.[2] The average person we meet is a potential friend, not an enemy (though some tiny fraction of the strangers we encounter may pose a discernable threat). The market, for Rothbard (1993, p. 102), is the opposite of the jungle. Absent markets we are forced to fight or to depend on the generosity of one another for the essentials of life. Neither struggle nor dependency of this sort, Rothbard argues, is conducive to the development of peaceful society let alone friendships.

As Storr (2008) describes, a variety of social bonds do often develop in markets or are strengthened because of markets. For instance, as we discuss above, coworkers often develop strong bonds because of their common experiences and circumstances (Zavella, 1985; Henderson and Argyle, 1995; Hodson, 1997). Bridge and Baxter (1992) consider that a specific social setting like the work environment may have a particular effect on how people who are already friends interact in a work space. The authors posit three categories of benefits that can derive from working alongside a friend – two friends who work with each other have more opportunity for their friendship to flourish, working together may allow for the recognition of increased similarities, and finally, friends working together would be exposed to a variety of bonding opportunities that 'allowed the two parties to build, demonstrate or test one another's caring, loyalty or trust' (Bridge and Baxter, 1992, p. 216).

Similarly, when discussing small-scale textile production in Trinidad, Rebecca Prentice (2009, p. 126) writes that 'the shop floor is an active social field in which gaining the aid of fellow workers is always part of the process'. The trust that mutual aid engenders can facilitate social friendships. Furthermore, office romance (which should not be confused with harassment) is a common phenomenon in the contemporary workplace (Pierce et al., 1996; Williams et al., 1999). Additionally, principal-client, seller-buyer relationships can develop into deep friendships (Price and Arnould, 1999; Butcher et al., 2002; Haytko, 2004). And master-apprentice and mentor-protégé relationships can sometimes grow into social friendships and even father-son, mother-daughter type relationships (Kram, 1983; Gardiner, 1998). The individual who met his wife at work, whose coworker is his child's godfather, who plays golf with his clients and who has a great deal of affection for his mentor is a familiar figure in contemporary creative cities.

Again, there is no reason to believe that these relationships that developed within and because of the market are any less meaningful than the connections made outside the market. Additionally, by making geographically dispersed communities possible, the market and the technological developments it spurs allow individuals to maintain the relationships that they value most if they become separated by distance and to be more selective about whom they want to engage with locally. Markets allow us to find and maintain relationships with the individuals who are most like us. This attraction to and search for similar people, however, is not antithetical to diversity. While people often do have intrinsic desires to associate with others who are similar to them on at least one demographic parameter, like race, nationality, gender or age group (Byrne, 1971; Tajfel and Turner, 1986), it is equally true that people often migrate to bigger cities to escape the very homogeneity of 'small-town life' and that they perceive that being exposed to 'foreign' persons and ideas is healthy and refreshing. Furthermore, because of the market, social bonds can be maintained with individuals back home even if you leave the village for the city. But, importantly, social bonds need not be exclusively with the other villagers. While markets allow us to maintain social bonds when we leave, they also make it possible for us to sever those relationships in favour of relationships that fit better.

Individuals thus come to see the market as not just a space for competition and exchange but also as a social space where social content often overlays economic dealings, and where friendships are developed and maintained.

Storr (2009) also maintains that virtuous behaviour is rewarded in well-functioning markets and that the market is a moral space where individuals learn to be virtuous. Following Smith ([1759] 1976a), Storr (2009) argues that morality is not something that is innate but instead develops through social interactions. Since our moral sentiments are learned and are not inborn, Storr (2009) contends that 'it makes sense to worry about the virtues and vices, the good and bad habits that individuals develop as a result of their experiences in the market'. The market, he argues, promotes virtue and mitigates vice.[3]

Adam Smith also highlighted the virtue-encouraging aspects of markets. He believed, for instance, that markets engender positive virtues both by harnessing individual prudence for the social good and by rewarding virtuous behaviour. Prudence directed merely at the preservation of the individual may not be considered the noblest of virtues but it is still a virtue (Smith [1759] 1976a, p. 216). And it is certainly a virtue that is rewarded in the market. As Smith ([1776] 1976b, p. 26) describes, we appeal to the baker's prudence (his self-regard) rather than his benevolence when seeking our daily bread. Moreover, as Smith stresses, markets not only reward prudence they also reward trustworthiness. As he writes, the wages of labour vary according to the small or great trust which must be reposed in the workmen. The wages of goldsmiths and jewelers are every-where superior to those of many other workmen, not only of equal, but of much superior ingenuity; on account of the precious materials with which they are [*sic*] intrusted. (Smith [1776] 1976b, p. 122)

Smith also believed that individuals in commercial societies tended to be more virtuous than individuals living in other kinds of nations. As he ([undated] 1978, pp. 486–7) writes, '[t]he establishment of commerce and manufactures, which brings about this independencey, is the best police for preventing crimes. The common people have better wages in this way than in any other, and in consequence of this a general probity of manners takes place thro' the whole country.'

William Casebeer (2008) interestingly argues that it is possible to tell a positive narrative of markets that stresses how they promote virtue. Market activity is often accused, he writes, of being 'selfish' or 'exploitative' or 'harmful' to the environment or to the poor or to ourselves. But, he (Casebeer, 2008, p. 3) contends, these stories 'leave off the considerable moral presuppositions and ethical benefits that free exchange assumes and enables'. Markets, Casebeer (2008, pp. 11–12) writes, 'can themselves evolve creatures that are prone to cooperation as much as competition, . . . [that] afford critical opportunities for cultivation of the classic virtues, . . . [and that] afford incentives to develop and maintain moral standards'. If markets sometimes promote moral bad, that bad must be weighed against the moral good that they promote if we are going to make a fair assessment of their positive and negative attributes.

Michael Novak (1993, p. 179) similarly argues that 'commerce . . . teaches care, discipline, frugality, clear accounting, providential forethought, . . . respect for reckonings . . . fidelity to contracts, honesty in fair dealings, and concern for one's moral reputation'. In her *Bourgeois Virtues*, McCloskey (2006) extends Novak's analysis and describes the market as a sphere where ethical and even virtuous behaviour is given scope, promoted and honed. According to McCloskey, the market does not make us greedy or materialistic but, in fact, makes us ethically better. As she writes (McCloskey, 2006, p. 29), 'capitalism has not corrupted the spirit. On the contrary, had capitalism not enriched the world by a cent nonetheless its bourgeois, anti-feudal virtues would have made us better people than in the world we have lost. As a system it has been good for us.' Love, faith, hope, courage, temperance, justice and, of course, prudence, McCloskey (2006) writes, both enable and are promoted by and developed through markets. Indeed, she insists, to succeed in the market we must act virtuously. Take, for instance, the virtue of prudence. The market participant who lacks 'good judgement' or 'practical wisdom' will fail. McCloskey writes that 'prudence as practical know-how is a virtue' (McCloskey, 2006, p. 254).

Also consider, for example, courage and hope. Entrepreneurship, the driving force of the market, is dependent on these two virtues. The would-be entrepreneur who does not have the hope that a better way of doing things can be discovered will never innovate. Similarly, the would-be entrepreneur who does not have the courage to test their new concepts in the marketplace or to persevere in the face of early failures will not transform the status quo. The market rewards these virtues and, in so doing, encourages them. As McCloskey summarizes, 'the bourgeois virtues . . . have been the causes and consequences of modern economic growth and modern political freedom'. Again, by rewarding virtue and punishing vice, the market teaches us to be virtuous (McCloskey, 2006, p. 22).

The market is thus not only a space where we are able to satisfy our material desires; it is also a space where we can satisfy our demands for conviviality and learn to be better people. The market is a space that satisfies our material desires as well as our ethical and social aspirations. This capacity of markets to be more than just sites for commercial dealings is precisely why cities can be more than just cold sterile spaces. Arguably, creative cities are possible because markets can be more than spaces for soulless materialism, self-seeking and greed. Creative cities depend on the fact that markets can be places that speak to our aspirations, support our friendships and allow for the expression of our values.

Recall that there is a deep relationship between cities and markets. The growth of cities depends on the economic prosperity generated in markets. Additionally, the development of thriving markets depends on the interactions and knowledge spillovers that occur within cities. Also recall that cities have always relied on creativity. As Landry and Bianchini (1995, p. 11) write, 'creativity has always been the lifeblood of the city. Cities have always needed creativity to work as markets, trading and production centres with their critical mass of entrepreneurs, artists, intellectuals, students, administrators and power brokers.' Cities, they assert, have always been places where individuals from different cultures interact and where these interactions lead to the creation of new ideas.

Charles Landry (who coined the term 'creative city') did not begin by focusing on the role of creativity within cities to suggest that creativity is now important to cities but was not important before. Instead, he wanted to highlight that creativity had become even more important in somewhat different ways than previously. He focused on creativity as a way of discussing the transitions that many cities were going through from old industrial centres to nodes within the knowledge economy. Whereas in previous centuries the successful cities were the ones that attracted manufacturing industries, in the twenty-first century the cities that thrive will be the ones that attract and nurture the creative class of knowledge creators who fuel these new creative knowledge-based industries (Landry and Bianchini, 1995, p. 12).

In *The Rise of the Creative Class,* Richard Florida (2002, p. 68) discusses the emergence of the new economic class which occupies creative cities and 'consists of people who add economic value through their creativity'. Included in this class would be individuals who work in knowledge-intensive industries from information technology to thought leaders such as non-fiction writers to artists such as poets, novelists and actors. As traditional industries increasingly rely on the application of knowledge and knowledge-based technologies, many workers in these industries are also members of the creative class. Members of this class, Florida (2002, p. 77) reports, tend to value individuality, merit, diversity and openness. According to Florida (2002, p. 76), over 25 per cent of US workers belonged to this class by the end of the twentieth century.

The creative class is a market phenomenon. The creative class emerged because of a change in the nature of work within markets. The creative class is also a market phenomenon, however, because its existence is made possible because markets are social and moral spaces. The sociability and morality of markets, which gives members of this creative class the opportunity to satisfy their desires for a particular type of conviviality and to express a particular set of values, is critical to the existence of this new class and the cities that support them. Stated another way, markets are sites of creative expression and cater to the people as a whole (and not just to their material wants). Consequently, urban spaces (because they are linked with markets) can and will be creative cities.

The next section will discuss how markets mitigate some of the problems associated with urban living by extending the opportunities for meaningful and civil social interactions.

CAN MARKETS MITIGATE SOME OF THE SOCIAL PROBLEMS ASSOCIATED WITH CITY LIVING?

There are undoubtedly many problems associated with urban living. Quotidian hassles include traffic congestion, air pollution, and fewer open and green spaces compared with rural areas. Sharp inequalities in access to social services also present challenges. Housing and public infrastructure tend to be derelict in some areas (Diamond, 1991, p. 219). Poor education is also a problem in poor communities. Teachers in poorer urban districts tend be less qualified, because in some parts of cities, wages are too low to compensate more capable teachers (Lankford et al., 2002, p. 38). Students in the low-income parts of cities tend to be low-achieving and the quality of education never reaches parity with the richer neighbourhoods. Furthermore, depending on the region or country in which cities are located, cities may also display peculiar patterns compared with the rest of the country or to cities in other countries.

For example, certain groups residing in urban areas in Latin America have a high rate of home rental as opposed to home ownership, as well as a greater density of persons per room (Bromley and Jones, 1996, p. 189).[4] As an illustration of the inequalities in service provision within cities, Magadi et al. (2003) find that in African countries with relatively good maternal health care, the urban poor receive ante-natal and delivery care that is worse than the standard received by the urban non-poor and even rural residents.

Other serious and more general social ills also disproportionately affect cities. These include higher rates of crime, poverty and social exclusion compared with rural areas. These issues cannot be ignored. Crime rates tend to be much higher in big cities than in rural areas (Cullen and Levitt, 1999). Two explanations provided for the observed high crime rates in big cities are that the benefits to criminality are higher and the likelihood of getting caught are lower in big cities (Glaeser and Sacerdote, 1999). Crime does seem to affect the costs of city life for inhabitants. Cullen and Levitt (1999, p. 159) estimate that for every 10 per cent increase in a city's crime rate, the population size declines by 1 per cent. Members of educated households are typically the first to leave in response to rising crime. The result of high urban crime rates may therefore be a reduction in the very human and social capital that is crucial to the growth and development of cities.

Within urban spaces, poverty also tends to be concentrated in particular pockets which increases the likelihood that poverty will persist (Kempen, 1994, 1997; O'Regan and Quigley, 1998). Generally high levels of poverty in urban areas are already linked with adverse social outcomes such as high infant and child mortality and poor-quality housing (UNDP, 2005). Unfortunately, concentrated poverty is said to be an increasing phenomenon in ethnic and racial minority neighbourhoods within cities (Burton and Jarett, 2000).

Social distance between groups within cities can also be quite high (UNDP, 2005). Spatial segregation within cities can occur along lines of income, class, ethnicity or race (Krivo et al., 1998; Wassmer, 2005).

'Ethnic ghettos' arise when communities of people who are united by such characteristics as West Indian heritage or Russian-speaking ability cluster into specific enclaves in cities (Bromley et al., 1996, p. 180). These spatial differences come with worrisome social stigmas, as evidenced by that fact that people often lie in filling out job applications about the neighbourhood in which they live. Globalization is sometimes blamed for the increased social stigmatization, exclusion of minority groups from political or judicial processes, and the erosion of human rights that are said to characterize cities (Smets and Salman, 2008).

Again, the social exclusion that occurs in cities, it is argued, is inevitable given the large groups of people that dwell within cities. As Wassmer (2005) claims, spatial segregation in cities may be a consequence of the process of 'Tiebout sorting'. Members of diverse groups who continually migrate into cities demand the formation of local governments that will represent each of their (relatively similar) interests. Local governments are bound by geographically defined districts, and therefore these groups spatially sort themselves according to the district they get representation in.

While acknowledging some positive attributes of cities as market settlements, Bookchin (1986) is quite critical of the modern city and seeks to highlight some of the psychic costs associated with city living and the social problems discussed above. As Bookchin (1986, p. 1) writes, 'cities embody the most important traditions of civilization. Owing to the size of their marketplaces and the close living quarters they render possible, cities collect those energizing forces of social life that country life tends to dissipate over wide expanses of land and scattered populations.' But Bookchin also believes that the modern 'bourgeois city' has not lived up to or, in fact, has betrayed its potential. 'Just as there is a point beyond which a village becomes a city', Bookchin (1986, p. 2) writes, 'so there is a point beyond which a city negates itself, churning up a human condition that is more atomizing – and culturally or socially more desiccated – than anything associated with rural life.' Bookchin (1986, p. 92) believes that large metropolitan cities such as Los Angeles have reached that point and actually describes them as the 'antithesis of an authentic community'. Even so-called cosmopolitan cities like New York are beginning to suffer from a similar crisis of authentic community (Bookchin, 1986, p. 96). As cities have become 'massive', Bookchin (1986, p. 102) complains, urban life becomes alienating and 'the urban ego, which once celebrated its many-faceted nature owing to the wealth of experience provided by the city, emerges with the bourgeois city as the most impoverished ego to appear in the course of urban development'.

In general (even when true), these types of social problems that are found in cities have less to do with cities being market settlements and more to do with cities (even modern cities) being only partially market settlements. For example, crime, poverty and social exclusion occur when people respond to incentives that are often only indirectly generated by the expansion of markets. Government intervention and other non-market processes are shown to be more likely to contribute to social ills than markets. Furthermore, world cities display wide variation in average income levels, population, poverty levels, crime rates and so on, which implies that we cannot always expect that the growth of a city will be accompanied by greater poverty or increased inequality – these problems may actually improve as cities grow. Finally, because market interactions can bring out the best in society in terms of fostering sociability and morality, a number of these problems are mitigated by the growth and development of markets.

Consider the level of crime within cities. The high incidence of crime within cities would seem to be at odds with the claims that we made earlier about market settlements being spaces which promote community and morality. It would seem that either we are mistaken (and market settlements in fact promote criminality as well) or that there are real limits to the ability of markets and so cities to engender virtuous behaviour or to facilitate the transforming of strangers into friends. Crime does have the potential to undermine markets, both directly by challenging the stability of property rights necessary for functioning markets, and indirectly by challenging the trust that undergirds market activities. It is important to note, however, that markets, and by extension cities, flourish in spite of crime. Although criminals are attracted to the riches available in big and prosperous market settlements, and a high level of criminal activity detracts from the experience of the peaceful inhabitants living there, significant material benefits can still accrue to individuals in cities as a result of the market process at work. Additionally, market settlements do promote beneficial and benign social behaviours such as kindness and restraint among larger numbers of people than is possible without a market. Arguably, crime is not a consequence of markets but instead a consequence of insufficient markets. That the incidence and severity of crimes are higher in poorer than in richer communities suggests that crime is not a market phenomenon but is instead a phenomenon that can be reduced as markets expand. Similarly, that many cities are still thriving suggests that for many the benefits of escaping crime can be outweighed by the cost of doing so (Becker, 1968).[5]

Similarly, the concentration of urban poverty is arguably the indirect and unfortunate result of anti-poverty government policies intended to level the playing field within cities (Kempen, 1994; Strait, 2001). Welfare programmes such as housing subsidies and eligibility criteria frequently target low-income areas within cities. However, these programmes often provide incentives to individuals to spend less time searching for work, to have children out of wedlock and to group themselves in certain districts or neighbourhoods (Strait, 2001, p. 273). Inasmuch as those behaviours exacerbate city poverty, poverty is not so much the result of market action as of government action.

Likewise, by stressing the social exclusion and spatial segregation that is said to characterize cities, it is possible to lose sight of the potential for greater interaction among diverse individuals within market settlements and the benefits of those interactions. It is important to stress here that our argument should not be thought of as an effort to say that the social ills that sometimes plague cities are irrelevant or non-existent. Instead, it is an effort to highlight some of the positive aspects of markets and cities that are often overlooked and to suggest that markets and cities have in some cases and may in many if not all cases work to solve social exclusion.

Indeed, throughout history, as new markets were discovered, opportunities to trade with foreigners presented themselves and were not ignored by merchants. Barrington Moore (2001) explains how markets were able to remove barriers to desired exchange including shackles that stemmed from human ignorance or distrust of other cultures. 'In early modern European cities', Moore writes, foreign trade did have certain liberating consequences, though these were not the only ones. A European trader was willing to disregard the religion, skin color, and odd habits of a potential customer or supplier for the sake of a good bargain. What brought them together was Marx's 'callous cash nexus' and very little else. (Moore, 2001, p. 716)

In places like Amsterdam and Genoa, Moore (2001, p. 716) argues that 'it is hard to believe that the experience of contact with foreigners left no traces on the trader's pattern of thinking'. This example illuminates an important consequence of markets. People's regard for their own advantages means that they are able to look past their differences if focusing on them would have blocked an improved state of their personal affairs. Stated another way, markets raise the cost of discrimination and so reduce it (Friedman, 1962, p. 110). Moore explicitly points out than in non-urban areas, where markets were less well developed, personal biases were not so easily overcome. Moreover, he claims that port cities, like Genoa, performed better not just economically but in terms of reduced violence. There is a real connection, Moore argues, between maritime city trade and the freedom of conscience that upholds tolerance, civility and reduced violence toward outsiders.

In addition to making discrimination more costly, markets give people experience with members of other groups. When people begin to trade, for instance, they come to realize that stereotypes (for example, beliefs that suggest that the trustworthiness of a trading partner is related to his ethnic background) are more difficult to sustain. Social distance and so the animosity between the various racial, ethnic and social groupings may be high within cities but personal experience with members of different racial, ethnic and social groups is also more likely within cities than elsewhere.

The social aspects of markets as they relate to cities extend beyond increased trust and civility. As noted earlier, cities are often viewed as places where strangers are fearful of one another and act rudely. Elijah Anderson (2004, p. 15) argues, however, that markets promote politeness and that marketplaces can 'offer a respite from this wariness, settings where a diversity of people can feel comfortable enough to relax their guard and go about their business more casually'. It is not surprising, therefore, that despite the conventional wisdom, advanced market settlements like New York City are often considered to be some of the most polite cities in the world.[6] Anderson chalks up the sociability apparent in cities to the proliferation of marketplaces and other public spaces.

One of these 'cosmopolitan canopies', as he calls them, is Philadelphia's historic farmers market, the Reading Terminal Market (Anderson, 2004, p. 15). In this relatively busy, quasi-public setting, under a virtual cosmopolitan canopy, people are encouraged to treat others with a certain level of civility or at least simply to behave themselves. Within this canopy are smaller ones or even spontaneous canopies, where instantaneous communities of diverse strangers emerge and materialize – the opportunities or openings provided by fascinating titbits of eavesdropped (or overheard) conversation. Here, along the crowded aisle and eating places, visitors can relax and feel relatively safe and secure. Although they may still avoid prolonged eye contact or avert their glances to refrain from sending the 'wrong' messages, people tend to positively acknowledge one another's existence in some measure. At times, strangers may approach one another to talk, to laugh, to joke, or to share a story here and there. Their trusting attitudes can be infectious, even spreading feelings of community across racial and ethnic lines.

Anderson suggests that bars, parks, mass transit systems, sporting arenas as well as the international restaurants and groceries that are so common in large cities can also act as 'cosmopolitan canopies'. Whatever notions we may have about city-dwellers in developed countries being persons who, out of fear, ignore strangers, racial minorities and the homeless, the fact is that people meet and interact with one another in market spaces.

Persons living in cities are simply forced to deal with others. Anderson (2004) claims that individuals within public spaces such as markets actively engage in 'folk ethnography' or people-watching – studying the behaviour of others and even actively participating in the culture of others by talking with them, eating their food, and even speaking their language in order to appear more cosmopolitan. People often understand more about themselves by observing others. In this way, people become more human and have more meaningful social interactions. According to Anderson,

> this kind of exposure to a multitude of people engaging in everyday behaviour often humanizes abstract strangers in the minds of these observers. The existence of the canopy allows such people, whose reference point often remains their own social class or ethnic group, a chance to encounter others and so work toward a more cosmopolitan appreciation of difference. (Anderson, 2004, p. 28)

The significance of markets for the development of diverse and creative cities and the capacity of markets to mitigate some of the problems often associated with urban life cannot be overstated. As persons of different cultures and ethnicities find that they are treated more civilly in cities, they will migrate there more and only increase the diversity of cities. This acceptance is arguably most visible in cities such as Montreal and Toronto – where nearly half of the inhabitants were born outside Canada (Smart and Smart, 2003, p. 276). Firms located in such cities will find that they have no shortage of workers who are able to meet the innovative demands of a global economy. Workers will tend to have more specialized skills, such as being able to differentiate between the different accents of foreign-language-speaking customers. The demands of international markets will therefore be met at lower costs by firms which are located in these diverse and creative city centres.

The supply and demand for employees with diverse backgrounds and experiences will continue to increase in these cities. This is evidenced by the high wages and fast accumulation of human capital that occurs within cities (Glaeser and Mare, 2001) as well as the increasing number of major transnational companies that are headquartered in creative cities around the world (Beaverstock and Boardwell, 2000, p. 279).

Although the social and moral dimensions of market settlements render positive economic consequences, it is also the case that the creativity, diversity and tolerance engendered by markets yield cultural benefits. Expressions of art – including art exhibitions, movies and museums – are increasingly dedicated to the experience of minorities and outsiders. This is as true of developed country cities like Washington, DC as it is of developing country cities like Accra, Ghana. The exposure of city-dwellers to all things foreign encourages a cosmopolitan sensibility within them. Hence the multitude of opportunities for interaction between urbanites of different backgrounds supplies them with more creative fodder. As Terry Nichols Clark recognizes in his edited volume, *The City as an Entertainment Machine* (2004, p. 306), Chicago's 'number one industry has become entertainment'. This suggests, he writes, that 'cultural activities are increasingly crucial to urban economic vitality' (Clark, 2004, p. 291). Cities become known as much for their ethnic diversity, cosmopolitan mindset, artistic innovations and inspired cultural expressions as for their high wages and economic prosperity.

Landry's modern creative cities peopled by Florida's creative class therefore have very little in common with the bourgeois cities that Bookchin describes. Although they are talking about the same geographical locations, their perspectives are almost wholly distinct. We have reason to believe that the modern city is not as bleak as Bookchin paints it. Even if Bookchin's (1986, p. 92) contention that the city is now 'merely a place in which to work' were correct, it does not signal the death of community as he infers. As we suggested above, the workplace is also a place where meaningful social interactions occur.

Similarly, as Storr (2010) argues, we do not experience the market as an anonymous other. We do not shop for groceries at a food store. We shop for groceries at the Whole Foods or the Giant down the street or at the co-op on the corner. Likewise, we do not work for a business. We work for a particular business. Moreover, while Bookchin may be right that the enormousness of the bourgeois city produces certain challenges, it also produces certain advantages that should not be overlooked (for example, diversity and a greater selection of communities to belong to and activities to participate in).

CONCLUSION

Historically, urban areas emerged as a consequence of the actions of individuals participating in market transactions. Due to the market process at work, cities have become the world's epicentres of economic prosperity, entrepreneurship and technological innovation. Some of the greatest thinkers in political economy and urban planning have stated that this relationship is a necessary one. Markets are inseparable from cities. Indeed, Weber maintained that the main feature of a city is that it has a market. And cities, in turn, provide fertile ground for the expansion of markets. Knowledge spillovers proliferate in large cities due to the sheer diversity of agents in close proximity with one another. As a consequence, cities become hotbeds of creative innovation.

While almost everyone will acknowledge that markets and so cities produce wealth, the negative social and moral consequences of markets and the social and moral ills associated with living in cities are often given much attention. To be sure, while the power of markets to generate economic success is well known, not everyone is convinced that markets engender morality or the 'greater good'. Markets have been accused of causing widening social and economic inequalities, of promoting vices like selfishness and greed, of destroying communities and their values, and generally of purging us of our spirituality, morality and culture. Gudeman (2001, p. 144), for instance, warns that by 'spreading rapidly and on a global scale, markets are subsuming greater portions of everyday life. Increasingly, we commoditize things, leisure, body parts, reproductive capacities, DNA, and social relationships. As people flock to cities, sell their hardwood trees, change clothing styles, and watch television, community . . . shrinks.'

This pessimistic take on markets is unfortunate, though unsurprising, given that even market enthusiasts tend to sing the virtues of anonymous exchange, competition and spontaneous orders while treating as vapid or dangerous the notions of building community, promoting sociality and remedying social ills through the deliberate design of policies (Storr, 2009).

City life it is sometimes argued is plagued by social problems. Besides the day-to-day inconveniences of living in urban areas, inequalities between different ethnic, racial and income groups are often observed to be exacerbated in cities. Much of the literature on urban planning focuses on disparities in the quality of housing, education and health care (to list a few) provided in urban areas. Furthermore, disproportionately high rates of crime, poverty and segregation in many cities imply that cities are places in desperate need of reconfiguration and intervention, and that markets have somehow precipitated breakdowns in the social order.

There is something in the way that we discuss this that glosses over the obvious differences between different cities. New York is very different from Paris and both are very different from smaller less cosmopolitan cities such as Richmond, Virginia; the social ills that plague one may not affect the other. Generally, however, markets and so cities are social spaces where social relationships matter. Likewise, they are also moral spaces where being virtuous is rewarded. Indeed, the interaction of people within markets gives rise not only to pecuniary benefits but also social and moral benefits. A positive mitigating consequence of the development of cities through markets is therefore that trust, civility and politeness increase among different social groups within cities. Furthermore, cities have become creative and diverse communities of people.

Local knowledge within cities goes beyond economic knowledge, in that individuals in cities also accumulate and transmit vast personal knowledge – knowledge of a diversity of backgrounds, experiences and cultures. Hence a striking feature of the development of cities is not only that they accumulate human capital rapidly, but also that they accumulate social capital at a faster pace than rural areas. Much of the literature surrounding creative cities concerns how local governments can transform their communities into creative cities. Although this chapter does not focus on this concern, it certainly follows from our analysis that one key strategy is to allow thriving markets.

NOTES

1. For Smith ([undated] 1978, p. 183), individuals are more likely to treat each other like friends the smaller the social distance between them, the more they are engaged in the same kind of labour and the more time that they spend working together. Smith believed feelings of friendship were even possible between slaves and masters wherever masters also toiled in the field alongside their slaves. He points to the brutal treatment that slaves received in the West Indies as opposed to elsewhere to suggest that where slaves and masters lived similar lives the slaves were treated better. This would suggest that friendships between supervisors and subordinates as well as between providers of services and their clients are possible and even likely as long as they belong to the same social stratum and are engaged in the same kind of work.
2. Friedrich Hayek, in Volume I of *Law, Legislation and Liberty* (1973), deals with the notion of the evolution of rules of conduct in society; rules which persist because they have historically assured our success in markets or elsewhere. As he summarizes, 'man is as much a rule-following animal as a purpose-seeking one. And he is successful not because he knows why he ought to observe the rules which he does observe, or is even capable of stating all these rules in words, but because his thinking and acting are governed by rules which have by a process of selection been evolved in the society in which he lives, and which are thus the product of the experience of generations' (Hayek, 1973, p. 11). Abstract rules, which in the past developed spontaneously, continue to guide us today, without us knowing why we abide by them or even that we do. While we can often instinctively recognize the benefits of forming a particular friendship or of treating a certain stranger with respect, Hayek's line of reasoning suggests that acting civilly has become a general

conditioned response for us, which we do not need to relearn with every new person that we meet. This is no less true of the people we meet within markets than the people we meet elsewhere. Acting with morality as a rule often ensures success not only in our personal lives, but also in our professional lives which play out in markets.

3. As Hayek (1973, p. 11) explains, what is moral is not objective and was not pre-chosen for us or declared by special individuals throughout history. Rather, morality, tradition and law have evolved historically through a process of selection. Those actions which a society deem as 'moral' at a particular point in history are, therefore, referred to as such because those actions have contributed to the success of that society. For example, in so far as being generous is regarded as being 'moral' in a society, this is because a majority of individuals within that society found that generosity persistently brought success in their personal and professional relations.

4. Bromley and Jones (1996) refer to Latin American inner cities such as that in Quito, Ecuador, where families that rent are also likely to be living in substandard living conditions compared with those that own their own homes.

5. The problem of crime cannot sensibly be mitigated by requiring cities to be smaller in size, as crime is a complex and ubiquitous social problem. As Jane Jacobs (1961) notes, '[t]he reasons for Los Angeles' high crime rates are undoubtedly complex, and at least in part obscure. But of this we can be sure: thinning out a city does not insure safety from crime and fear of crime' (Jacobs, 1961, pp. 32–3).

6. According to a 2006 *Readers Digest* survey.

REFERENCES

Anderson, E. (2004), 'The cosmopolitan canopy', *Annals of the American Academy of Political and Social Science*, **595**, 14–31.

Beaverstock, J.V. and J.T. Boardwell (2000), 'Negotiating globalization, transnational corporations and global city financial centres in transient migration studies', *Applied Geography*, **20**, 277–304.

Becker, G. (1968), 'Crime and punishment: an economic approach', *Journal of Political Economy*, **76**(2), 169–217.

Bookchin, M. (1986), *The Limits of the City* (2nd edn), Montreal, QC: Black Rose Books.

Bridge, K. and L.A. Baxter (1992), 'Blended relationships: friends as work associates', *Western Journal of Communication*, **56**, 200–25.

Bromley, R.D.F. and G.A. Jones (1996), 'Identifying the inner city in Latin America', *Geographical Journal*, **162**(2), 179–90.

Burton, L.M. and R.L. Jarrett (2000), 'In the mix, yet on the margins: the place of families in urban neighborhood and child development research', *Journal of Marriage and Family*, **62**(4), 1114–35.

Butcher, K., B. Sparks and F. O'Callaghan (2002), 'On the nature of customer-employee relationships', *Journal of Organizational Behavior*, **20**(5), 297–306.

Byrne, D.E. (1971), *The Attraction Paradigm*, New York, NY: Academic Press.

Casebeer, W.D. (2008), 'The stories markets tell: affordances for ethical behavior in free exchange', in P. Zak (ed.), *Moral Markets: The Critical Role of Values in the Economy*, Princeton, NJ: Princeton University Press, pp. 3–15.

Clark, T.N. (2004), *The City as an Entertainment Machine*, Oxford, UK: Elsevier.

Cullen, J.B. and S.D. Levitt (1999), 'Crime, urban flight, and the consequences for cities', *Review of Economics and Statistics*, **81**(2), 159–69.

Desrochers, P. (2001), 'Geographical proximity and the transmission of tacit knowledge', *Review of Austrian Economics*, **14**(1), 25–46.

Diamond, D.R. (1991), 'Managing urban change: the case of the British inner city', in R. Bennett and R. Estall (eds), *Global Change and Challenge*, London: Routledge, pp. 217–41.

Duranton, G. and D. Puga (2001), 'Nursery cities: urban diversity, process innovation, and the life cycle of products', *American Economic Review*, **91**(5), 1454–77.

Fischer, C. (1975), 'Toward a subcultural theory of urbanism', *American Journal of Sociology*, **80**(May), 1319–41.

Fischer, C. (1995), 'The subcultural theory of urbanism: a twentieth-year assessment', *American Journal of Sociology*, **101**(November), 543–77.

Florida, R. (2002), *The Rise of the Creative Class*, New York, NY: Basic Books.

Friedman, M. (1962), *Capitalism and Freedom*, Chicago, IL: University of Chicago Press.

Gardiner, C. (1998), 'Mentoring: towards a professional friendship', *Mentoring & Tutoring: Partnership in Learning*, **6**(1–2), 77–84.

Glaeser, E.L. and D.C. Mare (2001), 'Cities and skills', *Journal of Labor Economics*, **19**(2), 316–42.
Glaeser, E.L. and B. Sacerdote (1999), 'Why is there more crime in cities?', *Journal of Political Economy*, **107**(6), Part 2, S225–S58.
Glaeser, E.L., H.D. Kallal, J.A. Scheinkman and A. Shleifer (1992), 'Growth in cities', *Journal of Political Economy*, **100**(6), 1126–52.
Gudeman, S. (2001), *The Anthropology of Economy*, Malden, MA: Blackwell Publishers.
Hayek, F.A. (1973), *Law, Legislation and Liberty, Volume I: Rules and Order*, Chicago, IL: University of Chicago Press.
Haytko, D.L. (2004), 'Firm-to-firm and interpersonal relationships: perspectives from advertising agency account managers', *Academy of Marketing Science Journal*, **32**(3), 312–28.
Henderson, M. and M. Argyle (1995), 'Social support by four categories of work colleagues: relationships between activities, stress, and satisfaction', *Journal of Occupational Behavior*, **6**(3), 229–39.
Hodson, R. (1997), 'Group relations at work: solidarity, conflict, and relations with management', *Work and Occupations: An International Sociological Journal*, **24**(4), 426–52.
Jacobs, J. (1961), *The Death and Life of Great American Cities*, New York, NY: Random House.
Jacobs, J. (1969), *The Economy of Cities*, New York, NY: Random House.
Jacobs, J. (1984), *Cities and the Wealth of Nations*, New York, NY: Random House.
Kempen, E.T. van (1994), 'The dual city and the poor: social polarisation, social segregation and life chances', *Urban Studies*, **31**(7), 995–1015.
Kempen, E.T. van (1997), 'Poverty pockets and life chances on the role of place in shaping social inequality', *American Behavioral Scientist*, **41**(3), 430–49.
Kram, K.E. (1983), 'Phases of the mentor relationship', *Academy of Management Journal*, **26**(4), 608–25.
Krivo, L.J., R.D. Peterson, H. Rizzo and J.R. Reynolds (1998), 'Race, segregation, and the concentration of disadvantage: 1980–1990', *Social Problems*, **45**(1), 61–80.
Landry, C. and F. Bianchini (1995), *The Creative City*, London: Demos.
Lankford, H., S. Loeb and J. Wyckoff (2002), 'Teacher sorting and the plight of urban schools: a descriptive analysis', *Educational Evaluation and Policy Analysis*, **24**(1), 37–62.
Magadi, M.A., E.M. Zulu and Martin Brockerhoff (2003), 'The inequality of maternal health care in urban Sub-Saharan Africa in the 1990s', *Population Studies*, **57**(3), 347–66.
McCloskey, D.N. (2006), *The Bourgeois Virtues: Ethics for an Age of Commerce*, Chicago, IL: University of Chicago Press.
Moore Jr, B. (2001), 'Ethnic and religious hostilities in early modern port cities', *International Journal of Politics, Culture, and Society*, **14**(4), 687–727.
Novak, M. (1993), *The Catholic Ethic and the Spirit of Capitalism*, New York, NY: Free Press.
O'Regan, K.M. and J.M. Quigley (1998), 'Where youth live: economic effects of urban space on employment prospects', *Urban Studies*, **35**(7), 1287–305.
Pierce, C.A., D. Byrne and H. Aguinis (1996), 'Attraction in organizations: a model of workplace romance', *Journal of Organizational Behavior*, **17**(1), 5–32.
Prentice, R. (2009), '"Thieving a chance": moral meanings of theft in a Trinidadian garment factory', in K. Browne and B.L. Milgram (eds), *Economics and Morality: Anthropological Approaches*, New York, NY: Altamira Press, pp. 123–96.
Price, L.L. and E.J. Arnould (1999), 'Commercial friendships: service provider-client relationships in context', *Journal of Marketing*, **63**(4), 38–56.
Rothbard, M.N. (1993), *Man, Economy and State: A Treatise on Economic Principles*, Auburn, AL: Ludwig von Mises Institute.
Smart, A. and J. Smart (2003), 'Urbanization and the global perspective', *Annual Review of Anthropology*, **32**, 263–85.
Smets, P. and T. Salman (2008), 'Countering urban segregation: theoretical and policy innovations from around the globe', *Urban Studies*, **45**(7), 1307–32.
Smith, A. [1759] (1976a), *The Theory of Moral Sentiments*, Indianapolis, IN: Liberty Fund.
Smith, A. [1776] (1976b), *An Inquiry into the Nature and Causes of the Wealth of Nations*, Indianapolis, IN: Liberty Fund.
Smith, A. [undated](1978), *Lectures on Jurisprudence*, Indianapolis, IN: Liberty Fund.
Storr, V.H. (2008), 'The market as a social space: on the meaningful extra-economic conversations that can occur in markets', *Review of Austrian Economics*, **21**(2–3), 135–50.
Storr, V.H. (2009), 'Why the market? Markets as social and moral spaces', *Journal of Markets and Morality*, **12**(2), 277–96.
Storr, V.H. (2010), 'Hayek and Lefebvre on market space and extra-catallactic relationships', in R. Garnett, E. Olsen and M. Starr (eds), *Pluralism in Economics and Economies*, New York, NY: Routledge, pp. 181–93.
Strait, J.B. (2001), 'The disparate impact of metropolitan economic change: the growth of extreme poverty neighborhoods, 1970–1990', *Economic Geography*, **77**(3), 272–305.

Tajfel, H. and J.C. Turner (1986), 'The social identity theory of intergroup behavior', in S. Worchel and W. Austin (eds), *Psychology of Intergroup Relations*, Chicago, IL: Nelson Hall, pp. 7–24.

United Nations Development Programme: International Poverty Centre for Inclusive Growth (UNDP) (2005), 'Poverty and the city' (by Alejandro Grinspun), *Poverty In Focus*, **7**, 1–20.

Voltaire [1733] (2003), *Philosophical Letters: Letters Concerning the English Nation*, Mineola, NY: Dover.

Wassmer, R.W. (2005), 'An economic view of the causes as well as the costs and some of the benefits of urban spatial segregation', in D. Varady (ed.), *Desegregating the City: Ghettos, Enclaves, and Inequality*, New York, NY: State University of New York Press, pp. 158–74.

Weber, M. [1921] (1978), *Economy and Society: An Outline of Interpretive Sociology* (two volumes), Berkeley, CA: University of California Press.

Williams, C.L., P.A. Giuffre and K. Dellinger (1999), 'Sexuality in the workplace: Organizational control, sexual harassment, and the pursuit of pleasure', *Annual Review of Sociology*, **25**, 73–93.

Zavella, P. (1985), '"Abnormal intimacy": the varying work networks of Chicana cannery workers', *Feminist Studies*, **11**(3), 541–57.

21 Creative environments: the case for local economic diversity
Pierre Desrochers and Samuli Leppälä

Whether specialization or diversity of economic activities should be a regional development policy goal is a long-standing debate (Rodríguez-Pose and Crescenzi, 2008). On the one hand, as Hoover and Giarratani (1984, chapter 12, non-paginated) observed in their classic textbook, regional economic diversification has long been viewed as a '"healthy" structural feature worth striving for' although 'the grounds for this view . . . have never been clearly articulated'. In their opinion, this case can ultimately be traced back to the assumptions that 'a region with a diversified structure (many different kinds of activities and an absence of strong specialization) is necessarily less vulnerable to cyclical swings of general business conditions and demand' and that multiple employment and investment opportunities create more opportunities for workers, entrepreneurs and investors, thus providing 'a better chance for new kinds of business to get a start and to survive the hazardous years of infancy'. In the last two decades, however, Michael Porter's (1990) influential cluster-based prescription managed to successfully reorient most local development officials' goal towards regional specialization. More recently, the continual decline of poorly diversified regional economies once again reminded numerous policy makers of the dangers of putting all of one's economic eggs in the same basket (Chapman, 2005).

While the benefits derived from the geographical concentration of related firms are strong, our objective in this chapter is to expand upon the traditional arguments made on behalf of economically diversified regions by illustrating how such a setting inherently facilitates the emergence of new innovative and profitable activities. The chapter is structured as follows. The first section briefly reviews the traditional case on behalf of local diversity. We then examine the greater entrepreneurial opportunities provided by a more diversified local economic environment through a discussion of 'industrial symbiosis', that is, the creation of recovery linkages between diverse local industries through which the waste of one is turned into the valuable input of another. The third section illustrates how a diverse regional setting facilitates the creation of new technological combinations. In order to deliver both additional historical perspective and a description of the underlying mechanisms at the individual level, we supplement the current 'Jacobs spillovers' literature with additional insights from the scholarly study of human creativity and illustrative evidence collected in a qualitative survey of Canadian individual inventors. The last section is our conclusion.

THE TRADITIONAL CASE FOR LOCAL DIVERSITY

Following the writings of David Ricardo on comparative advantage, most economic analysts have considered local specialization as both a natural and desirable outcome of trade liberalization. While close scrutiny reveals important differences between regional and individual specialization (Leppälä and Desrochers, 2010), it has long been thought that by concentrating on the production of what they do relatively better than others and through subsequent exchange, all individuals enjoy a greater standard of living than if they were attempting to produce a wider range of goods and services in their local community. Regional economic specialization also allows producers to tap into a combination of natural advantages, such as a skilled labour pool possessing specific expertise, asset sharing and the provision of highly specialized intermediate inputs. Other traditional arguments supporting this case are that dense regional networks of similar or related firms encourage innovative behaviour and the diffusion of new know-how through both intense competition and the development of trust relationships resulting from frequent face-to-face communication (Marshall, 1920; Porter, 1990).

While the advantages that similar or directly related firms derive from close geographical proximity are obvious, it has also long been recognized that other factors militate against absolute regional specialization, and that such a setting is inherently problematic. The former considerations include transport costs; the undeniable (if difficult to prove) existence of a class of externalities, urbanization economies, by which the geographical concentration of a wide variety of firms generates significant benefits across different lines of work; and the inherently greater 'multiplier effect' of a more diverse setting when new productive activities are added to the local economic mix, in the process providing new customers to a whole range of (as opposed to a few) local producers (Hoover and Giarratani, 1984; Wheeler et al., 1998; Rosenthal and Strange, 2004; Polese, 2005). The latter considerations include the inevitability over time of the obsolescence of whatever output an economically specialized region might be producing or the emergence of better and/or cheaper competitors in other regions. As a result, a regional economy that fails to continually renew itself through the development of new activities will suffer at best stagnation and at worst decline and economic extinction (Jacobs, 1969). For example, in the nineteenth century Pittsburgh successively lost its salt, waggon, cotton textile and refined petroleum product industries to other regions. Despite these setbacks, the local economy thrived because of the addition of new activities such as steel, glass, electrical equipment and coal mining. Significant later losses in these industries, however, were not compensated by the parallel emergence of new profitable activities on a similar scale, therefore ushering in its well-known economic decline (Hoover and Giarratani, 1984).

Of course, a specialized region can experience faster and more significant employment and wealth creation than a more diversified local economy when there is a high demand for its main product (Polese, 2005). As Hoover and Giarratani (1984, chapter 12, non-paginated) further observe, 'diversification per se is roughly neutral in its effect on cyclical stability. What really makes a region especially vulnerable to cyclical swings is specialization in cyclically sensitive activities.' The same authors, however, quickly add that local diversity is always more desirable 'when we consider stability and other desirable attributes *over a longer period*' (Hoover and Giarratani, 1984, our emphasis). As the economist Alfred Marshall (1920, p. 273) had observed decades earlier, 'a district which is dependent chiefly on one industry is liable to extreme depression, in case of a falling-off in the demand for its produce, or of a failure in the supply of the raw material which it uses', but that this problem was 'in a great measure avoided by those large towns or large industrial districts in which several distinct industries are strongly developed'.

While the previous arguments are frequently raised in policy discussions, the particular processes through which local economic diversity contributes to the emergence of new activities and technological innovations are more rarely discussed. We now turn to a more detailed examination of how, *ceteris paribus*, a more diversified economic base inherently provides more entrepreneurial and innovative opportunities than a more specialized one.

LOCAL DIVERSITY AND ENTREPRENEURIAL OPPORTUNITIES: THE CASE OF INDUSTRIAL SYMBIOSIS

The argument that more a diverse local economic setting provides greater opportunities for the emergence of new activities seems commonsensical. While any selection of historical references is bound to be subjective, illustrating that the topic was already a familiar one to earlier generations of scholars sheds additional light on current controversies (see also Desrochers and Leppälä, 2010). Detailed discussions of the issue can be traced back at least to the work of the social theorist Herbert Spencer (1864, p. 52), who viewed the 'evolution of a homogeneous society into a heterogeneous one' as the inevitable result of innovative activities and of an ever-increasing division of labour. Spencer (1864) thus observed that when 'there grows up a fixed and multiplying community', such differentiations 'become permanent, and increase with each generation'. Among other causes driving this process was the fact that

> [c]ompeting workers, ever aiming to produce improved articles, occasionally discover better processes or raw materials. The substitution of bronze for stone entails on him who first makes it a great increase of demand; so that he or his successor eventually finds all his time occupied in making the bronze for the articles he sells, and is obliged to depute the fashioning of these articles to others; and, eventually, the making of bronze, thus differentiated from a pre-existing occupation, becomes an occupation by itself. But now mark the ramified changes which follow this change. Bronze presently replaces stone, not only in the articles it was first used for, but in many others – in arms, tools, and utensils of various kinds: and so affects the manufacture of them. Further, it affects the processes which these utensils subserve, and the resulting products – modifies buildings, carvings, personal decorations. Yet again, it sets going manufactures which were before impossible, from lack of a material fit for the requisite implements. And all these changes react on the people – increase their manipulative skill, their intelligence, their comfort, – refine their habits and tastes. (Spencer, 1864, p. 52)

From this and later examples, Spencer (1864, p. 55) inferred a widespread pattern of outcome, that is, that a developing society had been 'rendered more heterogeneous in virtues of the many new occupations introduced, and the many old ones further specialized' and that in areas which were already more heterogeneous, 'the results are in a yet higher degree multiplied in number and kind'.

More than a century later, Jan Lambooy similarly observed that

> specialization into complementary units creates a more stable structure and at the same time a more flexible one for adaptation to changing exogenous factors. In certain spatial entities in which specialization between complementary objects exists, it is, *ceteris paribus*, much easier to develop new specializations than in entities with the same population and a less diversified economic structure. Diversification and the possibility for specialization of the component parts

are highly correlated. In this case an analogy exists with biotic ecosystems in which mature entities are characterized by high levels of diversification and productivity, a low energy requirement for maintaining or expanding the system, and a high level of adaptability in response to changes. (Lambooy, 1973, pp. 149–50)

Although this was not their original goal, in the last two decades many analysts have provided much illustrative evidence of these processes through discussions of the development of localized exchanges of production residuals between geographically proximate and economically diverse factories and plants, or so-called 'industrial symbiosis' (Chertow, 2000; Ayres and Ayres, 2002; McManus and Gibbs, 2008). This line of research was originally triggered by the 'discovery' of numerous linkages of this type in the Danish city of Kalundborg. To summarize, the city and its surrounding region were recently hosts to numerous water (seven), energy (six) and solid waste (six) symbiotic relationships. Among other cases is a pipeline installed in 1972 that brought an excess amount of gas from the local oil refinery to a nearby plaster board factory to dry their production. Fly ash from a coal-fired power station is sold to cement companies. In 1976, managers at a local insulin and industrial enzymes plant began selling its sludge-like biomass made up of dead micro-organisms to local farmers for use as fertilizers. A few years later, power station employees got their hands on the refinery's spent cooling water when they needed to expand their operations.

The most relevant feature of the Kalundborg case for our purpose is that these developments resulted from decentralized entrepreneurial actions that built on readily existing industrial diversity. In each case, some local managers and entrepreneurs were confronted with a particular problem – either the (often costly) disposal of potentially valuable resources or the constant need for better and/or cheaper inputs – and saw opportunities in the diversified local economy to improve the competitive stance of their operations (Jacobsen and Anderberg, 2004; Jacobsen, 2006).

As knowledge about the Kalundborg case spread, later research uncovered similar spontaneous linkages in various regions of Europe and the United States (Wolf et al., 2007). Furthermore, because the incentives and conditions faced by Danish managers – the search for increased profitability and/or the necessity of removing nuisances to other parties while being located in a diverse economic setting – are probably as old as economic development itself, it is no surprise that historical evidence of the phenomenon is abundant (Simmonds, 1876; Koller, 1918; Kershaw, 1928; Lipsett, 1963). Interestingly, many early twentieth-century economic geographers addressed the issue through more or less detailed illustrations taken from a wide range of industries (Russell Smith, 1922; Galloway Keller and Longley Bishop, 1928; Weber, 1929; Whitbeck, 1929; Landon, 1939; Ostrolenk, 1941).

In the words of Keir (1919, pp. 39–40), large industrial operation often attracted 'plants whose business is the utilization of waste products. In order to insure a plentiful supply of raw material upon which to work, these shops must be where there are many factories creating the same sort of waste. For the factories, the presence of the waste-using shops turns a loss into a profit, a charge into a credit or a liability into an asset.' He further added: 'Whenever such waste-using plants appear, they add an increment to the importance of a locality as the center of an industry; for by transforming liabilities into assets, and turning costs into profits, they aid in the defense of the community against the onslaughts of outside competition. Hence they augment the growth of the industry in the location where it is already rooted.' He illustrated the regional nature of some of these processes through, among others, the cases of the cap shops of New York City that were usually located next door to clothing factories in order to have easy access to their remnants; a glue and mucilage manufacturer in Gloucester, Massachusetts, whose main supply was the heads and tails of fish in abundant supply in what was then one of the most important fishing ports in the world; and a great cement plant in Buffington, Indiana, that fed upon the slag of the largest steel mill in the United States located in the nearby town of Gary.

Interestingly, the observation of such linkages even led some economic geographers to anticipate the concept of 'industrial symbiosis'. The pioneer in this respect was Columbia's George T. Renner (Langdon White and Renner, 1936, p. 18), who further distinguished between 'disjunctive symbiosis', where 'unlike industries are situated within the same locality without there being any organic connection between them', and 'conjunctive symbiosis' where 'unlike industries exist together within an area because of organic relationship between them' (Langdon White and Renner, 1936, p. 18). The latter case included not only industries that existed side by side because one was the supplier of another or because they used a common source of raw materials, but also 'those industries which utilize waste products of other industries' (Langdon White and Renner, 1936, p. 18).

Industrial symbiosis provides a compelling illustration of the inherent benefits of local economic diversity in terms of generating new and different profitable entrepreneurial ventures that build on existing diverse activities, but in principle the same processes apply to almost any type of start-up activities that builds on urbanization economies. Perhaps just as fundamental in this context, but again less obvious to most observers, is the impact that a diversified local economy can have on nurturing the creative abilities of its inhabitants. While it is widely acknowledged that, even in this age of advanced communication technologies, urban agglomerations and their high population density are critical for creativity, the issue is either discussed in very broad terms, through assessments of the economic impact of specific 'creative industries', or more tangentially through the greater quality of life – and therefore greater appeal to highly mobile talent – that a thriving cultural scene gives to a specific location (Audretsch, 2003; Gertler, 2003; Stolarick and Florida, 2006). Local interactions between individuals with different expertise and modes of thought, we will now argue, should be given at least as much importance as these arguments in discussions of creative cities.

LOCAL DIVERSITY AND HUMAN CREATIVITY: THE CASE OF JACOBS EXTERNALITIES

In the last two decades, the argument that internally diverse regions are better incubators of innovative activities has been subsumed by growth economists under the label of 'Jacobs externalities', in reference to the work of urban theorist Jane Jacobs (1969) (Lucas, 1988; Glaeser et al., 1992). These researchers, however, have typically limited Jacobs's contribution to the diffusion of ideas across different lines of work in a diversified local economy, even though one could argue that her framework was broader and put much emphasis on the importance of traditional urbanization economies for entrepreneurial activities. There is, however, a general concern that the econometric studies that link together regional measures, like the degree of specialization and growth, do not yield any direct proof of the existence of these knowledge spillovers and thus that studies at a more individual level are desirable (Breschi and Lissoni, 2001; Hansen, 2002; Beaudry and Schiffauerova, 2009). Furthermore, it has often been pointed out that while regional specialization can afford many advantages to specific firms, both specialization and diversity have been found to have a positive effect on economic growth (Beaudry and Schiffauerova, 2009); economic diversity is not the absence of specialization, but rather the presence of multiple specializations based on comparative advantages at the individual or firm level (Wagner, 2000; Leppälä and Desrochers, 2010).

Be that as it may, the basic idea underlying 'Jacobs spillovers' as now understood in the economics literature is that the crucial externalities do not come from the reuse or diffusion of knowledge among immediate competitors, but rather from different lines of work altogether. The crucial insight in this case is therefore not that creative individuals are only found in economically diverse environments, but rather that in such an environment creative individuals are constantly faced with new problems and are given more opportunities to address them, including the possibilities of interacting more easily with people who possess different expertise than their own. These interactions take place at the individual level rather than between industries as such, and can be formal or informal, either within or between organizations.

Of course, the fact that all innovations are the result of new combinations of pre-existing and different know-how, skills, ideas, processes, materials and artefacts has long been known and discussed by students of human creativity and technological innovation (Desrochers, 2001). As Babbage (1832, p. 206) pointed out almost two centuries ago: 'The power of inventing mechanical contrivances, and of combining machinery, does not appear, if we may judge from the frequency of its occurrence, to be a difficult or a rare gift.' A century later, Carter (1939, p. 24) observed that 'one of the most frequent methods of employing inventive talent' is for an 'expert in one branch of technology [to] intelligently investigate another field with the objective of discovering some application for his specialized knowledge'. Barber (1952, p. 194) defined inventions as 'those imaginative combinations which men make of previously existing elements in the cultural heritage and which have emergent novelty as combinations'. According to Lampard (1955, p. 87), the 'mechanical inventions of the last two centuries . . . are a class of innovations representing new syntheses of technical and intellectual elements made available in the cultural stream of western Europe'. More recently, Fores (1979, p. 853) wrote that the main thrust of an engineer or a creative technician is 'to gather knowledge from diverse places in order to help solve technical problems'. In short, according to Berkun (2007, p. 92), 'no ideas are 100% new: they're all combinations of something and something'.

It is also generally admitted that multidisciplinary teams, by helping individuals overcome the blinders created by their particular expertise, most efficiently link concepts developed in one technology to problems arising in another (Schroeder et al., 1989). Brian Twiss thus explains:

> One of the reasons for the effectiveness of the multidisciplinary team is that it brings together people working within different mental constraints. An extreme case of this comes from a large

American research organization where one of the most creative members is a former theologian. Inevitably many of his ideas cannot be translated into practical terms, but, occasionally, however, he does come up with a proposal which would not have resulted from the normal thought processes of his technological colleagues and yet proves to be technically feasible. (Twiss, 1980, p. 69)

Not surprisingly in light of the importance of new combinations in any creative act, some social scientists have addressed the inter-industrial diffusion of technological knowhow through frameworks and concepts such as 'technological convergence', 'techno-economic paradigms', 'general purpose technologies' and 'recombinant growth' (Lipsey et al., 1998; Weitzman, 1998), while students of human creativity have written much on 'associative ability', 'bisociation', 'lateral thinking' and 'analogical reasoning', among others (Koestler 1969, de Bono, 1992; Weber and Perkins, 1992; Csikszentmihalyi, 1997; Sternberg, 1999; Berkun, 2007).

Conversely, the negative impact of a highly specialized local economy on the creative potential of its inhabitants was obvious to Malcolm Keir:

From the point of view of employees, [geographically specialized] localization is bad because it also tends toward narrowing the minds of the townspeople. A young man brought up in Fall River [Massachusetts], say, has but little choice of occupation; he must become a weaver or a loom-fixer or some other artisan connected with cotton manufacture, because by upbringing, education and example he is forced into that path, and furthermore he goes to work at an early age. It may happen that many a square peg is rammed into a round hole in this way, or a life constricted which might under better conditions have expanded. There is something deadening to the human mind in uniformity; progress comes through variation, therefore in a town of one industry a young man loses the stimulus for self-advancement. (Keir, 1919, p. 47)

Empirical studies that provide support for the connection between diversity and technological change are numerous (for example, Glaeser et al., 1992, Feldman and Audretsch, 1999). Nonetheless, due to their regional and aggregate perspective, they are unable to tell us why that is. In her original contribution, Jacobs (1969, p. 57) suggested more specifically that new goods or services are created after individuals have come up with new ideas that were suggested by (1) the materials or skills already being used or by (2) the particular problems encountered in the course of their work.

To gain a better understanding of the circumstances underlying these processes, we set out to study individual inventors in a 'population' whose propensity to move frequently between different lines of work and/or regularly borrow ideas from fields other than their own is well documented (Jewkes et al., 1969; Brown, 1988).

Our qualitative survey consisted of two rounds of semi-structured interviews covering the life history, formal education and training, work experience, creative thought processes and habits, and specific inventions of individuals based in Canada's two most economically diverse regions. The interviews were conducted face-to-face, recorded and transcribed. If needed afterwards, interviewees were contacted by phone or email to seek additional information or clarification. The first part of the survey was conducted between 1997 and 1999 and involved 45 inventors in southern Quebec. Forty-three out of the 45 interviewees were Francophone Canadians and, as can be expected, the majority of these individuals were, for linguistic reasons, reluctant to engage in any form of long-distance business relationships elsewhere in North America. The two English-speaking interviewees belonged to social and commercial networks whose geographical scale dwarfed anything observed among the rest of the sample. In order to gain further insight into this apparent discrepancy, another set of interviews was conducted between 2006 and 2009 with a group of 30 Anglophone Canadian inventors located in the province of Ontario.

The evidence presented in the remainder of this chapter is the result of a constant iterative process between scholarship and other literature, which helped sharpen lines of questioning and topics brought to light during the interviews. We are confident that, despite undeniable limits or local peculiarities, the evidence collected illustrates both the universality of human creative processes and the recurring problems faced by most individual inventors. Consequently, we identified three broad, although not mutually exclusive, sets of circumstances through which individuals found new uses or applications for existing products and created new combinations of existing products, processes and materials: (1) by adding to, switching or adapting specific know-how to other lines of work; (2) by observing something in another line of work and incorporating it into one's own line of work; and (3) through formal and informal multidisciplinary teams working towards the creation of new products and processes. The following will provide illustrative examples of these circumstances.

Adding to, Switching or Adapting Specific Know-how to Other Lines of Work

Benefiting from knowledge gained from previous jobs and tasks was one of the main knowledge spillover mechanisms we observed, as many inventors had very diverse professional backgrounds. A representative case is of an individual who had worked with electronics, digital devices, early IT and telephone technologies and eventually moved to other fields in search of new challenges. An industrial technician worked in the steel, chemical, aeronautical and armament industries before launching his own ceramic-making business. This widespread pattern of employment across different lines of work seems to be attributable at least in part to the fact that technically creative individuals tend to get bored very quickly with routine work.

Gaining knowledge from other lines of work need not always imply moving between firms, and therefore the mechanism is broader than job mobility as generally understood. Employees may acquire useful knowledge by moving between different divisions within a large firm or when a firm expands into new lines of business. Whatever the cause, however, this observed, widespread pattern of job mobility facilitates the spontaneous transfer of know-how across otherwise seemingly unrelated lines of work.

One interesting case involved the transfer of some basic know-how from the newspaper printing business to asphalt production. A recurring problem in the latter line of work was how to clean up residual asphalt found sticking inside tanks after long periods of inactivity. In a particular asphalt firm, people actually climbed in the tank to scrape the residual, a laborious and equipment-damaging process. After noticing this, an individual interviewee pointed out to his then new employer that, in the printing business where he was formerly employed, large tanks were cleaned by pouring hot water in them. Why couldn't a similar approach be tried in the asphalt tank? This technique was tried and proved successful, in the process saving a significant amount of resources.

Of course, in many cases, implementing know-how or ideas in new contexts would typically be but one step towards the creation of a new or improved product or process. Several other ideas as well as a significant amount of development work will also be required along the way.

Observing Know-how and Materials and Incorporating Them in a Different Production Setting

Sometimes observation and subsequent learning can be sufficient for the creation of inter-industrial knowledge spillovers. One such instance among our interviewees is a chemical engineer who once worked for a company with plants in remote locations. At the time, his employer needed to reduce his manpower, but was reluctant to do so in isolated plants for fear that employees working alone would be left unattended for several hours if hurt. This individual knew of devices that alerted emergency response personnel when a button was pushed, but this approach would obviously be inadequate if a worker was knocked unconscious. The engineer contacted a company supplying this service and requested that motion detectors be incorporated in their system so that an emergency call would automatically be placed if no motion was detected after a predetermined amount of time. As a result of this new combination, the company was able to save a considerable amount of money without risking the safety of its employees. An additional feature was then added to the system to allow it to work as a burglar alarm when activated by the employee. Our interviewee doesn't know if similar safety systems are now being used elsewhere, but an article on this particular invention was published in a trade magazine.

We documented numerous similar cases where an individual observed something new to him and incorporated it in the context of his previous expertise. For example, a shower brush was inspired by a car wash brush. A mouse pad arm rest was combined with an office chair after an individual had been inspired by some classroom furniture. A controllable sled was inspired in part by the movements of ice skates. A female inventor who set up a production shop for a new type of baby bag was inspired by the division of labour in a friend's restaurant kitchen. A device to conduct time studies drew on ideas from chess clocks, stop watches and computers, among others.

Multidisciplinary Team Made Up of Individuals Possessing Different Skills

One important role that firms have for technological development is that they are social environments where people with very different backgrounds can interact on a regular basis for the specific purpose of creating new combinations. From the perspective of one inventor interviewed: 'If you have experience with one thing, if you are inventor, this is very useful for you. But most useful thing from maybe . . . last five years was that I have knowledge, I receive knowledge from other people.' After having worked in a number of different firms and industries, he found that learning from colleagues with different skills significantly improved his creative capacities.

On other occasions though, multidisciplinary teams can be composed of individuals working for different employers and collaborating or providing input on a project, either formally or informally. Thus, the interaction can take place within inter-firm or social networks (Kogut, 2000; Balconi et al., 2004) as well as within intra-firm teams. Again, this basic insight has a long history. For example, John Stuart Mill (1848, Book

III, chapter XVII) considered the interaction among persons with dissimilar modes of thought and action one of the primary sources of progress.

One interesting case is a bicycle rack for domestic use. The inventor interviewed originally got the idea from a friend, who pointed out that no such thing existed yet. The reasons for this soon became obvious as the inventor began researching the topic. The rack needed to be light enough to be carried, heavy enough to hold the bicycles and prevent thefts, have a nice design, be maintenance-free and suitable for four bicycles (two adult and two children's bicycles), be they racing or mountain bikes. Finally, its price should not exceed 40 dollars. A metallic structure would have met most of these requirements, but would have been too heavy to carry. Aluminium was a lighter option, but was too expensive. The inventor then thought of using plastic, but realized quickly that it would be too light. He contacted an industrial draughtsman with whom he had worked with in the past on a specially designed water container for long-distance running. His former collaborator suggested that the rack should be made by blowing rather than casting (that is, filling a plastic mould) plastic. That way it would be empty inside, which would make it light enough to carry, but heavy enough to hold the bicycles in place after it was filled with water. This solution would finally prove to be the best one. Interestingly enough, although this solution could be seen *post facto* as a direct implementation of the main principle involved in their previous collaboration, the inventor still needed his previous collaborator to think of this approach.

CONCLUSION

Economically diversified cities and regions have long been recognized as being more resilient and offering more opportunities than less diverse settings. Despite the fact that specific materials, products and processes have always cut across 'industrial sectors', however, economic specialization has long been held by students of regional growth as the optimal economic setting to promote development and growth. One of the few authors to strongly dissent from that view is Jacobs (1969) who argues, among other things, that local diversity increases the probability of combining different resources. Further study of human creativity and the history of technology suggests that a diversified city is likely to facilitate the transfer of know-how from one area of industry to others that are unrelated in terms of the uses of the final products. By offering a greater number and variety of problems to be solved, as well as a much wider pool of expert knowledge and other resources, a diversified city can only increase the probabilities of new combinations. Of course, this interpersonal and interdisciplinary aspect of creativity has long made firms interested in promoting cross-functional new product teams (Song et al., 1997). A better understanding of the ways by which creative individuals combine existing resources in different configurations, however, requires that familiar research designs be reconsidered and at the very least supplemented by insights derived from fields that have until now been unrelated.

To what extent were the documented inventions then results of local economic diversity? Assessing the specific impact of large and diversified metropolitan areas on inter-industrial knowledge spillovers is not straightforward. In most cases, the new combinations we documented could probably have been developed in many other large urban agglomerations, especially when they were inspired by 'non-local' observations such as watching television or travelling. Nonetheless, the greater facility of face-to-face interaction between individuals possessing different expertise made possible by close physical proximity was made abundantly clear to us. The reasons given in this respect ranged from establishing trust to making sure that individuals with different expertise truly understood each other. Another recurring theme was, not surprisingly, that a large urban agglomeration provides many unplanned learning opportunities by spontaneously allowing creative individuals to observe processes and ways of doing things in different contexts. The main channel in this respect seems to be job mobility between different lines of work, a process that is obviously facilitated by the fact that a large and diverse metropolitan area gives creative individuals the possibility to do so without having to relocate their family or lose their friends and social networks. Admittedly, the expertise and capabilities possessed by an individual influence the number of possible job opportunities available to him. But while many companies are limited to a specific sector or a few end products, many capabilities are generic in nature and can be applied in many different contexts.

Regional scientists have long tended to look at local diversity in relative rather than absolute terms, a tendency which has persisted in the literature on Jacobs externalities (Glaeser et al., 1992). From the perspective of an economic agent, however, relative diversity is most certainly less relevant, inasmuch as an individual looking for useful know-how or inputs with which he is unfamiliar is more likely to find it in a large but relatively specialized city like Detroit rather than in a much smaller, but relatively more diversified, town. The size of the urban agglomeration is clearly a factor, since as Adam Smith long ago observed, the degree of sustainable specialization depends on the extent of the market. Therefore, large urban agglomerations can facilitate multiple specialized industries and yet not be dependent on any single one of them.

REFERENCES

Audretsch, D.B. (2003), 'Innovation and spatial externalities', *International Regional Science Review*, **26**, 167–74.
Ayres, R.U. and L.W. Ayres (2002), *A Handbook of Industrial Ecology*, Cheltenham, UK and Northampton, MA, USA: Edward Elgar Publishing.
Babbage, C. (1832), *On the Economy of Machinery and Manufactures* (2nd edn), London: Charles Knight, available at http://books.google.com/books?id=4QWZq4FDoH4C&source=gbs_navlinks_s (accessed 18 March 2011).
Balconi, M., S. Breschi and F. Lissoni (2004), 'Networks of inventors and the role of academia: an exploration of Italian patent data', *Research Policy*, **33**, 127–45.
Barber, B. (1952), *Science and the Social Order*, Glencoe, IL: Free Press.
Beaudry, C. and A. Schiffauerova (2009), 'Who's right, Marshall or Jacobs? The localization versus urbanization debate', *Research Policy*, **38**, 318–37.
Berkun, S. (2007), *The Myths of Innovation*, Sebastopol, CA: O'Reilly Media.
Breschi, S. and F. Lissoni (2001), 'Knowledge spillovers and local innovation systems: a critical survey', *Industrial and Corporate Change*, **10**, 975–1005.
Brown, K.A. (1988), *Inventors at Work: Interviews with 16 Notable American Inventors*, Redmond, WA: Tempus Book of Microsoft Press.
Carter, H.D. (1939), *If You Want to Invent*, New York, NY: Vanguard Press.
Chapman, K. (2005), 'From "growth centre" to "cluster": restructuring, regional development, and the Teesside chemical industry', *Environment and Planning A*, **37**(4), 597–615.
Chertow, M. (2000), 'Industrial symbiosis: literature and taxonomy', *Annual Review of Energy and the Environment*, **25**, 313–37.

Csikszentmihalyi, M. (1997), *Creativity. Flow and the Psychology of Discovery and Invention*, New York, NY: Harper Perennial.

de Bono, E. (1992), *Serious Creativity: Using the Power of Lateral Thinking to Create New Ideas*, New York, NY: Harper Business.

Desrochers, P. (2001), 'Local diversity, human creativity and technological innovation', *Growth and Change*, **32**, 369–94.

Desrochers, P. and S. Leppälä (2010), 'Industrial symbiosis: old wine in recycled bottles? Some perspective from the history of economic and geographical thought', *International Regional Science Review*, **33**, 338–61.

Feldman, M.P. and D.B. Audretsch (1999), 'Innovation in cities: science-based diversity, specialization and localized competition', *European Economic Review*, **43**, 409–29.

Fores, M. (1979), 'The history of technology: an alternative view', *Technology and Culture*, **20**(4), 853–60.

Galloway Keller, A. and A. Longley Bishop (1928), *Commercial and Industrial Geography* (revised edn), Boston, MA: Ginn and Company.

Gertler, M. (2003), 'Tacit knowledge and the economic geography of context, or the undefinable tacitness of being (there)', *Journal of Economic Geography*, **3**, 75–99.

Glaeser, E.L., H.D. Kallal, J.A. Scheinkman and A. Shleifer (1992), 'Growth in cities', *Journal of Political Economy*, **100**, 1126–52.

Hansen, N. (2002), 'Dynamic externalities and spatial innovation diffusion: implications for peripheral regions', *International Journal of Technology, Policy and Management*, **2**, 260–71.

Hoover, E.M. and F. Giarratani (1984), *An Introduction to Regional Economics* (3rd edn), New York, NY: Alfred A. Knopf, available at http://www.rri.wvu.edu/WebBook/Giarratani/chaptertwelve.htm (accessed 18 March 2011).

Jacobs, J. (1969), *The Economy of Cities*, New York, NY: Random House.

Jacobsen, N.B. (2006), 'Industrial symbiosis in Kalundborg, Denmark. A quantitative assessment of economic and environmental aspects', *Journal of Industrial Ecology*, **10**(1/2), 239–55.

Jacobsen, N.B. and S. Anderberg (2004), 'Understanding the evolution of industrial symbiotic networks', in J. van den Bergh and M.A. Janssen (eds), *Economics of Industrial Ecology: Materials, Structural Change, and Spatial Scales*, Cambridge, MA: MIT Press, pp. 313–35.

Jewkes, J., D. Sawers and R. Stillerman (1969), *The Sources of Invention* (2nd edn), London: Macmillan.

Keir, M. (1919), 'The localization of industry: how it starts; why it grows and persists', *The Scientific Monthly*, **8**(1), 32–48.

Kershaw, J.B.C. (1928), *The Recovery and Use of Industrial and Other Waste*, London: Ernest Benn.

Koestler, A. (1969), *The Act of Creation*, London: Hutchinson.

Kogut, B. (2000), 'The network as knowledge: generative rules and the emergence of structure', *Strategic Management Journal*, **21**, 405–25.

Koller, T. (1918), *The Utilization of Waste Products: A Treatise on the Rational Utilization, Recovery, and Treatment of Waste Products of all Kinds* (3rd revised edn), translated from the 2nd revised German edn, New York, NY: D. Van Nostrand, available at http://www.archive.org/details/utilizationofwas00kollrich.

Lambooy, J.G. (1973), 'Economic and geonomic space: some theoretical considerations in the case of urban core symbiosis', *Papers in Regional Science*, **31**(1), 145–58.

Lampard, E.E. (1955), 'The history of cities in the economically advanced areas', *Economic Development and Cultural Change*, **3**(1), 81–136.

Landon, C.E. (1939), *Industrial Geography*, New York, NY: Prentice-Hall.

Langdon White, C. and G.T. Renner (1936), *Geography: An Introduction to Human Ecology*, New York, NY: D. Appleton-Century.

Leppälä, S. and P. Desrochers (2010), 'The division of labor need not imply regional specialization', *Journal of Economic Behavior & Organization*, **74**, 137–47.

Lipsett, C. (1963), *Industrial Wastes and Salvage. Conservation and Utilization* (2nd edn), New York, NY: Atlas Publishing.

Lipsey, R.G., C. Bekar and K. Carlaw (1998), 'General purpose technologies: what requires explanation', in E. Helpman (ed.), *General Purpose Technologies and Economic Growth*, Cambridge, MA: MIT Press, pp. 15–54.

Lucas, R.E. (1988), 'On the mechanics of economic development', *Journal of Monetary Economics*, **22**, 3–42.

Marshall, A. (1920), *Principles of Economics* (8th edn), London: Macmillan.

McManus, P. and D. Gibbs (2008), 'Industrial ecosystems? The use of tropes in the literature of industrial ecology and eco-industrial parks', *Progress in Human Geography*, **32**, 525–40.

Mill, J.S. (1848), *Principles of Political Economy with Some of their Applications to Social Philosophy* (7th edn), London: Longmans, Green & Co., available at http://www.econlib.org/library/Mill/mlP.html (accessed 18 March 2011).

Ostrolenk, B. (1941), *Economic Geography*, Chicago, IL: Richard D. Irwin.

Polese, M. (2005), 'Cities and national economic growth: a reappraisal', *Urban Studies*, **42**, 1429–51.

Porter, M. (1990), *The Competitive Advantage of Nations*, London: Macmillan.

Rodríguez-Pose, A. and R. Crescenzi (2008), 'Mountains in a flat world: why proximity still matters for the location of economic activity', *Cambridge Journal of Regions, Economy and Society*, **1**, 371–88.

Rosenthal, S.S. and W. Strange (2004), 'Evidence on the nature and sources of agglomeration economies', in V. Henderson and J. Thisse (eds), *Handbook of Urban and Regional Economics*, Vol. 4, Amsterdam: Elsevier, pp. 2119–72.

Russell Smith, J. (1922), *Industrial and Commercial Geography*, New York, NY: Henry Holt & Company.

Schroeder, R.G., A.H. Van de Ven, G.D. Scudder and D. Polley (1989), 'The development of innovation ideas', in A.H. Van de Ven, H.L. Angle and M.S. Poole (eds), *Research on the Management of Innovation: The Minnesota Studies*, New York, NY: Harper and Row, pp. 107–34.

Simmonds, P.L. (1876), *Waste Products and Undeveloped Substances: A Synopsis of Progress Made in Their Economic Utilisation During the Last Quarter of a Century at Home and Abroad* (3rd edn), London: Hardwicke and Bogue.

Song, X.M., M.M. Montoya-Weiss and J.B. Schmidt (1997), 'Antecedents and consequences of cross-functional cooperation: a comparison of R&D, manufacturing, and marketing perspectives', *Journal of Product Innovation Management*, **14**, 35–47.

Spencer, H. (1864), *Illustrations of Universal Progress; A Series of Discussion*, New York, NY: D. Appleton and Company, available at http://books.google.ca/books?id=9QIMAAAAIAAJ&printsec=frontcover&dq=spencer+illustrations+of+universal+progress (accessed 18 March 2011).

Sternberg, R.J. (ed.) (1999), *Handbook of Creativity*, Cambridge: Cambridge University Press.

Stolarick, K. and R. Florida (2006), 'Creativity, connections and innovation: a study of linkages in the Montréal Region', *Environment and Planning A*, **38**, 1799–817.

Twiss, B.C. (1980), *Managing Technological Innovation*, London: Longman.

Wagner, J.E. (2000), 'Regional economic diversity: action, concept, or state of confusion', *Journal of Regional Analysis and Policy*, **30**, 1–22.

Weber, A. (1929), *Theory of the Location of Industries* (2nd edn), Chicago, IL: University of Chicago Press.

Weber, R.J. and D.N. Perkins (1992), *Inventive Minds: Creativity in Technology*, New York, NY: Oxford University Press.

Weitzman, M.L. (1998), 'Recombinant growth', *Quarterly Journal of Economics*, **113**, 331–60.

Wheeler, J.O., P.O. Muller, G.I. Thrall and T.J. Fink (1998), *Economic Geography*, Hoboken, NJ: Johh Wiley & Sons.

Whitbeck, R.H. (1929), *Industrial Geography: Production, Manufacture, Commerce*, New York, NY: American Book Company.

Wolf, A., M. Eklund and M. Söderström (2007), 'Developing integration in a local industrial system – an explorative approach', *Business Strategy and the Environment*, **16**(6), 442–55.

22 Does density matter?
Peter Gordon and Sanford Ikeda

Well-educated professionals and creative workers who live together in dense ecosystems, interacting directly, generate ideas and turn them into products and services faster than talented
people in other places can. (Richard Florida, 2009)

Since World War II, economic and demographic forces, possibly along with the consequences of earlier housing and infrastructural policies,[1] have flattened the population-
density gradient in metropolitan areas across the United States, while presumably
reducing the vitality and dense social networks associated with most traditional city
centres. In response, planning ideologies that are hostile to 'unplanned', low-density
development and that seek to promote high-density, pedestrian- and environmentally
friendly communities have been developed to combat these trends. But do scholars who
study cities even understand the nature of cities well enough to formulate policies that
impact cities in a positive way?

Economists do know that institutions matter, that human capital is important, and it
is almost a cliché that cities are 'engines of growth'. All three of these views are thought
to involve prompting the cultivation of ideas that contribute to entrepreneurship and
innovation. But is our understanding of the relationship among cities, human capital
and economic development sufficient to effectively guide top-down urban and regional
planning? We argue that the work of F.A. Hayek and Jane Jacobs strongly suggests the
answer is 'no'. Specifically, studies at the metro level that purport to show a positive correlation between density and economic growth, and between density and the migration
patterns of creative types, do not stand up to closer examination. But this is not to deny
that density, creativity and economic development are linked, and we offer a different
way of looking at density, 'Jacobs density', that is more helpful in highlighting the limits
of conventional land-use planning. We also argue that Hayek-Jacobs knowledge problems prevent even well-intentioned planners from solving many of the problems, some
of their own making, that plague many central cities. In this light, reliance on entrepreneurial solutions, emerging from congenial micro-environments, offer the best hope for
confronting urban land-use questions.

The outline of our chapter is as follows. We begin by briefly discussing how spontaneous or unplanned orders, such as cities and related institutions, remedy the so-called
knowledge problem without recourse to top-down direction. Next, we discuss the ways
in which 'smart growth' and some of the policies of New Urbanism, by failing to appreciate the nature of living cities as spontaneous orders,[2] at least to the extent that Jacobs
does, tend to adopt such a top-down approach in their land-use policies. We then offer
a different way of looking at density that implies a significantly less aggregated measure
of density, one that we feel is more consistent with the Hayek-Jacobs approach. Using
Public Use Microdata Sample (PUMS) data from the American Community Survey, we
re-examine the correlations between density and economic growth. Given the severity of

the knowledge problem, and thus what we don't know about the relation between human capital, cities and economic growth, we argue that economic growth is best facilitated by enabling the formation of 'congenial micro-environments', and that these cannot be the result of top-down planning. Finally, we offer some closing thoughts.

ORGANIZATION, CITIES AND EMERGENT ORDER

The role of organizations is fairly well understood, although much of economic activity involves building 'organizational capital' rather than 'widgets' (Kling, 2009). Moreover, there are other 'shells' involved in production. The built environment, meaning structures and their relations in urban space, is an obvious example. The nature of urban form has been studied for many years, giving rise to a rich set of ideas and hypotheses. But the interaction question we pose above – regarding cities, human capital and growth – is not easily treated via the canonical spatial equilibrium model of urban economics.[3]

On the other hand, from Adam Smith to F.A. Hayek and Jane Jacobs, from the Invisible Hand to the Emergent Order, economists have developed and honed the idea that the bottom-up flow of information facilitates social co-operation and co-ordination in markets and, in particular, in cities. This result remains counter-intuitive to many, who associate order with top-down control and are not ready to part with the idea that cities require some sort of top-down planning.[4] Urbanization does bring with it the potential for externalities and co-ordination problems, and an emphasis on these problems has pushed many analysts towards advocacy of strict land-use controls. But it is also true that many externality and co-ordination problems are resolved in land markets while others are resolved via private planning.

We are not, of course, the first to suggest that cities are spontaneous spatial orders (Jacobs, 1961, 1969; Webster and Lai, 2003). Cities have been recognized as places where entrepreneurial discoveries, transaction-cost economies and many potential positive externalities can be realized. Indeed, the popularity of the writings of Jane Jacobs (among others) has prompted the recognition that spatial arrangements can emerge that cause the positive externalities (agglomeration economies) to dominate, so that it is possible to see cities as an emergent spatial order whereby flexible land markets facilitate favourable spatial arrangements.

Jacobs (1961), for example, analyses how the character of public spaces can help or hinder the emergence of safety and the kind of land-use diversity that is the foundation for entrepreneurial discovery, especially in large cities. The object is to place 'eyes on the street' in large numbers around the clock so that people feel secure enough in public, where the majority of users are strangers to one another, to have the kind of informal contact that forms what Mark Granovetter (1973) terms 'weak ties' – the indispensible conduits through which knowledge of profit opportunities are transmitted. And this is achieved by allowing public spaces to create a diversity of interesting destinations, what Jacobs termed 'primary uses', to attract people from outside the locality into the district or neighbourhood and to encourage the population density to support this volume of traffic.

But such attractors presuppose that owners have the economic freedom to adjust land uses to unexpected changes in the socio-economic environment. That is, under normal circumstances local rules need to be flexible enough to enable owners to do this, even if it means a drastic departure from traditional uses or scales of operation. Converting old factories into mixed-use residential shopping centres is one common example, but razing a historic shopping district and erecting an office complex in its place is another, keeping in mind that both the factory and the stores were quite possibly in their own day considered by some to represent sharp breaks with past uses. It is all part and parcel of the competitive 'gales of creative destruction' at the heart of 'living cities',[5] which can be seen as a process in which entrepreneurs – both social and economic – cast aside established social ties in favour of newer, more profitable ones.

Again, in this light Jacobs (1961) – with her emphasis on the micro-foundations of cities – is remarkably similar to the ideas of Hayek with respect to how complex social networks emerge spontaneously to handle and cultivate dispersed local knowledge and human capital.[6] As human capital is widely recognized as the key to economic development, the main question involves identifying the spatial arrangements where it thrives through interaction and communication via social networks. This, however, does not favour centralized decision-making.

Top-down governmental planning at the local level is hobbled by the well-known limitations of central planning (Mises [1922]1981; Hayek [1945]1948): top-down planners have no way to tap into dispersed local knowledge, what Jacobs (1961) refers to as 'locality knowledge', and their actions are prone to politicization. In this way, private, non-governmental responses to collective action and public-good problems are instructive. For example, the fact that most Americans have the bulk of their assets (about two-thirds on average) tied up in their home has itself stimulated a demand for rules of neighbourhood land use and neighbourhood change, and so it is now standard practice in many places for developers to attach homeowner associations (HOAs) along with detailed governance documents to their residential developments (Nelson, 2005).

Of course, such rules can come from city councils and zoning boards as well as from developers, but some scholars have pointed to a recent trend in the form of the emergence of 'homevoter cities', typically small suburban municipalities with governments that are devoted to the maintenance of residential property values (Fischel, 2001), which in effect has blurred the distinctions between HOAs and homevoter cities. It is unclear that the differences are significant.[7] Suffice it to say that each emerges in response to a demand for property rights clarity. Each governance arrangement offers a trade-off of rights surrendered for protections gained; each of which are subject to competitive pressures, suggesting that market forces vet the trade-offs. This process can be seen as bottom-up planning, which is a source of flexibility as we have been discussing it.

But there is much more. Developers of shopping malls (and other planned unit developments) carefully plan and design all aspects, including use arrangements and common areas and facilities, to maximize rental incomes. This is simply planning in the pursuit of profit, benefiting from trial and error and very much dependent on local knowledge. It is a key aspect of what we may call bottom-up planning in order to highlight contrasts with the conventional association of 'planning' with a top-down activity. The usefulness of bottom-up planning could be enhanced if top-down planning were left as the default, where private planning is least likely, perhaps as a 'governance of last resort'. Randall Holcombe (2004) suggests such an approach. The actual division of responsibility between top-down and bottom-up planning would differ from place to place, although there are now significant efforts to strengthen the top-down role, in the name of 'sustainability' (Utt, 2009).

SMART GROWTH, DENSITY AND ALL THAT

Still, it is interesting that policy movements not known for their libertarianism, such as 'smart growth', 'new urbanism', 'sustainable development' and 'livable communities' now claim Jane Jacobs as their own. Indeed, Jacobs's once-controversial ideas seem to have become the new orthodoxy, including her emphasis on the importance of population density, and today's conventional planning employs the concepts of 'pedestrian-friendliness', 'diversity' and 'mixed use' as though they were taking their cue from Jacobs. Their interpretations of these concepts, however, tend to be off the mark.

DENSITY OR DIVERSITY?

In the present discussion, it is crucial to understand that for Jacobs high population density is important because it helps to generate land-use diversity, and diversity in turn is the key factor in fuelling dynamic economic development. That is, density alone is not sufficient to generate economic development or land-use diversity. If it could, county prisons or the streets around Yankee Stadium as fans crowd into and out of games would be economically diverse and dynamic places – they are not. The former is not dynamic for obvious reasons while the latter lacks dynamism because it fails to provide the foundation for dynamic long-term growth, although it may sustain businesses such as baseball cap and hotdog sales.

At the same time, long-term growth cannot take place without relatively high levels of population density. This is not only to generate high levels of demand for local products and services, but more importantly, again, to encourage 'eyes on the street' in high concentrations at various times of the day, promote security, and the formation of social networks (Granovetter, 1973) and social capital. These constitute the foundations of great cities, according to Jacobs, because they facilitate the informal flows of knowledge that entrepreneurs use to appropriately adjust land uses. Sustaining this diversity requires more economic activity than local residents can provide, which is why the ability to attract people, via primary uses, from outside the immediate area is so important for long-term development.

As areas grow economically, whether downtowns or suburbs, local population density rises, and as areas decline (again, whether downtown or suburbs), density falls. There is positive feedback as the expectation of economic opportunity in an area itself acts as an attractor.[8] People then attract more people, and this tends to create more economic opportunities, which in turn increases density.[9]

PRIMACY OF DIVERSITY

For Jacobs, 'diversity' refers mainly to the uses of public space.[10] We have already noted how population density is but one of the factors that Jacobs identified as 'generators of diversity', and that her primary concern was with diversity rather than density per se, and with how density and diversity work together to promote the foundations of long-term entrepreneurial development. Diversity for her is diversity of land use, especially diversity in primary uses/attractors into a given area, as well as in the form of special-ized shops (for example, the Tokyo electronics district, *Akihabara*). This is 'supply-side diversity'.

Although not the same as ethnic diversity, but related to it, is an equally important 'demand-side diversity', or a diversity in tastes. Jacobs (1969) argues that in order to sustain a diversity of uses that generate products on the supply side, there needs also to be a diversity of tastes to consume them. Fortunately, because great cities – cities with, say, populations in excess of one million – tend to attract misfits from smaller communi-ties, one tends to find in them a disproportionately wide range of backgrounds and tastes as compared with smaller cities and towns. The consumers of unusual products can reside in other cities, of course, but selling to consumers locally entails lower transaction costs, especially, again, in a dense urban environment, and demand-side diversity makes that possible.

As noted, one of the conditions Jacobs mentions for generating land-use diversity is that lively neighbourhoods need 'two or more primary uses' in order to encourage people to spend time in public space (for example, on sidewalks, roads and plazas) at dif-ferent times of the day. This sounds similar to what developers and planners today call 'mixed uses', but Jacobs (1961) emphasizes that the uses in question be unique enough to attract people from outside the locality, which is why she distinguishes them from what she terms 'secondary diversity' – restaurants, dry cleaners, grocery stores – that merely service the people brought into an area by the primary uses (such as apartments, schools, office buildings, concert halls and notable restaurants).

Moreover, while there may be some justification for contemporary planners to describe planned developments that combine retail, entertainment, residential and commercial uses as 'mixed use', the kind of diversity Jacobs sees as characteristic of long-term economic vitality is largely, though perhaps not exclusively, the result of an 'organic' process, typically small scale and at the level of the individual entrepreneur (although she didn't object to large-scale development per se). Today, developers and smart-growth planners, inspired by New Urbanism,[11] seem to want to skip the organic, evolutionary process and instead construct what they regard as the ideal outcome of that process. While some of these developments are small scale, many are very large-scale developments (for example, Hudson Yards in New York or 'lifestyle communities') that purport to take advantage of the traditional downtown aesthetic. Many appear to be successful up to a point.

But as Jacobs points out, building on a large scale in a given location not only imposes a deadening visual homogeneity, but also a homogeneity in the age of buildings (Jacobs, 1961, chapters 10 and 19). New buildings require higher rents to cover construction costs compared with more aged buildings. Thus, what large-scale projects lack are cheap spaces in which to experiment with new ideas. Jacobs famously argued that 'new ideas need old buildings' because aged or run-down buildings represent cheap space for new, typically young and relatively cash-poor, entrepreneurs to experiment and, importantly, to fail without courting financial disaster. Unfortunately you can't build old buildings, which are the 'naturally subsidized spaces' of economic development.[12] These problems are multiplied when it comes to public-private 'mega-projects'. The combination of new construction over a very large area with homogeneous architecture (even when several architects are employed) rules out the kind of 'old buildings' (or their equivalent) that can serve as incubators of entrepreneurship. While their high-priced spaces may sell, mixed use or not, their prospects as engines of future economic growth are dim.[13]

WALKABILITY

Pedestrian-friendliness is another lesson smart growth and New Urbanism seem to have drawn from Jacobs. Yet, making an existing area or a new development 'pedestrian-friendly' is a virtue only insofar as people have somewhere interesting to go. Living cities are not full of pedestrians; they are full of people who are going somewhere. Mega-project developers often tout parks, sports complexes or esplanades that will give people a place to go, but the really interesting aspects of cities are the unplanned niches that appear in the interstices of someone's grand plan – the space between the buildings. Otherwise the result is places that have the feeling of a 'Disneyland' – nice places to visit but they lack the kind of real economic opportunity that comes with spontaneous diversity.

In sum, too many of those who claim Jacobs as a major influence have missed the spontaneous order message (Jacobs, 1961, chapter 22) and have instead interpreted her descriptions of successful living cities more prescriptively than she intended.

DENSITY, JACOBS AND DEVELOPMENT

Urbanization and economic development facilitate each other. Investigators study the nature of cities to identify which attributes make a difference – and how. But there is no agreement on what and how to measure. As an indicator of success, many have settled on some measure of city growth as the dependent variable. But what about the explanatory variables? How do we describe the nature of these cities and their built environment? Urban economists have looked for correlations between population (or employment) densities and growth – or with enhanced productivity or inventiveness. But this approach is undermined by the fact that average densities over large geographical areas mask considerable variation. Some authors even use a state's proportion of urbanized population as a proxy for density. But even the measurements well below the state level are inadequate. The Los Angeles urbanized area (Census definition) has had a higher average population density than the New York urbanized area since at least 1990, but this comparison is an artefact of the boundaries chosen. One can easily identify central areas of both urbanized areas such that New York has the higher density. But there is no science to guide the choice of boundaries. Table 22.1 summarizes recent research on this topic and highlights the geographical areas that investigators have studied.

All of these areas are too large. Their average densities tell us very little. Whereas the importance of human capital to economic growth is well known, and whereas the importance of urbanization is also clear, it is much more difficult to identify simple relationships between these two phenomena. We are unconvinced by the simple 'density' and human capital relationships suggested by the authors cited in Table 22.1.

Urban economists, including those who study creativity, simply define density as 'number of persons per square area' per time period. There are at least two problems with measures of this kind. First, as Jacobs (1961, p. 205) points out, it is easy using

Table 22.1 Density research

Authors	Year	Brief title	Publication	Density measure
Glaeser and Resseger	2010	The complementarity between cities and skills	*Journal of Regional Science*	State population density
Abel, Dey and Gabe	2010	Productivity and the density of human capital	Federal Reserve Bank of New York Staff Report	Metropolitan area weighted average of constituent counties' population densities
Decker, Thompson and Wohar	2009	Determinants of state labour productivity	*Journal of Regional Analysis and Policy*	Share of state population in metropolitan areas
Mcgranahan and Wojan	2007	Recasting the creative class to examine growth processes in rural and urban counties	*Regional Studies*	County population density
Knudsen, Florida, Gates and Stolarick	2007	Urban density, creativity and innovation	Unpublished	Metropolitan area population density
Gabe, Kolby and Bell	2007	The effects of workforce creativity on earnings in US counties	*Agricultural and Resource Economics Review*	County population density
Bettencourt, Lobo and Strumsky	2007	Invention in the city: increasing returns to scale in metropolitan patenting	*Research policy*	Metropolitan area density of network connections
Acs and Armington	2004	Employment growth and entrepreneurial activity in cities	*Regional Studies*	Labour market area establishment density
Carlino, Chatterjee and Hunt	2001	Knowledge spillovers and the new economy of cities	Federal Reserve Bank of Philadelphia Working Paper	Metropolitan area employment density
Glaeser, Kolko and Saiz	2001	Consumer city	*Journal of Economic Geography*	City population density
Glaeser and Shapiro	2001	Is there a new urbanism?	NBER Working Paper	City population density
Harris and Ionnades	2000	Productivity and metropolitan density	Unpublished	Metropolitan area population
Ciccone and Hall	1996	Productivity and the density of economic activity	NBER Working Paper	County population density

this approach to conflate high density with 'overcrowding', where the latter is based on 'number of persons per room per dwelling'. Thus, critics of density will point to poor, typically overcrowded cities with high density but low measured development to refute the density-development nexus. Indeed, overcrowding in this sense does occur in very low-income areas and does not promote economic development. But note that very high population density is consistent with the absence of overcrowding (for example, the

Upper East Side is one of the densest districts in New York City) and overcrowding is consistent with low population density (for example, Appalachia). In fact, rising density and economic prosperity go hand in hand, even in the suburbs, towards which it is well documented that economic activity has been shifting since at least World War II. That is, while the population-density gradient has been flattening – especially in the United States – in the past half-century, the right-hand side of the gradient, where economic activity has been shifting, has been rising as the left-hand side has been falling. In this way, high and rising densities, without overcrowding, may still be an indicator of prosperity.

But, second, we have already noted how the areas that form the denominator of the density ratio are typically far too large and fail to capture important differences at the neighbourhood level, especially where, as has been the case in post-World War II urban development, cities have multiple 'employment sub-centres'.[14] Typical measures cast too wide a net to capture meaningful relationships. One way to take these concerns into account is simply to select as a denominator the smallest areal unit for which credible recent data are available. American Community Survey data for the PUMS areas (PUMAs) refer to the smallest such areal unit in the United States, since the database incorporates areas that are significantly smaller and far less aggregated than the usual metropolitan or urbanized area measures.

NEIGHBOURHOOD DENSITIES AND HUMAN CAPITAL: THE DATA

In defence of the authors cited in Table 22.1, data for sub-city units are not easily found. For example, economic data for downtowns (Central Business Districts, CBDs) are hard to come by because there are no official or widely agreed on definitions, although there are some employment as well as employment density data for the 50 largest CBDs at *Demographia* (http://www.demographia.com/db-cbd2000.pdf). We also have 50-year (1950–2000) population growth rates for 46 of the 50 surrounding urbanized areas and find that the correlation between CBD job density and urbanized area growth was −0.26. The importance of strong downtowns is seemingly not a driver of growth.[15]

Therefore, in an effort to study the effects of population density at the level of the smallest geographical units for which we could find useful and near-recent data, we analysed the American Community Survey (ACS) migration data for 2005 (5 per cent sample). These are reported for areas as small as the PUMAs which are the closest spatial units we have that might approximate neighbourhoods (Murphy, 2007). In 2005, there were 2077 of them in the United States (excluding Alaska), of which 1722 were in metropolitan areas. Their minimum size is 100 000 inhabitants and their average population was just over 145 000. The PUMA-level migration data most useful for us involve moves between PUMAs, which accounted for 79 per cent of all (within one year) movers. The highest education level recorded in this file is MA+ (holders of all Masters and professional degrees and higher).

Table 22.2 shows the top 25 PUMAs in terms of MA+ arrivals. Substantial human capital (as measured by people with advanced degrees) can be seen to migrate to parts of Manhattan as well as to areas such as Silicon Valley. These people are seemingly attracted to opportunities found in 'low-density' as well as in 'high-density' places. Four

Table 22.2   Top 25 destination PUMAs of MA+ degree holders

Rank	State	County	PUMA	Area sq km	Population	Density (population/ square mile)	Total arrivals	MA+ arrivals
1	NY	New York	3806	12	216899	17408	26547	11188
2	NY	New York	3805	8	214455	27319	26743	10781
3	VA	Fairfax; Fairfax City; Falls Church City	305	304	264375	870	36021	9351
4	CA	Santa Clara	2701	258	185680	720	35747	8947
5	MD	Montgomery	1004	155	174117	1125	25684	7830
6	IL	Cook	3510	29	150243	5138	33549	7692
7	DC	District of Columbia	105	28	108693	3855	29097	7323
8	DC	District of Columbia	101	39	104343	2666	24272	7303
9	IL	Cook	3502	17	151344	9041	45236	7100
10	WA	King	2002	143	149639	1048	35843	7098
11	NY	New York	3810	17	147115	8825	28854	6904
12	VA	Arlington	100	67	199697	2965	26718	6837
13	CA	Los Angeles	6125	73	224065	3091	33149	6677
14	CA	San Diego	8101	135	249239	1845	68744	6649
15	MA	Boston City	3302	31	141566	4496	34165	6427
16	CA	Santa Clara	2703	129	122524	948	30731	6229
17	TX	Harris	4607	85	143399	1678	36193	6122
18	NY	New York	3807	7	131322	18014	21907	6094
19	TX	Hays; Travis	5304	175	162872	930	45451	5936
20	TX	Harris	4604	49	144982	2963	42617	5873
21	CA	Alameda	2409	112	184025	1645	25773	5661
22	CA	Los Angeles	5411	42	185997	4398	37467	5602
23	MD	Montgomery	1003	115	173551	1511	35605	5494
24	CA	Santa Clara	2702	44	144337	3281	26763	5476
25	TX	Hays; Travis	5303	187	194399	1039	42008	5443

of the top 25 (out of 2069 areas included after discarding ones with only partial data) were in Manhattan and four of the top 25 were in Silicon Valley; other top 25 destinations included West Los Angeles and suburban Washington, DC, suburban Seattle, Boston, suburban Chicago, Austin and San Diego. The densest receiving area (in Manhattan) was 38 times as dense as the most spread out (in Silicon Valley, California), yet each one succeeded in attracting highly educated (and presumably creative) people. Note that the sizes of areas in Table 22.2 vary from below ten square kilometres (in Manhattan) to one just over 300 square kilometres (in the Washington, DC suburbs) and one just over 250 square kilometres (in Silicon Valley). Even density at the PUMA level is apparently a poor predictor of the arrival of highly educated migrants.

We can look further by starting with an inspection of simple correlations in Table 22.3. These show correlations over the set of all 'metropolitan' US PUMAs, and suggest some

Table 22.3   Density/migration correlation matrices; metropolitan PUMAs in the United States and nine US Census Divisions

All metropolitan PUMAs, N=1720

	Total in	BA	MA+	Artists and entertainers
Area density	0.0142	0.1322	0.1805	0.2534
Area size (sq km)	−0.0894	−0.0960	−0.0934	−0.0400
Area population	0.4666	0.2795	0.2111	0.1800

(a)   New England (Census Division 1) metropolitan PUMAs, N=97

	Total in	BA	MA+	Artists and entertainers
Area density	0.6572	0.5794	0.4312	0.3568
Area size (sq km)	−0.0732	−0.0462	−0.0351	−0.0522
Area population	0.0175	−0.0096	0.0424	0.0159

(b)   Mid-Atlantic (Census Division 2) metropolitan PUMAs, N=273

	Total in	BA	MA+	Artists and entertainers
Area density	0.1448	0.2590	0.2810	0.4079
Area size (sq km)	−0.2828	−0.2528	−0.1995	−0.1946
Area population	0.4839	0.2537	0.2588	0.1019

(c)   East North-Central (Census Division 3) metropolitan PUMAs, N=266

	Total in	BA	MA+	Artists and entertainers
Area density	0.3749	0.3268	0.3084	0.2833
Area size (sq km)	−0.2644	−0.1345	−0.1489	−0.0974
Area population	0.3986	0.3329	0.2823	0.2835

(d)   West North-Central (Census Division 4) metropolitan PUMAs, N=93

	Total in	BA	MA+	Artists and entertainers
Area density	0.3779	0.4008	0.3876	0.3600
Area size (sq km)	−0.3109	−0.2731	−0.1737	−0.2500
Area population	0.2661	0.0961	−0.0221	0.0087

(e)   South Atlantic (Census Division 5) metropolitan PUMAs, N=318

	Total in	BA	MA+	Artists and entertainers
Area density	0.1560	0.1660	0.2318	0.2613
Area size (sq km)	−0.3685	−0.2848	−0.2317	−0.1763
Area population	0.3014	0.2698	0.2108	0.1540

(f) East South-Central (Census Division 6) metropolitan PUMAs, N=81

	Total in	BA	MA+	Artists and entertainers
Area density	0.5333	0.3245	0.2148	0.3809
Area size (sq km)	−0.5097	−0.3901	−0.2870	−0.2361
Area population	0.3615	0.3100	0.3772	0.0132

(g) West South-Central (Census Division 7) metropolitan PUMAs, N=187

	Total in	BA	MA+	Artists and entertainers
Area density	0.3498	0.2432	0.3063	0.1981
Area size (sq km)	−0.3480	−0.2858	−0.2730	−0.1917
Area population	0.5928	0.5026	0.3627	0.3128

(h) Mountain (Census Division 8) metropolitan PUMAs, N=112

	Total in	BA	MA+	Artists and entertainers
Area density	0.3016	0.0697	0.0473	0.0638
Area size (sq km)	−0.2718	−0.2054	−0.2187	−0.0004
Area population	0.4920	0.2072	0.1876	0.1898

(i) Pacific[a] (Census Division 9) metropolitan PUMAs, N=293

	Total in	BA	MA+	Artists and entertainers
Area density	−0.1619	0.0848	0.0295	0.2111
Area size (sq km)	−0.0338	−0.1785	−0.1488	−0.0702
Area population	0.6351	0.1430	0.1186	0.1719

Note: [a]Excludes Alaska.

of the complexity. We added data on migrants in PUMS occupation group 2600 ('Arts, design, entertainment, sports, and media occupations') as a proxy for people doing 'creative' work (an idea popularized by Richard Florida (2002) and others). The correlation between PUMA density and arrivals of 'creative' people was 0.25. But it was lower for the MA+ arrivals (0.18), even lower for arrivals with BA or BS degrees (0.13) and negligible for all arrivals (0.01). Nevertheless, one could argue that there were intriguing differences in the propensity to move to the denser places. But when we conduct the same analysis at the level of the nine Census Divisions (Table 22.3a–i) even this pattern disappears. For Divisions 1, 3, 6, 7 and 8 the correlations of density with arrivals are highest for all arrivals while for Divisions 2, 5 and 9 they are highest for 'creative' people; for Division 4, the highest correlation is for the BA holders. And magnitudes of the correlations vary greatly among the Divisions.

We can go a step further via multiple regressions. Tables 22.4 shows estimation results

Table 22.4   *PUMA in-migration as a function of population density, population, per capita income and census division; metropolitan PUMAs in the United States*

Independent variables	(a) Linear function			(b) Logarithmic function		
	coefficient	*t*-value	p-value	coefficient	*t*-value	p-value
Constant	16791			5.2039		
		Linear effects			Logarithmic effects	
PUMA density	0.2008	2.46	0.014	0.1299	15.32	0.000
Metropolitan population	$-4*10^{-6}$	−0.70	0.486	−0.0261	−2.77	0.006
Metropolitan per capita income	0.4248	6.81	0.000	0.4546	5.28	0.000
			Dummy variables			
New England	32531	5.95	0.000	1.6743	5.98	0.000
Mid-Atlantic	−14785	−12.54	0.000	−0.8664	−14.51	0.000
East North-Central	−9752	−8.54	0.000	−0.5681	−9.7	0.000
West North-Central	−10076	−7.29	0.000	−0.5069	−7.17	0.000
South Atlantic	−7340	−6.53	0.000	−0.3921	−6.83	0.000
East South-Central	−8890	−6.22	0.000	−0.4638	−6.34	0.000
West South-Central	−2072	−1.72	0.086	−0.1543	−2.48	0.013
Mountain	−530	−3.73	0.000	−0.0316	−4.53	0.000
R-squared	0.2113			0.3468		

Note: *N*=1719.

for a migration model for all 2005 (inter-PUMA) migrants – in raw data ((a) in Table 22.4) as well as in log-transformed form (all but dummy variables are logs) ((b) in Table 22.4). The model's explanatory variables are the population density of the receiving PUMA, the size (population) and per capita income of the metropolitan area surrounding that PUMA as well as dummy variables for the nine Census Divisions (Pacific, Division 9, is the reference area). The metropolitan area descriptors are included for the obvious reason that geographic context matters a great deal. All the independent variables are significant with the expected signs. People prefer to move to dense PUMAs located in high-income but small metropolitan areas; they prefer New England or the Pacific. The long-standing frostbelt-to-sunbelt migration is only partly in evidence.

Interestingly, this model breaks down when we use it to predict in-migration of our subgroups, those with BAs or with MA+ training or in the entertainment (ENT) occupations (Table 22.5 (a and b)); the model's explanatory power and the elasticities with respect to destination densities are much lower. The highly trained and the creative movers seemingly make more idiosyncratic choices than the general population.

More than one researcher has shown that the established universities are now the magnets for enterprises that employ creative people (see, for example, Anselin et al., 1997). But prominent universities are not quickly or easily created. This suggests that such magnets cannot be easily manufactured via policy measures, as Florida's idea suggests.

Table 22.5   PUMA in-migration of degree holders and artists/entertainers

(a)   As a linear function of PUMA density and other factors

Group	BA holders		MA+ holders		Artists/entertainers	
Variables	coefficient	t-value	coefficient	t-value	coefficient	t-value
Constant	−870		−1170		45	
PUMA density	0.082*	4.44	0.057*	5.45	0.033*	9.47
Metropolitan population	$3.56*10^{-7}$	0.31	$-4.84*10^{-7}$	−0.75	$6.65*10^{-7}*$	3.10
Metropolitan per capita income	0.182*	12.94	0.107*	13.41	0.012*	4.51
			Dummy variables			
New England	3789*	3.07	1484	2.12	454	1.96
Mid-Atlantic	−2075*	−7.79	−730*	−4.85	−197*	−3.94
East North-Central	−1256*	−4.87	−429*	−2.94	−146*	−3.02
West North-Central	−805	−2.58	−592*	−3.35	−87	−1.49
South Atlantic	−867*	−3.41	−208	−1.45	−69	−1.46
East South-Central	−1112*	−3.45	−337	−1.85	−142	−2.35
West South-Central	−438	−1.61	−158	−1.03	−51	−1.00
Mountain	−101*	−3.14	−32	−1.76	−3	−0.53
R-squared	0.1493		0.1486		0.1130	

Note: $N=1719$; $*p < 0.01$.

(b)   As a logarithmic function of PUMA density and other factors

Group	BA holders		MA+ holders		Artists/entertainers	
Variables	coefficient	t-value	coefficient	t-value	coefficient	t-value
Constant	−12.0109		−18.0064		−17.8771	
PUMA density (log)	0.1056*	6.41	0.0901*	3.56	0.2886*	6.96
Metropolitan population (log)	−0.0653*	−3.56	−0.0770*	−2.74	−0.0557	−1.21
Metropolitan per capita income (log)	2.0181*	12.06	2.5370*	9.87	2.1979*	5.22
			Dummy variables			
New England	2.1657*	3.98	3.0167*	3.61	5.0507*	3.69
Mid-Atlantic	−0.8744*	−7.53	−0.7762*	−4.35	−1.4858*	−5.09
East North-Central	−0.6846*	−6.01	−0.7833*	−4.48	−1.4698*	−5.13
West North-Central	−0.4274*	−3.11	−0.9819*	−4.65	−1.2622*	−3.65
South Atlantic	−0.4141*	−3.71	−0.3853	−2.25	−0.7155	−2.55
East South-Central	−0.5858*	−4.12	−0.5912*	−2.71	−1.0939*	−3.06
West South-Central	−0.4119*	−3.40	−0.4186	−2.25	−0.8278*	−2.72
Mountain	−0.0441*	−3.25	−0.0597*	−2.87	−0.0557	−1.63
R-squared	0.1711		0.1005		0.1023	

Note: $N=1719$; $*p < 0.01$.

While we believe that these findings cast serious doubt on the usefulness of stand-ard measures of density, they do not contradict the relation between development and density, *rightly understood.*

As we have seen, for Jacobs population density is important because it fosters the informal contact that creates complex social networks, the matrix of economic develop-ment, to form. Until recently the main source of this kind of contact was through foot-traffic. Today, of course, the car has perhaps irrevocably altered the shape of cities. But we believe that Jacobs's underlying idea is still relevant.

With the car, having a high concentration of residents, workers and users of public space within a particular area is not necessary. Thinking of density in terms of opti-mizing the number of potential informal contacts makes it consistent in principle with relatively low-density development and a car-dominated transport system. But what we will call 'Jacobs density' refers to 'the level of potential informal contacts of the average person in a given public space[16] at any given time'. This we believe captures the essence of the Jacobsian emphasis on density – that is, as one of the conditions that promote the diversity of use and taste that is needed for long-term economic development – without being constrained by any particular historical context – for example, Hudson Street in the Greenwich Village. The drawback to this measure is that data on Jacobs density may be hard to get, because it would have to combine measures of distance travelled per hour (say) of the average user of public space and the average number of public stopping points in which informal contacts could take place (this goes as well for the kind of data that could distinguish between the overcrowding of rooms from high density, although we suspect there may be real-estate data that could supply this).[17] However, we can say that the informal contacts that form social networks valuable for entrepreneurial discov-ery would be hard to imagine taking place absent an environment of economic freedom.[18]

CONGENIAL MICRO-ENVIRONMENTS

Congenial environments are micro-environments, perhaps smaller than PUMAs, and come in many 'flavours'. And although we would like to find a simple way to describe and summarize them, the available data do not permit it. Indeed, because urban environ-ments are 'spontaneous orders' par excellence (Ikeda, 2007), what an 'optimal' density looks like adapts over time in unpredictable ways, and this means that such a measure is unlikely to be found. Here then our discussion will necessarily be more descriptive than quantitative.

For example, the rise of the 'consumer city' is the logical response to the declining importance of location near prominent natural features, including ports, rivers and canals. The increasing 'footlooseness' of employment opportunities has meant that capital could follow labour, rather than the reverse, which had been the rule for centuries (Carlino and Mills, 1987). This means that the quality of urban life is more important than ever. As Florida (2002) has emphasized, successful and attractive urban forms, then, must inspire productivity at work, but they must also be satisfying for non-work activities.

Most non-work activities have a social side. Where and how are these activities facilitated? This question again causes us to ask: what is a meaningful 'centre'? And, once again, there are no easy answers. The International Council of Shopping Centers (ICSC) counts over 100 000 US shopping centres of many types, a large number of which can be described as places where social interaction can occur (http://www.icsc.org/srch/lib/2009_S-C_CLASSIFICATION_May09.pdf). Many of these are now referred to as 'neighbourhood lifestyle centres', where shopping as well as socializing occur. Virginia Postrel (2006) notes that Vienna émigré Victor Gruen had tried to fashion shopping malls that could fulfil the function of the European downtowns he grew up in, famous for providing coffee houses where people could meet. But Gruen's ideas, she writes, have only recently come to fruition with the more open modern lifestyle centres where people are actually encouraged to sit and to linger.[19] The developer Rick Caruso, who has achieved some acclaim for the centres that he has recently opened, reports that whereas the average mall visit is for about 80 minutes, people spend more than twice as much time when visiting his centres. The downside is that many of these new centres are populated with well-known franchise stores and restaurants. There are few surprises. Jacobs would remind us that the charm of cities involves the possibilities of surprise – the good kind. Nevertheless, the suburbs do have places where people congregate. For example, Joel Garreau (1991) identifies 'edge cities', which typically begin as mall-like development, as just such places where, responding explicitly to Jacobs, he has declared that 'density is back!' (Garreau, 1991, p. 37).

CONVENTIONAL URBAN PLANNING

Many planners and policy-makers have argued that low-density 'sprawl' (the latter often undefined) is inefficient and have prescribed plans and policies to prompt more 'compact' development. The commentator George Will has asked (of Al Gore and his fellow critics): 'Does he worry that unsustainable growth will be sustained?' And it is unclear that any blanket prescription can be useful across the board. As we have noted, the well-known Achilles heel of central planning is planners' inability to discover or manage the dispersed knowledge that would be required. It is no different for cities. A Hayekian critique of urban dirigisme would also be a Jacobsian one. Large metropolitan areas include millions of parcels of land. Any presumption that managing the land uses involved is within the grasp of planners is naïve and hubristic. Open-ended free markets cannot easily be replaced.

The historian Kenneth T. Jackson writes:

> Since World War II, America's northeastern and midwestern cities have been in both relative and absolute decline. Their once proud central business districts have typically slipped into retail and business irrelevance; their neighborhoods have lost their once dense networks of bakeries, shoe stores and pharmacies; and their streets have too often become dispiriting collections of broken bottles, broken windows and broken lives. After dark, pedestrians retreat from the empty sidewalks, public housing projects come under the sway of gangs and drug dealers, and merchants lower graffiti-covered metal gates. Too often, no one is home. (Jackson, 1985, quoted in Jackson, 2007)

The Lincoln Institute (Brachman, 2005) reported similar alarming findings in terms of vacant and abandoned housing. From the records of the 2000 Census, they found

Table 22.6   Population growth in urbanized areas and central cities in the US Northeast and Midwest, 1950–2000

Urbanized area (UZA) *Central city (CC)*	State(s)	Population size		Growth (%)
		1950	2000	
New York	NY, NJ	12 296 000	17 800 000	45
New York CC	NY	7 892 000	8 008 000	1
Chicago	IL, IN	4 921 000	8 308 000	69
Chicago CC	IL	3 621 000	2 896 000	−20
Philadelphia	PA, NJ	2 922 000	5 149 000	76
Philadelphia CC	PA	2 072 000	1 518 000	−27
Boston	MA	2 233 000	4 032 000	81
Boston CC	MA	801 000	589 000	−26
Detroit	MI	2 752 000	3 903 000	42
Detroit CC	MI	1 850 000	951 000	−49
Minneapolis-St. Paul	MN	987 000	2 389 000	142
Minneapolis CC	MN	522 000	383 000	−27
St. Louis	MO, IL	1 401 000	2 078 000	48
St. Louis CC	MO	857 000	348 000	−59
Baltimore	MD	1 162 000	2 076 000	79
Baltimore CC	MD	950 000	651 000	−31
Cleveland	OH	1 384 000	1 787 000	29
Cleveland CC	OH	915 000	478 000	−48
Pittsburgh	PA	1 533 000	1 753 000	14
Pittsburgh CC	PA	677 000	335 000	−51
United States	–	152 271 000	281 422 000	85

that in Cleveland there were 25 000 vacant and 11 000 abandoned residential properties; in Baltimore the numbers were 40 000 (14 per cent of the housing stock) and 17 000; in Philadelphia there were 27 000 abandoned residential structures (10 per cent of the housing stock), 2000 abandoned commercial structures and 32 000 vacant lots; in St Louis 29 000 units were vacant which was equivalent to 17 per cent of the housing stock.

Census data also show (Table 22.6) that for the set of ten largest central cities in these two regions 50-year population growth (1950–2000) was negative – while the US population grew by 85 per cent. Only one of the ten showed positive population growth and that was New York City, but by only an almost negligible 1 per cent. But it was another story for these areas' suburbs (here the respective urbanized areas – not the Metropolitan Statistical Areas (MSAs) – less the traditional central city). These suburban areas all grew; all but Pittsburgh's grew by more than the national population growth rate. To be sure, the older US central cities boast islands of vitality and rebirth, but these are apparently swamped by the conditions that Jackson describes.

The mix of companies and industries in the economy is always changing. Churn is widely recognized as part of normal economic activity. Schumpeter famously referred to 'gales of creative destruction'. Churn also occurs in cities and accompanies productivity growth. An interesting line of urban research by Gilles Duranton (2007) suggests that metropolitan areas' ability to 'churn' industries, letting go of the old and accommodating the new, accompanies their success. In his theoretical model, cross-industry innovations lead to the churning of industries across cities and cities grow or decline as a result of the realized local industrial churn. Edward Glaeser has shown how Boston (Glaeser, 2005) and New York (Glaeser, 2009) have survived repeated crises and declines triggered by technology shocks – such as the emergence of steamships, automobiles and information technology – by reinventing themselves and accommodating the newly flourishing industries. Among the key assets needed to successfully respond to the recast challenges were a rich base of human capital and entrepreneurship in the two cities. Unlike these 'reinventive' cities, Detroit may not survive the decline of the traditional US auto industry. Curtis Simon's (2004) cross-sectional analysis of 39 industries across 316 US cities also demonstrates the role of industrial churn in the growth and decline of cities between 1977 and 1997, a period of burgeoning knowledge-intensive economies. The presence of larger manufacturing shares and a sector's own employment share in the beginning year was associated with slower subsequent growth, especially in the newer and skill-intensive industries.[20]

Three conclusions emerge from this discussion. First, an almost uncountable number of federal state and local plans and policies were supposed to change the reality that Jackson describes, but it is hard to find their effect. Most labour and capital have for many years migrated to the suburbs of the older cities or to the sunbelt. Preferences have trumped policies. Yet (perhaps ironically) in the new era of 'sustainability' concerns, policy discussions elaborate the importance of even more of the standard politicized top-down policies. Second, it is meaningless to aggregate into metropolitan units of analysis because, in many cases, the cities and the suburbs are so different. Analysts who write about cities, but who conflate the health of metropolitan areas with the health of their central cities (Glaeser, 1998) are making a mistake. Third, many of the older metropolitan areas have survived by growing outward. Rather than abandoning certain physical and social infrastructures, these have been rearranged so that the high costs of abandoning and replacing central city building stock could be avoided. Glaeser and Gyourko (2005) point out that much of the old housing stock found in run-down areas of older cities can be maintained at low cost and can continue to provide housing services for the low-income population.

So critics of 'sprawl' are unhappy with auto-oriented development – as well as with automobiles – which is naturally different from the cosy street life that many reminisce over. But whereas this position has often been cast as a concern over negative externalities (highway congestion, air pollution and so on), a newer set of criticisms suggests a lack of opportunities for positive externalities (interactions at work or at play). But the 'market failure' view is once again overdone. Just as some investigators have found that there are spatial accommodations that mitigate the commuting costs of spread-out development (namely, job decentralization), there is also evidence, such as the suburban lifestyle centres described above, that innovative and creative interactions can occur in modern dispersed cities.

LESSONS

The various cities examined here reflect complex and somewhat durable peculiarities. Their infrastructures (broadly speaking) had at one time served as congenial social and economic environments. But as circumstances change, some cities adapt better than others. Are there specific principles that top-down planners can implement? Or is a trial-and-error bottom-up approach better suited? We have claimed that Jane Jacobs looked at cities and neighbourhoods in Hayekian fashion. She appreciated the immense complexities involved and was pessimistic that they could be fathomed and usefully manipulated top-down. We agree. Of course, density, as we have defined it, remains important, and the kind of face-to-face contact and informal network-building described by Jacobs still serves as the foundation of living cities today, as they always have. But relying on crude measures of density to fashion policy, whether to promote economic development in the traditional sense, or to foster growth by somehow attracting 'creative' denizens, is unhelpful. Finally, the way the physical environment of cities has evolved in the twentieth century has perhaps made it harder to appreciate the role that the social infrastructure continues to play in economic development, and how it has adapted over time to changing circumstances of time and place. How it will adapt in the future no one can know, but we do know that, with economic freedom, adapt it will.

NOTES

1. See Jackson (1985, chapter 11). However, Cox et al. (2008) challenge the idea that the Interstate Highway System caused US suburbanization.
2. A 'spontaneous order' – sometimes called an emergent order (Johnson, 2001) – is sometimes described as 'the result of human action but not of human design' (Hayek, 1967). That is, it is a set of complex social relations that tend to arise and evolve without the necessity of an overarching plan or supreme planner. In addition to markets and market prices, other examples include language, case law and scientific paradigms.
3. The recent survey of urban economics by Glaeser and Gottlieb (2009) describes some of the difficulties that urban economists have encountered when they address economic growth questions.
4. See, for example, Calthorpe and Fulton (2001).
5. We borrow the term 'living city' from Roberta Brandes Gratz (1989) and use it in the sense of Jane Jacobs's concept of a 'city' as 'a settlement that consistently generates its economic growth from its own local economy' (Jacobs, 1969, p. 262). This usage is also consistent with that of the sociologist Max Weber (1958) and the historian Henri Pirenne (1952).
6. See especially Jacobs (1961), chapter 22.
7. An interesting debate between Fischel and Nelson concerns the question of whether HOAs and homevoter cities are complements or substitutes; see Nelson (2004) and Fischel (2004).
8. The complementarity of the health of cities and their suburbs is articulated in Voith (2000).
9. As Jacobs (1961, chapter 13) explains, however, this 'virtuous spiral' can also work in reverse, generating a 'dynamics of decline'.
10. There have been various tests by urban economists of Jacobs's diversity idea (Quigley, 1998). The empirical evidence is seemingly mixed. Dumais et al., (1997) found evidence of significant localization and agglomeration economies among firms in the same industry. Henderson (1994) tried to assess the relative importance of four possibilities: static/between firms in the same industry; static/between firms in different industries; dynamic/between firms in the same industry; and dynamic/between firms in different industries. In the Rosenthal and Strange (2004) survey of ten recent empirical studies, they find evidence in support of urbanization and localization and diversity (Jacobs) economies. These categories describe the range of parties involved, but the authors emphasize that the geographic and temporal scope are also of great interest. Henderson (1994) found evidence for localization as well as urbanization economies. He also presented strong evidence of dynamic externalities that are realized over years and reports a five-year lag before the full effect of externality benefits are experienced.
11. *The Charter of the New Urbanism* is available at http://www.cnu.org/charter (accessed March 2011).
12. Of course, subsidized construction that is done privately as part of a larger development scheme (for example, the Walentas family in the DUMBO – Down Under the Manhattan Bridge Overpass – district of Brooklyn) or through government transfers may also accomplish this in some cases. The latter,

however, are especially subject to interest-group rent-seeking and political manipulation. Jacobs's emphasis on old buildings reflects her attempt to explain how cities don't necessarily have to deliberately plan the construction of entrepreneurial incubators, but that these are and have historically been part of successful urban development.

13. The recent economic woes in Dubai are testament to the risks of undertaking such colossal construction, where perhaps 'giga-project' would be a more apt description.

14. See, for example, Glaeser and Kahn (2001).

15. In light of the declining importance of traditional downtowns, urban economists have devoted substantial effort in recent years to (1) theorizing about the rise of metropolitan sub-centres – and moving beyond the monocentric model of cities; and (2) finding ways to identify them. McMillen and Smith (2003) summarize much of this work. Using 1990 data, they also report their own findings on sub-centre identification for 62 US urban areas. They use these to test and confirm the implications of the Fujita-Ogawa model, in which the expected number of sub-centres increases with metropolitan area population and commuting costs. Redfearn and Giuliano (2007) present a case study of the 20-year (1980–2000) evolution of sub-centres (that they identify) in the Los Angeles area. Generalized accessibility explains less than does historical importance. Lee (2006) describes a two-dimensional categorization of metropolitan areas which considers the number of employment sub-centres as well as the degree of employment dispersion. He identifies employment sub-centres for the largest metropolitan areas. The 14 areas with populations of more than three million in 2000 were shown to have 223 sub-centres; the range was from as few as six (Philadelphia, Atlanta, Miami) to as many as 53 (Los Angeles). But the proportion of jobs not in any centre (not in the downtown nor in one of the sub-centres) varied from a high of 86.9 per cent (Philadelphia) to a low of 68.4 per cent (Los Angeles). Lee found that, as a group, commuters in dispersed job locations had shorter duration commutes than those working in sub-centres or in CBDs. Lee and Gordon (2007) estimate a metropolitan area growth model and find evidence that jobs dispersal contributes to commuting economies among the largest metropolitan areas; they accommodate growth by dispersing.

16. We define 'public space' here, not in the sense of publicly owned, but as places where one expects to encounter strangers. These spaces can be either privately or publicly owned.

17. The 'contacts per hour' approach to density also would appear to depend on making a number of assumptions that would then enable us to connect (1) miles driven per day by the average user; (2) average number of people occupying the various spaces in which informal contact could be made; and (3) the likelihood of such contact.

18. See Gwartney et al. (2010), available at http://www.cato.org/pubs/efw/

19. See also Hardwick (2004, p. 131).

20. There is one more caveat to this discussion. Glaeser and Gottlieb (2009, p. 983) note that '[h]ousing supply elasticity will determine whether urban success reveals itself in the form of more people or higher income'. This is, of course, correct but it must be added that there is considerable research that demonstrates that housing supply elasticities have been substantially reduced in many areas because of local land-use and development restrictions. In addition, when we study post-2000 growth of the 30 largest US metropolitan areas, we see that eight of them (Dallas, Houston, Atlanta, Phoenix, Tampa, Denver, San Antonio, Indianapolis) experienced above-average population growth along with below-average income growth; eight others (New York, Los Angeles, Boston, San Francisco, San Diego, Baltimore, Pittsburgh, Providence) experienced above-average income growth and below-average population growth. But five metropolitan areas excelled in both (Miami, Washington, DC, Seattle, Portland, Sacramento); nine 'non-successes' underperformed in both (Chicago, Philadelphia, Detroit, Minneapolis, St Louis, Cleveland, Cincinnati, Kansas City, Milwaukee). The Brookings Pendall et al. review (2006) of land-use regulations suggests a typology of regulatory regimes. But the link between regulation, housing supply elasticity and the nature of growth is not clear in the 30-area analysis.

REFERENCES

Anselin, L., A. Varga and Z. Acs (1997), 'Local geographic spillovers between university research and high technology innovations', *Journal of Urban Economics*, **42**(3), 422–48.

Brachman, L. (2005), 'Vacant and abandoned property: Remedies for acquisition and redevelopment', *Land Lines*, **10**(October), 1–5.

Calthorpe, P. and W. Fulton (2001), *The Regional City: Planning for the End of Sprawl*, Washington, DC: Island Press.

Carlino, G.A. and E.S. Mills (1987), 'The determinants of county growth', *Journal of Regional Science*, **27**(February), 39–54.

Cox, W., P. Gordon and C.L. Redfearn (2008), 'Highway penetration of central cities: not a major cause of suburbanization', *Econ Journal Watch*, **5**(1), 32–45.
Dumais, G., G. Ellison and E. Glaeser (1997), 'Geographic concentration as a dynamic process', NBER working paper No. 6270.
Duranton, G. (2007), 'Urban evolutions: the fast, the slow, and the still', *American Economic Review*, **97**(1), 197–221.
Edward, L. (2001), 'Public ownership in the American city', Harvard Institute of Economic Research discussion paper No. 1930, October.
Fischel, W.A. (2001), *The Homevoter Hypothesis: How Home Values Influence Local Government Taxation, School Finance, and Land Use Policies*, Cambridge, MA: Harvard University Press.
Fischel, W.A. (2004), 'Revolution or evolution?', *Regulation* (Summer), 48–53.
Florida, R. (2002), *The Rise of the Creative Class*, New York, NY: Basic Books.
Florida, R. (2009), 'How the crash will reshape America', *Atlantic*, March, available at http://www.theatlantic. com/magazine/archive/2009/03/how-the-crash-will-reshape-america/7293/.
Garreau, J. (1991), *Edge City: Life on the New Frontier*, New York; NY: Random House.
Glaeser, E.L. (1998), 'Are cities dying?', *Journal of Economics Perspectives*, **12**(2), 139–60.
Glaeser, E.L. (2005), 'Reinventing Boston, 1630–2003', *Journal of Economic Geography*, **5**(2), 119–53.
Glaeser, E.L. and J. Gottlieb (2009), 'The wealth of cities: agglomeration economies and spatial equilibrium in the United States', *Journal of Economic Literature*, **47**(4), 993–1028.
Glaeser, E.L. and J. Gyourko (2005), 'Urban decline and durable housing', *Journal of Political Economy*, **113**(2), 345–75.
Glaeser, E.L. and M.E. Kahn (2001), 'Decentralized employment and the transformation of the American city', working paper 8117, National Bureau of Economic Research, Cambridge, MA.
Granovetter, M. (1973), 'The strength of weak ties', *American Journal of Sociology*, **78**(6), 1360–80.
Gratz, R.B. (1989), *The Living City: How America's Cities are Being Revitalized in a Big Way*, New York, NY: Wiley.
Gwartney, J., J. Hall and R. Lawson (2010), *Economic Freedom of the World: 2010 Annual Report*, Canada: Cato Institute and Fraser Institute.
Hardwick, M.J. (2004), *Mall Maker: Victor Gruen, Architect of an American Dream*, Philadelphia, PA: University of Pennsylvania Press.
Hayek, F.A. [1945] (1948), 'The use of knowledge in society', in *Individualism and Economic Order*, Chicago, IL: University of Chicago Press.
Hayek, F.A. (1948), *Individualism and Economic Order*, Chicago, IL: University of Chicago Press.
Hayek, F.A. (1967), 'The results of human action but not of human design', in F.A. Hayek, *Studies in Philosophy, Economics and Politics*, Chicago, IL: University of Chicago Press.
Henderson, V. (1994), 'Externalities and industrial development', NBER working paper No. 4730.
Holcombe, R.G. (2004), 'The new urbanism and the market process', *Review of Austrian Economics*, **17**(2/3), 285–300.
Ikeda, S. (2007), 'Urbanizing economics', *Review of Austrian Economics*, **20**(4), 213–20.
Jackson, K.T. (1985) *Crabgrass Frontier: The Suburbanization of the United States*, New York, NY: Oxford University Press.
Jackson, K.T. (2007), 'Robert Moses and the rise of New York: the power broker in perspective', in Hilary Ballon and Kenneth T. Jackson (eds), *Robert Moses and the Modern City: The Transformation of New York*, New York, NY: W.W. Norton, pp. 67–71.
Jacobs, J. (1961), *The Death and Life of Great American Cities*, New York, NY: Vintage Books.
Jacobs, J. (1969), *The Economy of Cities*, New York, NY: Vintage House.
Johnson, S. (2001), *Emergence: The Connected Lives of Ants, Brains, Cities, and Software*, New York, NY: Simon & Schuster.
Kling, A. (2009), available at http://econlog.econlib.org/archives/2009/11/price_discrimin_3.html.
Lee, Bumsoo (2006), 'Urban spatial structure, commuting, and growth in US metropolitan areas', Unpublished doctoral dissertation, University of Southern California, Los Angeles, CA.
Lee, B. and P. Gordon (2007), 'Urban spatial structure and economic growth in U.S. metropolitan areas', paper presented at the 46th annual meeting of the Western Regional Science Association, Newport Beach, California.
McMillen, D.P. and S.C. Smith (2003), 'The number of subcenters in larger urban areas', *Journal of Urban Economics*, **53**, 321–38.
Mises, L. von [1922] (1981), *Socialism: An Economic and Sociological Analysis*, Indianapolis, IN: Liberty Classics.
Murphy, A. (2007), 'A dynamic model of housing supply', Department of Economics working paper, Duke University, Durham, NC.
Nelson, R.H. (2004), 'The private neighborhood', *Regulation* (Summer), 40–6.

Nelson, R.H. (2005), *Private Neighborhoods and the Transformation of Local Government*, Washington, DC: Urban Institute Press.

Pendall, R., R. Puentes and J. Martin (2006), 'From traditional to reformed: a review of land use regulations in the 50 largest metropolitan areas', Research Brief, Metropolitan Policy Program, The Brookings Institution, Washington, DC, August.

Pirenne, H. (1952), *Medieval Cities: Their Origin and the Revival of Trade*, Princeton, NJ: Princeton University Press.

Postrel, V. (2006), 'City lite: shopping centers are fulfilling their destiny, not as escapes from the city but as places to experience urban pleasures', *Los Angeles Times*, December 10.

Quigley, J.M. (1998), 'Urban diversity and economic growth' *Journal of Economic Perspectives*, **12**(2), 127–38.

Redfearn, C. and G. Giuliano (2007), 'Employment concentrations in Los Angeles, 1980–2000', *Environment & Planning A*, **39**(12), 2935–57.

Rosenthal, S.S. and W.C. Strange (2004), 'Evidence on the nature and sources of agglomeration economies', in J.V. Henderson, P. Nijkamp, E.S. Milles, P.C. Cheshire and J.F. Thisse (eds), *Handbook of Regional and Urban Economics: Cities and Geography*, New York: Elsevier, pp. 2119–71.

Simon, C.J. (2004), 'Industrial reallocation across US Cities 1977–1997', *Journal of Urban Economics*, **56**, 119–43.

Utt, R. (2009), 'The Oberstar transportation plan: a costly exercise in lifestyle modification', Washington, DC: Heritage Foundation.

Voith, R. (2000), 'Has suburbanization diminished the importance of access to center city?,' *Business Review*, May, Federal Reserve Bank of Philadelphia, 17–29.

Weber, M. (1958), *The City*, translated and edited by Don Martindale and Gertrud Neuwirt, New York, NY: The Free Press.

Webster, C. and L. Wai-Chung Lai (2003), *Property Rights, Planning and Markets*, Cheltenham, UK and Northampton, MA, USA: Edward Elgar Publishing.

23 Creative milieus in the Stockholm region
Börje Johansson and Johan Klaesson

In this chapter the Stockholm metropolitan region is presented as an example of how novelty-creation activities and occupations may unfold in an urban agglomeration. Why should we expect to find a stronger concentration of creative individuals and creativity-driven firms in large urban regions than elsewhere? In response to the posed question, the chapter makes use of the Stockholm region to stress phenomena such as multiplicity of interaction opportunities among novelty creators, innovators and potential users of the innovations. Using an analogy, it could be that a creative theatre life requires that actors, directors and audiences are in place. It also requires inflows from playwrights and stimuli from other theatre milieus. We give a number of historical examples to support this view, but start by presenting the Stockholm region in this context.

THE STOCKHOLM REGION

A brief description of Sweden's economic geography in the year 2005 may take the following form. There are three metropolitan regions; Stockholm, Gothenburg and Malmö. The population in the Stockholm region equals the sum in the two other regions. Close to half of the total population is located in the three metropolitan regions, and just below 40 per cent reside in 17 medium-sized urban regions. The remaining geography consists of about 50 small urban regions, hosting a bit more than 10 per cent of the population.

Table 23.1 illustrates the development of the country's urban regions during the period 1950 to 2005. What we observe is a process of population concentration such that the three largest urban regions have grown much faster than the average for the country for more than half a century. The second observation is that the Stockholm region comprises one-quarter of the country's population.

In this chapter we will demonstrate that the Stockholm region for a very long period of time has remained the major centre for knowledge development, innovations and intellectual creativity in Sweden. It has maintained this position by hosting more diversity and versatility than other regions. Given this position, the region has been an attractor for individuals with ambitions and talents in political, economic and cultural life. At the same time, novel ideas and solutions have continued to diffuse from the Stockholm region to other regions of the country. To a large extent the region has functioned as a node that collects 'global news' for dissemination to the rest of the country. An illustrative example of this function of pioneering new developments is that in 1885 Stockholm had the greatest number of telephones of all cities in the world (Hult, 1989).

The aim of this chapter is to provide the reader with a sequence of images of the Stockholm region, which together can describe its role as Sweden's major node for creative processes and innovative activities. This node is characterized by a labour supply with diversified cognitive skills that match the requirements of dispersed knowledge-

Table 23.1   Population size 2005 and growth between 1950 and 2005

Regions and groups of regions	Change 1950–2005 (%)	Size 2005	Population share 2005 (%)
Stockholm	72.4	2 250 000	24.9
Gothenburg (Göteborg)	61.3	1 016 661	11.2
Malmö	43.6	1 005 712	11.1
17 medium-sized regions	17.7	3 532 431	39.0
Small regions	−12.4	1 242 638	13.8
Country as a whole	28.4	9 047 752	100.0

Note: The same regional boundaries have been used for the entire period.

handling tasks in different parts of its economy. Although knowledge-related activities are concentrated in the region, we find that a large share of the labour force consists of workers who are assigned to information-handling tasks. However, if knowledge and information activities are added together, they dominate the contemporary economy of the Stockholm region, with a share approaching two-thirds.

We also want to show that Stockholm has a very long history as the major node for the Swedish imports of ideas, technology and products (embodying new technical solutions) from the rest of the world. In addition, we claim that the Stockholm region has saddle-point properties, reflected by its gradual dissemination of novelties to the rest of the national economy. The chapter ends with a discussion of Stockholm's creative clusters and the region's success in attracting talents to these clusters and other knowledge-handling activities.

SOCIAL MILIEUS THAT FOSTER AND REPRESS CREATIVE PROCESSES

An act of creativity often implies that a new and surprising solution is found in the context of a certain problem or a complex of problems. To enrich this rather poor description of the meaning of creativity, we may recognize that a creative act also can have the form of redefining a given problem, such that it is replaced by a new and more solution-friendly formulation. Creativity is related to a playful propensity to reshape the structure of a system or problem cluster, and to recombine the elements of the system.

Åke Andersson (1985) suggests that an analysis of creativity may be approached by considering the following aspects of the human brain: heuristic ability, ability to remember, to detect deep structure, to perceive and use ambiguity, multiplicity and variety, to appreciate paradoxes and surprises, to use disequilibria and to use fundamental uncertainty. Gudmund Smith (1993) argues that a high level of creativity is a common phenomenon for young children, adding that constraints from the social environment tend to reduce the person's creative capacity, which implies that most people lose part of their creativity as they grow older and start to experience responses from an environment which rewards established rather than innovative traits of problem solving. The message from Smith may be reformulated as a conjecture that we may identify social environments that are effective in suppressing creative thinking. If this is true, it should also be possible to outline models of social conditions that foster and enable creative processes and novelty-generating interaction among individuals.

The above conclusion suggests that creative activities are more frequent among certain groups of individuals, and that such creative groups, in turn, can be found in greater numbers in certain regional environments. The hypothesis put forward in this chapter is that creative milieus are characterized by communication externalities, where novel ideas generate additional ideas through interaction. As a consequence, creative milieus should be more prevalent in large and dense urban regions, to the extent that such regions host knowledge-intensive inhabitants with cognitive occupations, reflecting knowledge-handling activities. The outcome of favourable creativity conditions in a region may take different forms such as creation of scientific and research-based knowledge, supply of artefacts and performances in the arts and in entertainment, and innovations in the form of new production routines and novel products (goods and services).

It is clear that an identification of the skills and tasks associated with an occupation may indicate the likelihood that creative processes will develop among workers. However, there is no one-to-one relation between the type of occupation and the degree of creativity. Consider research and development (R&D) and observe that research involves checking and testing preliminary solutions and established knowledge, and the related activities are normally prescribed to be based on routines rather than creativity. Furthermore, a large share of artistic work and entertainment has a routine nature, where the appreciation may spring from pattern recognition rather than from unexpected, surprise-loaded experiences. Thus, in all creative areas we can distinguish between initiators or innovators and followers or disciples.

Charlotta Mellander (2009) argues that one needs to understand how the occupational structure in creative and knowledge-based industries differs from that in other industries (Andersson and Johansson, 1984; Florida, 2002). According to Mellander, this literature emphasizes social and economic diversity as a critical factor for the creativity of urban regions. In the analyses of Florida (2002) and Florida et al. (2008), urban regions manage to develop as a consequence of lower barriers to entry, in-migration of creative and talented persons and a supply of lifestyle activities that are attractive to people with creative skills.

EXAMPLES OF CREATIVE AND INNOVATION-RICH URBAN REGIONS

A functional urban region is characterized by being an arena for frequent interaction between individuals and between organizations, making it a facilitator of face-to-face contacts. Following contemporary research, such a region should allow people to meet with time distances that are shorter than 45 minutes (Johansson et al., 2002). As a consequence, such regions were much smaller in the creative centres of earlier eras – for example in ancient Athens, Renaissance Florence or eighteenth-century Edinburgh – than in the present-day Boston or Cambridge regions.

Creative urban regions are recognized for hosting individuals and groups of individuals that create and develop new ideas, solutions and knowledge, but also for hosting producers that carry out innovations such as new routines and new products. This form of definition focuses on observed consequences of creativity, without shedding light on how the creation comes about – partly in line with Koestler's observation that great scientists reach their findings as if they were 'sleepwalkers' (Koestler, 1959, 1964). Andersson (1985) argues that the common features of creative regions are (i) supply of financial resources for novelty creation, (ii) deep original knowledge and competence, (iii) experience of tensions between needs and available resources, (iv) a regional milieu that offers diversity, (v) opportunities for frequent interaction and (vi) structural instability that causes genuine uncertainty. In our exposition and examination of the Stockholm region, we emphasize competence, diversity and interaction opportunities.

The above characterization can be applied to the so-called Scottish Enlightenment during the second half of the eighteenth century. In the 1720s, Edinburgh had reformed and developed its university in line with the faculty system. A similar change took place in Glasgow but with less remarkable consequences than in Edinburgh, where the milieu gave rise to an extraordinary intellectual and cultural flowering, later referred to as the Scottish Enlightenment. A characteristic of Edinburgh's Old Town in those days was its lack of segregation, owing to the habit of housing both the very poor and the rich on different floors of each multi-storey building, while at the same time hosting a tavern where the residents of each building ate and drank in common.

Edinburgh's outbreak of intellectual inquiry took place in the dense milieu of the Old Town, which encouraged conversation and debate. This environment inspired scholars to explain phenomena by isolating a first principle. David Hume elaborated the concept of causality and suggested that causal relations are confined to ideas (in a model), Adam Smith recognized the implications of the division of labour and William Robertson the degree to which environmental factors shaped economic history. Others such as Joseph Black presented ideas about latent heat while James Hutton claimed that the Earth revealed an enormous antiquity (EB, 1991).

From another angle we may observe that Edinburgh was the university of the poet James Thomson, of James Boswell (the biographer of Dr Johnson), of the novelist and poet Oliver Goldsmith, and of Benjamin Rush who is recognized as a signatory of the Declaration of Independence. From the nineteenth century one finds Sir Walter Scott, who developed the historic novel (EB, 1991).

One background feature of the Scottish Enlightenment was a long history of theological debate, which sharpened minds and argumentation. This background may also be a reason for the strong orientation towards European culture. David Hume, *le bon David*, became famous in his lifetime for his 'History of England', while *A Treatise of Human Nature* has remained a point of reference into our time, just like Adam Smith's *Wealth of Nations*. These are just some of the most well-known works from the Scottish universities of the time.

A related and even more magnificent story is presented in *Wittgenstein's Vienna* (Janik and Toulmin, 1973), which reports on an intellectual milieu, during the decades around 1900, that generated novelties in a diverse number of fields that included music, journalism, architecture, theoretical physics and philosophy. In Vienna, where the Habsburg monarchy was suppressing new political ideas, interaction between creative people was fostered by the café culture and inflows of ideas from the rest of Europe, just as the Scottish Enlightenment had strong links to French society.

In the preceding two examples diversity prevails. We find the same story in England with Cambridge and the Bloomsbury group, centred on names such as Russell, Keynes,

Whitehead and many others. More recently, Cambridge has been recognized as a resource concentration for both theoretical and applied research with impacts on the development of materials technology and biotechnology.

How do these examples relate to creativity in economic life? Do the developments in the arts and sciences follow the same pattern as innovative activities by entrepreneurs and firms? It seems that we have to look for other regions when the introduction of new routines of production and new products (goods and services) are our main concern. From a Swedish point of view we can observe how industrialists sent their sons (and other successors) to study technology in England during the eighteenth century and to New England during the nineteenth century (Rydberg, 1989; Johansson, 1993). Starting at the end of the nineteenth century, the Boston region offered a fragmented picture with much immigration that gave rise to ethnic diversity and intellectual multiplicity. The telephone was invented and transformed to an innovation in this region, which also was the birthplace of the great market success of the Gillette Safety Razor. In the twentieth century inventions and entrepreneurial efforts brought about a series of market novelties in the field of electrical engineering, radio technology and related fields, for example, power tubes, thermostats and rectifier tubes (Warner, 1989).

The observations from the Boston region stress diversity, elements of social unrest and the formation of a university milieu, with access to the concentrated demand on the American east coast. In a later wave, the Boston region also became a major location for digital information and communications technology (ICT), although it was eventually overshadowed by developments on the west coast that centred on Silicon Valley. The latter case has become iconic, and narrative research documentations have emphasized the knowledge, competence, diversity and knowledge spillovers that are generated by labour mobility and venture capital networking (Saxenian, 1996; Huffman and Quigley, 2002). In its own way, the Stockholm region has in recent decades made imprints in the field of ICT innovations.

OCCUPATIONS AND CREATIVE PROCESSES

The subsequent analysis of occupations is based on two different classifications. The first classification is inspired by a recent contribution by Bacolod et al., (2009), where occupations are recognized by the type of skills required: cognitive, managerial-administrative, social and motor skills. The second classification is based on what types of operations (tasks) people in each occupation actually carry out (Andersson and Johansson, 1984), leading to a division into knowledge-, information-, service- and goods-handling activities, where occupations are classified according to tasks.

Herzog and Schlottman (1989) make a clear distinction between the two different impressions that arise when the basis is high-technology occupations versus high-technology industries. The message, which was later stressed by Florida (2002), is that a classification of creative occupations has the capacity to reveal more aspects of the modern urban economy than a classification of creative industries. Inspired by this ambition, we also consider Andersson's classification of occupations into (i) knowledge-handling, (ii) information-handling, (iii) service-handling and (iv) goods-handling tasks.

As illustrated in Table 23.2, all knowledge-handling occupations are also classified

Table 23.2   Cross-classification of 94 occupations by skill and task

	Tasks			
	Knowledge handling	Information handling	Service handling	Goods handling
Skills				
Cognitive	20	2	0	4
Managerial-administrative	0	18	3	0
Social	0	4	13	0
Motor	0	3	2	25
Sum	20	27	18	29

Note: Classification of skills inspired by Bacolod et al. (2009); classification of tasks according to Andersson (1985) and Andersson and Johansson (1984).

as cognitive. However, information-handling tasks cover all four categories of skills, although most information-handling occupations are associated with managerial-administrative skills. In a similar way we can see a strong correlation between service-handling and social skills, as well as between goods-handling and motor skills.

Table 23.2 informs us that management competence is primarily assigned to information-handling activities and not knowledge handling. What is then the difference between knowledge and information? A first observation is that knowledge tends to be durable and information perishable. However, information can also be a carrier of knowledge messages. Using the terminology in the table, knowledge reveals itself in cognitive patterns that can be universally used in explaining phenomena and in designing instruments for controlling phenomena. Geometry provides an example of knowledge which may be appreciated as a set of consistent theorems. Geometry is also embedded in instruments to find the shortest route.

Knowledge is the result of creative efforts. Åke Andersson (Chapter 2) suggests that knowledge can be understood as an ordered structure. Thus, we may consider thematic creativity which can give birth to new fundamental (structural) knowledge, as well as creativity in the form of variations on a given theme. If this idea is applied to innovations, one may safely conclude that most innovations in economic life amount to variations on an established theme. This is illustrated in the following list of firms' innovation efforts: (i) internal R&D efforts inside the firm; (ii) commissioned R&D taking place outside the firm; (iii) acquisition of new equipment to be used by a firm; (iv) search and collection of external knowledge; (v) training of and investments in a firm's human resources; (vi) efforts to commercialize innovations and promote their market penetration; (vii) product development and product design; (viii) collaborative innovation efforts together with external actors.

EDUCATION, SKILLS AND TASKS IN THE STOCKHOLM REGION

This section starts with an exposé of the knowledge intensity of the economy of the Stockholm region, as compared with the rest of Sweden. It then shows that the cognitive

Table 23.3   Knowledge intensity in the entire economy; per cent of total employment

Urban region(s)	1993	2007	Change 1993–2007
Stockholm	17.3	28.1	10.8
Gothenburg	14.1	24.1	10.0
Malmö	13.0	23.4	10.4
Medium-sized regions	10.3	18.6	8.3
All regions	8.6	14.7	6.1

Note: Statistics refer to 72 Swedish labour market (FA) regions. Knowledge intensity refers to the share of employment with at least three years of higher education.

Source: Statistics Sweden; Johansson et al. (2010).

skill intensity is higher in the Stockholm region than elsewhere in the country. In addition, cognitive skills are shown to increase with the size of regions. The intention is to show that in contemporary knowledge economies many cognitive skills are associated with knowledge-handling tasks which require university education.

Education and the Growth of Knowledge Intensity

Education matters for the urban economy in the sense that knowledge-intensive workers (with at least three years of university studies) receive a wage premium. This premium is claimed to be greater in large urban regions than in smaller regions (Glaeser and Mare, 2001; Rosenthal and Strange, 2008).

The knowledge intensity of the Swedish economy increased by more than six percentage points between 1993 and 2007 (Table 23.3). The increase was faster in the metropolitan regions, where it grew by 10 percentage points. This difference reflects the bias inherent in household migration patterns, where labour with high education is attracted to the largest urban regions. For the Stockholm region we also observe that its knowledge intensity is twice the national average.

The knowledge intensity of an urban region can be related to the absorption capacity of firms in the region, implying that firms can make use of all sorts of novelties in the world economy as stimuli for their own imitations and innovations (Cohen and Levithal, 1990). Thus, high knowledge intensity facilitates the creative processes of firms. In this context we can refer to Table 23.4, which shows that the share of knowledge-intensive labour is close to 60 per cent among persons in cognitive skills occupations. This is more than double the knowledge intensity of occupations with management skills.

Are people in occupations that require cognitive skills more creative than people in other occupations? Are knowledge handlers more creative than people having other occupation tasks. As already recognized, cognitive skills and knowledge-handling tasks are oriented towards improving and enhancing our understanding of the world and towards creating new knowledge. Thus, when occupations are classified as cognitive and knowledge-handling, then the message is that these occupations are oriented towards knowledge creation, and to manage this, cognitive knowledge handlers use their creative capacity as a resource. New knowledge is the result of technology development, formula-

Table 23.4   Knowledge intensity of different types of occupation skills in per cent, Sweden, 2007

Knowledge intensity	Cognitive skills	Managerial-administrative skills	Social skills	Motor and other skills	Total
Low	41.5	72.0	85.3	96.1	77.9
High	58.5	28.0	14.7	3.9	22.1
Total	100	100	100	100	100

Source: Statistics Sweden. High knowledge intensity implies that more than 50 per cent of the workers in the occupation has completed at least three years of higher education.

Table 23.5   Employment share of skills in Stockholm and the rest of Sweden, 2007 (per cent)

	Cognitive skills	Managerial-administrative skills	Social skills	Motor and other skills	Total
Stockholm	22.8	24.1	30.6	22.5	100.0
Rest of Sweden	17.7	17.6	30.9	33.8	100.0

Source: Statistics Sweden.

tion of new models and creation of algorithms and so on. This includes inventions and innovations.

The empirical examination compares how total employment is subdivided into occupations in the Stockholm region and the rest of Sweden. For skills, we want to shed light on the following pattern:

- Cognitive skills and managerial-administrative skills are over-represented in large urban regions, and hence over-represented in the Stockholm region.
- Motor and other skills are strongly under-represented in the Stockholm region.
- Social skills are equally frequent in Stockholm and the rest of Sweden, and tend to be proportional to population size.

This pattern is illustrated in Table 23.5, which shows that the share of cognitive occupations is almost 30 per cent greater in the Stockholm region than in the rest of the country, while managerial-administrative skills are more than 35 per cent greater in the Stockholm region. The structure may reflect the attractiveness of the Stockholm region to people with cognitive skills, and this attraction may in turn be caused by (i) amenities of the region that are appreciated by persons with cognitive skills and (ii) by higher wages in cognitive occupations located in the region. In the latter case it is often assumed that the pertinent occupations are more productive in large urban regions – when compared with a location in other urban regions (Glaeser, 2008).

In Table 23.6 we can see that a similar picture emerges when occupations are classified according to tasks. The Stockholm region has a higher share of both knowledge handlers and information handlers. At the same time the region's share is lower for service

*Table 23.6   Employment share of tasks in Stockholm and the rest of Sweden, 2007
(per cent)*

	Knowledge handling	Information handling	Service handling	Goods handling	Total
Stockholm	20.7	40.5	22.2	16.7	100.0
Rest of Sweden	16.5	33.6	27.0	22.9	100.0

handlers and goods handlers. Taking Stockholm as an example of a large urban region, we may conjecture that there is a geographic division of labour, where large urban regions specialize in knowledge and information activities whereas other regions have a higher share of occupations that handle services and goods.

Table 23.5 shows that cognitive skills as well as managerial-administrative skills both have greater shares in the Stockholm region than the national average. In a similar way, Table 23.6 demonstrates that knowledge-handling and information-handling occupations dominate the labour market of the Stockholm region. We observe that the share of knowledge handlers with cognitive skills is size-dependent. To test for this we can examine to what extent the agglomeration of each occupation type depends on urban size.

In the analysis we consider all urban regions in Sweden and hypothesize that the share of the four skill types and the four task types depend on the size of the region. In the regression equation the number of people in an occupation in region r, E_r is related to the population size, P_r, of the same region. This linear regression equation thus has the following form:

$$\ln E_r = \alpha + \beta \ln P_r + \varepsilon_r \tag{23.1}$$

The results from the regressions are presented in Tables 23.A1 and 23.A2 in the Appendix. Our main interest is to show how the location of occupations depends on the size of each urban region. From the Appendix it is obvious that an urban region's occupation shares are strongly associated with the size of the region. The size dependency is summarized in Table 23.7, which shows that a 10 per cent increase of the total population of an urban region is associated with more than an 11 per cent increase in the number of workers in occupations with cognitive or managerial skills as well as in knowledge-handling occupations, indicating that those occupations in a clear way are more frequent in large urban regions. As population size grows, the share of occupations associated with cognitive skills and knowledge handling increases in a disproportionate way.

A less than 10 per cent increase as a response to a 10 per cent increase in urban size is recorded for occupations with motor skills as well as for service-handling and goods-handling occupations. The interpretation of this is that as a region grows, activities that make use of these occupations gradually find their location in other smaller regions. Finally, we can observe that total employment grows faster than population size, implying a higher labour market participation rate.

Table 23.7 *Occupation increase (per cent) caused by a 10 per cent increase in the population size of urban regions*

Type of occupation by skill	Occupation increase	Type of occupation by task	Occupation increase
Cognitive	11.8	Knowledge	11.9
Managerial	11.0	Information	10.9
Social	10.1	Service	9.5
Motor	9.7	Goods	9.9
All occupations	10.3	All occupations	10.3

Specialization of Urban Regions as Regards Occupational Skills

The results in Table 23.7 may be complemented by an analysis of how each region's specialization in different occupations co-varies with urban size. For this exercise, specialization is measured by the specialization quotient for each occupation. The quotient, y_{rj}, of occupation j in region r is calculated as follows:

$$y_{rj} = 100 \cdot [Y_{rj}/Y_r]/[Y_j/Y] \tag{23.2}$$

where Y_{rj} denotes the number of persons with occupation j in region r; Y_r denotes the total labour force in region r; Y_j denotes the total labour force with occupation j in the country; and Y denotes the country's total labour force. If y_{rj} is greater than 100 for region r, it implies that region r specializes in occupation j. The specialization quotient can be estimated as a function of urban size by means of the following specification:

$$y_{rj} = \alpha + \beta \ln P_r + \varepsilon_r \tag{23.3}$$

where P_r refers to the size of urban region r. From the diagrams in Figure 23.1 we can see that a region's specialization in cognitive occupations increases as the population increases. The same applies for managerial-administrative occupations, but in this case the specialization increases at a slower pace.

Turning to Figure 23.2, it is obvious that specialization in motor-skill occupations declines with the size of the urban region. The same applies to a very modest degree for social skills, which seem to approach the level 100 as urban regions become large enough; this observation is consistent with our earlier observation that social skills tend to be size-neutral.

Large urban regions are characterized by being able to afford a richer spectrum of specialized firms as well as a broader composition of specialized labour supply. In particular, a diverse supply from many differentiated firms can take place because of the greater number of diversified customers in large metropolitan regions such as Stockholm. When a firm is small its possibilities to develop intra-firm division of labour are limited. As a consequence it has to purchase cognitive skills as services from other firms, and such opportunities are more plentiful in metropolitan regions. Table 23.8 illustrates that small

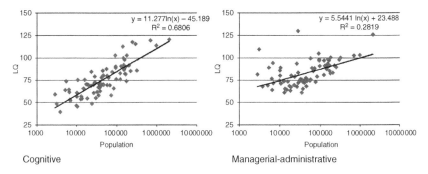

Figure 23.1   Specialization quotients as a function of urban labour market area size for cognitive and managerial-administrative occupations

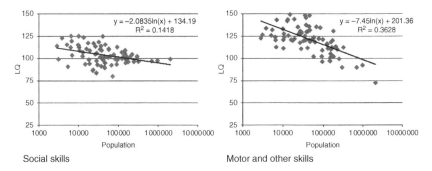

Figure 23.2   Specialization quotients as a function of urban labour market area size for social and motor-skill occupations

Table 23.8   Firm size and occupation types as a percentage of total firm employment, Sweden, 2007

Employees	Cognitive skills	Managerial-administrative skills	Social skills	Motor and other skills
1–4	13.0	23.7	21.9	41.4
5–9	9.3	20.8	26.1	43.8
10–19	10.8	20.5	24.1	44.6
20–49	13.8	19.9	23.3	43.0
50–99	15.9	20.3	23.0	40.8
100+	22.2	18.2	34.6	25.0
Mean	18.9	19.2	30.8	31.1

Source: Statistics Sweden.

firms have low shares of workers with cognitive skills. The share is an increasing function of the size of the firm, whereas managerial skills are roughly proportional to variations in size. Moreover, for firms with more than 100 employees, the share of workers in occupations with motor skills declines drastically.

KNOWLEDGE, R&D AND INNOVATION IN THE STOCKHOLM REGION

Innovations are generated by creative processes. There is a clear consensus in the innovation literature that the innovativeness of firms is affected positively by the individual firm's absorptive capacity as well as the corresponding capacity of the region where the firm is located. There is very little information about the creative capacity of innovative firms – as measured by the composition of occupations. Because of this, this section will focus on knowledge intensity.

Innovation Inputs and Outputs

The typical creative process in economic life is R&D activities, which by definition are designed to bring about new products and new routines. To emphasize that the verdict of a firm's creativity is made in the market place, the following exposition uses the term 'innovation activities', instead of R&D activities. This relates to the distinction between inventions and innovations, where the latter comprise those inventions and other novelties that are economically viable by generating revenues and profits in markets.

Figure 23.3 describes basic categories of inputs to innovation activities as well as basic outputs from these activities. The inputs include a firm's (i) interaction with other actors, (ii) import flows, (iii) inflow of labour from other firms, (iv) knowledge-intensive labour, (v) accumulated knowledge, (vi) R&D routines and heuristics, and (vii) innovation activities as measured by spending. As a first step we compare the Stockholm region with the rest of the country in terms of innovation inputs.

The second part of the figure considers the output from innovation activities. In this case we discuss the introduction of new products and new export products and the opening of new markets by firms in the Stockholm region.

Knowledge Intensity and Innovation Efforts by Firms in the Stockholm Region

Table 23.3 shows that the knowledge intensity of Swedish firms increased rapidly during the 1993–2007 period, with especially high growth in the Stockholm region. In Table 23.9 the same development is described for two sub-sectors of the economy – manufacturing and advanced services.

Table 23.9 shows that the knowledge intensity in the advanced services sector has grown fast in all three metropolitan regions and reached a very high level, which is about 100 per cent above the country average. Of course, this illustrates that knowledge intensity and creativity is strongly associated with service production. However, the values for the manufacturing industries show that their knowledge intensity is four times greater in the Stockholm region than in the country as a whole. The message from that

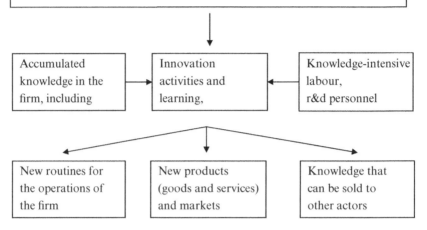

Figure 23.3   Categories of innovation inputs and outputs

Table 23.9   Knowledge intensity in manufacturing and advanced services

Urban regions	Manufacturing 1993	Manufacturing 2007	Advanced services 1993	Advanced services 2007
Stockholm	13.8	25.2	26.6	38.2
Gothenburg	9.4	19.9	25.1	36.9
Malmö	7.1	14.8	21.5	37.1
Medium sized	3.7	8.9	14.4	24.0
Rural areas	2.7	6.5	10.5	18.1

Note: The knowledge intensity of the labour force is the share of labour with at least three years of higher education; advanced services = SIC 65-74 and manufacturing = SIC 15-36.

Source: Johansson et al. (2010).

observation is that Stockholm's manufacturing sector has a markedly different orientation and activity composition than what applies to the non-metropolitan regions. The knowledge intensity of Stockholm's manufacturing firms reflects their focus on innovation efforts and knowledge creation. However, it is at this point impossible to substantiate these observations with firm-level data on occupation structure and its co-variance with innovation efforts.

The population size of the Stockholm region is about a quarter of Sweden's population. This may be compared with the region's share of the country's innovation efforts, which shows that the region has a much stronger orientation towards innovation than

Table 23.10   Innovation efforts in the manufacturing and service sectors, 2007

Regions	R&D man years, %	R&D spending, %
Stockholm	33.4	33.3
3 metropolitan counties[a]	76.0	78.0
The rest of the country	24.0	22.0
Total	100.0	100.0

Note: [a] The Country of Stockholm is approximately equal to the Stockholm region, whereas countries of Goteborg and Malmo are somewhat larger than the respective regions.

Source: Statistics Sweden; Johansson et al. (2010).

the country average. Another observation is that three-quarters of all innovation efforts in the country are associated with the three metropolitan counties.

THE ORIGIN OF IDEAS AND IMPORT DIVERSITY

In a widely cited contribution, Jane Jacobs (1984) outlines the mechanism behind the creativity and renewal of economic life in urban regions. Contrary to Marshall (1920), who stresses the importance of industry-specific localization economies of industry clusters, Jacobs suggests that creativity in economic life is stimulated by the diversity of large urban regions – metropolitan regions. Such regions offer their firms cross-fertilization of ideas that grow out of industrial diversity, with clusters of clusters and rich opportunities for novel combinations of seemingly unrelated fields.

In this context Jacobs points at a special feature of metropolitan regions: their interaction with the rest of the world economy by means of communication, export and import flows. In particular, metropolitan regions have a much richer composition of import flows than other regions, and such flows comprise products (goods and services) that add to the diversity that the region itself can produce. However, the important aspect is that the imports of metropolitan regions contain novelties from the world economy, and these novelties can stimulate existing and potential firms of the region to initiate their own product renewal and help the firms to detect new business opportunities. This picture can refer to Amsterdam in the seventeenth century or London in the nineteenth century. It also applies to the contemporary Stockholm region.

How can we verify that import of ideas, services and goods enriches the diversity of a region's economy so that it can function as a source of inspiration for creative processes? One approach could be to study how different urban regions grow in response to its import diversity. Here we will instead make use of a more direct Swedish study of how the arrival of innovation ideas to innovating firms affect the frequency with which they develop new export products and new links to foreign destination markets. Following Andersson and Johansson (2008, 2011), we can conclude that the frequency of innovation ideas increases as a consequence of the conditions enumerated below:

Table 23.11   Export shares of trading and manufacturing firms, 2004

Urban regions	Share of total export value; trading firms	Share of total export value; manufacturing firms
Stockholm	51	26
Gothenburg	14	18
Malmö	8	4
Medium-sized regions	18	34
Small regions	9	18
Total	100	100

Note: Manufacturing = SNI 15-36; trading firms = SNI 50-52.

Source: Statistics Sweden; Johansson et al. (2010).

1. The firm's experiences of previous product and market innovations and export activities.
2. Knowledge flows to the firm through import activities of the firm and its neighbouring firms.
3. Output diversity and scale of the firm.
4. Knowledge intensity of the firm, which reflects its absorption capacity.
5. Knowledge flows from the world to a firm belonging to a multinational corporate group via the internal network of the group.
6. The accumulated knowledge among firms in the region about export opportunities.

   With reference to the described conditions for export-product innovations, Table 23.11 presents export intensity in the Stockholm region and other Swedish regions. In the table we distinguish between exports that are carried out by trading companies (wholesale, agencies and so on) and by manufacturing firms. Trading firms are specialized to manage thin flows to a multitude of destinations. When flows are thicker they are exported by the manufacturing firms themselves. As shown in Table 23.11, more than 50 per cent of the exports by trading firms in Sweden are managed by firms in the Stockholm region. In contrast, direct exports managed by the producers themselves only account for about one-quarter of total exports, which is proportional to Stockholm's population share.

   For trading companies, we observe a strong concentration of their export value in the Stockholm region, matched by an even stronger concentration of their import value in the same region. As shown in Table 23.12, the import share of the Stockholm region's trading firms is close to 60 per cent. We can also verify that the import flows via trading firms is extremely diversified. When we distinguish import events by an eight-digit product code combined with an identification of the country origin of each import flow, the number of import events of trading firms reach the value 140 000 (Johansson et al., 2010). This can be compared with the corresponding diversity figures for the Gothenburg region with 65 000 and the Malmö region with just above 40 000.

Table 23.12   Import shares of trading and manufacturing firms, 2004

Urban regions	Share of import value; trading firms	Share of import value; manufacturing firms
Stockholm	57	21
Gothenburg	13	20
Malmö	8	5
Medium-sized regions	16	34
Small regions	6	20
Total	100	100

Note: Manufacturing = SNI 15-36; trading firms = SNI 50-52.

Source: Statistics Sweden; Johansson et al. (2010).

KNOWLEDGE FLOWS THROUGH LABOUR MOBILITY

A firm collects information about markets and technology through many channels as discussed previously. Some of the knowledge flows are paid for in the form of purchases from knowledge providers, including payments for patents. Still, an important part of knowledge flows seem to be pure knowledge spillovers. How do these spillovers take place? And why are these spillovers greater in metropolitan regions?

In large urban regions the labour market is denser than elsewhere, making the supply of labour more varied, with many specialized competences. Such thick labour markets can substantially increase the congruence between a heterogeneous supply and an equally differentiated demand for specialized labour from firms. In this way, people with specialized qualifications can more accurately be assigned to jobs which require their particular qualifications, causing improved productivity.

Labour market mobility is important also from a dynamic development point of view. When individuals shift employment from one firm to another, then the individual carries with him/her experiences and knowledge to the new firm. This evidently is an important mechanism for knowledge spillovers. The following observations illustrate how labour mobility affects knowledge flows in the Stockholm region (Andersson and Thulin, 2008; Johansson et. al., 2010):

- In a large and dense region like Stockholm, labour mobility has a higher frequency than in other Swedish regions. The greater knowledge intensity in the Stockholm region also implies that its labour mobility affects knowledge flows disproportionately.
- Econometric analyses show that labour productivity is higher in regions with greater labour-mobility intensity.
- The growth of labour productivity is faster in urban regions with large labour-mobility intensity.
- Labour mobility is greater than average for employees working in industries classified as advanced services (that is, SIC 65-74). In this context we observe that the

Stockholm region has both a high share of advanced services and high levels of labour mobility.

● Labour mobility is greater for knowledge-intensive labour, which favours the Stockholm region with its high knowledge intensity.

THE CREATIVE CLUSTERS OF THE STOCKHOLM REGION

The following sections examine four clusters with high specialization in the Stockholm region and present observations about their growth patterns. In the Swedish context, the pertinent industries have been labelled creative or innovative clusters.

Cluster Formation in the Stockholm Region

The preceding sections provided an introduction to the structural development of the Stockholm region. A major feature of this evolution has been a rapid expansion of the knowledge intensity and hence a growing share of knowledge handlers with cognitive skills. Knowledge intensity has increased in all sectors, but the intensity is far from evenly spread across sectors, and this may also imply that creative processes are more prevalent in some sectors than in others.

One way to organize the available data is to consider those sectors and sub-sectors for which the Stockholm region has a high specialization quotient (ratio) as specified in equation (23.2). Our hypothesis is that knowledge intensity and creativity in the region is primarily concentrated in industries with a high specialization quotient. As shown in Johansson et al. (2010), such an approach is supported by the fact that Stockholm's specialization pattern differs significantly from the pattern that can be found in the other two metropolitan regions, Gothenburg and Malmö.

We suggest that a cluster is identified as co-located firms in a group of associated industries with (i) a high specialization ratio, (ii) location in the region of suppliers that deliver to the firms in the cluster, (iii) location in the region of customers of the firms in the cluster, and (iv) tangible and intangible infrastructure endowments in the region (Figure 23.4). The cluster formation is strengthened when suppliers deliver distance-sensitive inputs to the cluster firms, and when the latter deliver distance-sensitive products (services) to their customers in the region. The observation is that distance dependency stimulates the co-location of cluster firms and 'environment' firms (Johansson and Forslund, 2008).

In a study from the 1990s, Johansson and Strömquist (1998) identify five major clusters in the Stockholm region. From these, we have selected four clusters that fit the label 'creative clusters'. In these clusters we find occupations that require cognitive skills of individuals working as knowledge and information handlers. The clusters are presented in Table 23.13, and they comprise (i) knowledge, information and market services to firms, (ii) financial services, (iii) media commodities and services, and (iv) ICT commodities and services. Specialization is recorded when the ratio is above 100, and hence the ratio 204 for financial services in 2008 means that these activities are over-represented by 104 per cent in the Stockholm region.

Table 23.13 shows that the four clusters increased their combined specialization quotient

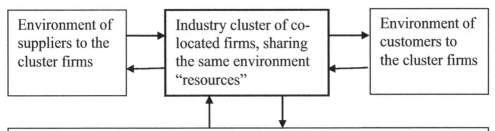

Figure 23.4   An industry cluster and its environment of suppliers, customers and endowments

Table 23.13   Four creative clusters of the Stockholm region

	Specialization 1993 (%)	Specialization 2008 (%)
Services to firms: legal including patents; accounting; market analysis; organization; advertising; design; fairs and conferences (25 SIC codes)	157	138
Financial services: banking; securities; insurance, and so on (16 SIC codes)	188	204
Media: printing; electronic mediation; video and films (21 SIC codes)	148	165
ICT products and services: production of and trade with office equipment; software and ICT services (23 SIC codes)	200	173
Remaining sectors of the economy	92	89

Source: Statistics Sweden.

between 1993 and 2008, since the remaining sectors of the economy reduced their joint ratio from 92 to 89. In this period financial services and media increase their specialization, whereas the ratio is reduced for ICT commodities and services, and for services to firms.

Specialization in the Stockholm Region and Diffusion to Other Regions

Following Karlsson and Johansson (2006), we can observe a global transformation of large urban regions from predominantly industrial economies to knowledge economies, which is changing the composition of industries, the location of production, the occupational structure, the education level, the variety of goods and services and the R&D

Table 23.14   Growth rates in the Stockholm region and in Sweden, percentages

	Stockholm		Sweden	
Year	1993–2000	2000–08	1993–2000	2000–08
Firm services	84.55	20.00	67.10	37.30
Financial	12.53	14.17	1.10	7.22
Media	0.39	11.44	−4.04	−4.94
ICT	17.80	78.11	37.30	56.85
The rest	9.77	9.72	4.27	8.03

Source: Statistics Sweden.

intensity. In this process, outsourcing of producer services plays a major role, allowing producers of both goods and services to decompose their production into sub-processes, which can be outsourced to new and separated suppliers of producer services (Klaesson and Pettersson, 2006). As shown in Table 23.14, firm services have continued to grow both in the Stockholm region and Sweden as a whole. This has happened across all regional sizes (Johansson et al., 2010). In a similar way the majority of industries in the ICT cluster have also diffused nationwide (Johansson, 2006; Johansson and Paulsson, 2009). There are some – albeit much weaker – signs of spatial diffusion of financial services. The final observation in Table 23.14 is, on the other hand, quite strong: industries in the media cluster do not display any general diffusion from the Stockholm region to other urban regions.

The growth of creative clusters as illustrated in Table 23.13 can be said to reshape the entire economy towards a stronger concentration of activities in the Stockholm region and other large urban regions. From Table 23.1 we also know that the three metropolitan regions grow much faster than other urban regions in the country. Does this mean that there is a conflict between metropolitan and other regions in the process of economic renewal? The question is essential because industries in the four clusters represent a growing segment of the contemporary economy in Sweden and other Organization for Economic Corporation and Development (OECD) countries. In the Stockholm region, total employment in the four clusters accounts for 24 per cent of total employment. The same figure for Sweden as a whole is 14 per cent.

To answer the above question we can refer to several studies, where Forslund (1997) refers to the 1980s, RTK (2003) to the 1990s and Johansson and Klaesson (forthcoming) to the period 1999–2006. All these studies confirm the picture provided by Table 23.15, which is that industries with high specialization in the Stockholm region can be expected to diffuse to other urban regions in the country. High specialization in Stockholm thus predicts that the industry is very likely to grow in a large number of other regions. The opposite holds true for industries with a low specialization in the Stockholm region. This indicates that structural change is initiated in the Stockholm region, while other urban regions follow the same path although with a clear delay.

Other smaller clusters in the Stockholm region, which follow the dynamic pattern seen in Table 23.15, comprise (i) marketing, advertising and conference activities, (ii) travel services and some transport services, and (iii) pharmaceuticals and medical equipment

Table 23.15 Diffusion regularity for industries with high and low specialization in the Stockholm region

Industries with:	Expansion in the rest of Sweden	Contraction in the rest of Sweden
High specialization in the Stockholm region	The pertinent industries (including the Stockholm clusters) increase their employment in most other regions.	
Low specialization in the Stockholm region		The majority of pertinent industries reduce their employment in most other regions.

Source: Forslund (1997, 1998); RTK (2003); Johansson et al. (2010).

industries. With few exceptions the industries with high specialization in the Stockholm region employ a large share of workers with cognitive skills and tertiary education in occupations that involve knowledge-handling tasks.

WHAT ATTRACTS HOUSEHOLDS TO THE STOCKHOLM REGION?

For a 35-year period, between 1970 and 2005, more than half of Sweden's population increase can be attributed to the growth of the Stockholm region. Such an expansion requires that both the number of jobs and the supply of labour grow. There is strong empirical evidence that this growth process satisfies a pattern where jobs follow people (Holmberg et al., 2003; Johansson and Klaesson, 2007). This finding is associated with theoretical arguments that show that large urban regions attract firms and create jobs by offering a superior labour supply, diverse input opportunities and a high local demand for distance-sensitive outputs, especially services.

Urban regions grow primarily as a result of having greater in-migration than out-migration flows. A positive net migration is often taken as a sign of a region's attractiveness. The choice of moving from one region to another is associated with a series of cost components such as the costs of transporting household members and equipment, finding new housing, finding a new job, breaking up old and establishing new social networks and so forth.

Do the migration flows bring about a gradual concentration of creative occupations in the largest urban regions? Available data do not allow for such an analysis. As a substitute, our interest is directed towards migration flows that make the knowledge intensity grow in the largest urban regions. In view of this, there are two major categories of inflows: (i) people who wish to pursue university studies and (ii) people who wish to find a job after completed university studies. For the latter type of flow, the literature recognizes the following two separate motives:

- The working life or job motive, with a focus on the career opportunities and the expected wage premium associated with changing one's location.
- The consumption motive, which includes the diversity of consumption alternatives, public goods and other amenities in the new location.

Comparing the Stockholm region with a typical medium-sized region in Sweden, we can conclude that the diversity of job opportunities is more than seven times greater in the Stockholm region (Johansson et al., 2010). The diversity advantage is especially pronounced with regard to knowledge-handling jobs that require cognitive skills.

ATTRACTIVENESS, WAGE PREMIUM AND AMENITIES OF THE STOCKHOLM REGION

The attractiveness of a region reveals itself in in-migration and generates high demand for land and housing, and this generates scarcity and increasing housing rent levels. As a consequence, household income needs to be higher than elsewhere in such a region, which should be reflected in higher wages. In turn, the latter requires that attractive urban regions have higher productivity. In view of this, one may contemplate an adjustment process as described in Figure 23.5 (Glaeser, 2008). Attractiveness as perceived by households and agglomeration advantages as perceived by firms bring about increasing wages and land values with higher rents for dwellings and premises. For Stockholm, this is reflected in housing prices that are about double the average for Sweden, and three to four times higher than in medium-sized and small regions. The rent level in Stockholm for Central Business District (CBD) floor space for retailing services is normally five to six times higher than CBD rents in medium-sized urban regions (Johansson et al., 2010).

Calculating an average wage index for all Swedish urban regions in 2006, we can conclude that the wage index of the Stockholm region was 22 per cent higher than the average for the country and 34 per cent higher than the average for medium-sized regions. Partly this is a reflection of the average education level having remained higher in the Stockholm region. However, we can also control for the education effect and instead calculate the average wage premium associated with a job in the Stockholm region for different occupation groups, as presented in Table 23.16. The premium is highest for managerial-administrative skills and there is about the same premium for social and cognitive skills. For motor skills there is barely any premium at all. The wage level for occupations with motor skills is approximately the same in the Stockholm region and the rest of Sweden. A similar result for motor-skill occupations is reported for the United States in Bacolod et al. (2009).

Why is the wage premium lower for occupations with cognitive skills than for occupations that require managerial and administrative skills? A primary reason can be that a large share of knowledge handlers with cognitive skills is employed by the public sector, where wages are on average lower than in the private sector. This may be complemented by the conjecture that knowledge handlers appreciate the location amenities of a large urban region, and that knowledge handlers may experience a creativity externality such as that other local knowledge handlers are a major attraction factor for knowledge handlers – all in jobs requiring cognitive skills.

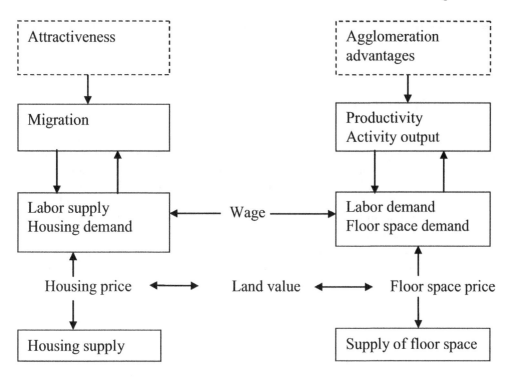

Figure 23.5   Location of households and firms and equilibrium adjustment of housing and floor area prices

Table 23.16   Average monthly wage (SEK), 2008

	Cognitive skills	Managerial-administrative skills	Social skills	Motor and other skills
Stockholm region	34 047	37 081	25 716	22 518
Rest of Sweden	29 526	29 100	21 916	22 085
Stockholm/Rest of Sweden (%)	115	127	117	102

Source: Statistics Sweden.

The overall attractiveness of the Stockholm region has been summarized in the following way (Johansson et al., 2010):

● Good accessibility to a wide range of job opportunities with many potential employers, in particular in occupations requiring cognitive skills.
● An infrastructure that increases households' accessibility to private and public services, and which makes public goods more accessible.
● A diverse and tradition-rich supply of cultural services.

- An infrastructure that provides an ample supply of waterfront locations, for housing as well as for workplaces.
- A great variety of housing and recreation milieus.

CONCLUDING REMARKS

This chapter illustrates the importance of the Stockholm region for the Swedish economy. For a long period of time, the Stockholm region has been the major centre for knowledge development, innovation and intellectual creativity in Sweden. It has maintained this position by being more diverse and versatile than other regions. Given this position, the region has been an attractor of individuals with ambitions and talents in political, economic and cultural life. At the same time novel ideas and solutions have continued to diffuse from the Stockholm region to other parts of the country.

The knowledge intensity of the Swedish economy has increased during the studied period. The increase was faster in the metropolitan regions, and in particular the Stockholm region. This development has been related to the well-established hypothesis that the knowledge intensity of an urban region reflects the absorption capacity of firms in the region, implying that firms can make use of all sorts of novelties in the world economy as stimuli for their own imitations and innovations (Cohen and Levinthal, 1990).

We have shown that occupations that require cognitive or managerial skills dominate the labour market of the Stockholm region, and that jobs with these skills correlate strongly with knowledge- and information-handling tasks. Descriptive statistics illustrate the associated wage premium. In this context, we also stress that Stockholm's manufacturing sector has a markedly higher share of knowledge-intensive labour than any other region of Sweden, reflecting the focus on innovation among Stockholm's manufacturing firms.

A major distinguishing feature of the Stockholm region is its interface with international import flows into the region. These flows are disproportionally large in terms of value as well as diversity. The important aspect is that the import flows contain novelties from the world economy. These novelties can stimulate existing and potential firms in the region to initiate the introduction of their own new products, and they can help the firms to detect new business opportunities. Based on these observations, this chapter suggests that the Stockholm region functions as a source of innovation and business renewal for the rest of the country, since novelties are disseminated through the regional hierarchy.

REFERENCES

Andersson, Å.E. (1985), *Kreativitet – Storstadens Framtid*, Stockholm: Prisma.
Andersson, Å.E. and B. Johansson (1984), 'Industrial dynamics, product cycles and employment structure', working paper 84-9, International Institute for Applied Systems Analysis, Laxenburg.
Andersson, M. And B. Johansson (2008), 'Innovation ideas and regional characteristics – product innovations and export entrepreneurship by firms in Swedish regions', *Growth and Change*, **39**, 193–224.
Andersson, M. and B. Johansson (2011 forthcoming), 'Heterogeneous distributions of firms sustained by innovation dynamics – a model with empirical application', *Journal of Industry Competition and Trade*, **X**(X).
Andersson, M. and P. Thulin (2008), *Globalisering, arbetskraftens rörlighet och produktivitet*, report, Stockholm: Globaliseringsrådet.

Bacolod, M., B.S. Blum and W.C. Strange (2009), 'Skills in the city', *Journal of Urban Economics*, **65**, 136–53.

Cohen, W.M. and D.A. Levinthal (1990), 'Absorptive capacity: a new perspective on learning and innovation', *Administrative Science Quarterly*, **35**,128–52.

EB (1991), *The New Encyclopedia Britannica*, Chicago, IL: Encyclopedia Britanica.

Florida, R. (2002), *The Rise of the Creative Class*, New York, NY: Basic Books.

Florida, R., C. Mellander and K. Stolarick (2008), 'Inside the black box of regional development', *Journal of Economic Geography*, **8**, 615–49.

Forslund, U.M. (1997), 'Studies of multiregional Interdependencies and change', TRITA-IP FR 97-31, Division of Regional Planning, The Royal Institute of Technology, Stockholm.

Forslund, U.M. (1998), 'Education intensity and interregional location dynamics', in A. Reggiani (ed.), *Accessibility, Trade and Location Behaviour*, Aldershot: Ashgate, pp. 97–120.

Glaeser, E.L. (2008), *Cities, Agglomeration and Spatial Equilibrium*, Oxford: Oxford University Press.

Glaeser, E.L. and D.C. Mare (2001), 'Cities and skills', *Journal of Labor Economics*, **19**, 316–42.

Herzog, H.W. Jr and A.M. Schlottman (1989), 'High-technology location and worker mobility in the U.S.', in Å.E. Andersson, D.F. Batten and C. Karlsson (eds), *Knowledge and Industrial Organization*, Berlin: Springer, pp. 219–32.

Holmberg, I., B. Johansson and U. Strömquist (2003), 'A simultaneous model of long-term regional job and population changes', in Å.E. Andersson, B. Johansson and W.P. Anderson (eds), *The Economics of Disappearing Distance*, Ashgate: Aldershot, pp. 161–89.

Huffman, D. and J.M. Quigley (2002), 'The role of the university in attracting high tech entrepreneurship: a Silicon Valley tale', *Annals of Regional Science*, **36**(3), 403–19.

Hult, J (1989), 'Bondeland blir industriland', in S. Rydberg (ed.), *Svensk teknikhistoria*, Hedemora: Gidlunds bokförlag, pp. 230–68.

Jacobs, J. (1984), *Cities and the Wealth of Nations*, New York, NY: Random House.

Janik, A. and S. Toulmin (1973), *Wittgenstein's Vienna*, New York, NY: Simon and Schuster.

Johansson, B. (1993), *Ekonomisk dynamik i Europa – Nätverk för handel, kunskapsimport och innovationer*, Malmö: Liber-Hermods.

Johansson, B. (2006), 'Spatial clusters of ICT industries', in B. Johansson, C. Karlsson and R.R. Stough (eds), *The Emerging Digital Economy – Entrepreneurship, Cluster and Policy*, Berlin: Springer, pp. 137–69.

Johansson, B. and U.M. Forslund (2008), 'The analysis of location, co-location and urbanization economies', in C. Karlsson (ed.), *Handbook of Research on Cluster Theory*, Cheltenham, UK and Northampton, MA, USA: Edward Elgar Publishing, pp. 39–66.

Johansson, B. and J. Klaesson (2007), 'Infrastructure, labour market accessibility and economic development', in C. Karlsson, W.P. Anderson, B. Johansson and K. Kobayashi (eds), *The Management and Measurement of Infrastructure*, Cheltenham, UK and Northampton, MA, USA: Edward Elgar Publishing, pp. 69–98.

Johansson, B. and J. Klaesson (forthcoming), 'Agglomeration dynamics of business services', *Annals of Regional Science*.

Johansson, B. and T. Paulsson (2009), 'Location of new industries: the ICT sector 1990-2000', in C. Karlsson, B. Johansson and R.R. Stough (eds), *Innovation, Agglomeration and Regional Competition*, Cheltenham, UK and Northampton, MA, USA: Edward Elgar Publishing, pp. 261–93.

Johansson, B., J. Klaesson and M. Olsson (2002), 'Time distances and labour market integration', *Papers in Regional Science*, **81**, 305–27.

Johansson, B., J. Klaesson, M. Andersson, U.M. Forslund and U. Strömquist (2010), 'Storstadsregionerna och ekonomins utveckling', JIBS Research Report Series No. 2010-1, Jönköping: Jönköping International Business School.

Karlsson, C. and B. Johansson (2006), 'Dynamics and entrepreneurship in a knowledge-based economy', in C. Karlsson, B. Johansson and R. Stough (eds), *Entrepreneurship and Dynamics in a Knowledge Economy*, London: Routledge, pp. 12–46.

Klaesson, J. and L. Pettersson (2006), 'Local and regional ICT service sector markets in Sweden', in B. Johansson, C. Karlsson and R.R. Stough (eds), *The Emerging Digital Economy – Entrepreneurship, Cluster and Policy*, Berlin: Springer, pp. 169–86.

Koestler, A. (1959), *The Sleepwalkers*, New York, NY and London: Macmillan.

Koestler, A. (1964), *The Act of Creation*, New York, NY and London: Macmillan.

Marshall, A. (1920), *Principles of Economics*, London: Macmillan.

Mellander, C. (2009), 'Creative and knowledge industries: an occupational distribution approach', *Economic Development Quarterly*, **23**(4), 294–305.

Rosenthal, S.S. and W.C. Strange (2008), 'The attenuation of human capital spillovers', *Journal of Urban Economics*, **64**, 373–89.

RTK (2003), *Växande branscher – Om Stockholmsregionens samspel med övriga landet*, Storstadspolitik 8:2003, Stockholm: Regionplane- och Trafikkontoret, Stockholms läns landsting.

Rydberg, S. (ed.) (1989), *Svensk teknikhistoria*, Hedemora: Gidlunds bokförlag.
Saxenian, A. (1996), *Regional Advantage: Culture and Competition in Silicon Valley and Route 128*, Cambridge, MA: Harvard University Press.
Smith, G.J.W. (1993), 'The creative person', in Å.E. Andersson, D.F. Batten, K. Kobayashi and K. Yoshikawa (eds), *The Cosmo-creative Society*, Berlin: Springer, pp. 31–44.
Warner, S.B. Jr (1989), 'The evolution of high technology in the Boston region 1920–1980', in Å.E. Andersson, D.F. Batten and C. Karlsson (eds), *Knowledge and Industrial Organization*, Berlin: Springer, pp. 133–42.

APPENDIX

Tables 23A.1 and 23A.2 present the results from estimating the regression equation

$$\ln E_r = \alpha + \beta \ln P_r + \varepsilon_r \qquad (23A.1)$$

where the dependent variable, E, measures the number of people in each urban region with different occupation skills (Table 23A.1) and with different occupation tasks (Table 23A.2).

The estimated parameters are highly significant for both skills and tasks. One interesting observation is that employment increases faster than population. A second observation is that cognitive skills as well as knowledge-handling occupations display a clearly higher threshold, as reflected by large absolute α-values (Table 23A.3).

Table 23A.1   Urban size and employment in different skill categories

Dependent variable	Total employment	Cognitive skills	Managerial skills	Social skills	Motor skills
Constant (α)	−1.25	−4.80	−3.81	−2.11	−1.51
t-value	(−16.1)	(−31.5)	(−22.8)	(−26.3)	(−11.3)
Population (β)	**1.03**	**1.18**	**1.10**	**1.01**	**0.97**
t-value	(144.0)	(83.6)	(70.9)	(135.6)	(78.0)
R^2	0.996	0.989	0.985	0.996	0.987
N	81	81	81	81	81

Table 23A.2   Urban size and employment in different task categories

	Total employment	Knowledge	Information	Service	Goods
Constant	−1.25	−4.95	−2.95	−1.6	−2.14
t-value	(−16.08)	(−31.39)	(−21.08)	(−15.89)	(−15.62)
Population	**1.03**	**1.19**	**1.09**	**0.95**	**0.99**
t-value	(143.97)	(81.21)	(83.83)	(102)	(77.63)
R^2	0.996	0.988	0.989	0.992	0.987
N	81	81	81	81	81

Table 23A.3   Definition of cognitive and knowledge-handling occupations

Knowledge handling	Cognitive occupations
1	Physicists, chemists and related professionals
1	Mathematicians and statisticians
1	Computing professionals
1	Architects, engineers and related professionals
1	Life science professionals
1	Health professionals (except nursing)
1	Nursing and midwifery professionals
1	College, university and higher education teaching professionals
1	Secondary education teaching professionals
1	Primary education teaching professionals
1	Special education teaching professionals
1	Other teaching professionals
1	Legal professionals
0	Archivists, librarians and related information professionals
1	Social science and linguistics professionals (except social work professionals)
1	Writers and creative or performing artists
1	Psychologists, social work and related professionals
1	Physical and engineering science technicians
0	Computer associate professionals
1	Optical and electronic equipment operators
1	Life science technicians
1	Artistic, entertainment and sports associate professionals
0	Potters, glass-makers and related trades workers
0	Handicraft workers in wood, textile, leather and related materials
0	Craft printing and related trades workers
0	Wood treaters, cabinet-makers and related trades workers

24 The creative city and its distributional consequences: the case of Wellington
Philip S. Morrison

I had a hunch that inequality in our society was being exacerbated by the rise of the creative economy. Indeed, inequality was highest in the creative epicenters of the U.S. economy. (Florida, 2005, pp. 4–5)

We find that the rhetoric of universal social potential accompanying creative city ideas continues to overlook those unable to participate in this new economy, as well as those who are more actively excluded. (Atkinson and Easthope, 2009, p. 64)

These concerns, which were raised in Richard Florida's (2005) *Cities and the Creative Class* and in a review of creative strategies in Australia's cities, do not take centre stage in Florida's argument. Rather, they linger as nagging doubts while the main thesis is being advanced. 'The underlying concern', Florida explains, 'is that our society continues to encourage the inventive talents of a minority while neglecting the creative capacities of the majority' (Florida, 2005, p. 5).

This is an opportune time to elevate these nagging issues by drawing evidence from Wellington City, which has been held up as a particularly creative city. The main point I wish to make in this chapter concerns the way in which successive concentrations of knowledge and creative workers in the central city of a metropolitan region runs the risk of increasing social inequality. The primary mechanism, I argue, is the way the spatial concentration of wealth at the centre steepens the housing rent gradient, leading to increasing suburbanization of the less competitive. The result is the addition of a geographic dimension to an existing inequality, one which through the externalities associated with social segmentation can negatively influence the social mobility of the relatively disadvantaged.

While the example I use is a small capital city in the southern hemisphere, the underlying process is present in the many countries used as examples in this book. Wellington City, the capital of New Zealand, has a population of less than 200 000 in a country of under five million people spread over a land area roughly equivalent to that of the United Kingdom. Since Wellington's public sector reforms in the 1990s – and the rise of the local film industry – the city has been heralded internationally as a creative city, as indeed it is.

Wellington City is cited by Richard Florida as an example of how a small city has been able to strengthen its economic competitiveness by luring the creative class and building on its creative industries; indeed, by becoming a 'world cultural capital' (Florida, 2003). Wellington was thrust onto the world stage largely as a result of the work of (now Sir) Peter Jackson, the creator of *The Lord of the Rings Trilogy*. Successive Wellington City mayors have used this attention to actively promote their city, adopting the external brand of 'Creative Wellington: Innovation Capital'.

What is important to recognize, however, is that Wellington City is part of the larger

Wellington Region, the population of which is almost two and a half times that of the city alone and whose propensity to share the benefits of the capital's creativity can be questioned. This chapter argues that investing in the urban physical and human infrastructure in order to attract skills to the city has its dual in the displacement of lower-income (often routine) service workers to the large suburban tracts and smaller towns within the larger region. The search for a harmonious balance between those who benefit from the steps taken to enhance human capital in the creative city and those who simply service its social and physical infrastructure complicates a holistic assessment of the benefits of spatially concentrating the creative class.

Although none of these points are new, they have usually been confined to discussions of gentrification – socio-economic displacement by neighbourhood (Peck, 2005; Atkinson and Easthope, 2009). What is instructive and possibly a little unusual about the case of Wellington is the way in which this process of displacement – through the workings of the local housing market – has spread to almost the whole of the city. The consequences of these market linkages are exacerbated in this city's case by its limited physical connection with the rest of the Wellington Region. Notwithstanding the economic linkages, the city – through its physical position in a region with a very complex topography – has a palpable degree of physical, cultural and political separation from its wider urban hinterland. It is this feature which renders Wellington something of a natural experiment with which to consider the distributional impacts of building a creative city.

I begin the chapter by reporting the conventional wisdom, the story line that accompanies the transformation of Wellington City into a highly creative city. I then turn to the social geography of the larger Wellington Region, of which Wellington City is the economic core although only a minor player in terms of land area and resident population. I trace some of the distributional consequences of the growth of the creative city, by arguing that the city's real estate price response to the growth of creative knowledge workers has made it increasingly difficult for those on low income to purchase (and in some cases even rent) within the boundaries of Wellington City. The result is a spatial exacerbation of the inequality inherent in the singular fostering of skill and creativity, without commensurate attention to addressing its distribution within the population as a whole. The chapter concludes with some reflections.

THE CONVENTIONAL WISDOM

From the poetry to the social surveys to the upbeat local radio, the City of Wellington is continually lauded for its multilayered and sometimes quirky amenities: natural as well as man-made. I must declare from the outset my own delight at the emergence of a vibrant exciting city out of what I recall from my youth was a dull collection of old grey buildings and sparsely inhabited streets. In those days, Wellington as a city was saved spiritually only by a harbour of rare natural beauty.

The natural beauty remains but most of the old grey buildings are gone. The city now has density, colour and innovative city planning. Thousands of inner-city apartments have been erected beside and above shops and offices within walking distance of the harbour front with its sculptures, buskers, coffee carts, skateboarders, unicyclists, fishermen and families on 'crocodiles'.[1] Wellington's citizens now join domestic and overseas tourists in crowding the city in the evenings and at weekends. The last 20 years have seen an extraordinary transformation of Wellington City into a place people want to go to and be part of rather than rush home and escape from. The visual evidence speaks for itself.[2]

Wellington's contemporary creativity is much more than *The Lord of the Rings Trilogy* or the technical effects that WETA Digital constructed for the film *Avatar* among many other films, impressive though these local pioneers have been. Everyday life in the City of Wellington is sustained by a creativity that extends well beyond the post-production facilities and related cinematic enterprises in the city's south-eastern suburb of Miramar. From the inspired science and arts on the six campuses of Wellington's three universities, several government-funded research institutes, through to an innovative computer software industry and a vibrant fashion industry, this compact 'walking city' squeezed within the 'horseshoe' of a town green belt has attracted many skilled people from within New Zealand and from overseas. They all rely on their creative capacity to survive in a highly competitive deregulated economy, where commercial spin-offs are sought as an integral consequence and even rationale for creativity.[3]

As well as the resident New Zealand National Symphony Orchestra, the New Zealand Opera Company and the New Zealand School of Dance, Wellington City also celebrates the arts through several annual events, including the Wearable Arts awards, a series of film festivals, the Festival of the Arts and the associated fringe festivals. Patronage comes from the same large core of well-paid professionals who frequent the city's cafés and high-rise offices. Not surprisingly, residents of Wellington City exhibit a level of pride in the look and feel of their city that is unsurpassed anywhere in the country (Quality of Life Team, 2008).

Wellington City's creativity also extends to its nightlife, much of which is affordable by the educated sons and daughters of the middle class for whom the recent decades have been so favourable. For this we have to thank former mayor Mark Blumsky, who made Courtenay Place his own, convincing New Zealand and a growing set of young tourist patrons that Wellington is a 24-hour party zone. Those who live in the city of Wellington may well party hard – young and old alike – for they constitute a concentration of the wealthiest and most highly educated people anywhere in the country.

THE CREATIVE CITY IN GEOGRAPHICAL CONTEXT

One way of appreciating the difference between the city and its much larger hinterland is through the map of population density, which reflects a complex interplay of geography and history (McConchie et al., 2000). As Figure 24.1 shows, residential densities are highest in the city, located in the south-west corner of the region surrounding the sea that penetrates inland from Cook Strait to form Wellington Harbour. According to the latest estimates (from 2009), 478 600 people lived in Wellington Region, of which only 40 per cent (195 500) live in Wellington City.

North of Wellington (City) lie the outlying cities of Porirua, Lower Hutt and Upper Hutt. Together the four cities collectively make up the Wellington Urban Area, north of which run a series of coastal settlements through to the Kapiti Coast and the neighbouring Horowhenua District. Inland, running north-north-east across the Rimutaka Range,

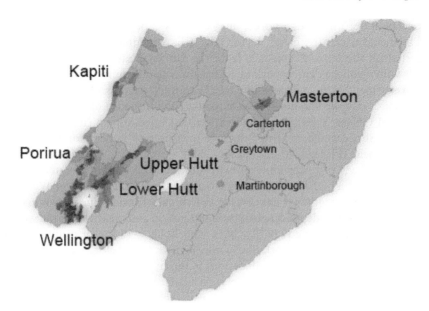

Figure 24.1   Population density by census area in the Wellington Region, 2001

are the largely rural Wairarapa settlements of Martinborough, Greytown, Carterton and Masterton. Separating all three settlement corridors are large stretches of mountainous country. It is within this highly variable and rugged typography that the social geography of the Wellington Region has developed.

Wellington's Creative Class

Attempts to identify a 'creative class' and to quantify its presence statistically in New Zealand are fraught with many of the same difficulties experienced elsewhere. Not only has the very concept of the creative class been questioned (Glaeser, 2004; Peck, 2005; Markusen, 2006; Scott, 2006, 2010), but there have been numerous difficulties in selecting appropriate forms of measurement. The main source available in New Zealand, the Census, suffers from the same restrictive and conservative boundaries identified by other researchers (Rosenfeld, 2004; Markusen, 2006).

Karen King (Chapter 9 in this volume) empirically defines creative occupations as those that have relatively high levels of autonomy and complexity: 'The creative class consists of occupations whose economic value is the creation of new ideas and forms, and includes occupations such as engineers, programmers and managers.' Many of these attributes are included within the 'knowledge worker' classification used in New Zealand to refer to those industries and occupations that are primarily based on highly skilled employment (Department of Labour, 2009).[4] These sectors represent an increasing share of the New Zealand economy's output and employment and are regarded as the most likely source of the future gains in innovation and knowledge that will be needed to improve productivity. One of the primary attributes of 'knowledge workers' is their high level of formal education.

The concept of the 'knowledge worker' may not fully capture the creativity component intended by the term 'creative class'. Todd Gabe (Chapter 7 in this volume), for example, has suggested on the basis of evidence from the United States that only two-fifths of individuals with a college degree work in occupations that require a high degree of creativity. No assessment of the marginal impact of creativity on wages has been undertaken in New Zealand, and we should acknowledge that the presence of such an effect may temper Edward Glaeser's empirical observation that once human capital is controlled for, much of what is deemed creative – through measures of 'bohemianism' for example – seems to disappear (Florida, 2002; Glaeser, 2004).

The remaining level of uncertainty notwithstanding, the present chapter does place considerable weight on higher qualifications to argue that in the context of Wellington's highly service-oriented economy, increases in individuals' formal education is associated with increasing levels of independence of thought, action and creativity in the work they perform. Other things being equal, a worker who holds a PhD, for example, is more likely to be engaged in creative work than someone with a bachelor's degree.

The importance of educational qualifications in the city notwithstanding, I also isolate occupations typically identified as 'creative' such as the arts, in demonstrating the greater presence of members of the creative class within Wellington City. While official statistics alone are unlikely to adequately capture the proportion of highly creative people who contribute to the local economy, what is important to note is that often those who have gained their creative skills through practice will work in a highly collaborative way with those with more formal qualifications. This is particularly the case in a small practical economy like New Zealand, in which small firms dominate.

The presence of an educated workforce in a small economy is certainly going to be a prerequisite for most knowledge work as well as for a high proportion of closely related work recognized as being creative. This is so within the arts and sciences but also within commerce and in entrepreneurial activities. On the basis of such measurable criteria, Wellington City stands out, not just within the wider Wellington Region but within the country as a whole. In 2006 an impressive 41.3 per cent of 25–60 year olds living in Wellington City had post-secondary degrees, compared with well under half that proportion in the rest of the Wellington Region and 18.9 per cent in New Zealand as a whole.

When it comes to higher degrees, the selectivity of Wellington City is even greater. While 3.3 per cent of New Zealand's 25–60 year olds hold master's degrees and doctorates, the corresponding figure for Wellington City is 8.9 per cent – the highest of any of the 73 local authorities in the country. None of the authorities in the Wellington Region even approaches half the proportion of advanced degrees that Wellington City residents hold.

More important for the argument about the distributional effects associated with the spatial concentration of talent is the change that has taken place in the city's workforce. It is a testimony to the city's ability to attract talent that Wellington City's proportion of degree-holders rose almost twice as fast among 25–60 year olds from 2001 to 2006 as that of any other local authority in the Wellington region (from 33 per cent to 41.3 per cent).

The spatial concentration of educated people is of course closely reflected in the city's occupational structure, with 34.3 per cent of those working in the city in 2006 being classified as professionals, compared to only 18.8 per cent in the country as a whole and 27.6

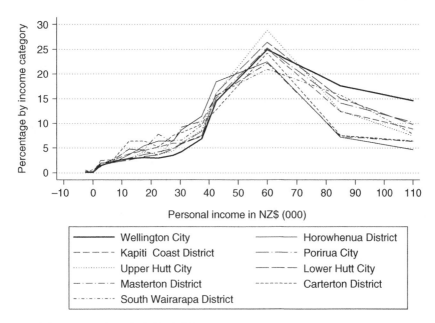

Source: Statistics New Zealand via Table Builder.

Figure 24.2   *Income distribution of usually resident professionals by local authority in the Wellington Region, 2006*

per cent in the Wellington Region. 'Arts and media professionals' made up 1.06 per cent of all those reporting occupations in the city, a higher proportion than all the other 72 local authorities (including Auckland City at 0.97 per cent). Wellington City housed over 12 per cent or 17 511 of all the arts and media professionals in the country. It is not just arts and media however; Wellington City is also home to an unusually high proportion of information and communications technology (ICT) professionals: 2.46 per cent of all workers in the city as compared with 0.79 per cent for the country as a whole. Over 16 per cent of all such workers lived in Wellington City in 2006.

More indicative still of the ability of Wellington to attract such creative workers is the income distribution of professionals living in different parts of the region. It is clear from Figure 24.2 that professionals living in Wellington City draw much higher salaries on average than those in other parts of the Wellington Region. Not only are there far fewer people in lower-income brackets (where part timers and women are over-represented), but among higher-income professionals Wellington City residents earn considerably higher incomes. In fact, the difference is probably understated in these Census data due to the bounding of the highest income category at NZ$100 000 and over.

The negative skewness of the regional income distribution is more marked for some professions than for others. The strong pull that Wellington City has on 'arts and media professionals' is evidenced by the higher proportion of low-income members of this group (the archetypal bohemians possibly) than is the case for other professionals. The income distribution of business, human resources and marketing professionals who live in the city is also more negatively skewed than is the rest of the region. The same is true of health professionals, ICT professionals and, most noticeably, legal, social and welfare professionals.

The cities of Wellington and Auckland share the most concentrated stores of knowledge in the country and this is reflected in their much higher average incomes (Rutherford, 2009).[5] However, an analysis of the geography of the income distributions of different New Zealand cities highlights the greater degree of residential sorting in more affluent cities and the consequently greater spatial concentration of low-income households (Martin, 2008a, 2008b).[6] As a population becomes more educated, the primary pool of the creative class becomes more geographically concentrated both within a country and within its major urban centres (Costa and Kahn, 2000; Whisler et al., 2008). Also, due to the application of an immigration points system, a high proportion of all immigrants coming into New Zealand have university degrees and other qualifications that are in high demand in what is a skill-deficient economy. This brings me to the central thesis of this chapter, namely that the relative concentration of creative talent in the main city of a region exacerbates competition for residential space, and for proximity to the workplace and to the service and recreational infrastructure of the city, a competition that favours those located at the centre.

Implications of the Creative City for Urban Form

The population of the inner cities of New Zealand's three main urban areas began to decline during the long boom following the end of the Second World War, a feature that was accelerated by the subsequent suburbanization of manufacturing itself and the accompanying income-elastic demand for housing space. The result was a steady decline in the residential population of the country's main central cities, by over three-quarters through to the early 1990s (Figure 24.3).

As the structure of the economy moved away from manufacturing towards a range of business and financial services in particular, so the advantages of agglomeration in the centre began to be recognized. Innovation in a wide range of services was increasingly viewed as the key to the growth of an economy that was opened up to worldwide competition through the deregulation phase of the late 1980s. Since the early 1990s, as Figure 24.3 shows, the resident populations of all three central cities have risen (Morrison, 2000).

What is historically and geographically unusual about the Wellington City case is the way in which the inner-city's population growth has exceeded its growth in employment. The ten years ending in 2006 saw a 38.5 per cent increase in the number of people living in the inner city, compared to only a 20.1 per cent increase in the number of employees working there each day. As a result, the ratio of the night-time to daytime population rose from 16.4 to 18.9 per cent within a decade. By 2006, the inner-city resident population of Wellington City alone had reached over 13 000 – the size of a small New Zealand town.[7] Similar trends have more recently been documented for Auckland City (Friesen, 2009).[8]

Reference to further academic research would at this point not capture what is of immediate importance about the above figures. A better indication of the energy associated with creativity is conveyed by a local journalist writing about a local Tweet-up – a face-to-face meeting in a local bar organized via Twitter:

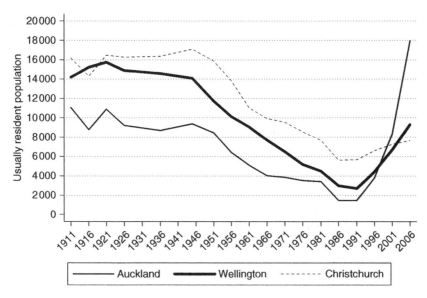

Source: Statistics New Zealand Census, 1991 to 2006.

Figure 24.3   *The decline and growth of usually resident population in the inner cities of Auckland, Wellington and Christchurch, 1911–2006*

> But Wellington is that kind of town. It amplifies communities. The single biggest reason for this could simply be Wellington's geography. It's a crescent of hills pressing the city against the harbour creating a densely packed urban atmosphere where cars intrude on pedestrians and you're never more than 100 metres from a café. . . . In summer, the bars with the afternoon sun teem with massive crowds and the earliest secure the best spots for late-working friends. . . . And everybody is connected. Large gatherings will descend on bars . . . drawn by messages and plans made via Twitter, Facebook, SMS and email. Wellington . . . it's a city built by geeks. . . . And if there's one thing geeks love, it's networks. (Green, 2010, pp. 6–7)

It is less clear whether the increased face-to-face contact that Wellington's increased urban concentration has allowed represents a shift in the fundamentals of the urban growth process. I was certainly not convinced of such a change 15 years ago and felt it was important 'not to let the change in direction of growth overwhelm the magnitudes involved' (Morrison, 2000, p. 280). Between 1996 and 2009, Wellington City still only increased its share of the region's population from 38.3 per cent to 40.8 per cent, so the growth of Wellington City did not involve a major redistribution of population within the Wellington Region. The important change is a qualitative one. The spatial redistribution of interest has to do with the way skill, talent and creativity has become more concentrated in Wellington City itself.

Distributional Implications of the Spatial Concentration of the Creative Class

The emergence of the 'knowledge and creative city' has had less effect on the spatial distribution of jobs and residences than it has had on the geographical distribution of human capital. The socio-economic structure of the Wellington Region in the early 1990s, before the population turnaround at the centre, already showed a disproportionately high residential concentration of people with university degrees living close to the heart of the city (Winchester, 2000, pp. 261–2). The latest layer of creative workers arriving over the last two decades has therefore augmented a pre-existing socio-economic geography in ways which have widened the gap between the city and the region.

Nowhere is this division between the city and the rest of the region more apparent than in the residential geography of those without a formal education; those among the 25–60 age group who have no educational qualifications of any kind. The difference between Wellington City and the rest of the region, already quite apparent in Winchester's maps from the early 1990s, had become even more marked 15 years later and are a striking indication of the exaggerating effect that the global competition for talent has on the residential mosaic. By 2006 the percentage of people without formal education in the regional local authorities outside Wellington City had reached 22.1 per cent, compared to the city's low figure of 7.6 per cent.[9] Labourers and machinery and plant operators, who were already under-represented in the city, showed an even higher tendency to reside in the smaller settlements on the periphery of the region.

Wellington's elite have always lived very close to the central business district (CBD), for historical reasons that reflect the strong challenge topography poses for physical access to the centre of commercial and political power (Hamer, 1990). The growing pressure from new waves of the contemporary elite wishing to live near the centre was led by a cadre of young knowledge and creative workers in the 1990s with the means to effect a supply response. A visual manifestation of that response has been a rapid growth in inner-city apartments (Morrison and McMurray, 1999), whose numbers has continued to rise beyond 6000 in the 20 years since an identifiable trend began in the early 1990s (Figure 24.4).

The growth of the inner-city apartment market reflects the way price differentials between the city and the rest of the region has increased; it is this real estate differential that is one of the main agents of contemporary socio-economic segmentation. In 2006, around 40 per cent of apartment dwellers in Wellington City's CBD were paying NZ\$450 or more per week in rent, with more than a quarter paying NZ\$500 or more per week (Statistics New Zealand, 2010, p.18). The three cities to the north of Wellington City (Porirua, Lower Hutt and Upper Hutt) hardly exceed 70 per cent of Wellington City's mean rental and as Figure 24.5 shows, the smaller towns in the Wairarapa – Masterton, Carterton and the South Wairarapa District – barely reached half the mean rent paid by Wellington City tenants. If these figures were adjusted for the size of dwellings, the difference would be considerably greater and real estate prices exhibit the same geography. The most important feature of Figure 24.5, however, is the way these trends in rent point to a widening gap between the cost of accommodation in the city and the rest of the region. The ratio of mean rents in Wellington City to those in Lower Hutt, for example, rose from 1.41 to 1.5 over the 15 years between 1991 and 2006.

The steeper rent gradient – the effect of a rise in the relative demand for accommodation in the city – means that people with lower bidding power have been redistributed towards the periphery of the city and beyond. They have increasingly moved into the lower rent fringes of the region including the smaller towns that service the rural areas

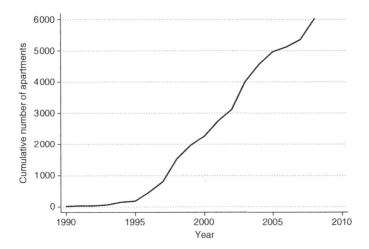

Note: Building consents consider apartments to be dwellings that include ten or more residential units. Consents will slightly overstate completions.

Source: Statistics New Zealand. Building consents.

Figure 24.4   *The cumulative growth of apartments in Wellington City, 1990–2008*

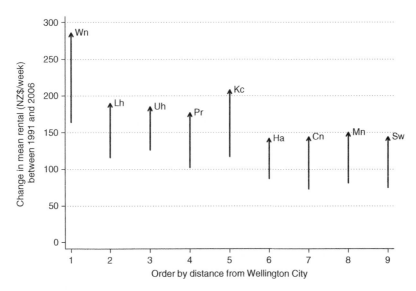

Note: 1. Wellington City, 2. Lower Hutt City, 3. Upper Hutt City, 4. Porirua City, 5. Kapiti Coast District, 6. Horowhenua District, 7. Carterton District, 8. Masterton District, 9. South Wairarapa District.

Source: Statistics New Zealand. Census of Population and Dwellings.

Figure 24.5   *The widening gap between mean rent levels in Wellington City and the other local authorities in the Wellington Region, 1991–2006*

of the Wellington Region, a feature initially documented in the case of beneficiaries (Morrison and Waldegrave, 2002). Ironically, many of those people now settling in the north-eastern periphery of the Wellington Region must now compete with rising demand for 'lifestyle' blocks by the relatively wealthy professionals who choose to commute to Wellington City. The combined effect has therefore been an increase in rents in some of the more sought-after locations close to the small towns in the rural parts of the region, a feature also visible in Figure 24.5.

While the greater preferences for cheaper land may be more typical of lower-income workers, presumably with larger families (as argued by a reviewer of this chapter), both anecdotal evidence and systematic analyses suggest that lower-income households are having to move still further down the rent gradient north of the city, particularly if they seek home ownership (Morrison, 2008). While a housing market in equilibrium may equalize the total costs of the residential package (housing and commuting costs), so that no household is worse off than any other as a result of their residential location, the particular combination of costs a household bears under these circumstances is for the most part a reflection of their highly constrained choice rather than a preference per se.

The regional decentralization of lower-income households that has accompanied the concentration of knowledge and creative workers in Wellington City housing has particularly marked ramifications in a settlement context in which regional employment is so highly centralized as it is in Wellington City. Although essentially excluded from the city as residents, many less-educated, low-wage workers are required to provide both infrastructural and personal services to those who do live there. The consequence is an unusually long commute (at least by New Zealand standards), often by the breadwinners of larger families – commutes which take their toll in terms of lost family time and additional stress (Stutzer and Frey, 2008). Meanwhile, many members of the new knowledge and creative classes, usually those with smaller families, live much closer to their place of work; they can either walk or cycle to work as well as being able to exercise discretion on exactly where to work and which hours of the day to work.

The primary thrust of the distributional thesis I am advancing in this chapter, therefore, is one in which the growth and centralization of the knowledge and creative classes – in a city designed to attract and retain them – has been accompanied by an accelerated decentralization of people with lower levels of formal education, lower incomes and often larger families. Yet the physical and social infrastructure investment in the central city that is believed to be so essential for raising the productivity of the creative class still has to be serviced; the cleaning, child-minding, shopping and other domestic tasks are increasingly being undertaken by service workers who live outside the city's invisible walls.

It may be tempting to counter this distributional thesis by appealing to the growth-inducing properties of the knowledge and creative classes. The argument here is that countries that face increased competition for their products will gain productivity benefits by physically concentrating skilled workers at higher densities in their central cities (McCann, 2009). According to this argument, the resulting economic growth will spill over into demand for workers at all levels. In this way, fostering the knowledge and creative city has the potential to raise employment levels of all workers within the metropolitan region.

The inter-industry and multiplier analysis necessary to test and quantify this connection is well beyond the scope of this chapter. However, existing economic impact studies by local consultants rarely go beyond aggregate returns to the regional economy as a whole. Few attempt to examine who actually benefits by occupation or skill set, let alone where the different categories live and work. This partly accounts for the scepticism present in the notion of 'creative trickle-down' (Peck, 2005, p. 759).

Finally, in light of the last observation it is instructive to ask how the presence of those with higher education has been associated with the relative growth of local authorities throughout the country. Although not confined to a narrower creative class as such, the results are instructive.

GROWTH AND THE CREATIVE CITY

Some critics of the creative city thesis have been quite direct in suggesting that the basic economics behind the ideas do not work. An example that refers to Florida's work is Steven Malanga (2004), who writes that '[f]ar from being economic powerhouses, a number of cities the professor identifies as creative-age winners have chronically underperformed the American economy' (p. 1).

Much has been written about the way in which the presence of educated and creative people in certain places acts as a magnet for others in a way that allows these places to gradually pull away from other parts of the country. Just how different Wellington City is in this respect can be gauged by plotting the percentage growth between 2001 and 2006 in the 25–60 age group against the proportion of people with degrees in 2001 across New Zealand's local authorities. The result in Figure 24.6 shows an initially close (cross-sectional) relationship. The circles are proportional to the population size of the local authority and clearly larger centres have a higher proportion of residents with university degrees. However, once the proportion of people with degrees reaches about 15 per cent, there appears to be only minimal association between the university-educated population share and population growth.[10] The relationship is also quite non-linear as the quadratic fit shows, and at least in cross-section, any extension of higher education into the working age population is associated with successively lower rates of population growth.[11]

In terms of specifics, Wellington City (46) and Auckland City (7) stand out as having the most highly educated working age groups, as does North Shore City (5) within the Auckland Region. Other examples include Palmerston North (39) and Hamilton (15), both university cities, and Christchurch (59). Outliers among fast-growing Territorial Local Authorities (TLAs) include a resort town, Queensland's Lake District (68), and the rapidly expanding ex-urban fringe of Christchurch, Selwyn (60).

In summary, while there is some prime facie evidence for a correlation between an educated population and the growth of the settlement in which they reside, the cross-sectional relationship at least is statistically rather weak and certainly not linear. Most of the variance in population growth remains unaccounted for by the proportion of degree-holders in its working age groups. In this respect, the New Zealand evidence would appear to be as unsettled as the American evidence, albeit on a much smaller scale.

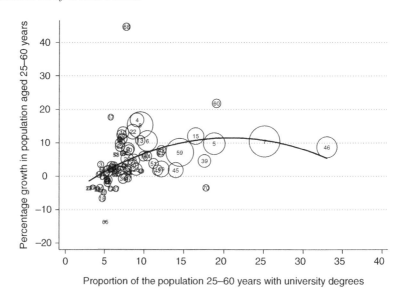

Note: Circles are proportionate to the period average of the 25–60 population.

Source: Statistics New Zealand. Table builder.

Figure 24.6 *The growth of the population (aged 25 to 60) in 73 Territorial Local Authorities in New Zealand from 2001 to 2006 against the proportion of people with university degrees in 2001*

CONCLUSIONS

The question raised in this chapter is whether (where and under what circumstances) the short-run economic returns to spatial concentration of the knowledge and creative classes might be outweighed by the longer-run social costs resulting from the geographic marginalization generated through a housing market which is particularly sensitive to both wealth and status. The Wellington City case is probably not unusual in terms of the underlying processes involved. What has made it an apt example is the way the segmented urban geography of the region has tended to spatially confine the benefits of concentrating the creative class within Wellington City itself.

The argument about the regressive distributional effects of fostering neighbourhoods of knowledge and creative workers is an intrinsically geographical one that is based on the pre-empting of space. In its quest for positional goods, the knowledge and creative class effectively deny the positive externalities they generate in both consumption and production to others, an increasing proportion of whom live on the periphery of the 'creative city'. The quest for more rapid economic growth and the investment in the schools and tertiary institutions through which it is nurtured, has reinforced a competition for – and a ranking of – residential space that has increasingly excluded less competitive members of the society from the knowledge and creative classes (Benabou, 1993).

A question that remains is therefore whether New Zealand is really one of those 'more nimble countries that have well established mechanisms for social cohesion . . . able both to mobilize their own creative energy from all segments of society, and to compete effectively for global talent' (Florida, 2005, p. 176). As most New Zealanders know, the distributional issues raised in this chapter have always been present. The social divisions in this country are quite apparent to those who have watched some of the films coming out of New Zealand; not fictitious movies such as *Lord of the Rings* or *Avatar* but the stark realism in films like *Once Were Warriors*, *This Way of Life* and, most recently, *Boy*. As these films indirectly assert, and as the country's prime minister has stated quite clearly, New Zealand 'simply can't afford a future where 20 percent of our workforce does not have the skills necessary for modern jobs' (Key, 2010). A central task ahead does indeed lie in developing new forms of social cohesion appropriate to the Creative Age (Florida, 2003, pp. 11–12). Until then, understanding the magnitude of the distributional consequences of fostering a 'creative class' through their geographic concentration remains one of the primary challenges facing the creative city movement.

ACKNOWLEDGEMENTS

I wish to thank one of our graduate students, Rene Rushton, for her thorough and creative sourcing of material for this chapter. Sadly, only a small proportion of the vast material Rene collected on this topic could be included. The salient points made by the two reviewers of this chapter were appreciated. Funding was made available by the School of Geography, Environment and Earth Sciences at Victoria University of Wellington.

NOTES

1. Crocodile is the name given to a two- or four-wheeled covered cycle that can be rented by groups to visit local sights; see http://www.travelpod.com/travel-photo/kevanna/11/1230175260/tour-on-the-crocodile-bike.jpg/tpod.html.
2. See http://www.wellingtonnz.com/.
3. At the same time, it is this link between creativity and commercialism that has disturbed most New Zealand critics of the creative cities thesis. The most comprehensive reaction to date has been by Michael Volkerling, then programme director of Leisure and Heritage Studies at Victoria University of Wellington (VUW). Volkering's first piece on the subject is a sympathetic critique of the application of the notion of a creative city to Wellington (Volkerling, 2006). His second article, however, is a broader reflection on the increasing pressure for the economic valuation of culture, including the notion of creativity (Volkerling, 2001). It is this explicit link between cultural policy and economic policy that has worried many of the people involved in cultural policy (McGuigan, 2009), not least because it represents one more potential victim of neo-liberalism (McGuigan, 2005). Deborah Jones from the Victoria Management School at VUW explores similar concerns over the relationship between creativity and national identity, using creative achievements such as *The Lord of the Rings Trilogy* to launch a national tourism campaign (Jones and Smith, 2005). This link between creativity and growth policy is further explored by Billy Matheson of the Centre for Creative Industries at the Wellington Institute of Technology (Matheson, 2006), whose concern has been the nature of the influence that the creative industries had on design education in New Zealand. Sociologist Anne de Bruin has also reflected on the links between entrepreneurship and creativity (de Bruin, 2005), while others have expressed concern over the growing proportion of New Zealand students who are enrolling in 'creative' courses offered by tertiary institutions (Bill, 2004).
4. See http://www.dol.govt.nz/publications/lmr/knowledge-economy/phase2/phase2_02.asp.
5. The main difference between the two cities is that 39.7 per cent of degree-holders in Wellington are employed by the public sector, compared with Auckland City's 26.8 per cent.

6. An index of deprivation cannot be treated simply as the inverse of an index of affluence. However, as Martin emphasizes, the publically available maps of neighbourhoods (area units) that are classified according to the New Zealand Deprivation Index highlight the spatial concentrations present in the two cities (White et al., 2008).
7. The term 'inner city' in New Zealand has a specific area 1 definition in each of the three main centres.
8. For similar trends in Australian cities, see http://www.environment.gov.au/soe/2006/publications/drs/ indicator/257/index.html.
9. Within the Wellington Region, the proportion of people with no qualifications ranges from a low of 7.6 per cent in Wellington City to a high of 31.4 per cent in the Horowhenua District. The next smallest proportion after Wellington is 16.6 per cent in the Kapiti Coast.
10. New Zealand's axis of growth is clearly considerably north of Wellington, along the Auckland-Tauranga axis. The Auckland Region as a whole grew much faster on an annual basis than Wellington City over the 1996–2009 period (2.22 per cent), as did the Bay of Plenty Region (1.39 per cent) and Tauranga City in particular (3.19 per cent). In regional terms, the country as a whole grew by 1.2 per cent per year from 1996 to 2009. The Auckland Region grew by 2.22 per cent and Christchurch by 1.26 per cent, compared to only 0.93 per cent per year for the Wellington Region during the same period (Statistics New Zealand). As noted, however, scale matters when talking about population growth. The Wellington Region is not Wellington City. Looking instead at the cities and districts captured in the 74 Territorial Local Authorities (TLAs) reveals that Wellington City itself grew at 1.51 per cent per year. This ranks it as the 15th fastest of the TLAs and the seventh fastest-growing city, just behind Auckland City at 1.74 per cent. The number of people living in Wellington City rose from 163 400 in 1996 to 195 500 in 2009, an overall rate of growth that was much faster than for the other cities in the region: Lower Hutt (0.23 per cent annual growth), Upper Hutt City (0.59 per cent) and Porirua City (0.52 per cent). Of the districts in the region, only the Kapiti Coast grew faster, at 1.85 per cent.
11. The linear regression, without the base population included, suggests that population increases at half the rate at which the number of people with degrees increases. However, when the population at the beginning of the period is added, the influence of the proportion of people with bachelor's degrees diminishes quantitatively (to under 19 per cent) and ceases to be statistically significant.

REFERENCES

Atkinson, R. and H. Easthope (2010), 'The consequences of the creative class: the pursuit of creativity strategies in Australia's cities', *International Journal of Urban and Regional Research*, **33**, 64–79.
Benabou, R. (1993), 'Workings of a city: location, education, and production', *Quarterly Journal of Economics*, **108**, 619–52.
Bill, A. (2004), '"Blood, sweat and tears": disciplining the creative in Aotearoa New Zealand', paper presented at the Third International Conference on Cultural Policy Research (ICCPR), Montréal, QC.
Costa, D. and M. Kahn (2000), 'Power couples: changes in the locational choice of the college educated: 1940–1990', *Quarterly Journal of Economics*, **115**, 1287–315.
De Bruin, A. (2005), 'Multi-level entrepreneurship in the creative industries: New Zealand's screen production industry', *International Journal of Entrepreneurship and Innovation*, **6**, 143–50.
Department of Labour (2009), *The New Zealand Knowledge Economy*, Wellington, NZ: Department of Labour.
Florida, R. (2002), 'Bohemia and economic geography', *Journal of Economic Geography*, **2**, 55–71.
Florida, R. (2003), *The Rise of the Creative Class*, Christchurch, NZ: Hazard Press.
Florida, R. (2005), *Cities and the Creative Class*, London: Routledge.
Friesen, W. (2009), 'The demographic transformation of inner city Auckland', *New Zealand Population Review*, **35**, 55–74.
Glaeser, E. (2004), 'Review of Richard Florida's "The Rise of the Creative Class"', available at http://www. creativeclass.com/Rfcgdb/Articles/Glaeserreview.pdf.
Green, H. (2010) 'A well-connected society', *Dominion Post*, 27 March.
Hamer, D. (1990), 'Wellington on the urban frontier', in D. Hamer and R. Nicholls (eds), *The Making of Wellington 1800–1914*, Wellington, NZ: Victoria University Press, pp. 227–54.
Jones, D and K. Smith (2005), 'Middle-Earth meets New Zealand: authenticity and location in the making of The Lord of the Rings', *Journal of Management Studies*, **42**, 923–45.
Key, J. (2010), 'Statement to parliament', presented to the House of Representatives in accordance with Standing Order 345, 9 February, pp. 1–23.
Malanga, S. (2004), 'The curse of the creative class', *City Journal*, Winter, 1–9.

Markusen, A. (2006), 'Urban development and the politics of a creative class: evidence from a study of artists', *Environment and Planning A*, **38**, 1921–40.

Martin, B. (2008a), *The Affluent Areas of New Zealand*, Auckland, NZ: Magnus Consulting.

Martin, B. (2008b), *Aspects of Affluence and Poverty in New Zealand: Pitfalls for the Unwary*, Auckland, NZ: Magnus Consulting.

Matheson, B. (2006), 'A culture of creativity: design education and the creative industries', *Journal of Management Development*, **25**, 55–64.

McCann, P. (2009), 'Economic geography, globalisation and New Zealand's productivity paradox', *New Zealand Economic Papers*, **43**, 279–314.

McConchie, J., D. Winchester and R. Willis (2000), *Dynamic Wellington*, Wellington, NZ: Institute of Geography, Victoria University of Wellington.

McGuigan, J. (2005), 'Neo-liberalism, culture and policy', *International Journal of Cultural Policy*, **11**, 229–41.

McGuigan, J. (2009), 'Doing a Florida thing: the creative class thesis and cultural policy', *International Journal of Cultural Policy*, **15**, 291–300.

Morrison, P.S. (2000), 'Turning inside out? Residential growth in the Wellington Region', in J. McConchie, D. Winchester and R. Willis (eds), *Dynamic Wellington*, Wellington, NZ: Institute of Geography, Victoria University of Wellington, pp. 271–86.

Morrison, P.S. (2008), 'On the falling rate of home ownership in New Zealand', Wellington, NZ: Centre for Housing Research Aotearoa New Zealand.

Morrison, P.S. and S. McMurray (1999), 'The inner city apartment vs. the suburb. Housing sub-markets in a New Zealand city', *Urban Studies*, **36**, 371–91.

Morrison, P.S. and C. Waldegrave (2002), 'Welfare reform and the intra-regional migration of beneficiaries in New Zealand', *Geoforum*, **33**, 85–103.

Peck, J. (2005), 'Struggling with the creative class', *International Journal of Urban and Regional Research*, **29**, 740–70.

Quality of Life Team (2008), 'Quality of life '07 in twelve of New Zealand's cities', Christchurch.

Rosenfeld, S. (2004), 'Art and design as a competitive advantage: a creative enterprise cluster in the Western United States', *European Planning Studies*, **12**, 891–904.

Rutherford, D. (2009), 'Measuring the New Zealand knowledge economy', in P.S. Morrison (ed.), *The Thirteenth Conference on Labour, Employment and Work*, Wellington, NZ: Victoria University of Wellington, pp. 394–8.

Scott, A.J. (2006), 'Creative cities: conceptual issues and policy questions', *Journal of Urban Affairs*, **28**, 1–17.

Scott, A.J. (2010), 'Cultural economy and the creative field of the city', *Geografiska Annaler*, **92**, 111–86.

Statistics New Zealand (2010), *Apartment Dwellers: 2006 Census*, Wellington, NZ: Statistics New Zealand.

Stutzer, A. and B.S. Frey (2008), 'Stress that doesn't pay: the commuting paradox', *Scandinavian Journal of Economics*, **110**, 339–66.

Volkerling, M. (2001), 'From cool Britannia to hot nation: "creative industries" policies in Europe, Canada and New Zealand', *Cultural Policy*, **7**, 437–55.

Volkerling, M. (2006), 'Wellington as a "creative city": after Florida – and before', *Asia Pacific Journal of Arts and Cultural Management*, **4**, 296–306.

Whisler, R.L., B.S. Waldorf, G.F. Mulligan and D.A. Plane (2008), 'Quality of life and the migration of the college-educated: a life-course approach', *Growth and Change*, **39**, 58–94.

White, P., J. Gunston, C. Salmond, J. Atkinson and P. Crampton (2008), *Atlas of Socioeconomic Deprivation in New Zealand* (NZDep2006), Wellington, NZ: Ministry of Health.

Winchester, D. (2000), 'The meaningful mosaic. mapping the social structure', in J. McConchie, D. Winchester and R. Willis (eds), *Dynamic Wellington: A Contemporary Synthesis and Explanation of Wellington*, Wellington, NZ: Institute of Geography, Victoria University of Wellington, pp. 233–70.

PART 6

VISIONS

25 Contract, voice and rent: voluntary urban planning
Fred E. Foldvary

'Creative' means both innovative and productive of greater value, production being the creation of economic value. Voluntary urban planning occurs when individuals are freely able to create: to design and operate their own buildings, environments and actions. Voluntary planning exists with contractual communities, which include both associations of co-owners and proprietary communities with renters. Purely voluntary development occurs when there is no imposed zoning and land-use restrictions; instead, covenants and easements provide flexible land-use agreements. Voluntary planning would seek to maximize the community land rent, which in turn provides an efficient source of funding for its collective goods, in contrast to distortionary taxation. Decentralized contractual development and governance would enable entrepreneurs, associations and proprietors to fully explore and apply their creativity to both shape and satisfy the desires of the household and business consumers.

VOLUNTARY ACTION AND PLANNING

Human action is voluntary in the absence of coercive harm, and when there is no restriction or imposed cost on peaceful and honest planning and human action. 'Harm' means, in this context, an invasion into the domain of others, excluding what may be merely disagreeable due to the recipients' beliefs and values. Hence, harm is distinct from offences that are displeasing but are not invasions (Foldvary, 1980).

A plan is a design and foundation for a construction or action. A building plan is the blueprint or map from which an edifice is constructed. A town or urban plan is a design for the physical elements of a city such as the streets, blocks, land usage and transit.

Human action that is anticipated necessarily involves a plan. Human action is purposeful, seeking means towards ends (Mises, 1966). Thus every human act is based on having chosen the best means, hence plan, towards one's end. But we can distinguish among time horizons. A longer-range plan looks farther into the future. Thus we can think of planning as choosing actions that have a longer time frame than the immediate reaction to happenings.

THE HOME DOMAIN

Urban planning will be analysed here in the direction of local to global contexts. We begin with the interior of one's house and garden. House interiors are for the most part decentralized. Traditionally, one's home is one's private domain. With voluntary planning, there is no restriction on the arrangements and activities inside one's home, even if others can observe it and disapprove.

Currently, governments sometimes intervene in creative interior decorating. For example, almost everywhere, one may not legally grow marijuana inside one's home or in one's garden. Thus, house flora must exclude illegal plants, and although in some American states recently, exceptions have been made for medical marijuana, these remain illegal by US law (although since 2009 the prohibition is reportedly not being enforced).

Governments also impose dress codes, even within dwellings. In Springfield, Virginia, for example, a man was seen nude in his kitchen, making coffee. A passer-by reported this to the police, who arrested the man for indecent exposure. This legal action had the backing of the Commonwealth's Attorney's Office (Thomas, 2009).

Such acts fall under the category of offences, and are not prohibited in a voluntary society. Creative cities imply creative individuals, implying that the human will is not restricted so long as others are not coercively harmed.

The interiors of dwellings can impose coercive harm when they involve danger and invasive nuisance. External effects such as noise can be coercively harmful to others. The concept of voluntary action implies an absence of master–slave relationships, hence human equality. One has a natural right to make some noise, since one cannot physically be completely silent, but one also has a natural right to be free from an invasion of high-decibel noise.

Whether light constitutes coercive harm depends on its origin. Sunlight reflected from one's property is neutral, but light originating from one's property is like noise, an invasion if its intensity is excessive.

The concept of a clear and present danger is similar to the ticking bomb. If one stores explosives in one's house, which could therefore blow up accidentally, then the very existence of the explosives is not hypothetical harm, but actual threat and thus a harm, just as aiming a loaded gun at a person is harmful as a threat.

Thus in a voluntary society, even the interiors of buildings are not subject to 'anything goes', but one may design the interiors as long as there is no coercive harm to others.

THE STREET

The modern street is the foundation of the local urban environment. Most streets today are provided by government, but there are also many privately provided streets (Roth, 2006). Voluntary urban planning could include government-provided streets and other infrastructure if they are provided in equal competition with private sector providers.

This is similar to schooling; the provision of schooling by government is not coercively harmful if private providers have the same opportunity, giving parents and students an equal choice. In schooling, the choice is equal only if the financing is equal, such as all schooling being financed by tuition, or if financed by government, with all parents being given vouchers for either private or governmental schools. With private and governmental schools having an equal financial status, the creativity of private teachers, students and administrators is not stifled.

Likewise, governmental streets are compatible with voluntary planning if the funding does not privilege government. In many private communities such as homeowners' associations or the private neighbourhoods of St Louis, the communities pay to maintain their streets, yet also pay the same taxes as neighbourhoods that have government-provided streets (Foldvary, 1994). For the governmental street to have an equal status, either the governmental street needs to be funded by the local property owners or tenants just as would be a private street, or else the members of the private place would get a tax credit equal to the expense avoided by the government.

A street is a territorial collective good, impacting the territory nearby. A normal street generates land rent, increasing the economic rent of the sites facing the street and also the rents of the neighbourhood. This generation of site rent is the economic basis for the financing of private communities. A hotel, for example, provides public transit in the form of elevators and escalators. The marginal cost of carrying one more rider is near zero, and the hotel practises marginal-cost pricing, charging nothing. The cost is paid by the room rental, as hotel guests will pay a greater rental for a hotel with elevators than one without.

Similarly, the hotel's other public goods are often offered without extra charge. These include its public park (the lobby), its security, fire protection and administrative services. Where there is a significant marginal cost, such as with room service, the hotel does charge the user. The swimming pool and exercise room are often gratis but some hotels charge extra; possibly the extra rental that the pool attracts may about equal the payment the hotels can get by charging. While a transient community such as a hotel has significant differences from a permanent residential neighbourhood, the economics of the collective goods is similar.

THE NEIGHBOURHOOD

Central planning by cities imposes a master plan and divides the city into zones, each with exclusive uses. Creative planning by developers has had to overcome zoning hurdles.

For example, the development of Reston, Virginia, required a change in the zoning ordinances. To Robert Simon, the developer, standard zoning laws were responsible for 'the diffusion of our communities into separate, unrelated hunks without focus, identity or community life' (Grubisich and McCandless, 1985, p. 41). Simon deplored the waste of land in typical suburban developments. Simon's team decided 'to plan Reston exactly the way we wanted it to be, as if there were no zoning ordinances at all'.

The result was a zoning innovation called 'residential planned community' (RPC) (changed to Planned Residential Community (PRC) in 1978), using 'density zoning' that left the overall density the same as with traditional zoning, but with heterogeneous density within the area (Grubisich and McCandless, 1985, p. 43).

A contractual community can provide its members with more public goods than cities provide, and can do so more efficiently. On the revenue side, their public finance is more efficient because it is based on benefits received rather than imposed taxes on unrelated sources such as one's general income and spending, taxes that create disincentives to produce and invest. Also conducive to creativity, an association of neighbours promotes camaraderie and community awareness, relative to atomistic households governed by a remote bureaucracy. On the spending side, in a study by Robert Deacon of 23 associations and 41 comparable towns, associations are reported as paying 58 per cent of what governments would spend for similar police services, and 70 per cent of similar sovereign expenditures for street maintenance (Frazier, 1980, p. 100). One factor accounting for the less efficient government service is the civil service, which may be less responsive to the residents.

The rationale for building codes is safety, but the codes often go beyond that to stifle creativity in buildings. They can subsidize status quo interests and pressure groups such as the labour unions engaged in construction. Rather than targeting performance standards to ensure safety, building codes usually specify materials that the planners think will meet these performance standards. As a result, builders cannot use innovative new materials that might achieve the same quality (Frieden, 1970, p. 203).

There are many other interventions that stifle creative development. While there has been great entrepreneurial creativity in technology in Silicon Valley, California, housing creativity has been restricted. The limitations include zoning, building codes, affordable housing requirements, development fees, urban growth boundaries, environmental review and requirements for 'open spaces' (Erin, 2001).

Another example of innovation tied to the elimination of building codes was Walt Disney World (WDW) in Florida. The company made an agreement with the State of Florida to have its own governing district, which WDW controlled (Foldvary, 1994). The exemption from building codes enabled WDW to use creative methods and building materials. WDW built what was at the time the tallest reinforced masonry building in the United States, the TraveLodge motel. No code in the United States would have allowed such a building of over 12 storeys (De Michael, 1973, p. 61). As a result of its freedom to innovate, the Disney Company became a patron of architecture, commissioning works by major architects. An example of innovation was the Team Disney office building at Lake Buena Vista, featuring an open cylinder fastened with a 74-foot beam at the rim, forming one of the world's largest sundials (Andersen, 1991, p. 66).

In *The Death and Life of Great American Cities* (1961), Jane Jacobs, a critic of governmental planning and 'urban renewal', identified four conditions needed for thriving, diverse cities: (1) high densities; (2) diversity in land uses; (3) pedestrian-friendly blocks and streets; and (4) old buildings co-existing with new ones. These conditions often conflict with zoning restrictions that mandate maximum density, separate the land uses and design streets to accommodate vehicle traffic rather than pedestrians. Urban renewal, in some cases, eliminated old, long-established low-income neighbourhoods.

The urban social or human ecology that Jacobs described for cities (Kinkella, 2009), and which motivated her opposition to massive imposed urban plans, is complementary to contractual market outcomes. Contracts prescribe what specific parties owe to one another, but cannot prescribe the interaction among the multitude of agents in the economy. A driver who has planned to go from A to B will encounter other drivers with different plans, and so the actual speed and lanes a driver will traverse cannot be predetermined. The outcome is a spontaneous order generated both by individual plans and contracts as well as by the reactions of drivers to other drivers. Urban design should establish institutions such as which side of the street to travel on, when to give way in intersections and payments for potential externalities such as congestion, without thereby prescribing outcomes such as is the case when 'urban renewal' involves massive destruction and redesign. The market, through signals such as prices and profits, and through rules both contractual and customary, creates order in co-ordinating individual plans.

Destruction takes place in a market when new structures have greater value than the old ones. The term 'creative destruction' was introduced by Werner Sombart (1913), a German sociologist and follower of Karl Marx. It became an economic 'grand term' (like Adam Smith's 'invisible hand' or Frédéric Bastiat's 'broken window') from its use by Joseph Schumpeter in *Capitalism, Socialism and Democracy* ([1942] 1976). The idea is that innovation replaces, hence destroys, the now obsolete capital goods. It is creative because innovation involves inventions and discoveries, but also because it creates a more productive or desired outcome than the previous methods and goods. It is reconstruction as well as destruction. The engineering creator is the inventor, but the economic creator is the entrepreneur who – in the face of the uncertainty of future demands – nevertheless recognizes the potential of new methods and products, organizes the factors of production and the marketing, and thereby creates a new economic reality.

Instead of the 'creative reconstruction' of market dynamics, which replaces old goods with better new ones, government policy has often resulted in destructive ruin in places such as Detroit. Although the automobile industry declined, entrepreneurship could have provided creative renewal, as it did in Pittsburgh, Pennsylvania. What contributed to the restoration of Pittsburgh was a split-rate property tax, a high rate on land and a low rate on buildings, a policy which is also followed by other municipalities in that state (Gaffney, 2007). Had Detroit and Michigan allowed new creative enterprise to flourish by levying only a tax on land value, the city might not be the ruin that it became. Besides taxes on income and sales, Michigan levies a business tax on gross receipts, a tax that cannot be passed on for firms competing in a global market, and thus cuts into profits, making marginal firms shut down and reducing new enterprise.

Purely voluntary urban planning precludes zoning and other land-use controls. Urban harmony is instead accomplished by the creativity of the developers and the residents and enterprises, implemented with contracts such as deeds, covenants and easements. A covenant is a binding promise to do or to not do something with the site. An easement is a contract to let another party use the land as if it belonged to that party.

Contracts are especially important for real estate and communities because the relationships are complex, have a long duration and are vulnerable to exploitation. For example, if a private company owns the street, it could charge the homeowners a large fee for access. The market remedy is integration and broad contracts. A common example of integration is a house with a yard. The owner of the house also wants to own the back yard to avoid being vulnerable to the power of the yard owner. In a private setting, the homeowner will tend to choose a location where the street is owned by a residential association so that the co-owners have the control, and they may have a complex contract in the form of a master deed and bylaws in addition to the partial horizontal integration. As analysed in the industrial organization literature, based on the work of Oliver Williamson (1985), the response to the problem of opportunism is an ongoing and detailed administrative contract.

The contracts of civic associations contains 'covenants, conditions and restrictions' (CC&Rs) that are enforced with fees, fines and liens on the property. Covenants and conditions run with the land, being included in the property encumbrances of the new owner.

During the nineteenth century, cities developed in an orderly manner without any visible hand to control the plans of the entrepreneurs. Britain had no governmental land-use controls until the Housing and Town Planning Act of 1909. Urban growth was directed by contracts (Davies, 2002, p. 19). The infrastructure was provided by the landlord or the developer. Covenants co-ordinated land-use rights, the types of materials used and the heights of the buildings.

To a member of an association, the CC&Rs may seem to restrict his creativity, since they specify the landscaping and architectural designs, but they provide for a collective creativity that originates with the developer, and this is explicitly agreed to when joining the community. Those who seek greater individual creativity can join communities such as the land trust of Arden, Delaware, where there are no architectural restrictions. In a free market, those who seek protection from the externality of adverse individual creativity may join a community with substantial restrictions, while those whose preference is greater individuality may also exercise their choice.

CREATIVE TRANSIT

The plan of a community includes not just the transit routes but also, for a large community, the transit system. Imposed government typically installs a rail and bus system which is inefficient in several dimensions. The vehicles often have many empty seats, the streets are congested for both parking and traffic, and the inefficient financing imposes deadweight losses on passengers and tax-payers.

In voluntary urban planning, the plan for urban transit works in harmony with the property rights of the owners of vehicles and real estate. The community would allocate and rent out 'kerb rights' to buses, jitneys and taxis (Klein et al., 1997), places where the vehicles may stop and pick up passengers without interfering with the other systems.

In a voluntary city governed by contractual communities, the owners of private communities would profit from renting these rights, along with metered parking. The optimal allocation of parking would use advanced metering technology that records the time electronically, with no time limit, the charge varying by hour to prevent congestion (Shoup, 2003). The optimal charge is just high enough to prevent congestion, thus zero in the times and places when empty parking spaces are plentiful.

As noted above, an example of the private provision of public transit is the hotel. As explained by Spencer Heath (1957), a pioneer in the study of proprietary communities, the hotel provides public transit in the form of elevators and escalators, and streets in the form of corridors and stairways. The marginal cost of one more user is close to zero, so the hotel practises marginal-cost pricing by letting the use be gratis. The presence of these collective goods makes the rooms more useful, and so the cost is paid from the room rentals.

We see here the close connection between contract and rent. The owners of the private place create a contract to provide collective goods that maximize the site rentals which pay for the goods. The contract is also tied to voice, as the hotel guest may voice his preferences when he contracts for a room, and may also voice any complaints later, to which the hotel is likely to be responsive, in order to maintain its reputation capital. Such voice is often much more productive in influencing outcomes in the direction that a specific individual desires than is a single vote in a large election.

COMMUNITY RULES

Developer entrepreneurs plan not only the physical elements of residential associations and condominiums, but also the rules. When the developer turns over control to the owners, the contract, bylaws and covenants become mixed with voice. The members may later alter the covenants.

The master deed also sets the financing of the public goods, in the form of periodic assessments which in effect amounts to charging a rental for the greater value that is due to the territorial goods. Thus the community's creative elements encompass contract, voice and rent, echoing Albert Hirschman's (1970) triad of exit, voice and loyalty.

Easement contracts facilitate a flexible decentralized land use. They can be used for long-term planning, such as an easement preventing a neighbour from blocking a view. They can also be used to change the previous plan, such as with an easement for access to one's property through the property of a neighbour, when this need was not previously foreseen.

Large cities usually have a master plan for the whole municipality, which then plans the land use for all the neighbourhoods. But many government services can be decentralized to the neighbourhoods, including local parks, streets, policing and land-use regulations. There are for many such services no economies of scale beyond a population of about 10 000. For example, an analysis of economies of scale in the municipalities of St Louis County found no significant diseconomies due to polycentric planning regarding service levels, a finding which is consistent with other studies of size effects (Parks and Oakerson, 1988, p. 122).

St Louis was selected as a case study of metropolitan organization by the Advisory Commission on Intergovernmental Relations because of its 'jurisdictional fragmentation'. In 1982, it had 151 government units and 427 'private places' (neighbourhoods that had privatized their streets). Another indication of the benefits of decentralized provision is that many communities in St Louis County incorporated as municipalities in order to avoid annexation by other cities and to shift control over local affairs from the county to the local area. In addition, many communities in the region are served by autonomous school and fire protection districts.

The private places of St Louis originated in the mid-1800s. They use deed covenants (or 'trust indentures') as a substitute for zoning; as residential associations, they are governed by boards of trustees. These communities are integrated within the city of St Louis and the towns of St Louis County, demonstrating the feasibility of consensual civic goods in the midst of the greater governmental infrastructure. The private places include communities in low-income and middle-class areas, demonstrating that private governance is not an exclusive phenomenon of wealthy areas. Some of these private places are in predominantly African-American neighbourhoods (Fitzgerald, 1988, p. 48).

Among the services provided by the private places are street maintenance, sewerage, snow removal, sweeping, mowing, tree trimming, street lighting, traffic control, access restriction, entrance signs and architectural covenants. A few also provide trash collection, a security patrol and park maintenance.

The front-end of law enforcement can be and is provided by private communities. Front-end services include guards, alarms that are connected to protective agencies and surveillance. The ability to restrict access is a key advantage of a private place; in many of them, one end of a street is closed off with gates, chains and barricades. Besides reducing traffic, the barriers provide protection against crime. Some subdivisions also restrict access through a layout of streets that avoids the typical grid pattern. A study by Oscar Newman found that restricted streets had lower crime rates and higher property values than similar housing in government streets (Parks and Oakerson, 1988).

Another example is an ethnically Italian neighbourhood called 'The Hill'. There, four organizations form an interlocking network: a church, a neighbourhood organization, a business club and a political party. Hill residents have a high degree of social control over their neighbourhood. Whereas other urban sections in St Louis experienced declining property values, valuations have increased in The Hill.

Another case, Lafayette Park, is a historically wealthy area that was formerly the site of some private places that had deteriorated but then underwent gentrification. New residents formed the Lafayette Square Restoration Committee. With increased surveillance crime decreased, and the park was restored as usable space. Another organization, the Lafayette Park Neighborhood Association, promotes youth employment and conducts clean-up campaigns. The city had abandoned the neighbourhood and intended to replace it with new development, but the restorationists revitalized the old land-use structure and restored it as a viable urban neighbourhood, serving as an example of a contractually provided public good.

Small communities can federate to provide public goods with economies of greater scale. For example, small municipalities have joined to provide greater-area police services such as dispatch centres. The fire districts of the St Louis metropolitan area practise mutual aid with first-response agreements. There are also metropolitan area organizations of school districts, offering joint purchasing of supplies. A cluster of small municipalities has formed a council to create a common agency to represent them in higher-level governments (Parks and Oakerson, 1988).

The most common method of raising revenue in the private places is a flat fee per residency. Some of the associations base their assessments instead on acreage or the value of the frontage to the street (Parks and Oakerson, 1988, p. 51; Beito, 1989, p. 32). Since these private places tend to have lots of similar value, the effect is that assessments are essentially based on the land rental generated by the locally provided civic goods, even when the payments are not specifically based on site value. In contrast, local property taxes vary also according to the value of improvements. The independence of the payments from the value of the buildings in the private places eliminates the disincentive effect that occurs when improvements are taxed, as is typical with property taxes in the United States (Foldvary, 2009).

The value of having such private places is shown by their existence despite tax disadvantages. Although a private community saves the city government the expense of maintaining the street and the other public goods that are owned by the community, in St Louis there is no tax rebate for such savings. In addition, association fees are not tax-deductible, while property taxes provide an income-tax deduction.

GOVERNANCE AND CONSTITUTIONS

'Government' in current practice consists of imposed rules. Even when the government is elected, it enacts rules imposed on unwilling minorities. When special interests influence legislation, the rules may even be imposed on unwilling majorities, exploiting their ignorance and apathy.

In contrast, voluntary governance consists of rules adopted by the consent of the members. The key contrast in organizational orders is not government versus market or governmental versus voluntary planning, but rather planning by imposed government versus planning by voluntary governance. Imposed government goes beyond prohibiting evil by controlling or altering acts that do not coercively harm others. An example of imposed planning is zoning that prohibits greater density. Greater density might be disagreeable to some, but as such it does not invade the domain of others.

Voluntary governance implies unanimous consent. Unanimity is not possible as regards the details of voluntary planning, but it is possible to implement it at the constitutional level of choice. A constitutional choice is the highest level of choice, which then sets the framework for subsequent operational choices.

An example of constitutional choice is a marriage. If both parties enter into a marriage by choice, they know that afterwards there will be many decisions in which they will have different opinions, and for which one or both spouses will have to compromise. There cannot be complete unanimity at the operational level of a marriage, the choices made within the constraint of the marriage agreement.

Likewise, becoming employed, enrolling in a university and joining a club are all constitutional decisions. In each case, there will be operational decisions that some of the parties disagree with, but they were aware of this when they entered into the organization, and they agreed to the operational rules. For example, the rules of a club may specify how the board of directors is elected, and how the directors make decisions by majority vote. One agrees to these rules when one joins.

Voluntariness exists at the constitutional level of choice. That is where a unanimous choice is made. The constitution is also the highest level of creativity. An architect, for example, creatively designs the structure of a building, and this becomes the constitutional constraint for the subsequent builder and construction workers.

The voice of the participant exists on both of the decision levels. First, a club member voices his approval when he agrees to the club rules. Second, the club member has a vote or other forms of participation according to the rules. The third voice is the most important: the member may exit the club. A club with no exit option constitutes slavery. For example, if divorce is prohibited, an unhappy spouse becomes a slave to the marriage. Exit is a constitutional choice, and voluntary governance implies both an agreement on entry and the possibility of exit. The absence of an exit option stifles creativity, since one is then precluded from applying new creativity in another direction.

Where feasible, a large association might also permit internal secession; the ability to withdraw from a territorial governance without moving out. But to be voluntary, the secession – as a constitutional choice – must be voluntary for all the adults affected by the seceding territory. For example, if Quebec were allowed to secede from Canada, voluntary secession would require those in Quebec who wish to remain Canadian, or to be independent of both Canada and Quebec, to do so. To avoid free riding, the seceding parties should also take with them their proportionate share of the debt of the organization from which they are seceding (Foldvary, 2005b).

Creativity is applied differently by proprietary communities and civic associations. A proprietary community has a single decision-maker. Even when the owner is a corporation, the chief executive is typically the operational entrepreneurial decision-maker, subject to the broad guidelines set by the board of directors. It is therefore important to carefully structure the incentives to make the chief executive a long-term owner who obtains some of the residual gains of the corporation, such as with shares of stock with long-term incentives.

The proprietor has the power to creatively alter the previous structure of the community. For example, if a shopping centre is no longer optimally designed for a population and its commerce has outgrown the old facility, the owner may apply creative reconstruction to tear down the old structures and erect new and better buildings.

A proprietary community empowers the chief executive, as the prime entrepreneur, to creatively destroy old plans and replace them with new ones. But the tenants of the proprietorship lack such creative power. They can seek to influence the entrepreneur, but the choice of the tenants is mostly constitutional: the decision to join or leave.

With a civic association governed by an elected board, the co-owners have a voice which lets them express and implement collective creativity. But they can lose the power of creative reconstruction. As analysed by Spencer MacCallum (2003), when property ownership is fragmented, holdouts can prevent a major redesign of an antiquated plan.

Generally, the aim of the civic entrepreneurs is the maximization of land value. The maximization of utility implies a greater demand to be located in the territory that generates maximum rent and site value. The rent or site value provides the source of the financing, without thereby imposing any deadweight loss. This is so because the rent is an annual fixed cost that is independent of the profits, wages, sales and personal property values of the individual tenants, customers and workers.

FORMS OF PROPERTY OWNERSHIP

Voluntary urban planning employs particular forms of property ownership. The most common in the countries that follow the English legal system is a 'freehold' title, providing the owner with a legal right to the possession of, and income from, the real estate during the life of the owner. In contrast, 'leasehold' provides rights of possession for a limited time, subject to the payment of a rental to the title holder. The most common form of freehold is 'fee simple'. Fee simple (absolute ownership) provides the greatest legal rights of ownership (Foldvary, 2005a).

Commercial real estate usually has leaseholds, although there are also some business condominiums and co-operatives. A plan that seeks to maximize the rental income of the property includes planning a mix of tenants that complement one another. The plan may also provide community services such as security, parking and bathrooms.

Urban creativity is usually best promoted when there is security of possession, and that can take place both with freehold and leasehold ownership, provided that the leasehold is for a long period of time, with contractual provisions preventing opportunism by the title holder. For example, the rental formula can be specified for a long period, such as being based on average local market rentals, but also with a provision for the lease-holder to exit either with a renewal clause or the ability to sublease.

POLICY AND POPULATION

While critics of government rightly point to taxes and restrictions that impede creativity (in contrast to private entrepreneurship), government can play a positive role in providing creative infrastructure and also with policies that do not get in the way of private creativity. The public finance most compatible with creative cities is a tax on land values. Unlike labour, land does not hide, shrink or flee when taxed. By taxing only the site and not the buildings and other improvements, the tax on land value does not penalize creative reconstruction, and it therefore promotes the efficient use of land (Foldvary, 2006).

If one were to engage in an empirical test of urban creativity, what variables would one measure? Mason Gaffney (2007, p. 3) suggests population growth. The growth of land value or land rent could also be used, but one would have to be careful to distinguish the increase in rent that is due to greater demand as opposed to the increase in prices that is due to development permit costs or to restricted supply, which occur when development is limited by zoning or other regulations. One could also use aggregate income growth relative to that of the whole economy and aside from population growth.

Population, writes Gaffney (2007, p. 4), 'is a sign of city health: . . . a thriving city attracts people, and people, viewed as human resources, help the city thrive. . . . It is noteworthy that most cities' growth spurts accompanied provision of vast parks, superior schooling, mass transit, and other such public goods.' Population growth has been responsive to urban policy: 'This rise and fall of growth rates is remarkably independent of external causes, and more responsive to internal reforms.'

Urban populations can also grow from perverse reasons, such as flight from poor rural areas where the poverty is not inherent but is created by land tenure (with much of the wealth absorbed by landlords or corrupt local officials), pollution, inadequate education or restricted opportunities for women. But in developed industrial economies, urban growth is usually due to economic opportunities.

In response to the Depression of 1920, New York Governor Al Smith got the legislature to enable New York City to exempt new buildings from the property tax. 'There ensued an extraordinary boom in both building and population, beginning immediately and with an "echo effect" to 1940, even during the Great Depression when most other cities' populations froze' (Gaffney, 2007, p. 7). The population of New York City grew five times faster than other east coast cities such as Philadelphia and Baltimore, despite the Immigration Act of 1924 that cut immigration to New York City sharply.

Another example of the effect of policy on population growth, and thus of creativity, was Cleveland from 1900 to 1920, during which time the population more than doubled. During this period, Cleveland's mayors, especially Tom Johnson, increased assessments on land and decreased them on buildings (Gaffney, 2007, pp. 15–16). But when 'old line' conservatives later replaced the reformist mayors, Cleveland 'began its long slide into its present torpor and mediocrity' (Gaffney, 2007, p. 17).

Another example of policy and growth was San Francisco after the earthquake of

1906. With the buildings destroyed, in effect the property tax fell de facto on the land value. The real estate owners quickly rebuilt in order to make the property tax worth paying. 'San Francisco bounced back so fast its population grew by 22%, 1900–10, in the very wake of its destruction; it grew another 22%, 1910–20; and another 25%, 1920–30, remaining the 10th largest American city' (Gaffney, 2007, p. 25). The political leadership was amenable to this tax system. In '1907 San Francisco elected a reform Mayor, Edward Robeson Taylor, with a uniquely relevant background: he had helped Henry George write *Progress and Poverty* in 1879' (Gaffney, 2007, p. 25).

The efficient collection of rent to finance public services can be and has been done contractually. Indeed, the village of Arden, Delaware, was founded in 1900 precisely to demonstrate this concept in practice. The village land is owned by a land trust, which collects rent from leaseholds. The residents own the buildings, and the county property tax is paid by the trust, so that the resident is not tax-penalized for improving his property (Foldvary, 1994).

Arden is the only village in the United States on the National Register of Historic Places in its entirety, placed there in 1973 for being a successful experimental community, an example of a garden city, a direct democracy, a centre of the arts and for the preservation of a 'true village feeling with a deep sense of community' (Liberman, 1974, p. 25).

Arden was founded in 1900 by followers of Henry George who wanted to build a model community which would test George's theory of public finance, in which land rent is an efficient and equitable source of public revenue. To those who question the feasibility of assessing and collecting public revenue from land rent or land value apart from the value of buildings and other improvements, Arden shows empirically that it can be done effectively. The concept of raising revenues through land rent has remained in the Arden Deed of Trust for 110 years, a testimony to its sound principles.

Many of the original settlers, not having to pay up-front costs for the leased land, built their own houses. Unlike many residential associations, there were no covenants or other restrictions imposed on the architecture. The houses were and remain different from one another: 'houses were placed randomly on their lots to give them privacy and room for gardens' (Liberman, 1974, p. 4). The predominant style is English Tudor, 'but aside from that, the place is the very definition of the term "radical diversity"' (Sayles, 1988, p. 27). This freedom of individual house style and placement on lots provides evidence that a residential association need not include restrictive covenants on the architecture. Reinke (1975, p. 53) goes so far as to say that 'Arden is known for its unkemptness; the fact that many residents cite as one of Arden's attractions the lack of pressure to keep up the lawn . . . makes for a great deal of variety in appearance'.

While the main inspiration for Arden was the thought of Henry George in financing the budget from land rent, a second source of inspiration was the garden-city idea of Ebenezer Howard ([1902] 1965). Howard's vision was to 'marry' city and country, so that city dwellers would not have to travel far to enjoy nature. Howard in turn was influenced by Henry George; his garden-city idea included a 'voluntary plan of public finance' using leaseholds of land: 'One essential feature of the plan is that all ground rents, which are to be based upon the annual value of the land, shall be paid to the trustees, who, after providing for interest and sinking fund, will hand the balance to the Central Council of the new municipality, to be employed by such Council in the creation and maintenance of all necessary public works – roads, schools, parks, etc.' (Howard [1920] 1965, p. 51).

Some 43 per cent of Arden (70 acres) was set aside as greens, forest and roads. A woodland perimeter separates Arden from the now-adjoining suburbia. The streets of Arden followed the contours of the land rather than being laid out in a straight-line grid. The Arden forests make the village land more desirable, adding to site rents, and the Arden rentals provide the funding for the maintenance of the forests.

The Arden leasehold system makes the carrying cost of unimproved land significantly higher in Arden than in surrounding areas. In 1965, for example, an acre of land in Arden would cost $328 in annual rent, whereas a similar acre outside Arden would only have been taxed $10, excluding sewer charges (Wynn, 1965, p. 32). There are therefore very few unimproved house sites in Arden.

The level of land rent provides evidence of the efficacy of the public finance system at Arden relative to neighbouring areas. The real estate in Arden has a higher market value than similar surrounding properties (Hamburger, 1991). This implies that the economic rent that is generated by the public goods exceeds their cost, with the premium retained by the leaseholders. It has been recognized in the minutes of the Board of Assessors that some of the value is due to a 'community value factor', arising from the community's artistic and social activities (Wynn, 1965, p. 49). This implies that the volunteer efforts generate further site value in addition to the goods funded by the rent.

If Arden is so successful, one would think that the model would be copied. And indeed, that is what has happened. Arden has been reproduced – twice – in neighbouring communities. In 1922, a committee headed by Frank Stephens founded a new Arden-type community, Ardentown, using funds lent by Fiske Warren, a friend of Stephens. It contains 110 acres, with a layout similar to Arden, including woodland owned by the trustees. In 1975, Ardentown became incorporated, with a town-meeting governance like Arden. A third community based on the Arden model, Ardencroft, was begun in 1950, bordering on Arden and Ardentown. It was founded by Donald Stephens, son of Frank Stephens, and attorney Phillip Cohen. With 63 acres, Ardencroft is intentionally racially integrated, and efforts to attract African-Americans have succeeded (Liberman, 1974).

There have also been other land-rent communities, such as Fairhope, Alabama. The viability of land-renting organizations has been further demonstrated by the recent development of land trusts that have been created for the purpose of leasing sites or preserving a particular type of land use. A residential type of community land trust (CLT) was developed by Ralph Borsodi in the 1960s, based on the Arden/Fairhope models. There are about 50 operating urban CLTs in the United States, and over 800 land trusts of various types (Naureckas, 1990, p. 115).

VOICE AND RENT SEEKING

The field of public choice in economics analyses collective decisions such as voting and legislation. Legislators respond to votes and money. Public choice theory states that legislators seek to satisfy the median voter – those in the centre of a political spectrum. But lawmakers also seek campaign funds and need to be responsive to the contributors.

The centralization of power in national governments has reduced the ability of localities to be self-governing and creative, as revenue sharing comes with federally imposed conditions. Schools, for example, need to conform to federal testing in order to get funds. The centralization of power and decision-making derives from the structure of voting: from the system of mass democracy.

Mass democracy exists when the number of voters is so large that candidates need to use the mass media to deliver their campaign messages. The need for mass media creates a demand for funds, which special interests supply in exchange for favours, a process economists call 'rent seeking'. Attempts to restrict campaign finance have been ineffective, as the interests find other ways to fund campaigns, and restrictions also clash with free speech, as the Supreme Court has ruled in the case of corporations and unions.

Since transfer seeking is inherent in the structure of mass democracy, it can only be eliminated by a change in the structure to its opposite; small-group voting. The need to use expensive media is greatly reduced, if not eliminated, when voters only elect a neighbourhood council. Groups of neighbourhood councils may then elect the next higher-level council, and the process continues up through the levels of government to the country's congress or parliament (Foldvary, 1999).

Such a bottom-up structure was proposed by anarchists in the nineteenth century for voluntary associations, a concept later adopted by the Bolsheviks who envisioned a union of councils, hence the Soviet Union, 'soviet' meaning council. Their slogan was 'all power to the soviets!'. But when they seized power the effect was that in practice the Communist Party ruled the country. In a genuine bottom-up democracy, any person may run for office.

Where contractual communities such as residential associations are already established, their boards of directors can serve as the local council. With power flowing bottom-up, the public choice dynamics would shift power towards local government. Each level of governance would be elected from the next lower level, and monitored by that level. Just having smaller local jurisdictions will not be so effective, as long as mass democracy exists for the greater jurisdictions.

Local creativity would be enhanced even more if the sources of public revenue were also decentralized. The property tax, especially a tax on land value, would be suitable as a local source of revenue, since a local income tax would be vulnerable to tax competition. Indeed, the American states use federal income taxation as a cartel, for the purpose of joint tax collection and revenue sharing. If the public revenue flowed up from the county level to the state and federal levels, that would empower localities to become more creative as cities and counties.

But political force evidently prevents governments from enacting efficient public finance, as the ownership of real estate, other than single-family homes, is highly concentrated (Wolff, 2007). The privatization of governance to civic associations would most likely meet less political resistance than a fundamental reform of taxation.

CONCLUSION

The concept of voluntary planning provides a basis for a comparative analysis of urban creativity in contrast to central governmental planning. Non-voluntary planning by definition implies that individuals are not able to fully make plans that provide them with the greatest expected utility for activities that do not harm others.

Voluntary planning is based on contract, voice and rent. Contracts include associations, easements and covenants. Voice is exercised at the constitutional level of entering and exiting a club, as well as at the operational level in voting for club leaders. Market rentals, including association assessments, provide an efficient financing of contractual communities, both in having no deadweight loss and in seeking to maximize rentals.

Creation includes both production and innovation, and voluntary planning and governance allow individual creativity the greatest opportunity to flourish.

REFERENCES

Andersen, K. (1991), 'Look, Micky, no kitsch!', *Time*, **138**, 66–9.
Beito, D.T. (1989), 'Owning the "commanding heights": historical perspectives on private streets', *Essays in Public Works History*, **16**(December), 1–47.
Davies, S. (2002), 'Laissez-faire urban planning', in D.T. Beito, P. Gordon and A.T. Tabarrok (eds), Ann Arbor, MI: University of Michigan Press, pp. 18–46.
De Michael, D. (1973), 'Engineered communities: inside Walt Disney World', *Actual Specifying Engineer*, **29**(February), 53–64.
Erin, A. (2001), *Why is Housing So Expensive in Silicon Valley?*, Santa Clara, CA: Civil Society Institute, available at http://www.scu.edu/civilsocietyinstitute/events/upload/SVHousing.pdf (accessed 15 February 2010).
Fitzgerald, R. (1988), *When Government Goes Private*, New York, NY: Universe Books.
Foldvary, F.E. (1980), *The Soul of Liberty*, San Francisco, CA: Gutenberg Press.
Foldvary, F.E. (1994), *Public Goods and Private Communities*, Aldershot, UK and Brookfield, VT, USA: Edward Elgar Publishing.
Foldvary, F.E. (1999), 'Recalculating consent', in online *Buchanan Festschrift*, http://publicchoice.info/Buchanan/files/foldvary.htm (accessed 2 February 2010).
Foldvary, F.E. (2005a), 'Planning by freehold', *Economic Affairs*, **25**(4), 11–15.
Foldvary, F.E. (2005b), 'The ethical, governmental, and economic elements of secession', *Santa Clara Journal of International Law*, **III**(2), available at http://www.scu.edu/scjil/archive/v3_FoldvaryArticle.shtml (accessed 31 January 2010).
Foldvary, F.E. (2006), *The Ultimate Tax Reform: Public Revenue from Land Rent*, Santa Clara, CA: Civil Society Institute, available at http://www.foldvary.net/works/policystudy.pdf (accessed 2 February 2010).
Foldvary, F. E. (2009), 'Urban planning: the government or the market', in R.G. Holcombe and B. Powell (eds), *Housing America: Building Out of a Crisis*, Oakland, CA: Independent Institute, pp. 323–42.
Frazier, M. (1980), 'Privatizing the city', *Policy Review*, **12**, 91–108.
Frieden, B.J. (1970), 'Housing and national urban goals: old policies and new realities', in J.Q. Wilson (ed.), *The Metropolitan Enigma: Inquiries in the Nature and Dimensions of America's 'Urban Crisis'*, Garden City, NY: Doubleday, pp. 170–225.
Gaffney, M. (2007), *New Life in Old Cities*, New York, NY: Robert Schalkenbach Foundation.
Grubisich, T. and P. McCandless (1985), *RESTON: The First Twenty Years*, Reston, VA: Reston Publishing Company.
Hamburger, A. (1991), telephone interview, 2 November for the chapter on Arden in Foldvary (1994).
Heath, S. (1957), *Citadel, Market and Altar*, Baltimore, MD: Science of Society Foundation.
Hirschman, A. (1970), *Exit, Voice and Loyalty: Responses to Declines in Firms, Organizations, and States*, Cambridge, MA: Harvard University Press.
Howard, E. [1902] (1965), *Garden Cities of To-Morrow*, Cambridge, MA: MIT Press.
Jacobs, Jane (1961), *The Death and Life of Great American Cities*, New York, NY: Random House.
Kinkella, D. (2009), 'The ecological landscapes of Jane Jacobs and Rachel Carson', *American Quarterly*, **61**(4), 905–28.
Klein, D., A. Moore and B. Reja (1997), *Curb Rights: A Foundation for Free Enterprise in Urban Transit*, Washington, DC: Brookings Institution Press.
Liberman, C. (1974), *The Arden Book*, Arden, DE: Community Planning Committee, Arden Town Assembly.
MacCallum, S. (2003), 'The entrepreneurial community in light of advancing business practices and technologies', in F.E. Foldvary and D. Klein (eds), *The Half-life of Policy Rationales*, New York, NY: New York University Press, pp. 227–42.
Mises, L. von (1966), *Human Action*, New Haven, CT: Yale University Press.
Naureckas, J. (1990), 'Land trusts offer American land reform', in *Intentional Communities*, Evansville, IN and Stelle, IL: Fellowship for Intentional Community and Communities Publications Cooperative, pp. 114–15.

Parks, R.B. and R.J. Oakerson (1988), *Metropolitan Organization: The St. Louis Case*, Washington, DC: Advisory Commission on Intergovernmental Relations.

Reinke, B. (1975), 'Utopian communities in America: potentials, promises, and perils', manuscript, Arden Archives, Arden, DE.

Roth, G. (ed.) (2006), *Street Smart: Competition, Entrepreneurship, and the Future of Roads*, Oakland, CA and New Brunswick, NJ: The Independent Institute and Transaction Publishers.

Sayles, T. (1988), 'Arden, Delaware', *Mid-Atlantic Country*, February, pp. 24–9.

Schumpeter, J.A. [1942] (1976), *Capitalism, Socialism and Democracy*, New York, NY: Harper.

Shoup, D. (2003), 'Buying time at the curb', in F.E. Foldvary and D. Klein (eds), *The Half-life of Policy Rationales*, New York, NY: New York University Press, pp. 60–85.

Sombart, W. (1913), *Krieg und Kapitalismus*, Leipzig: Duncker & Humblot.

Thomas, W. (2009), 'Man charged after making coffee naked', *My Fox*, 20 October, available at http://www.myfoxdc.com/dpp/news/local/101909_man_caught_making_coffee_naked_faces_charges (accessed 24 January 2010).

Williamson, O.E. (1985), *The Economic Institutions of Capitalism*, New York, NY: The Free Press.

Wolff, E.N. (2007), 'Recent trends in household wealth in the United States: rising debt and the middle-class squeeze', working paper No. 502, The Levy Economics Institute of Bard College, Annandale-on-Hudson, NY, available at http://www.levy.org/pubs/wp_502.pdf (accessed 15 February 2010).

Wynn, R.W. (1965), 'The full rental value: a study of the tax rate in Arden using single tax theory', master's thesis, Department of Business Administration, University of Delaware, Newark, DE.

26 A roadmap for the creative city
Charles Landry

I developed my first 'creative city' project in 1989 with 'Glasgow – the Creative City & its Cultural Economy'. This signalled an ongoing interest in how going with the culture of a place and its embedded resources can help reinvent a city and give it strategic advantage. Since then I have developed my ideas by working practically with several dozen cities. This work has focused on helping cities to identify and harness their assets, to assess how these can be used imaginatively, to think through their long-term aims and to suggest how they can be implemented. The text that follows comes from conclusions in reflecting on the lessons of this work as well as being inspired by other practitioners and authors.[1]

The primary conclusions are that the creative capacity of a place is shaped by its history, its culture, its physical setting and its overall operating conditions. This determines its character and 'mindset'. I evolved a contrast between the 'urban engineering paradigm' of city development focused on hardware with 'creative city making' which emphasizes how we need to understand the hardware and software simultaneously. Today the essential element of the personality of many cities is their 'culture of engineering' which is reflected in their mentality. The attributes to foster creativity associated with this mindset are both positive and negative. It is logical, rational and technologically adept; it learns by doing; it tends to advance step by step and through trial and error. It is hardware-focused. It gets things done. There is a weakness in that this mindset can become narrow, unimaginative and inflexible and forget the software aspect, which is concerned with how a place feels, its capacity to foster interactions and to develop and harness skill and talent. Mindsets either foster or hinder and block creative potential. The challenge, therefore, is to embed an understanding of the soft and creative thinking into how a city operates. Developing a 'creativity platform' is a main strategic tool in establishing a comprehensive 'creative ecology' within a city.

SETTING THE SCENE: THE ORIGINAL IDEA

The idea of the creative city, as contrasted to the 'creative milieu', emerged from the late 1980s onwards along a number of trajectories. When introduced in the late 1980s (Landry, 1990, 2000; Landry and Bianchini, 1995) it was seen as aspirational; a clarion call to encourage open-mindedness and imagination. Its intent was to have a dramatic impact on organizational culture. The philosophy was that there is always more potential in any place than any of us would think at first sight, even though very few cities – perhaps only London, New York, Amsterdam or Berlin – have been comprehensively creative over time.

It posits that conditions need to be created for people to think, plan and act with imagination in harnessing opportunities or addressing seemingly intractable urban problems.

These might range from addressing homelessness, to creating wealth or enhancing the visual environment. It is a positive concept; its assumption is that ordinary people can make the extraordinary happen if given the chance.

Creativity in this context is applied imagination using qualities like intelligence, inventiveness and learning along the way. In the 'creative city' it is not only artists and those involved in the creative economy who are creative, although they play an important role. Creativity can come from any source including anyone who addresses issues in an inventive way, be it a social worker, a business person, a scientist or public servant. It advocates the need for a culture of creativity to be embedded into how the urban stakeholders operate. By encouraging creativity and legitimizing the use of imagination within the public, private and community spheres, the ideas bank of possibilities and potential solutions to any urban problem will be broadened. This is the divergent thinking that generates multiple options, which needs to be aligned to convergent thinking that narrows down possibilities from which then urban innovations can emerge once they have passed the reality checker.

This requires infrastructures beyond the hardware – buildings, roads or sewage. Creative infrastructure is a combination of the hard and the soft, including too the mental infrastructure; the way a city approaches opportunities and problems; the environmental conditions it creates to generate an atmosphere; and the enabling devices it fosters that are generated through its incentives and regulatory structures. It requires thousands of changes in mindset, creating the conditions for people to become agents of change rather than victims of change, seeing transformation as a lived experience not a one-off event.

The built environment – the stage, the setting, the container – is crucial for establishing a milieu. The industrial city and its milieu looks, feels, operates and uses resources differently from a knowledge-intensive or creative city. The latter needs a different physical environment which fosters sociability, exchange and mixing in order to maximize its potential. In this way it becomes an accelerator of opportunities.

It needs to provide the physical preconditions or platform upon which the activity base or atmosphere of a city can develop. A creative milieu is a place that contains the necessary requirements in terms of 'hard' and 'soft' infrastructure to generate a flow of ideas and inventions. A milieu can be a building, a street or an area, such as the Truman's Brewery in Brick Lane, London, Rundle Street East in Adelaide, Queen Street in Toronto and SoHo in New York. In planning for a creative city a city needs to have:

● A definition of creativity and its scope.
● A mindset able to implement the idea.
● A conceptual tool – creativity as a resource.
● A benchmarking tool – the creativity index.

Each are described in turn. Since becoming and being a creative city is very much concerned with changing mindsets it is more a process than a plan, it is dynamic rather than static. There is no fixed point at which a city is creative. To maintain a creative position a city needs to be continually alert and strategically agile.

WHAT IS CREATIVITY: QUALITIES AND CHARACTERISTICS

Creativity is a general, all-purpose problem-solving and opportunity-creating capacity. Its essence is a multifaceted resourcefulness and the ability to assess and find one's way to solutions for intractable, unexpected or unusual problems or circumstances. Equally it helps a process of discovery through the supple capacity to imagine possibilities – to conceive and originate concepts and ideas and downstream to help bring them into being. In this way it enables potential to unfold. It is applied imagination, using qualities like intelligence, inventiveness and reflexive learning along the way. It is valuable in the social, political, organizational and cultural field as well as in technology and the economy. It can be applied to all spheres: from rethinking schools and teaching; inventing new systems of healthcare and delivery; recasting organizational structures. Crucially, it is now recognized that creative inputs add value to businesses which are not normally considered creative, such as engineering, facilities management or the hospitality industry as distinct from design, film or music. Creativity is both generic, a way of thinking and a mindset, and it has specific applications and is task-oriented in relation to particular fields.

Creativity requires certain qualities of mind, dispositions and attitudes. These characteristics include: curiosity, openness and a questioning attitude; the ability to stand back, listen and reassess; the courage not to take a given credo, practice or theory for granted and to dare to think outside of the box; and the gift of seeing relevance and connections between apparently different things. It involves fluency and flexibility and the ability to draw on ideas from across disciplines and fields of inquiry, to think laterally and to blend concepts from seemingly unrelated domains. It is based on divergent thinking, which opens out possibilities, reveals patterns and helps find solutions before prematurely closing in on a specific answer.

Creativity is not only concerned with the new, or a loose openness. To be effective in being creative means having the judgement and knowing when to be flexible and open, and when to be more focused and closed or tenacious and persistent. A misconception is that being creative is about being unconstrained. Being creative requires just as much attention as being a scientist or an engineer. The central point is that it is a different kind of attentiveness and approach. So in terms of education, as an instance, creative learners need four key qualities: to identify new problems, rather than depending on others to define them; to transfer knowledge from one context to another; to treat learning as an incremental process, in which repeated attempts will eventually lead to success; and to pursue a goal. The range of skills required include: self-organization; being interdisciplinary and to have personal and interpersonal abilities.

Everyone is in principle creative, but not everyone is equally creative, yet everyone can be more creative than they currently are. The same applies to organizations, neighbourhoods and city regions. Some aspects of creativity can be learnt but many individuals or organizations have default ways of thinking. Some flourish in a more free-ranging context; others find it threatening and destabilizing. It seems that most people and organizations prefer the comfort zone of the tried and tested, the known and apparently proven.

Creative behaviour and the ability to innovate occur when two types of mind are present. One is the exploratory, opportunity-seeking and connecting mind that can range horizontally across facts, issues and specialist knowledge and detect threads, themes and cross-cutting agendas. This is the enabling mind associated with being creative. This needs to be allied to the focused, vertical mind of someone who knows a topic, subject or discipline in profound detail. This is the instrumental mind.

INDIVIDUAL, ORGANIZATIONAL AND URBAN CREATIVITY

We can grasp quite easily what a creative individual might be like; for instance, their capacity to make interesting connections, to think out of the box (avoiding established theories) and to have sparks of insight. They have energy and courage as well as some sense of where they are going, although it is often unclear how. The same is true for a creative organization. But already the priorities are different and it adds a layer of complexity and a different dynamic takes place.

A creative organization probably has mavericks and creative individuals, but for the organization to work it needs other types too: consolidators, sceptics, solidifiers, balancers, people with people skills. Some people consider them as less interesting, but that is dangerous, because for the creative organization to work it needs mixed teams. How teams work together becomes significant. You need to achieve a series of balances, such as between being collaborative internally and perhaps using external competition to push you forward. And the organization needs a story and a proposed trajectory to give itself purpose in an attempt to make it more internally cohesive. The task is to align internally to face an outside world. Indeed it may be the case that a creative organization has quite 'ordinary' people in it, but because its spirit or ethos is open, exploratory and supportive this maximizes potential. This may then lead to greater, sustained organizational achievements. This often happens in sport where a team with no supremely gifted individuals wins, because it knows better how to make the most of its parts. The key is its open ethos. The value of ethos is incalculable.

Moving on to the next layer – the creative city – means that issues become very difficult as complexity rises exponentially. Cities involve a mass of individuals and an amalgam of organizations with different cultures, aims and attitudes. These can push in opposing directions. For example, it may be that some are pushing for urban expansion and extension, whereas others focusing on the sustainability agenda want to densify things. Or one organization may display great cultural understanding, whereas another may basically not get it. The challenge then is to discover where the lines of strong agreement can flow and to build on these so that similarities become more important than differences. The creative city notion does not imply there is a cosy consensus. Instead it stresses how rules of engagement between differences can be negotiated to move forward as in a mediation process. The overarching skill needed for a creative city, therefore, is that of the connectors, enablers and facilitators. These can be individuals or intermediary organizations which can stand above the nitty-gritty of the day-to-day, important as this is, and look at what really matters instead of getting stuck in detail.

'What really matters' in a city depends on circumstance, but increasingly, and this makes things extremely hard, it is being 'creative' itself: that is, 'providing the preconditions to think, plan and act creatively'. This means organizations changing their work culture. In other words we are only at the beginning of the 'creative city' journey. The notion has not embedded itself into the genetic code of the key institutions that make up cities.

WHAT IS A CREATIVE PLACE?

To plan a creative city we need to know what it is like. But first a reminder: a creative place can be a room, a building, a street or a neighbourhood. A creative city or city region is a good amalgam of all these. The qualities of each are rather similar: a sense of comfort and familiarity, usually a good blending of the old and new, variety and choice and a balance between the calm and the invigorating or risk and caution.

A creative city is a place where people feel they can fulfil themselves, because there are opportunities. Things get done. It is a place where people can express their talents which are harnessed, exploited and promoted for the common good. These talents act as a catalyst and role model to develop and attract further talent in a self-reinforcing cycle. Here there are myriad, high-quality learning opportunities, formal and informal, where self-development is easy, where learning programmes are forward-looking and adaptable and highly connected. There are ladders of opportunity and choices and a sense that ambition and aspirations can be met. There is a 'can do' mentality. The residents see that the city is an engine of possibilities.

There are places to meet, talk, mix, exchange and play. There is multicultural colour and diversity as this implies distinctiveness and varied insights. Yet even better it is an 'intercultural' place where the focus is on mixing different cultures, attitudes and experiences and sharing ideas and projects together.

The confidence to be outward-looking comes from residents having a sense of familiarity with people around them, in their family, their friendship networks, their neighbourhood or workplace or because of the physical landmarks in the city, be that a street, a cafe or a set of facilities. This anchors their sense of safety and security. The feeling of community is important, but it needs to be an evolving one that adapts to changes and so is resilient. Once people have confidence, they want to explore, discover, be curious and be surprised. This implies that the city has rich layers that do not reveal themselves immediately. The creative place exudes crucially a sense of a 'higher purpose'. This means that these are soulful places too, perhaps a gallery or a site of interest – a kind of cathedral of the post-industrial age.

In a successful creative city, the overall physical environment functions well for its inhabitants and it is easy to move around and connect with one another. Its high-level urban design inspires, stimulates and generates pride and affection. The architecture, old and new, is well assembled, and the street pattern is diverse and interesting. Webbed within the ordinary is the occasional extraordinary and remarkable or memorable. It is an environment in which creators of all kinds are content but not complacent, and where they are motivated to create; there are outlets and channels to communicate their ideas or research or sell their work. It is a natural market place, where people exchange ideas, develop joint projects, trade their products or work in its advanced industries. It offers a rich register of vibrant experiences through, for example, gastronomy, the arts, heritage and its natural surroundings, including thriving mainstream and alternative scenes and a healthy network of third spaces. Opportunities abound: the place is welcoming and encouraging. Its dynamism makes it a magnet and so generates critical mass and attracts people from outside and this guarantees longevity.

The political and public framework within which this exists has clarity of purpose and direction, and understands the importance of harnessing the potential of its people. It is lean, clear and focused. Its workings are easy to navigate and it is accessible, open and encourages participation. Public employees here are focused on the job at hand regardless of departmental boundaries. Differences are a natural part of this discussion culture. They are debated, accepted, negotiated and resolved without rancour. Its leadership has vision and is strategically agile yet is grounded in day-to-day reality. It is respected and trusted and recognizes its vital role in continuously identifying new opportunities and future-proofing. The society it rules over has a high degree of cohesion, is relatively open to incomers and to new ideas, even though these can sometimes be uncomfortable – indeed, creative places are often not that cosy and can be somewhat edgy. This society enjoys its status as a creative hub and the physical environment in which it exists. Levels of crime are in general low, the place feels safe and standards of living are relatively high. It is socially alert and seeks to avoid ghettoizing its poorest. Social organizations are active, well funded and constructive.

Industry is innovative and design-aware, with a strong focus on new trends, emerging technologies and fledgling sectors such as developing the green economy or creative industries. It is well networked and connected, and its commitment to research and development is well above average. Cross-fertilization across even the most diverse sectors occurs naturally. Public-private partnerships happen as a matter of course. The business community is entrepreneurial, has drive and is forward-thinking. It understands and utilizes well its natural resources, it harnesses existing talents and acts as a breeding ground for new skills. Business leaders are respected figures in their community and give something back. The community in turn is proud of their products and the reputation they bring to the place. Good use is made of its effective communications systems, including local and international transport, high-speed internet access and connectivity to the world at large.

Overall, as in all creative places, this place is unlike any other. You can feel and sense the buzz, it is obvious to residents and visitors alike. It accentuates its distinctiveness in a relaxed and unthreatening way. It is at ease with itself. Its history, culture and traditions are alive, receptive to influence and change, absorbing new ideas which in turn evolve and develop its distinctiveness and culture.

WHY IS THERE A CREATIVE CITY MOVEMENT? THE SHIFTING GLOBAL CITY REGION LANDSCAPE

The creativity notion has moved centre-stage to an extent that we can talk of a creativity and creative city movement. There are many triggers including the fierce nature of urban competition and because the old ways of doing many things do not work. Globally, over the last 20 years, cities have been searching for answers to re-establishing their purpose and creating new kinds of jobs, whilst their cities were physically often locked into their industrial past. This led to soul searching, which meant reassessing the old ways. Many concluded that education did not seem to prepare people for the demands of the 'new' world. Schools remained factories to drill in knowledge rather than communities of enquiry; they taught specific things rather than acquiring higher-order skills, such as learning how to learn, to create, to discover, innovate, problem-solve and self-assess. This means talent was not sufficiently unleashed, explored and harnessed. Second, hierarchical management systems in the public and private sectors were recognized as not efficient in a world where flatter, networked structures showed greater promise and new business models such as 'open innovation' were emerging.

In sum, *the world of cities and regions has changed dramatically* over the last 20 years. The reinvention of places like the Ruhr, Bilbao, Helsinki, Melbourne, Chicago or Vancouver is emblematic of this shift. Cities of every size in every location face periods of deep transition largely brought about by the vigour of renewed globalization and changes in the world's urban hierarchy. Each city region needs to reassess its role in this new configuration as they need to move their economy to one based on greater knowledge intensity.

Every city region of real ambition wants to move up the value chain and capture centrality. This is why city regions are continuously searching to be global niche centres of significance. The overall aim of these ambitious places is to increase their 'drawing power', by whatever means. This assesses the dynamics of attraction, retention and leakage of power, resources and talent. The right blend makes a city attractive and desirable, with different aspects tempting different audiences: power brokers, investors, industrialists, shoppers, tourists, property developers, thought leaders. Overall this creates the resonance of a city. Few places manage to develop the integrated and sophisticated city marketing that brings these elements together. Melbourne, Amsterdam and Berlin do it well. The consequence of achieving drawing power shows itself in economic, political and cultural power – the ability to shape things – and thus performance and wealth. New dimensions of competition are emerging, such as being 'green', and in that dimension places such as Zurich, Freiburg and Copenhagen have made a significant impact.

Cities now compete by harnessing every dimension of their asset base and practically all the major global city region players have recognized 'creativity' as a new multifaceted resource. Many have creativity strategies, for example, Singapore, Amsterdam, Berlin, Shanghai, London, Hong Kong, Osaka and Toronto. Increasingly, second- and third-tier cities are following in their wake.

The resources that city regions can creatively use can be hard, material and tangible or soft, immaterial and intangible; they can be real and visible or symbolic and invisible; they can be countable, quantifiable and calculable or they can concern themselves with perceptions and images. Ambitious cities seek to project and orchestrate their assets 'iconically'. The aim is to pull attention to the city, to create a richness of association and recognition and to grab profile. Icons are projects or initiatives that are powerfully self-explanatory, jolt the imagination, surprise, challenge and raise expectations. You grasp it in one. In time they become instantly recognizable and emblematic. Very few of these exist and the newest is likely to be the *Elbphilharmonie* in the HafenCity Hamburg built by Herzog de Meuron. Others that have caught the imagination include the Palm in Dubai. Most memorable are the physical ones. An icon, however, can be tangible or intangible: A building, an activity, a tradition, having a headquarters of a key organization in the city, the association of a person with a city, a plan or an event like the Olympics can be iconic. A city can even be iconic when it has many associations that build upon each other into a powerful composite picture. Most importantly, images and perceptions need to be grounded in reality.

There is a battle as to how to measure the significance of places as our measurement systems for assessing city dynamics are often out of date. We measure static quantities, such as population or gross domestic product, usually derived from the Census. As important as these measures are, they are distinct from relational measures, such as the power or information flows, connections, linkages, reputation, iconic presence and other less tangible factors. This is why a creativity index is proposed.

WHAT ARE THE DYNAMICS OF CREATIVITY? CREATIVITY AS A RESOURCE

The implication is that today there is a premium on creativity. For the first time in history, the imagination of the mind and its resulting knowledge is the primary source of economic productivity and problem-solving. We have evolved from a world where prosperity depended on *natural advantage* (arising from access to more plentiful and cheap natural resources and labour) to a world where prosperity depends on *creative advantage*, arising from being able to use and mobilize brainpower to innovate in areas of specialized capability more effectively than other places.

Success depends on a city's capacity to identify, nurture, harness, support, promote and orchestrate and mobilize their creative resources. It needs to develop its 'creative ecology'.

To fully harness creativity we need to think of resources more widely and draw on the history of places and their culture. In sum, these are cultural resources. They are the raw materials of the city and its value base; its assets replacing coal or steel. Creativity is the method of exploiting these resources and helping them grow. A city region has a vast array of these raw materials. They include unique resources embodied in people's inventiveness, skills and talents and the natural setting such as weather, topography, water and created landscapes like parks. They also include natural resources like coal and forests; history, heritage and tradition in the built fabric, in memories and rituals, and in acquired skills. It encompasses the quality of overall design, the pattern of streets and neighbourhoods, the balance between good ordinary buildings, the spectacular and iconic and representative structures. It consists of infrastructures from information technology (IT) to transport as well as how a city does its urban housekeeping. It contains specialist local industries and services and the skills and talent base as well as research and educational possibilities. Increasingly too the capacity within the cultural industries is important, from design to new media or film and the performance sectors. It involves furthermore activities cutting across trade fairs, sporting, the artistic arena and those that are community-based, as well as festivals and events. Finally, attitudes and attributes can be assets, such as whether there is a culture of curiosity or organizational competence.

Even the resulting regulations and incentives regime can act as a creative stimulus. For example, it is possible to use taxation in ways that encourage certain initiatives or behaviours.

The task of urban planners is to recognize, manage and exploit these resources responsibly. An appreciation of culture should shape the technicalities of urban planning and development rather than being seen as a marginal add-on to be considered once the important planning questions such as housing, transport and land use have been dealt with. A culturally informed perspective should condition how a city thinks of itself. Its vision for the future as culture helps us understand where a place comes from, why it is like it is now and how this might determine its potential. This focus draws attention to the distinctive, the unique and the special in any place.

CRITICAL MASS AND SIZE

Creativity potential is determined by context. These factors are often beyond the control of a city. They include the physical location, the geography, the size of the place, national politics or levels of centralization. Critical mass is key in achieving certain aims. Historically it was usually the larger places that became renowned for being creative. Looking at the acknowledged creative places from the past it is striking how many of them were hubs of empires such as Athens, Vienna or London or the centre of trading routes or entry points such as Venice or New York. Unsurprisingly, as poles of attraction they lured the best and the brightest from around their known worlds, which continually helped reinforce their positions, so helping to generate cultural and political power as well as complex specializations or industrial clusters through which they created their wealth.

Each of these famous creative hubs offered us something unique from which we can still learn today. Athens gave us an intellectual heritage that fostered debate, analysis and critique. Venice highlights to us the importance of specialization, expertise and trade networks. Florence reminds us how important new business models are, as exemplified by its invention of banking systems. Vienna shows us how a configuration of core ideas can affect a number of disciplines simultaneously. The rise of Paris as an arts and fashion leader was triggered and aided by royal sponsorship, which is in effect public investment. London of the swinging sixties hit a global Zeitgeist or mood of change, while the success of Silicon Valley helps point out the elements required – organizational, financial and legal – to turn ideas into reality.

The interesting question is whether smaller places, especially those with industrial traditions such as for producing coal, steel, manufactured goods or beer can be creative. In relative terms the answer is yes. Whilst they cannot compete with global hubs there is a vast range of global niches and strengths to be captured. And indeed very large places often become dysfunctional and so reduce their creativity potential.

What appear to be important are the forms of expertise that are agglomerated in a particular place. Here the idea of the quinary sector is helpful. The traditional breakdown into the primary, secondary and tertiary or service sector is well known. Yet the tertiary sector is immense and includes activities that are vastly different. Being a waiter or hairdresser is a service job, and cannot really be compared to being a lawyer or software engineer which requires different intellectual attributes. Some therefore define this as the quartenary sector. The quinary sector includes activities involving the highest levels of decision-making and strategic thinking and planning where often ideas, concepts, models and products and services themselves are rethought and reinvented. The creative city has a higher proportion of these people.

URGENCY AND WICKED PROBLEMS

The need for creativity should be seen in the light of new complex problems, such as greening and sustainability, which if treated seriously, will need to reshape how we think and behave. Some refer to this as the rise of wicked problems. Many public policy problems, such as obesity which cut across health and social issues, are severely complex. Called wicked problems they are seemingly intractable, made up of inter-related dilemmas, issues and interweave political, economic and social questions. Wicked problems cannot be tackled by traditional approaches, where problems are simply defined, analysed and solved in sequential steps. They have characteristics that make traditional hierarchical, top-down thinking less adept at solving them. There is no definite or unique 'correct' view of formulating the problem; and different stakeholders see the problem and solutions differently, often with deeply held ideological views. Data is frequently uncertain, difficult to acquire or missing. They are connected to other problems and every solution reveals new aspects of the problem that needs adjusting.

The greatest impact of creativity comes when it finds a way of solving wicked problems.

COST DISEASE

The particular challenge is for the public sector to attract talented people. The relative wages between the public and private sector are under pressure. This is because of the 'cost disease'. Many activities – especially within advanced manufacturing – can increase productivity dramatically through IT improvements or inventiveness and therefore justify salary increases. Making more with less is effectiveness in these contexts. In services and personalized services, which is largely the domain of the public sector, productivity increases are by contrast more difficult to achieve. If a teacher increases their productivity by having classes of 20 rather than 10, we deem this to be a loss of service. The same applies to a nurse or a social worker dealing with more patients or clients. Yet, their relative skill and wage expectations are the same as those working in advanced manufacturing. This upward cost pressure is the cost disease. For the public sector there are few choices. They will inevitably have higher salary demands and probably lower investment. This means that the public domain needs to be open to new and innovative ways of operating. It has to be imaginative in reinventing services in order to make its resources work harder.

SETTINGS AND MILIEU

Creativity needs physical and organizational environments, settings and a management ethos that encourages creativity to happen. Many organizations, institutions or cultures inadvertently kill their creativity by crushing their employees, or in the case of education their pupils' intrinsic motivation – the strong internal desire to do something based on passions and interests. Environments, firms or places that encourage individuals or organizations to become creative have a number of features, including: giving people the freedom and authority to act by delegating authority; presenting the right scope of challenge that is achievable but stretches people enough; providing sufficient time, human and financial resources to allow for trial and error as well as to make mistakes; creating a supportive team context where people are committed to the project, to each other and where ideas and different opinions can be shared to develop the potential of an idea, process or product; managerial and organizational support by creating an environment that publicly values and rewards creativity. Clearly this impacts on how companies, schools, universities or city regions operate.

A new organizational ethos is shaping up. It differs from the more simplistic efficiency and effectiveness paradigm associated with the late twentieth century. The characteristics and operating dynamics of the progressive early twenty-first-century corporate or public bureaucracy include being resourceful, strategically agile, responsive and imaginative.

The applications of creativity are context-driven. In the nineteenth century it was, for instance, the creativity of scientists in discovering the cure for cholera that advanced public health. In the twentieth century those that invented computers ultimately created the internet-based economy. In the twenty-first-century, two focuses for creativity are essential. The first is needed to advance the fourth lean, clean and green industrial revolution as well as to solve the problems of social integration or conviviality and to rethink healthcare and social services. The second is the ability to think holistically and across disciplines. In part this requires people to think differently because then they do things differently and ultimately, perhaps, different things.

CREATIVITY AND THE BUREAUCRACY

One arena for creative action is the public bureaucracy, as the twenty-first-century version will need to be different from and solve more complex problems than what was the case in the twentieth century. Our Western bureaucracies were developed to address issues of their time, and therefore reflect the culture of their age. At their best they sought systematic procedures to bring transparency, fairness and equity to decision-making. Yet as they evolved weaknesses appeared and combined with managerialism: they became convoluted. Changes are already afoot in the organizational practices of the public sector, commercial companies and in the wider world. They include a shift to involving users more as co-creators of policies, products or solutions; a shift from hierarchical to network thinking; a breakdown in traditional disciplinary boundaries; and cultural cross-fertilization. These have implications for how bureaucracies need to operate. The 'creative bureaucracy' idea is not a plan, but a proposed way of operating that helps create better plans and better future ways of operating. It is an adaptive, responsive and collaborative organizational form that in principle can harness the initiative, motivation and full intelligences of those working in them as well as respond to the changing demands of those they seek to serve.

CONTOURS OF THE NEW: WAVES OF CHANGE AND THEIR CONSEQUENCES

There is a curve that shows the movement over time from the agrarian to the creativity-driven economy. We were an agrarian society for millennia, an industrial one for 200 years, a society whose wealth creation was primarily driven by information for 30 years. We now talk of the knowledge- and innovation-driven economy and increasingly of a creativity-driven economy. Ever more speedily we have moved through phases where the dominance of a particular asset has changed.

Each metaphor such as 'the innovation economy' or 'the creativity-driven economy' provides a helpful lens from which to understand and gauge the shift in the primary means of wealth creation, the basis of competition, the social and cultural priorities, management style and operating systems, the role of the public sector and the measurement of success or failure. Now we have reached a stage where creativity and the capacity to imagine are seen as key.

Every shift in the means of economic wealth creation creates a new social order, new ways of learning and things to learn, new settings in which learning takes place and the demand for new kinds of facilities. It requires different cultural capabilities. For instance, looking at the economy, the capabilities and requirements to set up a Ford Motor Company or a WalMart are different from those thst create an Apple or a Google or a Kaos Pilots educational centre in Denmark or a Forum Virium in Helsinki.

The 'innovation or knowledge economy', for instance, is largely associated with technological innovation and the skills, attitudes and qualities of technologists, software engineers and other scientifically oriented people. Without wishing to generalize too much or fall into clichés, the personality characteristics of these groups is more logical, linear, rational, analytical and systematic. They of course have elements of creativity as well, but are less adept at social issues or communication. A survey of 103 engineers notes that engineers need to pay greater attention to interpersonal skills, communicative abilities and cultural literacy (Van der Molen et al., 2007).

There was a level of predictability about the foreseeable results of the former phases. Predicting exactly the 'emerging advantage' from creativity will be less easy. Put another way, we are moving from 'managing the known' to a design and innovation approach that is 'building the unknown'. Yet what is possible is to build capability and encourage the mindset for communities to have the foresight to identify the 'advantage' when it starts to emerge, and so to have the creative capacity to respond accordingly. This requires a governance ethos as well as management and learning systems that are aware of these needs and are willing to adapt to new demands.

OPENNESS AND DESIGN THINKING

The contours of the new wave are becoming much clearer as the nature and processes of technological innovation themselves are changing. The watchword 'open innovation system' encapsulates this movement. 'Collaborative service design' or 'co-production and co-creation' are other central themes rising in importance.

These underlying trends in the development of knowledge-intensive economies are evolving at a dramatic pace with user-driven product development and co-creation having a particular focus. The development of new IT platforms and web 3.0 with its immersive, interactive, ubiquitous and experiential focus will exacerbate this shift to co-creation. It changes how products and services are conceived and designed and how value-added is created. It has implications for both the public and private sectors. For instance, the trend for cities to get local people to come up with new ideas for public urban spaces fits this thinking perfectly. Another notion which expresses a deeper trend is the idea of the 'experience economy', which fits the idea that the world too is increasingly made up of more 'imagination-intensive industries'. Here businesses focus on orchestrating memorable products and events for their customers, which is the 'experience'. Sectors such as film, design, music and new media are central in this.

These trends will have powerful impacts on the desirable qualities in individuals and on the culture of organizations and how they need to work. Private or community sectors and public administrations need to ask themselves whether the skills are sufficiently present. The mental dispositions and skills required to be successful and rising to the fore more strongly include openness, creativity, communication ability, collaborative inter-disciplinary working, cultural literacy and lateral and holistic thinking. In organizational terms it means far more integrated working, the capacity to value the combined insights of different disciplines and the need to operate as task-oriented teams as distinct from operating in silos.

This is not to decry the strengths of the specialist or subject expert. However, to make the most of possibilities or to solve complex problems mostly requires the ability to work across boundaries and knowledge domains, especially since the structures and departments we usually operate with have come from a period where different priorities and a different global dynamic operated.

In this context 'design thinking', as part of the overall creativity paradigm, is seen as instrumental in coping with these shifts. Design thinking involves an ability to combine rationality, creativity with empathy in meeting needs. As a process it 'builds up' ideas while judgements are withheld for as long as possible. Thus more ideas and possibilities are generated and fear of failure is reduced. In principle this can increase lateral thinking and creativity. In contrast, analytical thinking – which predominated in the former phase of innovation – is more linear. It tends to break issues up into component parts, in order to understand its essential nature and inner connections and relationships. It is the world of 'who', 'what', 'where', 'when', 'why' and 'how'. Without wishing to denigrate these qualities, on their own they will not bring about the solutions to evolving problems or emerging opportunities.

MOVEMENTS OF CHANGE

Economies, societies and cultures evolve and new necessities emerge. Four movements over the last 30 years exemplify this: the quality imperative; the added value of design; the need for innovation; and now creativity. These four movements show the shifting focus in highlighting how organizations, cities and regions can become successful.

Together they form part of a new common sense. They are competitive tools. The aim is to embed these attributes into the genetic code of a city. Deeper drivers explain their significance. Quality requires conscientiousness, attention to detail and the maintenance of high standards. The threshold of necessary 'quality' has risen in overall terms. It highlights the ideal of *reliability, consistency and predictability* and the concept of continuous improvement and just-in-time production. Total quality management highlights the idea of *alertness, adaptability and responsiveness*. Now it is not simply continuous improvement that is required, but breakthroughs in how people think and solve problems. In the quality paradigm improvement is regarded as step by step or one-dimensional change, while innovation is seen as multidimensional, sometimes involving breakthroughs. Delivering a solution that is unique is becoming more important than delivering a standard solution with near perfect quality. The quality of design of the innovation becomes the differentiating factor. Design differentiation creates competitive advantage. Design links functionality and aesthetics. It is a bridge to turn creative ideas into innovations. The desire to generate rich experiences makes good design a prerequisite for success.

Firms have always needed to innovate. What has changed is the speed at which they must do so, which is driven by the pressures of global competition. In addition, the scope of innovations has broadened beyond product innovation in private companies to include innovations in the public sphere such as in healthcare or social services or new forms of service delivery or governance.

ALIGNMENT AND BRIDGING

Creativity and innovation are related. They connect but crucially they are not the same. First, there is a need for curiosity, with which it is possible to be imaginative and from which creativity can emerge. These first steps are divergent. Then, when the creativity is assessed by going through a reality checker, prototypes and inventions can emerge, which if generally applied become an innovation.

Yet the creativity and innovation agendas are aligning especially in considering how they are to be measured. Innovation thinking has moved from simply focusing on inputs to a systemic approach as it is clear that, for instance, levels of R&D on their own do not by definition involve creativity or lead to innovations. Wider conditions, namely the creative climate, it is recognized, determine the capacity of a place to be innovative within which specific attributes are necessary components such as good education and skills or research expenditure. Current discussions on innovation indices now include ideas such as 'total innovation' or 'hidden innovation'. This draws attention to how innovation needs to pervade a whole environment.

To capture the dynamics of innovation, analysts talk of a fourth generation of indicators, which stress the interactions and relationships of actors in the innovation system from firms to universities or public agencies to the culture, whilst bearing in mind the relative usefulness of formerly popular measures. The development of indicators lags behind how we understand the dynamics of reality. This is why the importance of the culture and creativity agenda was not seen.

THE CREATIVE CITY INDEX

I have developed a *Creative City Index* focusing on ten domains under which there are a raft of assessment questions and groups of indicators. These are:

- Political and public framework.
- Distinctiveness, diversity, vitality and expression.
- Openness, tolerance and accessibility.
- Entrepreneurship, exploration and innovation.
- Strategic agility, leadership and vision.
- Talent and the learning landscape.
- Communication, connectivity and networking.
- The place and place-making.
- Liveability and well-being.
- Professionalism and effectiveness.

Within each of these there are key traits that indicate creativity, and a series of questions has been designed to help assess the level of creativity under each of these headings. Collectively and in combination these represent the *creative ecology* of a place and assess whether there is a culture of creativity. Creativity is clearly not the preserve of any single sector and it is important to be wide-ranging in any programme of assessment. An assessment of creativity should focus on:

- The education and training system: primary, secondary and tertiary education, professional development, lifelong learning.
- Industry and business: small and medium-sized enterprises (SMEs) and large corporations, cluster initiatives, representative bodies such as chambers of commerce.
- The public administration and public bodies.
- The community and voluntary sector: local societies, social action groups.
- Cultural, tourism and leisure institutions: arts organizations, gastronomy, hospitality industry, sports.

While the ten domain headings generally speak for themselves, one would look for a strong showing in the following qualities: motivation, tenacity, awareness, clarity of communication, broad thinking, inspiration, aspiration, adaptability, dynamism, openness, participation, design awareness, sensory appreciation, professional pride, leadership and vision.

The judgements on the ten domains are drawn from four sources where scores range from 0 per cent to 100 per cent:

- A series of comparative benchmark data.
- Interviews with appropriate and representative groupings undertaken by outside experts.
- Assessments made by the city itself.
- A broader survey undertaken with a dedicated self-assessment software that has internal weighting mechanisms.

The judgements are a combination of objective data, external peer group assessment and internal self-assessment. On this basis an overall score is given for a city.

THE COMPETITIVE PLATFORMS FOR AMBITIOUS CREATIVE CITIES

City regions with the right strategic focus can punch above their weight in spite of global dynamics, but a series of factors are important. In essence they act as a roadmap for urban creativity.

Urban Leadership

The first of these is leadership and the six main qualities of urban leadership seem to be: foresight, which is the ability to imagine and vision and to assess how deeper trends will play themselves out. Strategic focus – the skill of concentrating on 'big-picture' and long-term future-oriented perspectives and within this the ability to be strategically principled and tactically flexible is important. There is a need to understand urbanism, city dynamics and iconics in a holistic way and the qualities and characteristics that make cities great. Framing this knowledge, a culture of openness and curiosity is essential, which involves adopting an ethos which values debate, critical thinking and learning. In order then to make things happen organizational agility is important, which is the ability to move from a controlling, centralizing, uniform, high-blame, low-risk culture to one which values responsiveness and flexibility. Yet this quality needs to be allied to a determined delivery focus, which is the motivation, will and ability to make what is promised happen – to 'walk the talk'.

An Ethical Development Perspective

Values-driven development has become more important. This is partly driven by ethics and also self-interest, thus merging the self-centred with the public good. This is because there is a profound yearning especially among the highly educated under-40s – which all aspirant creative cities want to attract – to give back to society or the world. This important shift I describe in *The Art of City Making* (Landry, 2006), where I discuss the need for cities to strive 'to be the most creative cities *for* the world' rather than 'to be the most creative cities *in* the world'. This one change of word – from 'in' to 'for' – has dramatic implications for its operating dynamics. It gives city-making an *ethical* foundation. It helps the aim of cities becoming *places of solidarity* where the relations between the individual, the group, outsiders to the city and the planet are in better alignment. This means that environmental and social justice issues rise to the fore. If cities want to attract the talented from the world this cannot be avoided. Indeed companies are increasingly driving the climate change agenda for mixed motives, but especially to keep an incoming flow of the most talented.

The same logic applies to city regions which want to be seen as leaders and role models. They therefore take on global responsibilities, especially in relation to sustainability issues. See how Singapore, London and soon New York have instituted congestion charging or how Stockholm and Copenhagen have taken a lead on the environment. Even China, in spite of the hitches around Copenhagen 2009, has hit the green road, a result of a major policy initiative agreed during the 17th National Congress of the Chinese Communist Party.

A consequence is that cities are attempting increasingly to bend the market through rethinking their regulatory and incentives regime to address imbalances. Social justice issues such as affordable housing become more significant as a creative city needs also to be liveable for all social groups. Many cities such as London demand a social housing component for key workers, for example, nurses or the police, in all their major developments. This reduces commuting times and helps promote the efficiency of the city dramatically.

INTEGRATED THINKING, PLANNING AND ACTING

The complexity of cities cannot be addressed through 'silo thinking' or departmentalism. Specialism still matters, but it needs to be framed within a mindset that recognizes how things are inextricably interwoven. It is difficult to see the whole by moving up from the parts. Yet in reverse it is easier to understand the detail having seen the interconnections and interdependencies.

At the highest level, there needs to be a conceptual shift, and thus the overarching paradigm for urban development would change from an urban engineering or infrastructure-driven approach to creative city making. This is the art of making places for people, including the connections between people and places, movement and urban form, nature and the built fabric, and the processes of building successful settlements. This involves the ability to combine hardware and software initiatives. How the physical city is put together in the creative city-making context now needs to serve social relations and networking dynamics. Cities must now understand the value of the latter by emphasizing issues such as atmospherics, liveability, well-being and the value and values of the public realm.

At a more day-to-day level many things are redefined, reconceived and operated. Even simple renaming can have dramatic longer-term effects as what we call things determines how we think about them and the priorities we set. The transport department, for instance, may be renamed and subsumed under a mobility and accessibility division, which is concerned as much with pedestrians as with cars or metro systems. Or waste or sewage issues may become part of a resource management system as new ecological thinking turns waste into an asset.

Strong concepts can change perspectives, especially when they force us to think horizontally and vertically at the same time. 'Seamless connectivity', for instance, seeks to ensure all transactions happen without friction or difficulty. This has not only a physical dimension, such as enhancing mobility so you can walk from A to B, or whether neighbourhoods easily connect and congestion and traffic jams are reduced. It also has economic and social dimensions. Here we ask 'how easy is it to transact and to get things done'; are the bureaucracies responsive, effective and flexible? Do immigration procedures work speedily? Do regulations encourage networking and transactions? Is IT connectivity ever-present?

Ultimately this implies rethinking governance for twenty-first-century needs, including the appropriate regulations and incentives structures that have this previously mentioned attribute of being strategically principled and tactically flexible. This also involves blending public, private and community-driven approaches, whilst ensuring that their best attributes are maintained, cherished and valued. In addition, unfortunately, city management has many blind spots since it is usually organized along traditional functional lines, such as housing, parks, health, police or transport. Other dimensions, which may be the things that 'really matter', such as responsibility for the overall atmosphere or social networking and bonding are often no one's responsibility.

FUTURE-PROOFING AND RESILIENCE

Cities that are punching above their weight, for example, Bilbao, Barcelona, Helsinki, Melbourne and Singapore, all have practical, long-term think tank organizations focusing on the 30-year horizon; they constantly monitor the best initiatives in the world and try to go beyond them. Only benchmarking against the best is being a follower, not a leader. This includes the capacity for high-level conceptual thinking and strategic planning to stay well ahead of trends. A useful metaphor is to see this as 'a collective thinking brain' for the city.

The aim is to future-proof the city and to make it resilient. When this perspective is embedded into forward planning it reflects the ability to imagine the implications of shallow and deeper trends and how these might play themselves out. It requires investing in future assets to safeguard against shocks, the unexpected and uncertainty. This helps develop strategic robustness and tactical flexibility.

Are current infrastructure developments, for instance, such as schools or universities, hospitals, police stations or museums being conceived within a future perspective? Schools at times look like factories for drilling in knowledge; hospitals rarely are built like centres for well-being. If education institutions are reconceived as centres for curiosity and imagination they would look, feel and operate differently. Hospitals conceived as centres for well-being and preventive medicine would too, as would police stations conceived of as centres for community engagement.

KNOWLEDGE AND THE LEARNING LANDSCAPE

The capacity to create knowledge through creativity lies at the heart of the creative city. This implies a varied mesh of formal and informal learning opportunities. This ranges from the obvious such as attracting knowledge and research generation centres from universities to science parks. The aim too is to attract thought leaders in many fields as well as renowned public sector and business leaders, who contribute to the creative city with their vast knowledge and experience but may have nothing to do with formal educational set-ups. Yet they may, for instance, be part of think tanks or be involved with them.

But there are many other forms of knowledge creation, exchange and transfer possibilities, which can be encapsulated under the heading 'open innovation'. Indeed many new forms of knowledge required for the creative city will not come out of the traditional learning institutions, since they involve issues such as 'enhancing network capacity' or developing new business models. In addition there are exchange forums such as *pecha kucha* or the First Friday concept which when managed well can act as accelerators of opportunity and new understandings. Furthermore there is the knowledge required to set up a creative milieu in the first place.

The focus on identifying, nurturing, harnessing, promoting, attracting and sustaining internal skills and talent as well as drawing these in from outside highlights issues like liveability. A 'CEOs for Cities' survey in the United States reports that whereas 15 years ago 80 per cent of educated people chose the company or the job before the city, now 64 per cent of these choose the city rather than the job. The creative knowledge-intensive city has a different look and feel from the industrial city.

This is why cities are raising the bar on infrastructure standards as part of overall urban design, such as airport quality, making public transport a delight to use, giving streets the feel of avenues and boulevards rather than thoroughfares. Great cities are seen less as a series of roads connecting disparate projects, but great streets uniting neighbourhoods and areas. At times too it requires courage and boldness and the ability to conceive of path-breaking or audacious initiatives such as the Guggenheim in Bilbao or the dramatic retrofitting of recycled buildings.

In the city that encourages learning and exchange educational institutions should be less islands operating in isolation but interwoven in multiple ways in the urban fabric.

A RICH URBAN EXPERIENCE

Most urban experiences are shallow, disappointing and increasingly homogenized. A creative city thus seeks to generate a rich, deep experience which is not pre-digested and over-branded where citizens feel they can be makers, shapers and co-creators of their experience rather than merely consumers of the pre-given. This requires the city to be confident in its identity, in order to develop cultural depth and sophistication as well as play off and be inspired by its history. Indeed creativity and history are great partners, both in terms of the physical fabric but also the intellectual depth that comes from having a past, which at its best triggers new thinking. Yet, crucially, a balance is needed. Valuing history, tradition and the tried and tested too much can hold places back. Being alert is essential, as the virtues that make places great or successful in the past may be precisely those that help it fail in the future. So a culture of considered and mindful openness is essential.

This richer experience involves combining a strong 'local buzz and global pipelines'. Local authenticity and the soul of a place need to come together with the best of the international. Yet the distinctively local and place-specific and its identity needs to be the overarching frame. Linked to this a good public realm is the encouragement of serendipity, so that chance encounters and face-to-face contacts occur easily and so you can 'bump into the fun' – central requirements to develop the creativity-driven knowledge-intensive economy.

When these things come together well a city can craft its centrality by becoming a transactional hub. This requires rethinking logistics beyond material factors, which is the art and science of managing product and service flows as well as ideas, creativity and knowledge. It helps a city have influence over global strategic networks whether physical, virtual or knowledge- and research-based.

Pulling these elements together, the dynamic and evolving creative city needs to move from brand-building to urban reputation management. In marketing, a brand is the symbolic embodiment of all the information connected with a product or service, such as a name, an image, symbol or expectation arising in the mind of people. Yet it is important to focus on tangible achievements rather than hype, as these can encourage a self-reinforcing and self-sustaining cycle of creativity. To be a creative city is an unfolding journey: an emergent process force-fed and accelerated by what has already been achieved.

NOTE

1. Five years after Glasgow – in working with Peter Hall – I encountered the work of Gunnar Törnqvist and Åke Andersson which helped me and was less known in the English-speaking world. They had discussed the context of knowledge, creativity and regional development, and drew attention to the role of the creative environment. In 1983 Törnqvist developed the notion of the 'creative milieu' while in 1985 Åke Andersson published an important account of creativity and city development using these insights and Stockholm as a case study. My collaboration with Klaus Kunzmann in 1993 where we compared the creativity of six German and six British cities was also important to me.

REFERENCES

Landry, C. (1990), *Glasgow: The Creative City & Its Cultural Economy*, Glasgow: Glasgow Development Agency.
Landry, C. (2000), *The Creative City – A Toolkit for Urban Innovators*, London: Earthscan Publications.
Landry, C. (2006), *The Art of City Making*, London: Earthscan Publications.
Landry, C. and F. Bianchini (1995), *The Creative City*, London: Demos.
Van der Molen, H.T., H.G. Schmidt and G. Kruisman (2007), 'Personality characteristics of engineers', *European Journal of Engineering Education*, **32**(5), 495–501.

Index

Abel, J.R. 65, 66, 129, 141, 142, 143
Abreu, M. 200, 203
Accra 416
Acemoglu, D. 129
Acs, Z.J. 232
Adelaide 518
adiabatic approximation 30
Africa 412, 416
agglomeration economies 7, 58, 59, 62, 296,
    334, 335, 387, 398–9, 402, 436
agoras 39, 40, 42, 47, 49
agrarianism 327–8
Alabama 513
Alberti, Leon Battista 31–2, 41–2
Allen, J. 98
Allen, P.M. 346
Allik, J. 118
Almeida, P. 233
Alonso, W. 58
Amabile, T.M. 89
amenities *see* scenes, innovation and urban
    development
Amsterdam 233, 289, 290, 302, 517, 523
    history 43–4, 287–8, 291, 292, 415, 469
    network cities *see* Randstad Holland
    Region 215, 218, 223, 227
analogies 26–7
anchoring 148–9
    higher education 146, 148, 367, 380, 399,
        446
Andersen, K. 504
Anderson, C.A. 122
Anderson, E. 415–16
Andersson, Å.E. 3–4, 7, 14, 15, 17, 20, 21, 39,
    43, 56, 85, 87, 91, 102–3, 104, 105–6, 286,
    330, 331, 457, 458, 459, 460, 461
Andersson, D.E. 330, 331, 334, 338, 339
Andersson, M. 469, 471
Anderstig, C. 286
Andreasen, N.C. 79
Angel, D.P. 172
Anselin, L. 59, 446
Antonovics, K. 136
Antwerp 43
Appadurai, A. 307
Archimedes 81, 88
architecture 27, 29, 192, 509, 521
    Arden (Delaware) 506, 512–13

classical Athens 39
    Enlightenment London 46
    Fin de Siècle Vienna 48, 50
    Renaissance Florence 41–2
    Walt Disney World in Florida 504
Arden (Delaware) 506, 512–13
Argote, L. 92
Aristophanes 39
Arnoldus, M. 289
Arthur, B. 291
artificial creativity 33–8
artificial intelligence (AI) 23, 33–8
artists 65, 76, 82, 123, 150, 231, 294
    arts: not just artists (and vice versa) *see*
        under arts
    Bohemian Index 61
    clusters 95–8
    concentrations of 233
    earnings penalty 139
    market system 394
    non-local interaction 101–2
    regeneration and growth 189
    social housing 383
arts 76, 82, 85, 91, 93
    not just artists (and vice versa) 259–61
        data limitations 261–4
        data, variables and methods 265–9
        implications for research and practice
            279–81
        research approach 264–5
        results 269–75
        thirty largest regions 275–8
ASEAN (Association of South East Asian
    Nations) 221
Asheim, B. 65, 147
astronomy 39
Athens, classical 39–40, 76, 458, 525
Atkinson, R. 68, 482, 483
Audretsch, D.B. 262, 311, 426
Austin 329, 402, 443
Australia 188, 218, 220, 298, 482, 518, 523,
    534
Austria
    Fin de Siècle Vienna 47–50, 459, 525
authenticity *see* scenes
aviation 27
    airports 302, 340, 535
Ayres, R.U. 425

Printed and bound by CPI Group (UK) Ltd, Croydon, CR0 4YY

16/04/2025

14658404-0001